ISBN 978-0-260-62730-8
PIBN 10960491

NINTH ANNUAL REPORT

OF THE

High Chief Ranger and High Standing Committee

AND

HIGH COURT SECRETARY-TREASURER

OF THE

Massachusetts Catholic Order of Foresters

TO THE

HIGH COURT,

APRIL 18, 1888.

BOSTON:

PRESS OF CASHMAN, KEATING & CO.

597 WASHINGTON STREET.

HIGH COURT OFFICERS.

For Term Ending April, 1889.

High Chief Ranger,

JEREMIAH G. FENNESSEY .   .   .   St. James Court No. 54

High Vice-Chief Ranger,

THOMAS SPROULES   .   .   .   .   St. Francis Court No. 4

High Court Secretary-Treasurer,

JAMES F. SUPPLE .   .   .   .   .   Columbus Court No. 9

High Senior Conductor,

EDWARD RILEY .   .   .   .   .   St. Joseph Court No. 11

High Junior Conductor,

*J. R. McLAUGHLIN, V. S.   .   .   .   Middlesex Court No. 60

P. A. MURRAY .   .   .   .   Charles River Court No. 55

High Inside Sentinel,

PHILIP SMITH .   .   .   .   .   .   Williams Court No. 19

High Outside Sentinel,

THOMAS J. DUNN   .   .   .   .   Cathedral Court No. 1

High Court Physician,

JOSEPH D. COUCH, M. D.   .   .   .   Benedict Court No. 39

High Court Chaplain,

REV. HUGH ROE O'DONNELL .   Star of the Sea Court No. 41

* Resigned.

ANNUAL REPORT

OF THE

High Chief Ranger and High Standing Committee,

For the-Year Ending April 18, 1888.

Representatives and Brothers of the High Court of the Massachusetts Catholic Order of Foresters.

It is with feelings of the greatest satisfaction that we welcome you to the Ninth Annual Convention of our Order. And in presenting our reports, we wish to congratulate you on the moral, physical, and financial condition of our Order.

Meetings of the High Standing Committee.

During the past year the High Standing Committee has held forty regular and forty-four special meetings, during which it has visited a number of the subordinate courts, and was greatly gratified to note the marked improvements, especially in attendance. Considerable of this success is due to the untiring zeal of the officers of these courts, and the increased interest taken in our Order by our clergymen, a large number of them having been admitted during the year.

Mortality.

During the past year there were thirty-four deaths, of which

2 were admitted in the year	. . .	1887
3 " " "	. . .	1886
1 " . " "	. . .	1885
1	. . .	1884
1	. . .	1883
5	. . .	1882
14	. . .	1881
7	. . .	1880

The foregoing tells the tale of the past more clearly than any other information can. It stands as the most effective arraignment of looseness in admissions, and of partial examinations. It is a full and complete answer to those who have so severely criticised the High Standing Committee during the past year, because of its close scrutiny of applications, and its watchfulness in guarding the out-door in order to reduce the death rate.

FINANCES.

In the report of the High Court Secretary-Treasurer will be found the receipts and disbursements in detail. We would recommend that the appropriation for the coming year should be such as would enable the High Standing Committee to go forward in the organization of new courts, increasing our membership, and establishing our institution as a permanent one among our people.

The action of the last convention in providing a permanent headquarters for the Order has been fully appreciated by the members, and the daily attendance of the High Court Secretary-Treasurer has given entire satisfaction, not only to those in the immediate vicinity of Boston, but to our brothers in the remotest part of the State.

NEW COURTS.

During the past year four new courts have been added to our number : St. Columbkill 65, Brighton ; Griffin 66, Franklin ; Canton 67, Canton ; St. Margaret 68, Beverly Farms.

The additions are of excellent material, the great majority being young men, and whose average age is 32.

CONSOLIDATION AND SUSPENSION.

It is very gratifying for us to be able to report that there have been no suspension nor consolidation of courts the past year ; and feeling assured that all of the courts are possessed of all of the elements favorable to prosperity, it only requires a prompt payment of all dues and a full attendance of members at regular meetings of the courts, to enable all future High Standing Committees to make a similar annual report.

ASSESSMENT CALLS.

During the past year the High Standing Committee has issued nine assessment calls ; and when call forty-four is received by the

High Court Secretary-Treasurer, we will have sufficient funds to adjust every death reported and found justly entitled to the same for the past year. This is very gratifying to us, and we know it is to every member of our Order, to be able to present a report which shows our organization second to no other in Massachusetts.

DISPUTED CLAIMS.

In the case of James L. Hennessey, of O'Connell Court, Winchester, the previous High 'Standing Committee refused to pay the claim, as the court was suspended four months before he died, and suit was brought by parties interested, and the case has been carried to the Supreme Court.

SECRET WORK.

The secret work, " as reported and accepted by the committee of last year," is working satisfactorily, and is sufficient to meet all the requirements of the members, such as recognition and grip.

RESERVE FUND.

The matter of a reserve fund is the one most important matter which your committee desires to impress upon your minds with all the force it possesses. We feel that our Order never was in a better condition to undertake the matter than at the present time, and the great necessity shows itself more clearly every day. We trust that you will give this your earnest consideration, that which it deserves, and that this convention before it adjourns, will have laid the foundation of a reserve fund, that will increase the confidence in our Order and the speedy payment of all just death claims.

CONSTITUTION AND BY-LAWS.

The High Standing Committee commends the present constitution as being ample for the government of our Order and worthy of further trial.

MEMBERSHIP.

During the year there have been admitted into the Order 574 new members and 97 rejected, and the High Standing Committee has labored to the utmost of its ability to strengthen the weakest points in the Order, and to that end a very close watch has been kept, guarding against the admission of men who were unfit to enter the Order, and while we were criticised, and considerable abuse has been heaped upon certain members of our body for so doing; still, we feel that we have performed our duties for the best interests of the Order, irrespective of personality, always having in mind that the interests of 3,300 men were of more importance then the personal desires of a few individuals.

Conclusion.

The members of the High Standing Committee return their most sincere thanks for the kind and courteous treatment received by them during their several visits to the different courts, and we trust that our acts will meet your approbation, and that the fruits of our labors, coupled with your wise enactments, will redound to the credit of the Massachusetts Catholic Order of Foresters.

JOHN H. WATSON,

High Chief Ranger.

Beverly Farms, April 13, 1888.

Report of High Court Secretary-Treasurer.

To the Representatives of the Massachusetts Catholic Order of Foresters :

BROTHERS : —

THE ninth convention of the Massachusetts Catholic Order of Foresters will open with splendid promise for the future of the Order.

With an organization comprising at present writing about 3,300 members we may well be proud of our position in the community, and our standing will bear comparison with any similar organization in the State.

We are no longer an experiment, looking in every direction for something to guide us; looking in every direction for some tangible support to which we might cling in our struggle for life; looking to this man or that for some idea, more or less new to its possessor, which we might adopt in the hope of strengthening our organization; no longer looking for remedies for the many evils which beset on all hands, from within as well as without our Order, — evils which were known to exist by the various High Standing Committees who have successively directed the affairs of the Order, but which with the limited experience enjoyed, they were powerless to guard the organization against.

We are no longer in that condition; we are on good, firm ground, and able to maintain our standing, if we only follow the dictates of prudence, and profit, not only by our own experience, but make use of the experience of others in the same connection, and apply ourselves to the perfection of the organization we have striven so long to preserve.

We can add much to give strength to our Order, and, under some circumstances, elimination would be of wonderful benefit to us; and while apparently a loss, would, in reality, increase our strength, and make us better able to provide for contingencies unseen which may at any time arise.

Commencing, then, our tenth year under such favorable auspices as now appear, we should be able to make rapid progress in the future. We know many of the evils which beset us within the Order, and, being forewarned, we have only ourselves to blame if we are not forearmed.

The subject of most interest to us, during the year just passed, has been the number of new applications for membership. From April 20, 1887, to March 31, 1888, the total number of new applications approved by the High Standing Committee is 521. This gratifying addition to our membership is pretty well distributed throughout the Order, and shows that a general interest has existed to increase our numbers.

The following list shows the number of new application papers approved for each court : —

No.	Court.					No.	Court.				
1	Cathedral				7	35	Sheil				2
3	Fenwick				6	37	Friendship				1
4	St. Francis				5	38	St. Joseph				6
5	Leo				13	39	Benedict				8
6	Cheverus				3	41	Star of the Sea				1
7	St. Patrick				1	43	St. Mary				—
8	Sherwood				27	44	St. Bernard				2
9	Columbus				1	45	Unity				2
10	Iona				8	46	St. Augustine				—
11	St. Joseph				5	47	St. Anne				9
12	Fulton				2	48	Sarsfield				13
13	Fitzpatrick				1	49	Constantine				26
14	Lafayette				15	51	Holy Trinity				3
15	SS. Peter and Paul.				2	52	Highland				—
16	Essex				17	53	Emerald				18
17	Hamilton				3	54	St. James				9
18	St. Peter				7	55	Charles River				5
19	Williams				7	57	Carroll				9
20	Mt. Pleasant				4	58	Prospect				3
21	St. Alphonsus				4	59	Worcester				16
23	St. John				—	60	Middlesex				23
24	St. Gregory				5	61	St. Lawrence				17
25	St. Francis				32	62	St. Catharine				7
26	St. Raphael				1	63	Shields				14
28	Erin				13	64	Gallagher				25
29	St. Thomas				—	65	St. Columbkill				53
30	Bass River				2	66	Griffin				21
32	Qualey				4	67	Canton				24
33	St. John				4						
34	Americus				5						521

This number includes

THREE NEW COURTS

which have been instituted during the year, viz: St. Columbkill No. 65 of Brighton, Griffin No. 66 of Franklin, and Canton No. 67 of Canton. It will be observed that the growth has been general;

and as the most applications have been in the latter part of the year, we have, in that alone, a sufficient indication that the Order generally approves of the course adopted by the High Standing Committee in disapproving all applications which were inimical to the good of the entire body.

A few in the Order, confined mainly to persons with some fancied grievance, have endeavored to belittle the efforts of the High Standing Committee, and have, as far as their limited influence extended, endeavored to neutralize the work which was being done by the High Standing Committee to improve the condition of the Order.

In nearly every such case which was called to the attention of the High Standing Committee, it was found that personal feeling was the real motive actuating the opposers of the men who were using their best endeavors, and all the experience which the various members of the High Standing Committee possessed, in conjunction with the experience of the Medical Examiners and the wise counsel and direction of the High Court Physician.

The labors of the latter gentlemen have been steady and constant. A regular attendant at meetings of the High Standing Committee, there were few matters of any importance which the High Court Physician did not discuss with the High Standing Committee, and the Order may well be congratulated on having the assistance of so able an advocate of healthy admissions only.

It seems to be the opinion of some members, and has been freely expressed by them, that when a man is proposed for membership he should be accepted because, 1st, they know him; 2d, they have known him one, two, five, or ten years, and they never knew him to die; 3d, each one of them knows more than the High Standing Committee about the applicant's general health. They completely ignore the fact that the applicant has been looked over by a Medical Examiner who forwards the result of his observations to the High Standing Committee.

These observations often assume a phase which would be alarming, if it were not pretty certain that every application gets a thorough scrutiny before being acted upon. To give an example: —

An application paper came to the High Standing Committee, with this result of the Medical Examiner's work:

"This man is a total wreck; he has consumption and heart disease." Yet the only charitable view of the matter would be to suppose that the persons who proposed the "wreck" really thought he was eligible for membership.

This is the charitable view; but it would take considerable argument to persuade the High Standing Committee that such was the case.

The total membership as given on report of fifty four courts Dec. 31, 1887, is 3,020, — not counting Nos. 14, 57, 58, 59. If we estimate the four courts mentioned at 180, the number would be 3,200 members Dec. 31, 1887. Add 179 approved from Dec. 30, 1887, to March 23, 1888, and we have 3,279 members, which is about the number now in the Order. Some suspensions have taken place; but the reports of such have been so slight and so manifestly incorrect as a whole, that no record has been kept of them beyond filing.

The membership a year ago was estimated at 2,868; but reports received show the membership to have been about 2,737.

The following table gives the membership, with Initiations, &c.: —

MEMBERSHIP.

No. of Court.	NAME OF COURT.	Dec. 31, 1886.	Dec. 31, 1887.	Initiated.	Admitted by Card.	Resigned and Withdrawn.	Rejected.	Suspended.	Reinstated.	Expelled.	Died.
1	Cathedral	128	131	10	.....	2	1	4	.....	.....	1
3	Fenwick	62	67	7	.....	1	.....	.....	.....	.....	1
4	St. Francis	110	114	8	.....	.....	5	3	.....	.....	1
5	Leo	79	104	16	15	.....	2	3	.....	.....	3
6	Cheverus	93	91	1	.....	.....	.....	1	.....	.....	2
7	St. Patrick	49	50	5	.....	1	.....	3	.....	.....	....
8	Sherwood	91	124	30	2	1	.....	.....	3	.....	....
9	Columbus	37	33	.....	.....	1	.....	1	.....	.....	2
10	Iona	59	63	7	.....	.....	2	3	1	.....	1
11	St. Joseph	134	135	7	1	1	6	5	.....	.....	1
12	Fulton	27	30	4	.....	.....	2	1	.....	.....	....
13	Fitzpatrick	62	60	1	.....	3	1	.....	.....	.....	....
14	Lafayette	.....	.....	.....	.....	.....	.....	.....	.....	.....	....
15	SS. Peter and Paul.	52	49	1	.....	1	.....	2	.....	.....	1
16	Essex	73	89	17	.....	.....	2	2	.....	.....	1
17	Hamilton	66	69	6	1	.....	2	2	.....	.....	2
18	St. Peter	57	66	12	.....	.....	1	3	.....	.....	....
19	Williams	67	70	3	4	.....	2	2	.....	2	1
20	Mt. Pleasant	62	68	6	1	.....	1	1	.....	.....	....
21	St. Alphonsus	44	47	7	.....	.....	3	3	.....	.....	1
23	St. John	29	27	.....	.....	.....	.....	2	.....	.....	....
24	St. Gregory	39	39	6	.....	2	.....	2	.....	.....	....
25	St. Francis	43	73	29	1	.....	1	.....	.....	.....	....
26	St. Raphael	39	40	1	1	.....	.....	1	.....	.....	....
28	Erin	55	59	6	.....	.....	2	.....	.....	.....	2
29	St. Thomas	73	73	.....	.....	.....	1	.....	.....	.....	....
30	Bass River	35	40	5..	.....	.....	1	.....	.....	.....	1
32	Qualey	22	27	6	.....	.....	1	1	.....	.....	....
33	St. John	63	63	10	.....	.....	2	2	.....	.....	2
34	Americus	.....	64	3	.....	2	2	1	.....	.....	1
35	Sheil	.....	24	.....	.....	.....	1	1	.....	.....	1
37	Friendship	65	47	1	.....	.....	.....	1	.....	.....	....
38	St. Joseph	42	42	3	.....	1	1	1	.....	.....	1
39	Benedict	19	22	6	.....	.....	.....	1	.....	.....	2
41	Star of the Sea	33	35	2	1	.....	1	1	.....	.....	....
43	St. Mary	24	23	.....	.....	1	.....	.....	.....	.....	....
44	St. Bernard	63	60	3	....	.....	.....	6	.....	.....	....
45	Unity	37	35	1	.....	.....	.....	3	1	.....	1
46	St. Augustine	32	29	1	.....	1	1	1	.....	.....	1
47	St. Anne	59	69	11	.....	.....	7	1	.....	.....	....
48	Sarsfield	49	58	12	.....	.....	1	3	.....	.....	....
49	Constantine	43	59	21	.....	2	5	2	.....	.....	1
51	Holy Trinity	54	54	2	.....	.....	.....	2	.....	.....	....
52	Highland	26	26	.....	.....	.....	1	.....	.....	.....	....
53	Emerald	37	54	19	.....	1	.....	1	.....	.....	....
54	St. James	25	33	7	1	.....	4	.....	.....	.....	....
55	Charles River	75	77	12	.....	5	5	5	.....	.....	....
57	Carroll	.....	.....	.....	.....	.....	.....	.....	.....	.....	....
58	Prospect	.....	.....	.....	.....	.....	.....	.....	.....	.....	....
59	Worcester	.....	.....	.....	.....	.....	.....	.....	.....	.....	....
60	Middlesex	47	64	17	5	1	3	4	.....	.....	....
61	St. Lawrence	27	42	16	.....	.....	5	1	.....	.....	....
62	St. Catherine	.....	31	32	.....	1	6	.....	.....	.....	....
63	Shields	.....	27	35	1	.....	.....	8	.....	.....	1
64	Gallagher	.....	57	64	.....	1	.....	5	.....	.....	1
65	St. Columbkill	.....	39	40	1	.....	.....	2	.....	.....	....
66	Griffin	.....	26	26	.....	.....	3	.....	.....	.....	....
67	Canton	.....	22	22	.....	.....	.....	.....	.....	.....	....
		2,580	3,020	567	35	29	81	95	5	2	33

The average age of the membership reported Dec, 31, 1887, is thirty-nine years—the addition of Lafayttte No. 14, Carroll No. 57, Prospect No. 58, and Worcester No. 59, not reported, would not materially change the result.

The average age of the applicants approved the past year is thirty-two years.

The occupations of the new members will form an interesting study as showing the class of risks the Order is now receiving. The list follows:—

Barber	4	Door Keeper	1	Marble Cutter	1
Baggage Master	2	Designer	1	Morocco Dresser	2
Base Ball Player	1	Dry Goods Dealer	2	Marketman	1
Baker	1	Expressman	1	Mill Supplies	1
Beef Dealer	1	Engraver	1	Mill Hand	3
Beamster	1	Engineer	4	Machinist	8
Book Binder	1	Farmer	6	Mason	6
Boot Fitter	1	Furniture Dealer	1	Overseer	2
Boot and Shoe Dealer	4	Fireman	6	Porter	8
Box Maker	1	Foreman	7	Produce Dealer	1
Book-keeper	3	Fish Dealer	1	Plumber	6
Blacksmith	11	Grocer	16	Packer	1
Bricklayer	3	Granite Polisher	2	Paper-Maker	1
Butcher	6	Granite Dealer	1	Paymaster	1
Butter Dealer	1	Gardener	4	Painter	1
Builder	1	Gate Tender	1	Printer	2
Clergymen	2	Horse Car Shifter	1	Physician	6
Chocolate-Maker	1	Hackman	3	Provision Dealer	7
Captain of Boat	1	Hostler	2	Policeman	6
Color Mixer	1	Harness-Maker	1	Quarryman	4
Cabinet-Maker	2	Horse Shoer	1	Rubber Worker	1
Car Driver	1	Insole Maker	1	Reporter	1
Cigar-Maker	2	Inspector of Prov.	1	Roofer	1
Collector	2	Iron Worker	1	Saloon Keeper	3
Clerk	33	Jeweller	3	Switchman	1
Coal Dealer	1	Junk Dealer	2	Sheepskin Washer	1
Carriage Washer	1	Lamplighter	3	Stone Cutter	18
Carpenter	12	Lawyer	3	Stone Dealer	1
Coachman	15	Law Student	1	Shoemaker	8
Currier	10	Laborer	80	Sexton	1
Contractor	3	Life Insurance Agent	1	Shipper	1
Car Inspector	1	Lithographer	1	Sculptor	1
Carriage Painter	2	Liquor Dealers	1	Salesman	3
Cooper	2	Lumber Dealer	1	Straw Blocker	1
Conductor	1	Laster	2	Superintendent	2
Caulker	1	Milk Dealer	2	Sawyer	1
Copper Roller	1	Moulder	2	Starchmaker	1
Die Rimmer	1	Merchant	2	Stableman	1

Teamster	22	Undertaker	5	Wheelwright	1
Tanner	2	Upholsterer	2	Wood Carver	1
Tailor	2	Weaver	1	Wood Worker	1
Telegraph Operator	2	Wire Drawer	1	Watchman	1
		Waiter	1		

The rejection of applicants, which has been such a fruitful subject during the year, will, perhaps, attract more attention than the approvals. The number rejected was 94, about 15 per cent. of the whole number. Many of these were by the medical examiners. In fact, if all who were rejected by the medical examiners, as positively unfit, were added to those whose rejection was recommended, or, to give it literally, those who were passed by the Medical Examiner, because he found nothing positive on which to base a rejection, yet whose general condition was so poor, or whose habits were so uncertain, that he could only report the facts as he found them, and leave the High Standing Committee to exercise its judgment in the case, it would be found to nearly equal the whole number.

The various occupations of those rejected are given below.

REJECTED.

Barber	2	Grocer	2	Piano Maker	1
Blacksmith	2	Hostler	1	Painter	1
Baker	1	Hairspinner	1	Pedler	1
Boiler Maker	4	Harness-Maker	1	Porter	1
Brakeman	1	Horse Shoer	1	Printer	1
Book-keeper	1	Janitor	1	Physician	1
Carpenter	5	Lamplighter	1	Pattern-Maker	1
Clerk	4	Laborer	9	Restaurant Keeper	1
Coachman	1	Liquor Dealer	1	Rectifier	1
Currier	1	Lithographer	1	Rubber Worker	1
China Decorator	1	Law Student	1	Shoemaker	3
Compositor	1	Laster	1	Saloon Keeper	3
Conductor, H. R. R.	1	Morocco Manuf'rer	1	Speculator	1
Engineer	1	Marble Worker	1	Teamster	6
Engraver	1	Mason	1	Tailor	6
Electrician	1	Machinist	4	Trader	1
Foreman	1	Miller	1	Telegraph Oberator	1
Gardener	1	Plumber	3	Wood Turner	1

The average age of those rejected is 33 years. Something has been said during the past year about the High Standing Committee being too strict in scrutiny of applications, and that certain persons would not be received under any circumstances. For the benefit of such critics, the following table is given. It is not large, and it appears as though it might be easily understood. It may be of benefit.

The average duration of life among drinkers of beer is 21 years; spirits, 16.7; both, 16.

It has been found that the average life of a man who became intemperate at 20, was 15 years; at 30, 13 years; at 40, 11 years; at 50, 10 years; at 60, 8 years. The rate of mortality in England (Registrar's Report, 1851) for 1,000 males, at or above 20 years was, Farmers, 28; Shoemakers, 18; Weavers, 17; Grocers, 11; Blacksmiths, 18; Carpenters, 19; Tailors, 19; Laborers, 21; Miners, 15; Bakers, 17; Butchers, 21; Innkeepers, 30. "The mortality of innkeepers, and keepers of beershops in any decade exceeds all other classes."

The following table gives the number of endowments paid, with the name, age at initiation, time of initiation, length of membership, time of death and cause, number of dependants or relatives, and to whom the endowment was paid. It will bear careful perusal, and it is now made as nearly correct as the limited records at the command of the High Court Secretary-Treasurer will permit. Further research may admit of further corrections in dates, &c.

NO.	NAME.	HT.	AGE.	INITIATED.	Yrs.	Mos.	Dys.	DATE OF DEATH.	CAUSE.	En-dow-ment.	NUMBER OF ES.	TO WHOM PAID.
1	Cornelius Cronin,	Iona, No. 10,	Malden 49	Mar. 14, 1880	1	7	5	Oct. 19, 1880	Typho-Malaria	$1,000	1, Widow	Wdw
2	Dennis	Leo, 5,			1	1		Nov., "	Phthisis	"	1, "	Exor
3	M. J. Kiley,	ark, 3,	Man 29	Nov. 14, 1879	1	9	6	Dec. 20, "	Pulmonary	"		Admini
4	D. J. Desmond,	Iona, 10,		Nov. 14, 1880	1	9	19	Jan. 3, 1881		"	1, "	Widow
5	P. H.	Cathedral, 4,	Boston 18	Sept. 3, 1879	1	3	8	Jan. 11, "		"	1, "	
6	Jeremiah			Oct. 15, 1880	1	3	12	Jan. 27, "		"	1, "	
7	A. Burbank,	6,		Feb. 11, 1880	0	11	24	Mar. 5, "	Typhoid	"	1, "	
8	John Dolan,	K, 13,		May 26, "	0	11	0	Apr. 26, "		"	1, "	
9	Patrick Kelley,	n, 17,		Aug. 3, "	0	10	14	June 17, "	Cancer in	"	1, "	
10	K y,	Iona, 10,	Malden	Apr. 21, "	1	1	27	June 18, "	Phthisis Pulmonalis	"	1, "	
11	Patrick C.	Americus, 34,	Man	Mar. 15, 1881	0	6	14	Aug. 29, "	Typhoid Pneumonia	"	1, "	
12	James L. Meagher,	Leo, 5,		Mar. 13, 1880	1	0	8	Aug. 23, "	Phthisis Pulmonalis	"	1, "	
13	Thos. F.	Leo, 5,		Aug. 10, 1881	1	1	24	Sept. 3, "	Intussus in Peritonitis	"	3, "	&
14	Archibald Morrison,			July 6, 1880	1	2	14	Sept. 3, "	Phthisis	"	1, "	
15	Michael	Leo, 5,		Aug. 16, "	1	2	14	Oct. 30, "	Bright's ase	"	4, "	& children
16	William Whitley,	St.		Apr. 12, "	1	8	5	Nov. 17, "	Chronic Catarrhal Pneumonia	"	1, "	
17	Daniel J. McDonald,	n, 17,		Apr. 21, 1881	0	9	1	Nov. 22, "	Chronic s & Pneumonia	"	1, "	
18	Henry	3,		Feb. 13, 1880	1	9	14	Nov. 27, "	Cancerous s. of Æsophagus	"	1, "	
19	David O'Callaghan,	d, 8,		Mar. 4, "	1	8	26	Nov. 30, "	ilar Pneumonia, sec'd stage	"	1, "	
20	Michael	n,		Dec. 27, "	1	9	9	Dec. 6, "	Pneumonia	"	1, "	
21	John M.	n, 11,		Jan. 10, 1880	1	7	26	Jan. 6, 1882	s and Cong. of n	"	2, Children	Guardian
22	Thos.T.McDonough,	St.		Mar. 22, "	1	9	17	Jan. 9, "	Inflammation of Bowels	"	1, Widow	Widow
23	James	St. Alphonsus, 21,		Feb. 15, "	1	3	10	Jan. 28, "	Phthisis	"	1, "	
24	Daniel	Cathedral, 1,		Oct. 15, 1879	2	3	16	Feb. 1, "	Pneumonia	"	1, "	
25	B. Mul y,	St. n, 38,		Mar. 29, 1881	1	1	19	Feb. 18, "	t	"	1, "	
26	John Boles,	Sullivan, 27,					18	Mar. 6, "	Ma a Potu	"		
27	Thos. Moore Bayley,	St. 7,		Jan. 18, "	1	10	26	Mar. 25, "	Colloid Cancer of Intestines	"	1, "	
28	Thos. Clark,	Leo, 5,		June 25, 1880	1	11	4	May 21, "	Cancer of Stomach	"	1, "	
29	des Purcell,	Benedict 3,	Somerville 35	June 24, 1881	1	10	17	May 28, "	Phthisis	"	1, "	
30	B. Mul y,	y, 40,		May 12, "	1	11	17	May 23, "	Pneumonia	"		
31	John Chambers,	1 x, 16,	Salem 40	June 23, 1880	1	11	17	June 10, "	Cirrhosis of Liver	"	1, "	
32	John Hayes,	St. Francis, 4,	33	June 1, 1882			26	June 27, "	Pneumonia	"	1, "	

ENDOWMENTS PAID— Continued.

NO.	NAME.	BY.	AGE.	INITIATED.	Yrs.	Mos.	Dys.	DATE OF DEATH.	BY.	Endow-ment.	NUMBER OF HEIRS.	TO WHOM PAID.
33	Wm. Miller,	Fenwick, 3,	25	Sept. 3, 1880	1	8	21	May 24, 1882	Delirium Tremens	$1,000	1, Father	Father
34	John Bentley,	13,	32	April 13, 1881		9	14	Jan. 27, "	at [Brain	"	1, Vw	Vw
35	Michael Leahey,	SS. Peter & Paul, 15,	34	Nov. 17, 1880	1	8	24	Aug. 11, "	of and Cong. of the	"	1, "	Father
36	Thos.	Cathedral, 1,	28	Mar. 12, "	2	5	6	Aug. 18, "	Typhoid Fever	"	1, "	"
37	Jno. B. M.D.	3,	37	Aug. 3, 1879	2	11	24	July 24, "	Pulmonary	"	1, "	"
38	Hugh	Fenwick, 3,	24	April 29, 1881	4	8	4	Sept. 7, "	Consumption	"	5, Widow	Vw
39	Wm.	Cheverus, 6,	24	Dec. 23, 1880	2	9	25	Sept. 27, "	of	"	1, Widow	Vw
40	Hugh Diver,	St. Francis, 6,	38	Mar. 21, "	2	7	5	Oct. 28, "	Crushed by stone falling	"	1, "	"
41	John	St. 4,	50	Jan. 8, "	1	11		Nov. 21, "	Pyæmia	"	1, Daughter	"
42	Henry	Leo, 5,	48	Feb. 11, "	2	10	13	Oct. 14, "	Pneumonia	"	1, Vw	Mother
43	Patrick Carroll,		22	April 26, 1882	2	8	10	Oct. 6, 1883	Pulmonary	"	1, Mr	Son
44	F.	Fitzpatrick, 13,	68	Feb. 11, 1880	3	11	28	Jan. 9, "		"	1, Son	Widow
45	James	St. 18,	23	Nov. 4, 1883	1	5	10	Jan. 22, 1882	Asthenia, Hip	"	1, Father	Vw
46	Ed. J. Burns,	St. Francis, 4,	29	May 26, 1881	1	10	1	Feb. 14, 1883	Typhoid Pneumonia	"	1, Father	Vw
47	Florence	St. Francis, 4,	32	Dec. 21, 1882	2	8	28	Feb. 14, "	Cirrhosis of	"	1, "	Guardian
48		Sheil, 35,	35	June 24, 1881		8	14	Feb. 28, "	Obstruction from Gall Stone	"	1, "	Widow
49		St. 8,	51	Mar. 4, 1880	3	10	14	Mar. 10, "	Catarrhal Pneumonia	"	2, Vw	"
50	Thos. A.	St. 38,	64	Mar. 29, 1881	2	2	18	Mar. 4, "	Meningitis	"	1, "	"
51	John	St. 13,	38	Mar. 30, "	2	1	18	Apr. 16, "		"	1, Sister	Mr
52	John		35	Nov. 3, 1850	2	6	23	Apr. 22, "	Phthisis	"	1, Widow	Vw
53	Neville,	Essex, 6,	41	Dec. 18, 1879	2	9	18	May 3, "	of the Brain	"	1, Child	Gh
54	Richard Collins,	Essex, 16,	42	July 8, 1880	2	10	9	May 5, "	Phthisis	"	1, "	Gh
55	James Carey,	St. Francis, 4,	31	Oct. 21, "	7	6	6	May 6, "	Drowning	"	1, Vw	Vw
56	P. H. McDevitt,	Sherwood, 8,	26	Dec. 22, 1882	9	2	9	May 8, "		"	1, Vw	Vw
57	Charles	St. Peter, 8,	24	April 2, 1880	2	2	1	May 28, "	Consumption	"	1, Father	Vw
58	John Kerrigan,	St. Anne, 47, Gl	24	Nov. 14, 1879	3	6	3	June 3, "	Pleuro-Pneumonia	"	4, "	Gh
59	John J. Whalen,	Fenwick, 3,	45	Nov. 14, "	3	1	7	Jan. 4, "	Pulmonary	"	1, Father	Nw
60	Callahan,	Cheverus, 6,	13	Dec. 1, 1880	3	6	20	May 17, "		"	3, Children	"
61	F	Fenwick, 3,	48	Feb. 10, "	2	4	18	May 13, "	Chronic Bronchitis	"	1, Vw	"
62	William B. Smith,	St.	37	April 13, "	3	2	17	June 21, "	Consumption	"	1, "	"
63	C. J. Sullivan,		50	April 27, 1882	1	2	24	June 28, "		"	1, "	"
64	John	St. 7,		Dec. 5, "	3	11	15	June 30, "	General	"	1, Vw	Heirs
65	Daniel Murphy,	50,	50	Dec. 12, 1879	3	8	28	July 2, "	Typhoid	"	1, Vw	"
66	Michael Brown,	Fenwick, 3,	31	Nov. 14, "	10	16		July 12, 1883		"	3, "	Mr
67	G.	3,	27	Sept. 16, 1880	3	1		Aug. 3, "		"	1, Mother	
68	John O'Brien,							Aug. 30, "				
69	James T.							Sept. 17, "				
70								Oct. 17, "				
71	J. A. Fleming, M. D.											
72	John J. Duffey,	Williams, 19,							Pulmonary Phthisis			

No.	Name	Court	Residence	Age	Date	Date of Death	Cause of Death	Amount	Beneficiaries	Relationship
73	M. H. Byrne,	..., 39,	...	28	Mar. 31, 1881	Sept. 17 28, 1883	Pulmonary Hemorrhage	$1,000	1, Widow	Widow
74	Bart. ...,	Essex 16,	Salem	35	Aug. 1, 1883	Oct. 2 1, "	Uremic ...	"	1, Mother	Mother
75	E. F. Dever,	..., 3,	Boston	22	Feb. 16, "	Nov. 8 4, "	His ...	"	1, Widow	...
76	John ...,	...,	"	47	Sept. 15, 1881	Nov. 18 6, "	Heart Disease	"	4, ...	Heirs
77	Patrick Monaghan,	St. Joseph, 11	Somerville	32	June 14, 1880	Sept. 3 14, "	Injury to Brain by fall	"	1, ...	
78	John Sweeney,	Benedict, 39,	Boston	46	Mar. 31, 1881	Nov. 5 25, "	Pulmonary Consumption	"		
79	Michael H. Murray,	Mt. Pleasant, 20,	Boston	42	Oct. 20, 1880	Dec. 3 1, "	Catarrhal Pneumonia, C'nsum'p.	"		
80	Michael Donahue,	Fenwick, 3,	"	40	Jan. 30, "	Dec. 10 22, "	Pleurisy	"		
81	John Murray,	Cathedral, 1,	"	39	Oct. 8, 1879	Dec. 2 25, "	His	"		
82	T. H. O'Rourke,	...,	"	25	July 2, 1883	Dec. 4 27, "	Pulmonary Phthisis	"	1, Sister	Sister
83	Philip McDonald,	St. Thos, 29	Brockton	23	Feb. 17, 1881	Feb. 5 21, 1884	Cerebral Paralysis	"	1, Widow	Widow
84	Jan B. Reagan,	... Riv. 55,	Watert'n	33	Nov. 5, 1883	Feb. 3 28, "	Pneumonia	"	1, Mother	Mother
85	Thos McDonough	... 7, 32,	...	40	Nov. 28, 1881	Feb. 5 21, "	Cong. of Lungs and Peritonitis	"	1, ...	Widow
86	...,	Americus, 34,	...	35	July 31, 1883	Mar. 4 29, "	Quick Consumption	"	1, ...	"
87	Denis Ahearn,	St. Patrick, 7,	So. ...	40	May 10, 1880	Mar. 2 25, "	Bright's Disease	"	4, 3 child'n	"
88	Frank A. Spitz,	St. Alphonsus, 21,	Boston	31	July 13, 1881	Mar. 4 27, "	Phthisis Pulmonalis	"	4, "	"
89	Alfred ...,	Cheverus, 6,	...	31	Feb. 25, "	Jan. 10 17, 1882	Pulmonary	"	3, 2	"
90	Jan A. McCarthy,	..., 10,	...	32	Oct. 12, 1882	Jan. 3 24, "	... Consumption	"	4, "	
91	John F. Cunningham	SS. Pet. & Paul, 15,	S. Bos'n	26	May 20, 1881	Feb. 10 6, "	Pneumonia	"	9, 8	Father & child'n
92	Stephen T. Sliney,	Fenwick, 3,	Boston	50	Mar. 7, "	Apr. 3 23, "	Bright's Disease of Kidneys	"	2, Parents	Guardian
93	...,	Essex 16,	Salem	29	Apr. 26, 1880	Mar. 11 19, "	Accident, falling off staging	"	5, Sister	Widow
94	John H. Matthews,	St. Joseph, 11,	Boston	28	Feb. 8, 1881	Mar. 2 2, "	Phthisis	"	5, ..., 4 child'n	"
95	John W. ...,	Erin, 28,	"	45	Jan. 8, 1880	Dec. 26 28, 1883	Phthisis	"	5, 4	"
96	John P. Duffin,	St. Francis, 4,	"		Apr. 26, "	June 4 18, 1884	Phthisis Pulmonalis	"	5, "	
97	Wm Meagher,	Cathedral, 1,	"	49	Sept. 8, 1880	May 16 24, "	Accid'nt, hhd. sugar fell on him	"	3, 2	"
98	Michael McCarthy,	Sherwood, 8,	"	30	Mar. 11, 1884	May 18 14, "	Diabetes	"	4, 3	"
99	Charles Lyons,	Iona, 10,	"	31	Apr. 22, 1880	May 7 3, "	Pneumonia, rt. lung & upp'r lt.	"	1, "	"
100	Daniel Bailey,	St. Francis, 4,	"	30	Apr. 22, "	Apr. 8 29, "	Phthisis	"	3, 2	"
101	Patrick A. Finn,	Sherwood, 8,	"	23	Apr. 4, 1881	June 17 9, "	Hemiplegia of Larynx	"	1, Daughter	Daughter
102	Edard W. Wright,	Williams, 19,	"	40	June 11, "	July 11 23, "	Shock, accident, ... of leg	"	1, ...	...
103	John J. Donovan,	... 40,	"	34	Mar. 23, 1882	July 22 15, "	Phthisis Pulmonalis	"	4, Widow, 3 child'n	Wid. and child'n
104	... Maguire,	Americus, 34,	"	33	Nov. 11, "	July 19 24, "	Chronic Bronchitis	"	1, Widow	Widow
105	Phil A. Cunningham	St. Joseph, 11	...	40	Mar. 31, 1881	Aug. 9 3, "	Pulmonary Consumption	"	1, "	"
106	James F. ...,	Star of Sea, 41,	E. Boston	37	Nov. 21, 1882	Aug. 2 10, 1883	... Consumption	"	1, Sister	Sister
107	Patrick Donohue,	St. Alphonsus, 21,	Boston	36	Dec. 13, 1881	Aug. 8 22, 1884	... of Stomach	"	1, Brother	Brother
108	Rev. Wm. J. Daly,	...,	"	29	Apr. 29, 1832	Aug. 1 9, "	Carcinoma of Liver	"	1, Widow	Widow
109	Rev. J. B. ...,	..., 6,	"	46	Mar. 11, 1882	June 22 18, "	Alcoholism	"	4, Mother	Mother
110	...,	SS. Pet. & Paul, 15,	S. Bos'n	29	Feb. 11, "	Aug. 5 24, "	Cirrhosis	"	4, Widow, 3 child'n	Wid. and child'n
111	M. J. Devine,	St. Thomas, 29,	Brockton	21	Mar. 31, 1881	Aug. 5 10, "	Phthisis	"	2, " 1 child	"
112	M. C. Boles,	Shiel, 35,	"	43	Jan. 28, 1882	Sept. 8 14, "	Hemorrhage of Lungs	"	1, "	"
113	P. H. Smith,	St. Peter, 18,	Dorchester	34	July 3, 1880	Oct. 4 1, "	Consumption	"	1, "	"
114	J. S. Tompkins,	St. Francis, 4,	Boston	30	Nov. 11, "	Oct. 10 23, "	Consumption	"	3, 3 child'n	child'n
115	B, A. Brown,						Killed by			"
116	...,						Consumption			

ENDOWMENTS PAID—Continued.

No.	NAME.	COURT.	AGE.	INITIATED.	Mem- bership. Yrs.	Mos.	Dys.	DATE OF DEATH.	CAUSE.	En- dow- ment.	NUMBER OF BENEFICIARIES.	TO WHOM PAID.
118	John Drury,	Shiel, 35, Boston,	25	Mar. 30, 1881	3	6	21	Oct. 21, 1884	Consumption	$1,000	1, Sister	Sister
119	T. H. Ahn,	Hamilton 17, Charlest'wn	24	Mar. 2, 1882	2	8	25	Nov. 27, "	Concussion of Brain	"	1, Nw	Nw
120	E. W. Bergen,	St. Francis, 4,	48	May 13, 1880	4	6	24	Dec. 7, "	Ptisis	"	1, Sister	Sister
121	Daniel Lynch,	St. Joseph, 11,	35	June 27, 1881	3	4	2	Nov. 4, "	Pneumonia	"	3, Children	Guardian
122	Matthew Cusack,	St. Alphonsus, 21,	43	Oct. 15, 1880	4	2	11	Dec. 17, "	Consumption	"	3, Nw chil'n	Wid. & children
123	J. M. Tirrell,	St. Patrick, 7, So. Boston	23	Jan. 24, 1882	2	11	27	Jan. 21, 1885	Phthisis	"	2 "	" "
124	John	Leo, 5,	24	Jan. 16, 1880	5	0	23	Feb. 9, "	Consumption	"	2 "	" "
125	Patrick	St. Joseph, 11,	32	Jan. 12, 1882	3	0	27	Jan. 8, "	Phthisis	"	3, Broth., wid., ch.	Broth., wid. & g.
126	J. W.	McGlew, 36,	35	Oct. 23, 1881	3	2	7	Jan. 30, "	Brt Disease	"	1, Widow	Widow
127	W. J. Barry,	Essex, 16,	25	Feb. 23, 1880	4	1	15	Feb. 8, 1885	Phthisis Pulmonalis	"	1, Sister	Sister
128	P. F. Hill,	Friendship, 37,	35	Feb. 6, 1882	3	1	11	Mar. 1, "	Ptisis	"	5, Nw, 4 chil'n	Wid. & guardian
129	Michael Ferrin,	Ny, 32,	44	Jan. 15, 1883	1	10	27	Dec. 12, 1884	Colis	"	2, Brothers	Brothers
130	Edward Doherty,	His, 6,	30	May 7, 1880	4	5	20	Oct. 27, "	Phthitis	"	6, Widow, 5 child'n	Wid. &
131	John Sullivan,	St. Patrick, 7, So.	48	Mar. 1, "	4	7	21	Mar. 17, 1885	Phthisis Pulmonalis	"	1, "	"
132	T. J. Flynn,	SS.Pet.&Paul,15, "	26	Aug. 18, "	4	8	10	Apr. 9, "	Phthisis Pulmonalis	"	1, Widow	Widow
133	Daniel Holland,	Connell,22, Winchester	39	Nov. 22, "	4	4	27	Apr. 15, "	Phthisis Pulmonalis	"	1, "	"
134	James Rice,	Ny, 32,	39	Feb. 15, "	4	1	20	Apr. 10, "	Accident, crushing h'd & sh'ld'r	"	1, "	"
135	John M. Perkins,	Erin, 28,	42	June 5, 1882	2	10	13	Apr. 18, 1885	Pneumonia	"	1, Nw,	Widow
136	Daniel M. Ellis,	Bass River, 30,	25	Feb. 5, 1885	3	1	1	May 1, "	Pneumonia	"	1, Father	Father
137	Joseph A. Kenny,	Fenwick, 3,	29	Mar. 19, 1880	5	0	28	Apr. 17, "	Consumption	"	2, Father & mother	Father & mother
138	John Schultz,	Holy Trinity,	32	Mar. 22, 1883	2	1	29	May 16, "	Accident	"	1, Nw, 2 chil'n	Widow
139	W. Neil,	McGlew, 36,	44	Mar. 21, 1881	4	1	25	May 23, "	Pneumonia	"	1, "	"
140	John Donovan,	Friendship, 37,	28	Apr. 2, 1882	3	1	23	May 4, "	Consumption	"	2, 1 child	1 child
141	J. S. MacCorry,	Columbus, 9,	35	Mar. 9, 1880	5	2	13	May 13, "	Brt Disease	"	1, Brother	Brother
142	Edward Gallagher,	Star of the Sea,41,E.	29	Dec. 13, 1881	3	5	24	June 7, "	Phthisis	"	4, Nw, 3 chil'n	Widow
143	Daniel R. McDonald,	Lyndon, 50,	26	Feb. 12, 1882	3	3	18	June 9, "	Brt	"	1, "	"
144	Dr. W. P. Kelley,	Liberty, 40,	25	May 12, 1881	3	10	27	Apr. 9, 1882	Inflammation of Cells	"	6, Sides & aunts	Sides & aunts
145	Peter Tracy,	Mt. Pleasant, 20,	48	Mar. 11, "	4	2	14	June 14, 1885	Congestion of Brain	"	5, Nw, 4 child'n	Wid. & child'n
146	Maurice O'Hearn,	Cheverus, 6,	39	Mar. 30, 1880	5	3	13	July 1, "	Bright's Disease	"	4, "	" "
147	Timothy Kg,	St. Patrick, 7, So.	32	Oct. 11, "	4	8	1	June 12, "	Uria	"	1, "	"
148	David Lane,	Cheverus, 6, Boston	40	Apr. 6, "	5	3	13	July 19, "	Phthisis	"	5, "	"
149	John F. Murphy,	Cheverus, 6,	22	Feb. 24, "	5	5	22	July 24, "	Apoplexy	"	1, Mother	Mother
150	Michael Reardon,	Sarsfield, 8,	47	Apr. 24, "	5	2	19	Aug. 4, 1884	Phthisis	"	1, Nw	Nw
151	Peter Hn,	Star of the Sea,41,E.	43	Dec. 13, 1881	3	10	8	Mar. 22, 1885	Pneumonia	"	3, Brothers	Brothers
152	P. W. Sweeney,	St. Bernard,44W.Newton	31	Sept. 25, 1881	3	11	27	Aug. 22, "	Phthisis	"	4, Father, 3 sisters	Father &
153	Thomas Daly,	Leo, 5, E.	30	Dec. 27, 1881	3	8	16	Sept. 15, "	Pyæmia	"	6, Children	Guardian
154	B. F. Harrington,	McGlew, 36, Chelsea	32	Mar. 21, "	4	6	10	Sept. 1, "	Phthisis	"	7, Nw, 6 child'n	Nw
155	John,	Cathedral, 1, Boston	40	Sept. 16, 1879	5	11	16	Sept. 21, "	Typhoid-Pneumonia	"	4, "	"
156	Timothy Leary,	Glark, 3,	37	Mar. 12, 1880	5	6	9	Sept. 21, "	Phthisis	"	7, "	"
157	James H. John,	Hamilton, 17,	38	July 6, "	5	2	24	Sept. 30, "	Neuralgia of Stomach	"	6, "	"

No.	Name	Court, No., Residence	Age	Date Initiated	Yrs.	Mos.	Days	Cause of Death	Date of Death	Amount	No.	Beneficiaries	Relationship
158	Timothy Dwyer,	Unity, 45, Bridgewater	44	Nov. 12, 1882	2	11	7	Pneumonia	Oct. 19, 1885	$1,000	6,	Widow, 5 child'n	Widow
159	John Sheehan,	Emerald, 53, Peabody	42	July 2, 1883	2	3	24	Phthisis Pulmonalis	Oct. 26, "	"	2,	1 child	Guardian
160	Hugh A. Carr,	Cheverus, 6, Boston	29	Feb. 11, 1880	5	8	6	Consumption	Oct. 17, "	"	6,	Widow, 5 child'n	Widow
161	D. M. Lynch,	Erin, 28,	31	Feb. 3, 1881	4	9	28	Phthisis and gen'l tuberculosis	Dec. 1, "	"	4,	"	Att'y for wid., g.
162	Michael Sullivan,	Essex, 16, Salem	40	May 4, 1880	5	6	0	Uremia	Nov. 4, "	"	9,	"	Widow & guar.
163	ohn Carney,	St. John, 33, Hyde Park	39	Dec. 14, 1880	4	10	22	Consumption	Nov. 5, "	"	6,	"	"
164	Patrick Prendergast,	Americus, 34, Boston	36	Nov. 21, 1882	3	0	23	Phthisis	Dec. 14, "	"	3,	"	"
165	J. R. Yendley,	St. Francis, 4,	38	Dec. 18, 1879	5	11	14	Chronic Interstitial Cirrhosis	Dec. 2, "	"	3,	1 child	"
166	John O'Day,	Erin, 28,	36	Apr. 6, 1881	4	8	14	Killed by Locomotive	Dec. 20, "	"	3,	2 child'n	"
167	James J. Quinn,	St. John, 33, E. Cambridge	33	Mar. 8, 1879	6	9	13	Pulmonary Phthisis	Dec. 21, "	"	2,	1 child	"
168	ohn H. Shea,	St. Francis, 4, Boston	56	Dec. 18, 1879	6	0	12	Valvular Disease of Heart	Dec. 30, "	"	3,	2 child'n	"
169	Peter Daly,	Erin, 28,	48	Feb. 3, 1881	4	10	19	Pyæmia	Dec. 22, "	"	4,	3	"
170	John Handran,	St. Anne, 47, Gloucester	33	July 6, 1885	0	4	28	Drowned	Dec. 4, "	177.50	4,	None	N'se, und'r, lawy. / Widow
171	Edward Brennan,	Cathedral, 1,	31	Oct. 15, 1879	6	2	12	Blood Poisoning	Dec. 27, "	"	1,	Widow, 2 child'n	Brother & sister
172	Michael Harvey,	St. Joseph, 11,	31	Oct. 11, 1880	5	2	15	Pneumonia	Dec. 26, "	"	3,	1,	"
173	W. H. Fitzgerald,	Mt. Pleasant, 20,	49	April 14, 1882	3	5	8	Heart Disease	Sept. 22, "	"	4,	Bros. & sisters	Widow
174	C. J. Hurley,	St. Patrick, 7,	31	Feb. 16, 1880	5	10	13	Congestion of Lungs	Dec. 29, "	"	3,	Widow, 2 child'n	Wid. & child'n
175	James J. McNealy,	St. Francis, 25,	45	Dec. 21, 1879	6	0	12	Heart Disease	Jan. 2, 1886	"	4,	"	"
176	John Kearney,	St. John, 23,	41	Dec. 14, 1880	5	0	24	Consumption	Jan. 7, "	"	5,	"	"
177	Francis P. Faten,	Fulton, 12,	48	July 14, 1883	2	5	26	Pneumonia	Jan. 9, "	"	8,	7	"
178	Patrick W. Sullivan,	Leo, 5,	40	Nov. 26, 1880	4	11	8	Pleuro-Pneumonia	Nov. 4, 1885	"	4,	5	Guardian
179	Edward J. Kenney,	Hamilton, 17,	35	July 6, 1880	5	6	4	Phthisis	Jan. 10, 1886	"	4,	4	Mother & widow
180	James W. Norris,	St. Joseph, 11,	33	Mar. 22, 1882	3	10	26	"	Feb. 17, "	"	4,	5	Wid. & children
181	William Logue,	Qualey, 32,	41	Jan. 2, 1882	4	1	17	Pulmonary Pneumonia	Feb. 19, "	"	2,	Mother & widow	Father
182	William Fay,	Hamilton, 17,	41	July 6, 1880	5	7	22	Paralysis	Feb. 28, "	"	4,	Widow, 3 child'n	Wid. & children
183	Michael Devine,	Essex, 16,	37	June 23, 1880	5	8	9	Catarrhal Pneumonia	Mar. 4, "	"	1,	Parents	"
184	Patrick Bellen,	St. Anne, 47,	47	Dec. 22, 1882	3	3	8	Acute Pulmonary Tuberculosis	Mar. 30, "	"	3,	Widow, 2 child'n	"
185	Michael McNeil,	St. Patrick, 18,	40	Mar. 3, 1881	5	1	3	Abscess of Lung from Injury	April 6, "	"	2,	1	"
186	Jeremiah Gull,	Iona, 10,	52	Feb. 10, 1880	6	1	23	Consumption	April 2, "	"	2,	1 child	"
187	Luke Kelley,	Mt. Pleasant, 20,	28	July 13, 1883	2	9	18	Chronic Catarrhal Pneumonia	May 1, "	"	6,	5 child'n	"
188	C. G. Kullburg,	Williams, 19,	38	Mar. 27, 1882	4	1	24	Drowning	May 21, "	"	4,	3	"
189	A. J. McGivney,	Sarsfield, 48,	40	Feb. 6, 1883	3	2	24	Pneumonitis	April 30, "	"	1,	Niece	Niece
190	Rev. C. McGrath,	St. Bernard, 44,	30	Feb. 26, 1882	4	3	3	Chronic Bronchitis	May 29, "	"	4,	Widow, 3 child'n	Widow
191	Richard A. Carroll,	Mt. Pleasant, 20,	37	April 10, 1884	1	11	26	Gastric Fever	April 5, "	"	7,	6	"
192	William Sullivan,	Fulton, 12,	26	Mar. 9, 1880	6	3	19	Pulmonary Phthisis	June 28, "	"	4,	3	"
193	William H. Sliney,	Americus, 34,	45	Mar. 15, 1881	5	2	28	Inflammation of Liver	June 13, "	"	2,	2	"
194	John McClure,	Sherwood, 8,	25	May 13, 1880	6	1	18	Cerebral Apoplexy	July 1, "	"	2,	Widow & child	Widow
195	Joseph R. Fenelon,	Leo, 5,	31	Jan. 16, 1881	5	6	5	Consumption of Lungs	July 21, "	"	2,	"	"
196	William Musler,	Cathedral, 1,	40	June 22, 1881	5	1	4	Phthisis	July 26, "	"	3,	2 child'n	Wid. & guardian
197	Hugh Harkins,	Sherwood, 8,	36	May 12, 1881	5	2	15	Inflam. of brain from sunstroke	July 27, "	"	3,	"	"
198	Thomas Maloney,	Fitzpatrick, 13,	34	Mar. 16, 1881	5	4	13	Typhoid Fever and Lung disease	July 29, "	"	3,	Wid. fath. moth.	Fath., moth., wid.
199	John Connors,	SS. Peter and Paul, 15,	45	Jan. 1, 1884	2	7	12	Laryngitis	Aug. 13, "	"			"
200	Daniel Gallivan,	St. Patrick, 7,	35	Jan. 28, 1881	5	8	1	Myelitis (Infl. of the spinal mar.)	Sept. 29, "	"	6,	Heirs	Heirs
201	John F. Daly,	SS. Peter and Paul, 15,	35	Sept. 15, 1880	6	3	1	Phthisis Pulmonalis	Dec. 16, "	"	7,	Widow, 6 child'n	Widow
202	William Pierce,	Shiel, 35,	36	Apr. 14, 1882	4	8	27	Pneumonia	Jan. 11, 1887	"			

ENDOWMENTS PAID—Continued.

NO.	NAME.	COURT.	AGE.	INITIATED.	Yrs.	Mos.	Dys.	DATE OF DEATH.	CAUSE.	Endowment.	NUMBER OF BENEFICIARIES.	TO WHOM PAID.
203	Edmund C. Keen,	St. Francis, 4,	30	Apr. 22, 1880	6	10	12	Mar. 4, 1887	Chronic Bronchitis	$1,000	3, Wid, 2 child'n	Ww
204	John J. Fenelon,	Benedict, 53,	42	Mar. 31, 1881	5	11	26	Mar. 27, "	Haemorrhage (from thor.)	"	5, " 4 "	"
205	James O'Toole,	Emerald, 53,	21	Sept. 6, 1883	2	11	16	Aug. 22, 1886	Unknown	"	2, Father & sister	Father & sister.
206	Michael Ledwith,	SS. Peter and Paul, 15,	34	Sept. 1, 1880	6	7	11	Apr. 12, 1887	Phthisis	"	6, Wid, 5 ch'n	Widow
207	Thos Hurley,	St. John, 33,	44	Mar. 8, 1881	6	0	3	Mar. 11, "	Inflammation of Brain	"	5, Widow, 2 child'n	Son
208	Dennis Crawford,	Erie, 19,	23	Oct. 3, "	5	6	26	Apr. 29, "	Consumption	"	3, Widow, 2 child'n	Ww
209	John,	Erin, 28,	39	Feb. 17, "	6	2	17	May 4, "	Pneumonia	"	6, " 5 "	Ww
210	Wm. F. Kean,	Leo, 5,	35	Nov. 19, 1886	2	7		May 30, 1885	Ac Meningitis	"	4, " 5 "	Guard'n & wid.
211	Michael	Hamilton, 17,	23	July 23, 1885	1	10	2	Jan. 26, 1887	Phthisis Pulmonalis	"	4, " 3 "	Wid
212	Jph Murray,	Bass River, 30,	38	Sept. 8, 1881	5	8	6	May 25, "	Progressive Paralysis	"	6, " 5 "	Wid. & guard'n
213	Patrick Murphy,	St. J 38,	30	Sept. 9, "	7	9	12	May 14, "	Haemoptysis	"	6, 1 child	"
214	Philip	Ham 17,	35	Apr. 6, 1882	7	2	18	June 21, "	Phthisis	"	2, " 1 child	"
215	John	Fenwick, 8,	50	Mar. 4, 1880	6	3	25	June 24, "	Liver,kidney&lung dis.—dropsy	"	6, 5 child'n	"
216	David Driscoll,	Shields, 3,	40	Jan. 21, 1881	6	2	13	June 29, "	Inflammation of her	"	5, " 5 "	"
217	Joseph Web,	Leo, 5,	28	Jan. 24, 1887	6	6	25	July 23, "	Malarial uses	"	5, " 4 "	"
218	William Ros,	Leo, 5,	38	Dec. 21, 1881	6	2	10	July 27, "	Typhoid-Pneumonia	"	2, Mth'r &	Mr & wid.
219	Wm J. Walsh,	St. John, 33,	34	Mar. 21, 1881	6	4	3	July 19, "	Consumption of Lungs	"	6, Widow & child	Widow & child
220	Michael J. Fennessy,	Essex, 16,	44	May 20, 1880	6	11	22	May 31, "	Phthisis Phthisis	"	6, Children	Guardian
221	J. J. Cunningham,	St. Ane, 46,	39	Aug. 14, 1880	2	4	11	Sept. 23, "	Drowned	"	1, Wid	Ww
222	Michael O'Keefe,	St. Joseph, 11,	44	Nov. 14, 1884	4	9	12	Aug. 25, "	Senile Marasmus	"	3, Father, 2	F. & at'y for 2 s.
223	John F. Rahl,	Cathedral, 1,	27	Dec. 8, "	5	7	12	July 6, "	Pneumonia	"	6, Widow, 5 child'n	G. of C., A. for W
224	B. H. Holthaus,	Columbus, 9,	39	Mar. 8, "	4	5	12	Oct. 3, 1887	Phthisis Pulmonary	"	4, " 3 "	Guard. of child'n
225	G. W.	Iona, 10,	23	April 23, 1883	5	27		Oct. 20, "	Dropsy, Heart Disease	"	1, Father	Widow
226	Patrick Connell,	Erin, 28,	49	Mar. 14, 1880	7	8	5	Oct. 20, "	Pneumonia	"	7, " 6 child'n	Father
227	B. J.	Unity, 45,	42	Feb. 3, 1881	6	9	25	Nov. 10, "	Degeneration of Lungs	"	4, Children	Son & guardian
228	Thos Sweeney,	St. 64,	49	Nov. 15, 1882	4	10	24	Nov. 28, "	Pneumonia	"	2,	Guardian
229	John F. Reavy,	cis, 6,	25	April 17, 1887	1	1	17	Nov. 6, "	Railroad Accident	"	2, Father &	Mr
230	M. J. Reagan,	cis, 6, 65,	28	Oct. 15, 1887	1	15	7	Dec. 4, "	Railroad	"	5, Widow, 4 child'n	Widow
231	D. F. McGilvray,	St.	35	May 7, 1880	7	7	1	Nov. 21, "	Fract. of Skull, blasting	adt	2, " 1 child	"
232	Walter Grace,	Columbus, 9,	27	May 26, 1881	7	21	21	Dec. 8, "	of Jaw	"	1, child	Father
233	John Martin,	Fin, 12,	36	May 12, 1881	6	27	8	Jan. 17, 1888	Chronic interst.	"	6, Wid, 5 ch'n	"
234	Timothy	Pat, 39,	45	April 27, 1880	7	8	10	Dec. 9, 1887	Paraplegia	na	1, "	Ww
235	Michael		49	Mar. 31, 1881	6	8	14	Jan. 7, 1888		"	11, " 10	" & child'n
236								Dec. 14, 1887		"		

The deaths unpaid are —

NAME.	COURT.	DIED.
J. J. Callahan	St. James, No. 54	Feb. 24, 1886
M. H. Kerrigan	St. Alphonsus, No. 21	April 22, 1887
T. J. Dacy	Americus, No. 34	Dec. 15, 1887
John Murray	St. Joseph, No. 11	Jan. 5, 1888
H. H. Sullivan	Cathedral, No. 1	" 13, "
•Peter Keliher	Leo, No. 5	Nov. 2, 1887
A. J. Harrington	Sherwood, No. 8	Jan. 5, 1888
P. C. Fennelly	St. Patrick, No. 7	" 23, "
Martin Brahenny	St. Joseph, No. 11	Feb. 22, "
Edward Ward	St. Alphonsus, No. 21	March 1, '·
Wm. J. McAleer	Fitzpatrick, No. 13	" 7, '·

In the Callahan case the Supreme Court has decided that Callahan's mother, who was named as the beneficiary, is entitled to the endowment.

In the Kerrigan case, the heirs are reported as unable to agree on a guardian.

In the Kelliher case, there is no widow or children, and the person named in the application as beneficiary is dead. There are about twenty odd relatives. Kelliher died in Salem, and members of Essex Court No. 16 looked after the remains, and had them forwarded to Boston for burial. Kelliher was originally a charter member of McGlew Court No. 36 (suspended), the remaining members having been admitted to Leo Court No. 5.

Of the number of deaths given in the table (1 to 236), the following shows : —

Initiated in 1879	. . . .	15
" " 1880	. . . .	95
" " 1881	. . . .	64
" " 1882	. . . .	32
" " 1883	. . . .	16
" " 1884	. . . .	3
" " 1885	. . . .	3
" " 1886	. . . .	2
" " 1887	. . . .	3

In three cases there is no record of initiation; but 1 died in 1880, 1 in 1882, 1 in 1885. So that the initiations may safely be credited to the early days of the Order.

Of the three in 1887 two were by railroad accident.

Taking the age at initiation the average age of those who died would be 35.7 years.

The expectation of life for a man 35 years is about 32 years.

The average length of membership of those who died was 3 1-3 years.

The expectation of life, according to the New York Mutual Life, is at 20, 42 years; at 30, 36 years; at 40, 28 years; at 50, 21 years; at 60, 14 years. Of the number in the table it appears that 126 died of consumption and other lung diseases, 53 per cent. of the number.

Since the organization of the Massachusetts Catholic Order of Foresters, the following list shows the number deceased in each year: 1880, 3; 1881, 17; 1882, 25; 1883, 40; 1884, 41; 1885, 48; 1886, 31; 1887, 34.

The above is, of course, merely an interesting statement of the mortality of the Order, and has no special value in a statistical sense, for the reason that our Order has only been in existence since 1879, and its duration is too short to enable us to determine with anything like certainty what the expected mortality may be.

Record of Membership.

During the year a book has been prepared to contain a record of all who have ever been members of the Order. An effort has been made to enter the names, commencing with the foundation of the Order; but, on account of the difficulty in getting in the original applications, but little progress has been made, and none can be made until all the applications are in possession of the High Standing Committee. A standing request has appeared on various calls during the past year that courts and individuals interest themselves in the matter, and forward the applications now out. It is, besides, more for the interest of the members to have the applications in one safe place, where reference may easily be had in case of necessity. It is earnestly hoped that no further urging will be needed in this connection.

FINANCIAL CONDITION OF COURTS.

No. of Court.	NAME OF COURT.	Bal. on Hand Dec. 31, 1886.	Total Receipts, 1887.	Total Expenditures, 1887.	Bal. on Hand Dec. 31, 1887.	Court Fund.	Contingent Fund.	Endowment Fund	Reserve Fund.	Special Fund.	Deficit.	Received Other Sources.
1	Cathedral	$463 90	$2029 45	$2194 19	$299 16	$287 66		$11 50				
3	Fenwick	55 84	1038 70	995 00	99 54	81 54				$18 00		
4	St. Francis	323 55	1773 68	1660 44	436 79	134 80	$136 05	101 00		$64 00		
5	Leo	325 74	1519 65	1599 80	245 59			*222 00		23 59		
6	Cheverus	113 66	1189 00	1149 73	152 83	152 83						
7	St. Patrick	87 56	756 55	750 71	93 40	79 65	8 75			5 00		
8	Sherwood	449 44	1888 82	2338 26	725 96	55 12	540 54		114 00	16 30		
9	Columbus	14 12	549 10	557 06	6 16	6 16						
10	Iona	55 18	1019 50	1050 83	23 85	74		9 11		14 00		
11	St. Joseph	221 73	1958 55	2071 67	108 61	83 11				25 50		
12	Fulton	60 51	445 60	434 07	72 04	55 04				17 00		
13	Fitzpatrick	110 85	856 90	859 43	108 32	80 82	27 50					
14	Lafayette											
15	SS. Peter & Paul	198 60	743 86	773 34	169 12	64 39	86 73			18 00		
16	Essex	201 43	1235 00	1412 22	24 21	24 21						
17	Hamilton	75 88	1084 75	1084 30	76 33							
18	St. Peter	188 08	956 90	874 84	250 14	177 09	24 29			48 01		
19	Williams	175 64	1201 10	1218 00	158 74	105 05	25 69	1 00		27 00		
20	Mt. Pleasant	254 61	1123 56	1037 14	341 03	102 02	216 21			†22 80		
21	St. Alphonsus	80 36	721 80	716 60	85 56		85 56					
23	St. John	27 80	300 10	303 88	24 02	24 02						
24	St. Gregory	82 59	546 44	546 44	82 59	82 59						
25	St. Francis	37 31	860 15	825 86	71 60	23 40	48 20					
26	St. Raphael	216 79	671 70	589 50	259 59	259 59						
28	Erin	37 30	912 50	939 96	9 84	9 84						
29	St. Thomas	327 50	937 73	946 65	318 58	76 70	46 88		75 00	120 00		
30	Bass River	139 70	560 81	546 88	153 63	87 63			42 00	24 00		
32	Qualey	60 09	455 17	448 27	66 99	66 99	6 00			10 00		
33	St. John	172 58	1025 25	1129 61	68 22	58 22				10 00		
34	Americus	209 38	918 45	922 26	205 57	80 00			72 40	23 17		30 00
35	Sheil	8 65	401 65	364 60	45 70	45 70						
37	Friendship		623 20	658 29							$35 09	$45 45
38	St. Joseph	8 23	649 45	644 05	72 63	13 63			28 00	31 00		
39	Benedict		290 20	24 50	16 50	16 50				‡19 90		
41	Star of the Sea	134 70	502 60	510 90	126 60	65 80	40 70					
43	St. Mary	29 72	320 20	341 90	8 02	8 02						
44	St. Bernard	41 77	811 74	826 31	40 00	40 00						
45	Unity	128 20	536 85	508 65	156 40	156 40						
46	St. Augustine	24 82	467 05	437 85	54 02	22 02	14 00			18 00		
47	St. Anne	469 86	1065 63	1057 82	477 67	247 77	160 00			†69 90		
48	Sarsfield	40 14	1078 80	1089 71	29 23					29 23		
49	Constantine	54 84	740 65	718 40	70 79	23 80	32 35			14 64		
51	Holy Trinity	296 71	920 29	1035 72	181 28	181 28	146 73		10 30	24 25		
52	Highland	68 43	320 65	347 10	41 98	41 98						
53	Emerald	62 40	721 15	593 70	189 85	36 85			134 00	19 00		
54	St. James	18 32	594 35	359 90	252 77		252 77					
55	Charles River	118 38	1015 15	1058 23	75 30	75 30						
57	Carroll											
58	Prospect											
59	Worcester											
60	Middlesex	104 31	952 56	888 63	168 24	92 09	72 00			4 15		
61	St. Lawrence	30 65	673 75	554 22	150 18	83 88			1 00	65 30		
62	St. Catherine		428 48	393 88	34 60	34 60						
63	Shields		411 70	396 96	14 74	14 74						
64	Gallagher		832 75	760 30	72 45	1 15	40 30			31 00		
65	St. Columbkill		478 90	361 65	117 25	23 85	10 00		40 00	43 40		
66	Griffin		150 87	95 05	55 82	7 75				48 07		
67	Canton								‖22 80			
		6407 85	44269 39	44005 26	7189 83	2757 03	2294 34	344 60	716 66	516 85	35 09	45 45

* Sick benefit.   † Assess. call relief.   ‡ For calls.   ‖ Feb. 15, 1888.

FNIANCIAL CONDITION OF COURTS.

Amounts Received for Initiation Fees, Court Dues, Assessments and Detailed Expenses.

No. of Court.	NAME OF COURT.	Received Initiation Fees.	Received Court Dues.	Received Assessments.	Received Other Sources.	Sick Benefits Paid.	Salaries Paid.	Court Physician Paid	Per Capita Paid.	Rent Paid.	Other Expenses.	Endowment Calls Paid.
1	Cathedral	$10 00	$393 50	$1464 00	$161 95	$43 95	$83 44	$155 00	$132 00	$87 00	$81 10	$1611 70
3	Fenwick	7 00	116 70	776 50	194 34	.....	49 00	64 00	63 00	24 00	18 50	776 50
4	St. Francis	24 00	325 75	1276 50	35 43	.....	49 00	.....	112 00	108 00	157 24	1234 20
5	Leo	51 00	267 00	1046 90	154 75	100 00	24 00	182 00	102 00	66 50	78 40	1046 90
6	Cheverus	2 00	151 80	989 20	58 75	9 00	36 48	.....	46 00	38 00	31 08	989 20
7	St. Patrick	5 00	164 00	528 80	.....	.....	40 00	62 50	50 00	46 00	22 11	530 10
8	Sherwood	30 00	332 50	1185 00	341 32	.....	22 95	104 75	91 00	75 00	110 40	1208 20
9	Columbus	.....	105 50	383 60	25 00	.....	27 00	.....	35 00	75 00	36 46	383 60
10	Iona	28 00	183 50	786 20	21 80	.....	40 00	81 75	59 00	66 00	67 28	726 80
11	St. Joseph	39 00	381 60	1404 95	.....	.....	36 00	135 00	138 00	60 00	123 85	1539 00
12	Fulton	4 00	88 00	352 80	80	.....	15 00	28 42	30 00	32 50	5 35	322 80
13	Fitzpatrick	3 00	183 50	663 50	6 90	.....	41 00	31 00	63 00	23 50	37 43	663 50
14	Lafayette											
15	SS. Peter & Paul	1 00	152 00	526 70	64 16	.....	15 00	.....	50 00	65 00	55 44	587 90
16	Essex	17 00	213 75	970 25	34 00	.....	.....	.....	64 00	129 15	285 77	933 30
17	Hamilton	.....	.....	.....	.....	.....	25 00	50 00	68 00	61 50	54 80	825 00
18	St. Peter	12 00	188 50	692 40	64 00	.....	14 25	60 50	64 00	41 00	22 89	692 20
19	Williams	2 00	393 00	704 40	101 70	190 00	34 00	101 25	65 00	66 00	58 35	704 40
20	Mt. Pleasant	16 00	201 00	681 90	156 66	.....	36 00	65 75	68 00	84 00	93 49	681 90
21	St. Alphonsus	31 00	135 75	549 80	5 25	3 75	45 30	.....	45 00	26 00	91 25	505 30
23	St. John	.....	50 10	250 00	.....	.....	.....	.....	29 00	19 00	7 58	248 30
24	St. Gregory	6 00	125 64	.....	50	.....	.....	38 00	37 00	36 00	.....	416 90
25	St. Francis	29 00	152 00	569 90	109 25	.....	.....	43 00	60 80	88 00	64 16	569 90
26	St. Raphael	3 00	114 60	419 05	135 05	.....	.....	.....	32 00	.....	99 80	457 70
28	Erin	18 00	150 50	738 00	6 00	.....	36 00	56 25	55 00	72 00	37 71	683 00
29	St. Thomas	2 00	173 80	757 50	4 43	.....	12 00	73 00	73 00	36 00	63 15	689 50
30	Bass River	3 00	112 25	432 90	12 66	18 00	.....	6 00	39 00	24 00	20 18	439 70
32	Qualey	6 00	102 70	285 70	60 77	.....	20 90	24 97	22 00	43 50	61 40	375 50
33	St. John	10 00	235 00	780 25	.....	145 00	24 00	67 25	56 00	30 00	27 11	780 25
34	Americus	3 00	175 50	642 85	97 10	.....	11 25	63 75	97 00	72 00	43 96	634 30
35	Sheil	.....	69 65	308 50	23 50	.....	.....	.....	25 60	24 00	39 00	276 00
37	Friendship	3 00	81 05	493 70	45 45	.....	60 00	35 00	46 00	.....	20 89	496 40
38	St. Joseph	9 00	121 25	473 20	46 00	.....	.....	40 75	44 00	74 00	12 10	473 20
39	Benedict	18 00	23 00	.....	.....	.....	.....	12 00	.....	12 50	.....	265 70
41	Star of the Sea	4 00	96 00	367 60	169 70	.....	.....	59 50	35 00	23 00	41 70	351 70
43	St. Mary	.....	41 40	278 80	.....	.....	.....	.....	23 00	25 00	15 10	278 80
44	St. Bernard	.....	.....	609 50	160 47	.....	.....	.....	59 00	75 00	.....	.....
45	Unity	3 00	99 85	395 00	.....	.....	.....	37 00	37 00	35 00	9 65	350 00
46	St. Augustine	1 00	91 75	321 80	52 50	.....	.....	13 00	30 00	46 00	27 05	321 80
47	St. Anne	19 00	191 00	633 40	188 23	55 00	.....	161 50	64 00	50 00	168 92	558 40
48	Sarsfield	36 00	145 50	566 40	330 90	.....	12 50	116 50	56 00	220 93	117 38	566 40
49	Constantine	21 25	149 80	521 60	48 00	.....	28 00	.....	51 20	72 00	22 80	544 40
51	Holy Trinity	2 00	.....	654 45	263 84	115 00	30 00	.....	54 00	38 00	95 52	703 20
52	Highland	.....	71 75	248 90	.....	.....	.....	26 00	27 00	27 00	14 20	252 90
53	Emerald	19 00	125 50	464 50	112 15	.....	.....	43 00	27 20	75 00	58 60	389 90
54	St. James	7 00	84 00	326 10	177 25	.....	.....	.....	30 00	44 00	29 60	256 30
55	Charles River	12 00	49 15	753 65	200 35	.....	.....	.....	77 00	60 00	105 63	815 70
57	Carroll											
58	Prospect											
59	Worcester											
60	Middlesex	17 00	77 64	554 90	293 02	.....	.....	28 00	60 00	197 98	37 25	565 40
61	St. Lawrence	16 00	104 50	411 20	100 05	.....	.....	19 00	45 40	70 00	55 02	364 80
62	St. Catharine	32 00	75 75	231 70	89 03	.....	.....	37 00	7 83	59 00	58 35	231 70
63	Shields	84 00	139 70	188 00	.....	.....	.....	13 50	27 00	34 25	91 11	231 10
64	Gallagher	222 00	121 25	324 00	107 50	.....	.....	140 00	58 00	35 25	135 85	391 20
65	St. Columbkill	40 00	70 00	200 90	168 00	.....	.....	84 00	35 00	27 50	57 65	157 50
66	Griffin	.....	10 40	123 20	17 27	.....	.....	.....	.....	.....	2 65	92 40
67	Canton											
		927 25	7409 33	29310 55	4445 78	679 70	868 07	2369 89	2765 03	2920 06	3072 16	30131 45

ENDOWMENT FUND.

Dr.

Balance on hand April 8, 1887			$5,787 60
Assessment call No. 27	$ 90		
" " " 30	3 00		
" " " 31	90		
" " " 32	9 40		
" " " 33	294 60		
" " " 34	1,385 00		
" " " 35	3,291 80		
" " " 36	3,425 90		
" " " 37	3,450 70		
" " " 38	3,511 30		
" " " 39	3,505 50		
" " " 40	3,536 80		
" " " 41	3,601 50		
" " " 42	3,503 40		
" " " 43	2,774 70		
			32,295 40
			$38,083 00

Cr.

Name		Branch		No.		Amount
Wm. F. Kean . .	of	Leo,	No.	5	. .	$1,000 00
John Conners . .	"	SS. Peter and Paul,	"	15	. .	884 20
James O'Toole . .	"	Emerald,	"	53	. .	900 00
Michael Connell .	"	Hamilton,	"	17	. .	1,000 00
John J. Fenelon .	"	Benedict,	"	39	. .	1,000 00
Michael Ledwith .	"	SS. Peter and Paul,	"	15	. .	1,000 00
Terence Griffin . .	"	Erin,	"	28	. .	1,000 00
Timothy Hurley .	"	St. John,	"	33	. .	1,000 00
Denis Crawford. .	"	Williams,	"	19	. .	1,000 00
Patrick Murphy .	"	Bass River,	"	30	. .	1,000 00
Joseph McGilvray.	"	Constantine,	"	49	. .	1,000 00
Philip Carney . .	"	St. Joseph,	"	38	. .	1,000 00
John Broderick. .	"	Hamilton,	"	17	. .	1,000 00
David Fahey. . .	"	Sherwood,	"	8	. .	1,000 00
Cornelius Driscoll .	"	Fenwick,	"	3	. .	1,000 00
Joseph Welsh . .	"	Shields,	"	63	. .	1,000 00
Wm. Brooks. . .	"	Leo,	"	5	. .	1,000 00
Thaddeus J. Walsh	"	Leo,	"	5	. .	1,000 00
Michael O'Keefe .	"	St. Augustine,	"	46	. .	1,000 00
John J. Cunningham	"	Essex,	"	16	. .	1,000 00
Michael J. Fennessy	"	St. John,	"	33	. .	1,000 00
J. F. Rahl . . .	"	St. Joseph,	"	11	. .	1,000 00
B. H. Holthaus . .	"	Cathedral,	"	1	. .	1,000 00
G. W. Cleary . .	"	Columbus,	"	9	. .	1,000 00
T. Sweeney . . .	"	Unity,	"	45	. .	1,000 00
P. Connell . . .	"	Iona,	"	10	. .	1,000 00
M. J. Regan . . .	"	Cheverus,	"	6	. .	1,000 00
B. J. O'Daly . .	"	Erin,	"	28	. .	1,000 00
John F. Reavy . .	"	Gallagher,	"	64	. .	1,000 00
D. F. McGilvray . .	"	Cheverus,	"	6	. .	1,000 00
Michael Durant. .	"	Benedict,	"	39	. .	1,000 00
Timothy Collins .	"	Fulton,	"	12	. .	1,000 00
Walter Grace . .	"	St. Columbkill,	"	65	. .	1,000 00
John Martin. . .	"	Columbus,	"	9	. .	1,000 00
						33,784 20
Balance						$4,298 80

GENERAL FUND.

Dr.

J. J. Lanigan, H. C. S.	$8 75
Sale of Stove	10 00
" " Settees	15 40
" " Safe	85 00
" " Box	1 50
Charter and Supplies, Courts 65, 66, 67 . . .	135 00
Sale of Certificates	22 00
" " Regalia	2 50
" " Postal Cards, by J. J. L.	63 77
" " " "	369 48
1886, Per Capita	95 43
1887, " "	2,928 00

$3,736 83

Cr.

SALARIES.

B. J. O'Daly, P. H. C., Secretary to April, 1887 . .	$185 00
J. F. Supple, H. C. Treasurer " " " .	400 00
J. J. Lanigan, Acting H. C. Secretary to April, 1887 .	200 00
J. F. Supple, H. C. Secretary-Treasurer to " 1888 .	800 00

$1,585 00

RENT.

H. H. Hunnewell, Hall, April 20, 1887	$10 50
G. R. Sneaden, " " 28, "	4 00
" " , " May 12, "	4 00
H. H. Hunnewell, " July 29, "	4 00
G. R. Sneaden, " Aug. 5, "	4 00
H. H. Hunnewell, " Oct. 9, "	4 00
Cashman, Keating & Co., for office of High Standing Committee for 11 months to April 1st, 1888 .	275 00

$305 50

Boston Post-Office Postal Cards	$315 00

PRINTING.

F. J. McQueeney, assessment call	$4 50
H. C. Treasurer Report, 1887	7 50
100 1-2 letter Circulars	3 00
4,000 Addressed Envelopes	17 00
600 Cards (notices)	3 50

.35 50

H. H. Sullivan:	
150 Circulars (Med. Ex.)	$2 25
Reports of Finance Com	21 00

23 25

Cashman, Keating & Co.:

1,000 Labels	2 00
1,000 Note Heads	4 50
2,000 Addressed Envelopes	6 00
200 Commissions (D. H. C. R.)	8 00
Book for Membership of the Order	27 75
100 Receipts (endowment)	5 00
	$53 25

Geo. B. Wilcox:

400 Credentials	2 50
200 Call of Convention	2 25
1 lot Postal Cards	65
800 Dup. Orders for Calls	4 00
100 Assessment Call	3 00
4 lots Postal Cards	2 60
1 lot Postal Cards	60
1 lot Postal Cards	60
Call of Convention	1 75
Assessment Call	3 50
6 lots Postal Cards	3 60
Per Capita Call	4 50
2 lots Postal Cards	1 20
2 lots Postal Cards	1 20
Notice of Meeting	1 00
3 lots Postal Cards	1 80
1 lot Postal Cards	60
5 lots Postal Cards	3 00
Assessment Call	3 50
3 lots Postal Cards	1 80
2,000 Beneficiary Blanks	6 50
Notice of Meeting	1 00
2 lots Postal Cards	1 20
Assessment Call	3 50
500 lists D. H. C. R. & Med. Ex	3 80
5 lots Postal Cards	3 00
Assessment Call	4 50
4 lots Postal Cards	2 40
Assessment Call	3 50
6 lots Postal Cards	3 60
Assessment Call	4 00
5 lots Postal Cards	3 00
5 lots Postal Cards	4 35
Assessment Call	4 00
2 lots Postal Cards	1 60
Assessment Call	5 00
200 Credentials	3 00
100 Call of Convention	1 50
	103 10

REGALIA.

F. Alford, Repairing Regalia.	$2 75	
" 2 sets "	16 00	
" 2 " "	16 00	
		$34 75

SEALS.

S. M. Spencer, 1 Seal	$3 50	
" 1 "	5 00	
" 1 "	5 00	
1 '.	5 00	
		18 50

POSTAGE.

Stamps, Envelopes (request)	$68 10	
Stamps (P. C. not for Assessment Calls), Plain Envelopes	26 43	
Stamps, J. J. Lanigan to April, 1887 . . .	2 00	
		96 53

TRAVELLING EXPENSES.

Deputy High Chief Rangers, —		
W. H. Rogers	$11 50	
Patrick McCarthy	1 50	
E. F. Chamberlain	18 70	
		31 70
High Standing Committee,—		
To Springfield	21 84	
Lanigan & Supple	2 50	
Sproules & Supple	1 00	
Lanigan & Supple	2 50	
H. S. Com. to Franklin	11 80	
H. S. Com. to Canton	1 90	
H. C. Secretary-Treasurer to E. Cambridge Court House, 3 days	4 25	
H. S. Com. to W. Quincy, Watson, Fennessey, Supple	1 66	
Watson, Supple & Daughn to Marlboro . . .	6 25	
H. S. C. Boylston Station	35	
High Standing Committee to Gloucester . . .	4 49	
High C. S. T. to Bridgewater	3 20	
Fennessey and Supple to Canton	80	
High Standing Committee to Canton . . .	9 90	
Fennessey and Supple to Marlboro	4 77	
Fennessey and Supple to Springfield. . . .	8 92	
Watson, Dore, McLaughlin and Supple to Providence	7 79	
High Standing Committee to Mount Benedict . .	6 00	
H. S. Com. to Brighton	5 00	
H. S. Com. to Brighton	6 00	
		110 92

MISCELLANEOUS.

Record Book, ...	$0 50	
D. Wilson & Co., Ballots	6 00	
S. Hobbs & Co., Seals	1 65	
J. T. Daly, " etc.	1 00	
Telegram to B. J. O'Daly	4 20	
Wm. Tufts, Dinner for Convention	50 25	
J. A. Gore, on account of Dinner	7 00	
S. Hobbs & Co., Stationery	11 49	
R. T. Purcell, 36 Batons, 12 Gavels	8 40	
T. J. Curtis, 6 Ballot Boxes	13 50	
M. R. Warren, 6 Record Books	4 20	
W. E. Fitzgerald, Expressing from Day St. to 597 Washington St.	1 50	
Expressing from 195 Dorchester Ave. to 597 Washington St.	3 00	
Expressing from Regent St. to 195 Dorchester Ave. .	2 00	
" " 68 Cornhill	75	
" " McGlew Court	15	
" " Worcester	15	
" to Northampton	25	
W. E. Fitzgerald	50	
Ellis & Lewis, Cuspadores, etc.	3 60	
Boston Directory	5 00	
Telegram from Holyoke	15	
Blotting Paper, Feather Duster, etc.	2 50	
Cashman, Keating & Co., Bookcase	50 00	
Owen A. Galvin, Professional Services	150 00	
Francis Supple, Safe	75 00	
T. Wholly, Carting Safe	8 00	
S. J. M. Gilbride, 1 office table, 4 chairs	18 00	
J. J. Lanigan, H.F.S., Postage, Envelopes, Paper, and Expressing.	10 00	
T. A. Jackson, Insurance of Office	18 00	
S. Hobbs & Co., Blank Book and Brush	3 45	
Telegram to H. C. R. Watson	35	
Messenger.	45	
S. J. M. Gilbride, 8 Crape Bows	4 95	
Howe Scale Co., Postage Scale	4 80	
Cleaning Office	1 00	
Wm. Costello for Portable Light and Labor on Gas Fixtures	8 00	
		479 81
Deficit to April, 1887		117 86
Balance on hand		421 08
		$3,736 83

Due on Postal Cards charged by J. J. L. . . . $ 63 77
Due on Postal Cards charged since April, 1887 . . 113 82

An endeavor has been made in the foregoing to give the condition of the Order impartially, and to show, as nearly as possible, the actual results of the work of the past year. If any imperfections exist, it is more owing to want of material than a lack of desire on the part of your secretary to prevent. Respectfully submitted,

JAMES F. SUPPLE,

High Court Secretary-Treasurer.

HIGH COURT OFFICERS.

MASSACHUSETTS CATHOLIC ORDER OF FORESTERS.

Organized April 9, 1879.   Charted July 30, 1879.

FOR TERM ENDING APRIL 5, 1880.

R. W. High Chief Ranger,
D. F. O'SULLIVAN.

R. W. High Vice-Chief Ranger,
H. H. SULLIVAN.

R. W. H. P. Secretary.
FLORENCE A. LAWLER.

R. W. H. Treasurer,
JEREMIAH J. SULLIVAN.

R. W. H. Senior Conductor,
MICHAEL EDMONDS.

R. W. H. Junior Conductor,
JOSEPH STEWART.

R. W. H. Inside Sentinel,
WILLIAM COOK.

R. W. H. Outside Sentinel,
JOHN McLAUGHLIN.

HIGH COURT OFFICERS.

FOR TERM ENDING APRIL 20, 1881.

R. W. High Chief Ranger,

D. F. O'SULLIVAN . . . . Cathedral Court No. 1

R. W. H. Vice-Chief Ranger,

H. H. SULLIVAN . . . . . Cathedral Court No. 1

R. W. H. P. Secretary,

MICHAEL EDMONDS . . . . Cathedral Court No. 1

R. W. H. Treasurer,

JAMES F. SUPPLE . . . . . Columbus Court No. 9

R. W. H. Financial Secretary,

WALTER C. GRANT . . . . St. Patrick Court No. 7

R. W. H. Senior Conductor,

THOMAS RAY . . . . . . Cathedral Court No. 1

R. W. H. Junior Conductor,

JOSEPH STEWART . . . . Cathedral Court No. 1

R. W. H. Inside Sentinel,

FLORENCE A. LAWLER . . . . Cathedral Court No. 1

R. W. H. Outside Sentinel,

JOHN J. McLAUGHLIN . . . Cathedral Court No. 1

R. W. H. C. Physician,

JOHN G. BLAKE, M. D. . . . . Columbus Court No. 9

R. W. H. C. Chaplain,

REV. WILLIAM J. DALY . . . St. Joseph Court No. 11

HIGH COURT OFFICERS.

High Chief Ranger,

D. F. O'SULLIVAN . . . . Cathedral Court No. 1

High Vice-Chief Ranger,

OWEN A. GALVIN . . . . Cheverus Court No. 6

High Court Secretary,

MICHAEL EDMONDS' . . . . Cathedral Court No. 1

High Financial Secretary,

JAMES C. KENNY . . . . . Fulton Court No. 12

High Court Treasurer,

JAMES F. SUPPLE . . . . Columbus Court No. 6

High Senior Conductor,

THOMAS RAY . . . . . Cathedral Court No. 1

High Junior Conductor,

J. S. O'GORMAN . . . . Friendship Court No. 37

High Inside Sentinel,

P. A. HARTNETT . . . . Sherwood Court No. 8

High Outside Sentinel,

JOHN MCCARTHY . . . . . Sullivan Court No. 27

High Court Physician,

JOHN G. BLAKE, M. D. . . . Columbus Court No. 9

High Court Chaplain,

REV. WILLIAM J. DALY . . . St. Joseph Court No. 11

HIGH COURT OFFICERS.

For Term Ending April 18, 1883.

High Chief Ranger,

HON. OWEN A. GALVIN . . . . Cheverus Court No. 6

High Vice-Chief Ranger,

F. A. LAWLER* . . . . . Cathedral Court No. 1

JAMES J. MCLAUGHLIN . . . Americus Court No. 34

High Court Secretary,

B. J. O'DALY . . . . . . Erin Court No. 28

High Financial Secretary,

P. A. HARTNETT . . . . . Sherwood Court No. 8

High Court Treasurer,

JAMES F. SUPPLE . . . . Columbus Court No. 9

High Senior Conductor,

J. C. CARSON . . . . . Fitzpatrick Court No. 13

High Junior Conductor,

F. A. STRANGE . . . . Mt. Pleasant Court No. 20

High Inside Sentinel,

P. J. SULLIVAN . . . . . Fenwick Court No. 3

High Outside Sentinel,

T. DONOVAN . . . . . Lafayette Court No. 14

High Court Physician,

JAMES A. FLEMING, M. D. . . . Fenwick Court No. 3

High Court Chaplain,

REV. W. DALY . . . . . St. Joseph Court No. 11

*Resigned during year.

HIGH COURT OFFICERS.

For Term Ending April 16, 1884.

High Chief Ranger,

Owen A. Galvin . . . . . Cheverus Court No. 6

High Vice-Chief Ranger,

James J. McLaughlin . . . Americus Court No. 34

High Court Secretary,

B. J. O'Daly . . . . . . Erin Court No. 28

High Financial Secretary,

James J. Lanigan . . . . Cathedral Court No. 1

High Court Treasurer,

James F. Supple . . . . Columbus Court No. 9

High Senior Conductor,

J. C. Carson . . . . . Fitzpatrick Court No. 13

High Junior Conductor,

T. Donovan . . . . . Lafayette Court No. 14

High Inside Sentinel,

T. Sproules . . . . . St. Francis Court No. 4

High Outside Sentinel,

C. J. Hurley . . . . . St. Raphael Court No. 26

High Court Chaplain,

Rev. Hugh Roe O'Donnell . Star of the Sea Court No. 41

High Court Physician,

James A. Fleming, M. D. . . . Fenwick Court No. 3

HIGH COURT OFFICERS.

For Term Ending April 28, 1885.

High Chief Ranger,

James J. McLaughlin . . . Americus Court No. 34

High Vice-Chief Ranger,

T. Sproules . . . . St. Francis Court No. 4

High Court Secretary,

B. J. O'Daly . . . . . . Erin Court No. 28

High Financial Secretary,

James J. Lanigan . . . . Cathedral Court No. 1

High Court Treasurer,

James F. Supple . . . . Columbus Court No. 9

High Senior Conductor,

T. Donovan . . . . . Lafayette Court No. 14

High Junior Conductor,

J. Torndorf* . . . . Holy Trinity Court No. 51

High Inside Sentinel,

C. J. Hurley . . . . St. Raphael Court No. 26

High Outside Sentinel,

Hon. Owen A. Galvin, P. H. C. R. . Cheverus Court No. 6

High Court Physician,

John B. Moran, M. D. . . . St. Francis Court No. 4

High Court Chaplain,.

Rev. Hugh Roe O'Donnell . Star of the Sea Court No. 41

*Resigned — never served.

HIGH COURT OFFICERS.

FOR TERM ENDING APRIL 28, 1886.

High Chief Ranger,
JAMES J. MCLAUGHLIN . . . Americus Court No. 34

High Vice-Chief Ranger,
JAMES J. BARRY . . . . St. Alphonsus Court No. 21

High Court Secretary.
B. J. O'DALY . . . . . . Erin Court No. 28

High Financial Secretary,
JAMES J. LANIGAN . . . . Cathedral Court No. 1

High Court Treasurer,
JAMES F. SUPPLE . . . . . Columbus Court No. 9

High Senior Conductor,
JOHN H. WATSON . . . . . Essex Court No. 16

High Junior Conductor,
EDWARD RILEY . . . . St. Joseph's Court No. 11

High Inside Sentinel,
JEREMIAH G. FENNESSEY . . . St. James Court No. 54

High Outside Sentinel,
EDWARD TRACEY* . . . . St. Patrick Court No. 7
T. SPROULES . . . .

High Court Physician,
JOHN B. MORAN, M. D. . . . St. Francis Court No. 4

High Court Chaplain,
REV. HUGH ROE O'DONNELL . Star of the Sea Court No. 41
*Resigned—never served.

HIGH COURT OFFICERS.

For Term Ending April 20, 1887.

High Chief Ranger,

John H. Watson . . . . . Essex Court No. 16

High Vice-Chief Ranger,

Thomas Sproules . . . . St. Francis Court No. 4

High Court Secretary,

Bernard J. O'Daly . . . . . Erin Court No. 28

James J. Lanigan . . . . Cathedral Court No. 1
Acting from Dec. 1, 1886.

High Financial Secretary,

James J. Lanigan . . . . Cathedral Court No. 1

High Court Treasurer,

James F. Supple . . . . Columbus Court No. 9

High Senior Conductor,

Edward Riley . . . . St. Joseph Court No. 11

High Junior Conductor,

Jeremiah G. Fennessey . . St. James Court No. 54

High Inside Sentinel,

James R. McLaughlin, V. S. . . Middlesex Court No. 60

High Outside Sentinel,

John Brant . . . . . . Leo Court No. 5

High Court Physician,

John B. Moran, M. D. . . . St. Francis Court No. 4

High Court Chaplain,

Rev. Hugh Roe O'Donnell . Star of the Sea Court No. 41

HIGH COURT OFFICERS.

FOR TERM ENDING APRIL 18, 1888.

High Chief Ranger,

JOHN H. WATSON . . . . . Essex Court No. 16

High Vice-Chief Ranger,

THOMAS SPROULES . . . . St. Francis Court No. 4

High Court Secretary-Treasurer,

JAMES F. SUPPLE . . . . . Columbus Court No. 9

High Senior Conductor,

EDWARD RILEY . . . . . St. Joseph Court No. 11

High Junior Conductor,

JEREMIAH G. FENNESSEY . . St. James Court No. 54

High Inside Sentinel,

JAMES R. McLAUGHLIN, V. S. . . Middlesex Court No. 60

High Outside Sentinel,

PHILIP SMITH . . . . . Williams Court No. 19

High Court Physician,

JOSEPH D. COUCH, M. D. . . . Benedict Court No. 39

High Court Chaplain,

REV. HUGH ROE O'DONNELL . Star of the Sea Court No. 41

DEPUTY HIGH CHIEF RANGERS.

For Term Ending April 18, 1888.

Dist.	Comprising Courts.	D. H. C. R.	Members of	No.
1....	1, 57........	W. E. Shay................	St. Francis...........	4
2....	3, 6........	M. Edmonds...............	Cathedral............	1
3....	4........	J. J. Donovan.............	St. James............	54
4....	5, 41........	M. J. Kelley............	Williams.............	19
5....	7, 38........	H. F. Scanlan...........	Fulton...............	12
6....	8........	M. J. Killion............	St. Francis...........	4
7....	9, 34........	A. F. Caldwell............	St. Patrick...........	7
8....	10, 33........	J. S. Kenney...............	St. John............	33
9....	11........	Andrew Golding..........	Cheverus.............	5
10....	12........	W. T. Maloney...........	Constantine..........	49
11....	13, 35........	Henry Griffin............	St. Joseph............	11
12....	14........	T. F. Lyons.............	Emerald............	53
13....	15, 46........	J. A. Berrill.............	Constantine............	49
14....	16........	Timothy Donovan........	Lafayette............	14
15....	17........	J. P. McEnany.............	Williams............	19
16....	18, 24........	H. P. Muldoon............	St. Patrick...........	7
17....	19........	T. F. Doherty............	Leo..................	5
18....	20, 37........	P. A. Donovan............	SS. Peter and Paul...15	
19 20	21, 23........	Thomas Mulcahy..........	St. John............	23
21....	25........	E. F. Chamberlain........	St. Peter.............	18
22....	26, 62........	C. J. Hurley...............	St. Raphael..........	26
23....	28, 52........	M. J. Fitzgerald..........	Sherwood............	8
24....	29........	P. McCarthy.............	St. Thomas..........	29
25....	30........	J. B. Harding.............	Essex................	16
26....	32........	D. F. Sullivan............	Sherwood............	8
27....	39........	W. A. Flaherty..........	Benedict............	39
28....	43........	W. W. Hurley............	St. Mary............	43
29....	44, 58........	P. A. Murray.............	Charles River........	55
30....	45........	Edward Brown..........	Unity................	45
31....	47........	J. J. Flaherty.............	St. Anne............	47
32....	48, 66........	W. H. Rogers.............	Sarsfield............	48
33....	49........	P. A. Sullivan............	Americus............	34
34....	51........	J. J. Stephan............	Sherwood............	8
35....	53........	O. P. Sullivan............	Bass River..........	30
36....	54........	M. A. Farrell............	Columbus............	9
37....	55........	P. A. Mulligan............	Middlesex............	60
38....	59........	J. B. Ratigan.............	Worcester............	59
39....	60........	W. F. Rooney.............	Prospect............	58
40....	61........	J. P. Cleary................	St. Francis...........	4
41....	63........	J. J. Leonard.............	Gallagher............	64
42....	64........	J. J. Callanan...........	Shields...............	63
43....	65........	John A. Gaw..............	St. Bernard..........	44
At large...........		Thomas J. Dunn..........	Cathedral............	1

MEDICAL EXAMINERS.

For Term Ending April 18, 1888.

DISTRICT.	MEDICAL EXAMINER.	COURTS.
1 Boston	W. G. MacDonald, 221 Shawmut Av.	1, 28, 49, 51
2 Boston	E. T. Galligan, 88 Warren Street	20, 21, 37, 38, 52
3 Boston	W. A. Dunn, 60 Chambers Street	3, 8, 9, 35
4 Boston, Brookline	S. A. Callanan, Dudley Street	11, 34, 54, 61
5 East Boston	M. W. O'Keefe, Maverick Square	5, 41
6 Boston, East Boston	James F. Ferrey, Chelsea Street	13, 19
7 Boston	James E. Dorcey, 181 Harrison Av.	4, 6, 12
8 South Boston	W. H. Devine, 597 E. Broadway, S. B.	7, 15, 46
9 Dorchester	E. C. Bullard, Harrison Square	18, 24
10 Malden	C. D. McCarthy, Malden	10
11 Woburn	J. H. Conway, Woburn	32
12 Lynn	C. A. Ahearne, Lynn	14
13 Salem	Francis E. Hines, Salem	16
14 Charlestown, Somerville, E. Cambridge	Joseph D. Couch, Somerville	17, 33, 39
15 Quincy	Joseph M. Sheahan, Quincy	25
16 West Newton, Waltham	C. J. McCormick, Waltham	44, 58
17 Jamaica Plain	J. P. Broidrick, Jamaica Plain	57
18 Newton, Brighton	M. J. Kelley, Watertown	60, 65
19 Watertown	F. M. O'Donnell, Newton	55
20 Hyde Park	C. E. Edwards, Hyde Park	23
21 Dedham	A. H. Hodgdon, Dedham	26
22 Peabody	J. Shannahan, Peabody	53
23 Norwood	Dr. Plympton, Norwood	62
24 Beverly	Charles Haddock, Beverly	30
25 Gloucester	P. Mooney, Gloucester	47
26 Randolph, Brockton	Benedict Donovan, Brockton	29, 43
27 North Attleborough,	T. F. McDonough, N. Attleborough	48
28 Bridgewater	G. H. Watson, Bridgewater	45
29 Worcester	Joseph H. Kelley, Worcester	59
30 Holyoke	F. P. Donoghue, Holyoke	93
31 Springfield	A. J. Dunne, Springfield	64
32 Franklin	J. C. Gallison, Franklin	66
33 Canton	T. D. Lonergan, Canton	67

REPRESENTATIVES.

	REPRESENTATIVES.	COURT.	PROXY REPRESENTATIVES.
1	Michael Edmonds	Cathedral 1	H. H. Sullivan.
2	James J. Lanigan.............	" 1	Jeremiah Sullivan.
3	Thomas J. Dunn.............	" 1	D. F. O'Sullivan.
4	John J. Irving...............	Fenwick 3	Daniel Gallagher.
5	Thomas Sproules	St. Francis............. 4	James P. Cleary.
6	William E. Shay	" 4	John E. Heslan.
7	Thomas F. Doherty..........	Leo...................... 5	Daniel T. McCallion.
8	John Gallagher..............	" 5	John Brant.
9	Owen A. Galvin.............	Cheverus.............. 6	D. J. Harkins.
10	Andrew Golding	" 6	W. T. Rich.
11	A. F. Caldwell	St. Patrick............ 7	E. Tracy.
12	D. F. Sullivan	Sherwood 8	M. J. Fitzgerald.
13	John P. Dore	" 8	A. J. Lill.
14	R. Farrenkopf	" 8	J. J. Stephan.
15	James F. Supple.............	Columbus.............. 9	M. A. Farrell.
16	Patrick H. Desmond........	Iona 10	Thos. F. Powell.
17	Edward Riley...............	St. Joseph 11	Patrick M. Keating.
18	Henry Griffin	" 11	Daniel A. Cronin.
19	P. O'Loughlin...............	" 11	Matthew Dolan.
20	H. F. Scanlan...............	Fulton 12	Denis Shea.
21	F. McFarland...............	Fitzpatrick 13	Thos. F. McCullough.
22	John Hayes.................	Lafayette 14	C. A. Ahearne, M. D.
23	P. A. Donovan..............	SS. Peter & Paul 15	John B. White.
24	John H. Watson	Essex 16	John B. Harding.
25	Daniel J. O'Brien...........	" 16	Michael A. Dodd.
26	John Hurley	Hamilton 17	James A. McGee.
27	Jeremiah Chamberlain	St. Peter 18	John F. Brooks.
28	M. J. Kelly.................	Williams 19	J. P. McEnany.
29	Frank J. McGrath..........	Mt. Pleasant 20	Fred J. Crosby.
30	J. T. Brickley..............	St. Alphonsus..........21	Cornelius McCarthy.
31	F. S. Sullivan..............	St. John...............23	Charles F. Morrison.
32	M. Dunican.................	St. Gregory 24	John Hogan.
33	John F. Cole...............	St. Francis............25	Thomas J. Foley.
34	C. J. Hurley................	St. Raphael 26	
35	John T. Daly	Erin 28	J. O'Mara.
36	Thomas F. Sullivan.........	St. Thomas.............29	Patrick McCarthy.
37	O. P. Sullivan..............	Bass River 30	J. Murphy.
38	T. D. Hevey................	Qualey 32	John Maguire.
39	J. C. Dwyer................	St. John...............33	B. J. Brogan.
40	P. A. Sullivan..............	Americus 34	J. J. King.
41	Joseph O'Hare..............	Sheil 35	W. H. Pierce.
42	H. C. Byrne................	Friendship.............37	T. H. Duggan.
43	Peter Morris...............	St. Joseph 38	J. P. Ego.
44	Wm. A. Flaherty	Benedict 39	Joseph D. Couch, M. D.
45	T. Hoey...................	Star of the Sea........41	N. Fairclough.
46	W. W. Hurley	St. Mary 43	M. P. O'Connor.
47	John A. Gaw...............	St. Bernard ... .44	F. Cox.
48	William Condon.............	Unity 45	Edward Brown.
49	John Doolin	St. Augustine..........46	P. H. Kerrigan.
50	John J. Flaherty...........	St. Anne 47	Wm. F. Moore.
51	P. Ryan...................	Sarsfield 48	W. H. Rogers.
52	William Daughn............	Constantine............49	W. T. Maloney.
53	G. Kranefuss	Holy Trinity 51	J. Torndorf.
54	Hugh H. Collins...........	Highland 52	John J. Corbett.
55	James Sherry..............	Emerald ... .53	John J. Bartlett.
56	Jeremiah G. Fennessey.....	St. James 54	John J. Donovan.
57	James J. Barnes	Charles River 55	Michael E. Conroy.
58	Thomas F. Gallagher.......	" " 55	J. A. Burns.
59	J. H. Morton..............	Carroll 57	J. H. Cronin.
60	W. F. Rooney.............	Prospect 58	
61	J. B. Ratigan..............	Worcester 59	J. W. Doone.
62	T. J. Hartnett.............	Middlesex 60	J. R. McLaughlin.
63	M. Driscoll................	St. Lawrence 61	Daniel Frawley.
64	George A. O'Bryan	St. Catherine 62	R. E. Oldham.
65	J. J. Callanan	Shields................63	F. F. O'Neill.
66	J. J. Leonard..............	Gallagher 64	
67	Wm. Mackin................	St. Columbkill 65	
68	A. F. Staples...............	Griffin 66	Matthew S. Conroy.
69	Thomas D. Lonergan, M. D..	Canton 67	Gerald A. Healy.
70	L. J. Watson	St. Margaret..........68	

DIRECTORY.

NAME OF COURTS, TIME AND PLACE OF MEETING, OFFICERS AND THEIR ADDRESSES.

NO. AND COURT NAME.	OFFICERS.		ADDRESS, ETC.	
1. Cathedral, Boston. Instituted Sept. 3, 1879. Meets 1st and 3d Wednesday at Garfield Hall, 1125 Washington St., Boston.	C. R. R. S. F. S. T.	A. M. Lanigan, W. P. Walsh, R. S. Bowman, Michael Edmonds,	656 Harrison Ave., 101 E. Brookline St., 24 W. Second St., 7 Elmwood Pl.,	Boston " So. Boston Roxbury
3. Fenwick, Boston. Inst. Nov. 14, 1879. Meets 2d Thursday of each month at Lusitana Hall, 164 Hanover St., Boston.	C. R. R. S. F. S. T.	Daniel Gallagher, Jeremiah J. Crane, John Keenan, John J. Irving,	528 Broadway, 9 N. Bennett St., Rear, 7 N. Hanover Ct., 193 Salem St., Rear,	So. Boston Boston " "
4. St. Francis, Roxbury. Inst. Dec. 18, 1879. Meets 1st and 3d Wednesday, Tremont Hall, Tremont St., Roxbury.	C. R. R. S. F. S. T.	Thomas F. Crosby, J. J. O'Brien, Thos. J. Firmeran, Michael J. Killion,	3 Worthington St., 4 Vernon Pl., 780 Parker St., 61 Terrace St.,	Roxbury " " "
5. Leo, E. Boston. Inst. Jan 16, 1880. Meets 2d and 4th Wednesday, at 144 Meridian St., East Boston.	C. R. R. S. F. S. T.	George F. Lowe, John W. Heenan, Patrick J. Glynn, Michael Killilea,	271 Sumner St., 142 Arlington St., 334 Sumner St., 74 Everett St.,	E. Boston Chelsea E. Boston "
6. Cheverus, Boston. Inst. Feb. 11, 1880. Meets 1st and 3d Monday at 9 Elm St.	. . R. C. S. R.	James Cashen. John E. Leonard, James O. Kane, Edward O'Hara,	47 Moulton St., 24 Arch St., 43 Commerce St.,	Charlestown Boston "
7. St. Patrick, So. Boston. Inst. Feb. 16, 1880. Meets 2d and 4th Monday at 376 Broadway.	. . C. R. R.	A. F. Caldwell, J. H. Pentoney. J. J. Mahoney, J. F. Carroll,	317 Broadway, 263 Fourth St., 304 Broadway, 263 Fifth St.,	So. Boston " " "
8. Sherwood, Boston. Inst. March 4, 1880. Meets 1st and 3d Friday at 616 Washington St.	R. S. C. S. R.	Rudolph Farrenkopf, M. J. Fitzgerald, James H. Mitchell, Thomas J. Lane,	107 Hudson St., 14 Melrose St., 38 Dennis St., 121 Centre St.,	Boston " Roxbury "
9. Columbus, Boston. Inst. Mar. 9, 1880. Meets 2d Wednesday at 616 Washington St.	C. R. R. S. F. S. T.	John F. Cleary, Wm. H. Murphy, M. T. Gleason, M. T. Milliken,	5 Pynchon St., 62 Allen St., 53 Harvard St., 282 E St.,	Roxbury Boston " So. Boston
10. Iona, Malden. Inst. Mar. 15, 1880. Meets 1st and 3d Thursday at Deliberative Hall, Pleasant St., Malden.	R. S. C. S. R.	Patrick H. Desmond, John F. Coleman, Michael J. Connelly, Paul J. McMahon.		Malden " " "
11. St. Joseph, Boston. Inst. Mar. 22, 1880. Meets 2d and 4th Wednesday, at Y. M. L. Hall, 60 1-2 Leverett St.	C. R. R. F. S. T.	Charles F. Dolan, James E. Kenely, C. W. Mullen, Daniel Carney,	10 Parkman St., 5 Spring St., 17 Parkman St. 5 Revere St. Pl.,	Boston " " "
12. Fulton, Boston. Inst. Mar. 18, 1880. Meets 1st Friday at Bay State Hall, 197 Shawmut Ave., Boston.	C. R. R. S. F. S. T.	Michael O'Brien, Henry F. Scanlon, Thomas Ward, Michael Nolan,	108 E. Canton St., 127 Union Park St., 546 Dorchester Ave., 64 Hampden St.,	Boston " So. Boston Roxbury
13. Fitzpatrick, Boston. Inst. May 5, 1880. Meets 2d and 4th Tuesday at Lusitana Hall, Hanover St.	C. R. R. S. F. S. T.	Antonio Thompson, James D. Mahoney, Frank J. McFarland, John M. Jordan,	5 Vernon Pl., 10 Henchman St. 425 Hanover St., 5 N. Hanover Court,	Roxbury " Boston "
14. Lafayette, Lynn. Inst. June 8, 1880. Meets 1st and 3d Wednesday, Emmett Hall, 65 Munroe St.	C. R. R. S. F. S. T.	J. J. Donahoe, J. D. Casey, G. A. Lemasney. T. Donovan,		Lynn " " "

15. SS. Peter & Paul, So. Boston. Inst. June 25, 1880. Meets 1st and 3d Tuesday at Lyceum Hall, 10 Broadway.	C. R. R. S. F. S. T.	Edward J. Leary. Patrick A. Donovan, John S. White, James Dempsey,	25 W. Fifth St., 292 D St., 83 Baxter St., 118 W. Fourth St.,
16. Essex, Salem. Inst. June 23, 1880. Meets 1st and 3d Wednesday at 199 Essex St.	C. R. R. S. F. S. T.	F. E. Hines, M. D., Wm. H. Morgan, John Chenery, Daniel Hallohan,	158 Washington St.,
17. Hamilton, Charlestown. Inst. July 8, 1880. Meets 2d and 4th Friday at 162 Main St.	C. R. R. S. F. S. T.	John Hurley, T. W. Murray, S. J. Cochrane, - William H. Breen,	13 Jerome Pl., 44 Warren St.,
18. St. Peter, Dorchester. Inst. July 22, 1880. Meets 1st and 3d Thursday at Blake's Hall.	C. R. R. S. F. S. T.	Henry McLaughlin, Eugene H. Buckley, Thomas Crowne, Edw. F. Chamberlain,	Dickens St., 1155 Dorchester Ave., Ashmont St., Norfolk St.,
19. Williams, E. Boston. Inst. Sept. 16, 1880. Meets 1st and 3d Thursday at O. F. Hall, Maverick Sq.	C. R. R. S. F. S. T.	F. S. Maloney, M. J. Kelley, Edward Hughes, Thomas Arthur,	123 Maverick St., 107 Paris St., 66 Adams St., 72 Marginal St.,
20. Mt. Pleasant, Roxbury. Inst. Oct. 20, 1880. Meets 2d and 3d Wednesday at 2319 Washington St.	C. R. R. S. S. T.	Garrett H. Keefe, Daniel F. Lynch, John J. Gately, F. J. Crosby,	63 Palmer St., 64 Regent St., 3 Jarvis Pl., 139 Eustis St.,
21. St Alphonsus, Roxbury. Inst. Oct. 13, 1880. Meets 2d and 4th Wednesday at Vernon Hall, cor. Tremont and Culvert Sts.	C. R. R. S. F. S. F.	James T. Brickley, Frank Walsh, John Killion, Cornelius McCarthy.	8 Oscar St., 101 Conant St., 8 Oscar St., 36 Elmwood St.,
23. St John, Hyde Park. Inst. Dec. 14, 1880. Meets 2d Monday at Lyric Hall.	C. R. R. S. F. S. T.	Charles F. Morrison, Thomas Murray, F. S. Sullivan, John Brady,	
24. St. Gregory, Milton. Inst. Dec. 20, 1880. Meets 1st Tuesday at Associates Hall.	C. R. R. S. F. S. T.	E. W. Daley, Wm. Brophy, C. J. Lyons, Patrick Fallon,	
25. St. Francis, W. Quincy. Inst. Dec. 21, 1880. Meets 2d and 4th Tuesday at Foresters' Hall.	C. R. R. S. F. S. T.	John C. Pendis, James L. Fennessey, John H. McGovern, John Hussey,	
26. St. Raphael, Dedham. Inst. Dec. 31, 1880. Meets 1st and 3d Sunday at Parochial Hall.	C. R. R. S. F. S. T.	John F. Reilly, John F. Barrett, Patrick Daley, P. O'Sullivan,	
28. Erin, Boston. Inst. Feb. 3, 1881. Meets 2d and 4th Tuesday at 1125 Washington St., Greystone Hall.	C. R. R. S. F. S. T.	Daniel Shannon, C. J. Lynch, W. A. Daly, J. O'Mara,	98 W. Dedham St. 10 Shelburn St., 10 Vinton St., 93 Pembroke St.,
29. St. Thomas, Brockton. Inst. Feb. 17, 1881. Meets 2d and 4th Thursday at Hibernian Hall, E. Elm St.	C. R. R. S. F. S. T.	T. F. Roach, Patrick Brennan, Fred. L. Smith, John W. Minton.	
30. Bass River, Beverly. Inst. Feb. 24, 1881. Meets 1st Thursday at Bells Hall, Cabot St.	C. R. R. S. F. S. T.	David H. Guinevan, Timothy Hennessey, Patrick Guinevan, Jeremiah Murphy,	
32. Qualey, Woburn. Inst. Mar. 2, 1881. Meets 1st and 3d Wednesday at Hibernian Hall, Main St.	C. R. R. S. F. S. T.	Thomas D. Hevey, Frank E. Tracey, Thomas Finnegan, Wm. O'Brien,	

33. St. John, E. Cambridge.	C. R.	Thomas Cawley,	E. Cambridge
Inst. Mar. 3, 1881.	R. S.	P. A. McCloskey,	19 Seventh St., "
Meets 3d. Monday at 115½ Cam-	F. S.	J. F. O'Connell,	"
bridge St.	T.	James Doherty,	"
34. Americus, Boston.	C. R.	John W. Brown,	792 Shawmut Ave., rear, Boston
Inst. Mar. 15, 1881.	R. S.	M. Hegarty,	26 W. Dedham St., "
Meets 1st and 3d Thursday at	F. S.	P. P. Sullivan,	13 Waltham St., "
Greystone Hall, 1125 Wash-	T.	Daniel Sullivan,	27 Laurel St., Roxbury
ington St.			
35. Sheil, Boston.	C. R.	John C. Carson,	6 Charter St., Boston
Inst. Mar. 18, 1881.	R. S.	C. J. Kelley,	2 Phipps Pl., "
Meets 1st Friday.	F. S.	Thomas Jacobs,	89 Chelsea St., Charlestown
	T.	Wm. Connolly,	24 Sheafe St., Boston
37. Friendship, Roxbury.	C. R.	Joseph W. Heenan,	5 Rochdale House, Burney St., Rox.
Inst. Mar. 25, 1881.	R. S.	Henry A. Kleh,	6 Willow Park, "
Meets 1st and 3d Monday at	F. S.	W. F. Arkinson,	141 Darmouth St., Boston
Old School Hse., Weston St.	T.	Jeremiah J. Hurley,	957 Tremont St., "
38. St. Joseph, Roxbury.	C. R.	Peter Morris,	Geneva Ave., Grove Hall, Dor.
Inst. Mar. 29, 1881.	R. S.	Wm. B. Reardon,	380 Warren St., Roxbury
Meets 1st and 3d Tuesday at	F. S.	John P. Ego,	411 " " "
Highland Hall, Warren St.	T.	M. Lennon,	Washington St., Dorchester
39. Benedict, Somerville.	C. R.	Joseph D. Couch M. D.,	Somerville
Inst. Mar. 31, 1881.	R. S.	James J. Muldoon,	"
Meets 2d Friday at Temper-	F. S.	Wm. F. Flaherty,	"
ance Hall, Hawkins St.	T.	Cornelius McGonagle,	"
41. Star of the Sea, E. Boston.	C. R.	Hugh Stewart,	Moore St., E. Boston
Inst. Dec. 13, 1881.	R. S.	C. H Cragin,	Leyden St,, "
Meets 1st Wednesday, School	F. S.	T. E. Cragin,	" " "
House Hall, cor. Saratoga	T.	N. Fairclough,	" " "
and Moore Sts.			
43. St. Mary, Randolph.	C. R.	W. W. Hurley,	Randolph
Inst. Sept. 4, 1882.	R. S.	Redmond P. Banett,	"
Meets 1st Sunday at Hibernian	F. S.	Charles S. Dolan,	"
Hall, North St.	T.	Patrick Brady,	"
44. St. Bernard, W. Newton.	C. R.	M. J. Duane,	W. Newton
Inst. Sept. 23, 1882.	R. S.	T. C. Donovan,	"
Meets 1st and 3d Monday at	F. S.	B. D. Farrell,	"
Foresters' Hall, Waltham St.	T.	John W. Gaw,	"
45. Unity, Bridgewater.	C. R.	William Condon,	Bridgewater
Inst. Nov. 12, 1882.	R. S.	David Cashon,	"
Meets 2d and 4th Tuesday at	F. S.	Edward Brown,	"
Masonic Hall, South St.	T.	James Clare,	"
46. St. Augustine, So. Boston.	C. R.	P. H. Kerrigan,	127 West Eighth St., So. Boston
Inst. Nov. 14, 1882.	R. S.	J. E. Murphy,	50 Lexington St., Charlestown
Meets 2d and 4th Thursday at	F. S.	J. M. Rigby,	44 Fifth St., So. Boston
376 Broadway.	T.	J. F. McNulty,	12 Woodward St., "
47. St. Anne's, Gloucester.	C. R.	John J. Flaherty,	Gloucester
Inst. Dec. 22. 1882.	R. S.	John F. Riley,	4 Sadler St., "
Meets 1st and 4th Tuesday at	F. S.	W. F. Moore,	"
G. A. R. Hall.	T.	Daniel Carroll,	"
48. Sarsfield, No. Attleboro.	C. R.	Thomas Kelly,	N. Attleboro
Inst. Mar. 6, 1883.	R. S.	M. Joseph Zilch,	"
Meets every Tuesday at Bar-	F. S.	Edward A. Irvine,	"
ton's Hall.	T.	John J. Casey,	"
49. Constantine, Boston.	C. R.	Wm. Daughn,	16 Bennett St., Boston
Inst. Apr. 5, 1883.	R. S.	M. J. Danehy,	138 Lexington St., "
Meets 2d and 4th Thursday at	F. S.	John J. Kilroy,	29 Marcella St., Roxbury
Greystone Hall, 1125 Wash-	T.	James T. Riley,	6 Chauncy St., Boston
ington St.			
51 Holy Trinity, Boston.	C. R.	Gerhard Kranefuss,	2 Acton St., Boston
Inst. Apr. 13, 1883.	R. S.	Joseph G. Mees,	4 Acton St., "
Meets 2d Sunday, at Casino,	F. S.	Thomas Gerhard,	29 Vernon St., Roxbury
133 Shawmut Ave.	T.	Adam Lorenz,	67 W. Sixth St., So. Boston

DIRECTORY — Continued.

No. and Court Name.	Officers.	Address, Etc.
52. Highland, Roxbury. Inst. Apr. 16, 1883. Meets 2d Monday at Vernon Hall, Tremont St., corner Culvert.	C. R. M. J. Driscoll, R. S. John P. Scannell, F. S. John J. Corbett, T. Thomas O'Flynn,	22 Hallock St., Roxbury 33 Prentiss St., " 300 Ruggles St., " Linden Park, "
53. Emerald, Peabody. Inst. July 2, 1883. Meets 1st Thursday at Main St., near the square.	C. R. James B. Carberry, R. S. Daniel J. Sweeney, F. S. Daniel J. O'Connor, T. Thomas F. Hutchinson,	Peabody " " "
54. St. James, Boston. Inst. July 2, 1883. Meets 1st and 3d Tuesday at 820 Washington St.	C. R. T. W. O'Rourke, R. S. D. J. Collins, F. S. J. J. Desmond, T. Jeremiah G. Fennessey,	Boston St., Dorchester 314 Fourth St., So. Boston 286 Third St., " Court House,
55. Charles River, Watertown. Inst. Oct. 8, 1883. Meets 2d and 4th Tuesday at Forester Hall, Main St.,	C. R. J. A. Burns, R. S. J. H. Carroll, F. S. T. F. Kelley, T. J. J. Barnes,	Watertown " " "
57. Carroll, Jamacia Plain. Inst. June 30, 1885. Meets 1st Friday K. of H. Hall, Centre St.	C. R. James Moulton, R. S. J. H. Lennon, F. S. J. H. Logan, T. Wm. Rooney,	1 Mount Hope St., Jamaica Plain Hyde Park Ave., " " "
58. Prospect, Waltham. Inst. Aug. 25, 1885. Meets 3d Sunday at A. O. H. Hall, Main St.	C. R. Michael J. Boland, R. S. Michael J. Lally, F. S. T. Timothy F. Buckley,	
59. Worcester, Worcester. Inst. Dec. 17, 1885. Meets 1st and 3d Thursday at I. C. B. S. Hall, 98 Front St.	C. R. Timothy H. Murphy, R. S. Charles G. Murray, F. S. James A. Fitzgerald, T. James Eaton,	19 Jaques Ave., Worcester 66 " " " Cor. Green and Gold St., " 16 Ingalls St., "
60. Middlesex, Newton. Inst. Feb. 19, 1886. Meets 2d and 4th Tuesday at Brackett's Block, Centre St.	C. R. P. A. Milligan, R. S. M. J. Joyce, F. S. R. Beard, T. G. E. Stuart,	Newton " " "
61. St. Lawrence, Brookline. Meets 1st and 3d Tuesday at Lyceum Hall, Wash'ton St.	C. R. Patrick Johnson, R. S. John Nolan, F. S. John M. O'Connor, T. James F. Donovan,	Davis Ave., Brookline Thayer Pl., " Fay Pl., " 35 Walnut St., "
62. St. Catharine, Norwood. Inst. Dec. 21, 1886. Meets 1st and 3d Wednesday at Casey's Hall.	C. R. John T. Brady, R. S. R. E. Oldham, F. S. Daniel Murray, T. John Gillooly,	Norwood " " "
63. Shields, Holyoke. Inst. Jan. 14, 1887. Meets 1st Wednesday and 4th Sunday at O'Niell's Hall, High St.	C. R. Jeremiah J. Callanan, R. S. John F. Riley, F. S. Jeremiah J. O'Leary, T. J. J. Burke,	107 Dwight St., Holyoke 159 Elm St., " 110 Dwight St., " 2 Dwight St., "
64. Gallagher, Springfield. Inst. April 17, 1887. Meets 2d and 4th Thursday at C. M. Hall, cor. Main and State Sts.	C. R. John J. Leonard, R. S. John J. Cruse, F. S. Wm. J. McCann, T. James J. Crean,	City Hall, Springfield " " "
65. St. Columbkill, Brighton. Inst. May 26, 1887. Meets 1st and 3d Tuesday at O. F. Hall, Brighton.	C. R. Wm. J. Van Etten, R. S. John Comerford, F. S. M. R. Murphy, T. Wm. J. Maguire,	Brighton " " "
66. Griffin, Franklin. Inst. Sept. 12, 1887. Meets 1st and 3d Tuesday in Basement of Church.	C. R. A. F. Staples, R. S. M. F. Conroy, F. S. D. W. Holloran, T. J. J. McCarthy,	Franklin " " "

DIRECTORY — Continued.

No. and Court Name.	Officers.		Address, Etc.
67. Canton, Canton. Inst. Jan. 26, 1888. Meets 1st and 3d Monday at Washington St. Hall.	C. R. R. S. F. S. T.	Edward C. Murphy, G. A Healy, James E. Grimes, Patrick E. Healey,	Ca " " . "
68. St. Margaret, Beverly Farms. Inst. April 14, 1888. Meets 1st and 3d Wednesdays, Marshall's Hall, cor. Hale and West Sts.	C. R. R. S. F. S. T.	Lawrence J. Watson, D. M. Linehan, Samuel A. Fogg, Patrick W. Brady.	Beverly Fa " " "
69. Stoughton, Stoughton. Inst. June 7, 1888. Meets 1st and 3d Wednesdays at K. of L. Hall, cor. Wash- ington St. and R. R. Ave.	C. R. R. S. F. S. T.	A. H. McDonald, James F. Cotter, John Madden, W. A. Welsh,	Stough " " "

NINTH ANNUAL CONVENTION

OF THE

Massachusetts Catholic Order of Foresters

HELD AT GARFIELD HALL, 1125 WASHINGTON STREET, BOSTON,

APRIL 18, 1888.

In compliance with the following call, the Representatives of the various Courts assembled in Garfield Hall, Wednesday, April 18, 1888.

MASSACHUSETTS CATHOLIC ORDER OF FORESTERS.

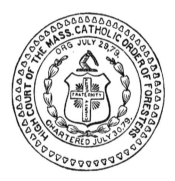

HIGH STANDING COMMITTEE.

597 Washington Street,

BOSTON, March 31, 1888.

To the Officers and Members of the Massachusetts Catholic Order of Foresters.

BROTHERS, — In accordance with the powers vested in the High Standing Committee of the Massachusetts Catholic Order of Foresters (under Art. IV. Constitution of the High Court, Page 11), a call is hereby issued for the assembling of Representatives of the Subordinate Courts of the Massachusetts Catholic Order of Foresters in Annual Session of the High Court of the Order, to be held at Garfield Hall, No. 1125 Washington Street, Boston, to be opened in regular form at 9.30 o'clock, A.M., on Wednesday, the eighteenth day of April A.D., 1888, as provided for in the High Court Constitution.

The basis of Representation shall be as laid down in Art. II., Sec. 3, Constitution of High Court, page 8.

Forms of Credential to the Annual Session of the High Court accompany this Call, one to be retained and held by the Representative for use at the Convention. If the Credential be transferred for cause, this should be stated on the back of Credential under the endorsements of Chief Ranger and Recording Secretary of the Court.

By order of the High Standing Committee,

JOHN H. WATSON,

High Chief Ranger.

JAMES F. SUPPLE,

High Court Secretary-Treasurer.

The hour having arrived, the High Chief Ranger, John H. Watson, called the Convention to order.

High Senior Conductor, Edward Riley, and High Junior Conductor, Jeremiah G. Fennessey, reported all the Officers of the High Court present and in their places.

High Chief Ranger Watson then opened the Convention in due form.

High Chief Ranger Watson announced the following: —

COMMITTEE ON CREDENTIALS.

Bros. James J. Lanigan	.	.	of Cathedral	No.	1
Andrew Golding	.	.	" Cheverus	"	6
Thomas Hoey.	.	.	" Star of the Sea	"	41
William Daughan	.	.	" Constantine	"	49
Rudolph Farrenkopf	.	" Sherwood	"	8
J. J. Barnes	.	.	" Charles River	"	55
John Hayes	.	.	" La Fayette	"	14

On motion of High Senior Conductor, Edward Riley, it was

Voted to take a recess of ten minutes to give the Committee on Credentials time to report.

At expiration of recess, the Chairman of the Committee on Credentials, Bro. James J. Lanigan, made the following report: —

Fifty-four Representatives were present from forty-six Courts, as follows: —

Cathedral, No. 1	.	.	.	James J. Lanigan.
" "	.	.	.	Michael Edmonds.
" "	.	.	.	Thomas J. Dunn.
Fenwick, No. 3	.	.	.	John J. Irving.
St. Francis, No. 4	.	.	.	Thomas Sproules.
" "	.	.	.	William E. Shay.
Cheverus, No. 6	.	.	.	Andrew Golding.
Sherwood, No. 8	.	.	.	D. F. Sullivan.
" "	.	.	.	R. Farrenkopf.
" "	.	.	.	John P. Dore.
Columbus, No. 9	.	.	.	James F. Supple.
St. Joseph, No. 11	.	.	.	Edward Riley.
" "	.	.	.	Henry Griffin.

St. Joseph, No. 11	Patrick O'Loughlin.
Fulton, No. 12	Henry F. Scanlan.
La Fayette, No. 14	John Hayes.
SS. Peter and Paul, No. 15	P. A. Donovan.
Essex, No. 16	John H. Watson.
St. Peter, No. 18	Jere. Chamberlain.
Mt. Pleasant, 20	F. J. McGrath.
St. Alphonsus, No. 21	J. T. Brickley.
St. John, No. 23	F. S. Sullivan.
St. Gregory, No. 24	Michael Dunican.
St. Francis, No. 25	John F. Cole.
St. Raphael, No. 26	C. J. Hurley.
Erin, No. 28	John T. Daly.
St. Thomas, No. 29	Thomas F. Sullivan.
Qualey, No. 32	Thomas D. Hevey.
St. John, No. 33	John C. Dwyer.
Americus, No. 34	P. A. Sullivan.
Shiel, No. 35	J. P. J. Ward.
Friendship, No. 37	H. C. Byrne.
St. Joseph, No. 38	P. Morris.
Benedict, No. 39	Joseph D. Couch, M.D.
St. Bernard, No. 44	John A. Gaw.
Unity, No. 45	William Condon.
St. Augustine, No. 46	John Doolin.
St. Anne, No. 47	John J. Flaherty.
Sarsfield, No. 48	Patrick Ryan.
Constantine, No. 49	William Daughan.
Holy Trinity, No. 51	Gerhard Kranefuss.
Highland, No. 52	H. H. Collins.
Emerald, No. 53	James Sherry.
St. James, No. 54	Jeremiah G. Fennessey.
Charles River, No. 55	J. J. Barnes.
" "	T. F. Gallagher.
Carroll, No. 57	James H. Morton.
Worcester, No. 59	J. B. Ratigan.
Middlesex, No. 60	T. J. Hartnett.
St. Catharine, No. 62	G. A. O'Bryan.
Shields, No. 63	J. J. Callanan.
Gallagher, No. 64	J. J. Leonard.
St. Columbkill, No. 65	William Mackin.
St. Margaret, No. 68	Lawrence J. Watson.

Voted to accept report of Committee on Credentials.

No. 4 in Order of Business was then taken up by High Chief Ranger, John H. Watson, and the High Court Secretary-Treasurer called the roll.

Fifty-three Representatives answered the roll call.

No. 5 in Order of Business was announced by the High Chief Ranger and it was

Voted to dispense with reading of the record of the last Convention.

No. 6 in Order of Business was announced by the High Chief Ranger, and on motion of Bro. John Hayes of La Fayette No. 14 it was

Voted to dispense with reading reports of High Standing Committee and High Court Secretary-Treasurer, as the printed reports were in the hands of the Representatives.

No. 7 in Order of Business was next taken up and High Chief Ranger, John H. Watson, announced the following Committees :

ON CONSTITUTION.

Hon. O. A. Galvin	. .	of Cheverus	No. 6
" John P. Dore	. .	" Sherwood	" 8
John B. Ratigan	. .	" Worcester	" 59
J. J. Callanan	. . .	" Shields	" 63
Gerald A. Healey	. .	" Canton	" 67
P. A. Donovan	. . .	" SS. Peter & Paul	" 15
A. F. Staples	. . .	" Griffin	" 66

ON FINANCE.

John J. Flaherty	. .	of St. Anne	No. 47
James J. Lanigan	. .	" Cathedral	" 1
W. F. Rooney	. .	" Prospect	" 58
John A. Gaw	. . .	" St. Bernard	" 44
A. F. Caldwell	. . .	" St. Patrick	" 7
J. J. Leonard	. . .	" Gallagher	" 64
John F. Cole	. . .	" St. Francis	" 25

ON APPEALS.

Michael Edmonds	. .	of Cathedral	No. 1
T. F. Sullivan	. . .	" St. Thomas	" 29
John J. Irving	. . .	" Fenwick	" 3
D. J. O'Brien	. . .	" Essex	" 16
James Sherry	. . .	" Emerald	" 53
Wm. Mackin	. . .	" St. Columbkill	" 65
Wm. Condon	. . .	" Unity	" 45

ON PETITIONS.

Thomas J. Dunn	. .	of Cathedral	No. 1
F. J. McFarland	. . .	" Fitzpatrick	" 13
L. J. Watson	. . .	" St. Margaret	" 68
Jere. Chamberlain	. .	" St. Peter	" 18
P. A. Sullivan	. . .	" Americus	" 34
W. A. Flaherty	. . .	" Benedict	" 39
H. H. Collins	. . .	" Highland	" 52

ON STATE OF THE ORDER.

Hon. T. F. Doherty	. .	of Leo	No. 5

P. H. Desmond .	.	.	of Iona	No. 10
J. T. Gallagher .	.	.	" Charles River	" 55
T. J. Hartnett	.	.	" Middlesex	" 60
G. A. O'Bryan .	.	.	" St. Catharine	" 62
Hon. W. W. Hurley .		.	" St. Mary	" 43
Jere. Murphy	.	.	" Bass River	" 30

ON SECRET WORK.

John T. Daly	.	.	of Erin	No. 28
John Gallagher .	.	.	" Leo	" 5
G. Kranefuss	.	.	" Holy Trinity	" 51
M. Driscoll .	.	.	" St. Lawrence	" 61
J. C. Dwyer	.	.	" St. John	" 33
M. J. Kelly .	.	.	" Williams	" 19
P. Ryan .	.	.	" Sarsfield	" 48

High Chief Ranger Watson announced No. 8 in Order of Business.

Bro. Ratigan, of Worcester No. 59, offered resolution relating to a badge for general use by members of the Order. ·

Referred to Committee on State of the Order.

Bro. Ryan, of Sarsfield No. 48, offered petition from his Court, asking for duplicate applications.

Referred to Committee on Petitions.

Bro. Lanigan, of Cathedral No. 1, offered following amendment to the Constitution: "Strike out four last lines on page 44, Art. V., Sect. 1."

Referred to Committee on Constitution.

Bros. Golding, Caldwell, Byrne, Griffin, McGrath, Sherry O'Loughlin, Ward, offered amendments to the Constitution.

All referred to Committee on Constitution.

Bro. Driscoll, of St. Lawrence No. 61, offered petition for change in Secret Work.

Referred to Committee on Secret Work.

Bro. McGrath offered various resolutions.

Referred to Committee on Constitution.

Bro. Hartnett, of Middlesex No. 60, offered a resolution.

Referred to Committee on State of the Order.

Bro. Lanigan, Chairman of Committee on Credentials, reported that Credentials had been presented by

Hon. T. F. Doherty	.	.	of Leo	No. 5
P. H. Desmond	.	.	" Iona	" 10
Thos. Hoey .	.	.	" Star of the Sea	" 41
Hon. O. A. Galvin	.	.	" Cheverus	" 6
M. J. Kelly .	.	.	" Williams	" 19

M. Driscoll	.	.	.	.	of St. Lawrence	No. 61
A. F. Staples	.	.	.	.	" Griffin	" 66
G. A. Healy	.	.	.	.	" Canton	" 67

Voted to accept the report of the Committee on Credentials.

Bro. Lanigan, Chairman of Committee on Credentials, reported that Bro. J. H. Cronin, of Carroll Court No. 57, presented a credential as regular Representative, although the Committee had already received the credential of James H. Morton as the regular Representative.

Voted to refer the matter to the Committee on Credentials, and said Committee retired to consider the case.

Bro. McGrath, of Mt. Pleasant No. 20, objected to the disposition made of his resolutions, and asked to have them sent to committee on State of the Order.

High Chief Ranger Watson declined to make the change.

Bro. McGrath moved to take the sense of the Convention on the disposition of his resolutions.

High Chief Ranger Watson stated the question. On the motion being put decided the motion lost.

Bro. McGrath doubted the vote.

High Chief Ranger Watson put the motion again, and asked for a standing vote; the result was 22 yea, 23 nay, and the motion was declared lost.

Bro. Edmonds, of Cathedral No. 1, raised the point of order that a committee was out and no business could be done.

High Chief Ranger Watson decided point well taken.

Voted to take a recess until Committee on Credentials were ready to report.

In a short time the Convention was called to order, and Bro. Lanigan, Chairman of the Committee on Credentials, reported that James H. Morton was entitled to the seat as regular Representative from Carroll Court No. 57.

Voted to allow the contestants five minutes each in which to make statements.

Bros. J. H. Cronin and James H. Morton then addressed the Convention, each giving his reasons for the contest.

Bro. Lanigan, for the Committee on Credentials, said "the committee had decided on the facts presented, and reported unanimously in favor of James H. Morton, on the ground that at the election held in March, no ballot was taken as the Constitution provides; at a subsequent meeting, specially called and held in due form, James H. Morton was constitutionally elected and the Committee so decide."

After some debate by Bros. Dunican, Morris, Byrne, and others, it was voted to accept the report of the Committee on Credentials, and High Chief Ranger Watson declared Bro. James H. Morton the regular Representative from Carroll No. 57.

No. 9 in Order of Business was taken up.

Bro. Thomas J. Dunn, Chairman of Committee on Petitions, reported on the petition of Sarsfield Court No. 48, for "duplicate applications for membership to be issued to members of the Order" as follows: .

"In the opinion of the Committee, some measure looking to the issuance of certificates of membership to the Order is necessary, and the Committee recommend that the drawing up of these certificates and their issuance to the Brothers of this Order, be referred to the High Standing Committee with full powers to act."

Voted to accept and adopt the report of the Committee on Petitions.

Bro. John T. Daly, Chairman of the Committee on Secret Work, reported as follows:

"The Committee on Secret Work beg leave to report that they have given the matter due consideration. In their opinion, new forms are not necessary, but practical workings of existing forms are requisite.

"Quarterly changes in pass-word should be made as required by Constitution, and Courts promptly notified.

"We recommend greater diligence by Deputy High Chief Rangers in transmitting the new pass-words, and the exemplification of such Secret Work as may from time to time be imparted them by the High Standing Committee."

Voted to accept and adopt the report of the Committee on Secret Work.

Bro. Galvin, Chairman of Committee on Constitution, said his Committee was ready to report on the matters referred to that Committee.

On the amendment offered by Bro. Ward "That the Constitution be so amended that the Annual Convention shall meet on consecutive days until it adjourned without day," the Committee reported ought to be adopted.

Bros. Ward, Callanan, C. J. Hurley, Ryan, Ratigan, and Daly debated the question.

On motion of Bro. Daly the previous question was ordered.

Voted to accept and adopt the report.

On the amendment offered by Bro. McGrath to retain a portion of each call to form a Reserve Fund, the Committee reported inexpedient.

Voted to accept the report.

On the amendment to take the power of approval or rejection of applications for membership in the Order, away from the High Standing Committee, the Committee reported inexpedient.

Voted to accept the report.

On the amendment offered by Bro. Kranefuss that in any month when no call was required, a sum equal to a call be collected and set aside as a Reserve Fund, the Committee reported inexpedient.

Voted to accept the report.

On the amendment offered by Bro. Lanigan to strike out in Art. V. Sect. 1, all assessment on ages over fifty, the Committee reported ought to be adopted.

Voted to accept and adopt the report.

On amendment offered by Bro. O'Loughlin to take away certain powers of the High Standing Committee during recess of High Court, the Committee reported inexpedient.

Bros. O'Loughlin, Galvin, Daly, and Ratigan discussed the question.

On motion of Bro. Ratigan the previous question was ordered.

Voted to accept the report of the Committee.

The vote was doubted, and High Chief Ranger Watson called for a standing vote. The count showed 42 yea, 13 nay, and the High Chief Ranger declared the motion carried.

On amendment offered by Bro. O'Loughlin to add a Finance Committee of five members to the High Standing Committee, the Committee reported inexpedient.

High Chief Ranger Watson said the question was on accepting the report of the Committee.

Bro. O'Loughlin spoke against the report.

Bro. Callanan rose to a point of order, that Bro. O'Loughlin was not speaking to the question.

High Chief Ranger Watson decided the point not well taken.

Bro. O'Loughlin continued and was again called to order by Bro. Callanan.

High Chief Ranger Watson decided that as Bro. O'Loughlin

claimed to be coming to the question he was in order and could proceed.

Voted to lay on the table.

On amendment offered by Bro. O'Loughlin to Art. VIII., Sect. 1, after the word "Court" in fourth line, "and all moneys shall be deposited in their joint names," the Committee reported ought to be adopted.

Voted to accept the report.

On amendment offered by Bro. O'Loughlin to Art. XIII., Sect. 3, after the word "shall" in fifth line, "every six months or oftener if a majority of them deem it necessary," the Committee reported inexpedient.

Voted to lay on the table.

On amendment offered by Bro. Golding to Art. III., Sect. 2, after "Court" in third line, "they shall be entitled to speak on any question submitted at the conventions of the Order, but not entitled to vote," the Committee reported inexpedient.

Voted to accept the report.

On amendment offered by Bro. O'Loughlin to Art. IV., Sect. 2, to strike out all after "Committee" in fourth line, the Committee reported inexpedient.

Voted to accept the report.

Dinner was announced in the lower hall, and a recess was taken till 1.30 P. M.

At 1.45 P. M. High Chief Ranger Watson called the Convention to order.

On amendment offered by Bro. Golding to combine the offices of Financial Secretary and Treasurer in each Subordinate Court, the Committee reported inexpedient.

Voted to accept the report.

On amendment offered by Bro. Byrne to Art. V., Sect. 8, "that all applications for membership be sent by the District Medical Examiner to the High Court Physician, his report shall be final and he shall be paid the sum of twenty-five cents for each examination to be deducted from the fee of the District Medical Examiner;" to Art. VII., Sect. 2, after the word "applicant" insert, "twenty-five cents of which shall be paid the High Court Physician," the committee reported a new draft, viz:

That each applicant shall pay as now two dollars on presenting his application; of this sum the Court shall retain twenty-five cents, which shall be forwarded at once to the High Standing

Committee, as the fee for the High Court Physician — the balance, $1.75, shall be paid to the District Medical Examiner, for examination of applicant, and, in all cases, must be forwarded with the application.

Voted to accept and adopt the report.

The vote was doubted, and the High Chief Ranger stated that the question was on accepting and adopting the report of the Committee on Constitution, a new draft of the amendment, and asked for a standing vote.

The count showed 39 yea, 8 nay, and the High Chief Ranger declared the motion carried, and the report of the Committee was accepted and adopted.

On amendment offered by Bro. Caldwell for relief of members who become sick or disabled, providing for payment of all dues of such members, the Committee reported inexpedient.

High Chief Ranger Watson said the question was on the acceptance of the report; the motion was put and declared carried; but the vote was doubted, and the High Chief Ranger asked for a count.

The count showed, 26 yea, 21 nay, and the High Chief Ranger declared the motion carried and the report of the Committee was accepted.

On amendment to Art. VIII., Sect. 3, page 31, after the word "shall," in first line "be elected at the Annual Convention of the Order;" after the word "money" in fifth line "every six months and oftener if a majority deem it necessary;" after the word "credentials" in third line, strike out the word "Finance" the Committee reported ought to be adopted.

Voted to accept the report.

Bro. J. J. Leonard offered motion to suspend the Order of Business and proceed to election of officers.

Voted to suspend Order of Business.

Voted that High Chief Ranger appoint a Committee of three to receive and count ballots.

High Chief Ranger Watson appointed,

Bros. Lanigan	of Cathedral No. 1
Healy	" Canton " 67
Hayes	" La Fayette " 14

Voted that High Chief Ranger appoint a second Committee.

High Chief Ranger Watson appointed,

Bros. Edmonds . . . . of Cathedral No. 1

Dore   .   .   .   .   .   of Sherwood No. 8

Hurley   .   .   .   .   " St. Raphael " 26

Voted that High Court Secretary-Treasurer call the roll, and that representatives proceed to centre of Hall and deposit ballots.

Voted to take an informal ballot for High Chief Ranger.

The ballot was taken and the Committee reported

Whole number of votes cast	66
Necessary for a choice	34
Jeremiah G. Fennessey	had 42
William E. Shay	" 22
John H. Watson	" 1
T. Sproules	" 1

A motion was made to make the ballot formal.

Bro. Golding raised the point of order that two thirds of the whole number had not voted for any one candidate.

High Chief Ranger Watson decided the point well taken.

High Chief Ranger Watson said a motion to take a formal ballot would be in order.

Voted to take a formal vote for High Chief Ranger.

Bro. Galvin offered a motion that the High Court Secretary-Treasurer cast one ballot for T. Sproules for H. V. C. R. Motion was carried.

On formal ballot for High Chief Ranger the committee reported

Whole number of votes cast	65
Necessary for a choice	33
Jeremiah G. Fennessey	had 43
William E. Shay	" 21
T. Sproules	" 1

High Chief Ranger Watson declared Jeremiah G. Fennessey elected High Chief Ranger for the coming year. On motion of Bro. Shay, it was voted to make the election unanimous.

High Chief Ranger Watson announced that one ballot had been cast for T. Sproules, for H. V. C. R., and declared T. Sproules elected H. V. C. R.

Bro. Ratigan nominated J. P. J. Ward for the office of High Court Secretary-Treasurer.

Bro. Galvin nominated James F. Supple, the present incumbent.

Bro. O'Loughlin seconded the nomination made by Bro. Ratigan, and said Bro. Ward was willing to perform the duties for less money than was now being paid.

Bros. J. J. Flaherty, John T. Daly, J. J. Lanigan, and Wm. Daughan, seconded the nomination of James F. Supple.

The Convention proceeded to ballot for the office of High Court Secretary-Treasurer. The committee reported

Whole number of votes cast	61
Necessary for a choice	32
James F. Supple	had 47
J. P. J. Ward	" 14

High Chief Ranger Watson declared James F. Supple elected High Court Secretary-Treasurer.

Voted that one ballot be cast by High Court Secretary-Treasurer for Edward Riley for High Senior Conductor.

High Chief Ranger Watson announced that one ballot had been cast by High Court Secretary-Treasurer for Edward Riley, for the office of High Senior Conductor, and he declared Edward Riley elected High Senior Conductor.

Voted that one ballot be cast by High Court Secretary-Treasurer for Dr. J. R. McLaughlin for High Junior Conductor.

High Chief Ranger Watson announced that one ballot had been cast by High Court Secretary-Treasurer Supple for Dr. J. R. McLaughlin for High Junior Conductor, and he declared Dr. James R. McLaughlin elected High Junior Conductor.

Voted that one ballot be cast by H. C. S. T. for Philip Smith for High Inside Sentinel.

High Chief Ranger Watson announced that one ballot had been cast for Philip Smith for High Inside Sentinel, and he declared Philip Smith elected High Inside Sentinel.

Two nominations were made for the office of High Outside Sentinel, viz:

Thomas J. Dunn,
Rudolph Farrenkopf.

The Convention proceeded to ballot.

The Committee reported on the ballot for High Outside Sentinel.

Whole number of votes cast	56
Necessary for a choice	29
Thomas J. Dunn	had 41
R. Farrenkopf	" 15

High Chief Ranger Watson declared Thomas J. Dunn elected High Outside Sentinel.

On motion of Bro. Farrenkopf, it was voted to make it unanimous.

Voted that High Court Secretary-Treasurer cast one ballot for Dr. Joseph D. Couch, High Court Physician.

High Chief Ranger Watson announced that one ballot had been cast for Dr. Couch for High Court Physician, and he declared Dr. Joseph D. Couch elected High Court Physician.

Voted that High Court Secretary-Treasurer, cast one ballot for Rev. Hugh Roe O'Donnell for High Court Chaplain.

High Chief Ranger Watson announced that one ballot had been cast for Rev. Hugh Roe O'Donnell for High Court Chaplain, and he declared Rev. Hugh Roe O'Donnell elected High Court Chaplain.

On motion of Bro. Galvin, it was voted that High Court Secretary-Treasurer cast one ballot for a Finance Committee of five members.

High Chief Ranger announced that one ballot had been cast for a Finance Committee of five members, viz:

William E. Shay	of St. Francis No. 4
Hon. John P. Dore	" Sherwood " 8
J. J. Lanigan	" Cathedral " 1
Andrew Golding	" Cheverus " 6
Wm. F. Rooney	" Prospect " 58

And he declared them elected.

Bro. Daly, Past Grand Registrar of the Knights of St. Rose, announced the Annual Mass under the auspices of the Knights of St. Rose would occur on May 30, next, and he hoped all the Representatives and other members of the Order would attend.

On motion of Bro. Ratigan it was voted:

Voted that it is the sense of the Convention that the High Standing Committee consider the expediency of calling the next Convention at Worcester.

Voted that items of interest to the Order and the public, be furnished to the newspapers.

Voted that the proceedings of the Convention be printed and distributed to the members of the Order.

Voted to proceed to installation of Officers.

High Chief Ranger John H. Watson called Past High Chief Ranger Hon. O. A. Galvin to the chair to act as the installing officer. Past High Chief Ranger Galvin appointed John T. Daly of Erin, No. 28, High Senior Conductor. H. C. Byrne, of Friendship, No. 37, H. J. Conductor, to assist in installation ceremonies, and J. P. Cleary, of St. Francis, No. 4, High Inside Sentinel. F. J. McGrath of Mt. Pleasant, No. 20, High Outside Sentinel, during ceremonies.

Past High Chief Ranger Galvin then called upon the outgoing officers to vacate their stations, and the officers elect to take places and prepare for installation.

Past High Chief Ranger Galvin then installed the officers of the High Court, for the ensuing year, as follows:

High Chief Ranger,
JEREMIAH G. FENNESSEY.

High Vice Chief Ranger,
THOMAS SPROULES.

High Court Secretary-Treasurer,
JAMES F. SUPPLE.

High Senior Conductor,
EDWARD RILEY.

High Junior Conductor,
DR. JAMES R. McLAUGHLIN.

High Inside Sentinel,
PHILIP SMITH.

High Outside Sentinel,
THOMAS J. DUNN.

High Court Physician,
JOSEPH D. COUCH, M. D.

Past High Chief Ranger Galvin then introduced High Chief Ranger Jeremiah G. Fennessey, who made a short address thanking the Representatives for electing him, and promising to do his whole duty.

Past High Chief Ranger Galvin then announced the officers of the High Court duly installed and in their places.

Bro. Hurley, of St. Raphael, No. 26, addressed the chair on a question of an applicant to his Court, whose application was, he claimed, delayed by the High Standing Committee until the applicant refused to come into the Order, and he (Hurley) thought a change was necessary, because such delays were bad for the Order. (The High Court Secretary-Treasurer had previously fully explained this matter to Bro. Hurley, showing him that no fault in the matter rested with the High Standing Committee.)

High Chief Ranger Fennessey explained the matter to the Convention, proving that the High Standing Committee were not in any way to blame.

Voted to take up the Order of Business.

Report of Committee on State of the Order on resolve to issue Assessment Calls once a month to accumulate a fund, the Committee reported inexpedient :

At this point supper was announced, and at 6.15 P. M. a recess was taken until 7.30 P. M., the Convention to re-assemble in Greystone Hall.

GREYSTONE HALL, 7.30 P. M., April 18, 1888.

High Chief Ranger Fennessey called the Convention to order; announced the first business, — the consideration of the report of the Committee on State of the Order, the Committee having reported inexpedient.

On motion of Bro. Sullivan, of St. John, No. 23, the previous question was ordered; High Chief Ranger Fennessey stated the question.

The vote was taken 15 yea, 17 nay, and the report of the Committee was not accepted.

Bro. Brickley of St. Alphonsus, No. 21, moved to indefinitely postpone.

Carried.

On motion of Bro. Daly, of Erin, No. 28,

Voted to extend the courtesies of the Convention to Past High Chief Ranger James McLaughlin, in order that he might present some matters relating to the Knights of St. Rose.

High Chief Ranger Fennessey appointed the High Conductors to escort Past High Chief Ranger McLaughlin to the platform.

Bro. McLaughlin was presented to the Convention and was warmly and enthusiastically received.

Bro. McLaughlin addressed the Convention at some length stating that by vote of the Knights of St. Rose, he, the Chief Consul, was instructed to announce to the Representatives that the Knights of St. Rose are desirous of securing a home for the Order. That the Knights of St. Rose stand ready to give the sum of $1,000 towards that object, and to ask that the Convention and the Order take it up and secure the necessary amount to ensure success.

Bro. Watson, Past High Chief Ranger, spoke in favor of the project.

Bro. Sproules, High Vice Chief Ranger, also spoke in favor and moved that the subject be referred to a Committee of seven to co-operate with such Committee as may be appointed by Knights of St. Rose.

Carried.

Report of Committee on State of the Order, on request of Worcester Court, No. 59, that a badge for general use be designed and adopted, the Committee reported to refer to the High Standing Committee.

Voted, on motion of Bro. Brickley of St. Alphonsus, No. 21, to accept the report.

Report of Committee on State of the Order, on instructions to High Standing Committee from Middlesex Court, No. 60, concerning report of finances, the Committee reported inexpedient.

Voted to amend the report by reference to the High Standing Committee.

Report of Committee on State of the Order, on Preamble and Resolutions offered by Bro. McGrath, of Mt. Pleasant, No. 20. Bro. O'Bryan, of St. Catharine, No. 62, on behalf of the Committee, read the matter considered, consisting of 3 Resolutions and a Preamble of 9 propositions, and reported that the vote of his Committee was inexpedient.

Voted to accept and adopt the report.

Voted that the High Standing Committee be instructed to consider the expediency of having the office of the High Standing Committee open at certain times, and that a placard to that effect be placed on the office.

Bro. McGrath moved that all amendments take effect May 1.

High Chief Ranger Fennessey ruled the motion out of order.

Under No. 13, Order of Business, Bro. Griffin of St. Joseph, No. 11, moved, that the thanks of the Convention be extended to Bro. John H. Watson, the retiring High Chief Ranger, for the able and efficient manner in which he has conducted the affairs of the Order.

Bro. McGrath, of Mt. Pleasant, No. 20, rose and said he would not vote for the motion, that it was not deserved, and should not be given.

Bro. Callanan, of Shields, No. 63, seconded the motion of Bro. Griffin. He also said he was astounded that any objection to the motion should be made, and that he could not understand how any brother could so far demean himself as to object to a vote of thanks to the retiring High Chief Ranger, and that a man who expressed himself as did the brother from Mt. Pleasant Court was unworthy of consideration

Bro. Daly of Erin Court, No. 28, said that he thought the motion did honor to the maker, because he knew that Bro. Griffin had not been in sympathy with the retiring High Chief Ranger. He said he also was surprised at the statement of Bro. McGrath, and he thought the proper place for such a brother (?) was on the other side of the door.

Bro. Maloney of Constantine Court, No. 49, said he endorsed the sentiments of the two previous speakers, and that he expected to find brotherly love instead of hate and ill-feeling, as expressed by the brother from Mt. Pleasant Court.

Bro. Griffin, of St. Joseph, No. 11, said he had attended seven Conventions, and he believed the retiring High Chief Ranger, Bro. Watson, was honest, faithful, just and true, and one of the most efficient High Chief Rangers ever elected, and Bro. Watson had his highest esteem.

On motion of High Senior Conductor Riley, the previous question was ordered.

Bro. Morris of St. Joseph Court, No. 38, rose, and desired to say something.

High Chief Ranger Fennessey asked for the consent of the Convention.

No objection was made, and the High Chief Ranger told Bro. Morris to proceed.

Bro. Morris said he had the same opinion as Bro. McGrath, and did not think Bro. Watson should get any thanks, and would vote against the motion.

The question was called for.

High Chief Ranger Fennessey stated the question, and it was carried by unanimous vote; there were no nays.

On motion of Bro. Brickley, of St. Alphonsus, No. 21,

Voted to thank all the members of the High Standing Committee for their efforts during the past year.

High Chief Ranger Fennessey extended the thanks of the Convention to Past High Chief Ranger John H. Watson.

Bro. Watson, P. H. C. R., feelingly responded, and expressed his delight at the progress the Order had made, and his confidence in the future of the Order; that in his administration he had acted for the best interests of all the members, and with the desire to advance the Order, and not the pet schemes or untried theories of any visionist, and that he retired from two years' service, as High Chief Ranger, with the consciousness that he had endeavored to do his duty. He had only the kindliest and most brotherly feeling for every member of the Order, and felt supremely honored by the motion just passed.

On motion of High Senior Conductor Riley,

Voted that when we adjourn, we adjourn to meet May 3, at 8 P. M.

Voted that the High Standing Committee procure a new set of Regalia for its own use.

Under No. 14, Order of Business,

Voted to admit to membership in the High Court, the following Past Chief Rangers:

Thomas Crosby	of St. Francis	No.	4
A. F. Caldwell	" St. Patrick	"	7
R. Farrenkopf	" Sherwood	"	8
M. A. Farrell	" Columbus	"	9
P. M. Keating	" St. Joseph	"	11
H. F. Scanlan	" Fulton	"	12
D. J. O'Brien	" Essex	"	16
John Hurley	" Hamilton	"	17
F. S. Maloney	" Williams	"	19
F. M. Kivenear	" "	"	"
John F. Dever	" Mt. Pleasant	"	20
J. T. Brickley	" St. Alphonsus	"	21
John Hogan	" " Gregory	"	24
T. Crowley	" Erin	"	28
T. D. Heavy	" Qualey	"	32
M. F. Leonard	" Americus	"	34
T. H. Duggan	" Friendship	"	37
Joseph Cahalan	" St. Joseph	"	38
P. H. Kerrigan	" " Augustine	"	46
Thomas Kelley	" Sarsfield	"	48
Wm. Daughan	" Constantine	"	49
Joseph Torndorf	" Holy Trinity	"	51
M. J. Driscoll	" Highland	"	52
T. W. O'Rourke	" St. James	"	54
T. F. Gallagher	" Charles River	"	55
J. H. Morton	" Carroll	"	57
M. Driscoll	" St. Lawrence	"	61
J. J. Callanan	" Shields	"	63
J. J. Leonard	" Gallagher	"	64
W. Mackin	" St. Columbkill	"	65
A. F. Staples	" Griffin	"	66

Bro. J. J. Flaherty, Chairman of Committee on Finance, said his Committee was prepared to make a report of the amount required for the expenses of the High Standing Committee for the coming year, and reported as follows:

For general printing	$300 00
" printing 4,000 copies of report of H. C. S. T., with proceedings of Convention	400 00
" salary of H. C. S. T.	800 00
" office rent	300 00
" travelling expenses, H. S. Com.	250 00
" " " D. H. C. R.	100 00

| For postage | . | . | . | . | . | . | . | . | 150 | 00 |
| " miscellaneous expenses | . | | . | . | . | . | . | | 400 | 00 |

$2,700 00

and suggest that a per capita of 75 cts. be ordered.

Voted to accept and adopt the report.

Committee on Finance also reported on resolution of Bro. McGrath, of Mount Pleasant, No. 20, that $500 be always kept on hand by the High Court Secretary-Treasurer, in the General Fund.

The Committee reported inexpedient.

Voted to refer back to the Committee on Finance to report at next session of the Convention.

On motion of Bro. Brickley of St. Alphonsus, No. 21,

Voted to adjourn.

Adjourned at 10.15 P. M.

Closed in due form by High Chief Ranger Fennessey.

JAMES F. SUPPLE,

High Court Secretary-Treasurer.

Second Session of Ninth Annual Convention.

Greystone Hall, May 3, 1888.

High Chief Ranger Fennessey called the Convention to order at 8.15 p. m.

The High Senior Conductor reported H. V. C. R. Sproules and H. J. Con. McLaughlin, absent.

High Chief Ranger Fennessey appointed Bro. Hurley of Hamilton, No. 17, H. V. C. R., and Bro. Hayes of LaFayette, No. 14, H. J. Con.

High Chief Ranger Fennessey then opened the session in due form.

High Chief Ranger announced the first business, the reading of records of last session.

High Court Secretary-Treasurer proceeded to read the records.

Bro. Golding moved to dispense with the reading of the records.

The vote was taken and the motion was declared lost.

The H. C. Secretary-Treasurer continued the reading of the records.

The High Inside Sentinel, Philip Smith, announced the arrival of the High Court Chaplain, Rev. Hugh Roe O'Donnell.

High Chief Ranger Fennessey appointed a committee to escort the High Court Chaplain to the platform.

High Court Chaplain, Rev. Hugh Roe O'Donnell, entered and was received with enthusiasm while proceeding to his station.

The H. C. Secretary-Treasurer continued the reading of the records.

Voted to dispense with further reading of the records.

Bro. J. J. Flaherty, for the Committee on Finance, reported as follows:

The Committee on Finance, having examined the books and accounts of the High Court Secretary-Treasurer, beg leave to submit the following report: —

General Fund.

Amount received since April 20, 1887	$3,732 83
" expended from April 20, 1887, to April 1, 1888 . . .	3,315 77
Balance in General Fund	$417 06

ENDOWMENT FUND.

Amount on hand, April 20, 1887	$5,787 60
Received from April 20, 1887, to April, 1888	32,295 40
	$38,083 00
Endowments paid	33,784 20
Balance in Endowment Fund	$4,298 80

The Committee found the books in excellent condition and well kept. Vouchers were presented for all expenditures, and the examination was rendered comparatively easy by the systematic and careful book-keeping of the High Court Secretary-Treasurer.   Signed,

J. J. FLAHERTY,

for the Committee.

Bro. Daly moved to accept and adopt report of the Committee on Finance.

Carried.

Bro. J. J. Flaherty, for Committee on Finance, read resolution, which was referred back to the Committee at last session, obliging the High Standing Committee to keep $500 on hand, etc. The Committee reported inexpedient.

Bro. Daly moved to accept and adopt the report.

Bro. McGrath said he offered the resolution, and desired very much to have it pass.

Bro. Daly hoped the report of the Committee on Finance would be accepted, and he then moved the previous question.

Bros. Shay and Byrne argued against the previous question being put.

Bro. Rogers, of Sarsfield, No. 48, expressed the belief that the High Standing Committee could get along without any instructions from Bro. McGrath.

High Chief Ranger Fennessey said the question was on the previous question. Vote was taken and declared lost.

Vote was doubted, and a count showed 22 yea, 20 nay, and the previous question was ordered.

High Chief Ranger Fennessey said the question was on the motion of Bro. Daly to accept and adopt the report of the Finance Committee. Vote was taken and motion declared carried.

Bro. McGrath moved a reconsideration of the vote accepting and adopting the report of the Committee on Finance.

High Chief Ranger Fennessey decided the motion not in order, Bro. McGrath not having voted with the majority.

Bro. Bryne, of Friendship Court, No. 37, moved to reconsider the vote accepting and adopting the report of Committee on Finance.

High Chief Ranger Fennessey decided Bro. Byrne was out of order, also.

Bro. Daly said he could make the motion, and be in order, and to accommodate the brothers who were in such distress to reconsider, he moved to reconsider the vote accepting and adopting the report of the Committee on Finance.

High Chief Ranger Fennessey stated question was on motion of Bro. Daly to reconsider the acceptance and adoption of report of Finance Committee.

The question was debated by Bros. Rogers, McGrath, Griffin, C. J. Hurley, T. F. Sullivan, J. Chamberlain, Hayes, Caldwell, and Lanigan.

Bro. T. F. Sullivan moved the previous question.

Vote was taken, and the previous question was ordered.

Vote was taken on the motion to reconsider the acceptance and adoption of the report of the Committee on Finance, and declared lost.

High Chief Ranger Fennessey announced " The Committee on Conference, on part of the Order, on Home for the Order."

A. T. Caldwell .	. . .	of St. Patrick,	No. 7
P. H. Desmond	. . .	" Iona,	" 10
John Hayes	. . . .	" LaFayette,	" 14
G. A. Healy	. . . .	" Canton,	" 67
M. Driscoll	. . . .	" St. Lawrence,	" 61
J. J. Barnes	. . . .	" Charles River,	" 55
Wm. Mackin	. . . .	" St. Columbkill,	" 65

Bro. Shay, of St. Francis, No. 4, said he was informed that H. C. Secretary-Treasurer Supple had paid some bills, contracted on account of the GUIDE, the organ of the Order, out of his own pocket, and he moved that the amount be paid to Bro. Supple from the surplus on hand in General Fund.

Bro. Lanigan, P. H. F. S., made a statement concerning the business of the GUIDE, and its failure through non-support by the members. That, as one of the managers of the GUIDE, he knew that in order to save the honor of the Order, Bro. Supple had paid out about $200, and he thought he should be reimbursed, as the labor performed gratuitously by the managers of the GUIDE was quite enough, without expecting any of them to lose any money on it, and he hoped the amount would be voted.

High Senior Conductor Riley stated that the High Court Chaplain could not remain long, and moved to lay on the table.

Vote was taken, and declared carried.

High Chief Ranger Fennessey, then introduced Rev. Hugh Roe O'Donnell, H. C. C., who said this was his fifth year of service, and that he was a member of the Order, as well as Chaplain of the High Court.

He thanked the Convention for his re-election, and said he would have renewed interest in the welfare of the Order. He was pleased to know that extra care was being taken in the admission of new members, and he hoped particular care would be taken about admission of applicants who dránk to excess. He said it augured well for the success of the Order.

It gave him pleasure to accept the position of High Court Chaplain of the Massachusetts Catholic Order of Foresters, and expressed the hope that the future of the Order would be as bright as the present. (Prolonged applause.)

The High Court Chaplain then withdrew.

High Senior Conductor Riley moved to take question from the table.

Vote was taken and declared carried.

High Chief Ranger Fennessey stated question.

Bros. Rogers and Riley spoke for the motion.

Bros. Morris and C. J. Hurley spoke against the motion.

High Chief Ranger Fennessey put the question.

Bro. McGrath asked the floor, and said he was sorry that he was always at sword's point with the High Court Secretary-Treasurer, but he could not vote for the motion.

Bro. Lanigan, P. H. F. S., asked Bro. McGrath if he did not know that the GUIDE was run on promises of members who never paid.

Bro. McGrath said he did not know, and would vote against the motion.

Bro. Watson, P. H. C. R., said that when we met and subscribed for the GUIDE, over $800 was promised, and about $500 only received, and he thought as the High Court Secretary-Treasurer had stood by the Order, and saved the honor of the Order, the amount lost by Bro. Supple should be repaid, and he hoped it would be done.

Bro. Griffin thought the debt should be paid.

Bro. Byrne raised a point of order which the H. C. R. decided not well taken.

Bro. Daly moved the previous question.

Vote was taken and declared carried, and the previous question was ordered.

High Chief Ranger Fennessey said question was on the motion of Bro. Shay to re-imburse Bro. Supple for money expended on the GUIDE, the organ of the Order.

Vote was taken, and declared carried.

Bro. Shay offered an amendment to the Constitution to strike out words "shall in person," in 2d line of Art. III, Sect. 2,

High Chief Ranger refused to receive the amendment.

Bro. Riley, H. S. Con., asked for a ruling on point of order.

High Chief Ranger decided point not well taken.

High Chief Ranger said that all amendments should be presented on first day of the Convention, and he would adhere to his decision that the matter could not be acted upon at this time. That the entire order of business was gone over at last session of the Convention.

Bro. Shay said the Section as it stood was an absurdity.

High Senior Conductor Riley said he wanted the same thing taken out at last Convention, but the Convention voted it down.

High Chief Ranger said he thought a change should be made, but could not allow it now.

Bro. Daly moved to suspend the regular order of business, so that we could go back to No. 8.

High Chief Ranger Fennessey ruled the motion out of order.

Bro. Shay appealed from the decision of the H. C. R. on his amendment.

High Chief Ranger Fennessey stated the decision and appeal. His decision was that new business cannot be introduced at this time, and that Bro. Shay appealed from his decision.

Bro. Rogers raised a point of order that the question between the H. C. Ranger and Bro. Shay should be decided.

High Chief Ranger Fennessey decided point not well taken.

Bro. McGrath spoke about certain amendments he offered one year ago, and said it seemed that nothing was acceptable that he offered.

Bro. Caldwell asked if the appeal was debatable.

Bro. Chamberlain raised a point of order. High Chief Ranger decided not well taken.

Bro. McGrath thought the decision of the High Chief Ranger should not be sustained.

Bro. Shay stated for Bro. McGrath's benefit, that he wanted to know which was the superior, the High Chief Ranger or the Convention.

High Chief Ranger Fennessey said the Convention was superior to the High Chief Ranger, but not to the Constitution.

Bro. Daly moved the previous question.

Vote was taken, and the previous question was ordered.

High Chief Ranger stated the appeal.

Vote was taken on sustaining the decision of the Chair, and declared carried.

Vote was doubted. A count showed 33 yea, 13 nay, and the High Chief Ranger declared "the decision of the Chair stands."

Vote was again doubted, and another count showed 32 yea, 15 nay, and the High Chief Ranger declared "the decision of the Chair stands."

Bro. Driscoll said his Court, St. Lawrence, No. 61, ignored some parts of the Constitution, and wanted to know what was going to be done about it.

High Chief Ranger Fennessey said the D. H. C. R. of that District would probably attend to the matter.

Bro. Rogers moved to adjourn.

High Chief Ranger declared motion not in order, as the records had not been read and acted upon.

High Court Secretary-Treasurer proceeded to read the records.

Bro. Rogers moved that the records be considered sufficiently read, and that further reading be dispensed with.

Vote was taken and declared carried unanimously.

Bro. Rogers moved to accept and adopt the records.

Vote was taken and declared carried.

Voted to adjourn *sine die*.

Closed in due form by High Chief Ranger Fennessey, at 10.20 P. M.

JAMES F. SUPPLE,

High Court Secretary-Treasurer.

MAY 3, 1888.

DEPUTY HIGH CHIEF RANGERS.

For Term Ending April, 1889.

DIST.	COMPRISING COURTS.	D. H. C. R.	MEMBERS OF	NO.
1...	1, 12....	JAMES P. CLEARY, Roxbury.......	St. Francis........	4
2...	3, 5....	MICHAEL EDMONDS, "	Cathedral	1
3...	4, 38....	P. A. DONOVAN, South Boston......	SS. Peter and Paul.	15
4...	6....	M. A. FARRELL, Roxbury..........	Columbus	9
5...	7, 34....	DANIEL A. CRONIN, Boston.., ...	St. Joseph.........	11
6...	8, 60....	A. F. CALDWELL, So. Boston.......	St. Patrick........	7
7...	9, 54....	GERHARD KRANEFUSS, Boston.....	Holy Trinity......	51
8...	10, 17....	D. F. SULLIVAN, "	Sherwood	8
9...	11, 13....	WILLIAM DAUGHAN, "	Constantine	49
10...	14, 30....	JAMES SHERRY, Peabody..........	Emerald..........	53
11...	24, 62....	RUDOLPH FARRENKOPF, Boston....	Sherwood	8
12...	16, 53....	JOHN HAYES, Lynn	Lafayette..........	14
13...	18, 19....	HENRY P. MULDOON, South Boston..	St. Patrick........	7
14...	20, 21....	P. A. SULLIVAN, Boston	Americus..........	34
15...	23, 55....	A. M. LANIGAN, "	Cathedral	1
16...	32, 61....	MICHAEL LEONARD, "	Americus..........	34
17...	25, 37....	E. F. CHAMBERLAIN, Mattapan.....	St. Peter..........	18
18...	15, 35....	GEORGE A. O'BRYAN, Norwood.....	St. Catharine......	62
19...	49....	P. A. MULLIGAN, Newton..........	Middlesex.........	60
20...	29, 43, 69....	THOMAS F. SULLIVAN, Brockton...	St. Thomas........	29
21...	44, 58....	JOHN T. DALY, Boston.............	Erin..............	28
22...	26, 67....	THOMAS MULCAHEY, Hyde Park....	St. John..........	23
23...	57, 51....	THOMAS W. O'ROURKE, Dorchester..	St. James	54
24...	33....	N. FAIRCLOUGH, Boston............	Star of the Sea.....	41
25...	28....	JOHN E. HESLAN, Roxbury........	St. Francis........	4
26...	65....	THOS. F. GALLAGHER, Watertown ..	Charles River.....	55
27...	41, 46....	JAMES CASHIN, Boston.............	Cheverus..........	6
28...	39....	WM. A. FLAHERTY, Somerville.....	Benedict	39
29...	45....	WILLIAM CONDON, Bridgewater.....	Unity.............	45
30...	52....	P. H. KERRIGAN, South Boston.....	St. Augustine......	46
31...	68, 47....	JOHN J. FLAHERTY, Gloucester.....	St. Anne..........	47
32...	48, 66....	WILLIAM H. ROGERS, Plainville....	Sarsfield..........	48
33...	59....	JOHN B. RATIGAN, Worcester	Worcester.........	59
34...	64....	JEREMIAH J. CALLANAN, Holyoke..	Shields.	63
35...	63....	JOHN J. LEONARD, Springfield......	Gallagher	64
		JOHN H. WATSON, Beverly Farms...	Essex	16
At large		HON. JOHN P. DORE, Boston......	Sherwood	8
		P. McGRATH, Watertown..........	Charles River.....	55

MEDICAL EXAMINERS.

For Term Ending April 18, 1889.

DISTRICT.	PLACE.	EXAMINER.	COURTS.
1	Boston	E.. G. McDonald, 221 Shawmut Av.	8, 11, 28, 49.
2	Boston	F. T. Galligan, 88 Warren Street.	20, 21, 37, 38, 52.
3	Boston	S. T. Mara, 266 Tremont Street	3, 9, 35.
4	Boston	S. A. Callanan, 179 Dudley Street	1, 18, 34, 51, 54.
5	Boston, Brookline	Joseph P. Murphy, 1607 Tremont St., Rox., also at Brookline	4, 61.
6	Boston	James E. Dorcey, 165 Harrison Av.	6, 12, 17.
7	East Boston	M. W. O'Keefe, 50 Maverick Square	5, 41.
8	Boston, East Boston	James F. Ferry, 10 Chelsea Street	13, 19.
9	South Boston	W. H. Devine, 599 Broadway	7, 15, 46.
10	Milton	J. A. Lanagan, 1186 Washington St.	24.
11	Malden	C. D. McCarthy	10.
12	Woburn	J. H. Conway	32.
13	Lynn	C. A. Ahearne	14.
14	Salem Beverly Farms	Francis E. Hines	16, 68.
15	East Cambridge, Somerville	J. A. Gregg	33, 39.
16	Quincy	Joseph M. Sheahan	25.
17	West Newton, Waltham	C. J. McCormick	44, 58.
18	Jamaica Plain	J. P. Broidrick	57.
19	Newton, Brighton	M. J. Kelley, Watertown	60, 65.
20	Watertown	F. M. O'Donnell, Newton	55.
21	Hyde Park	John C. Lincoln	23.
22	Dedham	A. H. Hodgdon	26.
23	Peabody	John Shannahan	53.
24	Norwood	L. H. Plympton	62.
25	Beverly	Charles Haddock	30.
26	Gloucester	Philip Mooney	47.
27	Randolph, Brockton	Benedict Donovan, Brockton	29, 43.
28	Bridgewater	G. H. Watson	45.
29	North Attleborough	T. F. McDonough	48.
30	Worcester	Joseph H. Kelly	59.
31	Holyoke	F. P. Donoghue	63.
32	Springfield	A. J. Dunne	64.
33	Franklin	J. C. Gallison	66.
34	Canton	Thomas D. Lonergan	67.
35	Stoughton	Michael Glennon	69.
36	Marlboro	James Campbell	

TENTH ANNUAL REPORT

OF THE

HIGH COURT SECRETARY-TREASURER

OF THE

MASSACHUSETTS CATHOLIC ORDER OF FORESTERS,

TO THE HIGH COURT, APRIL 17, 1889,

TOGETHER WITH

REPORT OF PROCEEDINGS OF THE

TENTH ANNUAL CONVENTION

AND

NEW LIST OF MEDICAL EXAMINERS AND D. H. C. R.s, AND
MEETINGS AND LIST OF OFFICERS, CORRECTED
TO JULY 19, 1889.

BOSTON:
PRESS OF CASHMAN, KEATING & CO.
597 WASHINGTON STREET.

TENTH ANNUAL REPORT

OF THE

HIGH COURT SECRETARY-TREASURER

OF THE

MASSACHUSETTS

CATHOLIC ORDER OF FORESTERS,

TO THE HIGH COURT, APRIL 17, 1889·

TOGETHER WITH

REPORT OF PROCEEDINGS

OF THE

TENTH ANNUAL CONVENTION

AND

NEW LIST OF MEDICAL EXAMINERS AND D. H. C. R.s, AND
MEETINGS AND LIST OF OFFICERS, CORRECTED
TO JULY 19, 1889.

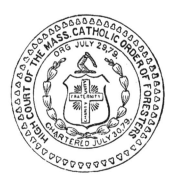

BOSTON:
PRESS OF CASHMAN, KEATING & CO.
597 WASHINGTON STREET.

HIGH COURT OFFICERS

For Term Ending April, 1890.

High Chief Ranger,

JEREMIAH G. FENNESSEY . . . St. James Court No. 54

High Vice-Chief Ranger,

PHILIP SMITH . . . . . Williams Court No. 19

High Secretary-Treasurer,

JAMES F. SUPPLE . . . . Columbus Court No. 9

High Senior Conductor,

EDWARD RILEY . . . . St. Joseph Court No. 11

High Junior Conductor,

P. A. MURRAY . . . . . Middlesex Court No. 60

High Inside Sentinel,

THOMAS J. DUNN . . . . Cathedral Court No. 1

High Outside Sentinel,

R. FARRENKOPF . . . . . Sherwood Court No. 8

High Medical Examiner,

JOSEPH D. COUCH, M. D. . . . Benedict Court No. 39

High Chaplain,

REV. HUGH ROE O'DONNELL . Star of the Sea Court No. 41

HIGH COURT OFFICERS

For Term Ending April 17, 1889.

High Chief Ranger,
JEREMIAH G. FENNESSEY . . . St. James Court No. 54

High Vice-Chief Ranger,
THOMAS SPROULES . . . . St. Francis Court No. 4

High Court Secretary-Treasurer,
JAMES F. SUPPLE . . . . Columbus Court No. 9

High Senior Conductor,
EDWARD RILEY . . . . St. Joseph Court No. 11

High Junior Conductor,
*J. R. McLAUGHLIN, V. S. . . . Middlesex Court No. 60
P. A. MURRAY .. . . . . " " " "

High Inside Sentinel,
PHILIP SMITH . . . . . Williams Court No. 19

High Outside Sentinel,
THOMAS J. DUNN . . . . . Cathedral Court No. 1

High Court Physician,
JOSEPH D. COUCH, M. D. . . . Benedict Court No. 39

High Court Chaplain,
REV. HUGH ROE O'DONNELL . Star of the Sea Court No. 41

*Resigned.

ANNUAL REPORT

OF THE

HIGH STANDING COMMITTEE,

For the Term Ending April 17, 1889.

Representatives to the Annual Convention of the High Court Massachusetts Catholic Order of Foresters.

BROTHERS: We meet in Tenth Annual Convention to hear what progress has been made in the extension of our Order, what increase in membership since the last Convention was held, and for the purpose of carefully devising and formulating such laws as will tend to increase the stability of our organization, so that it may be a permanent institution amongst our people whom it is principally intended to benefit; and who, to-day, are looking at, and examining our work in the past, and asking, will this work, that so far has received the approval and commendation of those who are most interested, be continued in the future? In order that you may have some basis to work on, the Constitution wisely provides that the High Standing Committee shall report to the Annual Session of the High Court, the general condition of, and all matters of interest relative to, the Order. Article IV., Section 3, High Court Constitution.

In obedience to this command, this report is herewith presented.

MEETINGS.

Since the last Annual Convention the High Standing Committee have held 46 regular meetings, at most of which all of the members were present; and the members of the Committee have in addition made many visits to the sessions of the Subordinate Courts, and in some instances made two or three visits to Courts that required the attention and supervision of the Committee. It has not been found practicable to visit all the Subordinate Courts during the past year; and, in fact, it was not required, because most of the Courts in the Order were and are doing well, and do not have to be compelled to comply with the provisions of the Constitution.

MEMBERSHIP.

During the year we have received and passed on 910 application papers for membership in our Order; of this number 817 were approved, 89 were rejected, and 5 were held over for further consideration.

I must not be understood that all that were rejected were so rejected by the High Standing Committee; many, very many, were rejected by the Medical examiners, and, in so doing, they were fully borne out by the facts in each case, after examination by the High Standing Committee.

NEW COURTS.

During the year six new Courts have been instituted. Stoughton 69, at Stoughton; St. Michael 70, South Boston; Phil Sheridan 71, at Newburyport; Merrimack 72, at Haverhill; Taunton 73, at Taunton; and Hendricken 74, at North Easton.

The average age of the members of these Courts is 31 years, and they are intelligent, active men, who will, undoubtedly, be of great benefit and strength to the Order.

We wish to return our thanks to Rev. Father Theodore Metcalf and Father M. P. O'Connor, of South Boston; Rev. A. J. Teeling, of Newburyport; Rev. Father O'Doherty, of Haverhill, for the great assistance and support given your Committee by them, in the formation of the Courts in their respective cities; also to D. H. C. R. Thomas F. Sullivan, of St. Thomas Court 29, for his untiring zeal in the formation of Stoughton and Hendricken Courts.

Your Committee hopes that, during the coming year, other brothers will show the same zeal and interest in extending your Order, and the propagation of its principles.

Taunton Court 73 was instituted with the largest Charter list, 80, of any Court ever formed in the Order, and it bids fair soon to be the largest Court in the State. This Court, and Hendricken Court 74, are in the diocese of Providence, so that we can now say, that our Order is no longer local, as it exists in the three dioceses in the State, and with a fair promise to grow more rapidly in the future, than it has in the past.

An attempt is being made, at the present time, to form Courts in Marlborough, Fitchburg, and Lowell, where nearly the requisite number for a Charter has been examined, and soon we expect to see Courts in each of these places.

FINANCES.

The Order has never been in better condition financially. At the last Convention we had 12 unpaid death claims, about which there was no question as to the liability of the Order. One claim, that of Hennessey, who was at one time a member of O'Connell Court, and which had been held in abeyance for some years, was then pending on the Superior Court of Middlesex County; a trial was had subsequently, and a decision was given adverse to the Order. An appeal was taken to the Supreme Court, and while pending there, your Committee was advised by the Counsel of the Order to settle the case by the payment of the endowment — the costs to be paid by the heirs of Hennessey.

During the year, we have had 43 deaths in the Order, and the endowment in each case has been paid except the last 8 — so that of all the deaths reported up to date, officially, we can say that they have been paid, or that sufficient money has been called for to pay them, and if no further deaths occurred, it would leave a balance in the Secretary-Treasurer's hands for the payment of at least one or two endowments.

This is a gratifying condition of affairs, and we think it is as perfect as it can be made under the present system of collecting the endowment money.

Of the money appropriated for the support of the High Standing Committee, there remains an unexpended balance that may be allowed to remain for the purpose of extending the Order during the coming year.

PER CAPITA TAX.

Your Committee would recommend that the sum of 75 cents per capita be the tax levied on the members for the coming year; and that it be made a general appropriation rather than for specific items. This recommendation is made for two reasons: first, because it will simplify the accounts; and second, because in the entire history of the Organization the amount appropriated for each specific item has generally been exceeded except for salaries, and formation of new Courts. The money is carefully managed, and, in the opinion of your Committee, it is not thought wise to hamper it by unnecessary resolutions.

No Suspension.

No Court has been suspended for the non-payment of the endowments during the year; although, in some cases. it might have been a salutary lesson to some of the Subordinate Court Officers who will not perform the duties assigned them under the Constitution, yet it was not deemed wise to suspend the Court, on account of the great injury that might be done the members, when they complied with all the laws of the Order.

Mortality.

During the year we had in the Order 43 deaths occurring in the following months.

January	.	.	4	June	.	.	3	November	.	.	5
February	.	.	2	July	.	.	4	December	.	.	3
March	.	.	3	August	.	.	5				—
April	.	.	1	September	.	.	1				43
May	.	.	5	October	.	.	7				

This is merely to show that it will be impossible to determine with any degree of accuracy what the death rate in any month will be, so that the assessment calls might be issued with any degree of regularity, in order that the number of assessments would not press too heavily on the members.

We find from an examination of the records, that of those who died from April 24, 1888, the first death after the 1st session of the Committee last year, to March 19, 1888,

That 4 were initiated in	.	.	.	.	1879
" 11 " " "	.	.	.	.	1880
" 7 " " "	.	.	.	.	1881
" 6 " " "	.	.	.	.	1882
" 9 " " "	.	.	.	.	1883
" 2 " " "	.	.	.	.	1884
" 2 " " "	.	.	.	.	1885
" 2 " " "	.	.	.	.	1886
" 1 " " "	.	.	.	.	1887
" 1 " " "	.	.	.	.	1888

—
43

and yet complaint has been made when men are rejected, by men, who, if they attempted to make any study at all in relation to mortality in fraternal organizations, must admit that it was owing to the loose system of admissions of members into the Massachusetts Catholic Order of Foresters, in the early years of its history, that has caused the death rate to be so high in the last few years, and that the policy inaugurated by the High Standing Committee, in 1885, was what saved the organization from wreck, — the place so many of the assessment and fraternal societies have reached in the past; and such loose and unwise admissions are undermining the stability of all such societies and organizations to-day, who seek mainly to gain members, that a few men may grow rich while the organization that they manage will die an untimely death.

The men who originated the present policy, in 1885, were abused and found fault with; they should receive, and are entitled to receive, the gratitude and thanks of all men who have made the affairs of the organization a study in order to improve it and strengthen it, because the way was made clear and plain for them by the men who held the lamp of experience in the past; and that lamp is burning brighter than ever to-day.

Your Committee has reason to thank the Committee of 1885–86, because we can say to-day that we have rejected a smaller percentage of applicants during the last three years than any of the so-called well-managed organizations; those that we can fairly claim are representative in the sense that they are good. We mean the Royal Arcanum, O. U. W., Legion of Honor; that our percentage of rejections is less than any of these organizations, and we can say what no other organization doing business in this State can say, that of the men admitted in the last two years we have not lost one from a chronic disease, and of the 800 men admitted into the organization in 1888–89, we have lost only one, and the death was caused by pneumonia.

You and the constituency which you represent, the 4,000 members that compose the Organization, are under great obligations to the Medical Examiners and the H. C. P. Dr. Joseph D. Couch for the care with which the applicants and application papers have been examined.

MEMBERSHIP.

To-day we number nearly 4,000 members, between 3,950 and 3,975; about a net increase of 700 hundred members; being a larger percentage of increase than that of any other fraternal organization doing business in the State whose reports we have been able to obtain.

The growth has been quite general in the Courts throughout the Order; some Courts have lost members or merely held their own; but the great majority have gained. Why have some gained and some lost? The question almost answers itself. Where the members attend the meetings, and see that the officers perform the duty properly assigned them by the Constitution, the Court prospers; but where the members and officers are careless and negligent, the Court must suffer as a result. We would recommend that the officers in all the subordinate Courts first hold the interests of the M. C. O. F. in view, and if they will accept duties in organizations of a similar nature, and neglect the duties assigned them and accepted by them in the M. C. O. F. that the D. H. C. R. should remove them. No man can serve two masters, and no officer can be true to the interest of one organization if he is an officer of another at the same time.

APPLICATION PAPERS.

For the last three years the High Standing Committee have been asking for the application papers of the members, so that they be retained in a safe place provided by the Order. Many of the members must have their application papers, and in the event of their decease it causes needless delay and unnecessary complication on account of the loss of the papers, when a little forethought would avoid it. The representatives to this Convention are earnestly urged to have the members yet holding their applications to forward them to the High Court Secretary-Treasurer.

Your Committee would urge the necessity of compelling Courts to have their meetings at least twice in each month. We find that when the Court will meet only once a month that quite frequently that means no meeting at all, and, as a result, the interest of the Order is neglected.

CERTIFICATE OF MEMBERSHIP.

Every member in the Order should have a certificate of membership, and you are asked to enact such legislation as will accomplish that end. Each new Court was furnished with certificates by the High Standing Committee and members of the Order, and all new applicants should be compelled to take one.

Pass-Word.

Your Committee considers that the provision of the Constitution which provides for a quarterly change of pass-word, should be changed so that it would be issued semi-annually. Where the meetings occur as they now do, — only once or twice a month, — it would be much better and more convenient for the members to have the pass-word issued only once in six months.

Secret Work.

The secret work of the Order seems to be satisfactory and no change is recommended.

Payment of the Endowment.

One great drawback to extension and growth of the Order is the delay on the payment of the endowment. It is, in fact, the only thing in the judgment of your Committee, that to-day hurts the Order; a brother dies; the D. H. C. R. is notified and he proceeds to examine the books of the Court to see if the deceased brother was financial at the time of his death. The D. H. C. R. then forwards the certificate to the H. S. Committee who proceed to investigate and ascertain whether the brother was financial and in good standing; this having been done the Committee issues a call; the members have 40 days in which to pay and as a general thing, they take it, and in many of the Courts, your Committee are inclined to think more; the Treasurer then has 15 days and it must take at least 55 days to get the amount in to pay the endowment. The family of the deceased brother are getting impatient at the delay, and inquire of the members of the Court; members, as a rule, say the blame is with the High Standing Committee, when they don't know, and will not take the trouble to find out.

But in the past the Courts have not paid the money promptly — some of the Courts, we mean; some always pay before it is due· The assessment should be made in advance, and the officers of the Court should communicate directly with the High Court Secretary-Treasurer. Your Committee would, therefore, recommend that the time be reduced from 40 to 30 days, and the time allowed the Treasurer, from 15 to 10 days; and that the supervision and examination of the Deputy High Chief Ranger in relation to the standing of a deceased member, be done away with; nothing comes from it but delay, and no additional safeguard is thrown around th rights of the Order. If the officers of a Court do not perform their duty in relation to suspensions, when death occurs their sympathy will be manifested so that when the books are examined by the Deputy, the deceased member will be found financial. We do not mean to say that the books would be tampered with; but we do say that no case has yet occurred where a member has been found in arrears after death, even where he did not attend a meeting for some time prior to death.

Salvation Fund.

One of the things that the Order should provide for in the Constitution is that when a member in good standing is taken ill through no fault of his own, that he should be kept financial; it is one of the most successful arguments advanced by other organizations, and is the means of attracting a great many men into them; we should do all that reason, justice, humanity, and brotherhood demand. Many of the Courts have provided for it in their by-laws: all should be compelled to.

Sick Benefit.

The Constitution should be so amended that the Courts who desire to have a sick benefit fund for their members could be allowed to do so. It would strengthen the Order and bring many men into it, who to-day go elsewhere because that part is entirely thrown out from our Constitution.

Visits.

We would urge on the delegates the necessity of impressing on their Courts the advisibility of frequent visitations between the Courts. It will give the members a chance to get acquainted with each other; it will make and cement many friendships, and it will enlarge the usefulness of the organization; it will often bring out latent talent, and it will cause emulation that cannot but be beneficial to the Order.

Parade.

The Order has been in existence for 10 years; as yet it has not had a public demonstration of any kind to let the people whom it intends to benefit know what it is. We would suggest the advisibility of having a general parade in the near future, so that the

Catholics of Massachusetts may know that they have a body of men that they can trust, rely on, and that they will not be injured either in purse, body, or soul by being connected with it.

RESIGNATION.

You are asked to deal with the matter of resignations by the members. By some it is contended that members can resign, and by others that they cannot; whether they have the right to do it or not, it has been done for the last 10 years, and it seems to us that the Convention should act on the matter so that the entire Order may know what steps a man may take to leave the Organization, if he wishes to.

FORMING A COURT WITH LESS THAN TWENTY MEMBERS.

It is desirable to have a Court of the Massachusetts Catholic Order of Foresters in every parish in Massachusetts, and the question has often been asked if 20 is not too many to demand for a charter. We would ask you to consider the matter, if it would not be advisable to have it regulated in the same manner that many other organizations do. Let a less number join the Order when they are prepared to pay the required fee for a charter, and do not drive them into an Organization that they would prefer to remain out of but cannot help themselves because they have no other to join.

INVESTIGATING COMMITTEE.

A matter of the greatest importance is the admission of men into the Order, who, while physically qualified, yet have habits of life such as would preclude them from getting into the organization. This cannot be found out unless the Investigating Committee, appointed to investigate into the character of a man, performs its whole duty. We must have temperate men in the Order, not necessarily total abstainers (while they would be the best material), but we cannot take men who are merely good fellows and yet who neglect all the duties incumbent on them as husbands, fathers, and sons. Investigating Committees can be of great assistance to the Order by properly performing the duty assigned them.

RESERVE FUND.

The gravest and most important question that will come before this Convention is that of a reserve fund. It has been under dis-

cussion for the last four years; it is under discussion in the other
fraternal beneficiary associations for a longer period. All agree
that a Reserve Fund will be of immense benefit to any society that
lays the foundation of one and adds something to it; all agree
that a certain amount should be on hand, so that deaths, as they
occur, should be met by the endowment, and the same paid upon
legal proof, and, without delay. Various High Standing Committees
of the Order commended it to the consideration of many Conventions, without any definite action having been taken./ High Chief
Ranger James J. McLaughlin said in his report of the High Standing Committee for 1884–85 : "In this, we are pleased to state
that there is a growing sentiment among the members that we
are sufficiently strong to undertake the erection of a building that
will at once be a home to our people and a source of income to
our Order." We suggest that this is a matter worthy of your consideration, and not an unlikely form of creating the reserve fund
spoken of above. And, again, in the report of 1885–86, he says:
"The matter of providing for a suitable reserve fund, and its
preservation and increase, is one that your Committee desires to
impress upon your attention with all the force they possess. It
is a question that has been talked upon in every Court in the
Order ; and your action on this subject is waited for with an
interest that surpasses that of any question before your body. We
trust that you will give it the benefit of your earnest and intelligent
consideration, — the consideration that it deserves ; and that, in
your adjournment, the ground-work will have been laid for the
establishing of a reserve that will increase the confidence of our
Order, and be a guarantee to all that permanency has at last been
obtained."

An attempt was made to carry the project through the Convention in one of those years, but the timid ones said, wait ; the
Courts do not understand it ; and it was defeated by a few votes,
only to be renewed by the successive High Standing Committees.
Last year High Chief Ranger Watson, for the High Standing Committee, said : "The matter of a reserve fund is the one most
important matter which your Committee desires to impress on your
minds with all the force it possesses. We feel that our Order
never was in a better condition to undertake the matter than at
the present time, and the great necessity shows itself more clearly
every day. We trust that you will give this your earnest con-

sideration, — that which it deserves, — and that this Convention, 'before it adjourns, will have laid the foundation of a reserve fund that will increase the confidence in our Order, and the speedy payment of all death claims." And Past High Chief Ranger McLaughlin appeared before the Convention as consul of the Knights of St. Rose body, and made a proposition from it to the Order donating the sum of one thousand dollars for the purpose of a building fund, subject to the action of the Convention. A Committee of seven was appointed from the Convention to meet a similar body from the Knights of St. Rose, and agree upon a plan, and that Committee will report to you to-day. We bespeak for it your most careful consideration and your best support, if the project the Committee should present is feasible. Many things must be taken into consideration ; but you must be governed mainly by three propositions, namely, Have we the right to form a reserve ? The law almost says that we must have one of a limited amount. Is it wise to risk ? It would be the part of prudence and wisdom to have at least sufficient money on hand, or suitably invested, so that, in case the organization ever ceased to exist, that every claim against the Order should be met and paid, and, if any person was injured by the fall or disruption of the organization, that at least the widow and orphan of those who had gone before would not be the ones to first feel the effect of the want of faith on the part of the members. Can we afford to ? The experience of kindred organizations all over the country say, yes. We have the faith, the ability, and the means ; and we will be recreant to every feeling of duty, false to the men who sent us here to represent them, unless in this Convention we lay the foundation of a reserve fund that will give the men in the organization something to stay for, — will be an induce- ment for those who are not in to join us ; and it may give the Order what it sadly needs, and what does more to strengthen organizations and elevate individuals than anything else, the knowledge that they have a home. Act wisely and well.

Soon after the Convention of last year, Dr. J. R. McLaughlin, of Middlesex Court No. 60, resigned his position on the High Order Committee, and Brother P. A. Murray, of the same Committee, was elected to fill the vacancy.

At the first session of the Convention of 1888, the High Standing Committee were requested to consider the expediency of holding the Convention for this year in the city of Worcester. After carefully considering the matter, and consulting many of the delegates, your Committee came to the conclusion that it would be much better for the Order, and for the convenience of the delegates who were to attend the Convention, to hold it in Boston; better for the Order, because it would not cost the Courts so much in having the delegates come to Boston, and then go to Worcester; and for the additional reason that the Constitution provides that, if a special session of the Convention should be called, it should be held, if practicable, where the annual session was held.

RECORDS AND OFFICE OF HIGH COURT SECRETARY-TREASURER.

During the year the High Court Secretary-Treasurer has constantly labored to perfect the records of the Order, so that they may be in a condition to at all times give such information as may be required. Few men can realize the amount of work that this task involves; but we can have the assurance that when it is done, we will have books and papers as perfect as human skill can make them. The office of the High Court Secretary-Treasurer and High Standing Committee has been open for a portion of every day in the year, except Sunday, and the High Court Secretary-Treasurer has been in daily attendance. Some of the brothers seem to desire to have the High Court Secretary-Treasurer in attendance all the time, and devote all his attention to the affairs of the Order. If the office is to be open all the time, and a suitable man is to occupy the office, he should receive compensation in accordance with his ability and work.

The High Court Physician, Dr. Joseph D. Couch, has been in attendance at nearly all of the meetings of the Committee, and has given his advice freely, and at all times. The position of the High Court Physician is no longer an ornamental one; and any future occupant of that office will have work to perform which must be attended to. Your Committee is under great obligation to the High Court Physician for his uniform kindness, as well as for the manner in which he has devoted his professional skill to the interests of the Order.

The Committee has received many invitations during the year to attend various entertainments given by the Subordinate Courts. When feasible they have been accepted; but all could not be accepted, especially when reasonable notice was not received, and when more pressing business of the Order had to be attended to.

CONSTITUTION.

Your Committee has suggested numerous changes to the Constitution, and many others may be presented to-day. We believe that the Constitution can be improved; but do not think that it can be decidedly improved without care, thought, and deliberation. We would, therefore, recommend that the amendment proposed and adopted last year, providing for a continuous session, be repealed, and that a permanent committee on Constitution be appointed who shall take into consideration the matter of revising the Constitution, and when they are ready to report that the convention be reconvened for the purpose of acting on the report of the committee. It may be said that the Constitution is good enough; that it has sufficed in the past, and, therefore, that a change is unnecessary. The matter ought to be fairly met; let each sacrifice his particular views, so that, as a result of the combined thought and wisdom of all, we may have something which will be of permanent value to the Order.

Your Committee returns its thanks for the many kindnesses shown it during the year; and for the hospitality that has been displayed towards it by brothers throughout the State, the members have been placed under lasting obligations.

During the year 15 clergymen have joined the Order, and we return our thanks to them, and the many other reverend gentlemen who have spoken so kindly of, and approved, our Order and the work it is doing.

Brothers! Ten years ago was formed an organization that promised to do much. It, at the time, was thought visionary and impracticable; but it has performed the work that its founders intended; and while it may have departed somewhat from the lines originally laid out, the principles and purposes have never been changed. We meet to-day, in tenth convention, stronger than ever before — stronger numerically, stronger financially, stronger physically. We have the experience of the past before us — let us profit by it. Let the bonds of Friendship, Unity, and true Christian charity, be so cemented by loyal adhesion to each other, that no man or men can do aught to impair the usefulness of our Order. Let us be loyal to the principles that govern our Order, and we will be loyal to our grand church, as good citizens as any in our common country, we will receive the approval and encouragement of our pastors, the prayers of the widow and orphan, and the blessing of God.

JEREMIAH G. FENNESSEY,

High Chief Ranger.

Boston, April 17, 1889.

Report of High Court Secretary-Treasurer,

To the Representatives of the Massachusetts Catholic Order of Foresters:

Brothers : —

The report of the business done the past year by the Subordinate Courts of the Massachusetts Catholic Order of Foresters is herewith submitted for your inspection.

The work of the Courts, as given in their reports, is here presented in such shape that each member of the Order may see for himself just what his own Court has done, and also see what a neighboring Court has accomplished or neglected to attempt. He may also see what has been done by Courts most distant from him, and may judge for himself whether the sentiment which pressed him on to advance the interests of the Order, and thereby himself, has kept pace with the same, or a similar, sentiment existing in the breast of a brother Forester fifty or one hundred, or more, miles away.

He may also judge whether (provided he has been negligent in his obligations as a member) he has not made a grave mistake in belonging to an organization which is advancing so rapidly as to make his almost wilful carelessness all the more glaring.

Such members, let us hope, are few; but that we have some, is only too true. And the experience of the Deputy High Chief Rangers show it only too clearly.

To such members only one word can be said, and that is: "Gentlemen, you are surely dropping behind, and unless you quicken your efforts you will not be missed when the Recording Secretary of your Court writes against your name the simple word — suspended."

Let us hope, then, that all such will see that in making ever so slight an effort to advance the interests of the Order, they are at the same time encouraging hundreds of others to do likewise, and are very materially advancing their own interests. It must be patent to every one that an act which strengthens the organization makes the standing of the most humble member much firmer.

To the courts which have shown extraordinary zeal in increasing membership and funds too much praise cannot be given, and the showing made of the work of the past year should redound to their lasting credit. We have had a year of unexampled prosperity, and the promising view which was opening for us a year ago has been well realized. Members generally have taken hold of the work of the order and carried it forward, and, to-day, instead of having a weak and indifferent membership waiting for something to turn up, we have a living, active membership, which has increased during the year passed far beyond expectation — increased, too, in the face of violent opposition at the beginning of the term, which, we are only too happy to state, has been negatived by the manly and conservative course which our esteemed High Chief Ranger has pursued in all his dealings with the members, both individually and collectively. Increased, too, in the face of active competition from other organizations, which have all promised more than they can or will perform, as the future will only too plainly show. Many, far too many, Catholics belong to other organzations, which, while claiming to treat all members alike, yet Catholics who are members of such, could if they would, tell of the strained feeling which appears if a Catholic member attempts to develop any more activity as a member than is necessary for the payment of dues.

To those we say, the Massachusetts Catholic Order of Foresters offers you superior inducements, because in our Order your activity may have full scope, and you are just as well received in one Court of the Order as another. We have a successful organization, composed of Catholics, and it is your duty to join it in preference to any other. Our membership Jan. 1, 1888, was 3,200 ; Jan. 1, 1889, was 3,644 — add 325 approved from Jan. 1, 1889, to April 1, 1889, and we have for our present membership, 3,969, from which are to be deducted the few suspensions and deaths since Jan. 1, 1889.

The following tables show the membership as given on returns received from Courts, with the gain from initiations, withdrawals, and reinstatements, and the loss from suspensions, withdrawals, and death : —

MEMBERSHIP.

No. of Court.	NAME OF COURT.	Membership Dec. 31, 1887.	Membership Dec. 31, 1888.	Initiated in 1888.	Admitted on W. Card in 1888.	Reinstated in 1888.	Average Age of Court Dec. 31, 1888.	Average Age of Court Dec. 31, 1887.	Withdrawn on Card in 1888.	Resigned Membership in 1888.	Suspended for Non-payment in 1888.	Expelled, 1888.	Died, 1888.	Rejected by Ballot in 1888.	Rejected by H.S.C. in 1888.
1	Cathedral	131	130	6	1	1	41.1	40.4	1	1	4		3	1	1
3	Fenwick	67	70	4		2	42.4	42	1		8		1		
4	St. Francis	114	110	5	1		42.2	41	1		1		3		1
5	Leo	104	106	7			40.6	39.5	1		4		3		3
6	Cheverus	91	86	4	1		43.3	44			3		4		6
7	St. Patrick	50	47				41.4	40			2		1		5
8	Sherwood	124	141	22			38.2	38.2			1		3		
9	Thos	33	34	2	3		32.7	36			2		2		2
10	Iona	135	69	10			40.5	42	1		6		3		1
11	St. Joseph	63	137	1			40.4	40			1		1		6
12	Fulton	30	29	1		1	42.7	42.3			2		3		3
13	Fitzpatrick	60	54	12	1		43.1	42.6	1		3		1		1
14	Lafayette	49	58	14			40.7	42.1	2	1	2		2		2
15	SS. Peter & Paul	49	62	15	1		40.4	41	2	2	3		3		1
16	Essex	90	99				38.5	37.4							
17	Hamilton	69	65	6	1	1	44.4	46.3	1		1		1		1
18	St. Peter	66	69	4			39.1	38			2		1		
19	Williams	70	71	11			37.4	38.6			1		1		1
20	Mt. Pleasant	68	76	2			44.4	38			2				
21	St. Alphonsus	47	46	5			38.3	43	4		3			1	
23	St. John	28	30	11			38.6	37.05	4	2	3		1		
24	St. Gregory	39	48	19			38.03	39	1		2		1		
25	St. Francis	73	88	1			41.7	37.2			3				
26	St. Raphael	40	37	17	1		41.7	40.7	3		6		1		
28	Erin	59	74	12			36.3	42.4			1				
29	St. Thomas	73	78	2			40.3	33.6					1		
30	Bass River	40	36	8			39.08	39.1	1	2	9				1
32	Qualey	27	35	8			42.03	38.4			1				1
33	St. John	64	59	3			36.4	41.5			1		1		1
34	Americus	64	77	14			38.2	37.2	1	1	1				
36	Sheil	24	24	4			37.3	38.2	1						
37	St. Joseph	47	47	2	2		44.6	35					2		1
38	St. Joseph	42	45	4	1		39	44.2	1						
39	Benedict	22	31	8			40.3		1				1		
41	Star of the Sea	35	33	3			37.6	37.15			4				

MEMBERSHIP—Continued.

No. of Court.	NAME OF COURT.	Mem'ership Dec. 31, 1887.	Mem'ership Dec. 31, 1888.	Initiated in 1888.	Admit'ted on W. Card in 1888.	Reins'ated in 1888.	Ave age Age of C'urt Dec. 3R, 1888.	Ave age Age of C'urt Dec. 3R, 1887.	Withdrawn on Card in 1888.	Resigned Membership in 1888.	Suspended for Non-payment in 1888.	Expelled, 1888.	Died, 1888.	Rejected by Ballot in 1888.	Rejected by H.S.C. in 1888.
43	St. M——	23	22	1			41·8	40			1				
44	St. Bernard	59	52	2			34·5	31			1		1		1
45	M——	36	38	1	1		41·08	40·5			1		1		6
46	St. ——	29	30	4	1		40·8	38		1	6				1
47	St. Anne	69	68	8		2	31·04	30			1		1		
48	Sarsfield	58	64	23		1	39·5	37·6			3		1		
49	Constantine	56	76	5			36·6	35·1							4
50	Holy Trinity	54	58	1			41·01	39·2	2	1	2				1
51	Highland	26	24	13			37·5	35·08	3	2	2				3
52	Emerald	54	63	19			35	33·02			4				
53	St. James	33	52	6			29·1	29·9		1	5	3			2
54	Charles River	77	76	12			34·4	33	2		1				
55	Carroll	28	39				37·7	37			1				1
56	Prospect	51	46	17		2	33·2			3	11			1	3
57	Worcester	53	70	13	3		34·5	34			4		1		
58	——	64	77	15	1		34·3	35·8			1				2
59	St. Catherine	42	57	8			30·6	31·7	1	1	1				1
60	Shields	32	40	14			33·3	35		2	3				
61	Gallagher	27	30	14			36·06	34·1			1				
62	St. Columbkill	57	62	21		1	31·9	31					1		7
63	Griffin	39	58	3	3		36·3	35							4
64	*Canton	26	28	24			33·7	31							
65	†St. Margaret		45	5			33·5								
66	‡Stoughton		27	5			31·6								
67	$St. Michael		32	7			31·2								
68	||Phil. Sheridan		26	13			30·7								
69	¶Merrimack		55	1			30·7								
			28												
		3,180	**3,644**	**508**	**23**	**10**			**30**	**22**	**129**	**3**	**46**	**5**	**78**

* Instituted Jan. 26, 1888.   † =   ‡ Instituted June 7, 1888. $ Instituted Sept. 14, 1888.

|| Instituted April 14, 1888.   ¶ Dec. 20, 1888.   Instituted Sept. 18, 1888.

It will be seen for the year ending Dec. 31, 1888, the largest addition to the Order was made by Canton Court, No. 67, with 24 initiations; next is Constantine, No. 49, with 23 initiations; next is Sherwood, No. 8, with 22 initiations, and St. Columbkill, No. 65, with 21 initiations. St. Francis, No. 25, and St. James, No. 54, have 19 initiations each, and Erin, No. 28, and Worcester, No. 59, initiated 17 each.

The percentage of increase is shown by the following table:

No. of Court.	NAME OF COURT.		No. of Court.	NAME OF COURT.	
1	Cathedral	.046	38	St. Joseph	.095
3	Fenwick	.06	39	Benedict	.363
4	St. Francis	.044	41	Star of the Sea	.085
5	Leo	.067	44	St. Bernard	.017
6	Cheverus	.044	45	Unity	.055
8	Sherwood	.177	46	St. Augustine	.034
9	Columbus	.06	47	St. Anne	.059
10	Iona	.16	48	Sarsfield	.138
11	St. Joseph	.074	49	Constantine	.41
12	Fulton	.033	51	Holy Trinity	.092
13	Fitzpatrick	.016	52	Highland	.038
14	Lafayette	.25	53	Emerald	.24
15	SS. Peter and Paul	.28	54	St. James	.58
16	Essex	.166	55	Charles River	.078
18	St. Peter	.09	57	Carroll	.43
19	Williams	.057	59	Worcester	.32
20	Mt. Pleasant	.16	60	Middlesex	.203
21	St. Alphonsus	.042	61	St. Lawrence	.357
23	St. John	.18	62	St. Catherine	.25
24	St. Gregory	.28	63	Shields	.52
25	St. Francis	.26	64	Gallagher	.245
26	St. Raphael	.025	65	St. Columbkill	.54
28	Erin	.29	66	Griffin	.115
29	St. Thomas	.137	67	Canton	1.14
30	Bass River	.05	68	St. Margaret	.209
32	Qualey	.296	69	Stoughton	.185
33	St. John	.047	70	St. Michael	.27¼
34	Americus	.22	71	Phil Sheridan	.309
35	Sheil	.166	72	Merrimack	.037
37	Friendship	.042			

The average age of the membership of the Order, as per returns, Jan. 1, 1888, was thirty-nine years; the average age of the Order, Jan. 1, 1889, was thirty-eight years.

Since April 18, 1888, the following new courts have been formed:

Stoughton . . . . No. 69 . . 27 charter members.
St. Michael . . . " 70 . . 20 " "
Phil Sheridan . . " 71 . . 42 " "
Merrimack . . . " 72 . . 27 " "
Taunton . . . . " 73 . . 80 " "
Hendricken . . . . " 74 . . 23 " "

The average age of the applicants approved the past year was thirty-two years, and the number applying to each Court is given below.

New applications received from April 17, 1888, to March 31, 1889 : —

No.	Court.		No.	Court.	
1	.. Cathedral	16	39	.. Benedict	4
3	.. Fenwick	3	41	.. Star of the Sea	1
4	.. St. Francis	7	44	.. St. Bernard	1
5	.. Leo	6	45	.. Unity	1
6	.. Cheverus	7	46	.. St. Augustine	1
7	.. St. Patrick	4	47	.. St. Anne	16
8	.. Sherwood	28	48	.. Sarsfield	15
9	.. Columbus	2	49	.. Constantine	20
10	.. Iona	17	51	.. Holy Trinity	21
11	.. St. Joseph	7	52	.. Highland	3
12	.. Fulton	1	53	.. Emerald	9
14	.. Lafayette	17	54	.. St. James	20
15	.. SS. Peter and Paul,	17	55	.. Charles River	4
16	.. Essex	15	57	.. Carroll	11
18	.. St. Peter	8	59	.. Worcester	18
19	.. Williams	8	60	.. Middlesex	7
20	.. Mt. Pleasant	18	61	.. St. Lawrence	11
21	.. St. Alphonsus	2	62	.. St. Catherine	22
23	.. St. John	9	63	.. Shields	8
24	.. St. Gregory	19	64	.. Gallagher	7
25	.. St. Francis	22	65	.. St. Columbkill	11
26	.. St. Raphael	1	66	.. Griffin	6
28	.. Erin	8	67	.. Canton	22
29	.. St. Thomas	30	68	.. St. Margaret	7
30	.. Bass River	1	69	.. Stoughton	42
32	.. Qualey	9	70	.. St. Michael	38
33	.. St. John	4	71	.. Phil Sheridan	77
34	.. Americus	19	72	.. Merrimack	41
35	.. Sheil	3	73	.. Taunton	86
37	.. Friendship	7	74	.. Hendricken	26
38	.. St. Joseph	1			

The average age of applications rejected, the past year, was 33.8 years.

The whole number of rejections, from April 18, 1888, to April 1, 1889, is ninety-four. Last year, the rejections, for the same period, were ninety-four,— or fifteen per cent. of the whole number received; this year, it is not quite eleven per cent. of the whole number received.

This may seem to imply that less care is used in scrutinizing applications; but such is not the fact. More care, if anything, is exercised than ever before. The High Court physician has attended constantly the meetings of the High Standing Committee, and all applications have received a careful examination at his hands,— many of them being sent to his office for that purpose, when an extraordinary number were to be acted upon.

The proper inference to be drawn is, that the members of the Order have used greater care in selection of applicants, having finally realized that it is useless to try to pass into the Order men who are not physically fit to become members.

The various occupations of new applicants do not differ much from last year; but, for easy reference, the list is given this year.

OCCUPATIONS OF APPLICANTS APPROVED FROM JANUARY 1, 1888, TO JANUARY 1, 1889.

Armorer	1	C. H. Inspector	1	Furniture Salesman	1
Baggage Master	1	Coachman	26	Fireman	3
Bookkeeper	3	Cutlery Grinder	1	" in Mill	1
Blacksmith	17	Cutler	1	" in Shop	1
" helper	1	Currier	14	Furnishing Goods	1
Builder	2	Carbuilder	1	Frt. Handler	1
Butcher	9	Carriage Smith	1	" Clerk	1
Barber	7	Collector	1	Fisherman	1
Bricklayer	6	Carpet Maker	1	Farmer	14
Bookseller	1	Carriage Painter	2	Farm Hand	2
Butter Salesman	1	" Driver	2	Gilder	1
" Dealer	1	Cigars and Tobacco	1	Grocer	18
Bell Hanger	1	Copper Worker	1	" Clerk	4
Brush Maker	1	Coal and Wood	1	Gardener	11
Bartender	1	D. M. D.	1	Gun Barrel Prover	1
Boot & Shoe Dealer	1	Dep. Sheriff	1	Granite Dealer	3
Boss Finisher	1	Dry Goods	3	" Cutter	8
Brass Finisher	2	Dining Saloon	1	" Polisher	2
Boiler Maker	1	Dealer in Paper Stock	1	" Man'f'r	1
Boot Maker	1	Drug Clerk	1	Glass Artist	1
Baker	1	Driver Baker's Wagon	1	Hotel Bellman	1
Boot Fitter	1	Doorkeeper	1	Harness M'k'r	4
Cooper	1	Engraver	1	Heel Man'f'r	1
Clergyman	15	Expressman	3	" Cutter	1
Clerk	30	Engineer	3	" Maker	2
Cabinet Maker	4	Foreman	3	Hay Clerk	1
Chaser	1	" for Contractor	1	Horse Shoer	5
Confectioner	1	" in Shoe Factory	1	Hatter	9
Civil Engineer	1	" in Quarry	1	Hackman	7
Carpenter	30	" in Silk Mill	1	Hostler	3
Cattle Dealer	1	" Laborer	1	Iron Worker	2
Cook	1	" B. W. Works	1	" Moulder	1
Conductor, H. R. R.	2	Furniture Finisher	1	Inner Sole Cutter	1

Insurance Agent	.	1	Pedler	. . .	2	Shipping Clerk	.	5
Jeweller	. .	5	Postal Clerk	. .	1	Store Keeper	.	1
Jewelry Trader	.	1	Polisher in Laundry		1	Stable "	.	5
Janitor	. .	3	Paper Hanger	.	1	Stiffening M'k'r.	.	1
Laster	. . .	2	" Maker	.	3	Steam Gauge "	.	1
Lithographer	.	2	" Salesman	.	1	Stock Fitter	.	1
Longshoreman	.	1	Provisions	.	7	" Broker	.	1
Life Insurance Agent	1	" Clerk	.	1	Starch Maker	.	2
Lamplighter	. .	1	Piano Maker	.	1	Stone Mason	.	3
Leather	. .	1	" String Winder	1	Silversmith	.	2
" Cutter	.	1	Plasterer	. .	1	Stitcher	.	1
Liquor Dealer	.	6	Painter	. .	7	Stone Polisher	.	1
" Clerk	.	1	Physician	. .	14	Switchman	. .	1
Letter Carrier	.	2	Porter	. . .	9	Tender in Grain Store	1
Laborer	. .	105	Printer	. . .	2	Teamster	. .	42
Lawyer	. .	7	Plumber	. .	11	Tailor	. . .	10
Mill Supplies	.	1	Policeman	. .	11	Tinsmith	. .	3
Master Painter	.	1	Quarryman	. .	1	Tanner	. . .	1
Marble Cutter	.	1	Rubber Cutter	.	1	Trader	. . .	1
Morocco Dresser	.	5	Restaurant	. .	1	Tel. Operator	.	1
" Finisher	.	2	Real Estate	. .	1	Upper Leather Cutter	1
Machinist	. .	14	Roofer	. . .	2	Upholsterer	.	2
" Helper	.	1	Supt. Water Dept.		1	U.S. Storekeeper	.	1
Moulder	. .	3	Shoe Stitcher	.	3	Undertaker	. .	3
Mill Hand	. .	1	" Fitter	. .	1	Varnisher	.	2
Milkman	. .	6	" Maker	.	51	Variety Store	.	1
Merchant	. .	4	" Finisher	.	4	Wire Drawer	.	1
Merchant Tailor	.	1	" Cutter	. .	6	Wool Spinner	.	1
Man'f'r.	. .	2	" Dealer	. .	6	" Grader	.	1
Mason	. .	10	" Merchant	.	1	" Sorter	.	1
Meat Cutter	. .	1	" Caster	.	2	" Dyer	.	1
Night Watchman	.	2	Sta. Engineer	.	3	Watchman,		
" " in mill	1	Shovel Maker	.	2	B. & M. R. R.	.	1
Nail Maker	. .	1	Salesman	. .	58	Waiter	. . .	1
Overseer Farm	.	1	" Goods	.	3	Weaver	. . .	3
Officer House of Cor.	1	" Jewelry	.	1	Wheelwright	.	1
" Custom House	1	Stone Cutter	.	10			
Oil Merchant	.	1	Seal "	.	1	Total	. .	783
Pharmacist	. .	1	Student	. .	5			

OCCUPATIONS OF APPLICANTS REJECTED FROM JANUARY 1, 1888, TO JANUARY 1, 1889.

Apothecary	. .	1	Furniture Polisher	.	1	Painter	.	1
Brakeman	. .	3	Fisherman	. .	1	Packer	.	1
Bottle Dealer	.	1	Flour Inspector	.	1	Plumber	.	1
Britannia Smith	.	1	Grocer	. . .	2	Quarryman	.	1
Barber	. . ,	1	Horseshoer	. .	1	Rubber Worker	.	2
Bartender	. .	1	Hostler	. . .	1	" Boot Maker	1
Blacksmith	. .	1	Hatter	. . .	1	Roofer	. .	1
Boarding House K'p'r.	1	Junk Dealer	. .	1	Ship Carpenter	.	1
Compositor	. .	1	Loco. Engineer	.	1	Stone Cutter	.	4
Currier	. .	2	Laborer	. .	8	Silversmith	. .	1
Conductor R. R.	.	1	Lawyer	. .	1	Salesman	.	1
Carpenter	. .	1	Laster	. .	2	Shoemaker	. .	2
Coal Dealer	. .	1	Moulder	. .	2	Shoe Finisher	.	1
Cook	. . .	1	Machinist	. .	1	Switch Tender	.	1
Clerk	. . .	1	Printer	. .	1	Tobacco Dealer	.	1
Clerk in Liq. Sal.	.	1	Paving Cutter	.	1			
Engineer	. .	1	Policeman	. .	1	Total	. .	72
Furniture Dealer	.	1	Piano Maker	.	2			

The following table gives the number of endowments paid to April 1, 1889:—

ENDOWMENTS PAID.

NAMES OF DECEASED MEMBERS. DATE AND CAUSE OF DEATH. COURT OF WHICH THE DECEASED WAS A MEMBER, AND BENEFICIARIES, AGE, LENGTH OF MEMBERSHIPS.

No.	NAME.	COURT.	AGE.	INITIATED.	Membership Yrs.	Mos.	Dys.	DATE OF DEATH.	CAUSE.	Endowment.	NUMBER OF BENEFICIARIES.	TO WHOM PAID.
1	Cornelius Cronin,	ola, No. 10, Men	49	Mar. 14, 1880	7		5	Oct. 19, 1880	Typho-Malia	$1,000	1, Widow	Administratrix
2	Dennis McCarthy,	b, 5, Boston			1	1	6	Nov. 20, "	Phthisis	"	1, "	dow
3	M. J. Kiley,	ck, 3,	31	Nov. 14, 1879	1	9	19	Dec. 3, 1881	Pulmonary Consumption	"		Executor
4	D. J. Desmond,	Iona, 10, Halen	29	Mar. 14, 1880	1			Jan. 11, "	Typhoid Pneumonia	"	1, "	Administrator
5	P. H. McGrath, A,	nal, 1, Boston	48	Sept. 3, 1879	1	3	8	Jan. 11, "	Aky	"	1, "	dow
6	Jeremiah A,	atal, 1,	33	Oct. 15, "	1	3	12	Jan. 27, "	Pneumonia	"	1, "	
7	Edward A. Burbank,	Cheverus, 6,	38	Feb. 11, 1880	1		0	Mar. 5, "	Typhoid Pneumonia	"	1, "	"
8	ohn lm,	Fitzpatrick, 13,	42	May 26, "		10	24	April 26, "	Pneumonia	"	1, "	"
9	Patrick My,	Hamilton, 17,	43	Aug. 3, "	0	10	11	June 17, "	Cancer in Groin	"	1, "	"
10	Patrick Murray,	Iona, 10, Malden	46	April 21, "	1		14	June 18, "	his Pulmonalis	"	1, "	"
11	Patrick C. Dailey,	Americus, 34, Boston	26	Mar. 15, 1881		6	27	Aug. 29, "	Typhoid Pneumonia	"	1, "	"
12	James L. Mr,	b, 5,	27	Aug. 13, 1880	1		14	Aug. 23, "	Phthisis Pulmonalis	"	1, "	"
13	Thomas F. Simpson,	b, 5,	24	Aug. 10, 1881	1	0	8	Aug. 24, "	Intussus Ception Peritonitis	"	3, & children	" & guardian
14	Archibald Morrison,	Min, 17,	47	July 6, 1880	1	1	27	Sept. 3, "	Ate Phthisis	"	1, "	"
15	Michael McCarthy,	Leo, 5, ank, 7,	36	Aug. 16, "	1	8	5	Oct. 30, "	Bright's Disease	"	4, "	" & children
16	William Whitley,	St. Sh, 11,	40	April 21, 1881	1		1	Nov. 5, "	Chronic Catarrhal Pneumonia	"	1, "	"
17	Daniel J. McDonald,	Hamilton, 17,	49	April 21, 1880	1	9	14	Nov. 22, "	Chronic his & Pneumonia	"	1, "	"
18	thy St,	Fenwick, 3,	23	Mch. 4, "	1	11	26	Nov. 30, "	Cancerous Dis. of Æsophagus	"	1, "	"
19	David lan,	nd, 8,	26	Dec. 27, "	1	11	9	Dec. 6, "	Lobular Pneumonia, sec'd stage	"		"
20	Mhael O'Brien,	St. Joseph, 11,	23	May 10, "	1	7	26	Jan. 6, 1882	Pneumonia,	"	3, Children	Guardian
21	John M. Galvin,	St. Sh, 11,	31	Mar. 22, "	1	9	17	Jan. 9, "	Bronchitis and Cong. of Brain	"	1, Widow	dow
22	Thos. T. McDonough,	St. Alphonsus, 21,	28	Oct. 15, "	1	3	10	Jan. 25, "	Inflammation of his	"	1, "	"
23	James My,	Cathedral, 1,	25	Oct. 15, 1879	2	3	16	Feb. 1, "	Phthisis	"	1, "	"
24	Daniel od,	St. Joseph, 38,	46	Mar. 29, 1881	1	10	19	Feb. 18, "	Pneumonia	"	1, "	"
25	lark B. Mulvey,	Shin, 27,	36		1	1	18	Mar. 6, "	Heart Disease	"		"
26	John Boles,	St. Patrick, 7,	40	Jan. 18, "				Mar. 25, "	Mania a Potu	"		
27	Thos. ohre Bayley,	Leo, 5,	21	June 25, 1880	1	10	26	May 25, "	Colloid Cancer of	hes	1, "	"
28	Thos. Clark,	Hut, 39, Somerville	35	June 24, 1881	1	4	4	May 21, "	Cancer of Stomach	"	1, "	"
29	James Fell,	Liberty, 40, Boston	39	May 12, "	1	0	17	May 28, "	Phthisis	"		"
30	ok kn,	Essex, 16, Salem	40	June 23, 1880	1	11	17	May 29, "	Pneumonia	"	1, "	"
31	John Chambers,	St. Francis, 4, Boston	33	June 1, 1882	1	11		June 10, "	Cirrhosis of Liver	"	1, "	"
32	John Hayes,						26	June 27, "	Pneumonia	"		"

ENDOWMENTS PAID — Continued.

NO.	NAME.	COURT.	AGE.	INITIATED.	Yrs.	Mos.	Dys.	DATE OF DEATH.	CAUSE.	Endowment.	… OF …	TO whom PAID.
33	… Miller,	Fenwick, 3, …	25	Sept. 3, 1880	1	8	21	May 24, 1882	… at Sea	$1,000	1, …	Father
34	…	…	32	April 13, 1881	1	9	14	Jan. 27, "		"	1, Widow	"
35	… Devenny,	SS. … & Paul, 15, "	34	Nov. 17, 1880	2	5	6	Aug. 11, "	Rheumatism	"	1, Father	…
36	Jo. B. Foley, M.D.,	… 3, "	28	Mar. 12, "	2	11	6	Aug. 18, "	… of … Cong. of the [Brain	"		"
37	… McDade,	… 1, 3,	27	Aug. 3, 1879	2	11	24	July 27, "	… Fever	"		…
38	Wm. Fitzgibbon,	Fitzpatrick, …	24	April 20, 1880	2	4	8	Sept. 7, "	Pulmonary Hyperæmia	"	5,	…
39	Hugh Diver,	Fenwick, 3,	24	Dec. 23, 1881	2	9	25	Sept. 27, "	… Consump …	"	1,	…
40	…	… 6,	38	Mar. "	2	7	5	Oct. 28, "	… of …	"	1,	…
41	…	St. Francis, 25, W.	40	Dec. 21, "	1	11		Nov. 21, "	… by … falling	"	1,	"
42	…	St. … 4,	50	Jan. 8, "	2	10	13	Nov. 3, "	…	"	1, Widow	…
43	… Gill,	… 5, … 6,	48	Feb. "	2	8	10	Oct. 14, "	Pneumonia	"	1,	…
44	… F. Decker,	…	22	April 26, 1882	2	10	8	Jan. 6, 1883	…	"	1, Son	Son
45	James …	…	08	Feb. 11, 1880	2	10	28	Jan. 9, "	… Hip	"	1, …	Father
46	Ed. L. Burns,	Fitzpatrick, 13,	34	Nov. 17, "	1	11	5	Oct. 22, 1882	…	"	1, …	Widow
47	Florence …	St. … 18,	23	Jan. 26, 1881	1	10	18	Feb. 14, 1883	…	"	1, …	…
48	… McCormick,	St. … 4,	28	May 26, 1882	1	8	18	Feb. 14, "	… of …	"	1, …	…
49	…	St. … 4,	32	Dec. 21, "	1	2	28	Feb. 19, "	… Gill …	"	1,	…
50	… A. Breen,	Sheil, 35, … 8,	24	June 24, 1881	1	8	10	Mar. 4, "	…	"	2, …	Son
51	David Horan,	St. …	35	Mar. 4, 1880	3	14		Mar. 18, "	…	"	1, …	…
52	…	… 13,	18	Mar. 30, 1881	3	18		April 16, "	… of …	"	1, …	…
53	…	Essex, 16,	64	"	3	16		April 22, "	…	"	1, Sister	Sister
54	Richard Collins,	…	38	Nov. 3, 1880	2	6		May 3, "	… of … Brain	"	1, …	…
55	James …	Ex., 16,		Aug. 4, "	2	9	1	May 6, "	…	"	1, Her	…
56	P. H. …	St. … 4,	41	Dec. 18, 1879	3	4	18	May 8, "	…	"	1, Child	Child
57	… Doherty,	St. … 8,	12	July 8, 1880	2	10		May 30, "	… Pyæmia	"	4, …	…
58	… J. …	St. … 8,	21	Oct. 21, "	2	7	6	June 28, "	…	"	1, …	…
59	…	St. Anne, 47,	33	Dec. 22, 1882	2	9	1	June 2, "	…	"	1, Her	…
60	James Callahan,	… 3,	26	April 2, 1880	2	2		Jan. 3, "	…	"	1, …	…
61	… F. Daly,	… 6,		Mar. "	2	3	2	May 4, "	…	"	3, Children	…
62	William B. Smith,	… 3,	37	Nov. 14, 1879	3	7		June 13, "	…	"	1, …	Widow
63	C. J. Sullivan,	… 13,	45	Nov. 14, "	2	6	20	June 28, "	…	"	1, …	"
64	John …	St. … 7,	13	Dec. 1, 1880	3	4	18	June 28, "	…	"	1, …	"
65	…		18	Feb. 10, "	3	2	17	June 30, "	…	"	1, …	"
66	… G. …	… 6,	37	April 13, "	3	2	24	July 12, 1883	…	"	1, …	"
67	… T.	St. … 23, Hyde	27	April 8, 1883	1		15	July 5, "	… Debility	"	1, …	…
68	…	Star of the Sea, 41, Boston	49	May 27, 1882	1			July 24, "	Septicæmia	"	1, …	…
69	… Nee,	…	50	Dec. 5, "	3	8	11	Aug. 23, "	… … fever	"	1, …	Widow
70	…	… 3,	37	Dec. 12, 1879	3	3	16	Sept. 30, "	… … fever	"	3, …	Heirs
71	L. A. …, M.D.,	… 3,		Nov. 14, "	3	3		Oct. 17, "	…	"	1, Mother	…
72	… J.	Willia … 9,	27	Sept. 16, 1880	3	1		"				

No.	Name	Address	Age	Date		Cause of Death	Amt.	Beneficiaries	Relation
73	M. H. Byrne,	Benedict, 39, Somerville	28	Mar. 31, 1881	2 5 17 Sept. 28, 1883	Pulmonary Hemorrhage	$1,000	1, Widow	Widow
74	Bart. Whalen,	Essex, 16, Salem	35	Aug. 1, 1883	2 2 Oct. 1,	Uremic [illegible]	"	1, Mother	Mother
75	E. F. [illegible],	Fenwick, 3, Boston	22	Feb. 16, 1881	8 18 Nov. 21,	Phthisis	"	1, Widow	Widow
76	John O'Brien,	Hamilton, 17,	47	Sept. 15, 1881	2 6 Sept. 6,	Heart Disease	"	4, Heirs	Heirs
77	Patrick Monaghan,	St. Joseph, 11,	32	June 14, 1880	3 1 7 Nov. 24,	Injury to Brain by fall	"	1,	
78	John Sweeney,	[illegible], 39, Somerville	40	Mar. 31, 1881	3 2 Nov. 25,	Pulmonary Consumption	"	"	
79	Michael H. Murray,	Mt. Pleasant, 20, Boston	42	Oct. 30,	3 2 10 Dec. 11,	Catarrhal Pneumonia, C'nsum'p.	"	"	
80	Michael Donahue,	Fenwick, 3,	40	Jan. 30,	4 Dec. 22,	Pleurisy	"	"	
81	John Murray,	Cathedral, 1,	39	Oct. 8, 1879	5 Dec. 25,	Phthisis	"	1, Sister	Sister
82	T. H. O'Rourke,	St. [illegible], 54,	25	July 2, 1883	4 Feb. 25,	Pulmonary Phthisis	"	1, Widow	Widow
83	Philip McDonald,	St. Thomas, 29, Brockton	39	Feb. 17, 1881	3 4 Feb. 27, 1884	[illegible] Paralysis	"	1, Mother	Mother
84	John B. Reagan,	Chas Riv. 55,	33	Nov. 28, 1881	3 23 Feb. 21,	[illegible]	"	1, Widow	Widow
85	Thos McDonough	[illegible], 32, Woburn,	30	July 10, 1883	2 5 Feb. 28,	[illegible] of [illegible] and Peritonitis	"	"	
86	Jhs Welsh,	Americus, 34, Boston	35	May 30, 1880	3 9 Jan. 29,	Quick Consumption	"	1,	
87	Enis Ahearn,	St. Patrick, 7, So.	31	Oct. 13, 1881	4 10 17 Mar. 10,	Bright's Disease	"	4, 3 child'n	
88	Frank A. Spitz,	St. [illegible], 21,	31	Feb.	3 10 Jan. 12,	Phthisis [illegible]	"	3, 3 "	
89	Al[fred] Green,	[illegible], 6,	41	Oct. 14, 1882	3 7 Feb. 6,	Pulmonary Consumption	"	3, 2 "	
90	John A. McCarthy,	Fitzpatrick, 13,	32	Mar. 14, 1880	3 24 Jan. 21,	Pulmonary [illegible]	"	1,	
91	John F. Cunningham	Iona, 10,	32	May 20, 1881	3 10 7 April 23,	[illegible]	"	2, Parents	Parents
92	Stephen T. Sliney,	SS.Pet.&Paul,15, S.Bos'n	50	April 7,	3 11 3 April 19,	Bright's Disease of Kidneys	"	1, Sister	Sister
93	Thos Garvey,	Fenwick, 3,	38	Mar.	3 11 12 Mar. 2,	[illegible], falling off staging	"	5, Widow, 4 child'n	Widow
94	John H. [illegible],	Essex, 16, Salem	32	April 26, 1880	8 2 Dec. 28, 1883	Phthisis	"	5, 8	
95	John W. Lynch,	St. Joseph, 11,	49	Feb. 3, 1881	3 5 June 18, 1884	Phthisis Pulm [illegible]	"	5, 4	
96	John P. Duffin,	Erin, 28,	45	Jan. 8, 1880	4 16 May 24,	Heart Disease	"	3, 2 "	
97	William Meagher,	St. Francis, 4,	43	April 26,	4 18 May 14,	Accid'nt, hhd. sugar fell on him	"	3, 3 "	
98	Michael McCarthy,	[illegible], 13,	49	Sept. 8,	3 7 25 May 2,	Diabetes Melletus	"	4,	
99	Charles Lyons,	Cathedral, 8,	30	Mar. 24, 1881	3 1 8 May 9,	Pneumonia. r. lung & [illegible] lt.	"	4, 2 "	
100	[illegible] Bry,	Iona, 10,	31	April 11,	3 18 April 29,	Phthisis	"	3,	
101	Patrick A. Finn,	St. Francis, 4,	30	April 22, 1880	4 17 June 9,	Hemphlegia of Larynx	"	1, Daughter	Daughter
102	Edward W. Wright,	Sherwood, 8,	40	April 22,	4 11 May 23,	[illegible], [illegible] of leg	"	1, Mother	Mother
103	John J. Donovan,	Williams, 19,	23	April 4, 1881	3 11 July 15,	Phthisis Pulmonalis	"	4,	
104	Michael Maguire,	Liberty, 10,	40	June 23,	4 1 June 24,	Chronic Bronchitis	"	4, [illegible] 3 child'n	
105	Phil A.,	Americus, 34,	34	Mar. 11,	3 4 22 July 3,	Pulmonary Consumption	"	1,	
106	[illegible] F. Lynch,	Americus, 34,	33	Nov. 21, 1882	3 9 19 Aug. 10,	Pulmonary Consumption	"	1, Sister	Sister
107	Patrick Donohue,	[illegible], 11,	40	Mar. 22, 1880	2 9 22 Dec. 14, 1883	[illegible] of Stomach	"	1, Brother	Brother
108	Rev. Wm. J. Daly,	Star of Sea, 41, E. Boston	37	Dec. 13, 1881	2 8 9 Aug. 22, 1884	Carcinoma of Liver	"	1, Widow, 3 child'n	Widow
109	Rev. J. B. O'Donnell,	St. [illegible], 21, Boston	36	April 26, 1883	2 1 22 June 18,	[illegible]	"	1, Mother	Mother
110	Thos Toohey,	Fitzpatrick, 13,	29	Mar. 29, 1882	4 5 15 Aug. 24,	Cirrhosis	"	4, Widow, 4 child'n	Wid. and child'n
111	M. J. Devine,	Cheverus, 6,	46	Feb. 11, 1880	4 5 29 Aug. 10,	Phthisis	"	2, 1 child	
112	M. C. Roles,	SS.Pet.&Paul,15, S.Bos'n	21	Mar. 7, 1882	2 5 Sept. 5,	[illegible] of Lungs	"	1,	
113	Thomas Cahill,	St. Thomas, 29, Brockton	21	Mar. 31, 1881	3 13 Sept. 14,	Consumption	"	9, 3 child'n	
114	P. H. [illegible],	Shiel, 35,	43	Jan. 13, 1882	4 1 Oct.	Cholera-Morbus	"	1,	
115	J. S. [illegible],	St. Peter, 18, Dorchester	30	July 3, 1880	3 1 Oct. 4,	Killed by locomotive	"	1,	
116	B. A. [illegible],	St. Francis, 4, Boston	30	Nov. 11,	3 10 23 Oct. 4,	Consumption	"	9, 3 child'n	
117	Martin	Shiel, 35,	37	Nov. 11, 1881	2 2 25 Oct. 21,	Consumption	"	1,	
118	John Drury,	Hamilton,17,Charlest'wn	24	Mar. 2, 1882	3 2 Nov. 27,	Concussion of Brain	"	1, Sister	Sister
119	T. H. Martin,	St. Francis, 4, Boston	48	May 13, 1880	4 6 24 [illegible] 7,	Phthisis	"	1, Widow	Widow
120	E. W.,						"	1, Sister	Sister

ENDOWMENTS PAID — Continued.

No.	NAME.	COURT.	AGE.	INITIATED.	Yrs.	Mos.	Dys.	DATE OF DEATH.	CAUSE.	Endowment.	NUMBER OF BENEFICIARIES.	TO WHOM PAID
121	Thomas Lynch,	St. Joseph, 11, Boston	35	June 27, 1881	3	4	7	Nov. 4, 1884	Pneumonia	$1,000	3, Children	Guardian
122	Matthew Cusack,	St. Alphonsus, 21, So. Boston	43	Oct. 15, 1880	4	2	2	Dec. 17, "	Consumption	"	5, Widow, 4 child'n	Wid. & children
123	J. M. Tirrell,	St. Patrick, 7, So. Boston	23	Jan. 24, 1882	2	11	27	Jan. 21, 1885	Phthisis	"	3, "	"
124	John Delaney,	Leo, 5, E. Boston	24	Jan. 16, 1880	5	3	23	Feb. 9, "	Consumption	"	2, "	Guardian
125	Patrick O'Gorman,	St. Joseph, 11, Boston	32	Jan. 12, 1882	3	11	26	Jan. 8, "	Phthisis	"	3, Broth., wid., ch.	Broth., wid. & g.
126	J. W.	McGlew, 36, Chelsea	35	Oct. 23, 1880	4	3	27	Jan. 30, "	Heart Dis.	"	1, Widow	Widow
127	W. J. Barry,	Essex, 16, Salem	25	June 23, 1880	3	11	15	Feb. 8, 1885	Phthisis Pulmonalis	"	1, Sister	Sister
128	P. F. Welsh,	Friendship, 37, Boston	6,	Feb. 15, 1882	3	1	1	Mar. 7, "	Paralysis	"	5, Widow, 4 child'n	Widow
129	Michael Ferrin,	Gray, 32, Woburn	44	Mar. 15, 1883	1	10	27	60, "	Enteritis	"	4, " 3 "	Wid. & guardian
130	Edward Doherty,	Gray, 6, Boston	30	May 7, 1880	4	5	20	Oct. 27, "	Phthisis	"	9, Heirs	Heirs
131	John Sullivan,	St. Patrick, 7, So. Boston	48	Mar. 1, "	5	1	16	Mar. 17, 1885	Phthisis Pulmonalis	"	6, Widow, 5 child'n	Wid. & guardian
132	T. J. Flynn,	SS. Pet. & Paul, 15, "	26	Aug. 18, "	4	7	21	April 9, "	Phthisis Pulmonalis	"	1, "	"
133	Daniel Holland,	O'Connell, 22, Winchester	39	Nov. 22, "	4	4	23	April 15, "	Pneumonia	"	1, "	"
134	Jas Rice,	Qualey, 32, Woburn	39	Feb. 15, "	5	1	20	April 10, "	Accident, crushing h'd & shl'd'r	"	1, "	"
135	John M. Perkins,	Erin, 28, Boston	42	June 5, 1882	2	10	13	April 18, 1885	Pneumonia	"	1, Father	Father
136	Daniel M. Gillis,	Bass River, 30, Beverly	25	Feb. 19, 1880	3	1	1	April 17, "	Pneumonia	"	2, Father & mother	Father & mother
137	Joseph A. Devenny,	Fenwick, 3, Boston	22	Mar. 13, 1883	2		29	May 16, "	Consumption	"	3, Widow, 2 child'n	Widow
138	John Schultz,	Holy Trinity, "	39	April 21, 1881	4		28	May 17, "	Kent	"	1, "	"
139	W. O'Neil,	McGlew, 36, Chelsea	44	Mar. 9, 1880	3	4	25	May 16, "	Pneumonia	"	1, "	"
140	John Donovan,	Friendship, 37, Boston	28	April 2, 1880	3	1	23	May 25, "	Consumption	"	2, 1 child	1 child
141	J. S. MacCorry,	Columbus, 9, "	35	Mar. 13, 1883	2	3	4	May 13, "	Heart Disease	"	1, Brother	Brother
142	Edward Gallagher,	Star of the Sea, 41, E. "	29	Dec. 14, 1881	3	5	24	June 7, "	Drowned	"	4, Widow, 3 child'n	Widow
143	Daniel R. McDonald,	Star of the Sea,	26	Feb. 14, 1882	3	3	18	June 3, "	Phthisis	"	1, "	"
144	Dr. W. P. Kelley,	Liberty, 40, Boston	25	May 12, 1881	4		27	April 9, 1882	Inflammation of Bowels	"	6, Uncles & aunts	Uncles & aunts
145	Peter Tracy,	Mt. Pleasant, 20, "	48	Mar. 10, "	4	2	26	June 14, 1885	Congestion of Brain	"	5, Widow, 4 child'n	Widow & child'n
146	Maurice O'Hearn,	Cheverus, 6, "	39	Mar. 30, 1880	5	3	14	July 14, "	Bright's Disease	"	4, " 3 "	"
147	Timothy Long,	St. Patrick, 7, So. "	32	Oct. 11, "	4	8	1	June 12, "	Pneumonia	"	1, "	"
148	David Lane,	Cheverus, 6, Boston	49	April 6, "	5	3	13	July 19, "	Phthisis	"	5, " 4 "	"
149	Joseph F. Murphy,	Cheverus, 6,	22	Feb. 24, "	5	5		July 24, "	Apoplexy	"	1, Mother	Mother
150	Michael Reardon,	Sherwood, 8, "	47	April 22, "	5	3	22	Aug. 14, "	Phthisis	"	1, Widow	Widow
151	Peter Hawkins,	Star of the Sea, 41, E. "	43	Dec. 13, 1881	2	2	19	Mar. 2, 1884	Pneumonia	"	3, Brothers	Brothers
152	P. W. Sweeney,	St. Bernard, 44, W. Newton	25	Sept. 25, 1882	2	10	27	Aug. 22, 1885	Phthisis	"	4, Father, 3 sisters	Father & sister
153	Thomas Daly,	Leo, 5, E. Boston	39	Sept. 27, 1881	3	8	18	Sept. 15, "	Pyæmia	"	6, Children	Guardian
154	B. F. Harrington,	McGlew, 36, Chelsea	32	Mar. 21, "	4	5	10	Sept. 1, "	Phthisis	"	7, 6 child'n	Widow
155	Owen McCarthy,	Cathedral, 1, Boston	40	Sept. 3, 1879	6		16	Sept. 19, "	Typhoid Pneumonia	"	4, "	"
156	Timothy Leary,	Fenwick, 3, "	37	Mar. 12, 1880	5	5	9	Set. 24, "	Phthisis	"	6, "	"
157	James H. Phalan,	Hamilton, 17, "	38	July 12, 1882	3	2	24	Sept. 21, "	Phthisis	"	7, " 6 "	"
158	Timothy Dwyer,	Unity, 45, Bridgewater	44	Nov. 12, 1882	2	11	7	Oct. 19, 1885	Pneumonia	"	6, " 5 "	"
159	John Sheehan,	Emerald, 53, Peabody	42	July 2, 1883	2	3	24	Oct. 26, "	Phthisis Pulmonalis	"	1, child	"
160	Hugh A. Carr,	Cheverus, 6, Boston	29	Feb. 11, 1880	4	7	26	Oct. 17, "	Consumption	"	2, Sisters	Guardian

No.	Name	Society	Date Admitted	Date of Death	Cause of Death	Amount	Beneficiary	Relation
161	D. M. Inch,	Erin, 28, Boston	31	Feb. 3, 1881	9 28 Dec. 1, 1885	Phthisis and Gen'l	$1,000	6, 5 child'n	Widow
162	John Sullivan,	40	May 4, "	3 5 29 Nov. "	4, 2 "		Att'y for wid, g.
163	John Roy,	St. John, 23, Hyde Park	40	Dec. 14, 1880	20 14 Dec. "	9, 8 "	Widow & guar.
164	J. R. Yendley,	St. Francis, 4, Boston	39	April 18, 1879	6 18 Dec. 21, "	Chronic Interstitial	3, 5 "	"
165	John O'Day,	"	36	April 8, 1881	4 4 Dec. 30, "	Killed	3, 1 child	"
166	Jmes J. Shea,	28, E. Cambridge	33	Mar. 8, "	9 22 Dec. 22, "	Pulmonary	2, 2 child'n	"
167	Jn H. Shea,	St. Francis, 4,	56	Dec. 18, 1879	4 Dec. 27, "		3, "	"
168	Peter Daly,	Erin, 28,	48	Feb. 3, 1885	10 24 Dec. "		4, "	"
169	John Handran,	St. Jane, 47,	33	July 6, 1885	11 20 Dec. 26, "	Bld Poisoning	177.50	3	Ne, und'r a'wy
170	Edward Brennan,	Cathedral, 1,	35	Oct. 15, 1879	11 22 Sept. 22, "		$1,000	One	Widow
171	W. H. Fitzgerald,	St. Joseph, 11,	31	Oct. 11, 1880	2 18 Dec. 29, "		3, Widow, 2 child'n	Brother & sister
172	C. J. Hurley,	Mt. Pleasant, 20,	49	April 14, 1882	8 18 Jan. 2, 1886	Heart Dise	1, "	Widow
173	Jnes J. Smith,	St. Patrick, 7,	31	Feb. 16, 1880	5 10 Jan. 7, "	Congestion of Lungs	4, Bros. and sister	Widow & child'n
174	Francis P. Paten,	St. 25,	45	April 4, 1881	4 10 June 25, 1886	Heart Dise	4, Widow, 2 child'n	"
175	Patrick W. Davis,	Fulton, 12,	41	July 14, 1883	2 20 Jan. 10, 1886		4, 3 child'n	"
176	Edward J. Kenney,	Leo, 5,	48	Nov. 6, "	5 11 Jan. "	Pleuro-Pneumonia	8, 7 "	Guardian
177	Jmes W. Davis,	Hamilton, 17,	40	July 6, "	5 13 Feb. 19, "		3, 5 "	
178	Jim Logue,	Qualey, 32,	33	Jan. 2, 1882	2 21 Feb. 28, "	Phthisis	4, 4 "	Wid. and child'n
179	Jim Fay,	Hamilton, 17,	35	Mar. 1, 1880	5 17 Mar. 30, "	Pulmonary Pneumonia	4, Widow, 3 child'n	Father
180	Michael Devine,	Essex, 16,	45	July 23, "	4 2 April 6, "	Paralysis	1, Parents	Wid. and child'n
181	Patrick Dolan,	St. Anne, 47,	37	Mar. 22, 1882	9 13 April 4, "	Pneumonia	3, "	"
182	Josiah Gill,	St. Peter, 18,	47	Mar. 1, 1881	5 10 May 21, "	Injury	2, 2 child'n	"
183	Luke Kelley,	Mt. 10,	40	Feb. 10, "	3 11 May "		2, 1 child	
184	C. G. Kullburg,	Mt. 19,	52	July 13, 1883	9 17 May 29, "	Drowning	6, 5 child'n	Niece
185	Rev. C.	St. 48,	28	Mar. 27, 1882	4 2 May "		8, 3 "	"
186	Daniel A. Doell,	St. Bernard, 44,	38	Mar. 6, 1883	2 29 April 5, "	Bronchitis	1, 7 "	
187	William Sullivan,	Mt. Saint, 20,	40	Feb. 26, 1882	18 June 13, "	Gastric Fever	4, Nece	Widow
188	William H. Riley,	Fulton, 12,	30	April 10, 1884	3 18 June 28, "	Pulmonary Phthisis	4, Widow, 3 child'n	Mow
189	John McClure,	St. 8,	37	Dec. 22, 1880	6 22 July 1, "		4, 6 "	"
190	Joseph B. Mer,	Sherwood, 8,	26	Mar. 15, 1881	5 6 July 21, "	Cerebral	2, 3 "	"
191	Wm Harkins,	Leo, 5,	45	May 13, 1880	6 13 July 26, "		2, 2 "	Widow
192	Thomas Mccoy,	Cathedral, 1,	31	Jan. 16, "	5 1 July 27, "		2, Wdw & child	"
193	John Gallivan,	Sherwood, 8,	40	May 22, 1881	3 1 July 29, "	Inflam. of Brain from sunstroke	3,	Widow
194	John F. Daly,	Fitzpatrick, 13,	36	Mar. 16, "	2 7 Aug. 13, "	Typhoid Fever and Lung Dis.	3, 2 child'n	
195	William Free,	SS. Peter & Paul, 15,	34	Jan. 1, 1884	2 15 Sept. 29, "	Laryngitis	3, 2 "	Heirs
196	Patrick C. Green,	St. Patrick, 7,	45	Mar. 28, 1881	11 15 Dec. 16, "	Myelitis (Inf. of the Spinal Cr.)	6, "	Widow
197	John J. O'Toole,	SS. Peter & Paul, 15,	35	Sept. 15, 1880	11 26 Aug. 24, "	Phthisis	7, "	
198	Michael Edith,	Shiel, 35,	36	April 14, 1882	8 10 Aug. 26, "	Pneumonia	5, 4 "	Father & sister
199	Timothy Hurley,	St. 4,	30	April 11, 1882	6 12 Mar. 11, 1887	Bronchitis	5, "	Widow, 5 child'n
200	Daniel Gallivan,	St. 39,	42	Mar. 31, 1881	4 12 Mar. 27, "	Haemorrhage (from	3, 4 "	Children
201	John F. Daly,	St. 53,	21	Sept. 6, 1883	11 16 Aug. 22, 1886	Unknown	2, Widow, 5	Widow
202	William Free,	SS. Peter and Paul, 15,	44	Sept. 1, 1880	6 3 Mar. 11, 1887	Phthisis	5, Children	
203	Dennis Crawford,	St. John, 33,	23	Mar. 11, "	6 11 April 12, "	Bronchitis	5, "	
204		Williams, 19,		Oct. 3, "	6 26 April 29, "	Inflammation of Brain	3, Widow, 2 child'n	Widow

ENDOWMENTS PAID—Continued.

No.	NAME.	COURT.	AGE.	INITIATED.	Yrs.	Mos.	Dys.	DATE OF DEATH.	CAUSE.	Endowment.	NUMBER OF BENEFICIARIES.	TO WHOM PAID.
209	Terence Griffin,	Erin, 28,	39	Feb. 17, 1881	6	2	17	May 4, 1887	Pneumonia	$1,000	6, Wi dw, 5 child'n	Widow
210	Wm. F. Kean,	Leo, 5,	35	Nov. 19, 1886		2	7	May 30, 1885	Acute Meningitis	"	4, 3 "	Guardian & wid.
211	Michael Connell,	Hamilton, 17,	35	July 23, 1885	1	10	2	Jan. 26, 1887	Phthisis Pulmonalis	"	4, 3 "	Widow
212	Joseph McGilvray,	Constantine, 49,	23	Sept. 8, 1881	5	5		May 25, "	Progressive Paralysis	"	3, 2 "	"
213	Patrick Murphy,	Bass River, 30,	33	"	5	6	8	May 14, "	Hæmoptysis	"	6, 5 "	Wid. & guardian
214	Philip Casey,	St. ... h, 38,	30	April 6, 1882	5	2	18	June 21, "	Phthisis	"	6, 1 child	"
215	John Broderick,	Hamilton, 17,	35	"	5	3	25	June 24, "	Liver, Kidd., & Lung Dis., Dropsy	"	6, 5 child'n	"
216	David Fahey,	Sherwood, 2,	40	Mar. 4, 1880	7	6		June 29, "	Inflammation of Liver	"	5, 4 "	"
217	Cornelius Driscoll,	Fenwick, 3,	23	Jan. 21, 1881	6	6	13	July 2, "	Malarial Causes	"	2, Mother & widow	Mother & wdw
218	Joseph Ahin,	Shields, 63,	28	Jan. 14, 1887		6	25	July 27, "	Typhoid-Pneumonia	"	2, Widow & child	Widow
219	William Ellis,	Leo, 5,	38	Dec. 24, 1880	6	4		July 19, "	Consumption of Lungs	"	6, Children	Guardian
220	Thos J. Walsh,	St. J h, 33,	34	Mar. 21, 1881	6	2	10	May 31, "	Pulmonalis Phthisis	"	2, Kw	Widow
221	Michael J. Fennessy,	Essex, 16,	39	May 21, 1881	6	11	22	Sept. 23, "	Drowned	"	2, Father, 2 sisters	F. & At'y for 2s.
222	J. J. Cunningham,	St. Augustine, 46,	27	Aug. 14, 1880	2	8	11	July 25, "	Senile Marasmus	"	6, Widow, 5 child'n	G. of C A. for W.
223	Michael O'Keefe,	St. Joseph, 11,	27	Nov. 14, 1884	5	7	9	Oct. 3, "	Pneumonia	"	2, 1 child	Guard. of child'n
224	John F. Rahl,	Cathedral, 1,	45	Dec. 27, 1882	4	5	6	Oct. 20, "	Phthisis, Pulm dis	"	4, 3 child'n	Widow
225	B. H. ...,	Columbus, 2,	39	Mar. 8, "	4	7	12	Oct. 19, "	Dropsy, Heart Disease	"	7, Father	Father
226	G. W. Cleary,	Iona, 10,	23	April 23, 1883	8	8	5	Nov. 5, "	Pneumonia	"	7, Kw, 6 child'n	Widow
227	Patrick Connell,	Erin, 28,	49	Mar. 14, 1880	4	9	25	Nov. 28, "	Degeneration of Lungs	"	4, Children	Father
228	B. J. Ilty,	Unity, 45,	49	Feb. 3, 1881	10	4	17	Oct. 6, "	Pneumonia	"	2,	Son & guardian
229	Thomas Sweeney,	Gallagher, 64,	42	Nov. 6, 1881	1	15		Dec. 4, "	Railroad Accident	"	2, Father & mother	Guardian
230	John F. Reavy,	Cheverus, 6,	25	April 17, 1887	1	11		Dec. 6, "	Railroad Accident	"	5, Wi dw, 4 child'n	Widow
231	M. J. Reagan,	Cheverus, 6,	28	Oct. 15, 1886	7	7	1	Dec. 1, "	Pneumonia	"	2, 1 child	Widow & child
232	D. F. McGilvray,	St. Columbkill, 65,	35	May 7, 1880	7	6	27	Jan. 17, 1888	Fract. of Skull, Blasting Accident	"	1,	Father
233	John Martin,	Columbus, 9,	36	May 26, 1881	6	8	10	Jan. 9, 1887	Cancer of Jaw	"	6, Widow, 5 child'n	Widow
234	Timothy ...,	Fulton, 12,	45	May 12, 1881	8	14		Jan. 7, 1888	Chronic Int. Pneumonia	"	1, "	"
235	Michael Durant,	Benedict, 39,	55	April 27, 1880	7	10	1	Jan. 8, "	Paraplegia	"	8,	& child'n
236	A. J. Harrington,	Sherwood, 8,	49	Mar. 31, 1881	2	7	22	Jan. 14, 1887	Cerebral Paresis	"	1, 10 "	"
237	T. J. Callahan,	St. James, 54,	55	Mar. 4, 1880	7	10	24	Jan. 5, 1888	Phthisis Pulm dis	"	8, 7 "	"
238	T. J. Dacey,	Americus, 34,	38	July 2, 1883	5	8	10	Feb. 24, 1886	Peritonitis	"	1, Mother	Mother
239	M. Brahenny,	St. Joseph, 11,	29	Jan. 21, 1886	1	10	22	Dec. 15, 1887	Dropsy	"	1, Brother	Brother
240	H. H. Sullivan,	Cathedral, 1,	56	Mar. 13, 1882	8	11	27	Feb. 22, 1888	Heart Disease	"	6, Children	Widow
241	John Murray,	St. Alphonsus, 21,	34	Sept. 13, 1879	4	10	9	Jan. 5, "	Bright's dise	"	5, Widow, 4 child'n	Children
242	I Kw,	St. Joseph, 11,	34	Feb. 13, 1884	6	1	17	Jan. 10, "	Consumption	"	1, Mother	Mother
243	Wm. J. ...,	Fitzpatrick, 13,	31	May 4, 1882	9	15		Jan. 22, "	Phthisis	"	4, Widow, 3 child'n	Widow
244	John J. Craig,	Leo, 5,	32	June 22, 1881	8	1	16	Mar. 5, "	Hemorrhage of Lungs	"	1, Mother	Mother
245	Peter Kelliher,	Leo, 5,	41	Feb. 21, 1881	6	3		Mar. 7, "	Phthisis Pulmonalis	"	10, Relatives	Relatives
246	Peter Kilroy,	St. Louis, 4,	56	Mar. 21, 1881	7	11	17	Mar. 14, "	Chronic Bronchitis	"	2, Widow, 1 child	Widow
247	John Collins,	St. Louis, 29,	28	Dec. 18, 1879	8	3	16	Nov. 2, 1887	Typhoid Fever	"		
248				Nov. 8, 1883	4	5	16	April 24, "				

No.	Name	Branch	Age	Joined	Died	Cause	Amount	Beneficiaries	Relation
249	James Goodf kw,	, 6,	45	April 28, 1882	6 5 May 3, 1888	Erysipelas	$1,000	4, Wdw, 3 child'n	Widow
250	M. A. Fox,	Essex, 16,	33	Feb. 10, 1881	6 24 May 4, "	Laryngeal Tumor	"	2, Mother & aunt	Mother & aunt
251	M. H. Kerrigan, an,	St. Alphonsus, 21,	53	Oct. 15, 1880	7 1 Apl 22, 1887	Pneumonia	"	8, Children	Guardian
252	John J. ,	Leo, 5,	46	Feb. 9, 1887	3 1 May 10, 1888	Car. idc Neuralgia	"	8, Widow, 7 child'n	Widow
253	T. F. Powell,	Cheverus, 6,	40	May 26, 1882	6 8 de 4, "	Val. Disease of Heart	"	4, " "	"
254	John Hines,	Essex 16,	49	Oct. 4, 1883	6 7 May 25, "	Catarrhal Pneumonia	"	1, Widow	"
255	J. J. Callaghan,	Lafayette, 14,	56	April 20, 1881	6,11 21 April 3, "	Septicemia	"	4, Bro. and sisters	Sister-in-Law
256	Joseph ay,	Cheve rs, 6,	36	May 27, "	7 13 June 29, "	Peritonitis	"	6, Wid ow, 5 chil'n	"
257	James Gorman,	Williams, 19,	33	May 2, "	7 2 June 30, "	Pleuritis	"	6, " 5 "	"
258	Patrick Dowd,	St. Francis, 25,	42	July 12, "	1 28 July 12, "	Phthisis Pulmonalis	"	2, Children	Guardian
259	A. A. Vogel,	Holy Trinity, 51,	34	April 13, 1883	5 2 July 15, "	Bright's Disease	"	5, Widow, 4 child'n	Guardian & wid.
260	James J. Whalen,	St. ave, 47,	28	Dec. 22, 1882	5 11 May 3, "	Phthisis Pulmonalis	"	1, moth. wid. & ch.	Moth. wid. & ch.
261	J. J. McKernan,	Iona, 10,	27	Mar. 17, 1887	1 12 July 29, "	Cancer of Liver	"	1, ther	Mother
262	James H. Hurley,	Sarsfield, 48,	52	Mar. 6, 1883	5 Aug. 6, "	Ascites	"	3, " 2 child'n	Wid. and child'n
263	el McGuire,	Fenwick, 3,	46	Jan. 16, 1880	5 14 July 30, "	Typhoid Fever	"	4, Son	Son
264	John Kelly,	St. Francis, 4,	64	Dec. 18, 1879	8 16 Aug. 14, "	Apoplexy	"	4, Widow, 3 child'n	Wid. and child'n
265	D. Doherty,	Sherwood, 8,	28	Oct. 23, 1884	3 22 Aug. 15, "	Phthisis Pulmonalis	"	4, " 2 "	Widow
266	P. C. Fennelly,	St. Patrick, 7,	38	May 10, 1880	7 13 Aug 23, "	Consumption	"	3, " 3 "	Widow & child'n
267	J. L. Hennessy,	l 22,	26	Oct. 26, 1882	3 6 May 2, 1886	Consumption	"	1, M ther	Guardian
268	J. ,	, 8,	35	Aug. 10, "	6 16 Aug. 26, "	Fracture of Skll	"	2, Children	Guardian
269	T. R. Fallon,	Essex, 16,	50	Oct. 6, 1880	7,11 11 Sept. 17, "	Scelerosis	"	1, Widow	Widow
270	Wm. Lynch,	Cheverus, 6.	45	April 8, 1883	8 25 Oct. 9, "	Pleurisy	"	4, Wdw, 2 child'n	Widow & child'n
271	James Smith,	Shell, 35,	53	June 18, 1879	5 1 Aug. 9, "	Phthisis	"	3, " 2 child'n	Widow & daugh.
272	James Fay,	St. Francis, 4,	48	Oct. 15, 1880	9 15 Oct. 3, "	Bright's Disease	"	9, " 8 "	Widow
273	James Connell,	Iona, 10,	68	Oct. 3, 1879	9 1 Oct. 14, "	Phthisis	"	1, Wdw	"
274	W. Manning,	Cathedral, 1,	39	Sept. 12, 1883	9 13 Oct. 16, "	Paralysis	"	1, " 3 "	"
275	John Burke,	Cathedral, 1,	36	June 12, 1886	5 4 Oct. 24, "	Phthisis	"	1, Wdw 4	"
276	A. M. Cuffe,	SS. Peter and Paul, 15,	35	Oct. 5, 1884	2 21 Oct. 26, "	Pneumonia	"	5, " "	"
277	M. Hogan,	St. Joseph, 38,	31	Feb. 2, 1858	4 9 Nv. 6, "	Chr. Catar. Pneumonia	"	1, Mother	Father
278	M. H. Ryan,	SS. Peter and Paul, 15,	32	Mar. 26, 1880	8 18 Nov. 20, "	Typhoid Pneumonia	"	1, Father	Father
279	J. F. Bradley,	Fitzpatrick, 13,	54	May, "	5 15 Nov. 11, "	Peritonitis	"	5, Children	Child'n & guard.
280	Bartley Feeney,	Fitzpatrick, 13,	56	Aug. 18, "	8 3 Nov. 25, "	Drowning	"	5, " 4	Widow & child'n

The following deaths are also reported : —

NAME.	COURT.	DIED.
Thomas F. Kelly	Highland, No. 52 .	Nov. 25, 1888.
C. O'Melia	Leo, No. 5	Dec. 25, "
T. L. Silk	Mt. Pleasant, No. 20 .	Dec. 30, "
J. H. McDowell .	St. Joseph, No. 11 .	Dec. 31, "
M. Neville	Iona, No, 10 . . .	Jan. 17, 1889.
Edward Millin	St. Alphonsus, No. 21	Jan. 23, "
Patrick McGee .	Erin, No. 28 . . .	Jan. 25, "
Timothy Sheehan	Iona, No. 10 . . .	Jan. 31, "
James Dorgan	St. Thomas, No. 29 .	Feb. 7, "
M. D. Sullivan	Sherwood, No. 8 . .	Feb. 21, "
Charles Shortell .	Essex, No. 16 . . .	Mar. 17, "
P. H. Kerrigan .	St. Augustine, No. 46	Mar. 18, "
J. F. Carroll . . .	St. John, No. 33 . .	Mar. 19, ".

Of the number given in the table (1 to 281), and those reported to present writing, the following summary will be found interesting : —

Initiated in 1879 21
1880 112
1881 73
1882 39
1883 . . . . . - 25
1884 6
1885 3
1886 5
1887 5
1888 1

Since the organization of the Massachusetts Catholic Order of Foresters, the number deceased each year is as follows : —

1880 3
1881 17
1882 25
1883 40
1884 41
1885 47
1886 32
1887 34
1888 46

RECORD OF MEMBERSHIP.

A book was prepared especially for entering the names of all who have ever been members of the Order. But little progress has been made on account of the holding of applications by various members. It is earnestly hoped that another appeal will not be necessary, and that any member who holds his own application, or any other, will forward the same at once, in order that the work of arranging and entering in proper order may go on. Notwithstanding the length of time this request has been before the members, some are believed to be still in their possession, or the possession of the Courts. Within a week two packages have been received containing over one hundred such papers. Officers of Courts are requested to interest themselves in the matter, and see that none of the applications are laid away with property of their Courts, where they are seldom or never seen, and where the chance of finding them, unless by special search, is very slight.

FINANCIAL CONDITION OF COURTS.

AMOUNTS RECEIVED FOR INITIATION FEES, COURT DUES, ASSESSMENTS AND DETAILED EXPENSES.

No. of Court.	NAME OF COURT.	Received for Initiation Fees 1888.	Received for Court Dues 1888.	Received for Endowment Fund 1888.	Per Capita for High Court Received 1888.	Received for Withdrawal Cards 1888.	Received from Other Sources 1888.
1	Cathedral.........	$24 00	$313 50	$1,680 80	$100 50	$0 25	....
3	Fenwick...........	4 00	81 60	908 60	52 50	......	$34 70
4	St. Francis.......	15 00	324 50	1,399 20	81 75	......	6 25
5	Leo..............	23 00	320 50	1,392 40	....	......	148 50
6	Cheverus.........	4 00	156 60	1,145 10	....	......	......
7	St. Patrick.......	....	139 75	596 90	35 25	......	130 15
8	*Sherwood	87 00	405 60	1,560 40	....	......	286 78
9	Columbus	2 00	101 00	388 00	25 50	......	37 00
10	*Iona.	32 00	190 25	814 20	47 25	......	8 35
11	St. Joseph........	29 00	409 50	1,695 85	98 25	0 25	10 42
12	Fulton	1 00	88 25	387 90	21 75	......	......
13	Fitzpatrick	1 00	170 75	754 90	42 00	0 25	4 20
14	*Lafayette	12 00	153 50	627 20	41 25	......	64 25
15	SS. Peter & Paul..	52 00	174 32	426 70	....	0 25	......
16	Essex	12 00	260 75	1,044 22	128 00	......	15 00
17	Hamilton	2 00	201 50	915 05	51 00	0 50	......
18	*St. Peter	6 00	197 50	830 70	50 25	......	21 10
19	Williams.	16 00	409 50	861 90	53 25	......	22 15
20	Mt. Pleasant.....	47 00	210 50	869 10	52 50	36 54	......
21	St. Alphonsus.....	6 00	136 15	638 70	35 25	0 25	3 64
23	St. John.........	5 00	52 90	267 50	....	......	......
24	St. Gregory......	36 00	112 25	476 60	....	......	......
25	St. Francis.......	19 00	251 00	990 20	....	......	217 00
26	St. Raphael	5 00	61 10	476 50	27 00	1 00	25 92
28	Erin..............	49 00	179 50	879 05	44 25	0 25	......
29	St. Thomas.......	24 00	175 60	852 61	54 75	......	138 08
30	Bass River.......	2 00	92 75	428 60	....	0 75	......
32	Qualey	26 00	119 85	356 40	18 00	......	48 37
33	St. John.........	3 00	232 80	737 50	46 50	......	......
34	Americus	48 00	208 00	808 90	48 75	......	2 70
35	Sheil	4 00	60 20	302 35	17 25	......	......
37	Friendship........	15 00	148 50	551 00	34 75	......	35 09
38	St. Joseph........	6 00	132 25	565 50	33 00	0 25	13 85
39	Benedict	24 00	27 90	360 30	34 50	......	......
41	*Star of the Sea..	3 00	73 50	397 60	24 00	......	......
43	St. Mary	....	50 90	304 70	....	......	......
44	St. Bernard	3 00	....	601 20	39 75	......	104 93
45	Unity	4 00	115 60	478 20	27 75	......	......
46	St. Augustine.....	1 00	88 50	383 20	22 50	......	......
47	St. Anne	26 00	200 25	719 50	48 75	......	53 40
48	Sarsfield	26 00	229 35	776 30	44 25	......	128 30
49	Constantine.......	23 00	203 75	871 20	49 50	......	121 61
51	Holy Trinity	5 00	82 85	665 65	43 50	......	269 15
52	Highland	......	....	....	....	......	....
53	Emerald	13 00	172 75	660 20	38 75	0 50	119 23
54	St. James	19 00	119 65	425 40	31 50	......	0 50
55	Charles River.....	15 50	108 05	838 65	53 75	1 25	88 64
57	Carroll	39 00	101 25	371 40	24 00	.....	60 40
58	Prospect	....	100 60	429 05	27 00	......	78 27
59	Worcester	17 00	176 00	791 90	50 25	......	168 67
60	Middlesex.........	13 00	8 73	849 75	54 40	......	466 85
61	St. Lawrence.....	45 00	151 25	622 30	41 50	......	207 90
62	St. Catherine	8 00	94 25	392 30	51 75	... ..	235 00
63	Shields...........	38 00	91 75	318 25	....	......	28 20
64	*Gallagher	45 00	178 75	602 30	45 75	......	205 11
65	St. Columbkill	68 00	161 00	594 80	38 25	0 25	132 04
66	Griffin	15 00	31 80	313 90	18 75	......	15 45
67	Canton	25 00	93 00	356 10	24 75	......	137 65
68	St. Margaret......	8 00	28 65	169 50	18 00	......	49 30
69	Stoughton........	5 00	40 60	155 70	20 25	......	167 63
70	St. Michael	23 00	17 75	77 10	....	......	......
71	Phil. Sheridan	55 00	35 50	165 40	....	......	....
72	Merrimack........	148 50	11 50	....	....	......	....
		1,332 00	9,067 65	40,321 38	3,113 65	42 54	4,061 73

* Error in returns.

FINANCIAL CONDITION OF COURTS.

No. of Court.	NAME OF COURT.	Paid Endowment Calls 1888.	Paid H.C. Per Cap. 1888.	Paid for Rent 1888.	Paid for Salaries of Officers &.	Paid for Medical Ex. &.	Paid H.C.P. 1888.	Paid for Sick Benefits 1888.	Paid Court Physician for Attendance on Members 1888	Paid for Other Expenses 1888.
1	Cathedral.........	$1558 10	$100 50	$74 60	$82 75	$17 00	$1 00	$39 00	$97 50	$78 25
3	Fenwick	908 60	52 50	24 00	49 00				34 00	12 93
4	St. Francis......	1391 35	81 75	108 00	49 00				167 50	112 00
5	Leo..............	1392 40	80 25	60 00	12 00			130 00	66 65	43 20
6	Cheverus........	1145 10	109 75	55 00	31 20					40 65
7	St. Patrick......	555 60	35 25	48 00	15 00				48 50	19 08
8	*Sherwood	1594 50	95 25	79 25	75 00	50 75	7 25		132 16	327 19
9	Columbus	375 20	25 50	75 00	27 00					16 25
10	*Iona.............	814 20	47 25	51 00	40 00	17 75	2 25		70 75	59 95
11	St. Joseph........	1524 60	99 00	53 50	40 00	16 75	1 75		99 75	134 40
12	Fulton............	387 90	21 75	30 00	15 00				7 50	11 75
13	Fitzpatrick......	754 90	44 25	38 00	41 00	4 00			29 00	81 72
14	*Lafayette........	632 20	41 25	45 00		34 50	1 50		59 00	8 65
15	SS. Peter & Paul..	426 70	43 50	62 50	30 00	36 25	1 25			66 82
16	Essex............	946 00	128 00	181 00						142 54
17	Hamilton.........	824 60	51 00	60 00	25 00				120 00	35 11
18	*St. Peter	843 20	50 25	56 50	15 00	14 00	2 00		33 50	28 37
19	Williams	861 90	53 25	78 00	17 50	9 75	0 25	65 00	71 75	47 71
20	Mt. Pleasant	869 10	52 50	84 00	52 39	29 00	3 00		71 25	77 28
21	St. Alphonsus....	638 70	35 25	48 00	49 70	3 75	0 25			2 00
23	St. John..........	267 50	20 25	30 00						23 16
24	St. Gregory.......	476 60	33 75	36 00		21 00	3 00		19 00	25 68
25	St. Francis.......	991 60	57 00	100 00		37 50	3 25		73 00	123 99
26	St. Raphael......	476 50	35 00	25 00					34 50	71 45
28	Erin	815 60	44 25	72 50	36 00	31 75			68 50	18 06
29	St. Thomas.......	844 20	54 75	48 00	12 00	12 00		31 75	72 50	65 50
30	Bass River	439 00	27 00	24 00		4 00	0 50		70 00	5 46
32	Qualey............	379 75	20 25	33 00	20 90	15 75	1 75	2 50	14 95	8 25
33	St. John..........	737 50	46 50	30 00	24 00			165 00	65 00	45 70
34	Americus	841 10	48 75	77 00		31 00	3 00	30 10	67 00	11 15
35	Sheil.............	321 90	19 50	24 00						26 00
37	Friendship.......	492 90	33 75	44 00	40 00	1 75	1 50		23 00	49 44
38	St. Joseph........	537 40	30 75	51 00				22 90	36 25	17 85
39	Benedict	360 30	34 50	25 00		8 25	1 25			8 00
41	*Star of the Sea...	387 90	24 00	24 00					35 00	32 85
43	St. Mary..........	304 70	17 25	31 35						8 25
44	St. Bernard	577 00	39 75	45 50	7 50	4 00				98 56
45	Unity	480 00	27 75	35 00		4 00			37 00	23 15
46	St. Augustine....	383 20	22 50	52 50					14 75	8 43
47	St. Anne..........	719 50	48 75	50 00	5 00	21 25	1 50	97 50	136 50	171 11
48	Sarsfield.........	776 30	44 25	172 16		15 75	1 75		75 00	99 52
49	Constantine......	867 00	49 50	72 00	28 10			40 00		132 05
41	Holy Unity.......	661 80	43 50	36 00	30 00			222 00		62 05
52	Highland									
53	Emerald	727 30	84 75	118 75				15 00	57 00	78 27
54	St. James.:.......	408 00	32 25	54 00				42 40		22 20
55	Charles River.....	815 40	57 75	60 00	11 00	7 75				45 15
57	Carroll	416 70	24 00	54 00		17 75	2 25			26 06
58	Prospect..........	597 80	36 00	60 00		40 25	1 00			42 40
59	Worcester.........	791 90	50 25					31 09		69 54
60	Middlesex.........	884 40	55 50	184 59		22 00				300 55
61	St. Lawrence......	622 30	41 50	80 09		29 00	1 00	29 05	48 90	193 19
62	St. Catherine.....	341 70	51 75	51 00		18 50	1 50			135 04
63	Shields	321 40		40 50		26 00				89 65
64	Gallagher	741 00	45 75	55 30	102 00	31 75	0 25			128 36
65	St. Columbkill	596 30	38 25	96 00		42 50	1 75			130 76
66	Griffin.:.........	313 90	18 75	28 96		3 00	0 75			19 12
67	Canton	300 60	24 75	26 02				10 50		30 95
68	St. Margaret	169 50	18 00					6 00		3 10
69	Stoughton........	155 70	20 25	12 32		8 75	1 25		15 50	105 52
70	St. Michael.......	77 10				14 00	2 00			61 04
71	Phil. Sheridan.....	166 40		18 00	7 50					63 15
72	Merrimack			5 00		54 25	8 00			3 55
		40031 50	2670 75	3393 88	990 54	757 00	57 75	979 79	2072 16	3968 07

* Error in returns.

FINANCIAL CONDITION OF COURTS.

No. of Court	NAME OF COURT	Bal. on Hand Dec. 31, 1887.	Total Receipts 1888.	Total Expenditures 1888.	Total Balance on Hand Dec. 31, 1888.	Deficit from business of 1888	Balance from business of 1888	Endowment Fund on Hand Dec. 31, 1888.	Court Fund on Hand Dec. 31, 1888.	A.C.R. Fund on Hand Dec. 31, 1888.	Contingent Fund on Hand Dec. 31, 1888.	Special Fund on Hand Dec. 31, 1888.	Reserve Fund on Hand Dec. 31, 1888.
1		$299 16	$2 19 05	$2 48 70	$9 51		$0 35	$84 10	$285 31				$25 00
3	St. Francis	99 54	1 91 40	1 91 03	99 91		0 37		74 91	$43 00	$17 65		79 00
4	Leo	436 79	1 81 60	1 64 60	353 89	$82 90		110 25	121 64	86 00	138 90	$188 00	23 00
5		245 59	1 84 70	1 44 50	345 49		99 90		48 49	39 00			
6	St.	152 83	95 70	31 70	76 83	76 00			20 18	5 00			
7		93 40	42 50	21 43	274 02	71 57	0 62	41 30	88 82		476 24	34 40	136 00
8	...is	725 96	89 78	2 35	654 39								2 00
9		6 16	53 00	93 96	40 71		34 55	12 80			2 10		2 40
10	*Iona	23 85	43 05	93 15	12 75	11 10			25 91		55 97	8 35	36 25
11	St. ...h	108 61	43 27	43 75	382 13		273 52	171 25					18 00
12	Fulton	72 04	98 20	43 90	97 04	19 77	25 00		118 66	1 00	31 70		
13	Fitzpatrick	9 27	93 10	92 87	88 55		76 10		79 04				
14	*Laf...e	169 12	82 02	82 10	85 37	13 75			55 85				
15	SS. Pet & Paul	24 21	63 27	67 02	155 37		62 43	90 45		32 00	73 06		
16	Essex ...	76 33	97 54	1 97 54	86 64		54 34		56 31				
17		249 99	10 05	15 71	130 67		62 73		86 64	33 00	20 84		
18	*St. Peter	158 74	95 55	92 82	312 72	22 88	157 69	1 00	40 22	37 80	112 87	56 63	
19	Mt. ...	341 03	82 90	11 80	316 43				261 59	9 00	85 56		
20	St. ...t	85 56	25 64	43 52	318 15	15 51	42 34		110 85				
21	St. John	24 02	89 99	77 65	127 90				33 34				75 00
23	St. Gregory	82 59	85 40	90 91	8 51		9 82		8 51	19 00	48 20		70 35
24	St. Francis	71 60	44 85	85 03	92 41		90 86	63 95	95 26		242 71	210 46	8 00
25	St. Raphael	298 99	77 20	86 34	162 46		14 07	8 41	11 28	72 00	46 88		
26	Erin	9 84	86 02	82 45	313 06		65 39		10 09		107 77		75 00
28	St. ...	318 50	12 05	40 66	75 23		104 34				54 37		
29	...s River	153 63	91 04	69 96	422 84	45 86	71 52	56 90	76 14	30 00			8 00
30	...ley	66 99	84 62	13 70	107 77	93 90	7 25		102 75	2 00	31 00	28 00	23 17
32	St. John	100 67	68 80	69 10	138 51				38 32				
33		205 57	16 35		6 77		98 00	68 10	27 90				
34		45 70	83 80	66 34	212 82		54 70	28 10	27 85				
35	Shell		84 34	66 15	98 00								
37	Friendship	60 25	50 85		114 96								
38	St. Joseph												

*Error in returns.

FI NCIAL CONDITION OF COURTS— Ont' nd.

No. of Court	NAME OF COURT	Bal. on Hand Dec. 31, 1887	Total Receipts 1888	Total Expenditures 1888	Total Bal'nce on Hand Dec. 31, 1888	Deficit from business of 1888	Balance from business of 1888	Endowm't Fund on Hand Dec. 31, 1888	Court Fund on Hand Dec. 31, 1888	A. C. R. Fund on hand Dec. 31, 1888	Contingent Fund on Hand Dec. 31, 1888	Special Fund on Hand Dec. 31, 1888	Reserve Fund on Hand Dec. 31, 1888
39	Benedict	$126 40	$6 70	$7 80	$8 90	$5 65	$8 90	$4 80	$62 30	$1 00	$21 00		$3 00
41	*Star of the Sea		08 10	63 75	120 75	5 85			2 17				
43	St. Mary	8 02	55 60	81 45	2 17	23 43		90	141 27		11 25		
44	S. d.	06 60	748 88	772 31	143 17		18 65			19 00	93 05		
45	Unity	36 40	36 59	606 90	175 05		13 82		37 59	19 10			49 75
46	S. ne	54 02	95 30	481 38	67 84	199 01			85 51		45 85		15 30
47	S. Anne	47 67	94 20	1,251 11	278 66		19 47	4 20	97 60	3 55	148 68	$28 10	
48	Sarsfield	30 79	04 20	1,188 73	49 75		80 41						32 00
49	S. e	70 79	89 06	1,188 65	151 20		10 80		57 31		289 97		
51	...ly	181 28	1,06 15	1,055 35	192 08	76 64	37 20	23 90	89 34	85 00	49 00		32 10
52	...ity						08 79	94 75	100 33				
53	Highland	89 85	1,04 43	1,087 07	113 21		55 29		115 72		122 42	8 00	
54	Emerald	32 77	56 05	558 85	289 97	41 28	49 79	92 00	20 93			74 82	
55	S.	75 30	95 84	997 05	184 09		22 92		98 28	44 00	14 71		
56	Charles River	26 14	56 05	540 76	181 43	54 31	81 81	35 60	94 25	26 49	107 38		86 21
57	Cal	37 31	64 92	676 20	96 03				15 89	59 32			
58	Prospect	70 35	03 82	1,014 03	330 14		88 78		48 16	25 00		137 65	
59	Worcester	68 24	32 73	1,447 04	113 93	1 35	10 42	55 50	6 92			47 38	
60	Middlesex	30 18	07 95	1,045 03	173 10	17 50	43 68		25 53	7 00	24 75		
61	S. nce	34 18	81 30	599 49	216 06		76 85			27 00			
62	S. le	17 24	46 20	477 55	15 89		69 89		15 51				
63	Shields	72 45	96 91	1,104 41	54 95		24 75		2 95				
64	*Gallagher	93 25	94 34	1,905 56	282 03		0 85						
65	*Gallagher ll	55 82	94 90	384 48	66 24		44 20						
66	...th		66 50	392 82	243 68								
67	Canton		81 95	205 10	76 85								
68	S. t		89 18	319 29	69 89								
69	S. th		117 85	93 10	24 75								
70	S. Michael		35 90	235 05	0 85								
71	m.		60 00	115 80	44 20								
72	rt.												
		8,119 46	57,462 65	55,059 95	9,848 66	877 26	2,933 16	1,078 26	3,017 42	06 26	2,473 88	821 79	716 53

* Error in r ts.

ENDOWMENT FUND.

Dr. 4641

Assessment Call No. 41 .			. . . . . .		$ 13 40
" " " 42 .			. . . . . .		101 20
" " " 43 .			. . . . . .		859 90
" " " 44 .			. . . . . .		3,719 10
" " " 45 .			. . . . . .		3,728 90
" " " 46 .			. . . . . .		3,771 05
" " " 47 .			. . . . . .		3,839 65
" " " 48 .			. . . . . .		3,799 85
" " " 49 .			. . . . . .		3,874 95
" " " 50 .			. . . . . .		4,022 00
" " " 51 .			. . . . . .		4,010 35
" " " 52 .			. . . . . .		3,878 60
" " " 53 .			. . . . . .		3,931 30
" " " 54 .			. . . . . .		3,728 45
" " " 55 .			. . . . . .		1,439 50
" " " 56 .			. . . . . .		14 50

$44,732 70

Balance, April 1, 1888 . . . . .   4,298 80

$49,031 50

Cr.

A. J. Harrington,	of Sherwood,	No.	8 . .	$1,000 00
J. J. Callahan,	" St. James,	"	54 . .	1,000 00
T. J. Dacey,	" Americus,	"	34 . .	1,000 00
M. Brahaney,	" St. Joseph,	"	11 . .	1,000 00
H. H. Sullivan,	" Cathedral,	"	1 . .	861 00
John Murray,	" St. Joseph,	"	11 . .	1,000 00
Edward Ward,	" Alphonsus,	"	21 . .	1,000 00
W. J. McAleer,	" Fitzpatrick,	"	13 . .	1,000 00
John J. Craig,	" Leo,	"	5 . .	1,000 00
Peter Kelliher,	" Leo,	"	5 . .	1,000 00
Peter Kilroy,	" St. Francis,	"	4 . .	1,000 00
John Collins,	" St. Thomas,	"	29 . .	1,000 00
James Goodfellow,	" Cheverus,	"	6 . .	1,000 00
M. A. Fox,	" Essex,	"	16 . .	1,000 00
M. H. Kerrigan,	" St. Alphonsus,	"	21 . .	1,000 00
John J. Sullivan,	" Leo,	"	5 . .	1,000 00
Thomas F. Powell,	" Cheverus,	"	6 . .	1,000 00
John Hines,	" Essex,	"	16 . .	1,000 00
John J. Callahan,	" Lafayette,	"	14 . .	1,000 00
Joseph Carley,	" Cheverus,	"	6 . .	1,000 00
James Gorman,	" Williams,	"	19 . .	1,000 00
Patrick Dowd,	" St. Francis,	"	25 . .	1,000 00
A. A. Vogel,	" Holy Trinity,	"	51 . .	1,000 00
James J. Whalen,	" St. Anne,	"	47 . .	1,000 00
John J. McKernan,	" Iona,	"	10 . .	1,000 00
James H. Hurley,	" Sarsfield,	"	48 . .	1,000 00
Michael Maguire,	" Fenwick,	"	3 . .	1,000 00
John Kelly,	" St. Francis,	"	4 . .	1,000 00
Daniel Doherty,	" Sherwood,	"	8 . .	1,000 00
P. C. Fennelly,	" St. Patrick,	"	7 . .	1,000 00
J. L. Hennessy,	" O'Connell,	"	22 . .	1,000 00
James Keohane,	" Sherwood,	"	8 . .	1,000 00
T. R. Fallon,	" Essex,	"	16 . .	1,000 00

ENDOWMENT FUND — *Continued.*

Cr.

Wm. Lynch,	of Cheverus,	No. 6 . .	$1,000 00	
James Smith,	" Sheil	" 35 . .	1,000 00	
James Fay,	" St. Francis,	" 4 . ,	700 00	
James Connell,	" Iona,	" 10 . .	1,000 00	
Wm. Manning,	" Cathedral,	" 1 . .	1,000 00	
John Burke,	" Cathedral,	" 1 . .	1,000 00	
A. M. Cuffe,	" SS. Peter and Paul,	" 15 . .	1,000 00	
Michael Hogan,	" St. Joseph,	" 38 . .	1,000 00	
M. H. Ryan,	" SS. Peter and Paul,	" 15 . .	1,000 00	
J. F. Bradley,	" Sheil,	" 35 . ,	1,000 00	
Bartley Feeney,	" Fitzpatrick,	" 13 . .	1,000 00	
Michael McDonough,	" Fitzpatrick,	" 13 . .	1,000 00	

Held for proper papers in H. H. Sullivan case . . .   139 00
  "   "   "   James Fay case 300 00
—————— $45,000 00
Balance on hand 4,031 50

GENERAL FUND.

Dr.

Balance, April, 1888	$417 06
Charters and Supplies to Courts No. 68, 69, 70, 71, 72, 73, 74	315 00
Per Capita, 1887	78 00
" " 1888	2,471 00
Sale of Postal Cards, Books and Regalia . . .	456 49
" Benefit Certificates	142 00
Conscience Money Received	2 00

$3,881 55

Cr.

RENT.

G. R. Sneaden:
  Hall for Convention $15
   "   " 3 00
   " D. H. C. R. Meeting 3 00
Cashman, Keating & Co.:
  Office of High Standing Committee to April, 1889 300 00
$321 50

TRAVELLING EXPENSES.

High Standing Committee:
  Beverly Farms $7 22
  Hyde Park 2 10
  Stoughton 3 75
  H. C. S. T. 1 70

TRAVELLING EXPENSES.

High Standing Committee:

Stoughton	$13 55
H. C. S. T.	1 00
"	75
"	75
Randolph	3 79
Haverhill	4 00
H. C. S. T.	1 00
H. I. S. to Haverhill	2 25
H. C. R. "	3 45
Salem and Gloucester.	2 59
Newburyport	10 00
"	9 85
South Boston	48
H. C. S. T.	30
1,000 Mile Ticket, B. & M. R. R. . . .	20 00
Newburyport	16 25
1,000 Mile Ticket, B. & M. R. R . . .	20 00
Salem, H. C. S. T.	70
Malden	80
Newburyport and Haverhill	1 20
Foxboro, H. O. S.	1 25
Lowell	3 60
Foxboro	12 80
Lowell	3 66
Stoughton	3 05
1,000 Mile Ticket, O. C. R. R.	20 00
Haverhill	16 00
1,000 Mile Ticket, B. & M. R. R. . . .	20 00
Newburyport	1 20
1,000 Mile Ticket	20 00
Jamaica Plain	25
Marlboro, Springfield, Holyoke . . .	9 25
Taunton	2 10
Marlboro	4 49
Canton	9 50
Salem	70
Taunton	1 55
Newburyport	6 75
1,000 Mile Ticket, B. & M. R.R. . . .	20 00
Taunton	9 55
Lowell	50
Newton	97
Taunton	16 75
1,000 Mile Ticket, O. C. R. R.	20 00
North Easton and Brockton . . .	18 95

                                                         $350 35

Boston Post-Office:

Postal Cards	$422 50
Stamped Envelopes, printed . . .	67 90
Postage and Stamped Envelopes, plain . .	37 06

                                                         $527 46

TRAVELLING EXPENSES.

Deputy High Chief Rangers:

W. H. Rogers, to April, 1888	$10 00
"	3 50

T. F. Sullivan, to April, 1888 . . . . $10 50
      " 7 00
      " 7 00
      " 7 50
T. J. Dunn, to April, 1888 . . . . 33 60
D. Leahy 5 00
J. W. Davis 6 00
C. J. Hurley 6 25
A. F. Caldwell 2 15
                                                  ————— $98 50

REGALIA.

F. Alford, 2 Sets Regalia $17 00
    "   1   " 8 50
    " .   " 7 73
    "   1   " 10 25
                                                    ————— $43 48

SEALS.

S. M. Spencer, 1 Seal $5 00
  .   "   1 " 5 00
     "   1 " 5 00
          1 ' 5 00
          1 ' 5 00
                                                    ————— $25 00

PRINTING.

G. B. Wilcox:
        Assess. Call $4 50
     8 lots Postal Cards 80 6 40
     1 lot   "   "   H. C. R. . . . 1 50
     3 lots "   "   . . 80 2 40
        Assess. Call 4 50
     1 lot Medical Examiner Circulars . . . 4 50
     1 lot Duplicate Orders 6 00
     2 lots Postal Cards 80 1 60
     1 lot Notice of Appointment, Med. Ex. . . 3 25
     1 lot Lists of D. H. C. R. . . . 4 80
     9 lots Postal Cards 80 7 20
        Assess. Call 4 50
        Per. Cap. Assess. Call 2 50
     1 lot Duplicate Orders 2 50
     9 lots Postal Cards 80 7 20
     1 lot Officers Cards 6 10
        500 Rituals, Comp. and Printing . . 41 80
        Assess. Call 4 50
     2 lots Postal Cards 80 1 60
        50 Circulars 2 00
     3 lots Postal Cards 80 2 40
        Assess. Call 5 50
     2 lots Postal Cards 80 1 60
        5,000 Suspension Blanks 8 75
     4 lots Postal Cards 80 3 20
        Assess. Call 5 50
     4 lots Postal Cards 80 3 20
        Assess. Call 4 50
     3 lots Postal Cards 80 2 40
        1,000 Rejection Notices 3 50

PRINTING.

1 lot	Postal Cards	. . . . . .	$ 80	
	Assess. Call	. . . . . .	4 50	
" "		. . . . . .	5 50	
" "		. . . . . .	5 50	
				$176 20

J. F. McCarthy & Bro., 1,000 Envelopes and Printing $5 00

Cashman, Keating & Co.:

1 lot	Ballots	$3 00	
1 lot	Letterheads	12 00	
1 lot	Notice of Meeting, H. S. C. . . .	2 50	
1 lot	P. C. R. Blanks	2 25	
150	Postals and Printing	3 00	
300	Reports	163 88	
500	Bill Heads	6 00	
1 lot	Notice of Meeting	2 50	
1,000	Receipts	5 00	
4,500	Reports of Proceedings of Convention .	273 62	
1,000	Envelopes and Printing	3 00	
1 lot	Postal Cards	80	
1 lot	" "	80	
1 lot	" "	80	
1,000	Envelopes and Printing	3 00	
2,000	Blank Assess. Notices (Cards) . . .	5 00	
1 lot	Postal Cards	80	
300	Financial Statements	10 50	
300	Report of Membership	7 50	
200	Roll of Officers	4 00	
200	Circulars to D. H. C. R.	3 50	
50	Ribbon Badges, D. H. C. R., Printing .	1 50	
12 lots	Postal Cards 80	9 60	
175	Circulars, Meeting in Marlboro . .	2 50	
3 lots	Postal Cards 80	2 40	
13 lots	" " 80	10 40	
			$539 85

MISCELLANEOUS.

E. J. Shaw, for Lettering Signs at 597 Washington St.	$12 39	
Expenses of Convention	19 60	
Francis Supple, 1 Sitting Desk	10 00	
Boston Gas Light Co. . . $2 08, $2 73	4 81	
H. N. Hatch, Tin Boxes for Safe . . .	5 50	
William Tufts, Catering for Convention . .	75 00	
E. J. Shaw, for Lettering Slab, 597 Washington Street	4 80	
T. D. Poole, for Dating Stamp	5 00	
Francis Supple, 1 Standing Desk . . .	7 00	
" " Bench for Large Seal Press . .	5 00	
H. Dodd, Subscription to Dial	2 50	
Robert Carrington, Binding Rituals . . .	62 00	
Samuel Hobbs & Co., Stationery . . .	19 46	
J. F. Supple, on account of "Guide" . . .	185 00	
Boston Gas Light Co.	4 29	

MISCELLANEOUS.

Expressing to Haverhill and Fitchburg	. . .	$ 30
" "		15
" from N. Attleboro	. . . . .	15
" to N. Rutland .	. . . . .	25
Samuel Hobbs & Co., Stationery	. . . .	3 90
Expressing to Cohasset & Plymouth	. . . .	30
Messenger Service, 7 times .	. . . .	2 02
D. Wilson & Co., Ballot Box	. . . . .	1 42
" " Ballots	. . . . .	1 43
" " "	. . . . .	1 50
" " Ballot Box	. . . . .	1 20
Wrapping Paper and Twine	. . . . .	1 00
Six pcs. Ribbon for Cert.	. . . . .	3 00
500 Gold Seals	. . . . . .	1 87
S. M. Spencer, 1 Rubber Die	. . . . .	40
F. Alford, 1 Ballot Box	. . . . .	1 75
M. R. Warren, 6 Record Books	. . . . .	3 75
R. T. Purcell, 6 Gavels, 24 Batons	. . . .	8 10
Expressing to So. Framingham	. . . . .	30
Catholic Directory	. . . . . .	1 10
Francis Supple, 2 Filing Books	. . . . .	4 50
" " 3-lbs. Rubber Bands	. . . .	5 00
Extra Keys for Office and Building	. . . .	1 30
Cashman, Keating & Co., for Gas	. . . .	6 11
S. J. M. Gilbride, Ribbon for D. H. C. R. Badges	.	3 00
Cleaning Office, 7 times	. . . . .	7 50

$483 65

SALARY.

H. C. S. T. .	. . . .	800 00
Balance on hand .	. . . .	510 56

$3,881 55

Due on Postal Card Account, J. J. L.	. . .	$54 70
" " " " to April, 1888	. .	57 51
" " " " since April, 1888 .	.	155 69

DEPUTY HIGH CHIEF RANGERS.

For Term Ending April, 1890.

Comprising DIST.	COURTS.	D. H. C. R.	MEMBERS OF	NO.
1	1, 12	GEORGE A. O'BRYAN, Norwood . .	St. Catherine	. 62
2	3, 11	MICHAEL EDMONDS,Elmwood Pl.,Rox.	Cathedral . . .	1
3	4, 38	HENRY P. MULDOON, 52 Gates Street, South Boston	St. Patrick	. . 7
4	5, 19, 41	G. H. KEEFE, 63 Palmer St., Roxbury,	Mt. Pleasant . .	. 20
5	6, 49	T. F. GALLAGHER, Watertown . .	Charles River . .	. 55
6	7, 15	FRANCIS M. KIEVENAAR, 306 Sumner Street, East Boston	Williams . . .	. 19
7	8	P. A. MULLIGAN, Newton	Middlesex . .	. 60
8	9, 54	G. KRANEFUSS, 2 Acton Street,Boston,	Holy Trinity	. 51
9	10, 67	D. F. SULLIVAN, 25 Hndson Street, Boston	Sherwood . .	. . 8
10	13, 17	P. M. KEATING, 42 Court St., Boston,	St. Joseph	. . 11
11	14, 26	H. C. GRIFFIN, 8 Eaton Street, Boston	St. Joseph	. . 11
12	16, 30	JOHN HAYES, Lynn	La Fayette	. . 14
13	18, 23	WM. T. MALONEY, W. Roxbury .	Constantine	. . 49
14	24, 44	M. LEONARD, 2 Bush Street, Boston,	Americus . .	. . 34
15	25, 34	E. F. CHAMBERLAIN, Mattapan . .	St. Peter . .	. 18
16	28, 70	JOHN E. HESLAN,Arklow St., Roxbury,	St. Francis	. . 4
17	29	A. H. MCDONALD, Stoughton . .	Stoughton . .	. 69
18	32, 62	A. M. LANIGAN, 664 Harrison Ave.,	Cathedral . . .	1
19	33, 35	N. FAIRCLOUGH, 108 Chauncy Street,	Star of the Sea	. 41
20	39	W. A. FLAHERTY, Somerville . .	Benedict . . .	39
21	43, 58	P. A. SULLIVAN, Wareham Street, Boston	Americus . . .	34
22	45	WM. CONDON, Bridgewater . . .	Unity	. 45
23	46, 51, 57	T. W. O'ROURKE, 108 Boston Street, Dorchester	St. James . . .	54
24	47, 68	WM. F. MOORE, Gloucester . .	St. Anne . . .	47
25	48, 66	WM. H. ROGERS, Plainfield . . .	Sarsfield . . .	48
26	52, 65	P. A. DONOVAN, 292 D Street South Boston	SS. Peter & Paul	15
27	20, 21	JNO. C. PENDIS, W. Quincy . . .	St. Francis . .	25
28	37, 55	MICHAEL MORRISSEY, Watertown .	Middlesex . .	. 60
29	53	DR. T. E. HINES, Salem	Essex	. 16
30	59	T. H. MURPHY	Worcester . . .	59
31	60, 61	WM. MACKIN, Brighton	St. Columbkille .	65
32	63	J. J. LEONARD, Springfield. . . .	Gallagher . . .	64
33	64	J. J. CALLANAN, Holyoke . . .	Shields . . .	63
34	69, 73, 74	THOS. F. SULLIVAN, Brockton . .	St. Thomas . .	29
35	71, 72, 75	JAS. F. CARENS, Newburyport . .	Phil Sheridan	. 71

JOHN H. WATSON, P. H. C. R., Beverly Farms.

At large   HON. JOHN P. DORE, Boston.

MARTIN J. O'BOYLE, Taunton.

MEDICAL EXAMINERS.

FOR TERM ENDING APRIL, 1890.

DIST.	PLACE.	EXAMINER.	COURTS.
1	Boston	W. G. McDONALD, M. D., 221 Shawmut Av.,	6, 8, 11, 28, 49.
2	Boston, Milton	E. T. GALLIGAN, M. D., 88 Warren St., Roxbury,	20, 21, 24, 37, 38, 52.
3	Boston	F. T. MARA, M. D., 266 Tremont St.. . .	3, 9, 35.
4	Boston, Dorchester . . .	S. A. CALLANAN, M. D., Warren St., cor. Warren Pl., Rox.	1, 12, 18, 34, 51, 54.
5	Boston, Brookline . . .	JOSEPH P. MURPHY, M.D., 1607 Tremont St., Rox., also at Brookline . .	4, 61.
6	Boston, East Boston . . .	JAMES F. FERRY, M. D., 10 Chelsea St., E. B. .	5, 13, 19, 41,
7	South Boston	WM. H. DEVINE, M. D., 599 Broadway, S. B. .	7, 15, 46, 70.
8	Malden	C. D. McCARTHY, M. D.	. 10.
9	Woburn	J. H. CONWAY, M. D.	. 32.
10	Lynn	C. A. AHEARNE, M. D.	. 14.
11	Salem, Beverly Farms, Beverly .	FRANCIS E. HINES, M. D.	16, 68, 30.
12	Charlestown, E.Camb., Somerville,	J. A. GREGG, M. D.	. 17, 33, 39.
13	Quincy	JOS. M. SHEAHAN, M. D.	. 25.
14	West Newton, Waltham . .	C. J. McCORMICK, M. D.	. 44, 58.
15	Jamaica Plain	J. P. BROIDRICK, M. D.	. 57.
16	Watertown, Newton, Brighton .	M. J. KELLEY, M. D., Watertown .	. 55, 60, 65.
17	Hyde Park	JOHN C. LINCOLN, M. D.	. 23.
18	Dedham	A. H. HODGDON, M. D.	. 26.
19	Peabody	JOHN SHANNAHAN, M. D.,	53.
20	Norwood	L. H. PLYMPTON, M. D.	. 62.
21	Gloucester	PHILIP MOONEY, M. D.	. 47.
22	Randolph, Brockton . . .	BENEDICT DONOVAN, M.D., Brockton .	. 29, 43.
23	Bridgewater	G. H. WATSON, M. D.	. 45.
24	North Attleborough . . .	T. F. McDONOUGH .	. 48.
25	Worcester	H. P. KELLEY, M. D.	. 59.
26	Holyoke	F. P. DONOGHUE, M. D.	. 63.
27	Springfield	A. J. DUNNE, M. D. .	. 64.
28	Franklin	J. C. GALLISON, M. D.	. 66.
29	Canton	THOS. D. LONERGAN, M.D.	67.
30	Stoughton, North Easton .	MICHAEL GLENNON, M. D.	69, 74.
31	Newburyport	J. J. HEALY, M. D. .	. 71.
32	Haverhill	W. D. COLLINS, M. D.	. 72.
33	Taunton	M. C. GOLDEN, M. D.	. 73.
34	Amesbury	J. H. O'TOOLE, M. D.	. 75.

REPRESENTATIVES.

	REPRESENTATIVES.	COURT.	No.	PROXY REPRESENTATIVES.
1	A. M. Lanigan	Cathedral	1	N. M. Williams.
2	Thomas J. Dunn	"	1	Jeremiah Sullivan.
3	Michael Edmonds	"	1	John M. Singler.
4	Daniel Gallagher	Fenwick	3	John J. Irving.
5	Wm. E. Shay	St. Francis	4	James P. Cleary.
6	Thomas F. Crosby	"	4	John E. Heslaw.
7	John Brant	Leo	5	George F. Lowe.
8	James F. McCloskey	"	5	D. T. McCallion.
9	Owen A. Galvin	Cheverus	6	William T. Rich.
10	Andrew Golding	"	6	D. J. Harkins.
11	Augustus F. Caldwell	St. Patrick	7	Henry P. Muldoon.
12	John P. Dore	Sherwood	8	A. J. Lill.
13	D. F. Sullivan	"	8	M. J. Fitzgerald.
14	R. Farrenkopf	"	8	C. E. Colbert.
15	James F. Supple	Columbus	9	John F. Cleary.
16	James B. Buckley	Iona	10	P. H. Desmond.
17	Edw. Riley	St. Joseph	11	Charles F. Dolan.
18	Daniel A. Cronin	"	11	Patrick M. Keating.
19	Patrick O'Loughlin	"	11	Henry Griffin.
20	Henry F. Scanlan	Fulton	12	Michael O'Brien.
21	Antonio Thompson	Fitzpatrick	13	John D. Mahoney.
22	Jeremiah J. Donohue	Lafayette	14	Dr. C. A. Ahearne.
23	Edw. J. Leary	SS. Peter & Paul	15	Patrick A. Donovan.
24	Dr. F. E. Hines	Essex	16	J. H. Watson.
25	M. A. Dodd	"	16	W. J. McGee.
26	John Hurley	Hamilton	17	L. J. Lyons.
27	Henry McLaughlin	St. Peter	18	Jeremiah Chamberlain.
28	F. S. Maloney	Williams	19	Philip Smith.
29	John F. Dever	Mt. Pleasant	20	John J. Gately.
30	Frank J. McGrath	"	20	Fred J. Crosby.
31	Jas. T. Brickley	St. Alphonsus	21	Charles Mahan.
32	Charles F. Morrison	St. John	23	Thomas Murray.
33	Edw. W. Dailey	St. Gregory	24	Joseph H. Blake.
34	J. C. Pendis	St. Francis	25	Thomas Foley.
35	P. F. Lacey	"	25	Michael Dumphy.
36	Charles H. Riley	St. Raphael	26	John F. Riley.
37	John T. Daly	Erin	28	Jeremiah O'Mara.
38	Timothy F. Roach	St. Thomas	29	Patrick Gilmore.
39	Thomas F. Sullivan	"	29	Patrick McCarthy.
40	Patrick Stanton	Bass River	30	Owen P. Sullivan.
41	Thomas D. Hevey	Qualey	32	John Maguire.
42	John C. Dwyer	St. John	33	John S. Kenney.
43	Jas. J. McLaughlin	Americus	34	J. J. Cuddihy.
44	Michael Leonard	"	34	J. J. King.
45	John C. Carson	Sheil	35	William Connolly.
46	T. H. Duggan	Friendship	37	J. W. Keenan.
47	Peter Morris	St. Joseph	38	Luke Riley.
48	Joseph D. Couch	Benedict	39	William A. Flaherty.
49	W. F. O'Donnell	Star of the Sea	41	Nicholas Fairclough.
50	W. W. Hurley	St. Mary	43	M. P. O'Connor.
51	Frank T. Cox	St. Bernard	44	
52	William Condon	Unity	45	Edward Brown.
53	John Doolin	St. Augustine	46	James J. Hughes.
54	John J. Flaherty	St. Anne	47	William F. Moore.
55	Thomas Kelly	Sarsfield	48	Patrick Ryan.
56	William Daughan	Constantine	49	James A. Berrill.
57	William T. Maloney	"	49	David Leahy.
58	Joseph Tondorf, Jr	Holy Trinity	51	Gerhard Kranefuss.
59	H. H. Collins	Highland	52	J. J. Corbett.
60	James B. Carbrey	Emerald	53	Jas. Sherry.
61	Jeremiah G. Fennessey	St. James	54	Thomas W. O'Rourke.
62	J. A. Burns	Charles River	55	T. F. Gallagher.
63	Peter McGrath	"	55	M. E. Conroy.
64	J. H. Morton	Carroll	57	J. H. Cronin.
65	William F. Rooney	Prospect	58	M. J. Boland.
66	John B. Ratigan	Worcester	59	T. H. Murphy.
67	P. A. Murray	Middlesex	60	R. J. Morrissey.
68	P. A. Mulligan	"	60	T. F. Glennon.
69	Michael Driscoll	St. Lawrence	61	Patrick Johnson.
70	John T. Brady	St. Catherine	62	George A. O'Bryan.

REPRESENTATIVES.—Continued.

	Representatives.	Court.	No.	Proxy Representatives.
71	J. J. Callanan...............	Shields 63		
72	J. J. Leonard	Gallagher 64		Edward A. Hall.
73	William Mackin............	St. Columbkill........65		William J. Van Etten.
74	Albert F. Staples	Griffin 66		Matthew F. Conroy.
75	Edw. C. Murphy	Canton 67		Gerald A. Healy.
76	Laurence J. Watson	St. Margaret.........68		Patrick W. Brady.
77	Archibald H. McDonald....	Stoughton 69		Dr. Michael Glennon.
78	T. J. Giblin, D. M. D.......	St. Michael 70		Robert Dwyer.
79	James F. Carens...........	Phil. Sheridan 71		Frank McGrath.
80	Richard Dwyer.......... ...	Merrimack 72		
81	M. J. O'Boyle..............	Taunton..............73		John S. Conaty.
82	George F. Brammer.......	" 73		James P. Corr.
83	D. F. Buckley..............	Hendricken 74		Francis Jackson, Sr.

DIRECTORY.

NAMES OF COURTS, TIME AND PLACE OF MEETING, OFFICERS AND THEIR ADDRESSE

No. AND COURT NAME.	OFFICERS.		ADDRESS.	
1. Cathedral, Boston. Instituted Sept. 3, 1879. Meets 1st and 3d Wednesday, Garfield Hall, 1125 Washington St., Boston.	C. R. R. S. F. S. T.	Jere. McSweeney, W. P. Walsh, John W. Sweeney, Michael Edmonds,	100 E. Dedham St., 101 E. Brookline St., 94 Mercer St., 7 Elmwood Pl.,	Bosto " So. Bosto Roxbur
3. Fenwick, Boston. Inst. Nov. 14, 1879. Meets 2d Thursday of each month, Lusitana Hall, 164 Hanover St., Boston.	C. R. R. S. F. S. T.	Thos. P. Burke, Jeremiah J. Crane, John Keenan, John J. Irving,	9 N. Bennett St., Rear, 9 N. Bennett St., Rear, 7 N. Hanover Ct., 193 Salem St., Rear,	Bosto " " "
4. St. Francis, Roxbury. Inst. Dec. 18, 1879. Meets 1st and 3d Wednesday, Tremont Hall, Tremont St., Roxbury.	C. R. R. S. F. S. T.	Jere. J. O'Brien, Michael J. O'Connor, John M. Lehan, Michael J. Killion,	4 Vernon Pl., Burney House, Burney St., 106 Conant St., 61 Terrace St.,	Roxbur " " "
5. Leo, E. Boston. Inst. Jan. 16, 1880. Meets 2d and 4th Wednesday, 144 Meridian Street, East Boston.	C. R. R. S. F. S. T.	George F. Lowe, John W. Heenan, E. J. McLaughlin, Michael Killilea,	271 Sumner St., 142 Arlington St., 625 Saratoga St., 163 Webster St.,	E. Bosto Chelse E. Bosto "
6. Cheverus, Boston. Inst. Feb. 11, 1880. Meets 1st and 3d Monday, 9 Elm St.	C. R. R. S. F. S. T.	James Cashen, D. J. Harkins, James O. Kane, Edward O'Hara,	22 Thacher St., 52 S. Margin St., 90 Bunker Hill St., 24 Mt. Vernon St.,	Bosto " Charlestow "
7. St. Patrick, So. Boston. Inst. Feb. 16, 1880. Meets 2d and 4th Monday, 376 Broadway.	R. S. S. C.	Joseph F. Carroll, J. H. Pentoney, J. J. Mahoney, James Cahill,	263 Fifth St., 265 Fourth St., 47 Gates St., 317 Silver St.,	So. Bosto " " "
8. Sherwood, Boston. Inst. March 4, 1880. Meets 2d and 4th Tuesday, 616 Washington St.	C. R. R. S. F. S. T.	Rudolph Farrenkopf, M. J. Fitzgerald, A. J. Lill, Thomas J. Lane,	147 Hudson St., 14 Melrose St., 3 Champny Pl., 121 Centre St.,	Bosto " Roxbu "
9. Columbus, Boston. Inst. March 9, 1880. Meets 2d Monday, Carroll Hall, 275 Harrison Avenue.	C. R. R. S. F. S. T.	Wm. H. Bodfish, Wm. H. Murphy, M. T. Gleason, M. T. Milliken.	15 Euclid St., 62 Allen St., 53 Harvard St., 282 E St.,	Dorchest Bostc " So. Bostc
10. Iona, Malden. Inst. March 15, 1880. Meets 1st and 3d Thursday, Deliberative Hall, Pleasant St., Malden.	C. R. R. S. F. S. T.	James B. Buckley, Dennis Kelliher, M. A. Devver, Paul J. McMahon,	14 Middlesex St., 1 Willow Pl., 69 Cedar St., 28 Main St.,	Mald " " "
11. St. Joseph, Boston. Inst. March 22, 1880. Meets 2d and 4th Wednesday, Y. M. L. Hall, 60 1-2 Leverett St.	C. R. R. S. F. S. T.	Christopher J. Fay, James E. Kenely, Charles W. Mullen, Daniel Carney,	8 Eaton St., 5 Spring St., 17 Parkman St.. 5 Revere St. Pl.,	Bost " " "
12. Fulton, Boston. Inst. March 18, 1880. Meets 1st Friday, Bay State Hall, 197 Shawmut Avenue, Boston.	C. R. R. S. F. S. T.	Denis Shea, H. F. Scanlan, Thomas Ward, Michael Nolan,	Cor. Albany and Dover Sts., 117 Union Park, 546 Dorchester Ave., 38 Hampden St.,	Bost Bost " Roxbu
13. Fitzpatrick, Boston. Inst. May 5, 1880. Meets 2d and 4th Tuesday, Lusitana Hall, Hanover St.	C. R. R. S. F. S. T.	John Feeney, Patrick F. Reynolds. Frank J. McFarland, Antonio Thompson,	364 Hanover St., 14 N. Bennett St., 425 Hanover St., 5 Vernon Pl.,	Bost " " "
14. Lafayette, Lynn. Inst. June 8, 1880. Meets 1st and 3d Wednesday, Emmett Hall, 65 Munroe St.	C. R. R. S. F. S. T.	James D. Casey, Geo. E. Monroe, G. A. Lemasney, T. Donovan,	72 Highland Ave., 147 Broad St., 37 Robinson St., 105 Adams St.,	Ly " " "

DIRECTORY— Continued.

No. and Court Name.	Officers.	Address.
15. SS. Peter & Paul, So. Boston. Inst. June 25, 1880. Meets 1st and 3d Friday, 376 Broadway.	C. R. Edward J. Leary, R. S. John S. McGann, F. S. John B. White, T. James Dempsey,	25 W. Fifth St., So. Boston 70 Tudor St., " 83 Baxter St., " 118 W. Fourth St., "
16. Essex, Salem. Inst. June 23, 1880. Meets 1st and 3d Wednesday, 199 Essex St.	C. R. Jas. J. Murphy, R. S. Andrew J. Byrne, F. S. Peter F. E. Carney, T. Dennis F. Hallohan,	8 1-2 Allen St., Salem 2 Parker's Ct., " 30 Hancock St., " 328 Essex St., "
17. Hamilton, Charlestown. Inst. July 8, 1880. Meets 2d and 4th Friday, 162 Main St.	C. R. John Hurley, R. S. T. W. Murray, F. S. S. J. Cochrane, T. William H. Breen,	28 Mt. Vernon St., Charlestown 164 Main St., " 22 Soley St., " 295 Bunker Hill St., "
18. St. Peter, Dorchester. Inst. July 22, 1880. Meets 1st and 3d Thursday, Blake's Hall.	C. R. Edw. F. Chamberlain, R. S. Eugene H. Buckley, F. S. Thomas Crowne, T. Henry McLaughlin,	Norfolk St., Mattapan 1155 Dorchester Ave., Dorchester Off Newhall St., " Dickens St., "
19. Williams, E. Boston. Inst. Sept. 16, 1880. Meets 1st and 3d Thursday, O. F. Hall, Maverick Sq.	C. R. F. S. Maloney, R. S. M. J. Kelley, F. S. D. J. O'Regan, T. Thomas Arthur,	123 Maverick St., E. Boston 107 Paris St., " 247 Sumner St., " 72 Marginal St., "
20. Mt. Pleasant, Roxbury. Inst. Oct. 20, 1880. Meets 2d and 4th Wednesday, 2319 Washington St.	. R. Garrett H. Keefe, . S. Daniel F. Lynch, C. S. John J. Gately, R. David O'Brien,	63 Palmer St., Roxbury 64 Regent St., " 5 Clarence St., " 30 Mall St., "
21. St. Alphonsus, Roxbury. Inst. Oct. 13, 1880. Meets 2d and 4th Wednesday, Vernon Hall, cor. Tremont and Culvert Sts.	. R. Francis A. Mahan, . S. Frank Walsh, C. S. John Killion, R. Cornelius McCarthy,	85 Longwood Ave., Roxbury 62 Bumstead Lane, " 8 Oscar St., " 12 Cottage Pl., "
23. St. John, Hyde Park. Inst. Dec. 14, 1880. Meets 2d Monday, Lyric Hall.	C. R. John Brady, R. S. Thomas Murray, F. S. R. J. Sullivan, T. F. S. Sullivan,	Readville 78 Water St., Hyde Park " " " Garfield St., "
24. St. Gregory, Milton. Inst. Dec. 20, 1880. Meets 1st Tuesday, Associates Hall.	C. R. John O'Callaghan, R. S. Michael Dunican, F. S. C. J. Lyons, T. Patrick Fallon,	Milton Lower Mills E. Milton Milton "
25. St. Francis, W. Quincy. Inst. Dec. 21, 1880. Meets 2d and 4th Tuesday, Foresters' Hall.	C. R. John Vogel, R. S. James L. Fennessey, F. S. John H. McGovern, T. John Hussey,	W. Quincy " " "
26. St. Raphael, Dedham. Inst. Dec. 31, 1880. Meets 1st and 3d Sunday, Parochial Hall.	C. R. John F. Reilly, R. S. John F. Barrett, F. S. Jas. J. Gaffney, T. P. O'Sullivan,	Dedham " " "
28. Erin, Boston. Inst. Feb. 3, 1881. Meets 2d and 4th Tuesday, 1125 Washington St., Grey- stone Hall.	C. R. Daniel Shannon, R. S. C. J. Lynch, F. S. W. A. Daly, T. J. O'Mara,	98 W. Dedham St., Boston 10 Shelburn St., Dorchester 10 Vinton St., So. Boston 93 Pembroke St., Boston
29. St. Thomas, Brockton. Inst. Feb. 17, 1881. Meets 2d and 4th Thursday, Hibernian Hall, E. Elm St.	C. R. John E. Saxton, R. S. Michael P. Corcoran, F. S. John Shea, T. John W. Minton,	Campbello Forest Ave., Brockton Eliot St., " "
30. Bass River, Beverly. Inst. Feb. 24, 1881. Meets 1st Thursday, Bell's Hall, Cabot St.	C. R. David H. Guinevan, R. S. Timothy Hennessey, F. S. Patrick Guinevan, T. Jeremiah Murphy,	Beverly " " "
32. Qualey, Woburn. Inst. March 2, 1881. Meets 1st and 3d Wednesday, Hibernian Hall, Main St.	C. R. John Bowler, R. S. Frank E. Tracey, F. S. Thomas Finnegan, T. Wm. O'Brien,	Shamrock St., Winchester 7 Glenwood St., Woburn 13 Carter St., " 20 Church Ave., "

33. St. John, E. Cambridge.
Inst. March 3, 1881.
Meets 3d Monday, 115½ Cambridge St.

C. R.   Daniel J. Donovan,
R. S.   John S. Kenney,
F. S.   J. F. O'Connell,
T.   James Doherty,

34. Americus, Boston.
Inst. March 15, 1881.
Meets 1st and 3d Thursday, Greystone Hall, 1125 Washington St.

C. R.   John W. Brown,
R. S.   R. T. Purcell,
F. S.   P. P. Sullivan,
T.   Michael Leonard,

35. Sheil, Boston.
Inst. March 18, 1881.
Meets 1st Friday, Washington Hall, cor. Hanover and Blackstone Sts.

.   John C. Carson,
.   C. J. Kelley,
C. R.   Thomas Jacobs,
E.   Wm. Connolly,

37. Friendship, Roxbury.
Inst. March 25, 1881.
Meets 1st and 3d Monday, Old School-House, Weston St.

C. R.   Joseph W. Keenan,
R. S.   Geo. F. Shine,
F. S.   W. F. Arkinson,
T.   Jeremiah J. Hurley,

38. St. Joseph, Roxbury.
Inst. March 29, 1881.
Meets 1st and 3d Tuesday, Highland Hall, 191 Warren St.

C. R.   Peter Morris,
R. S.   Wm. B. Reardon,
F. S.   John P. Ego,
T.   M. Lennon,

39. Benedict, Somerville.
Inst. March 31, 1881.
Meets 2d Friday, Temperance Hall, Hawkins St.

C. R.   Jas. J. Muldoon,
R. S.   John A. Gregg, M. D.,
F. S.   Wm. A. Flaherty,
T.   Cornelius McGonagle,

41. Star of the Sea, E. Boston.
Inst. Dec. 13, 1881.
Meets 1st Wednesday, School-House Hall, cor. Saratoga and Moore Sts.

C. R.   Wm. R. Fairclough,
R. S.   C. H. Cragin,
F. S.   Jas. W. Prest,
T.   N. Fairclough,

43. St. Mary, Randolph.
Inst. Sept. 4, 1882.
Meets 1st Sunday, Hibernian Hall, North St.

R.
C. S.
R. S.
T.

44. St. Bernard, W. Newton.
Inst. Sept. 23, 1882.
Meets 1st and 3d Monday, Foresters' Hall, Waltham St.

C. R.
R. S.
F. S.
T.

45. Unity, Bridgewater.
Inst. Nov. 12, 1882.
Meets 2d and 4th Tuesday, Young Men's Benevolent Hall, Centre St.

C. R.   William Condon,
R. S.   David Cashon,
F. S.   Patrick A. Reynolds,
T.   James Cleare,

46. St. Augustine, So. Boston.
Inst. Nov. 14, 1882.
Meets 2d and 4th Thursday, 376 Broadway.

C. R.   Francis M. Hughes,
R. S.   Jas. J. Hughes,
F. S.   Chas. H. Doolin,
T.   J. F. McNulty,

47. St. Anne's, Gloucester.
Inst. Dec. 22, 1882.
Meets 1st and 4th Tuesday, G. A. R. Hall.

R.   John J. Flaherty,
S.   John F. Riley,
C. S.   Daniel F. Hiltz,
E.   Daniel Carroll,

48. Sarsfield, No. Attleboro.
Inst. March 6, 1883.
Meets every Tuesday, Barton's Hall.

C. R.   Edw. A. Irvine,
S.   M. Joseph Zilch,
R. S.   John P. Zilch,
T.   John C. A. Dieble,

49. Constantine, Boston.
Inst. April 5, 1883.
Meets 2d and 4th Thursday, Greystone Hall, 1125 Washington St.

C.   David Leahy,
R. R.   John J. Dolan,
F. S.   John J. Kilroy,
T.   James T. Riley,

DIRECTORY — Continued.

No. and Couet Name.	Officers.		Address.	
51. Holy Trinity, Boston. Inst. April 13, 1883. Meets 2d Sunday, Casino, 133 Shawmut Ave.	C. R. R. S. F. S. T.	Frederick Schwaab, Francis Funke, Henry Wessling, Jos. Spang,	13 Avon Pl., 139 Shawmut Ave., 35 E. Springfield St., 31 Warwick St.,	Roxbury Boston " Roxbury
52. Highland, Roxbury.. Inst. April 16, 1883. Meets 2d and 4th Wednesday, Gurney St.	C. R. R. S. F. S. T.		22 Hallock St., 33 Prentiss St., 300 Ruggles St., Linden Park,	Roxbury " " "
53. Emerald, Peabody. Inst. July 2, 1883. Meets 1st Thursday, Main St., near the Square.	C. R. R. S. F. S. T.	David J. Horrigan, Francis J. Turner, John J. Sweeney, Daniel J. Sweeney,	131 Boston St., 106 " " 	Salem " Peabody "
54. St. James, Boston. Inst. July 2, 1883. Meets 1st and 3d Tuesday, 820 Washington St.	C. R. R. S. F. S. T.	T. W. O'Rourke, D. J. Collins, J. J. Desmond, Michael J. Noonan,	118 Boston St., 314 Fourth St., 286 Third St., 214 South St.,	Dorchester So. Boston " Boston
55. Charles River, Watertown. Inst. Oct. 8, 1883. Meets 2d and 4th Tuesday, Forester Hall, Main St.	C. R. R. S. F. S. T.	E. J. Burke, J. J. Herlihy, M. E. Conroy, J. J. Barnes,	Chapel St., 	Newton Watertown " "
57. Carroll, Jamaica Plain. Inst. June 30, 1885. Meets 1st Friday, K. of H. Hall, Centre St.	C. R. R. S. F. S. T.	John D. Fallon, J. H. Lennon, Wm. Rooney, Dr. J. P. Broidrick,	Centre St., Hyde Park Ave., Centre St., South St.,	Jamaica Plain " " "
58. Prospect, Waltham. Inst. Aug. 25, 1885. Meets 3d Sunday, A. O. H. Hall, Main St.	C. R. R. S. F. S. T.	Michael J. Boland, Michael Bergin, John E. Burke, Timothy F. Buckley,	57 Oak St., 14 Common St., Main St., 105 Cushing St.,	Waltham " " "
59. Worcester, Worcester. Inst. Dec. 17, 1885. Meets 1st and 3d Thursday, I. C. B. S. Hall, 98 Front St.	C. R. R. S. F. S. T.	Jas. H. Fitzgerald, Michael J. Madden, P. J. Meade, James Eaton,	7 Gold St., 61 Eastern Ave., 32 Pleasant St., 22 Ingalls St.,	Worcester " " "
60. Middlesex, Newton. Inst. Feb. 19, 1886. Meets 2d and 4th Tuesday, Brackett's Block, Centre St.	C. R. R. S. F. S. T.	R. J. Morrisey, Michael Morrisey, P. R. Mullen, G. E. Stewart,	Boyd St., Cross St., Washington St., Pearl St.,	Newton Watertown Newton "
61. St. Lawrence, Brookline. Meets 1st and 3d Tuesday, Lyceum Hall, Washington St.	C. R. R. S. F. S. T.	Francis F. Muldowney, Daniel Frawley, Thomas F. McMahon, Michael O'Day,	12 Juniper St., Chestnut St., Kerrigan Pl., Elm Pl., Harrison Pl., Davis Ave.,	Brookline " " " "
62. St. Catharine, Norwood. Inst. Dec. 21, 1886. Meets 1st and 3d Wednesday, Casey's Hall.	C. R. R. S. F. S. T.	Michael E. Hayden, R. E. Oldham, Daniel Murray, John Gillooly,		Norwood " " "
63. Shields, Holyoke. Inst. Jan. 14, 1887. Meets 1st Wednesday and 4th Sunday, O'Niell's Hall, High St·	C. R. R. S. F. S. T.	Jeremiah J. Callanan, John F. Riley, Jeremiah J. O'Leary, J. J. Burke,	107 Dwight St., 159 Elm St., 110 Dwight St., 2 Dwight St.,	Holyoke " " "
64. Gallagher, Springfield. Inst. April 17, 1887. Meets 2d and 4th Thursday, C. M. Hall, cor. Main and State Sts.	C. R. R. S. F. S. T.	John J. Toomey, John T. Lovett, John J. Leonard, John J. Cruse,	97 Willow St., 171 E. Liberty St., 118 Greenwood St., 95 St. James Ave.,	Springfield " "
65. St. Columbkill, Brighton. Inst. May 26, 1887. Meets 1st and 3d Tuesday, O. F. Hall, Brighton.	C. R. R. S. F. S. T.	George F. Mitchell, John Comerford, John H. Greenleaf, Chas. E. Sanderson,	Washington St., Eastburn St., Winship St., Parsons St.,	Brighton " " "
66. Griffin, Franklin. Inst. Sept. 12, 1887. Meets 1st and 3d Tuesday Basement of Church.	C. R. R. S. F. S. T.	A. F. Staples, M. F. Conroy, D. W. Holloran, J. J. McCarthy,		Franklin " " "

DIRECTORY — Concluded.

No. and Court Name.	Officers.		Address.
67. Canton, Canton. Inst. Jan. 26, 1888. Meets 1st and 3d Monday, Washington-St. Hall.	C. R. R. S. F. S. T.	Patrick F. Brady, G. A. Healy, James E. Grimes, Patrick E. Healey,	Canto: " " "
68. St. Margaret, Beverly Farms. Inst. April 14, 1888. Meets 1st and 3d Wednesday, Marshall's Hall, cor. Hale and West Sts.	R. S. C. S. R.	Lawrence J. Watson, Thos. M. Dix, Jr., Samuel A. Fogg, Michael J. Riordan,	Beverly Farm " Box 54, " "
69. Stoughton, Stoughton. Inst. June 7, 1888. Meets 1st and 3d Thursday, Hall, cor. Washington and Wyman Sts.	. . . C R. R.	A. H. McDonald, James F. Cotter, John S. Madden, W. A. Welsh,	Stoughto " " "
70. St. Michael, So. Boston. Inst. Sept. 14, 1888. Meets 1st and 3d Tuesday, Gray's Hall.	C. R. R. S. F. S. T.	Jas. P. Duffey, Jas. T. Costello, John J. Barry, Timothy F. Shea,	508 E. Sixth St., So. Bosto 599 Broadway, " 187 Bowen St., " 144 K St., "
71. Phil Sheridan, Newburyport. Inst. Sept. 18, 1888. Meets 1st and 3d Tuesday.	C. R. R. S. F. S. T.	Jas. F. Carens, Albert E. Moylan, Jeremiah Healy, Wm. C. Cuseck,	20 Fair St., Newburypor 33 Olive St., " 16 Dove St., " 25 Merrimack St., "
72. Merrimack, Haverhill. Inst. Dec. 20, 1888. Meets 2d and 4th Thursday, 78 Merrimack St.	C. R. R. S. F. S. T.	Richard Dwyer, John P. O'Brien, John T. Desmond, M. P. Fitzgerald,	Blossom St., Bradfor 28 Franklin St., Haverhi 81 Merrimack St., " "
73. Taunton, Taunton. Inst. March 12, 1889. Meets	C. R. R. S. F. S. T.	Benjamin Morris, John J. McGinty, J. T. Claffey, G. F. Brammer,	Taunto " " "
74. Hendricken, No. Easton. Inst. March 29, 1889.	C. R. S. R. S. T.	Daniel F. Buckley, P. F. A. Long, D. J. Dineen, James Dermody,	No. East " " '

The figures, as given in the tables Financial Condition of Courts, are taken from the returns made by the Courts and certified to by the D. H. C. R.

Where glaring errors have been discovered, they have been corrected; but no effort has been made to verify the accounts generally, or to make the figures agree. This would entail such an immense amount of labor that it was useless to think of it. One of your D. C. H. R.'s has undertaken to make the accounts of a Court in his district balance, and, in order to do so, had to make an audit of the books himself, running back for a year.

That he and the Court will be well repaid in the satisfaction found in putting the Court in the position of knowing just where it stood, there can be no question; but it is not possible to do this in every case, and there are few D. H. C. R.'s who can give the time to the work.

It is hoped that in the near future a new form of book for the financial matters of the Courts may be issued. The present seems too complicated to ready auditing, and a simpler form can be devised. With this in view, several forms have been drawn up, and are now under consideration. One of the chief difficulties is the multiplicity of accounts — there are too many to look after and keep separate, and the Financial Secretaries, who are, in the main, hard-working officers, can hardly be blamed much if matters get a little mixed. With books for Subordinate Courts of simpler form, the financial officers of the Courts would take new life.

Assessment Calls.

During the year 1888, eleven Assessment Calls were issued — viz., 43, 44, 45, 46, 47, 48, 49, 50, 51, 52, 53. One more call might have been issued if we had known that deaths had occurred to warrant its issuance. Our increased membership, of course, increases the amount received on a Call, so that now about four thousand dollars is collected on each Call.

Increasing membership has not increased our death rate, as, with a membership approaching four thousand, our deaths for last year were forty-six, of which number only one was initiated in 1888, three in 1887, one in 1886, and three in 1884.

Without any question, our Order, as now constituted, is the best physically, of any, and we can show what it is safe to say has never been equalled, an increasing membership and a decreasing average age.

With the same care in the future in the admission of new applicants, we may confidently look forward to a brilliant career for the Massachusetts Catholic Order of Foresters.

Respectfully submitted,

JAMES F. SUPPLE,
High Court Secretary-Treasurer.

TENTH ANNUAL CONVENTION

OF THE

Massachusetts Catholic Order of Foresters

HELD AT THE BOSTON TAVERN, 347 WASHINGTON STREET, BOSTON,

APRIL 17, 1889.

In compliance with the following call, the Representatives of the various Courts assembled. at the Boston Tavern, Wednesday, April 17, 1889.

MASSACHUSETTS CATHOLIC ORDER OF FORESTERS.

HIGH STANDING COMMITTEE,

597 Washington Street,

BOSTON, March 30, 1889.

To the Officers and Members of the Massachusetts Catholic Order of Foresters.

BROTHERS, — In accordance with the powers vested in the High Standing Committee of the Massachusetts Catholic Order of Foresters (under Art. IV., Constitution of High Court, Page 11), a call is hereby issued for the assembling of Representatives of the Subordinate Courts of the Massachusetts Catholic Order of Foresters in Annual Session of the High Court of the Order, to be held at the Boston Tavern, No. 347 Washington Street, Boston, to be opened in regular form at 9.30 o'clock, A.M., on Wednesday, the seventeenth day of April A.D., 1889, as provided for in the High Court Constitution.

The basis of Representation shall be as laid down in Art. II., Sect. 3, Constitution of High Court, page 8.

Forms of Credential to the Annual Session of the High Court accompany this Call, one to be retained and held by the Representative for use at the Convention. If the Credential be transferred for cause, this should be stated on the back of Credential under the endorsements of Chief Ranger and Recording Secretary of the Court.

By order of the High Standing Committee,

JEREMIAH G. FENNESSEY,

High Chief Ranger.

JAMES F. SUPPLE,

High Court Secretary-Treasurer.

The hour having arrived, High Chief Ranger, Jeremiah G. Fennessey, called the Convention to order.

High Senior Conductor, Edward Riley, and High Junior Conductor, P. A. Murray, reported that all the Officers of the High Court were present except Vice High Chief Ranger, T. Sproules, and High Inside Sentinel, Philip Smith.

High Chief Ranger Fennessey appointed Bro. A. F. Caldwell, of No. 7, to act as Vice High Chief Ranger, and Bro. M. Driscoll, of No. 61, to act as High Inside Sentinel.

High Chief Ranger Fennessey then opened the Convention in due form, and prayer was offered by High Court Chaplain, Rev. Hugh Roe O'Donnell.

High Chief Ranger Fennessey announced that the High Court Chaplain had engagements which called him away, and as he was obliged to go soon, he would at this time ask the Rev. gentleman to say a few words of encouragement and advice.

Father O'Donnell then briefly addressed the Convention, saying that he was very glad to be able to be present at the opening of the Convention, and expressed his regrets at his inability to remain all through the proceedings. He said he was glad that this Order was called Catholic because none but Catholics could belong to it. He recommended holding the Convention at some other time than Holy Week, as the High Court Chaplain was very busy at such time as was everybody connected with the Church. He hoped the Convention would be harmonious and deal wisely with the questions presented.

Father O'Donnell was frequently applauded, and at the close of his remarks departed under escort of the High Conductors.

High Chief Ranger Fennessey appointed following

COMMITTEE ON CREDENTIALS:

Bros. J. J. Leonard	.	of Gallagher	No.	64
A. H. McDonald	.	" Stoughton	"	69
Dr. T. J. Giblin	.	" St. Michael	"	70
J. F. Carens	.	" Phil Sheridan	"	71
R. Dwyer	.	" Merrimack	"	72
M. J. O'Boyle	.	" Taunton	"	73
D. F. Buckley	.	" Hendricken	"	74

The Committee reported (Bro. Caldwell, of No. 7, in the chair) that sixty-seven Representatives were present representing fifty-one Courts.

Voted to accept report of Committee on Credentials.

High Chief Ranger Fennessey announced No. 4 of Order of Business. Bro. J. T. Daly, of Erin No. 28, moved to dispense with roll call.

Voted to dispense with calling the Roll.

High Chief Ranger Fennessey announced No. 5 Order of Business.

Bro. Pendis, of St. Francis No. 25, moved to dispense with reading Records of last Convention.

Bro. Ratigan, of No. 59, objected, as he did not know what was in the records.

Bros. Callanan, of No. 63, and Morris of No. 38, wanted the records read.

Bro. Caldwell, of No. 7, moved the previous question.

High Chief Ranger Fennessey stated the question.

The previous question was ordered.

Voted to not dispense with reading the records.

The High Court Secretary-Treasurer proceeded to read the records

Bro. Shay, of St. Francis No. 4, moved to dispense with further reading as every member of the Order had a printed copy of the records.

Bro. Callanan, of No. 63, said he had no copy.

Bro. Daly, of No. 28, said the Convention had nothing to do with the matter as it was in the Order of Business.

High Chief Ranger Fennessey stated the question.

Voted to dispense with further reading of the record.

Under No. 6 of the Order of Business the High Chief Ranger called attention to the report of the High Court Secretary-Treasurer which was in the hands of the Representatives, and then

proceeded to read his report of the work of the High Standing
Committee during the year, and his review of the condition of the
Order.

Reading of the report was listened to with great interest, and at
its conclusion was enthusiastically applauded.

Bro. Daly moved that report be divided, and the various matters
referred to the appropriate Committees.

Motion was carried.

High Chief Ranger Fennessey appointed the following Committees:

On Constitution.

P. H. C. R.	Hon. Owen A. Galvin	of Cheverus	No. 6
" " " "	James J. McLaughlin	" Americus	" 34
	Jeremiah J. Callanan	" Shields	" 63
	Dr. F. E. Hines	" Essex	" 16
	John B. Ratigan	" Worcester	" 59
	W. E. Shay	" St. Francis	" 4
	Daniel A. Cronin	" St. Joseph	" 11

On Appeals.

Andrew Golding	of Cheverus	No. 6
Jas. F. Carens	" Phil Sheridan	" 71
George F. Brammer	" Taunton	" 73
E. J. Leary	" SS. Peter & Paul	" 15
E. C. Murphy	" Canton	" 67
M. W. O'Rourke	" St. James	" 54
L. J. Watson	" St. Margaret	" 68

On Petitions.

A. F. Caldwell	" St. Patrick	No. 7
M. Edmonds	" Cathedral	" 1
Charles H. Riley	" St. Raphael	" 26
William Daughan	" Constantine	" 49
J. A. Burns	" Charles River	" 55
H. F. Scanlan	" Fulton	" 12
J. H. Morton	" Carroll	" 57

On State of the Order.

Hon. John P. Dore	" Sherwood	" 8
M. Driscoll	" St. Lawrence	" 61
W. Mackin	" Columbkille	" 65
Dr. C. A. Ahearne	" Lafayette	" 14
John T. Daly	" Erin	" 28
J. C. Pendis	" St. Francis	" 25
T. F. Sullivan	" Thomas	" 29

ON SECRET WORK.

P. A. Mulligan	" Middlesex	No. 60
William F. Moore	" St. Anne	" 47
Frank S. Maloney	" Williams	" 19
John F. Dever	" Mount Pleasant	" 20
J. B. Buckley	" Iona	" 10
John C. Carson	" Sheil	" 35
John C. Dwyer	" St. John	" 33

High Chief Ranger Fennessey announced No. 8 in Order of Business.

Amendments to the Constitution were offered by

Bro. Driscoll	of St. Lawrence	No. 61
" Morrison	" John	" 23
" Caldwell	" Patrick	" 7
" Pendis	" Francis	" 25
" Dever	" Mount Pleasant	" 20
" McGrath	" " "	" 20

All referred to Committee on Constitution.

Bro. McGrath, of Mount Pleasant No. 20, offered a resolution.

Referred to Committee on Constitution.

Bro. Cronin, of St. Joseph No. 11, offered a resolve for a reserve fund.

Referred to Committee on Constitution.

Bro. Gallagher, of Fenwick No. 3, offered an amendment to Constitution.

Referred to Committee on Constitution.

Bro. McGrath, of Mount Pleasant No. 20, offered a resolution.

Referred to Committee on Constitution.

Bro. Morrison, of St. John No. 23, offered an amendment to Constitution.

Referred to Committee on Constitution.

Bro. McGrath, of Mount Pleasant No. 20, rose to ask a question but was called to order by Bro. Leary of No. 15.

Bro. Morrison, of St. John No. 23, offered an amendment to Constitution.

Referred to Committee on Secret Work.

Bro. Daughan, of Constantine No. 49, called attention to the A. C. R. Fund, and moved to incorporate with Court Fund.

High Chief Ranger Fennessey stated that an amendment to that effect had been offered and referred.

Bro. O'Loughlin, of St. Joseph No. 11, rose and stated that he had something to offer.

Bro. Morris, of St. Joseph No. 38, said he would like to hear what Bro. O'Loughlin was saying, but he could not hear him.

Bro. O'Loughlin continued, and said the approaching Centennial Celebration in New York would be a fit occasion to prove that, as Catholics, we were as good citizens as any, and moved that a Committee of five be appointed to consider what the sentiment of Catholics really is on the subject.

Bro. Callanan, of Shields No. 63, said he hoped politics would be kept out of the Order, and that it was not necessary for us, as Catholics, to prove that we were good citizens.

Bro. O'Loughlin thought the matter would do no harm, and hoped the Committee would be appointed.

Bro. Daly, of No. 28, moved previous question.

Previous question was not carried.

Bro. Cronin, of St. Joseph No. 11, hoped the resolution would not be received, and that the Committee would not be appointed.

Bro. Ratigan moved a recess for dinner.

Voted to take a recess for dinner at 1.10 P. M.

Reassembled at 3 P. M.

Bro. O'Loughlin, of St. Joseph No. 11, withdrew his motion, and offered a substitute.

High Chief Ranger Fennessey stated question.

Vote was taken and declared carried.

Bro. Shay, Chairman of Committee on Finance, reported for his Committee that books and accounts of High Court Secretary-Treasurer were found correct, and recommended per capita tax of seventy-five cents. Also read the bond of High Court Secretary-Treasurer to the Convention.

The report follows.

BOSTON, April 15, 1889.

To the Officers and Members of the Massachusetts Catholic Order of Foresters.

Your Committee, appointed to examine the books of the High Court Secretary and Treasurer, have attended to their duty, and would report that they found the books all correct and in perfect order.

We find the total receipts in General Fund	$3,881 55
Expenses	3,367 39
Balance	$514 16
Total receipts in Endowment Fund	$49,032 10
Expenses	44,561 00
Balance	$4,471 10

, The Committee recommend that the per capita tax be kept at the present rate of seventy-five (75) cents.

WM. E. SHAY,
JNO. P. DORE,
ANDREW GOLDING.

Brother Shay also said that the Committee on Finance was surprised that the High Court Secretary-Treasurer kept matters so straight, when the work was made so difficult by the Courts.

Bro. Morrison, of St. John No. 23, asked for explanation about Endowment Table, where it showed No. 176 and No. 193, both Jno. Carney.

High Court Secretary-Treasurer said that was an error of the types, and that one should read Joseph Donovaro, of Williams No. 19.

Bro. Leary, of No. 15, asked if any Courts were allowed to pay in instalments.

High Chief Ranger Fennessey said he had covered that point in his instructions to Deputy High Chief Rangers.

Past High Chief Ranger J. J. McLaughlin moved to accept report of Committee on Finance.

Voted to accept.

Bro. J. J. McLaughlin reported for Committee on Constitution recommending that the part of Constitution calling for continuous sessions be stricken out.

Also that Committee on Constitution be permanent, and that the recommendation of High Chief Ranger to have the Committee on Constitution consider the amendments offered, and report later, be adopted.

High Chief Ranger stated the question on acceptance of report of Committee on Constitution.

Voted to accept.

Bro. McLaughlin moved that the recommendation for striking out the words in Art. XI. Sect. 1: — "It shall meet on consecutive days until it be adjourned without day " be adopted.

High Chief Ranger stated the question.

Voted to adopt.

High Chief Ranger stated question on adoption of report of Committee on Constitution to make Committee on Constitution a permanent Committee.

Voted to adopt.

Bro. Mulligan asked leave for Committee on Secret Work to retire to consider the matters referred to it.

High Chief Ranger ruled that Committee could retire, and the business of the Convention go on.

Bro. Caldwell, for Committee on Petitions, reported no petitions.

Voted to accept report.

Voted to discharge Committee.

Bro. Golding reported for his Committee.

No business.

Voted to accept report.

Voted to discharge Committee.

High Chief Ranger announced No. 11 in Order of Business, viz., Reports of Special Committees.

Bro. Caldwell, for Committee on behalf of the Order to establish a home, reported as follows : —

To the High Chief Ranger, Officers, and Brothers.

Your Committee, appointed at the last Annual Convention as the Committee on the "Home for the Order," to confer with a like Committee from the Knights of St. Rose, met and organized as a Joint Committee, — Bro. William E. Shay, Chairman; Bro. A. F. Caldwell, Secretary, — and it was —

Voted that this Committee recommend the creation of a reserve fund, and that such portions as this Convention, in its judgment, see fit may be set apart for a Home for the Order.

Voted that, provided the Convention accept and adopt this recommendation, that the offer of the Knights of St. Rose be accepted as a nucleus for the Home,

Voted that the Chairman and Secretary sign report for their Committee.

W. E. SHAY, *Chairman.*
A. F. CALDWELL, *Secretary.*

High Chief Ranger asked for the will of the Convention on the matter before it.

High Chief Ranger stated the question on accepting the report of the Committee.

Dr. Hines moved to accept the report of the Committee; also to refer to Committee on Constitution.

Voted to accept the report.

Bro. O'Loughlin thought that we, with only four thousand members, should not have a Home, as the members of the Order had something else to do besides going into a building scheme; that it was a big undertaking to put a building up.

Dr. Hines thought anything of the kind should be referred to Committee on Constitution, because it would, in his opinion, facilitate business.

Bro. Ratigan thought the Committee on Constitution had enough to do without considering a Home.

High Chief Ranger stated the question on reference to Committee on Constitution.

Voted not to refer to Committee on Constitution.

Bro. Golding moved a Special Committee.

Voted to refer to Special Committee.

Voted to make Committee seven in number.

Past High Chief Ranger McLaughlin moved to suspend the rules and proceed to election of officers.

Voted to suspend the rules.

High Chief Ranger Fennessey announced that the next business in order was the election of officers.

Past High Chief Ranger McLaughlin then nominated Bro. Jeremiah G. Fennessey, of St. James No. 54, for the position of High Chief Ranger.

Bro. Griffin, of No. 11, seconded the nomination, saying he was glad of the opportunity to say that he was wrong in so strenuously opposing the present incumbent at the beginning of the term just ended.

High Chief Ranger Fennessey appointed following Committee to collect and count ballots : —

Bros. O'Loughlin	.	.	.	.	of St. Joseph No. 11
Golding .	.	.	.	.	" Cheverus " 6
Caldwell	.	.	.	" St. Patrick " 7

Bro. McLaughlin moved that the High Court Secretary-Treasurer cast one ballot for Jeremiah G. Fennessey for High Chief Ranger.

Motion put and declared carried.

The Committee reported that the High Court Secretary-Treasurer had cast one ballot as directed, and the High Chief Ranger announced that Jeremiah G. Fennessey was elected High Chief Ranger for the coming year.

Bro. Golding moved to nominate W. E. Shay for High Vice Chief Ranger.

Dr. Hines said that he was pleased to present the name of one whom all knew as a hard worker, and that he presented the name of Philip Smith, of Williams No. 19, for Vice High Chief Ranger.

Bro. O'Loughlin nominated Bro. Thos. Sproules for Vice High Chief Ranger.

Bro. Sproules thanked the Bro. from No. 11, and declined the nomination.

Bro. Shay presented name of Edward Riley.

Bro. O'Loughlin seconded the nomination.

Bro. Gallagher, of Fenwick No. 3, presented name of Thos. J. Dunn.

Bro. Dunn declined.

Bro. Golding moved to close the nomination.

Voted to close.

High Chief Ranger instructed the Committee to collect ballots for Vice High Chief Ranger.

Bro. Shay stated that he served one year on Finance Committee, and knew something of the work done by the High Court Secretary-Treasurer and its difficulties, and moved that one ballot be cast by Committee to receive votes, for James F. Supple for High Court Secretary-Treasurer.

High Chief Ranger stated the question and declared that it was a unanimous vote.

Bro. O'Loughlin of Committee to receive ballots reported

Whole number votes cast for V. H. C. R.	71
Necessary for a choice	36
Philip Smith of Williams No. 19	42
Edw. Riley of St. Joseph No. 11	28
Thomas Sproules of St. Francis No. 4	1

High Chief Ranger declared Philip Smith elected Vice High Chief Ranger.

The Committee reported that Bro. Caldwell of the Committee had cast one vote for James F. Supple for High Court Secretary-Treasurer, and High Chief Ranger declared James F. Supple elected High Court Secretary-Treasurer.

Bro. Driscoll moved that High Court Secretary-Treasurer cast one ballot for Edward Riley for High Court Senior Conductor. High Chief Ranger stated question and declared the motion carried. High Court Secretary-Treasurer cast the ballot, and High Chief Ranger declared Edward Riley elected High Senior Conductor.

Bro. Caldwell moved that High Court Secretary-Treasurer cast one ballot for P. A. Murray for High Junior Conductor. High

Chief Ranger stated question and declared the motion carried. High Court Secretary-Treasurer cast the ballot, and High Chief Ranger declared P. A. Murray elected High Junior Conductor.

Bro. Sullivan, of No. 29, moved that High Court Secretary-Treasurer cast one ballot for T. J. Dunn for High Inside Sentinel. High Chief Ranger stated question and declared the motion carried. High Court Secretary-Treasurer cast the ballot, and High Chief Ranger declared T. J. Dunn elected.

Bro. Maloney, of Constantine No. 49, nominated, in a few well-chosen words, William Daughan of Constantine No. 49, for High Outside Sentinel.

Bro. Shay nominated R. Farrenkopf of No. 8.

Bro. Leary nominated P. A. Donovan of No. 15.

Voted to close nomination.

The Convention proceeded to ballot for High Outside Sentinel.

Bro. Shay moved that High Court Secretary-Treasurer cast one ballot for Dr. Joseph D. Couch for High Court Physician.

Voted.

High Chief Ranger declared ballot cast as directed and that Dr. Joseph D. Couch was elected High Court Physician.

Bro. Daly moved that High Court Secretary-Treasurer cast one ballot for Rev. Hugh Roe O'Donnell for High Court Chaplain.

Voted.

High Chief Ranger declared ballot cast, and that Rev. Hugh Roe O'Donnell was elected High Court Chaplain.

Committee to collect ballots reported on vote for High Outside Sentinel.

Whole number of votes cast	70
Necessary for a choice	36
Bro. Daughan, of No. 49	11
" Donovan, " 15	16
" Farrenkopf, " 8	43

High Chief Ranger declared Bro. R. Farrenkopf elected High Outside Sentinel.

Bro. Shay moved to proceed to installation of Officers.

Voted.

High Chief Ranger invited Past High Chief Ranger McLaughlin to perform the installation ceremonies.

Bro. Daly, of Erin No. 28, moved that High Court Secretary-

Treasurer cast ballot of Convention for Committee on Finance, to be composed of same brothers who served last term.

Voted; and High Chief Ranger declared that one ballot had been cast as directed for the following brothers to serve on the Finance Committee: —

Bros. W. E. Shay	of St. Francis No.	4
Hon. Jno. P. Dore	" Sherwood "	8
Jas. J. Lanigan	" Cathedral "	1
Andrew Golding	" Cheverus "	6
W. F. Rooney	" Prospect "	58

On the invitation of High Chief Ranger Jeremiah G. Fennessey, Past High Chief Ranger James J. McLaughlin then took the chair, and appointed Bro. Donovan, of La Fayette No. 14, to act as High Inside Sentinel; Bro. Caldwell, of St. Patrick No. 7, to act as High Senior Conductor; Bro. Daley, of Erin No. 28, to act as High Junior Conductor; Bro. Cleary, of St. Francis No. 4, to act as High Court Secretary-Treasurer.

Past High Chief Ranger McLaughlin then installed, in a most impressive manner, the following as officers of the High Court for the term ending April, 1890: —

High Chief Ranger,
JEREMIAH G. FENNESSEY.

Vice High Chief Ranger,
PHILIP SMITH.

High Court Secretary-Treasurer,
JAMES F. SUPPLE.

High Senior Conductor,
EDWARD RILEY.

High Junior Conductor,
P. A. MURRAY.

High Inside Sentinel,
THOMAS J. DUNN.

High Outside Sentinel,
R. FARRENKOPF.

High Court Chaplain,
REV. HUGH ROE O'DONNELL.

High Court Physician,
JOSEPH D. COUCH, M. D.

Past High Chief Ranger McLaughlin then introduced High Chief Ranger Jeremiah G. Fennessey, who warmly thanked the Convention for the confidence displayed by its vote, and briefly referred to the work of the Order, and the glorious future before us if we are united and true to ourselves.

High Chief Ranger then called for report of Committee on State of Order.

Bro. Dore, Chairman of Committee, stated that Bro. Driscoll, Secretary of Committee, would report.

Bro. Driscoll submitted a report that Committee could not consider the matters referred to it in the short time it had had, and asked for further time.

Vice High Chief Ranger Smith, in the chair, announced that next business in order was reports of Committees.

Bro. Mulligan, for Committee on Secret Work, reported as follows :

The Committee beg leave to report that it is inexpedient to make any change in the secret work of the Order.

P. A. MULLIGAN,
F. S. MALONEY,
J. B. BUCKLEY,
J. C. DWYER.

Bro. Shay hoped the report would not be accepted.

High Senior Conductor Riley moved a new Committee of five on Secret Work, to be nominated by the Convention.

Motion was carried.

Bro. J. T. Daly moved that Brother Shay, of No. 4, and Past High Chief Ranger McLaughlin, of No. 34, be on the Committee.

Bro. Riley also nominated J. J. McLaughlin.

Voted to place Past High Chief Ranger McLaughlin, of No. 34, on Committee.

Bro. Shay nominated J. T. Daly.

Voted to place J. T. Daly, of No. 28, on the Committee.

Bro. Pendis nominated W. E. Shay.

Bro. Shay declined.

Bro. Callanan nominated J. H. Watson Past High Chief Ranger.

Voted to place Past High Chief Ranger Watson, of No. 16, on the Committee.

Bro. M. Edmonds was nominated.

Voted to place Past High Chief Secretary Michael Edmonds, of No. 1, on the Committee.

Bro. Driscoll nominated M. Leonard of No. 34.

Voted to place M. Leonard, of No. 34, on the Committee.

High Chief Ranger Fennessey announced the Committee on Secret Work complete, as follows: —

> Past High Chief Ranger James J. McLaughlin of Americus No.'34.
> John T. Daly of Erin No. 28.
> Past High Chief Ranger John H. Watson of Essex No. 16.
> Past High Court Secretary Michael Edmonds of Cathedral No. 1.
> Michael Leonard of Americus No. 34.

High Chief Ranger Fennessey announced as Committee on Constitution: —

W. E. Shay.	.	.	.	.	of St. Francis	No.	4
Andrew Golding.	.	.	.	" Cheverus	"	6
Dr. F. E. Hines .	.	.	.	" Essex	"	16
Joseph Tondorf, Jr.	.	.	.	" Holy Trinity	"	51
Jno. T. Daly	.	.	.	. .	" Erin	"	28
Jno. B. Ratigan .	.	.	.	" Worcester	"	59
Jeremiah J. Callanan	.	.	" Shields	"	63

Bros. Hines and Callanan declined, and High Chief Ranger appointed, in place of them, Daniel A. Cronin, of St. Joseph No. 11, M. J. O'Boyle, of Taunton No. 73, and announced the permanent Committee on Constitution complete, as follows: —

W. E. Shay	.	.	.	.	of St. Francis	No.	4
Andrew Golding .	.	.	.	" Cheverus	"	6
Daniel A. Cronin	.	.	.	" St. Joseph	"	11
Joseph Tondorf, Jr.	.	.	.	" Holy Trinity	"	51
Jno. T. Daly	.	.	.	.	" Erin	"	28
Jno. B. Ratigan .	.	.	.	" Worcester	"	59
M. J. O'Boyle	.	.	.	.	" Taunton	"	73

On motion of High Senior Conductor Riley, a vote of thanks was tendered to retiring Vice High Chief Ranger Thomas Sproules.

Past Vice High Chief Ranger Sproules thanked the Convention for its kind remembrance of his services.

Bro. Shay suggested that High Court Secretary-Treasurer formulate an uniform system of book-keeping for all the Courts.

Bro. Riley asked if it would not cause expense.

Bro. Daly said his experience was that whether or not expense was caused, he believed a new system should be adopted, and that the High Court Secretary-Treasurer could do that from his experience.

Voted that such a system be adopted as suggested.

High Chief Ranger Fennessey appointed following Committee on Building:

Thomas Sproules P. V. H. C. R.	of St. Francis No. 4
Hon. John P. Dore	of No. 8
M. Driscoll	" " 61
H. C. Griffin	" " 11
John C. Pendis	" 25
John J. Leonard	" " 64

Bro. Daly, of Erin No. 28, said he wanted a ruling on the question whether a man could resign from the Order. In his experience as Deputy High Chief Ranger he said he found a number of members were entered on the books of Courts he had charge of, as resigned.

High Chief Ranger Fennessey said the matter was worth discussing and asked for opinions.

Bro. Callanan said "if a man could not resign, what could be done with him, let him run in arrears and be suspended?" He thought it was not an honorable way to treat a man.

Bro. Cronin said his experience was same as Bro. Daly. His own opinion was that a member could resign. •

Bro. Caldwell asked if a man should not be as free to leave as to join.

Dr. Hines said he believed if a man paid his dues he had a right to resign his membership.

Bro. Callanan related a case which came under his own observation.

Bro. Shay called attention to the report of High Court Secretary-Treasurer showing that twenty-nine had resigned membership.

Bro. McLaughlin of St. Peter, No. 18, said some had resigned from his Court.

Bro. O'Loughlin said he thought a man could resign.

High Chief Ranger said he was ready to give a decision, and then gave a lengthy statement covering the question, and he decided that a member could resign because resignation had been made in sufficient number to establish a custom; that, in his opinion a Catholic could not take an obligation from which he could not free himself, and he therefore ruled that a member could resign.

Bro. Shay notified the Convention that the Committee on Constitution would meet one week from April 17, at rooms of High Standing Committee.

Bro. Tondorf wished to know about the standing of a member with a withdrawal card.

High Chief Ranger decided that the standing of a member with a withdrawal card depended on the member himself. He should take sufficient interest in his own business to see that his dues were paid to some one.

Bro. Caldwell asked to have the duties of Vice Chief Ranger defined.

High Chief Ranger decided that the Vice Chief Ranger had charge of the door and should give permission to enter.

Bro. Callanan suggested that this conflicted with Sect. 7, page 58, of the Constitution.

High Chief Ranger decided that it did not conflict.

Bro. Golding suggested that the Convention proceed to the next matter in Order of Business.

Bro. Daly moved to adopt the report of the Committee on Finance.

Voted to adopt.

Bro. O'Rourke asked a question about presenting an application in person.

High Chief Ranger said the matter was already in possession of the Committee on Constitution.

Bro. Driscoll moved that proceedings of Convention be printed as soon as possible after dissolution of Convention.

Bro. Shay amended to include High Chief Ranger's address.

Amendment was accepted by Bro. Driscoll.

Voted to print.

Bro. Brant asked about presenting the proposition fee.

High Chief Ranger said he would decide at next meeting of Deputy High Chief Rangers.

High Chief Ranger announced No. 14 in order of business.

Past High Chief Ranger John H. Watson spoke of recommendation of High Chief Ranger concerning labors of High Court Secretary-Treasurer.

High Chief Ranger Fennessey said he knew something of the work of the Order, and that, when he was in the city, he spent a couple of hours in the office every day. That he found the High Court Secretary-Treasurer there, and trying to straighten out the carelessness of ten years. That, owing to want of records, the Order had paid dearly, and that the High Court Secretary-Treasurer should be paid a proper compensation.

Bro. Tondorf said he was surprised at the growth of the Order, and thought the extra labor was great; he was surprised that the salary was at the old figure, and he moved that the amount be raised to a thousand dollars.

Bro. Harkins seconded the motion, and gave the Convention reasons why he thought more compensation should be given.

Bro. Doolin, of St. Augustine No. 46, moved to amend, — to make the amount twelve hundred dollars.

Bro. Tondorf accepted the amendment; no objection was made.

High Chief Ranger stated the question.

Bro. Duggan, of Friendship No. 37, said he represented a Court in which were a number of kickers, and he himself believed that the salary should be fifteen hundred dollars, but did not think his Court would stand it.

Bro. Daly said he represented a Court which delegated full power to him. He knew what the work was, and he knew that there was no man in the hall who, if able to do the work of High Court Secretary-Treasurer, would do it for twelve hundred dollars. He had a fair idea what the work was from his experience with the the late lamented High Court Secretary B. J. O. Daly, in occasionally assisting him in the work of the order.

High Outside Sentinel Farrenkopf announced supper.

Bro. O'Loughlin said there was one who did not believe that twelve hundred dollars should be paid; that no praise should be given to a man who did his duty, and he must vote and speak against the motion; that he thought the secretary of other organizations did very much more work. He thought the Order was not in condition to pay any more money; he opposed the raising of the salary from good motives, and he felt bound to oppose it.

Bro. Watson, Past High Chief Ranger, asked if Bro. O'Loughlin would, provided the amount of per capita was sufficient, object to the increase.

Bro. O'Loughlin said the duties of the office did not require it.

Bro. Doolin asked Bro. O'Loughlin if he would do the work for a thousand dollars.

Bro. O'Loughlin said he would under some circumstances, but his income was now such he would not.

Bro. O'Rourke asked what constitutes a day's work; and he thought the High Court Secretary-Treasurer worked ten hours a day for the Order.

High Chief Ranger Fennessey said Bro. O'Loughlin's position reminded him of this: That we might just as well say to Owen A. Galvin, J. J. McLaughlin, or Jno. H. Watson, here is an office, — what will you do the work for?

He was surprised at the statements made about what other men would do the work for. He understood how it was that men could offer to do the work for less than the present incumbent was getting.

He called attention to the report, and asked how many men in the Order, who could write the report, would do it for eight hundred dollars or a thousand dollars.

High Outside Sentinel Farrenkopf announced supper.

Voted to lay on the table.

Voted to take a recess till eight o'clock.

The Convention reassembled at 8.10.

High Chief Ranger stated question.

Bro. Doolin moved to take from table.

Voted to take from the table.

Bro. Daughan spoke at length on the subject, and said twelve hundred dollars was not sufficient to compensate the High Chief Secretary-Treasurer for the work he had performed; that he knew some men would object to anything. Even though a man did offer to do the work for nothing, some men would object. He represented a Court which had as much interest in the Order as any other, and his Court would have confidence in what he did. That in the past the High Court Secretary-Treasurer had given his time without compensation in the early days of the Order, and he deserved just compensation now. That it honestly belonged to him, and he could go back to his Court with confidence that he would receive commendation for his action.

Bro. Hevey said the matter was discussed enough, and moved the previous question.

Previous question was not seconded.

Bro. Duggan said he wished to express the feeling of the Court he represented, and thought, for the good of the Order, it should be held over. He appreciated the noble work of the High Officers the past year, and he thought the laborer worthy of his hire.

Bro. Cronin said that, as his associate from his Court was opposed to the matter, he was sorry to differ from him.

He thought St. Joseph Court No. 11 was desirous of being in the front rank, and, when the work was well done, salary was no consequence. That we should be just to our officers, and his Court would not object, because his Court was now paying their Financial Secretary three hundred dollars per year, and the brother doing the work was earning three hundred dollars, and ought to get it.

Bro. Dwyer, of St. Michael No. 70, said he was a new member; but he was always an advocate of good salary for good work, — cheap salary meant cheap work. That he thought the per capita was ample for it, and it should be passed ; and, from what he heard since he came into the Convention, lawyers seemed to be offering themselves cheap for the position of High Court Secretary-Treasurer, but he judged some of them were left.

Bro. Shay said he knew from his experience on the Finance Committee that the work of the office called for it, and we were not paying our High Court Secretary-Treasurer the proper amount for the labor performed, and he hoped the motion would prevail.

Bro. Sullivan, of No. 8, said he was surprised that any one should object to the increase of salary of the High Court Secretary-Treasury, because he believed the labor warranted it, and, in his opinion, every Court of the Order would coincide with his view. As a representative from Sherwood Court, he was satisfied that his doings at the Convention would be ratified, and moved the previous question.

Bro. Maloney, of Constantine No. 49, asked for time to make a few remarks, and proceeded to say he could see no objection to increasing the salary, and knew that the same class of work in mercantile houses was paid far better. He hoped the vote would be unanimous, and said he agreed with Bro. Dwyer, of No. 70, that cheap salary meant cheap work.

Bro. Dwyer, of Merrimack No. 72, moved the previous question, which was seconded.

High Chief Ranger stated the question.

High Senior Conductor Riley asked for the floor.

High Chief Ranger decided debate out of order.

Bro. O'Loughlin rose to a question of privilege.

High Chief Ranger Fennessey asked Bro. O'Loughlin to state his question of privilege.

Bro. O'Loughlin proceeded and was soon called to order by the High Chief Ranger who stated that Bro. O'Loughlin was not speaking to a question of privilege, and had obtained the floor under a subterfuge.

Bro. Driscoll appealed from the decision of the High Chief Ranger.

High Chief Ranger stated the appeal.

Bro. Driscoll stated his reasons for appealing.

High Chief Ranger stated the appeal.

Bro. O'Loughlin spoke on the appeal, giving his reasons why the decision of the High Chief Ranger should not be sustained.

Bro. O'Rourke hoped the decision of the Chair would be sustained, and said the proper way was to vote down the previous question.

Bro. Duggan said the previous question was debatable.

Bro. Cronin said he thought the High Chief Ranger right.

High Chief Ranger stated the question on the appeal: " Shall the decision of the Chair stand?" and it was

Voted to sustain the decision of the Chair.

High Chief Ranger Fennessey stated that question was on ordering the previous question.

Vote was taken and High Chief Ranger declared the previous question was ordered.

The vote was doubted.

High Chief Ranger requested members to stand and be counted. A count showed 39 yea, 10 nay, and the previous question was ordered.

High Chief Ranger stated the question.

Bro. Caldwell rose to a question of privilege because he wanted a chance to speak on the question.

High Chief Ranger again stated the question: " On the motion of Bro. Tondorf, amended by Bro. Doolin, that salary of the High Court Secretary-Treasurer be made $1200 for the ensuing year," and declared the motion carried.

High Inside Sentinel Dunn wanted a record in figures and doubted the vote.

High Chief Ranger requested the brothers to stand and be counted.

High Chief Ranger requested Bro. McGrath, of Mt. Pleasant No. 20, to make the count. Bro. McGrath declined, saying that the Order had a paid officer whose duty it was to count.

High Chief Ranger then requested Bro. O'Loughlin to make the count.

Bro. O'Loughlin complied, and reported 40 yea, 7 nay, and the High Chief Ranger declared the motion carried.

Bro. Cronin moved to make the vote unanimous.

High Chief Ranger asked if there was any objection.

Bro. Shay thought that was forcing gentlemen to do something they did not wish to do.

Bro. Daly said he thought the members voted as they felt, and jit was as well to leave the vote as it was declared.

High Chief Ranger called for names of Past Chief Rangers.

PAST CHIEF RANGERS.

A. M. Lanigan	.	.	.	.	.	.	of No.	1
T. F. Crosby	.	.	.	.	.	.	" "	4
G. F. Lowe	.	.	.	.	.	.	" "	5
Jas. Cashin	.	.	.	.	.	.	"	6
M. F. Farrell	.	.	.	.	.	.	"	9
C. F. Dolan	.	.	.	.	.	.	.. "	11
M. O'Brien	.	.	.	.	.	.	.. "	12
Dr. F. E. Hines	.	.	.	.	.	.	"	16
Henry McLaughlin	.	.	.	.	.	.	"	18
G. H. Keefe	.	.	.	.	.	.	"	20
J. T. Brickley	.	.	.	.	.	.	"	21
C. F. Morrison	.	.	.	.	.	.	.. "	23
E. W. Daly	.	.	.	.	.	.	"	24
T. F. Roach	.	.	.	.	.	.	"	29
Thos. Cawley	.	.	.	.	.	.	.. "	33
J. W. Brown	.	.	.	.	.	.	.. "	34
J. W. Keenan	.	.	.	.	.	.	"	37
J. J. Muldoon	.	.	.	.	.	.	"	39
W. R. Fairclough	.	.	.	.	.	.	.. "	41
Michael Taafe	.	.	.	.	.	.	.. "	44
John A. Gaw	.	.	.	.	.	.	"	44
John Hargedon	.	.	.	.	.	.	"	44
W. W. Hurly	.	.	.	.	.	.	.. "	43
W. Condon	.	.	.	.	.	.	.. "	45

T. C. Kelly	. . . .	" 48
W. Daughan	. . . .	" 49
G. Kranefuss	. . . .	" 51
J. A. Burns	. . . .	" 55
M. Boland	. . . .	" 58
R. A. Morrisey	. . . .	" 60
P. Johnson	. . . .	" 61
J. T. Brady	. . . . "	" 62
Wm. J. Van Etten	. . . .	" 65
A. F. Staples	. . . . . . "	" 66
Ed. C. Murphy	. . . . . .	" 67
L. J. Watson	. . . . . : "	" 68
A. H. McDonald	. . , ...	" 69
Dr. T. J. Giblin	. . . . . .	" 70
J. F. Carens	. . . .	" 71

Bro. Golding moved to adjourn *sine die.*

Bro. O'Loughlin thought it better to adjourn subject to the call of the High Standing Committee.

Voted to adjourn subject to call of High Standing Committee.

Voted to adjourn.

Closed in due form by High Chief Ranger Fennessey, at 9.30 P.M.

Second Session of the Tenth Annual Convention,

Called to order by Vice High Chief Ranger Smith at 8 P. M.

High Conductors reported High Court Officers all present.

Opened in due form.

High Chief Ranger Fennessey announced, as first business, reading of roll call.

Roll call was read by High Court Secretary-Treasurer, and showed that forty-seven Representatives were present, representing thirty-nine Courts, as follows: —

Cathedral, No. 1 . . .	Michael Edmonds.
" " . . .	Thomas J. Dunn.
Fenwick, No. 3	Daniel Gallagher.
St. Francis, No. 4 . . .	William E. Shay.
Cheverus, No. 6	Andrew Golding.
St. Patrick, No. 7 . . .	A. F. Caldwell.
Sherwood, No. 8 . . .	A. J. Lill.
" " . . .	R. Farrenkopf.
" " . . .	C. E. Colbert.
Columbus, No. 9 . . .	James F. Supple.
St. Joseph, No. 11 . . .	Edward Riley.
" " . . .	D. A. Cronin.
Fulton, No. 12	Henry F. Scanlan.
Fitzpatrick, No. 13 . . .	J. D. Mahoney.
La Fayette, No. 14 . . .	Dr. C. A. Ahearne.
SS. Peter and Paul, No. 15 .	P. A. Donovan.
Essex, No. 16	M. A. Dodd.
Hamilton, No. 17 . . .	John Hurly.
Williams, No. 19 . . .	F. S. Malony.
" " . . .	P. Smith.
Mt. Pleasant, No. 20 . . .	F. J. McGrath.
St. John, No. 23 . . .	T. Murray.
St. Gregory, No. 24 . . .	E. W. Daily.
St. Raphael, No. 26 . . .	J. F. Riley.
Qualey, No. 32	Thomas D. Hevey.
St. John, No. 33 . . .	John C. Dwyer.
Americus, No. 34 . . .	M. Leonard.

Shiel, No. 35	J. C. Carson.
Benedict, No. 39 . . .	Joseph D. Couch, M. D.
St. Bernard, No. 44 . . .	F. T. Cox.
St. Augustine, No. 46 . .	John Doolin.
St. Anne, No. 47 . . .	W. F. Moore.
Sarsfield, No. 48 . . .	T. Kelly.
Constantine, No. 49 . . .	W. T. Maloney.
" " . . .	D. Leahy.
Highland, No. 52 . . .	H. H. Collins.
Emerald, No. 53 . . .	J. B. Carbrey.
St. James, No. 54 . . .	Jeremiah G. Fennessey.
Charles River, No. 55 . .	J. A. Burns.
Middlesex, No. 60 . . .	P. A. Murray.
" " . . .	P. A. Mulligan.
St. Catharine, No. 62 . . .	J. T. Brady.
St. Margaret, No. 68 . . .	Lawrence J. Watson.
Phil Sheridan, No. 71 . .	J. F. Carens.
Merrimack, No. 72 . . .	R. Dwyer.
Taunton, No. 73 . . .	M. J. O'Boyle.
" " . . .	G. F. Brammer.

High Chief Ranger announced the reading of the records.

High Court Secretary-Treasurer proceeded to read the records.

High Senior Conductor Riley asked to suspend the reading.

Bro. McGrath, of No. 20, objected.

High Senior Conductor Riley asked if the records must not be read at some time before final adjournment.

High Chief Ranger Fennessey ruled that records must be read; but the Convention could, by majority vote, suspend the reading.

Bro. McGrath thought the records should be read.

Bro. Maloney, of No. 49, thought it was a waste of time.

Bro. Daly, of No. 28, moved previous question.

Seconded.

Voted to put the previous question.

Voted to suspend reading of records.

High Chief Ranger Fennessey announced and read a communication from Hon. O. A. Galvin, relating to the R. J. Downey case, saying the heirs were willing to take five hundred dollars.

High Chief Ranger explained the circumstances of the case, that Downey was once rejected for heart disease on application to St. Joseph No. 11. He shortly afterward applied to Cheverus Court No. 6, and was admitted. Afterward died of heart disease. Claim was made, and two Conventions have refused to pay. He ruled the matter not properly before the Convention, and ruled it out of order.

High Chief Ranger announced that the five-minute rule would be enforced.

High Chief Ranger called for report of Committee on Washington Centennial.

No report was offered.

High Chief Ranger called for report of Committee on Constitutional Amendments.

Bro. Shay, Chairman of Committee, introduced the Secretary of the Committee, Bro. Daly, of No. 28.

Bro. Daly said the Committee had devoted a great deal of time to consideration of the amendments offered, and had used its best judgment in every case.

Bro. Daly read amendment offered by Bro. Caldwell, of No. 7.

Bro. Pendis, of No. 25, suggested that all the matters reported on favorably by the Committee be read first.

Bro. Shay said the Committee recommended striking out Court in the titles of High Court Secretary-Treasurer and High Court Chaplain, and to change High Court Physician to High Medical Examiner.

High Chief Ranger stated question to change titles of High Court Secretary-Treasurer and High Court Chaplain to High Secretary-Treasurer, and High Chaplain, and High Court Physician to High Medical Examiner. No objection was made, and the High Chief Ranger declared it carried.

The Committee reported amendment concerning Trustees of High Court, to elect three now who shall give bonds, — one to be elected every year subsequently.

High Chief Ranger suggested that all amendments relating to a Reserve Fund be laid aside until the question of a Reserve Fund be settled.

The Committee reported in favor of a resolve of Bro. D. A. Cronin for an assessment of fifty cents to create a Reserve Fund, with a minority recommendation of an assessment of one dollar for the same purpose.

High Court Ranger asked pleasure of the Convention.

Bro. Pendis, of No. 25, moved to adopt.

High Chief Ranger stated question.

Bro. Duggan asked for an explanation.

Bro. Daly, of the Committee, explained.

High Senior Conductor Riley thought a Reserve Fund necessary.

Bro. Mackin, of No. 65, asked for a reading.

Bro. Daly, of the Committee, read the resolve.

Bro. Kelly, of No. 48, objected, and thought a Reserve Fund not necessary, and moved to refer to next Convention.

Bro. Sullivan, of No. 29, thought a Reserve Fund was necessary.

Bro. McGrath, of No. 20, asked how fund was to be used. He said that he offered an amendment a year ago that would have been better.

Bro. Carbrey, of No. 53, said he was instructed to vote against the Reserve Fund; but he would like to see it started, and he moved to strike out the one-dollar assessment.

High Chief Ranger stated the question.

Bro. Cronin, of No. 11, asked if Bro. Carbrey, of No. 53, would vote for the first part if the Convention accepted his amendment.

Bro. Golding stated that, if the calls were necessary, no assessment would be made for the Reserve Fund.

Bro. Pendis wanted a Reserve Fund, and thought it was imperative.

Bro. Gallagher, of No. 3, thought it would be a benefit to the Order to have a Reserve Fund.

Bro. Daughan, of No. 49, thought it was our duty to advance the interests of the Order, but he could not agree to more than a fifty-cent assessment.

Bro. Cronin, of No. 11, hoped the recommendation of the Committee would be adopted.

Bro. Farrenkopf said he felt obliged to speak on the question, and he hoped the Reserve Fund would be adopted, as it was a provision for our own endowments.

Bro. Maloney, of No. 49, thought we should be proud of being a State organization, and should have a Reserve Fund and be able to stand for all time.

Bro. McGrath, of No. 20, asked for more explanation.

Bro. Pendis moved previous question.

High Chief Ranger stated the question to be, the adoption of a Reserve Fund, on the resolve offered by Bro. D. A. Cronin, of No. 11 — "That it is the sense of this Convention that a Reserve Fund be created forthwith, and it is voted that an assessment of fifty cents be levied on all members in good standing on first day of

October in each year. Said assessment to be known as Reserve Fund Assessment; and that each new member admitted after said date be also assessed fifty cents for said fund," and amendment to make the assessment one dollar, and amendment to strike out one dollar.

High Chief Ranger then put the question,

" Shall the main question be now put " — and High Chief Ranger declared it was not a vote.

Bro. Shay asked for division of question.

High Chief Ranger ruled that it was divided by the amendment.

Bro. Daly, of No. 28, called attention of delegates that the assessment was only for a one-dollar assessment in a year to take the place of a death call.

High Senior Conductor Riley said he was only in favor of fifty cents.

Bro. Mackin, of No. 65, was in favor of an assessment every year for a Reserve Fund so that all would fare alike in future.

Bro. Carson, of No. 35, thought the recommendation of the Committee was good.

Bro. Dwyer, of No. 72, wished to know if it was necessary for every member who was in favor to speak.

The question was called for.

High Chief Ranger stated question on amendment to strike out one dollar.

Voted to strike out.

High Chief Ranger stated question on the resolve for fifty-cent assessment.

Vote declared carried.

Vote was doubted.

High Chief Ranger order a count, which showed 47 yea, 5 nay.

High Chief Ranger announced it carried, and report accepted and adopted.

The Committee reported amendment to Art. VIII. to strike out first five lines as far as " shall " in sixth line, and insert " the trustees " before " shall " in sixth line, and add to end of the Section "no portion of the Reserve Fund shall be drawn upon except by vote of Convention."

High Chief Ranger asked for objections to its adoption.

None being made, High Chief Ranger declared it carried and adopted.

The Committee reported amendment to duties of Deputy High Chief Ranger, Art. 9, Sect. 1, in tenth line, after " thereof," strike out as far as " Deputy " in 6th line, page 23.

High Chief Ranger declared it carried and adopted, no objection being made.

The Committee reported amendment in 5th line, page 24, to strike out " Past Chief Ranger," and insert "members of the Order." High Chief Ranger declared it was carried and adopted, no objection being made.

The Committee reported amendment to strike out in Sect. 2, page 24, in third line, " frequently," and insert " semi-annually, in months of April and October, and such other times as may be necessary."

High Chief Ranger declared it carried and adopted, no objection being made.

The Committee reported amendment about deposing an officer, and recommended to strike out in third line, page 25, after " final," as far as " in," in the sixth line.

High Chief Ranger declared it carried and adopted, no objection being made.

The Committee reported an amendment to insert "forthwith " on page 25 after " shall " in sixteenth line.

High Chief Ranger declared it carried and adopted.

The Committee reported amendment to hold the annual session on fourth Wednesday in April.

High Chief Ranger declared it carried and adopted.

The Committee reported amendment to duties of Committee on State of the Order, to strike out all after " shall " in second line, Sect. 7, page 32, as far as " report " in fifth line, and add after " proper," in last line, " for the advancement of the Order."

High Chief Ranger stated question.

Bro. Mackin, of No. 65, asked for explanation.

Bro. Daly gave the explanation.

Bro. Mackin, of No. 65, thought it should not be stricken out.

High Chief Ranger again stated the question.

Vote was taken and declared carried by two-thirds vote.

The Committee reported amendment, page 37, Sect. 2, in second line, to strike out after " Court " " each applicant shall, in person, present the," and after " membership," in first line, page 38, insert " must be forwarded "; in second line, page 38, strike out words " at a regular meeting "; in sixth line, page, 38, after "inclusive," alter so as to read " It must bear the recommendation of two members in good standing in the Court to which the applicant applies, and must be accompanied with a fee of not less than $2 " ; in nineteenth line, page 38, strike out " health," and insert " habits."

Dr. Hines thought the Investigating Committee should look after applications more closely, and that the Medical Examiner should not be expected to look into the character of applicants.

Bro. Shay differed from Dr. Hines, and thought the Medical Examiner ought to be expected to examine. Bro. Shay thought no Chief Ranger could oblige the Investigating Committee to report on a man's health.

High Chief Ranger asked Bro. Shay if it was not the duty of the Investigating Committee to find out if the applicant's health was formerly good.

Bro. Shay hoped the word " health " would be stricken out.

Dr. Ahearn, of No. 14, objected to the statement, that the Medical Examiner who made proper examinations did receive proper compensation; he denied that and wanted it understood.

Bro. Riley, High Senior Conductor, thought that the Medical Examiner should see that the report of the Investigating Committee is signed to each application.

Dr. Hines thought it was the duty of the Investigating Committee to report on applicant's statements.

Bro. Driscoll, of No. 61, moved to amend to investigate habits.

High Chief Ranger stated the question.

Bro. Mackin objected to striking out the words " in person."

Bro. Driscoll said he was instructed to present the amendment.

Bro. Collins, of No. 52, thought the Investigating Committee should investigate, and that every applicant should be seen at the Court.

Bro. Caldwell, of No. 7, thought our Investigating Committees in all the Courts were careless, and that ours was the only Order obliging applicants to present paper in person.

Bro. Donovan, of No. 15, hoped the amendment would not prevail.

Bro. Murray, of St. John, No. 23, said that the clause in the Constitution requiring applicant to appear, was not enforced, and he thought it could not be enforced.

Bro. Brickley, of No. 21, moved previous question.

High Chief Ranger put the question and declared previous question ordered.

High Chief Ranger stated the question.

Vote was taken and declared carried, and amendments adopted.

Vote was doubted and a count showed 31 yea, 16 nay.

High Chief Ranger declared it was not a vote.

On motion the roll was called and showed 35 yeas, 15 nays, and it was declared carried.

The Committee reported amendment, page 41, after "left," in first line, insert "and contain thereon his age at initiation, birthplace, occupation, residence, date of initiation, and to whom endowment is to be paid."

High Chief Ranger declared as there was no objection the amendment was carried and adopted.

Bro. Morris moved to adjourn to one week from to-night.

High Chief Ranger put the question, and declared it was not a vote.

The Committee reported amendment to strike out Sect. 6, page 42.

High Chief Ranger stated question, and declared it was a vote.

The Committee reported amendment raising Initiation Fee, and explained why it should be done.

Bro. Duggan, of No. 37, objected and thought the Initiation Fee high enough.

Bro. Maloney, of No. 49, thought we should be careful, and hoped the amendment would be passed.

Bro. O'Rourke, of No. 54, was opposed to the amendment.

Bro. Driscoll, of No. 61, moved that when we adjourn, we do so subject to call of the High Standing Committee.

High Chief Ranger put the question on the adjournment, and declared it a vote.

Bro. Riley moved to adjourn.

High Chief Ranger stated the question.

Vote was taken and declared carried.

Closed in due form at 11 P. M.

JAMES F. SUPPLE,
High Secretary-Treasurer.

Third Session of the Tenth Annual Convention

Held at the Boston Tavern, June 26, 1889.

High Chief Ranger Fennessey called the Convention to order at 8 P. M.

High Conductors reported all the High Court officers present except High Senior Conductor Edward Riley, and High Outside Sentinel R. Farrenkopf.

High Chief Ranger Fennessey appointed Bro. Leonard, of No. 64, High Senior Conductor, and Bro. Murphy, of No. 67, High Outside Sentinel.

Opened in due form.

Roll call was read.

Forty-six representatives were present representing 35 Courts, as follows :—

Roll Call. Third Session.

T. J. Dunn	of Cathedral	No.	1
M. Edmonds	" "	"	1
J. Sullivan	" "	"	1
D. Gallagher	" Fenwick		3
N. E. Shay	" St. Francis	"	4
T. F. Crosby	" "		4
J. F. McCloskey	" Leo		5
A. Golding	" Cheverus	"	6
Hon. J. P. Dore	" Sherwood	"	8
R. Farrenkopf	" "		8
A. J. Lill	" "		8
J. F. Supple	" Columbus	"	9
D. A. Cronin	" St. Joseph	"	11
H. C. Griffin	" "	"	11
M. O'Brien	" Fulton	"	12
A. B. Thompson	" Fitzpatrick	"	13
J. D. Mahoney	" "	"	13
Dr. C. A. Ahearne	" La Fayette	"	14
M. A. Dodd	" Essex	"	16
J. H. Watson, P.H.C.R.	" "	"	16
P. Smith	" Williams	"	19
J. F. Dever	" Mt. Pleasant	"	20
F. J. McGrath	" "	"	20
C. F. Morrison	" St. John	"	23
E. W. Daily	" St. Gregory	"	24
J. T. Daly	" Erin	"	28

T. F. Roach	.	.	.	.	of St. Thomas	No.	29
T. D. Hevey	.	.	.	.	" Qualey	"	32
J. J. McLaughlin, P.H.C.R.	.		.	.	" Americus	"	34
M. Leonard	.	.	.	.	" "	"	34
W. F. O'Donnell	.	.	.	.	" Star of the Sea	"	41
F. T. Cox	.	.	.	.	" St Bernard	"	44
J. Doolin	.	.	,	.	" St. Augustine	"	46
T. Kelly	.	..	.	.	" Sarsfield	"	48
J. Torndorf, jr.	.	.	.	.	" Holy Trinity	"	51
H. H. Collins	.	.	.	.	" Highland	"	52
J. B. Carbrey	.	.	.	.	" Emerald	"	53
J. G. Fennessey	.	.	.	.	" St. James	"	54
P. A. Murray	.	.	.	.	" Middlesex	"	60
P. A. Mulligan	.	.	.	.	" "	"	60
J. T. Brady	.	.	.	.	" St. Catharine	"	62
J. J. Leonard	.	.	,	.	" Gallagher	"	64
W. Mackin	.	.	.	.	" St. Columbkille	"	65
E. C. Murphy	.	.	.	.	" Canton	"	67
R. Dwyer	.	.	.	.	" St. Michael	"	70
M. J. O'Boyle	.	.	.	.	" Taunton	"	73

High Chief Ranger announced the first business in order, reading of records.

Records were read by High Secretary-Treasurer.

High Chief Ranger declared records approved, no objection being made.

High Chief Ranger asked for the report of Committee on " Good of the Order."

Dr. Ahearne said he could not say anything, although he wished to, but as his secretary was absent he could do nothing.

Bro. McGrath, of No. 20, asked leave to introduce some new amendments.

High Chief Ranger said he had ruled that the amendments as adopted became part of the Constitution at time of adoption, and ruled that the business now before the Convention was the unfinished report of the Committee on Constitution.

Committee on Constitution reported, Amendment to raise initiation fee to $6.

Bro. Watson, Past High Chief Ranger, said he was opposed to any change in the amount of initiation, and we should be careful to do nothing to prevent members coming in — that raising the amount would prevent members from coming in — and because we were now doing well, we should be satisfied and let the Initiation Fee remain as it is.

Bro. Mulligan said he was opposed to the amendment, that he believed very few in the Order wanted it.

Bro. Tondorf explained how it was that the Committee on Constitution reported this amendment. That his Court wished it, and out of courtesy to No. 51, the Committee reported in favor of it.

Bro. Doolin, of No. 46, said he was instructed to vote against the amendment.

Past High Chief Ranger McLaughlin moved the previous question.

Previous question was ordered.

High Chief Ranger stated the question, and vote being taken, declared it was not a vote.

Committee on Constitution reported an amendment to Sect. 3, page 43, line three, after " treasurer," in the third line, to strike out " of," and insert " in," and after " Court," in same line, strike out " in a," and after " fund," in third line, strike out rest of the section.

Bro. Caldwell, of St. Patrick No. 7, said many Courts now had only one Fund, and he could not see the necessity of putting money into a fund which could not be used, and he wished to know what were the legitimate expenses of a Court.

Bro. Gallagher, of No. 3, was opposed to the amendment.

Past High Chief Ranger McLaughlin said he could not see how any injury could be done by adopting.

Bro. Shay, for the Committee, said he wished the Brother who offered these amendments would get up and defend them.

Bro. Caldwell, of No. 8, said money placed in the A. C. R. Fund would be locked up and could not be touched.

High Chief Ranger stated the question, and declared it was a vote.

The Committee reported amendment to Sect. 5, page 44, to strike out " day " in second line, and insert " meeting "; strike out " 40 " in fifth line, and insert " 30 "; strike out " after becoming payable " in fifth line; strike out " be " in fifth line, and insert " stand," and strike out in 6th line all after " Order."

High Chief Ranger stated the question.

Vote was taken and declared carried.

The vote was doubted and a count showed 20 yea, 23 nay.·

High Chief Ranger declared it was not a vote.

Committee reported an amendment to Sect. 7, page 44, in first line, to strike out " 40," and insert " 30."

Bro. Mackin asked if Committee were to report 30 days on Endowment Calls.

Bro. Daly said it was.

Bro. Mackin moved to reconsider vote refusing to adopt amendment to Sect. 5, page 44.

Question was stated.

High Chief Ranger declared reconsideration was carried.

High Chief Ranger stated the question to amend Sect. 5, page 44, as stated above.

Vote was taken and declared carried and adopted.

Committee again reported amendment to Sect. 7, page 44 (stated above).

High Chief Ranger stated the question, and declared it was a vote, and was adopted.

Committee reported amendment to Sect. 9, page 45, in fifth line, to strike out " 40," and insert " 30."

High Chief Ranger stated the question, and declared it was a vote, and was adopted.

Committee reported amendment to Sect. 2, page 47, in second line, to strike out " 40," and insert " 30."

High Chief Ranger stated the question, and declared it was a vote, and was adopted.

The Committee reported amendment to strike out " immediately," and insert " within 3 days after notification" after " shall," in second line of Sect. 5, page 48.

Bro. Crosby, of No. 4, said it sometimes happened that a Recording Secretary did not know of a death in 3 days.

Question was stated and declared carried and adopted.

The Committee reported amendment to last four lines of Sect. 5, page 49, after " dying," strike out " of delirium tremens," and insert " from the excessive use of alcoholic drinks, habitual use of opium, hydrate of chloral, or any other narcotics, tobacco excepted."

Question was stated and High Chief Ranger declared it was carried and adopted.

Committee reported amendment to Sect. 6, page 49, to strike out in second line " 55 " and insert " 35."

High Chief Ranger stated question and declared it carried and adopted.

Dr. Ahearne moved to reconsider vote amending last 4 lines of Sect. 5, page 49.

Point of order was raised that Dr. Ahearne voted in negative.

High Chief Ranger ruled point well taken.

Bro. Driscoll moved to reconsider.

Dr. Ahearne spoke to the question that he thought suicides should not be debarred.

Past High Chief Ranger McLaughlin wished to know if the addition would stand in law.

High Chief Ranger related two cases within his knowledge where law courts refused to order payment.

Past High Chief Ranger McLaughlin thought we were courting litigation by addition to this section.

Bro. Daly, of No. 28, read question 15 of the application which all new applicants agree to on entering the Order.

Bro. Caldwell thought the contract of the application would not stand.

Dr. Ahearne said his point was on matter of suicides. He thought we were liable to pay for suicides.

High Chief Ranger related cases in other organizations of deaths by intemperance or suicide.

Dr. Couch asked if insane persons could make a contract.

High Chief Ranger decided no.

· Bro. Gallagher, of No. 3, said we were wasting time on the question; that we ought to try and get through our business.

High Chief Ranger stated the question.

Dr. Ahearne and Bro. Dore also spoke on question.

High Chief Ranger stated the question, and declared reconsideration carried.

Vote was doubted and a count showed 27 yea, 9 nay.

High Chief Ranger declared reconsideration carried, and question was on the report of the Committee and adoption of amendment.

Bro. Tondorf thought it was just to oblige members to live up to their contract, and if it was in the Constitution, all who applied would know what to expect.

Bro. Daughan, of No. 49, thought suicide should be struck out.

High Chief Ranger stated the question.

High Chief Ranger declared it was not a vote.

Vote was doubted and a count showed 23 yea, 22 nay.

High Chief Ranger declared it was not a vote.

Dr. Ahearne moved to strike out suicide.

High Chief Ranger put the question and declared it was not a vote.

Vote was doubted and a count showed 20 yea, 28 nay, and it was not a vote.

Committee reported amendment striking out all of Sect. 10, page 51.

Bro. McGrath, of No. 20, objected, and thought it was a good thing and worked well in his Court.

High Chief Ranger stated the question.

Vote was taken, declared not a vote, doubted, and a count showed 13 yea, 25 nay, and it was not a vote.

Bro. Dwyer, of No. 70, moved to amend, to strike out 40 and insert 30 in the 6th line, Sect. 10, page 51.

High Chief Ranger declared it was a vote and was adopted.

Committee reported amendment to Sect. 1, line 2, page 51, strike out "once" and insert "twice."

Bro. McGrath thought it should be optional.

Bros. Murphy, of No. 67, Collins, of No. 52, Crosby, of No. 4, Cronin, of No. 57, Leary, of No. 15, Dailey, of No. 24, spoke on the question.

High Chief Ranger stated that he thought it was for the good of the Order to have the Courts meet twice a month.

Bros. Griffin and Cronin also spoke on question.

Bro. Brickley moved previous question.

Previous question was ordered.

High Chief Ranger stated the question.

Vote was taken and declared carried and adopted.

Vote was doubted, a count showed 35 yea, 7 nay, and High Chief Ranger declared it was a vote.

Committee reported amendment to first line, Sect. 4, page 53, after "Chief Ranger" strike out "shall" and insert "may," and after office in second line strike out "appoint a chaplain who shall be a Roman Catholic priest," and insert "request the parish priest to appoint a chaplain."

Bro. Tondorf spoke in favor of the amendment.

High Chief Ranger stated the question.

Vote was taken and declared carried and adopted.

The Committee reported amendment to page 54, in first line strike out "close of each term," and insert "last meeting in June and December."

High Chief Ranger put the question and declared it was a vote and was adopted.

Committee reported amendment to duties of Chief Ranger, strike out "declare suspended all members in arrears for" in ninth line, Sect. 1, page 56, and insert, "read at every meeting the names of members who have suspended themselves by non-payment of," and after " Tax " in the 11th line insert "since the preceding meeting."

High Chief Ranger stated the question and declared it was a vote and was adopted.

Committee reported amendment to duties of Vice-Chief Ranger, to strike out after " members " in sixth line of Sect. 2, page 57, " suspended and expelled, and the names of rejected applicants for membership," and insert " in good standing."

High Chief Ranger stated question and declared it was a vote and was adopted.

Committee reported amendment to duties of Recording Secretary, strike out after " money " in fifth line, Sect. 3, page 57, " he shall upon receipt of a notice of an assessment from the High Secretary-Treasurer, immediately present the duplicate orders to the Financial Secretary and to the Treasurer, and."

High Chief Ranger put the question and declared it was a vote and was adopted.

Committee reported amendment to duty of Financial Secretary in Sect. 4, page 58, to strike out in second and third line "receiving the notice of the issue," and insert "receipt," also strike out " Recording " in fourth line and insert " High," also to insert " Treasurer " after " Secretary " in fourth line, also after " Committee," in second line, page 59, to insert " He shall forward to the Recording Secretary the assessment calls received by him in order that they may be read at the first meeting following their ·receipt."

The High Chief Ranger put the question and declared it was a vote and was adopted.

The Committee reported amendment to page 60, seventh line, — " strike out fifty-five, insert thirty-five days."

High Chief Ranger put the question, and declared it was a vote and adopted.

The Committee reported amendment striking out after " Court " in first line, page 61, " in the name of the Trustees."

High Chief Ranger put the question, and declared it was a vote and adopted.

The Committee reported amendment striking out " property " in fourth line, Sect. 6, page 61, and inserting " paraphernalia."

High Chief Ranger declared it was a vote and adopted.

The Committee reported amendment to duties of Trustees, page 61, to strike out all Sect. 8, and substitute therefor "It shall be the duty of the Trustees to have charge of all money and property not otherwise provided for in the Constitution."

High Chief Ranger put the question, and declared it was a vote and adopted.

The Committee reported amendment on page 63, striking out Sect. 2.

High Chief Ranger put the question, and declared it was a vote and adopted.

The Committee reported amendment to Sect. 1, page 68, striking out all after "Endowment" in third line, and insert "and General Funds."

High Chief Ranger put the question, and declared it was a vote and adopted.

Bro. Caldwell moved to amend, — strike out "Court," and insert "General" in any place in the Constitution where Court Funds were spoken of.

Bro. Brickley moved previous question.

Previous question was ordered.

High Chief Ranger stated the question on Bro. Caldwell's amendment, and declared it was a vote.

Vote was doubted. The count showed it was a vote, and High Chief Ranger declared it was a vote and adopted.

The Committee reported an amendment to Sect. 3, page 69, — strike out all after "Secretary" in fourth line.

High Chief Ranger declared it was a vote and adopted.

Committee reported amendment that all amendments go into effect Aug. 1.

High Chief Ranger ruled that all amendments go into effect on adoption.

Bro. Driscoll asked leave to present the report of Committee on State of the Order.

Leave was granted.

Bro. Driscoll read report.

To the Officers and Members of the Tenth Annual Convention, M. C. O. F.

BROTHERS, — Your Committee on the State of the Order would report that they have examined the reports of the Deputy High Chief Rangers, and find that the condition of the Order, as shown by these reports, is generally good, but in some of the Courts much improvement is needed. From one Court no return whatever has been made, and we learn that no stated meetings of this Court are held, but that the dues are simply collected and paid over. Such a condition of things should not be allowed, and the Deputy High Chief Ranger should promptly call the attention of the High Standing Committee to such cases. Your Committee learns, with regret, that unhappy differences exist between at least one Court and the pastor of the parish. They recommend that, in this and similar cases, the High Standing Committee request the High Court Chaplain, or other Clerical members of the Order, to aid them in restoring friendly relations between pastors and Courts of the Order.

Your Committee would recommend that only those brothers who are willing to devote sufficient time to the proper performance of the duties of the office be appointed Deputy High Chief Rangers. They also recommend that the examining physicians be called together occasionally, in order that some uniformity may be secured in the method of examining candidates for membership. They also suggest that applicants for admission to the Order should not be rejected when the sole disability consists in a reducible and retainable rupture.

For the Committee.

M. DRISCOLL, Secretary.

High Chief Ranger stated the question to be the acceptance of report of the Committee on State of the Order.

Bro. Brickley moved to accept.

Dr. Ahearne spoke on the part of report relating to rupture, that such men should be accepted.

Bros. Shay and Brickley spoke to the question.

High Chief Ranger stated the question and declared the report accepted.

The Committee on Constitution also reported inexpedient to legislate on the following resolves and amendments referred to it.

To set apart 5 cents a month from Court dues to pay for negligent members.

To pay $500 to members on total disability — balance at death.

To report on general fund each call.

On assessment for Court fund.

On Sect. 2, Art. 13, funds, etc.

On third line Art. 5; Sect. 8, after " forwarded," to strike out " at once.".

On Endowment Law making two classes.

To establish a Reserve Fund by assessing members for each death reported and putting such money as the Order is not obliged to pay (if any) aside.

On paying certain bills, and keeping $500 on hand.

On Courts to pay dues for sick members.

The Convention voted to accept the report of the Committee on Constitution.

On Honorary members—offered by Bro. McGrath, of No. 20.

" That honorary members be allowed all the privileges of active members, except those pertaining to Endowment, of which they shall not in any way be entitled to benefit from, either in voting for High Court membership, or being candidates for the same, neither shall they be allowed to hold the offices of Chief Ranger, Vice Chief Ranger, Recording or Financial Secretaries, or Treasurer, and that they shall not have a voice or vote in anything pertaining to Endowment and the fee for honorary membership shall be $3.00 and the dues shall be 25 cts per month."

Committee reported inexpedient.

Amended to refer to next Convention.

Voted to refer to next Convention.

High Chief Ranger announced next business election of 3 trustees.

Bro. Dever wanted to have all inconsistencies remedied.

Bro. Daly so moved.

High Chief Ranger stated question and declared it was a vote.

Bro. Driscoll moved that amendments be printed as soon as possible.

Bro. Shay moved to proceed to nomination of Trustees for Reserve Fund.

Bro. Golding nominated J. Tondorf. Bro. Shay nominated D. A. Cronin. Bro. Brickley nominated W. E. Shay.

Bro. Shay declined.

Vice High Chief Ranger Smith nominated Bro. O'Boyle.

Bro. Shay moved to close list.

Declared a vote.

Bro. Shay moved that High Secretary-Treasurer cast one ballot for the three named.

Bro. Cronin said he wanted to have the terms graded.

On motion of Bro. Daly voted to have the trustees hold in the order named.

High Secretary-Treasurer cast the ballot as follows:

J. Tondorf, of No. 51,	. . . .	for 3 years.
D. A. Cronin, " " 11,	. . . .	" 2 "
M. J. O'Boyle," " 73,	. . . .	" 1 year.

and High Chief Ranger declared those brothers elected.

Bro. McGrath moved to change name of organization.

High Chief Ranger ruled motion out of order.

Bro. Cronin moved to adjourn.

Bro. Daly moved to read records for approval of same and so that Convention might adjourn *sine die.*

Bro. McGrath raised point of order.

High Chief Ranger ruled point not well taken.

Bro. Golding asked about printing Constitution.

High Chief Ranger said it was in power of High Standing Committee to print.

High Secretary-Treasurer proceeded to read records.

After reading a portion Bro. Daly, of No. 28, moved to suspend further reading and approve the records.

Bro. McGrath objected; said it was a violation of the Constitution not to read the records in full.

High Chief Ranger ruled that rules could be suspended.

Bro. McGrath raised a point of order.

High Chief Ranger asked Bro. McGrath to state his point of order.

Bro. McGrath read from Cushing's Manual.

High Chief Ranger ruled it was not a point of order.

Bro. Daly moved previous question.

High Chief Ranger stated question.

High Chief Ranger ruled again that after a portion of the records are read, the Convention can suspend further reading.

Bro. Leary, of No. 15, wanted to know what became of the previous question.

High Chief Ranger said that he wished all to have a chance to speak, and for that reason had given Bro. McGrath the floor.

Bro. McGrath appealed from decision of the Chair on suspension of rules.

Bro. Golding wanted to know what benefit it was to us to listen to all this talk about Cushing's Manual.

Bro. McGrath said he thought it was not right to decide against him, and we ought to go according to Cushing.

High Chief Ranger stated the manner in which he looked at the question, and read last paragraph of Cushing on pages 159-160, paragraph No. 315.

High Chief Ranger stated the appeal from his decision.

Voted to sustain the decision of the Chair.

High Chief Ranger stated question on suspension of reading the records and approval of the records.

Vote was taken and High Chief Ranger declared records read and approved.

Bro. Daly, of No. 28, moved to adjourn *sine die.*

High Chief Ranger stated the question.

Vote was taken and declared carried.

Closed in due form. Adjourned at 11.35 P. M., and High Chief Ranger Fennessey declared Tenth Annual Convention of the Massachusetts Catholic Order of Foresters closed.

JAMES F. SUPPLE,

High Secretary-Treasurer.

ELEVENTH ANNUAL REPORT

OF THE

HIGH SECRETARY-TREASURER

OF THE

MASSACHUSETTS CATHOLIC ORDER OF FORESTERS,

TO THE HIGH COURT, APRIL 23, 1890.

WITH

REPORT OF PROCEEDINGS

OF THE

ELEVENTH ANNUAL CONVENTION

AND

LIST OF MEDICAL EXAMINERS AND D. H. C. R.s, AND MEETINGS
AND LIST OF OFFICERS.

BOSTON:

PRESS OF CASHMAN, KEATING & CO.

597 WASHINGTON STREET

ELEVENTH ANNUAL REPORT

OF THE

HIGH SECRETARY-TREASURER

OF THE

MASSACHUSETTS CATHOLIC ORDER OF FORESTERS,

TO THE HIGH COURT, APRIL 23, 1890.

WITH

REPORT OF PROCEEDINGS

OF THE

ELEVENTH ANNUAL CONVENTION

AND

A LIST OF MEDICAL EXAMINERS AND D. H. C. R.s, AND MEETINGS
AND LIST OF OFFICERS.

BOSTON:
PRESS OF CASHMAN, KEATING & CO.
597 WASHINGTON STREET

HIGH COURT OFFICERS

For Term Ending April, 1891.

High Chief Ranger,

JEREMIAH G. FENNESSEY . . . St. James Court No. 54

High Vice Chief Ranger,

PHILIP SMITH . . . . . Williams Court No. 19

High Secretary-Treasurer,

JAMES F. SUPPLE . . . . Columbus Court No. 9

High Senior Conductor,

EDWARD RILEY . . . . . St. Joseph Court No. 11

High Junior Conductor,

P. A. MURRAY . . . . . Middlesex Court No. 60

High Inside Sentinel,

JOHN T. DALY . . . . . . Erin Court No. 28

High Outside Sentinel,

R. FARRENKOPF . . . . . Sherwood Court No. 8

High Medical Examiner,

JOSEPH D. COUCH, M. D. . . . Benedict Court No. 39

High Chaplain,

REV. HUGH ROE O'DONNELL . Star of the Sea Court No. 41

HIGH COURT OFFICERS

For Term Ending April, 1890.

High Chief Ranger,

JEREMIAH G. FENNESSEY . . . St. James Court No. 54

High Vice-Chief Ranger,

PHILIP SMITH . . . . . . Williams Court No. 19

High Secretary-Treasurer,

JAMES F. SUPPLE . . . . Columbus Court No. 9

High Senior Conductor,

EDWARD RILEY . . . . . St. Joseph Court No. 11

High Junior Conductor,

P. A. MURRAY . . . . . Middlesex Court No. 60

High Inside Sentinel, ,

THOMAS J. DUNN . . . . Cathedral Court No. 1

High Outside Sentinel,

R. FARRENKOPF . . . . Sherwood Court No. 8

High Medical Examiner,

JOSEPH D. COUCH, M. D. . . . Benedict Court No. 39

High Chaplain,

REV. HUGH ROE O'DONNELL . Star of the Sea Court No. 41

ANNUAL REPORT

OF THE

HIGH STANDING COMMITTEE,

FOR THE TERM ENDING APRIL 22, 1890.

Representatives to the Annual Convention of the High Court Massachusetts Catholic Order of Foresters.

BROTHERS : Another year has gone by since we last met, and we are now assembled to legislate for the coming year; to avoid the mistakes of the past, if any, and to draw new inspiration and courage, so that the work of love and charity that we are engaged in may be continued by our successors, and that the mistakes we may have made may, by your wisdom and prudence, be avoided in the future.

We meet with the knowledge that our organization has not deteriorated during the year; that our membership has not been diminished, and that the faith of the members in the ultimate success of the objects that we have in view is stronger than at any time heretofore in its history.

We also meet, with some sadness in our hearts, because we know that a number of our members, who were active in the work of our society have been called before the great white throne of God; and we have reason to feel assured that in part, by their connection with this, a Catholic society, they were prepared for that summons which all will receive, rich and poor alike, and that when least expected. And yet in their decease we can find some consolation, when we know that the purpose for which they were members of our organization has been carried out ; and that the organization has made provision to meet that promised to them in life, and to pay to their family the endowment, that we expect ours at some time to receive.

It was provided in the early years of the organization that " the High Standing Committee shall report to the annual session of the

High Court, the general condition of, and all matters of interest relative to the order." Article IV., Section 3, High Court Constitution.

In accordance with this provision this report is respectfully presented for your careful consideration.

MEETINGS.

Since the first session of the last Annual Convention the High Standing Committee have held (41) forty-one regular meetings, at nearly all of which each member of the committee was present; and in addition to this, visits were made by the members to Courts in all parts of the State, and when the occasion required it, as often as necessary.

The average length of the sessions of the High Standing Committee was about four hours.

APPLICATIONS FOR MEMBERSHIP.

During the year we have received and passed on 877 new applications for membership in the Order. 813 were approved; 68 were rejected; 6 were held over from last year. There are no applications waiting action by the Committee. By this you will see that the percentage of rejection is getting less each year; and not because the medical examiners are getting careless in their work, or that the High Standing Committee is less careful in its supervision, but that a better class of men are applying for membership, with the knowledge that if anything is wrong in their physical or moral condition it will be ascertained, and they cannot become members. Men have been rejected for both causes. We would call your attention to some remarks made by members about the delay in acting on applications. Each application is acted on at the meeting following its receipt by the High Secretary-Treasurer; and, if found to be a safe risk, is immediately forwarded to the Subordinate Court, for the initiation of the applicant. If rejected, notice is sent to the Recording Secretary of the Subordinate Court at once; and if any doubt should exist as to the advisability of accepting the risk, the application is laid over for further examination and investigation. All doubts are always given to the Order.

NEW COURTS.

During the year four new Courts have been established. St. Jarlath 75, at Amesbury; Quincy 76, at Quincy; Mystic 77, at

Medford, and St. Monica 78, at Lawrence. Each of the Courts are established in thriving and prosperous localities; and, with proper energy and activity on the part of the officers and members, will be a desirable acquisition to the Order.

Attempts have been made to form Courts in other localities, but by reasons that your committee were not able to offset, they have not yet been formed.

A sufficient number of applicants to form a Court in the city of Lowell had been examined; but, owing to the death of the doctor who had the examinations in charge, a delay has been made. We expect to get the Court in a short time.

An attempt is now being made to form Courts in New Bedford and Fall River; and in a short time it is hoped that Courts will be established in each of those cities.

Suspensions.

Highland Court, No. 52, was suspended for non-payment of the endowment calls, Friday, March 21, 1890 ; and on the same being paid, was reinstated on Friday, March 28, 1890.

We would again remind the officers of a number of the Courts, that they should promptly forward all moneys collected for the endowment, within the time provided by the Constitution, or else they should be dealt with as circumstances would demand.

The members generally pay promptly, and their interest should not be endangered or jeopardized by the carelessness or neglect of the financial officers of some of the Courts. A constant supervision of the affairs of each Court, by its Chief Ranger, especially in relation to its finances, would be of great assistance to the High Standing Committee, and of great benefit to each Court, and it would materially assist in the prompt payment of the endowment.

Mortality.

During the year we had 55 deaths in the Order, occurring in the following months :

April 4	October 4
May 5	November 7
June 1	December 8
July 5	January 8
August 4	February 4
September 2	March 3

And this is to remind you that it will be impossible to approxi-
mate with any certainty what the death-rate will be, or when the
assessment calls will be sent out. When the deaths occur the calls
will be issued, and their prompt payment will be beneficial to the
Order, and doubly beneficial to the heirs of the deceased members
who are entitled to receive the endowment.

From an examination of the records, we find that of those who
died, from the date of the Convention last year, and reported up
to date

1 was initiated in	. . . . .	1879
12 were initiated in	. . . . .	1880
11 were initiated in	. . . . .	1881
4 were initiated in	. . . . .	1882
7 were initiated in	. . . . .	1883
3 were initiated in	. . . . .	1884
2 were initiated in	. . . . .	1885
7 were initiated in	. . . . .	1887
6 were initiated in	. . . . .	1888
2 were initiated in	. . . . .	1889

55

The mortality has been unusually heavy during the past year.
Part of it we can readily account for. The disease called " La
Grippe," that swept over the entire civilized world, left its mark on
our organization; and not on ours alone, because all fraternal
organizations suffered from it, some of them in a marked degree.
We have reason to be thankful that our loss was not greater;
and we should return our thanks to God for his mercy to us. It
should be a lesson to us that we should constantly keep in mind,
and be prepared for the final summons when it comes.

ENDOWMENT CALLS.

Fifteen calls have been issued since the last convention; and
the amount that will be collected from them, if paid in within the
constitutional limit, thirty-five days, would see the Order, on the first
day of June next, entirely out of debt, with a balance on hand of
about two thousand dollars, to meet any liability that might be
incurred before that time.

This is certainly encouraging, because it has been constantly
stated by all the members, that if the calls would average only

one a month that no fault could reasonably be found ; and since the Convention of 1884, when the present system went into effect, only 71 assessment calls have been issued, when the average called for 72, or 12 each year. We can rest assured of one thing, that all money collected is honestly administered and promptly paid ; and that profit by the officers of the Order is not sought for. But when death comes its consequences must be met ; and no Catholic worthy the name will shirk his duty or try to evade the responsibility.

Disputed Claims.

The claim of the heirs of Richard J. Downey, who was formerly a member of Cheverus Court, has been settled since the last Convention. Richard J. Downey applied for membership in St. Joseph Court, No. 11, Oct. 21, 1881. He was rejected by the Court Physician at that time. Some four months later he applied to Cheverus Court, No. 6, Jan. 27, 1882, and was admitted to membership. He died of heart disease, March 24, 1885. The High Standing Committee of 1885 refused to pay the claim, because of an evasion in his second application, wherein he stated that he never applied for membership before. The Convention of 1886 sustained the action of the High Standing Committee. Suit was then brought in the Superior Court of Suffolk County, and postponed, for various causes, to the time of holding the last convention of the Order, when the claim was again presented to the Convention, but not received.

The suit was then pressed. The counsel of the Order advised the settlement of the claim, as Downey had complied with all the financial requirements of our laws, and as it would be impossible to prove whether he knowingly misstated that he had not applied for membership before his application to Cheverus Court. Neither application had been signed by him ; and after considering the matter with great care, it was deemed advisable by the High Standing Committee, after many consultations with the Counsel of the Order, to settle the claim. This was done, and $400 was paid to the heirs ; all costs to be borne by them.

Frank P. Hansen was admitted a member of Sarsfield Court 48, on the 8th of February, 1884, and was found dead in a pond near his house, in that town, on Nov. 8, 1889. The Medical Examiner of Bristol County reported the cause of death to be drowning.

The cause, on the death certificate, was reported to be temporary insanity.

We find that he went home from work on the third day of November, sick; and remained at home until the night of Nov. 7; when, it is presumed, that about 12.30 o'clock, on the morning of Nov. 8, he went to the pond, and cut himself in the abdomen, with some sharp instrument, supposed to be a razor, and either fell, or threw himself into the pond, where he was found during the day. He was at the time undoubtedly laboring under melancholia, and the probabilities are that he was not responsible for his act. If this is so, his heirs would, undoubtedly, be entitled to recover, in Court, the endowment.

The Constitution of our Order, Article 5, Section 5, provides that, "In no case shall any endowment be paid to the heirs or dependants of a member committing suicide, or dying of delirium tremens." Under this provision the High Standing Committee are absolutely prohibited from paying, and report the facts to you for your consideration.

MEMBERS.

At the time of holding the First Session of the Tenth Convention we had about thirty-nine hundred and fifty members in the Order; to-day we have about forty-five hundred — a few less, perhaps, not more than fifty. This, under the trying circumstances of the year, is something of which we have reason to be proud; because we can again say that we have more than held our own. We have disappointed those who are anxious to speak ill of us, but cannot; because, if anything is said, it must be in commendation.

We should not be satisfied with even a proportionate increase for the coming year; we have the material to draw from; we have the men to advance the interests of the Order, and they are the men that you represent. We do not expect our members to turn themselves into insurance agents; but, occasionally, at odd moments, by presenting, and recommending to their friends and acquaintances our society, they not only do the whole order a valuable service, but they assist in spreading the good work of the organization in their immediate localities, and would be instrumental in getting many to avail themselves of the benefits it confers. We have an immense Catholic population to draw from, — something like 800,000 in the State of Massachusetts, — and, with proper exertion on the part of the officers and members, we should easily obtain a sufficient number to make our membership in a few years at least 10,000. You can assist in this work by applying a little of that zeal that you are possessed of to the furtherance of the end we have in view.

DEATH CERTIFICATES.

It is of the utmost importance that the Death Certificates should be properly filled out, and that all facts that are of interest to the members at large should be furnished to the proper officers. Payment is often postponed by the inexcusable neglect of some of the Subordinate Court officials; and then the High Standing Committee receives all the blame. An improvement has been noticed this last year; but there is room for more.

APPLICATION PAPERS.

Some of the members yet hold their papers of membership, notwithstanding that, for the last three years, they have been asked to return them to the High Court Office. In the report of the High Standing Committee last year, the attention of the delegates was called to the danger of delay in presenting them. Where death occurs, and the paper cannot be found, delay in the payment is sure to occur; and sometimes litigation is caused between members of the deceased brother's family. This has occurred, and may again, unless the members provide against it in advance. We hope that you will bring this matter before the members of your Courts, and urge on them the necessity of providing against trouble.

PER CAPITA TAX.

The Per Capita Tax to be levied this year, we would recommend, be the same as last year, seventy-five cents. We think that it will be sufficient to meet the current expenses of the Order, and leave a balance on hand at the end of the year. While the expense of conducting the Order the past year has, apparently, been larger than the amount allowed by the Convention, it will, in fact, leave a balance in favor of the Order, when the amounts outstanding and due the High Standing Committee, from the various Subordinate Courts for supplies, are paid. In addition to this the printing account was much larger last year than usual, caused by the extra printing authorized by the Convention.

New Account Books.

At the first session of Tenth Convention, it was voted, " That the High Secretary-Treasurer formulate a uniform system of books for all the Courts." (Pages 71, 72, Report of Convention.) After an immense amount of labor on his part this was done, and the books forwarded to the Courts. Some of them returned the books. This was contrary to the wish of the Convention; and all must take and keep them, so that we may be able to have some system. Under the old method it was impossible to tell when the members paid their dues; and on more than one occasion, the payment of the endowment was endangered by the loose and careless manner in which the accounts were kept. We hope to see the trouble remedied now; and, with a proper spirit manifested on the part of the officers, what was a source of annoyance will become a pleasure.

Legitimate Expense.

The question that has caused most discussion in the meetings of the Subordinate Courts, during the past year, is that of legitimate expense. Opinions of various kinds have been given; but, so far as we are aware, by no one in authority to give one. We would suggest that the matter be brought before the Convention to-day, and that a decision be made in accordance with the provisions of the Constitution, so that all the Courts will know what action to take when the question comes up again.

Salvation Fund.

It was suggested last year, by the High Standing Committee, that a Salvation Fund be established in each Court, for the care of members who are taken sick, or injured, through no fault of their own. The Convention did not look kindly on the matter, and defeated it. We would renew the recommendation, and suggest that each Court adopt a by-law, providing that in the event of the sickness of a member, through no criminal fault of his own, he shall be retained financial by the Court of which he is a member. We talk of charity. When the occasion arises where it may be needed, let us be prepared for it. Many of the Courts do this cheerfully now; all should do it. If we are brothers, in the true sense of the word, let us show that we appreciate the blessings of health and prosperity that God has given us, and that at the same time we can sympathize with those who may be afflicted, and that we come cheerfully to the assistance of those in distress. By doing this at all times we would, indeed, be a brotherhood of men under the Fatherhood of God.

Deputy High Chief Rangers.

Two years ago, on the appointing of the Deputy High Chief Rangers, they were assigned to districts away from their homes. We think that it has worked well. As a rule the deputies take more interest in the labor assigned them, and the members of the Courts in their jurisdiction appreciate them more. It would be advisable to continue this method in the future. They are entitled to, and receive, the thanks of the High Standing Committee for the labor of love performed by them.

Reserve Fund.

On the recommendation, last year, of the High Standing Committee, the Constitution was amended to provide for a Reserve Fund. (Section 2, Article 8, High Court Const.) It provided that an assessment of fifty cents should be levied on each member in the Order, on the first day of October last; and that each new member should pay, on his initiation, the same amount.

No time was named for the issuing of the call for its collection; and the High Chief Ranger, hearing of the number of deaths that had occurred, and some of which were not reported, thought a delay in the collection might with safety be made. This was done, but things did not improve. Extra calls had to be issued; and, finally, the call for the Reserve Fund was issued on the 2d day of January, 1890. If fault is to be found for the delay, the High Chief Ranger assumes the entire responsibility for it. Nearly all of the Courts have paid the amount due by them; so that we have to-day, in the Reserve Fund of our Order, a sum exceeding two thousand dollars, with a balance of about two hundred and fifty dollars yet to be paid. We have reason to feel gratified that this sum is collected. It is something that the thoughtful members of the Order have been looking forward to for years; and it proves that the prophecy made by them, in advocating it, when they stated that the rank and file would heartily respond, if called on to establish a Salvation Fund for the payment of the endowment, was correct.

All are now satisfied that the step taken was a wise one; all are
aware that if it had been taken some years ago that we need not
fear an epidemic of any ordinary proportions, and all realize that
the continuance of it will enable us to attract men to our ranks,
who care for something more than even the promise of honest men.
It should be laid sacredly by; and I hope that the Convention will
not have occasion to call on it for many years. The Trustees have
organized, and will report to you to-day.

MEDICAL EXAMINATION.

The Medical Examiners have, as a rule, given satisfaction to the
High Standing Committee and the Order, and they realize that
their reputations, while such, must go hand in hand with it. One
thing we would suggest to them, and that is, that the rule of
secrecy, so far as the examination goes, must be strictly lived up
to. Much mischief may be accomplished by an intimation to an
applicant, or his friends, whether he has or has not passed, when
he may have to be rejected for other reasons afterwards.

The Standing Committee is under great obligations to the High
Medical Examiner, Dr. Joseph D. Couch, for his constant attendance at the meetings of the Committee, and the performance of
any duty that may be assigned him. It is done at great inconvenience to himself, at times; and we are sure that the entire
Order appreciates the work done by him.

CONSTITUTION.

The Constitution of the Order was adopted July 30, 1879. Since
then it has been amended, altered, revised, and changed in various
ways, at nine different Conventions. We would suggest that no
changes be made at this. We have too much rather than too little
legislation; and it would, in the judgment of your Committee, be
advisable to let time decide what is necessary, rather than attempt,
at the present Convention, to change until it can be ascertained
what changes are necessary. More amendments have been made
in the eleven years of our existence than to the Constitution of the
United States for the last one hundred years.

RECORDS AND OFFICE OF THE HIGH SECRETARY-TREASURER.

The Office of the High Standing Committee has been open daily
during the year just past, and some person has been in attendance

all the time. Work has been pushed in the records of the Order, and we can expect that soon the papers relating to the History of the Organization will be in such a condition that it will require but very little effort to get what information is necessary, in relation to any member or Court in it. The accumulated papers of ten years had to be straightened out, and no person unless he has been in constant attendance can realize the amount of labor performed.

The High Secretary-Treasurer has been at all times at the service of the Order, and on several occasions has been away from his home more than one day at a time. His labors could be much lightened with a little care on the part of the Subordinate Court Officers. If blanks were properly filled out it would, in many instances, save hours of careful labor.

INVESTIGATING COMMITTEE.

One of the most important committees appointed to the Subordinate Court, is the committee appointed to investigate to the character and habits of the applicants for memberships. Their appointment should be something more than a matter of form, as the very life of the Order depends on the character of the men taken into it. The habits of men desirous of connecting themselves with us should be closely scrutinized, and if they are not fit to be introduced into the families of the members, they should not be allowed to come into the Organization. Members are at times lenient, perhaps too much so, and while it is at all times desirable to assist a man who may require care, and sometimes reformation, yet the *interest of the members should first be attended to*, and the families of the men in the Order have the greatest claim on it for sympathy and watchfulness. We would also suggest that if there are any men in the Organization who by their mode of life bring any scandal on it, that they should be brought before the Arbitration Committee and dealt with as the case might require.

The interest of every member in the Organization is the same, the amount of benefit to be derived is the same, and the amount of good accomplished will depend on the individual effort of each brother. We are all equal, and all should be willing to bear an equal burden, and then the labor of all will be lightened.

During the year your committee has made many visits to various Courts throughout the State, and has been received with uniform kindness by the members, and at times with great inconvenience to themselves. We can assure them that it will always be appreciated by us, and that on account of the kind treatment received during the year 1888–90, it will be cherished as a memorable period in our lives, and always will be remembered with feeling of pleasure and gratification.

We return our sincere thanks to the many clergymen that have assisted in furthering the interests of the Massachusetts Catholic Order of Foresters during the year, and we feel grateful to them for the interest taken in our work.

The Committee especially desires to return its thanks to P. H. C. R. John H. Watson for the valuable assistance given by him at various times. Whenever he was called on to do anything, he willingly responded.

About twelve years ago organizations like this first came into life in any number, and from that time to this the Old Line Insurance Companies have seen fit to attack them; some have justly deserved it, because the men who originated them merely formed them in order that they might receive the benefit of them, and cared little whether the organizations would prosper or not. We have, with many other good and sound Fraternal societies, outlived the storm, because we have been actuated only by a desire to bring insurance so cheap and yet have it good, that all might avail themselves of it. The late Insurance Commissioner of Massachusetts, Hon. John K. Tarbox, said in his report, for 1886, " The death-rate in the Fraternal Orders, about ten in a thousand (and ours has been less than that), is lower than in the other societies. Speaking generally of these societies, the fit word is one of cordial commendation. Aside from the gracious benefits they dispense through the insurance plan, they unite the people in sympathetic association and foster a worthy social spirit. The law should not impede, but protect them in their liberty to pursue their benevolent objects."

These words, coming from one of the purest of Massachusetts' sons, should have weight with you, and impel you on to greater work in behalf of your organization.

We need more protection against possible want, and if we are alive to the demands of the day, we can confer the benefits that so many have already received, on those of our people who need it as much, if not more, than those who have received it.

The present commissioner, Major George S. Merrill, says in his report published this year, speaking about the Fraternal associations that " The consideration of the permanency of these associations is in no degree essential to an opinion upon their present usefulness, when well conducted in providing benefits from which pecuniary obstacles would otherwise shut out thousands of families, or their worth as educators of the mass of the people in the value of the more staple and permanent forms of life insurance. They are cultivating fields into which the great life companies could not profitably enter, and their beneficence flows in channels that would be otherwise parched and dry."

Words, indeed, well spoken, and we are sure that he meant them. With the cost much less than half what it would cost in the old line companies they realize the danger they are in, and therefore attack all.

The Hierarchy speaking from the Third Plenary Council said, " It is not enough for Catholics to shun bad or dangerous societies : they ought to take part in good and useful ones. If there ever was a time when merely negative goodness would not suffice, such, assuredly, is the age in which we live ;" and again : " We also esteem, as a very important element in practical Catholicity, the various forms of Catholic beneficial societies, and kindred associations of Catholic working men."

" It ought to be, and we trust is, everywhere their aim to encourage habits of industry, thrift, and sobriety ; to guard the members against the dangerous attractions of condemned or suspicious organizations, and to secure the faithful practice of their religious duties, in which their temporal as well as their eternal welfare so largely depends."

" With paternal affection we bestow our blessing upon all these various forms of combined Catholic actions for useful and holy purposes ; we desire to see their number multiplied and their organization perfect."

What more is wanted ? We have the best authority in our State commending societies similar to our own. We have the approval of our clergy, who realize the necessity of combined action, so that good may come of it. We have the knowledge that during the last eleven years the Massachusetts Catholic Order of Foresters has been tried and never been found wanting. We have been the benefactors of nearly two thousand persons ; we have kept the families of many of our deceased brothers together ; we have aided the widow in the hour of need, and saved many children to the faith of our fathers. We have shown the people of this commonwealth that we are throughly capable of making provision for the protection and education of our own people, and we are stronger and better to-day than ever before because we are united, because we are not met with taunts of broken promises, and because we have faith in the future. Brothers, you are called to do your share in forwarding this good work; you have assumed the responsibility, and on you will depend, in a great measure, what will be the future history of the Massachusetts Catholic Order of Foresters.

JEREMIAH G. FENNESSEY,

High Chief Ranger.

Boston, April 23, 1890.

Report of High Secretary-Treasurer.

To the Representatives of the Massachusetts Catholic Order of Foresters:

BROTHERS,— It is with great satisfaction and pleasure that I submit to you the report of the work performed by the Subordinate Courts of the Massachusetts Catholic Order of Foresters during the year 1889.

We commenced 1889 with a roll of 63 Courts and membership as given on the returns of the Courts of 3,644. We had in 1888, as in 1887, a year of prosperity and a very gratifying increase of membership. Our membership Jan. 1, 1888, was 3,230, and during 1888 we added 444 to our rolls.

Starting Jan. 1, 1889, we seem to have taken on a new life, and from all sides came words of encouragement to the High Chief Ranger and High Standing Committee, assuring them that the year then commencing would be one of good feeling to all, and that each and every member, who had anything to do with the direction of affairs in the various Subordinate Courts, would do all he could to advance the interests of the Order, and make it what all wished it to be, a first-class Catholic organization.

How well these promises and assurances have been fulfilled you can now judge for yourselves. Much satisfaction and pleasure may be had by contemplating the fact, that on all sides members have endeavored to keep the promises made, and that those who took no special interest in the advancement of the Order were content to look on and aid by not interfering with the work of those who were actively engaged in building up the membership. In this connection we may call attention to the fact, that it is not the largest Courts in the Order which have done the best in the past year, but the growth has been pretty well spread throughout the Courts. Eighteen Courts have suffered a loss in membership, and thirty-seven Courts have gained in membership. The others remain as they were. Of those Courts which made a gain, St. Thomas Court, No. 29, of Brockton, made the largest addition, 39 having been added in the year.* Sarsfield, No. 48, comes next with 21 initiations, Iona No. 10, and St. Francis No. 25, have 20 each, Cathedral, No. 1, and Phil. Sheridan, No. 71, have 19 each, Lafayette, No. 14, St. John, No. 23, and St. Michael, No. 70, have 17 each, St. Gregory, No. 24, and Emerald, No. 53, have 16 each, St. Catharine, No. 62, has 15, Stoughton, No. 69, has 13, Merrimack, No. 72, has 11, Mt. Pleasant, No. 20, St. Anne, No. 47, St. James, No. 54, have 10 each.

The percentage of increase is shown by the following table:

No. of Court.	NAME OF COURT.		No. of Court.	NAME OF COURT.	
1	Cathedral	.192	39	Benedict	.064
3	Fenwick	.029	41	Star of the Sea	.03
4	St. Francis	.036	43	St. Mary	.045
5	Leo	.056	45	Unity	.16
6	Cheverus	.023	47	St. Anne	.206
7	St. Patrick	.128	48	Sarsfield	.375
8	Sherwood	.092	49	Constantine	.146
9	Columbus	.059	52	Highland	.083
10	Iona	.478	53	Emerald	.254
11	St. Joseph	.022	54	St. James	.25
14	Lafayette	.327	55	Charles River	.079
15	SS. Peter and Paul	.112	57	Carroll	.158
16	Essex	.11	59	Worcester	.2
17	Hamilton	.046	60	Middlesex	.093
18	St. Peter	.072	61	St. Lawrence	.21
19	Williams	.098	62	St. Catherine	.4
20	Mt. Pleasant	.208	63	Shields	.17
21	St. Alphonsus	.109	64	Gallagher	.08
23	St. John	.6	65	St. Columbkill	.051
24	St. Gregory	.388	66	Griffin	.214
25	St. Francis	.25	67	Canton	.104
26	St. Raphael	.216	68	St. Margaret	.22
28	Erin	.094	69	Stoughton	.44
29	St. Thomas	.52	70	St. Michael	.75
30	Bass River	.194	71	Phil Sheridan	.37
32	Qualey	.171	72	Merrimack	.59
34	Americus	.182	74	Hendricken	.23
37	Friendship	.042	75	St. Jarlath	.33
38	St. Joseph	.023			

* Holy Trinity, No. 51, gained about the same number, but report is not in.

MEMBERSHIP.

No. of Court	NAME OF COURT	Membership Dec. 31, 1888	Membership Dec. 31, 1889	Initiated in 1889	Admitted on W. Card in 1889	Reinstated in 1889	Average age of Court Dec. 31, 1889	Average age of Court Dec. 31, 1888	Withdrawn on Card in 1889	Resigned Membership in 1889	Suspended for Non-payment in 1889	Expelled, 1889	Died, 1889	Rejected by Ballot in 1889	Rejected by H. S. C. in 1889
1	Cathedral	130	149	25	1		40.1	41.1	1	1	6		1	1	2
3	Fenwick	70	68	2	1		43.2	42.4			3		3		1
4	St. Francis	110	109	4			43	42.2			3		2		1
5	Leo	106	101	6	2		42.1	40.6	1		8		2		3
6		86	84	2			43.8	45.3	2		3				1
7	St. Patrick	47	48	6			42	41.4			2		4		2
8	Sherwood	141	148	13	1		38.6	38.2			3		1		
9		34	33	2							1		7		3
10	Iona	69	89	33			39.1	40.5			6		2		1
11	St. Joseph	137	133	3			41.2	40.4	2		3		1		2
12	Fulton	29	28				44.2	42.7			1				
13	Fitzpatrick	54	52				45	43.1			3		2		
14	Lafayette	58	75	19	1		41.1	40.7			2		3		3
15	SS. Peter & Paul	62	66	7			41.5	40.4	1	3	3		3	1	1
16	Essex	99	104	11	2		38.1	38.5		1	1		3		2
17	Hamilton	65	66	3			47.1	44.4					2		1
18	St. Peter	69	69	5			39.8	39.1	2		1		2		
19	Williams	71	70	7			40.8	39.4							1
20	Mt.	76	86	16			38.2	37.4			5		1		2
21	St.	46	50	5			43.9	44.4			7			1	1
23	St.	30	47	18	1		34.5	38.3							1
24	St. Gregory	48	64	19			37.1	38.6			1		1		2
25	St. Francis	108	108	22			37.6	38.03			3		2		1
26	St. Raphael	37	45	8			39.08	41.7			2				4
28	Erin	74	78	7	1		42.7	41.7							2
29	St.	78	117	41			34.4	36.3	1		1		1		1
30	Bass River	36	41	7			38.9	40.3			1		2		2
33	St. John	35	35	6			38.7	39.08			2				1
34	Americus	59	60	8			42	42	1		3		1		1
35	Sheil	77	86	14			36.1	36.4			3		2		1
37	Friendship	24	24	1			39.4	38.3			1		1		
38	St. Joseph	45	47	2			38.3	37.3			1		1		1
39	Benedict	31	33	1	1		46.8	44.6	1		2		1		1

MEMBERSHIP — *Continued.*

No. of Court	NAME OF COURT	Membership Dec. 31, 1888	Membership Dec. 31, 1889	Initiated in 1889	Admitted on W. Card in 1889	Reinstated in 1889	Average Age of Court Dec. 31, 1889	Average Age of Court Dec. 31, 1888	Withdrawn on Card in 1889	Resigned Membership in 1889	Suspended for Non-payment in 1889	Expelled, 1889	Died, 1889	Rejected by Ballot in 1889	Rejected 1 y. H. S. C. in 1889
41	Star of the Sea	33	33	1			38.3	37.6	1	1	2		1		
43	St. Mary	22	23	1			42.4	41.8	1	1	1		2		
44	St. Bernard	52	51	6			36.	34.5			8		1		1
45	Trinity	38	44	14	1		39.5	41.08	1		51	7			2
46	St. Augustine	30	28	24	1	3	42.1	40.8	1		3	1	1		1
47	St. Anne	68	78	11		1	31.4	31.04			1				
48	Sarsfield	64	85	40			38.4	39.5			3				
49	Constantine	76	81	2			37.7	36.6			2				
51	Holy Trinity	58	93	16		7	36.	41.01		1	20		1		1
52	Highland	24	73	13			38.7	37.5		2	3		1		2
53	Emerald	63	72	6			30.4	35.		1					1
54	St. James	52	62	6			35.3	29.1	1	2	14			1	
55	Charles River	76	76				37.7	31.4			3			1	
57	Carroll	39	44	14			37.7	37.7			7				
58	Prospect	46	48	7			37.4	33.2			2				2
59	Worcester	70	72	12	1		34.6	34.5	1		1				3
60	Middlesex	77	81	16	2		35.1	34.3			3				6
61	St. Lawrence	57	65				30.2	30.6			2				1
62	St. Catherine	40	55	5			35.6	33.3			1				1
63	Shields	30	27	3			38.6	36.06			8				
64	Gallagher	62	52	6			32.9	31.9							
65	Columbkille	58	55	5			34.4	36.3							
66	Griffin	28	33	6			35.4	33.7	1						
67	Canton	45	43	14			33.4	33.5	1						
68	St. Margaret	27	30	19			30.8	31.6							
69	Stoughton	32	45	21			30.5	31.2							
70	St. Michael	26	43	16			30.5	30.7	1						
71	Phil. Sheridan	55	39	107			31.7								
72	Merrimack	28	39	6			34.1								
73	Taunton		106	81			27.6				8				6
74	Hendricken		29	33			30.6								1
75	St. Jarlath		73				31.3								1
76	Quincy		33				28.4								
77	Mystic		23												
	Total.	3,614	4,270	836	20	14			21	21	174	8	55	12	67

The average age of the membership of the Order as per returns was Jan. 1, 1888, 39 years.

Jan. 1, 1889, 38 years.

Jan. 1, 1890, 38.7 years.

Five Courts are not included in this; but the addition will not materially change the figures either way.

The average age of applications approved the past year is 30.9 years.

The following table gives the number applying to each Court:

New applications received from April 17, 1889, to March 31, 1890:

No.	COURT.		No.	COURT.	
1	Cathedral	24	44	St. Bernard	0
3	Fenwick	2	45	Unity	8
4	St. Francis	4	46	St. Augustine	0
5	Leo	3	47	St. Anne	28
6	Cheverus	2	48	Sarsfield	18
7	St. Patrick	6	49	Constantine	10
8	Sherwood	13	51	Holy Trinity	29
9	Columbus	11	52	Highland	4
10	Iona	23	53	Emerald	30
11	St. Joseph	3	54	St. James	9
12	Fulton	2	55	Charles River	12
14	Lafayette	10	57	Carroll	2
15	SS. Peter and Paul	7	59	Worcester	10
16	Essex	13	60	Middlesex	1
17	Hamilton	4	61	St. Lawrence	9
18	St. Peter	10	62	St. Catherine	15
19	Williams	6	63	Shields	8
20	Mt. Pleasant	13	64	Gallagher	10
21	St. Alphonsus	4	65	St. Columbkill	7
23	St. John	15	66	Griffin	11
24	St. Gregory	10	67	Canton	3
25	St. Francis	14	68	St. Margaret	2
26	St. Raphael	11	69	Stoughton	16
28	Erin	16	70	St. Michael	14
29	St. Thomas	41	71	Phil Sheridan	12
30	Bass River	8	72	Merrimack	11
32	Qualey	6	73	Taunton	32
33	St. John	6	74	Hendricken	13
34	Americus	13	75	St. Jarlath	90
35	Sheil	1	76	Quincy	49
37	Friendship	0	77	Mystic	33
38	St. Joseph	2	78	St. Monica	26
39	Benedict	2			
41	Star of the Sea	1			832
43	St. Mary	4			

NEW COURTS.

The following are the new Courts established since April 17 1889 :

St. Jarlath, No. 75, Amesbury, 60 charter members. Instituted June 14. 1889.

Quincy No. 76, Quincy, 22 charter members. Instituted Oct. 24, 1889.

Mystic, No, 77, Medford, 23 charter members. Instituted Dec. 12. 1889.

St. Monica, No. 78, Lawrence, 20 charter members. March 26, 1889.

The average age of applicants rejected the past year was 33.5 years.

The whole number of applications received between April 17, 1889, and April 1, 1890, was 834. Of this number 65 were rejected, 7 per cent. of the whole number received.

From April, 1888, to April, 1889, 11 per cent. were rejected, and from April, 1887, to April, 1888, 15 per cent. were rejected.

It is gratifying to note here that the Medical Examiners generally have exerted themselves to give the Order good examinations, and, in the opinion of the High Standing Committee, we have as good examinations as are possible.

The Medical Examiners realize that recommending a poor risk is not a safe business, as they now know that the High Standing Committee will not approve a paper even if recommended by the Medical Examiner, unless fully satisfied that the applicant is in perfect health.

The High Medical Examiner has been a constant attendant at the meetings of the High Standing Committee, and, as in the past, has given the High Standing Committee the benefit of his advice and experience on every occasion when it was needed. The services of so conscientious an officer cannot be too highly estimated, and it is hoped that the members generally appreciate his labors.

OCCUPATIONS OF APPLICANTS APPROVED

FROM JANUARY 1, 1889, TO JANUARY 1, 1890.

Book-keeper	9	Cone Maker	1
Boot maker	2	Cardriver	3
Boot-crimper	1	Cook	1
Boot and shoe dealer	2	Carriage Trimmer	7
Blacksmith	32	" Worker	12
Boiler maker	5	" Painter	12
" helper	1	" Maker	1
Box maker	1	" Blacksmith	1
Baggage-master	1	" Driver	1
Brush-maker	3	Diver	1
Baker	4	Druggist	4
Barber	11	Driver	1
Butcher	11	Drug Clerk	2
Butter dealer	1	Dentist	1
Bartender	1	Expressman	3
Burnisher	1	Elevator Conductor	1
Bricklayer	2	Engineer	2
Bottler	1	Edge Setter	1
Carpet worker	1	Farmer	8
Carpenter	24	Florist	2
Cutter	2	File Manufacturer	1
Coal and Wood	1	Foreman	3
Cornice-maker	1	Furnishing Goods	1
Copper-worker	1	Freight Handler	1
Contractor	5	Fish Dealer	3
Clerk	18	" Cutter	3
Clo.-trimmer	1	" Shipper	1
Clergyman	3	Frame Gilder	2
Coachman	20	Furniture Dealer	1
Card Grinder	1	Fireman	5
Currier	9	Fresco Painter	1
Cattle Dealer	1	Grocer	16
Cooper	1	" Clerk	3
Coppersmith	1	Gas Fitter	1
Comb-Maker	1	Gardener	10
Collector	1	Glass Silverer	1
Caterer	1	German-silver Worker	1
Cotton Spinner	1	Granite Polisher	4
China Dealer	1	" Dealer	5
Cabinet-Maker	1	" Cutter	6
Cutler	1	Glass Artist	1
Crayon Artist	1	Grinder	1
Cloth Inspector	1	Hinge Maker	1

Hotel Keeper	.	.	.	2
" Bellman		.	.	1
" Clerk		.	.	2
Horse Shoer	.	.	.	2
Hatter	.	.	.	6
Hostler	.	.	.	7
Hardware Clerk		.	.	2
Hair Dresser	.	.	.	3
Hack Driver		.	.	3
H. R. R. Conductor		.		1
Harness Maker	.		.	4
Instrument Maker	.		.	1
Iron Slitter		.	.	1
" Moulder			.	2
" Polisher		.	.	1
Insurance Clerk		.		1
Jeweller	.		.	14
Janitor	.	.	.	2
Junk Dealer		.	.	1
Jewelry Manufacturer		.		1
Laborer	.	.	.	102
Letter Carrier		.	.	4
Longshoreman	.		.	1
Loom Fixer	.		.	2
Lithographer		.	.	1
Leather Dealer		.	.	1
" Cutter	.		.	1
" Salesman	.		.	1
Laster	.		.	6
Lamplighter	.		.	1
Lawyer	.	.	.	3
Liquor Clerk	.		.	1
" Dealer	.		.	3
Merchant	.	.	.	2
Morocco Dresser		.	.	10
" Finisher	.		.	1
Master Painter	.		.	1
Metal Worker		.	.	1
Moulder	.		.	2
Mason	.	.	.	11
Mill Hand	.		.	1
Marble Dealer		.	.	1
Machinist	.		.	19
Machine Agent		.	.	1
Mule Spinner	.		.	1
Melter in Foundry		.		1
Marketman		.	.	1
Milkman		.	.	2

Medical Student	.		.	1
Meat Cutter	.		.	1
Operator in Bleachery		.		1
Overseer	.		.	1
Polisher	.	.	.	3
Plumber		.	.	7
Pharmacist		.	.	1
Physician		.	.	12
Postmaster		.	.	1
Printer	.	.	.	4
Provision Dealer		.	.	11
" Salesman		.		2
Painter	.		.	23
Piano Tuner	.		.	3
" Maker		.	.	3
" Finisher		.	.	1
Postal Clerk		.	.	1
Porter	.	.	.	5
Potter	.	.	.	3
Policeman		.	.	9
Paper-maker		.	.	4
" Hanger		.	.	1
Plasterer	.	.	.	3
Pedler	.	.	.	2
Periodical Dealer		.	.	1
Produce	.	.	.	1
Quarryman		.	.	3
Rumseller		.	.	1
Rubber-boot Maker	.		.	1
" Worker		.	2
" Cutter	.		2
" Packer		.	1
Restaurant Keeper	.		.	4
Roofer	.	.	.	1
R. R. Freight Agent		.		1
Reporter		.	.	1
Silversmith		.	.	2
Shoemaker	.		.	66
Stovemounter		.	.	2
Stone cutter	.		.	17
" Polisher	.		.	1
" Pointer		.	.	4
" Mason		.	.	5
" Merchant		.	.	1
Salesman	.		.	15
Shoe Treer	.		.	1
" Stitcher		.	.	5
" Finisher		.	.	1

Shoe Fitter	.	.	.	1
" Dealer	.	.	.	4
" Cutter	.	.	.	5
Sole Cutter	.	.	.	5
Stableman	.	.	.	2
Stablekeeper	.	.	.	1
Silk Merchant	.	.	.	1
Store-keeper	.	.	.	2
Stevedore	.	.	.	1
Shipper	.	.	.	4
Soapmaker	.	.	.	1
Stockbroker	.	.	.	1
Sexton	.	.	.	1
Stationary Engineer	.	.		3
Shovelmaker	.	.	.	3
Student	.	.	.	1
Saloonkeeper	.	.	.	3
Teamster	.	.	.	35
Tack polisher	.	.	.	1
Telegrapher	.	.	.	2
Tinsmith	.	.	.	3

Tailor	.	.	.	4
Tanner	.	.	.	1
Trader	.	.	.	1
Tobacco Dealer	.	.		2
Undertaker	.	.	.	5
Veterinary Surgeon	.	.		1
Wire Drawer	.	.		1
Waiter	.	.	.	2
Weaver	.	.	.	3
Wool Sorter	.	.	.	2
Wine Clerk	.	.	.	2
Wood Turner	.	.	.	1
" Worker	.	.		1
" Jointer	.	.	.	1
Watchman	.	.	.	7
Woollen Dyer	.	.	.	1
" Spinner	.	.		1
" Kapper	.	.		1
" Carder	.	.		1
				920

OCCUPATIONS OF APPLICANTS REJECTED

From January 1, 1889, to January 1, 1890.

Brick-mason . . . 1	Grocer 2
Bricklayer . . . 2	" Clerk . . . 2
Blacksmith . . . 1	Gardener 1
Boarding-house Keeper . 2	Hackman . . . 1
Bottler 1	Insurance Agent . . 2
Bartender . . . 2	Janitor 2
Baker 1	Laborer 8
Brass Polisher . . 1	Laster 1
Clerk 2	Liquor Dealer . . . 2
Coachman . . . 2	" Clerk . . . 1
Carpet Worker . . . 1	Milkman 1
Carriage Washer . . 1	Machinist . . . 2
Carpenter 2	Mechanic 1
Cabinet-maker . . 1	Master of fishing schooner, 1
Compositor . . . 1	Marketman . . . 1
Contractor . . . 1	Merchant 1
Currier 1	Morocco Dresser . . 1
Cooper 1	Musician 1
Confectioner . . . 1	Music Teacher . . 1
Dry Goods Pedler . . 1	Plumber 2
Fish Salesman . . . 1	Piano Maker . . . 3
Gilder . . . 1	Photographer . . . 1
Painter 3	Shipper 1
Paper Maker . . . 1	Silversmith . . . 1
Provision Dealer . . 1	Telegrapher . . . 1
Quarryman . . . 1	Tailor 1
Rubber-boot Maker . 1	Upholsterer . . . 1
Railroad Conductor . . 1	Varnish Salesman . . 1
Saloonkeeper . . 2	
Shoemaker . . . 6	90
Stonecutter . . . 2	

NAMES OF ██████ ██s. DATE ██ █████ ██s. ██ OF DEATH, COURT OF ██ ██ DECEASED ██S A ██, ██D

BENEFICIARIES, ██E, LENGTH OF ██s.

NO.	NAME.	COURT.	AGE.	INITIATED.	Membership Yrs.	Mos.	Dys.	DATE OF DEATH.	██E.	En-dow-ment.	██ ██s.	MR OF ██S.	TO	██M PAID.
1	██s ██n,	██da, No. ██,	49	Mar. 14, 1880		7	5	Oct. 19, 1880	Typho-Mal ██ia	$1,000	██w		Widow	██x
2	M. J. Kiley,	██b, 5, ██lk, 3,	31	Nov. 14, 1879	1	1	9	Nov. 20, "	██s	1,	"		Executor	
3	██ed,	Iona, ██,	██	Nov. 29, "	1	6	19	Dec. 3, 1881	██ly	"			Athm	██r
4	D. I. ██h,	██l, 1,	48	Sept. 3, 1879	3	3	8	Jan. 11, "	██ia	1,	"		Wid ow.	
5	P. I. ██,	██d, 1,	33	Oct. 15, "	1	3	8	Jan. 27, "	██y	"	"		"	
6	Edward A.	██s, 6,	38	Feb. 11, 1880	0	10	24	Mar. 5, "	██ia	"	"		"	
7	██n ██n,	██k, 13,	42	May 26, "	0	11	0	Mar. 26, "	██ia	"	"		"	
8	██k ██y,	██n, 17,	43	Aug. 3, "	0	10	14	April 17, "	Cancer in	1,	"		"	
9	██k ██y,	██, ██,	46	April 21, "	1	1	27	June 18, "	██s	1,	"		"	
10	██tick C. Dailey,	██d, ██,	26	Mar. 15, 1881	0	6	14	Aug. 29, "	██d	1,	"		"	
11	██s L. Meagher,	Leo, 5,	24	Aug. 10, 1881	0	0	8	Aug. 23, "	██s	1,	"		"	&
12	██s F.	██b, 5, ██n, 17,	47	July 6, 1880	1	1	24	Sept. 3, "	██s	1,	"		"	&
13	██ld	██,	36	Aug. 16, "	1	2	14	Oct. 30, "	██e Phthisis	3,	" & ██il		"	
14	██l	██y,	40	April 12, 1881	1	8	5	Nov. 17, "	Bright's	4,	"		"	
15	██m ██ly, ██d,	St. ██n, 1,	31	April 21, 1881	1	7	1	Nov. 22, "	██c	1,	"		"	██n
16	██l J.	Fenwick, 3,	49	Feb. 13, 1880	1	9	14	Nov. 27, "	██s ██s. ██	1,	"		"	
17	██y ██le,	██8,	23	Mch.	1	8	26	Nov. 30, "	██br	██e			Gna.	
18	██el O'Brien,	██h, 11,	26	Dec. 27, "	1	11	9	Dec. 6, "	██dia, ad Cong. of ██n	1,	██n		Widow	██d
19	██ M.	██h, 1,	31	May 10, "	1	9	17	Jan. 9, 1882	██n d	2,	Widow		"	
20	Thos. T. McDonough,	██s.	28	Mar. 22, "	1	3	10	Jan. 25, "	██s	1,	"		"	
21	██es	██s, ██s, 2,	46	Oct. 15, 1879	2	3	16	Feb. 1, "	██a		"		"	
22	Mark B. ██y,	██n, 38,	36	Mar. 29, 1881	1	10	19	Feb. 18, "	██e		"		"	
23	██n ██s,	St. Sullivan, 2,	40	Jan. 18, "	1	2	18	Mar. 6, "	██a a ██n		"		"	
24	██s. Mc Bayley,	St. ██k, 7,	36	June 25, 1880	1	10	26	Mar. 25, "	Colloid ██ of ██n	1,	"		"	
25	██es. Clark,	██b, 5, ██dt, 39, Somerville	35	June 24, 1881	1	11	4	May 21, "	██s	1,	"		"	
26	██nes Pell,	██ty, 40,	39	May 12, "	1	0	17	May 28, "	██ia		"			
27	██k ██n,	██k, ██,	40	June 23, 1880	1	11	10	May 29, "	██s of ██ia	1,	"		"	
28	██h Hayes,	St. Francis, 4,	33	June 1, 1882	1	11	17	June 27, "	██ia	1,	"		"	

ENDOWMENTS PAID — Cont' ued.

NO.	NAME.	COURT.	AGE.	INITIATED.	Membership Yrs.	Mos.	Dys.	DATE OF DEATH.	CAUSE.	Endowment.	NUMBER OF Ms.	TO WHOM PAID.
33	nas Miller,	Mr, 3, E,	25	Sept. 3, 1880	1	8	21	May 24, 1882	Delirit m Tremens	$1,000	1, Father	Mr
34	John M F,		32	April 13, 1881	1	9	14	Jan. 27, "	st at Sea	"	1, Mw	Widow
35	M Leahey,	r & Paul, E,	34	Nov. 17, 1880	1	8	24	Aug. 11, "	n of t [Brain	"	1, Father	Father
36	is Devenny,	Fenwick, 3,	28	Mar. 12, "	2	5	6	Aug. 18, "	m ard Cong. of the	"	1, Father	"
37	Jno. B. y, M.D.,	1,	27	Aug. 3, 1879	2	11	24	July 27, "	Fever	"	1, s	s
38	Wm. e,	, 3,	37	April 20, 1880	2	4	8	Sept. 7, "	Hy Hyperamia	"	5, Mw	Widow
39	n,	K, 3,	28	Dec. 2, 1881		9	25	Sept. 7, "		"	1, "	"
40	th Diver,	h 3, 6,	38	Mar. 23, 1880	1	7	5	Oct. 28, "	of Brain g	"	1, "	"
41	h Joyce,	M,	40	Dec. "	1	11		Nov. 3, "	t by lg	"	1, "	"
42	k y,	Quincy		Jan. 8, "	2	10	13	Nov. 3, "	P	"	1, Widow r	Mr
43	h F.	l,	48	Feb. 11, "	2	8	10	Jan. 6, 1883	Tid Pneumonia	"	1, Mr	Son
44	r,	Leo, 5,	22	April 26, 1882	2	10	28	Jan. 22, 1882	g	"	1, Son	"
45	Ed. L. Burns,	s, 6,	68	Feb. 17, 1880	1	11	5	Oct. 22, 1882	t Disease	"	1, Mw	Mw
46	e	, 8,	23	Jan. 4, 1883		1	10	Feb. 14, 1883	g	"	1, Father	r
47	N	s, 4,	28	May 26, 1881	1	8	18	Feb. 14, "	t	"	1, Mw	Mw
48	,	St. Francis, 4,	29	Dec. 21, 1882	1	1	28	Feb. 19, "	m m ll Stone	"	1, "	"
49	s.A. m,	Mil, 35,	35	June 24, 1880	1	8	10	Mar. 4, "	l Pneumonia	"	2, lg	lg
50	David lm,	l, 8,	51	Mar. 20, 1881	3	3	14	Mar. 18, "	s	"	1, Mw	Widow
51	h ay,	n, 8,	30	Mar. "	3	7		April 16, "	t	"	1, "	"
52	s Neville,	x, 0,	35	Nov. 3, 1880	2			April 22, "	t of	"	1, Sr	Widow
53	s Collins,	y,	22	Aug. 18, 1879	2	6	1	May 3, "	Phthisis	"	1, Mw	"
54	P. H.	St. Francis, 4,	34	Dec. "	2	9	18	May 5, "	e of the Brain	"	1, Child	
55	John Kerrigan,	l, 8,	41	July 8, 1880	2	10		May 6, "		"	1, Mw	Mw
56	h J. m,	St. Peter, 18,	42	Oct. 21, "	2	7	9	May 8, "	Drowning	"	1, Child	s
57	s F. Daly,	St. ee, 47,	33	Dec. 22, 1882	2	6	6	June 28, "	c	"	4, Father	r
58		s, 4,	26	Mar. "		1	1	June 3, "	a	"	1, Father	
59	William B. h,	k, 3,	37	Nov. 14, 1879	3	1	2	May 4, "		"	3, Child n	Wi dw
60	C. L. m,	Fenwick, 3,	45	Nov. 14, "	3	6	3	May 13, "		"	1, Mw	"
61	n Rickard,	Fitzpatrick, 13,	13	Dec. 1, 1880	2	7	20	June 21, "	Carditis	"	1, "	"
62	l m,	k, 7,	28	Feb. 10, "	2	4	18	June 28, "	Chronic Bronchitis	"	1, "	"
63	s G. n,	m, 6,	48	April 13, "	2	2	17	June 30, "	Constm n	"	1, "	"
64	John m,	m, 23, Hyde Park	37	April 8, 1883		2	24	July 2, "	e	"		
65	s T. Walker,	Sar d e Sea,41,	27	May 27, 1882	1	1	15	July 12, 1883	Septi ia	"	1, Mw	W dw
66		Fenwick, 3,	49	Dec. 3, "	2	7	28	Aug. 3, "	Typh td Fever	"	3,	Heirs
67	L A. M, M.D.,	Fenwick, 3,	50	Nov. 14, 1879	3	8	11	Aug. 23, "	Typhoid Fever	"	3, "	"
68	John J. y,	Williams, 19,	27	Sept. 16, 1880	3	10	16	Sept. 30, "	Pulmonary Phthisis			
71			31	Nov. "	3	1		Oct. 17, "		"	1, Mr	Mr
72												

No.	Name	Council, No.	Town		Admitted		Died		Cause of Death	Amount	Beneficiary	Relation
73	M. H. [Rose], [Ilun],	; [Eat], 39,	Somerville	28	Mar. 31, 1881	2	Sept. 17	Sept. 28, 1883	Pulmonary Hemorrhage	$1,000	1, Widow	Ww
74	Bart. [Ilun],	Essex. 16,	Salem	35	Aug. 1, 1883	2	Oct. 1,		Uremic Coma	"	1, Mother	Mother
75	E. F. [der],	[Fnk], 3,	Boston	22	Feb. 16, "	8	Nov. 4,		Phthisis	"	1, Mw	Mw
76	John O'Brien, [M],	[Fin], 17,	"	47	Sept. 15, 1881	2	Nov. 6,		Heart Disease	"	4,	Mw
77	Patrick	St. Joseph, 17,	So.	32	June 14, 1880	3	Sept. 14,		Injury to Brain by fall	"	1,	Heirs
78	John Sweeney,	[Fnk], 39,	Somerville	46	Mar. 31, 1881	1	Nov. 24		Pulmonary Consumption	"	1,	
79	Michael H. Murray,	Mt. Pleasant, 20,	Boston	42	Oct. 20, 1880	7	Dec. 11		Catarrhal Pneumonia, C'nsum'p.	"	4,	
80	Michael [B],	Fenwick, 3,	"	30	Jan. 30, "	2	Dec. 22,		[Phy]	"	1,	Sister
81	John Murray,	Cathedral, 1,	"	39	Oct. 8, 1879	4	Dec. 25, "		Phthisis	"	1, Sister	
82	T. H. O'Rourke,	St. James 54,	"	25	July 17, 1881	5	Dec. 27,		Pulmonary Phthisis	"	1, Mw	Mw
83	Philip	St. [ ], 29,	Brockton	39	Feb. 5, 1883	1	Feb. 4, 1884		Cerebral Paralysis	"	1, Mother	Mother
84	Jas. B. Reagan,	Charles Riv.55,	Water't'n	23	Nov. 31, 1881	2	Feb. 28,		Pneumonia	"	1, Mw	Widow
85	Thos McDonough	1 [Ray], 32,	[Wn],	33	Nov. 31, 1883	1	Feb. 21,		Cong. of Lungs and Peritonitis	"	1,	"
86	Thos [Mh],	Americus, 34,	Boston	40	July 25, 1880	3	Jan. 23,		Quick Consumption	"	1,	"
87	Denis Ahearn,	St. Patrick, 7,	So.	35	May 10, 1880	9	Mar. 29,		Bright's Disease	"	4, 3 child'n	"
88	Frank A. Spitz,	St. [ ], 21,	"	31	Oct. 13, 1881	4	Mar. 10,		Phthisis Pulmonalis	"	4, 3 "	"
89	[Mh]d Green,	[ns], 6, 13,	"	31	Feb. 25, "	2	Jan. 12,		Pulmonary Consumption	"	4, 2 "	"
90	John A. McCarthy,	[ns]k, 13,	"	41	Oct. 17, 1882	10	Jan. 24,		[ ] ry Consumption	"	1,	
91	John F. Cunningham	Iona, 10,	"	32	Mar. 14, 1880	7	Jan. 6,		Pneumonia	"	1, 8	
92	Stephen T. Sliney,	SS. Pet.& Paul,15,	S.Bos'n	26	May 20, 1881	11	April 23,		Bright's Disease of Kidneys	"	9, 8	Father & child'n
93	Thos [ ]	[ ]k, 3,	Boston	50	April 7, "	11	Mar. 19,		[Mr], falling off staging	"	2, Parents	Father & [ther]
94	John H.	Essex, [ ],	Salem	29	Mar. 2, "	3	Mar. 2,		Phthisis	"	1, Sister	Guardian
95	John W. Lynch,	St. [ ]h, 11,	Boston	32	April 26, 1880	8	Dec. 28, 1883		Phthisis	"	2,	Widow
96	John P. Duffin,	Erin, 28,	"	39	Feb. 3, 1880	2	April 15, 1884		Phthisis Pulmonalis	"	5, 4 child'n	"
97	[Wm] Meagher,	St. Francis, 4,	"	43	Jan. 26, "	4	April 16		Heart Disease	"	5, 4	"
98	Michael McCarthy,	[ ]k, 13,	"	49	April 26, "	3	May 14,		Acid'nt, hhd. sugar fell on him	"	4,	"
99	Charles Lyons,	Cathedral, 1,	"	30	Sept. 8, 1881	1	May 25		Diabetes [Mis]	"	3, 2 "	"
100	Daniel Ba[i]gy,	Sherwood, 8,	"	40	Mar. 8, "	7	May 2,		Pneumonia. r.lung & upper lt.	"	3, 3	"
101	Patrick A. Finn,	Iona, 10,	Malden	31	April 11, "	3	April 29,		Phthisis	"	1,	"
102	Edward W. Wright,	St. Francis 4,	Boston	40	April 22, 1880	0	June 9,		Hemphlegia of Larynx	"	2, 2	Daughter
103	John J. Donovan,	v [ ]d, 8,	"	24	April 22, "	4	May 1,		[Sak], accident, crushing of leg	"	1, Daughter	Mr
104	Michael Maguire,	Williams, 19,	"	23	April 4, 1881	1	July 23,		[Mis] Pulmonalis	"	1, Mother	Widow
105	Phil A. Cunningham,	Liberty, 40,	"	40	June 23, "	3	July 15,		Chronic Bronchitis	"	4, [Mw], 3 child'n	Wid. and child'n
106	James F. Lynch,	Americus, 34,	"	34	Mar. 11, "	4	June 24,		Pulmonary Consumption	"	1,	Widow
107	Patrick Donohue,	St. Joseph, 11,	"	33	Nov. 21, 1882	1	Aug. 10,		Pulmonary Consumption	"	1,	"
108	[Rev] Wm.J. Daly,	St. Francis 4,	Boston	40	Mar. 23, 1880	9	Aug. 9,		Cancer of 1 [Sh]	"	1, Daughter	Sister
109	Rev. J.B. O'Donnell,	St. Alphonsus,21,	Boston	36	April 26, 1883	2	Aug. 22, 1884		Alcoholism	"	4, [Mw], 3 child'n	Brother
110	Thos [Ray],	Fitzpatrick, 13,	"	29	Mar. 29, 1882	1	June 18,		Carcinoma of Liver	"	4, Mother	Widow
111	M. J. Devine,	[ns], 6,	"	46	Feb. 11, 1880	5	Aug. 24,		Cirrhosis	"	1, [Ster]	[Mr]
112	M. C. [ds],	SS.Pet.& Paul,15,	S.Bos'n	29	Mar. 7, 1882	3	Aug. 10,		Phthisis	"	1, Widow, 4 child'n	Wid. and child'n
113	Thos Cahill,	St.Thomas, 29,	Brockton	24	Mar. 31, 1881	3	Sept. 5,		Consumption	"	2, 1 child	"
114	P. H. Smith,	Shiel, 35,	"	43	Jan. 3, 1882	8	Sept. 14,		[Sh]-Morbus	"	1,	"
115	J. S. Tompkins,	St. Peter, 18,	Dorchester	31	July 3, 1880	8	Oct. 1,		Killed by [ ]tive	"	1,	"
116	B. A. Brown, [Msh],	St. Francis, 4,	Boston	34	Nov. 30, 1881	3	Oct. 4,		Consumption	"	3, 3 child'n	"
117	Martin	Shiel, 35,	Boston	25	Mar. 31, "	10	Oct. 21,		Consumption	"	1, Sister	Sister
118	John Drury, [n],	Hamilton,17,	Charlest'wn	24	Mar. 2, 1882	6	Nov. 27,		Concussion of Brain	"	1, Widow	Widow
119	T. H. [An],	St. Francis, 4,	Boston	48	May 13, 1880	4	Dec. 7,		Phthisis	"	1, Sister	[Ster]
120	E. W. [Bergen],											

ENDOWMENTS PAID—Continued.

No.	NAME.	MBR.	AGE.	INITIATED.	Yrs.	Mos.	Dys.	DATE OF DEATH.	CAUSE.	Endowment.	NUMBER OF BENEFICIARIES.	TO WHOM PAID
121	Thos Lynch,	St. Joseph, 11, Boston	35	June 27, 1881	3	4	7	Nov. 4, 1884	Pneumonia	$1,000	3, Children	Guardian
122	Mw 1 ask,	St. Alphonsus, 21, "	43	Oct. 15, 1880	4	2	2	Dec. 17, "	Consumption	"	5, Widow, 4 child'n	Wid. & children
123	J. M. Tirrell,	St. Patrick, 7, So. Boston	23	Jan. 24, 1882	2	11	27	Jan. 21, 1885	Phthisis	"	3, 2 "	Guardian
124	John Delaney,	Leo, 5, E. Boston	24	Jan. 16, 1880	5	1	23	Feb. 9, "	Consumption	"	2, "	Widow
125	Patrick O'Gorman,	St. Joseph, 11, Boston	32	Jan. 12, 1882	2	11	26	Jan. 8, "	Phthisis	"	3, Broth., wd, ch.	Broth., wid. & g.
126	J. W. McClellan,	Chelsea	36	Oct. 23, 1881	3	3	27	Jan. 30, "	art Disease	"	3, Zww	Widow
127	W. J. Barry,	Essex 16, Salem	25	June 23, 1880	4	7	15	Feb. 8, 1885	Phthisis Pulmonalis	"	1, Sister	Sister
128	P. F. Welsh,	Friendship, 37, Boston	35	Feb. 6, 1882	3	1	1	Mar. 7, "	Paralysis	"	4, Widow, 4 child'n	Mw
129	Michael Ferrin,	Jay, 32, Woburn	44	Jan. 10, 1883	2	10	27	Dec. "	Enteritis	"	4, 3 "	Wid. & g ardian
130	Edward Doherty,	Cheverus, 6, Boston	30	May 7, 1880	4	5	20	Oct. 27, "	Phthisis	"	3, Brothers	Brothers
131	John Sullivan,	St. Patrick, 7, So. Boston	48	Mar. 17, 1883	1	16	Mar. 17, 1885		Phthisis	"	6, Mw, 5 child'n	Wid. & guardian
132	T. J. Flynn,	SS. Pet.&Paul,15, " "	26	Aug. 18, "	4	7	21	April 9, "	Phthisis Pulmonalis	"	1, "	"
133	Daniel Holland,	O'Connell,22, Winchester	39	Nov. 22, "	4	4	23	April 15, "	Pneumonia	"	1, "	"
134	James Rice,	1 May, 32, Woburn	39	Feb. 15, "	5	1	20	April 10, "	Accident, crushing h'd & shl'd'r	"	1, "	"
135	John M. Perkins,	Erin, 28, Boston	42	June 5, 1882	2	10	13	April 18, 1885	Pneumonia	"	1, Father	Father
136	Daniel M. Gillis,	Bass River, 30, Beverly	25	Feb. 19, 1880	3	1	May 1, "		Pneumonia	"	2, Father & Motner	" & mother
137	John Schultz,	Holy Trinity, "	39	Mar. 21, 1883	1	29	April 17, "		Consumption	"	2, Widow, 2 child'n	Widow
138	W. Neil,	Gea. 36, "	44	April 21, 1881	4	1	28	May 16, "	Pneumonia	"	1, "	"
139	John Donovan,	Friendship, 37, Boston	28	April 9, 1880	5	1	29	May 25, "	Consumption	"	2, 1 child	Brother
140	J. S. MacCorry,	Columbus, 9, "	35	Dec. 13, 1882	2	3	2	May 4, "	Heart Disease	"	1, Brother	Widow
141	Edward Gallagher,	Star of the Sea,41, E. "	29	Feb. 14, 1882	3	5	24	June 7, "	Drowned	"	4, Mw, 3 child'n	
142	Daniel R. McDonald,	1 Jno, 50, Boston	25	May 12, 1881	3	18	June "		Phthisis	"	4, 3 child'n	
143	Dr. W. P. Kelley,	Liberty, 40, "	48	Mar. 11, 1880	10	27	April 9, 1882	Imflammation of Bowels	"	6, Uncles & uats	Xhes & mts
144	Peter Tracy,	Mt. Pleasant, 20, "	35	Mar. 30, 1880	4	26	June 14, 1885		Congestion of Brain	"	5, Widow, 4 child'n	Widow & child'n
145	Maurice O'Hearn,	Cheverus, 6, "	38	Oct. 11, "	4	8	1	June 12, "	Bright's Disease	"	4, " 3	"
146	Timothy Long,	St. Patrick, 7, So. "	32	April 6, "	5	3	13	July "	Pneumonia	"	5, " 4	"
147	David Lane,	Mrs, 6, Boston	49	Feb. 24, "	4	6	July "		Phthisis	"	1, "	"
148	Joseph F. Murphy,	Mrs, 6, "	22	April 22, "	5	5	July 24, "		Apoplexy	"	1, Mother	Mother
149	Michael Reardon,	Sherwood, 8, "	47	Dec. 13, 1881	3	2	19	Aug. 14, "	Phthisis	"	1, Widow	Widow
150	Peter Hawkins,	Star of the Sea,41, E. "	43	Sept. 25, 1882	2	10	27	Mar. 2, 1884	Pneumonia	"	3, Brothers	Brothers
151	P. W. Sweeney,	St.Bernard,44, W. Newton	25	Dec. 27, 1881	2	8	18	Aug. 22, 1885	Phthisis	"	4, Father, 3	Father & sister
152	Thomas Daly,	Leo, 5, E. Boston	32	Mar. 21, "	4	5	10	Sept. 1, "	Pyæmia	"	6, Children	Guardian
153	B. F. Harrington,	Mw, 36, Gea. "	40	Sept. 12, 1879	6	16	Sept. "		Phthisis	"	7, Mw, 6 child'n	Widow
154	Owen McCarthy,	Cathedral, 1, Boston	37	Mar. 12, 1880	6	9	Sept. 21, "		Typhoid Pneumonia	"	4, 3	"
155	Timothy Leary,	Fenwick, 3, "	38	July 6, "	2	11	7	Sept. 30, "	Neuralgia of Stomach	"	7, 8	"
156	James H. Phalan,	Unity, 45, Bridgewater	42	Nov. 12, 1882	2	3	24	Oct. 19, 1885	Phthisis Pulmonalis	"	6, 5	"
157	John Sheehan,	Emerald, 53, Peabody	29	July 2, 1883	2	4	7	Oct. 26, "	Pneumonia	"	6, 1	"
158	Timothy Dwyer,	Cleverus, 6, Boston		Feb. 11, 1880				Oct. 17, "	Consumption	"	2, Sisters	Guardian
159												
160	Hugh A. air,											

No.	Name	Society, No.	Place	Date	Age	Death Date	Cause of Death	Amount	Beneficiary	Relation
161	D. M. Lynch,	Erin, 28,	Boston	Feb. 3, 1881	9 28	Dec. 1, 1885	Phthisis and Gen'l tuberculosis	$1,000	Ww, 5 ldn	Atty for wid, g.
162	Michael Sullivan,	St., 16,	Salem	May 40, 1880	4 3	Nv. 4, "	Uremia	"	" 2 "	Ww & guar.
163	John My.,	St. John, 23,	Hyde Park	Dec. 14, 1880	11 20	Nv. "	Consumption	"	" 3 "	" "
164	Patrick Prendergast,	Americus, 34,	Boston	Nov. 21, 1882	14	Dc. "	Chronic Mal Cirrhosis	"	" 8 "	" "
165	J. R. Yeulley,	St. Francis, 4,	"	Dec. 18, 1879	6 2	Dec. 20, "	Ed by the	"	" 5 "	" "
166	John O'Day,	Erin, 28,	"	April 6, 1881	8 15	Dec. 60, "	Pulmonary Phthisis	"	1 child	" "
167	James J. Quinn,	St. John, 23, E. Cambridge	Mar. 8, "	4 9	Dec. 30, "	Mar Disease of Heart	"	2 child'n	" "
168	John H. Shea,	St. Francis, 4,	Boston	Dec. 18, 1879	4	Dec. 22, "	Pyæmia	"	" "	" "
169	Peter Daly,	Erin, 28,	"	Feb. 3, 1881	4 10 24	Dc. 26, "	Ed	"	" 3	" "
170	John Handran,	St. Anne, 47,	Gloucester	July 6, 1885	5 11	Dc. 27, "	Bd Poisoning	177.50	None	N'se, adr lawy
171	Edward Brennan,	Cathedral, 1,	"	Oct. 3, 1881	5	Sept. 22, "	Pneumonia	$1,000	Wiw, 2 child'n	Widow
172	Mel Hrvey,	St. Joseph, 11,	"	Oct. 15, 1879	1 22	Dec. 29, "	Heart Disease	3,	Bros. and sster	Brother & sster
173	W. H. Fitzgerald,	St. Patk, 20,	"	April 14, 1882	2 18	Jn. 2, 1886	Heart Disease	4,	Wiw, 2 child'n	Widow
174	C. J. Hurley,	St. Pk, 7,	"	Feb. 16, 1880	8 1	Jan. 7, "	Congestion of Lungs	4,	" 2 child'n	" & child'n
175	James J.	St. Francis, 25,	"	April 21, "	5 10	Jan. 18, "	Heart Disease	4,	" "	" "
176	John Donovaro,	Williams, 19,	"	April 14, 1881	4 10	June 25, 1886	Consumption	8,	4 "	" "
177	Francis P. Paten,	Fulton, 12,	"	July 14, 1883	6 2	Jan. 10, 1886	Pneumonia	5,	4 "	" "
178	Patrick W. Sullivan,	Leo, 5,	"	Nov. 26, 1880	3 21	Feb. 17, "	Pleuro-Pneumonia	7,	5 "	" "
179	Edward J. Kenney,	Hamilton, 17,	"	July 6, "	5 7 13	Feb. 19, "	Phthisis	6,	4 "	Guardian
180	James W. Norris,	St. Joseph, 11,	"	Mar. 2, "	1 6	Feb. 28, "	Phthisis	4,	4 "	Mother &
181	William Logue,	Quiney, 32,	"	Jan. 2, 1882	4 2	Mar. 4, "	Pulmonary Pneumonia	4,	Mother & widow	Widow & widow
182	William Fay,	Hamilton, 17,	"	July 6, 1880	5 1	Mar. 30, "	Paralysis	4,	Widow, 3 child'n	Wid. and child'n
183	Michael Devine,	St. Anne, 47,	"	June 23, "	9 13	April "	Catarrhal Pneumonia	1,	Parents	Father
184	Patrick Bellen,	Essex, 16,	"	Dec. 22, 1882	3 10	April 2, "	Acute Pulmonary Tuberculosis	3,	Ww, 2 child'n	Wid. and child'n
185	Jeremiah Cahill,	St. Peter, 18,	"	Mar. 7, 1881	5 2	May 21, "	Abcess of Lung from Injury	3,	1 child	" "
186	Pe Kelley,	Leo, 10,	"	Feb. 10, "	5	May 21, "	Consumption	6,	5 child'n	" "
187	Pe Kelley,	M., St., 20,	"	July 23, 1883	5 7	April 30, "	Chronic Catarrhal Pneumonia	4,	3 "	" "
188	C. G. Kullburg,	Williams, 19,	"	Mar. 17, 1882	4 2	May 29, "	Drowning	2,	3 "	" "
189	A. J. McGivney,	Sarsfield, 48,	"	Mar. 6, 1883	4 1	May 5, "	Pneumonitis	8,	7 "	Niece
190	Rev. C. McGrath,	St. Bernard, 44,	"	Feb. 26, 1882	4 29	April 5, "	Chronic Bronchitis	4,	Niece	Niece
191	Richard A. Carroll,	Mt. Pleasant, 20,	"	April 10, 1884	3 18	June 13, "	Gastric Fever	4,	Ww, 3 cill'n	Widow
192	William Sullivan,	Fulton, 12,	"	Dec. 9, 1880	6 22	June 28, "	Pulmonary Phthisis	4,	6 "	" "
193	William H. Sliney,	Americus, 34,	"	Mar. 16, 1881	5 4	July 1, "	Inflammation of liver	4,	" "	" "
194	John McClure,	Sherwood, 8,	"	May 16, 1880	6 2	July 26, "	Consumption of Lungs	2,	Widow & child	Widow
195	Joseph B. Fenelon,	eff, 5,	"	Jan. "	6 13	July 27, "	Phthisis	3,	Widow & child	Widow
196	William Musler,	Cathedral, 1,	"	June 22, 1881	5 1	July 29, "	Inflam. of Brain from sunstroke	3,	2 kn'n	Widow & guar.
197	Hugh Harkins,	Sherwood, 8, 13,	"	May 12, "	1 1	Aug. 13, "	Typhoid ever and dng Dis.	3,	2 "	" "
198	Thomas My.,	Pk, 13,	"	Mar. "	6 13	Sept. 29, "	Myelitis (Inf. of the spinal cr.)	3,	Wd. ftth. moth.	Fath., th., wid.
199	John Connors,	SS. Peter & Paul, 15,	"	Jan. 1, 1884	2 11 15	Dc. 16, "	Laryngitis	6,		Heirs
200	Daniel Gallivan,	St. Patrick, 7,	"	Jan. 28, 1881	8 26	Dec. 24, "	Phthisis Pulmonalis	7,	6 child'n	Widow
201	John F. Daly,	SS. Peter & Paul, 15,	"	Sept. 15, 1880	5 11	Aug. 26, "	Pneumonia	5,	" "	" "
202	William Pierce,	Shiel, 35,	"	April 14, 1882	8 27	Jan. 4, 1887	Chronic Bronchitis	5,	" "	" "
203	Edmund C. Pn,	St. Francis, 4,	"	April 30, 1880	6 10 12	Mar. 27, "	Hæmorrhage (from abn. aneur.)	5,	4 "	" "
204	John J. Pn.,	det, 39,	"	Mar. 31, 1881	5 11 26	Mar. 4, "	Phthisis	2,	Father & sster	Father & sister
205	James O'Toole,	Emerald, 53,	"	Sept. 6, 1883	2 11 16	Aug. 22, 1886	Unknown	6,	Ww, 5 cill'n	Widow
206	Michael Pn,	SS. Per and Paul, 15,	"	Sept. 8, 1880	6 7 11	April 12, 1887	Phthisis	5,	Children	Children
207	Thy Hurley,	St. John, 33,	"	April 8, 1881	6 0 3	Apr. 11, "	Inflammation of btin	6,	Children	Children
208	Dennis Bnford,	Williams, 19,	"	Oct. 3, "	6 5 26	April 29, "	Consumption	3,	Widow, 2	Widow

ENDOWMENTS PAID— Continued.

NO.	NAME.	COURT.	AGE.	INITIATED.	Membership Yrs. Mos. Dys.	DATE OF DEATH.	CAUSE.	Endowment.	NUMBER OF BENEFICIARIES.	TO WHOM PAID.
209	Terence Kean,	Erin, 28,	39	Feb. 17, 1881	6 - 2 17	May 4, 1887	Pneumonia	$1,000	6, Widow, 5 child'n	Widow
210	Wm. F. Kean,	Leo, 5,				May 30, 1885			4, " 9	Guardian & wid.
211	Michael Hall,	Hamilton, 17,	35	Nov. 19, 1886	2 7	Jan. 26, 1887	Acute Meningitis		4, " 3	Widow.
212	Joseph McGilvray,	Constantine, 49,	23	July 23, 1885	1 10	Jan. 25, "	Phthisis Pulmonalis		3, " 2	"
213	Patrick Roy,	Bass River, 30,	30	Sept. 8, 1881	5 4	May 14, "	Progressive Paralysis		6, " 5	Wid. & guardian
214	Philip Casey,	St. Joseph, 38,	30	Sept. 9, "	5 8	June 21, "	Hæmoptysis		2, " 1 child	"
215	John Broderick,	Hamilton, 8,	35	April 6, 1882	5 9	June 24, "	Phthisis		6, " 5 child'n	"
216	Riley,	Sherwood, 8,	50	Mar. 4, 1880	7 3	June 29, "	Liver, Kid., & Lung Dis., Dropsy		6, " 5	"
217	Cornelius Driscoll,	3,	40	Jan. 14, 1881	6 6	July 2, "	Inflammation of Liver		5, " 4	"
218	Ah,	Shields 63,	28	Jan. 14, 1887	2 6	July 13, "	Malarial Causes		2, Mother &	Mother &
219	William Brooks,	Leo, 5,	38	Dec. 24, 1880	6 6	July 27, "	Typhoid-Pneumonia		2, Widow & child	Widow
220	J. Walsh,	Leo, 5,	44	Mar. 21, 1881	6 4	July 31, "	Consumption of Lungs		6, Children	Guardian
221	Michael J. Messy,	St. John, 33,	44	May 20, 1881	6 2	May 31, "	Pulmonalis Phthisis		1, Widow	Widow
222	J. J. Cunningham,	Essex, 16,	39	Aug. 14, 1880	6 11	Sept. 3, "	Drowned		3, Father, 2 sisters	F. & At'y for 2s.
223	O'Keefe,	St. Augustine, 46,	44	Nov. 14, 1884	3 8	Aug. 6, "	Senile Marasmus		5, Widow, 5 child'n	G. of C. A. forW.
224	John F. Rahl,	St. Joseph, 11,	27	Dec. 27, 1882	4 9	July 25, "	Pneumonia		2, " 1 child	Guard. of child'n
225	B. W. Holthaus,	Cathedral, 1,	23	Mar. 8, "	5 7	Oct. 3, "	Phthisis Pulmonalis		4, " 3 child'n	"
226	G. W. Curry,	Columbus, 9,	23	April 23, 1883	4 5	Oct. 20, "	Dropsy, Heart Disease		1, Father	Father
227	Patrick Hall,	Iona, 10,	49	Mar. 14, 1880	7 8	Nov. 5, "	Pneumonia		4, Widow, 6 child'n	Widow
228	B. J. Daly,	28,	42	Feb. 3, 1881	6 9	Nov. 25, "	Degeneration of Lungs		4, Children	Son & guardian
229	Thomas Sweeney,	Unity, 45,	49	Nov. 1, 1882	4 10	Oct. 6, "	Pneumonia		2, Children	Guardian
230	F. Reavy,	Gallagher, 64,	25	April 17, 1887	1 7	Oct. 4, "	Railroad Accident		2, Father & mother	Mother
231	M. J. Reagan,	Cheverus, 6,	28	Oct. 15, 1886	1 15	Nov. 21, "	Railroad Accident		5, Widow, 4 child'n	Widow
232	D. F. McGilvray,	Cheverus, 6,	35	May 26, 1887	7 21	Dec. 17, 1888	Pneumonia		2, " 1 child	"
233	Walter Grace,	St. Columbkill, 65,	27	May 12, 1881	6 27	Jan. 7, 1887	Fract.of Sk ull,BlastingAccident		6, Widow, 5 child'n	Father
234	John Martin,	Columbus, 9,	45	April 27, 1880	7 10	Jan. 9, "	of Jaw		"	"
235	Timothy Collins,	Fulton, 12,	49	Mar. 31, 1881	6 8	Jan. 14, "	Chronic		6, Widow, 5 child'n	"
236	Michael Butt,	30,	55	Mar. 4, 1880	7 10	Dec. 7, "	Paraplegia		11, " 10	& child'n
237	A. J. Harrington,	Sherwood, 8,	29	July 2, 1883	2 7	Feb. 5, 1888	al Paresis		8, " 7	"
238	A. J. Callahan,	St. James, 54,	38	Jan. 13, 1886	1 10	Dec. 24, 1886	Phthisis Pulmonalis		1, Mother	Mother
239	T. J. Dacey,	Americus, 34,	38	Mar. 13, 1882	5 11	Dec. 15, 1887	Peritonitis		1, Brother	Brother
240	M. Brahenny,	11,	56	Sept. 13, 1879	8 4	Feb. 22, 1888	Dropsy		1, Widow	Widow
241	H. H. Shin,	Cathedral, 1,	38	Feb. 13, 1884	3 10	Jan. 13, "	Heart Disease		5, Children	Children
242	John Murray,	St. Joseph, 11,	34	May 4, 1882	5 9	Jan. 5, "	Bright's dis		1, W, 4 child'n	Mother
243	Edw.	St. Alphonsus, 21,	32	Feb. 22, 1881	8 9	Mar. 1, "	mption		1, 3 child'n	Widow
244	Wm. J. Craig,	Fitzpatrick, 13,	31	June 22, 1881	8 9	Mar. 7, "	Phthisis		1, Mother	Mother
245	John J. Craig,	Leo, 5,	32	Mar. 17, 1880	8 11	Mar. 14, "	Hemorrhage of Lungs		1, "	"
246	Peter Kelliher,	Leo, 5,	41	Mar. 18, 1881	8 7	Nov. 7, 1887	Phthisis Pulmonalis		19, Relatives	Relatives
247	Peter Kilroy,	St. Francis, 4,	56	Dec. 18, 1879	8 3	April 4, 1888	Chronic Bronchitis		1, Widow, 1 child	Widow
248	John Collins,	St. 29,	28	Nov. 8, 1883	4 5	April 24, "	Typhoid Fever		1, "	"

No.	Name	Church	Age	Date		Cause of Death	Year	Amount	Beneficiaries	Relation
49	James ..w,	Cheverus, 6,	45	April 28, 1882	6	Erysipelas	3, 1888	$1,000	4, Widow, 3 child'n	Widow
250	M. A. Fox,	Essex, 16,	33	Feb. 9, 1881	7	Laryngeal Tumor	4,	"	2, Mother & aunt	Mother & aunt
251	M. H. Kerrigan,	St. Alphonsus, 21,	53	15, 1887	6	Pneumonia	22, 1887	"	8, Children	Guardian
252	John J. Sullivan,	5,	46	Feb. 15, 1882	3	Cardiac Neuralgia	1, 1888	"	8, Widow, 7	Widow
253	T. F. Well,	6,	40	May 26, 1882	6	Val. Disease of Heart	8 June 4,	"	4, Widow, 7	Widow
254	Jno Hines,	Essex, 16,	49	April 24, 1883	6	Catarrhal Pneumonia	25,	"	5, Widow	Widow
255	J. J. Callaghan,	Lafayette, 14,	56	April 20, 1881	11	Sep nia	3,	"	4, Bro. and sisters	Sister-in-Law
256	Joseph Carley,	Cheverus, 6,	36	May 27,	1	Peritonitis	29,	"	6, Widow, 5	Widow
257	James Gorman,	Williams, 19,	33	July 2,	7	Pleuritis	30,	"	6,	
258	Patrick Dowd,	St. Francis, 25,	42	July 12,	7	Phthisis Pulmonalis	12,	"	2, Children	Children
259	A. A. Vogel,	Holy Trinity, 51,	34	April 13, 1883	3	Bright's Disease	15,	"	5, Widow, 4 child'n	Widow, 4 child'n
260	James J. W.,	St. Anne, 47,	28	Dec. 22, 1882	5	Phthisis	2,	"	3,	
261	J. J.,	Iona, 10,	27	Mar. 17, 1887	4	Cancer of liver	29,	"	3, mother	mother
262	James H. Key,	Sarsfield, 48,	52	Aug. 6, 1883	12	Ascites	6,	"	3, Widow, 2 child'n	Wid. and child'n
263	Michael Maguire,	Fenwick, 3,	46	16, 1880	5	Typ bid fever	30,	"	4, Son	Guardian
264	John Kelly,	St. 4,	28	23, 1884	8	Apoplexy	14,	"	3,	Widow
265	D. Roy,	Sherwood, 8,	38	May 16, 1880	3	Phthisis Pulmonalis	15,	"	4,	Widow &
266	P. C. Fennelly,	St. Patrick, 7,	26	Oct. 26, 1882	6	Consumption	23,	"	2, Mother	Mother
267	J. L. Hennessy,	O'Connell, 22,	35	Aug. 10,	3	Fracture of Skull	26, 1886	"	2, Children	
268	J. Keohane,	Sherwood, 8,	50	Oct. 6, 1880	4	Scelerosis	16, 1888	"	1, Widow	Widow
269	T. R. Im,	Essex, 16,	46	April 6,	7	Pleurisy	17,	"	1,	
270	Wm Lynch,	6,	45	June 8, 1883	8	Phthisis	1,	"	4, Widow, 2	
271	James Smith,	Sheil, 35,	53	Dec. 18, 1879	8	Phthisis	9,	"	3,	
272	James Fay,	St. 4,	48	Oct. 3, 1880	8	Bright's Disease	3,	"	3,	
273	James Connell,	Iona, 10,	68	Oct. 7, 1879	9	Phthisis	13,	"	9, Widow	
274	W. Manning,	Cathedral, 1,	39	Nov. 12, 1883	1	Paralysis	14,	"	3,	
275	John Burke,	Sheil, 1,	35	12, 1883	4	Phthisis	16,	"	3,	
276	A. M. Cuffe,	SS. Peter and Paul, 15,	66	June 12, 1883	2	Pneumonia	24,	"	4,	
277	M. Hogan,	St. Joseph, 38,	35	Feb. 5, 1886	4	Chr. Catar. Pneumonia	26,	"	5, Mother	Mother
278	M. H. Ryan,	SS. Peter and Paul, 15,	32	Mar. 2, 1888	1	Pneumonia	6,	"	1, Father	Father
279	J. F. Bradley,	Sheil, 35,	54	Nov. 26, 1880	8	Typhoid Pneumonia	20,	"	5, Children	Children
280	Bartley Roy,	Mark, 13,	56	Aug. 18,	5	Peritonitis	11,	"	9, Wid. 4 children	Widow & child'n
281	Michael McDonough Fitzpatrick, 13,	Mt. Pleasant, 20,	44	Aug. 16, 1880	20	Drowning	30, 1888	"	1,	
282	Thos L. Silk,		47	Jan. 16, 1880	19	Apoplexy	25, 1888	"	1, Wid. 2 children	Wid. &
283	John O'Melia,	Iona, 10,	48	20,	27	Tumor of Bowels	31,	"	2, Wid. 1 son	Wid. & son
284	Me M,	5,	53	Jan. 10, 1881	11	Heart Disease	31, 1888	"	1, Wid. 1 son	
285	James H. McDowell,	St. Joseph, 11,	35	Jan. 16, 1883	21	Consumption	8 Nov.	"	1, Sister	Sister
826	Thos F. Kelly,	Highland, 52,	40	May 23, 1883	5	Phthisis Pulmonalis	2, 1889	"	1,	
287	Patrick Magee,	Erin, 28,	38	Feb. 6, 1881	7	Consumption	24,	"	1, Mother	Mother
288	James Dorgan,	St. Thomas, 29,	50	Oct. 15, 1880	10	Phthisis	25, 1889	"	1, Widow	Widow
289	Edward Millin,	Alphonsus, 21,	36	May 7, 1886	8	Consumption	7,	"	1, Widow	Widow
291	P. H. Kerrigan,	Sherwood, 8,	45	Nov. 14, 1882	2	Phthisis Pulmonalis	23,	"	1, Widow	Widow
292	Timothy Sheehan,	Iona, 10,	51	Nov. 23, 1880	4	Hemorrhage from Lung	21,	"	1, Wid. & daugh.	Wid. & guard.
293	Charles Shortell,	Essex, 16,	54	June 23,	8	Phthisis	31,	"	2, Widow	Widow
924	Jno F. C Carroll,	St. John, 33,		Mar. 8, 1881	11	Heart Disease	19,	"	2, Wid. & daugh.	W. & daugh.

ENDOWMENTS PAID—Continued.

No.	NAME.	COURT.	AGE.	INITIATED.	Yrs.	Mos.	Dys.	DATE OF DEATH.	CAUSE.	Endowment.	NUMBER OF BENEFICIARIES.	TO	WM PAID.
295	Van der Mey	Friendship, 37,	40	Mar. 25, 1881	8	8	22	April 17, 1889		$1,000	1, Widow	Widow	
296	Peter H. Curley,	Iona, 4,	52	Dec. 18, 1879	9	3	22	April 10, "		"	1, Widow	Widow	
297	Jas. Cunningham,	Iona, 10,	58	Mar. 14, 1880	8	11	29	April 13, "	Hemorrhage of Stomach	"	1, Widow	Widow	
298	William Lynch,	Mack, 13,	35	May 5, "	8	11	11	April 16, "		"	7, 5	Sons and bos.	
299	Mk H. Devine,	Essex, 16,	52	June 29, "	8	9	10	April 9, "	Sons of L and	"	1, Bror	Daughter	hFru
300	John Mullen,	St. Francis, 4,	50	June 1, 1882	6	10	27	April 28, "		"	1, New	Widow	
301	Oge Sullivan,	Williams, 19,	46	Feb. 26, 1884	5	2	16	May 12, "	Gal Hemorrhage	"	4, Sin	Gin	
302	Chas Hoy,	St. Gregory, 24,	32	Feb. 16, 1880	5	3	1	May 27, "	This Pulmonalis	"	1, Wew	Widow	
303	J. Clary,	Leo, 5,	53	Jan. 16, 1880	9	2	16	April 2, "		"	1, Widow	Widow	
304	Me Sheehan,	St. Ther, 18,	52	July 22, "	8	10	5	May 27, "		"	1, Widow	Ay	
305	E. C. Ladd,	Sherwood, 8,	49	Mar. 4, "	9	1	9	April 13, "	His dom this	"	1, Widow	Ay	
306	Wis J. Daly,	Cheverus, 6,	34	Mar. 2, "	9	1	19	April 21, "	His of hr	"	1, Uncle	Guard.	
307	Thos. E. Atherton,	Iron 5,	45	Feb. 13, "	9	3	14	May 27, "		"	1, Wew	Widow	
308	Denis O'Connor,	SS. Ther and Jul, 15,	47	Mar. 2, 1881	8	1	1	July 3, "		"	1, Wid. & dhn	Wid. & Widow	hFru
309	John Donohue,	Sherwood, 8,	52	Mar. 11, 1880	9	3	15	June 26, "		"	7, Wid. & mild'n	Wid. & guard.	
310	John Curley,	St. Columbkille, 65,	41	Nov. 15, 1887	1	7	16	July 8, "	His and el. dhis	"	1, Mr	Mr	
311	George B. Duffy,	St. Lawrence, 61,	24	April 5, "	2	3	3	July 8, "	Hy and die	"	1, Widow	Widow	
312	Thomas Downey,	St. Alphonsus, 21,	45	Mar. 14, 1888	1	4	6	July 20, "	Ma Morbus	"	1, Ser	Ser	
313	John H. O'Dea,	Canton, 67,	29	Sept. 17, "	10	14	14	Aug. 1, "	Ad	"	1, His	His	
314	R. J. Downey,	Cheverus, 6,	26	Jan. 27, 1882	3	1	27	Mar. 24, 1885	Htt Disease and My	400	1, Bror	Guardian	
315		Williams, 19,	44	Mar. 20, 1880	4	18	18	July 27, 1889	Htt caused by bl. mb.	1,000	1, Bror	Bror	
316	Ed J. Franey,	Cheverus, 6,	25	Jan. 20, 1888	1	7	5	Aug. 25, 1889	His dhis	"	8, Wid. & Bror	Wl. &	gat
317	Min J. Ford,	St. Joph, 38,	43	Mar. 29, 1881	8	4	4	Aug. 3, "	Diabetes	"	2, Sirs	Sin	git
318	John J. Carm,	St. Ther, 18,	51	July 22, 1880	9	13	13	Aug. 5, "	Ay	"	2, Gin	Gin	
319	Key Seits,	St. Francis, 4,	40	Jan. 6, 1881	8	3	27	Oct. 10, "	Phthisis Pulmonalis	"	1, Widow	Widow	
320	Charles Haney,	Qualey, 32,	45	May 12, 1880	9	4	9	Oct. 15, "	Pleumo ia	"	3, Sin	Gin	
321	Wms,	Columbus, 9,	42	Mar. 6, "	8	7	4	Sept. 16, "	At	"	1, Sw	Widow	
322	Jw Jw	Iona, 10,	57	Mar. 14, 1880	9	7	12	Oct. 16, "	His and Heart Failure	"	6, Wid. & Sin	Widow	
323	Jas. P. McEnaney,	Williams, 19,	36	Sept. 16, 1881	8	1	22	Nov. 8, "	Paralysis and Heart Failure	"	1, Widow	Wl. & guard.	
324	Timothy Gall	Iis, 34,	42	June 5, 1883	6	5	28	Nov. 13, "		"	1, Widow	Widow	
325	John H. Cuddihy,	Iis, 34,	33	Mar. 15, 1881	8	7	5	Nov. 23, "	His causing Septicæmia	"	1, Widow	Widow	
326	Thos. H. Clary	St. James, 54,	39	Sept. 18, 1883	6	1	2	Nov. 20, "	Phthisis	"	1, Widow	Mother	
327	Hry J. Duggan,	Cly, 32,	48	Apr. 4, 1888	9	7	16	Nov. 20, "	Bd Fever and Pneumonia,	"	1, Widow	Widow	
328	Min Bn,	Mack, 3,	57	Mar. 19, 1880	8	8	27	Dec. 16, "	His Anaemia	"	1, Ser	Ser	
329	John McNamara,	Iona, 10,	32	Dec. 8, "	9	8	24	Dec. 8, "	His	"	1, Mr	Sister	
330	John T. Coleman,	Ina, 10,	32	April 7, 1889	9	7	22	Nov. 29, "	His	"	1, Mr	Mother	
331	Wkd F. Min,	St. Ther, 18,	50	Aug. 16, 1883	2	2	4	Oct. 20, "	Phthisis	"	10, Wid. & child'n	Wid. & child'n	
332	Mk I. Hallisey,	Shields, 63,	39	Jan. 14, 1887	2	7	22	Sept. 6, "	Typhoid Fever	"	1, Wew	Attorney	

ENDOWMENTS PAID — Continued.

No.	NAME.	COURT.	Age.	INITIATED.	Membership. Yrs.	Mos.	Dys.	DATE OF DEATH.	CAUSE.	Endowment.	NUMBER OF BENEFICIARIES.	TO WHOM PAID.
333	T. ...	Benedict, 39,	47	Dec. 27, 1883	5	11	16	Dec. 13, 1889	Heart Di sase	$1,000	1, Wdw	Wdw
334	John Sheehan,	St. Joseph, 11,	51	Dec. 22, 1882	6	11	23	Dec. 15, "	Phthisis	"	1, Wdw	"
335	Lawrence Andrews,	St. Thomas, 29,	39	Mar. 12, 1885	4	9	7	Dec. 19, "	Phthisis	"	1, Wdw	"
336	Jeremiah Daly,	Iona, 10, ... 49,	33	Aug. 18, 1887	2	4	2	Dec. 20, "	Phthisis	"	2, Wid. & child'n	Wd. as guard'n
337	James Wholly,	St. ...s, 4,	44	June 14, 1888	1	5	18	Dec. 2, "	Phthisis	"	1, Son	Wd. as guard'n
338	James P. Mulvey,	St. ...h, 11,	31	June 9, 1881	8	6	23	Jan. 2, 1890	Phthisis	"	1, Mther	Mther
339	John J. Sheehy,	St.	37	Dec. 27, 1883	6	1	13	Jan. 10, "	Phthisis	"	3, Wd. & 2	Wd'n Widow

The following deaths are also reported :

NAME.	COURT.	DIED.
James McGinn	Sarsfield, No. 48	Nov. 3, 1889.
F. P. Hansen	" "	Nov. 8, 1889.
Michael Keyes	Sherwood, No. 8	Dec. 27, 1889.
Daniel Manning	St. Francis, No. 25	Jan. 8, 1890.
Michael B. Murphy	Hamilton, No. 17	Jan. 12, 1890.
Patrick T. Clark	Mt. Pleasant, No. 20	Jan. 13, 1890.
John Breslin	Qualey, No. 32,	Jan. 19, 1890.
Bernard McLaughlin	Cathedral, No. 1,	Jan. 22, 1890.
Thomas Dugan	Benedict, No. 39,	Feb. 4, 1890.
John McCarthy	St. Peter, No. 18,	Jan. 2, 1890.
Edmond Boylan	Constantine, No. 49,	Feb. 17, 1890.
Christopher Morrissey	St. Francis, No. 25	Feb. 19, 1890.
James E. Doherty	St. Joseph, No. 38	March 22, "
William H. O'Connor	Erin, No. 28	Feb. 23, "

Initiated in 1879	. . . . . .	23
1880	. . . . . .	125
1881	. . . . . .	86
1882	. . . . . .	45
1883	. . . . . .	37
1884	. . . . . .	8
1885	. . . . . .	5
1886	. . . . . .	6
1887	. . . . . .	10
1888	. . . . . .	6
1889	. . . . . .	2

Since the organization of the Massachusetts Catholic Order of Foresters, the number deceased each year is as follows :

1880	. . . .	3
1881	. . . .	17
1882	. . . .	25
1883	. . . .	40
1884	. . . .	41
1885	. . . .	48
1886	. . . .	32
1887	. . . .	34
1888	. . . .	46
1889	. . . .	54

Work on the book containing the record of membership has been necessarily slow; and although as much care has been exercised as is possible, we still believe there are some applications yet to come in, of members initiated in the early years of the Order. We have only reached the end of 1881, and do not desire to enter any more until satisfied that all who entered the Order previous to Jan. 1, 1882, are entered. Thus far about 2,800 names are entered, and this work, although seemingly simple, has taken almost the entire time of an assistant the past year. Numberless requests have been made for return of applications, to this office; and it is difficult to understand why members should not feel that the applications are safe in the possession of the High Standing Committee. The possession or holding of an application by a member does not strengthen his membership, or make his claim on the Order, in the event of death, any stronger than if the application was in the care of the High Standing Committee. If the members desire a complete record of the membership it is absolutely necessary that every application should be sent in; and members who know of any case in which a member still holds his application are earnestly requested to interest themselves and have the papers forwarded.

FINANCIAL CONDITION OF COURTS.

AMOUNTS RECEIVED FOR INITIATION FEES, COURT DUES, ASSESSMENTS AND DETAILED EXPENSES.

No. of Court.	NAME OF COURT.	Received for Initiation Fees 1889.	Received for Court Dues 1889.	Received for Endowment Fund 1889.	Per Capita for High Court Received 1889.	Received for Withdrawal Cards 1889.	Received from Other Sources 1889.
1	Cathedral	$36 00	$423 25	$2,079 65	$98 25		$23 18
3	Fenwick	6 00	52 50	982 90	51 00		34 00
4	St. Francis	12 00	352 50	1,557 60	81 00		
5	Leo	18 00	327 75	1,541 40			130 90
6	Cheverus	6 00	81 20	1,321 20	34 00		71 25
7	St. Patrick	18 00	148 75	694 45	36 75		52 25
8	*Sherwood	39 00	411 65	1,919 50			175 06
9	Columbus	2 00	97 00	489 50	26 25	$0 25	3 13
10	*Iona	114 00	274 50	1,318 40	62 25		67 78
11	St. Joseph	10 00	393 25	1,904 10	95 25	25	
12	*Fulton	2 00	84 50	441 50	21 00		
13	Fitzpatrick		158 25	821 40	39 00		
14	Lafayette	57 00	198 00	944 70	54 00		75 36
15	SS. Peter & Paul	23 00	193 00	977 70			58 10
16	Essex	33 00	369 35	1,383 40	79 50		26 30
17	Hamilton	9 00	197 75	1,054 20	48 75		
18	St. Peter	5 00	203 50	935 20	51 00	50	31 80
19	Williams	27 00		429 00	53 25		54 50
20	Mt. Pleasant	52 00	245 00	1,162 30	60 00		23 35
21	St. Alphonsus	19 00	141 25	760 61	36 00		68 00
23	St. John	54 00	106 50	466 90			19 00
24	St. Gregory	57 00	162 75	861 30	34 50	25	1 25
25	St. Francis	66 00	291 25	1,430 20			
26	*St. Raphael	26 00	111 75	575 75			29 70
28	Erin	7 00	248 25	1,224 75	55 50	25	
29	St. Thomas	123 00	235 00	1,353 05	75 00		96 01
30	Bass River	21 00	100 75	490 35	26 25		2 35
32	Qualey	18 00	134 00	458 45	20 25	25	2 25
33	St. John	24 00	226 20	879 10	42 50		33 30
34	Americus	42 00	238 20	1,073 80	54 00	,	29 60
35	Sheil	3 00	65 50	302 80	16 50		
37	Friendship						
38	*St. Joseph	1 00	132 75	690 80	32 25	25	
39	Benedict	3 00	52 55	376 60	45 75	25	
41	Star of the Sea	1 00	80 50	440 30	22 50		36 50
43	St. Mary	3 00	40 65	354 10	17 25		
44	St. Bernard			650 50	39 00		73 31
45	Unity	18 00	120 15	591 30	30 20		72 21
46	St. Augustine		85 50	436 60	21 00	25	32 20
47	St. Anne	62 00	220 50	964 90	57 00		254 03
48	*Sarsfield	76 00	230 75	1,055 50	57 00		295 80
49	Constantine	33 00	238 50	1,180 30	57 75	25	5 95
51	Holy Trinity	120 00	141 95	1,100 70	59 25		227 85
52	Highland	12 00	66 50	315 70	15 75		
53	Emerald	44 00	211 00	957 10	59 25	25	164 02
54	St. James	12 00	160 65	701 25	40 50		
55	Charles River						
57	Carroll	18 00	74 15	530 10	32 25		160 12
58	Prospect		96 50	477 50	18 75		
59	Worcester	42 00	165 75	889 90	51 75		76 65
60	Middlesex	7 00	59 25	1,033 00	57 75		766 25
61	St. Lawrence	36 00	180 25	824 00	47 25		321 50
62	St. Catherine	36 00	148 50	715 40	37 50	25	97 96
63	Shields	27 00	136 70		18 00		214 55
64	Gallagher	10 00	180 40	822 00	44 25		213 61
65	St. Columbkille	13 90	167 65	778 00	40 50		129 25
66	Griffin	30 00	38 00	442 50	24 00		
67	*Canton	5 00	134 75	653 00	34 50		22 00
68	St. Margaret	6 50	75 90	406 10	21 75	25	22 00
69	Stoughton	42 00	98 80	554 10	32 25	25	510 36
70	St. Michael	57 00	103 25	486 10	27 00		6 30
71	Phil. Sheridan	21 00	154 45	957 10	54 00	25	467 35
72	Merrimack	45 00	108 00	423 70	28 50	25	213 80
73	Taunton	339 00	137 45	1,048 80	64 50		435 64
74	Hendricken	61 25	40 50	236 20	20 25		108 09
75	*St. Jarlath	270 00	54 50	523 45	46 50		113 73
76	Quincy	93 00	19 25	61 40			8 00
77	Mystic						
	Total	$2,473 65	10,229 05	53.513 16	$2.507 45	$4 25	$6.157 45

* Error in returns.

FINANCIAL CONDITION OF COURTS.

No. of Court.	NAME OF COURT.	Paid Endowment Calls 1889.	Paid H. C. Per Cap. 1889.	Paid for Rent 1889	Paid for Salaries of Officers 1889.	Paid for Medical Ex. 1889.	Paid H. C. P. 1889.	Paid for Sick Benefits 1889.	Paid Court Physician for Attendance on Members 1889.	Paid for Other Expenses 1889.
1	Cathedral........	$2044 00	$98 25	$77 75	$82 75	$7 00	$1 00	$79 75	$199 50	$66 10
3	Fenwick.........	982 90	51 00	26 00	49 00	3 50	50			23 45
4	St. Francis.....	1303 00	81 00	110 50	68 00	7 00	1 00		140 25	151 59
5	Leo.............	1583 60	77 25	65 00	36 00	10 50	1 50	105 00	109 00	37 82
6	Cheverus........	1321 20	63 00	65 00	55 80	3 50	50			31 55
7	St. Patrick......	733 70	36 75	56 25	65 00	10 50	1 50	20 00	71 50	25 09
8	*Sherwood.......	1833 40	109 50	100 50	75 00	22 75	3 25		142 75	119 28
9	Columbus.......	499 40	26 25	44 50	27 00					19 40
10	*Iona...........	1330 90	63 00	48 00	40 00	89 50	7 75	10 00	84 35	54 24
11	St. Joseph......	1877 70	101 25	84 00	60 13	5 25	1 25		169 75	93 17
12	*Fulton..	441 50	21 00	40 50	15 00	1 75	25	2 00	29 50	75
13	Fitzpatrick.....	821 40	40 50	32 50	41 00				26 75	61 10
14	Lafayette.......	950 70	54 00	36 00		33 25	4 75		77 00	57 16
15	SS. Peter & Paul	977 70	48 75	57 00	30 00	14 00	2 00			72 24
16	Essex...........	1224 00	76 50	143 00		21 00	1 00			208 56
17	Hamilton.......	1134 10	48 75	60 00	57 75	7 00	1 00		60 00	27 20
18	St. Peter........	1025 00	51 00	71 00	15 00			19 40	68 50	65 22
19	Williams........	922 90	53 25	71 00	21 00	15 75	2 25	75 00	75 75	139 89
20	Mt. Pleasant....	1136 10	60 00	83 50	55 00	33 25	6 50		79 00	206 21
21	St. Alphonsus...	760 60	36 00	69 00	59 35	12 25	1 75			91 74
23	St. John........	466 90	21 00	30 00		35 00	5 00		39 50	30 01
24	St. Gregory.....	799 10	45 00	63 00		40 25	5 75		56 00	98 16
25	St. Francis......	1430 20	73 50	100 00		38 50	5 25		88 00	89 73
26	*St. Raphael.....	609 40	30 75	25 00					36 00	18 45
28	Erin.	1264 80	55 50	72 00	36 00				74 25	19 85
29	St. Thomas......	1360 90	75 00	72 00	12 66	71 75	10 25	94 14	107 00	164 85
30	Bass River......	490 35	26 25	26 00		12 25	1 75		34 42	28 53
32	Qualey.........	522 00	26 25	26 50	23 80	10 50	2 50		43 45	19 63
33	St. John........	847 80	43 25	40 00	244 00	14 00	2 00	70 00	55 00	44 00
34	Americus	1158 40	54 00	95 25	2 875	24 50	3 50	24 00	59 50	63 55
35	Sheil	324 70	18 00	24 00		1 75	25			5 15
37	Friendship......									
38	*St. Joseph......	741 10	32 25	54 00				7 80	63 00	11 90
39	Benedict	376 60	45 75	25 00		1 75		25		6 35
41	Star of the Sea..	474 50	22 50	30 50						15 40
43	St. Mary.......	354 10	17 25	22 90		2 00				8 70
44	St. Bernard.....	662 70	39 00	65 00	15 00				39 00	15 12
45	Unity....	608 10	30 00	35 00					31 79
46	St. Augustine...	436 60	21 00	50 50					16 75	15 20
47	St. Anne	950 50	57 00	50 00	5 00	40 25	6 50	147 50	184 00	120 81
48	*Sarsfield	1154 50	57 00	190 40	4 50	43 75	6 25		154 50	88 92
49	Constantine.....	1187 70	57 75	72 00	31 50	19 25	2 75	10 00		58 44
51	Holy Trinity....	1093 80	60 00	36 00	30 00	70 00	10 00	112 42		89 15
52	Highland.......	325 70	17 25	35 75		8 75	1 25		24 00	3 60
53	Emerald	945 90	59 25	150 00		24 50	3 50		65 00	127 80
54	St. James	830 60	45 75	60 00	31 50					92 17
55	Charles River...									
57	Carroll.........	629 60	32 25	37 50		8 75	1 50			37 80
58	Prospect.......	674 90	29 25							23 00
59	Worcester......	986 80	51 75	62 50	34 70	21 00	3 00	2 70		68 72
60	Middlesex	1103 10	59 25	185 21				5 25		533 11
61	St. Lawrence....	905 40	47 25	39 50	35 20	21 00	3 00		59 90	399 05
62	St. Catharine....	715 40	37 50	54 00		36 75	5 25	16 00	62 10	108 59
63	Shields..........		40 50	89 00		14 00	2 25		31 00	147 70
64	Gallagher.......	888 40	44 25	43 30	100 00	10 50	1 50			186 87
65	St. Columbkille..	778 00	40 50	96 00	33 70	7 00	1 00			204 38
66	Griffin..........	480 00	24 00	30 00		10 50	1 50			4 65
67	*Canton........	611 30	34 50	38 34						65 85
68	St. Margaret....	394 50	21 75	45 00				75	31 00	34 62
69	Stoughton.......	554 10	32 25	112 50		24 50	3 50	2 00	41 50	300 36
70	St. Michael......	499 80	27 00	92 00		33 25	4 75			41 57
71	Phil. Sheridan ..	957 10	54 00	72 00	30 00			31 00		346 74
72	Merrimack......	458 75	28 50	59 00		24 50	4 75			84 73
73	Taunton........	930 60	64 50	33 79		197 75	30 00	216 00	100 50	119 29
74	Hendricken.....	236 20	20 25	7 50				75		156 33
75	*St. Jarlath	523 45	46 50		2 70	157 50	22 50			75 65
76	Quincy.........	62 36		21 00		54 25	7 75		.	45 00
77	Mystic									
	Total...........	54710 25	$2963 00	$3908 99	$1331 79	$1377 75	198 25	849 96	$2798 97	$5803 02

* Error in returns.

FINANCIAL CONDITION OF COURTS.

No. of Court.	NAME OF COURT.	Balance on Hand Dec. 31, 1888.	Total Receipts 1889.	Total Expenditures 1889.	Total Balance on Hand Dec. 31, 1889.	Deficit from Business of 1889.	Balance from Business of 1889.	Endowment Fund on Hand Dec. 31, 1889.	General Fund on Hand Dec. 31, 1889.	Contingent Fund on Hand Dec. 31, 1889.	Special Fund on Hand Dec. 31, 1889.	Court Reserve Fund on Hand Dec. 31, 1889.
1	Central	$9 41	$2,660 33	$2,656 10	$373 64	$9 95	$4 23	$9 75	$253 89		$59 00	$ .50
3	Fenwick	.99 91	1,126 35	1,136 35	89 96		140 76		30 25	$106 90	183 00	4 25
4	St. Francis	353 89	2,003 10	1,862 34	494 65	7 62		63 40	131 25	8 93	41 00	58 00
5	Leo	345 49	2,018 05	2,025 67	337 87	26 90			47 97	123 35		
6	Cheverus	76 83	1,513 65	1,540 55	49 93	70 09				480 92		
7		274 02	90 20	1,020 29	203 93			25 20			40 00	
8		646 74	2,545 21	2,406 43	785 52		138 78	86 10	217 90			
9		40 71	68 13	66 55	42 29	25	1 58	2 90	35 14	10 93		
10	*Iona	12 85	1,836 93	1,727 74	122 04	3 25	109 19		53 21	112 07		
11	St. ?ph	382 13	2,402 85	2,392 50	392 48	4 60	10 35	197 65	42 76			
12	*Fulton	97 04	49 00	52 25					93 89	27 95		
13	?ick	86 55	1,018 65	1,023 25	81 95		116 20		54 00	85 57		
14		112 10	1,329 06	1,212 86	228 30		50 11		142 73	110 87		
15	S. ?er & Paul	155 37	1,251 80	1,201 69	205 48		217 49		94 61		16 44	
16	Essex	86 64	1,891 55	1,674 06	304 13			1 40	304 13		5 43	
17		130 67	1,309 70	1,309 70	44 57			26 20	44 57			
18		293 42	1,227 00	1,315 12	205 30	86 10	110 26		69 35	37 22		
19		316 93	1,557 05	1,46 79	427 19	88 12			32 39			
20	Mt. Pleasant	318 15	1,542 65	1,542 56	201 24	116 91		62 20	06 59			
21	St. Alphonsus	127 90	1,024 85	1,030 69	106 59	5 84	18 99		27 50	67 00	57 44	
23	St. ?nn	8 77	66 40	67 41	27 50		9 79		44 55			
24	St. Gregory	96 96	1,117 05	1,07 26	106 75	37 73		6 90	57 73	46 88		24 00
25	?ncis	162 46	1,787 45	1,85 18	124 73		23 60	69 15	90 96	45 82		75 00
26	?el	313 06	43 20	39 60	336 66	86 49	13 35		57 68	29 75		
28	Erin	75 23	1,535 75	1,522 40	88 58		21 15		87 88			14 00
29	?s	422 84	1,882 06	1,88 55	336 55	41 43		31 30	14 03	31 00	36 60	50
30	?s iter	92 88	40 70	69 55	14 03		65 08	12 85	37 26		28 00	37 17
32		138 51	83 20	64 63	97 08	73 85			10 30			
33		6 77	1,205 13	1,40 05	71 85				52 35			
34		212 82	1,437 60	1,31 45	138 97		22 45		52 27			
35	Sheil	38 32	87 80	33 85	52 27	53 00						1 00
37	?p								1 70			
38	*St. Joseph	114 95	857 05	910 05	61 95				25 35	31 00		
39	Benedict	2 90	478 15	455 70	25 35	18 30			78 80	1 00		
41	*Star of the Sea	99 10	580 80	599 10	80 80							

* Error in returns.

FINANCIAL CONDITION OF COURTS—Contin'ed.

No. of Court.	NAME OF COURT.	Balance on Hand Dec. 31, 1888.	Total Receipts 1889.	Total Expenditures 1889.	Total Balance on Hand Dec. 31, 1889.	Deficit from Business of 1889.	Balance from Business of 1889.	Endowment Fund on Hand Dec. 31, 1889.	General Fund on Hand Dec. 31, 1889.	Contingent Fund on Hand Dec. 31, 1889.	Special Fund on Hand Dec. 31, 1889.	Court Reserve Fund on Hand Dec. 31, 1889.
43	St. Mary	$2 17	$415 00	$404 95	$12 22	$34 01	$10 05		$12 22			
44	St. Bernard	126 10	762 81	796 82	92 09		35 50		92 09			
45	Unity	175 05	831 86	743 89	263 02	17 53	15 23		40 89	$43 45		$19 00
46		67 84	575 55	540 05	103 34			$1 20	128 50	132 63		
47	St. Anne	278 66	1,715 05	1,561 56	261 13		76 36		218 48	69 85	$34 25	55 30
48	*Sarsfield	54 32	1,515 05	1,699 82	69 55	6 35	148 38			7 88	41 77	48 00
49	Gee.	151 20	649 75	1,501 37	227 56					250 91		
51	Holy Trinity	192 08	409 95	416 30	340 46		59 17	32 10	40 58	144 35		
52	Highland	46 93	1,435 62	1,376 45	40 58	45 62			50 51	110 87		80
53	Emerald	113 21	914 14	690 02	172 38							
54	St. James	289 97			144 35				136 98			
55	Eles River		814 62	747 40	248 65	134 40	67 22	20 50	130 87	157 40	50 00	50
57	Carroll	181 43	592 75	727 15	727	5 12			92 00	9 26		
58	Prospect	96 03	1,226 25	1,231 17	308 77		37 33	3 30	68 00		234 38	
59	Ber.	313 89	1,923 25	1,685 92	151 26	101 30	02			4 74		
60	Middlesex	113 93	1,409 00	1,510 30	71 80		72 05			101 41	79 29	
61	St. Lawrence	173 10	1,035 61	1,035 59	234 38				45 65		116 65	
62	St. Catherine	234 36	396 50	324 45	87 94	4 56		39 82	70 06			
63	Shields	15 89	1,270 26	1,160 57	50 39	31 27	99 26	97 20	10 27			
64	Gallag dr	54 59	1,129 30	550 65	250 76	16 15	4 88	11 60	86 09			
65	St. Columbkille	282 03	534 50	749 99	50 09			19 00	70 13			
66	Griffin	66 24	849 25	527 62	342 26		167 05		217 94		118 06	1 00
67	*Canton	243 68	532 50	1,070 71	81 73				6 03	31 00	†125 00	
68	St. Met	76 85	1,237 76	698 37	236 94	18 72	163 31		15 10		‖70 15	
69	Saughton	69 89	679 05	1,490 84	6 03		159 02	145 50	77 22			
70	St. M' Insel	24 75	819 25	660 23	164 16		332 96		97 31			
71	Phil. Sheritan	85	2,025 39	1,692 43	203 22		45 26		45 26	‖74 68		37 00
72	Merrimack	44 20	466 29	421 03	332 96				21 15			
73	Mon		1,028 18	828 30	45 26	8 65						
74	Hendricken		181 65	190 80	199 88							
75	*St. Jarlath											
76	Quincy											
77	Mystic											
	Total	$9,601 66	$883 92	$40 33	$11,252 99	$1,154 83	$2,566 41	$1,395 22	$4,903 48	$2,473 69	$1,336 46	$376 02

*Error in returns.   ‖Sick Benefit.   †Hall Fund held by Chief Ranger.

ENDOWMENT FUND.

Dr.

Assessment Call No. 48	:	. .	. . . . .		$1	00
"	"	" 50	. . . .			90
"	"	" 51	. . . .		28	15
"	"	" 52	. . . .		127	60
"	"	" 53	. . . .		138	40
"	"	" 54	. . . .		‑ 421	90
"	"	" 55	. . . .		2,719	95
"	"	" 56	. . . .		4,243	05
"	"	" 57	. . . .		4,492	95
"	"	" 58	. . . .		4,466	75
"	"	" 59	. . . .		4,580	20
"	"	" 60	. . . .		4,550	75
"	"	" 61	. . . .		4,551	80
"	"	" 62	. . . .		4,620	59
	"	" 63	. . . .		4,715	80
"	"	" 64	. . . .		4,737	59
"	"	" 65	. . . .		4,693	86
"	"	" 66	. . . .		4,626	60
"	"	" 67	. . . .		4,158	75
"	"	" 68	. . . .		3,289	40
"	"	" 69	. . . .		5	20

	$61,171 19
Balance, April, 1889	4,471 10
	$65,642 29

Cr.

H. H. Sullivan,	of Cathedral,	No.	1 . .	$139	00
M. Phelan,	" Fenwick,	"	3 . .	1,000	00
P. H. Curley,	" St. Francis,	"	4 . .	**1**,000	00
John Mullen,	" St. Francis,	"	4 . .	1,000	00
Henry Seits,	" St. Francis,	"	4 . .	1,000	00
James P. Mulvey,	" St. Francis,	"	4 . .	1,000	00
James Fay,	" St. Francis,	"	4 . .	300	00
Coleman O'Melia,	" Leo,	"	5 . .	1,000	00
Thomas Atherton,	" Leo,	"	5 . .	1,000	00
Jere McCarthy,	" Leo,	"	5 . .	1,000	00
F. J. Daly,	" Cheverus,	"	6 . .	1,000	00
James Cavenagh,	" Cheverus,	"	6 . .	1,000	00
R. J. Downey,	" Cheverus,	..	6 . .	400	00
M. D. Sullivan,	" Sherwood,	"	8 . .	1,000	00
John Donohoe,	" Sherwood,	..	8 . .	1,000	00
E. C. Bullard, M. D.,	" Sherwood,	..	8 . .	1,000	00
T. F. McFarland,	" Columbus,	"	9 . .	1,000	00

Cr. — Continued.

Maurice Neville,	of Iona,	No. 10	. .	1,000 00
T. Sheehan,	" Iona,	" 10	. .	1,000 00
J. Cunningham,	" Iona,	" 10	. .	1,000 00
Andrew McKinney,	" Iona,	" 10	. .	1,000 00
J. T. Coleman,	" Iona,	" 10	. .	1,000 00
John McNamara.	" Iona,	" 10	. .	1,000 00
Jere Daly,	" Iona,	" 10	. .	1,000 00
J. H. McDowell,	" St. Joseph,	" 11	. .	1,000 00
J. J. Sheehy,	" St. Joseph,	" 11	. .	1,000 00
John Sheehan,	" St. Joseph,	" 11	. .	1,000 00
Wm. Lynch,	" Fitzpatrick,	" 13	. .	1,000 00
D. O'Connor,	" SS. Peter & Paul,	" 15	. .	1,000 00
P. H. Devine,	" Essex,	" 16	. .	1,000 00
Charles Shortell,	" Essex,	" 16	. .	1,000 00
John J. O'Brien,	" St. Peter,	" 18	. .	1,000 00
E. F. Hallahan,	" St. Peter,	" 18	. .	1,000 00
M. Sheehan,	" St. Peter,	" 18	. .	1,000 00
E. J. Franey,	" Williams,	" 19	. .	1,000 00
J. P. McEnany,	" Williams,	" 19	. .	1,000 00
Eugene Sullivan,	" Williams,	" 19	. .	1,000 00
Thomas L. Silk	" Mt. Pleasant,	" 20	. .	1,000 00
Thomas Downey,	" St. Alphonsus,	" 21	. .	1,000 00
Edward Mellin,	" St. Alphonsus,	" 21	. .	1,000 00
C. J. Lyons,	" St. Gregory,	" 24	. .	1,000 00
Patrick McGee,	" Erin,	" 28	. .	1,000 00
James Dorgan,	" St. Thomas,	" 29	. .	1,000 00
L. Andrews,	" St. Thomas,	" 29	. .	1,000 00
C. Haney,	" Qualey,	" 32	. .	1,000 00
H. J. Duggan,	" Qualey,	" 32	. .	1,000 00
J. F. Carroll,	" St. John,	" 33	. .	1,000 00
T. Driscoll,	" Americus,	" 34	. .	1,000 00
J. J. Cuddihy,	" Americus,	" 34	. .	1,000 00
A. Mahoney,	" Friendship,	" 37	. .	1,000 00
M. Ford,	" St. Joseph,	" 38	. .	1,000 00
Thomas Griffin,	" Benedict,	" 39	. .	1,000 00
P. H. Kerrigan,	" St. Augustine,	" 46	. .	1,000 00
James Wholly,	" Constantine,	" 49	. .	1,000 00
T. F. Kelly,	" Highland,	" 52	. .	1,000 00
T. H. Brennan,	" St. James,	" 54	. .	1,000 00
G. B. Duffy,	" St. Lawrence,	" 61	. .	1,000 00
P. J. Hallisey,	" Shields,	" 63	. .	1,000 00
John Curley,	" St. Columbkille,	" 65	. .	1,000 00
John H. O'Dea,	" Canton,	" 67	. .	1,000 00

$57,839 00

Balance on hand 7,803 29

$65,642 29

GENERAL FUND.

Dr.

Balance, April, 1889	$514 16
Charter to Courts No. 75, 76, 77, 78	180 00
Per Capita, 1888	36 .75
" " 1889	2,957 85
Sale of Postal Cards, Books, &c.	958 67
" Benefit Certificates	57 00

$4,704 43

Cr.

RENT.

G. R. Sneaden:	
Meeting D. H. C. R.	$3 50
Cashman, Keating & Co.:	
Office of High Standing Committee to April, 1890	275 00

$278 50

TRAVELLING EXPENSES.

High Standing Committee:	
Easton to Stoughton	$2 50
H. S. C.	20
To Essex	1 ·60
1,000 Mile Ticket B. & A. R. R. . . .	20 00
H. S. C.	1 00
To North Easton	2 00
H. S. C.	2 75
To Newburyport	80
1,000 Mile Ticket	20 00
To Canton	7 65
To Brighton	2 30
1,000 Mile Ticket O. C. R. R.	20 00
H. C. P. & H. C. R.	2 00
High Chief Ranger	95
H. S. C.	2 70
J. H. Watson, P. H. C. R. . . . ,.	5 00
To Amesbury	4 26
1,000 Mile Ticket B. & M. R. R. . . .	20 00
To Amesbury	19 50

High Standing Committee— *continued.*

H. C. R. and High Medical Examiner	3 30
H. S. C.	2 00
H. S. C.	1 00
H. S. C., Quincy	6 70
To Lawrence	5 05
H. S. C.	4 95
H. S. C., to Lawrence	3 16
H. S. C., to Springfield	9 11
H. S. C., to Beverly	4 85
1,000 Mile Ticket B. & M. R. R.	20 00
H. S. C., New Bedford, Fall River and North Attleboro	8 40
1,000 Mile Ticket O. C. R. R.	20 00
H. S. C. Lawrence, Newburyport and Amesbury	2 03
1,000 Mile Ticket B. & M. R. R.	20 00
1,000 Mile Ticket B. & M. R. R.	20 00
H. S. C., Lawrence, Haverhill, and Newburyport	21
To Lawrence, two trips	16
To Medford	5 88
H. M. E. & V. H. C. R.	4 50
V. H. C. R., to Newburyport	1 00
H. S. C.	4 50
H. S. C.	35
H. S. C., Salem and Peabody	4 05

Deputy High Chief Rangers:

T. F. Sullivan	5 00
"	7 50
"	20 00
A. H. McDonald	7 00
John T. Daly	6 80
Wm. H. Rogers	7 00
"	7 00
Thos. J. Dunn	16 80
P. A. Donovan	2 00
A. M. Lanigan	28 85
"	4 00
James Sherry	4 00
Rudolph Farrenkopf	10 00
John Hayes	5 00
N. Fairclough	4 50
E. F. Chamberlain	4 00
Daniel F. Sullivan	10 00
P. A. Sullivan	21 75
J. F. Carens	2 50
	$173 70

REGALIA.

Frederick Alford:

Regalia, etc.	$21 22	
"	17 00	
"	8 50	
. . . .	4 05	
	$50 80	

SEALS.

S. M. Spencer:

1 Seal	$5 00	
1 "	5 00	
1 "	5 00	
1 " and Rubber Wheel	5 75	
1 "	4 00	
	$24 75	

PRINTING.

Cashman, Keating & Co.:

2,000 Letter heads	$11 00	
200 Circulars	2 00	
200 Notices	2 00	
300 Circulars to Deputies	3 50	
1,000 copies Constitution	107 48	
300 Reports	188 21	
4,500 " of Proceedings of Convention .	271 16	
6,000 Constitutions	203 52	
600 Account Books	371 48	
1,000 Envelopes	3 00	
23 Lots Postal Cards	18 40	
10 " " "	8 00	
13 " " "	10 40	
13 " " "	10 40	
6 " " "	4 80	
39 " " "	31 20	
4 " " "	3 20	
	1,249 75	

Geo. B. Wilcox:

Assessment Calls	$5 50	
" "	4 50	
Assessment Blanks	6 00	$16 00

J. F. McCarthy & Bro.:

Applications and Envelopes	$151 00	

Boston Post Office:

Postal Cards	$585 00	
Stamped Envelopes	151 85	736 85

W. F. & P. B. Dunham:

Assessment Calls	$4 25
D. H. C. R. Badges	1 75
Financial Statements	
Report of Membership	
Roll of Officers	13 00
Roll of Members	4 50
Assessment Call	4 25
" "	3 75
" "	4 25
1,000 Blanks	3 00
1,000 Withdrawal Cards	5 00
Assessment Call	4 25
" "	4 25
200 D. H. C. R. lists	4 75
Assessment Call	4 75
2 Cuts of Seal	2 25
Assessment Call	5 25
300 Medical Examiner Lists	2 50
Assessment Call	7 00
Ballots	1 50
Letter heads	1 52
4,000 Medical Examiner Slips	6 00
Assessment Call	2 75
7,500 Receipts	20 00
Calls for Convention	3 00
400 Credentials	5 00
Assessment Call	4 25
" "	4 25
1,000 Receipts to Sherwood No. 8 . . .	0
Assessment Call	3 2_{0}
Endowment Receipts	3 50
26 Lots Postal Cards	20 80

$156 30

MISCELLANEOUS.

Messenger Service, 23 Times	7 40
Telegram and Telephone Service, 11 times . . .	5 92
1 Gross Pencils	1 20
Expressing	30
" to Amesbury	15
" from Lynn	47
.. . .	15
" to New Bedford	25
" from Lawrence	15

Travelling Bag for H. S. C.	$5 00
Cleaning Office	6 00
Preliminary Expenses in Medford.	5 00

H. W. Upham:

Binding Court Reports	6 00
" Receipt Books	21 20
" Reports	29 12
" Constitutions	52 80

Stone & Forsyth:

Twine	3 55

M. R. Warren:

Stationery	4 00

Samuel Hobbs & Co.:

Stationery	16 27

Boston Regalia Co.:

3 Ballot Boxes	3 70

Cashman, Keating & Co.:

Gas	29 60

R. T. Purcell:

Ballots, Gavels and Batons	20 00
500 Gold Seals	1 88

S. J. M. Gilbride:

Ribbon	5 40
"	10 00
" Pins, etc. for D. H. C. R. Badges .	3 75

Francis Supple:

Wrapping Paper	10 50

Expenses of Meeting of D. H. C. R.	7 00
" " Convention, April 17	14 00

Boston Tavern:

Hall for Convention, Dinners and Suppers, Apr. 17	161 00

Boston Tavern:

Hall for Convention and Expenses . . .	23 65

Boston Tavern:

Hall for Convention	10 00	
	———	$455 41

Salary High Secretary-Treasurer to Feb. 15, 1890	$1,050 00	
Balance on hand	30 91	
	———	$4,704 43

Received for Reserve Fund	$1,979 95
Due from Courts for Books and Cards . . .	469 83

DEPUTY HIGH CHIEF RANGERS.

For Term Ending April, 1891.

DIST-RICT	COURTS	NAME & RESIDENCE OF D. H. C. R.	COURT OF WHICH D. H. C. R. IS A MEMBER.
1	Cathedral, No. 1 St. Joseph, " 11 Quincy, " 76	**A. F. Caldwell,** 317 Broadway, So. Boston.	St. Patrick, No. 7
2	Sherwood, " 8 St. James, " 54	**Geo. A. O'Bryan,** Norwood.	St. Catharine, " 62
3	Leo, " 5 Williams, " 19 Star of the Sea, " 41	**Garrett, H. Keefe,** 63 Palmer St., Roxbury.	Mt. Pleasant, " 20
4	Highland, " 52 St Catherine, " 62 St. John's, " 33	**Henry C. Griffin,** 8 Eaton St., Boston.	St. Joseph, " 11
5	St. Margaret, " 68 Cheverus, " 6 Bass River, " 30	**John Hayes,** Munroe and Market Sts., Lynn.	Lafayette, " 14
6	St. Raphæl, " 26 Lafayette, " 14	**A. M. Lanigan,** 664 Harrison Ave., Boston.	Cathedral,
7	St. Gregory, " 24 Fulton, " 12	**Daniel Shannon,** 98 W. Dedham St.	Erin, " 28
8	Fenwick, " 3 St. Joseph, " 38	**Michael Edmonds,** Roxbury.	Cathedral, " 1
9	St. Francis, " 4 St. Michæl, " 70	**James Cashin,** 52 Nashua St., Boston.	Cheverus,
10	Columbus, " 9 Erin, " 28 St. Francis, " 25	**E. F. Chamberlain,** Mattapan.	St. Peter, " 18.
11	Iona, " 10 Cannon, " 67	**D. F. Sullivan,** 25 Hudson St., Boston.	Sherwood, " 8
12	St. Patrick, " 7 Ss. Peter & Paul " 15	**John E. Heslin,** Arklow St., Roxbury.	St. Francis, " 4
13	Fitzpatrick, " 13 Hamilton, " 17	**N. Fairclough,** 108 Chauncy St., Boston.	Star of the Sea, " 41
14	Constantine, " 49 Americus, " 34	**R. J. Morrissey,** Newton.	Middlesex, " 60
15	St. Peter, " 18 St. John, " 23	**Henry P. Muldoon,** 52 Gates St., South Boston.	St. Patrick, " 7
16	Middlesex, " 60 St. Lawrence, " 61	**Wm. Mackin,** Brighton.	St. Columbkille, " 65
17	Friendship, " 37 Charles River, " 55	**James P. Duffy,** 508 E. Sixth St., South Boston.	St. Michael, " 70
18	Mt. Pleasant, " 20 St. Alphonsus, " 21	**M. E. Conroy,** Watertown.	Charles River, " 55
19	St. Bernard, " 44 Shell, " 35	**Wm. F. Rooney,** Waltham.	Prospect, " 58
20	St. Benedict, " 39 Mystic, " 77	**Wm. A. Flaherty,** Somerville.	St. Benedict, " 39
21	St. Mary, " 43 Prospect, " 58	**P. A. Sullivan,** 19 Wareham St., Boston.	Americus, " 34
22	Qualey, " 32 Carroll, " 57 Holy Trinity, " 51	**Thos. W. O'Rourke,** 108 Boston St., Dorchester.	St. James, " 54

DEPUTY HIGH CHIEF RANGERS— *Continued.*

DIST-RICT	COURTS		NAME & RESIDENCE OF D. H. C. R.	COURT OF WHICH D. H. C. R. IS A MEMBER.	
23	Essex, .	No. 16	**Lawrence J. Watson,** Beverly Farms.	St. Margaret,	No. 68
24	Emerald,	" 53	**F. E. Hines, M. D.** Salem.	Essex,	" 16
25	St. Columbkille, St. Augustine,	" 65 " 46	**J. W. Brown,** 792 Shawmut Ave., Boston.	Americus.	" 34
26	Sarsfield, Griffin,	" 48 " 66	**William H. Rogers,** North Attleborough.	Sarsfield,	" 48
27	Merrimack, St. Jarlath,	" 72 " 75	**James F. Caréns,** Newburyport.	Phil. Sheridan,	" 71
28	Phil. Sheridan, St. Monica,	" 71 " 78	**Richard Dwyer,** Haverhill.	Merrimack,	" 72
29	Stoughton, Hendricken,	" 69 " 74	**Thomas F. Sullivan,** Brockton.	St. Thomas,	" 29
30	St. Thomas,	" 29	**A. H. McDonald,** Stoughton.	Stoughton,	" 69
31	Unity,	" 45	**William Condon,** Bridgewater.	Unity,	" 45
32	Worcester,	" 59	**T. H. Murphy,** Worcester.	Worcester,	" 59
33	Shields,	" 63	**Capt. John J. Leonard,** Springfield.	Gallagher,	" 64
34	Gallagher,	" 64	**J. J. Callanan,** Holyoke.	Shields,	" 63
35	Taunton,	" 73	**Philip Smith, H. V. C. R.** East Boston.	Williams,	" 19
36	St. Anne,	" 47	**John J. Flaherty,** Gloucester.	St. Anne,	" 47
	AT LARGE,		**John H. Watson, P. H. C. R.** Beverly Farms. **Hon. John P. Dore,** Boston. **Thos. Sproules, P. H. V. C. R.** Roxbury. **E. A. Irvine,** North Attleborough. **Geo. F. Brammer,** Taunton.		

MEDICAL EXAMINERS.

For Term Ending April, 1891.

Dist.	Place.	Examiner.	Courts.
1	Boston	Wm. G. McDonald, M. D., 221 Shawmut Av.,	8, 11, 28, 49, 51.
2	Boston	E. T. Galligan, M. D., 88 Warren St., Roxbury,	20, 21, 37, 38, 52.
3	Boston	J. A. Coogan, M. D., 39 Chambers St.	3, 6, 13, 35.
4	Boston	F. T. Mara, M. D., 93 Broadway, S. B.	9, 54.
5	Boston, Dorchester	S. A. Callanan, M. D., Warren St., cor. Warren Place.	1, 12, 18, 24, 34.
6	Boston, Brookline	Joseph P. Murphy, M. D., 1607 Tremont St., Rox., also at Brookline	4, 61.
7	Boston, East Boston	James F. Ferry, M. D., 10 Chelsea St., E. B.	5, 19, 41.
8	South Boston	Wm. H. Devine, M. D., 599 Broadway, S. B.	7, 15, 46, 70
9	Malden	C. D. McCarthy, M. D.	10.
10	Woburn	J. H. Conway, M. D.	32.
11	Lynn	C. A. Ahearne, M. D.	14.
12	Salem, Beverly Farms, Beverly	Francis E. Hines, M. D.	16, 30, 68.
13	Charlestown, E. Camb., Somerville	J. A. Gregg, M. D.	17, 33, 39.
14	Quincy	Jos. M. Sheahan, M. D.	25.
15	West Newton, Waltham	C. J. McCormick, M. D.	44, 58.
16	Jamaica Plain	J. P. Broidrick, M. D.	57.
17	Watertown, Brighton	M. J. Kelley, M. D., Watertown	55, 65.
18	Newton	F. M. O'Donnell, M. D.	60.
19	Hyde Park	John C. Lincoln, M. D.	23.
20	Dedham	A. H. Hodgdon, M. D.	26.
21	Peabody	John Shannahan, M. D.	53.
22	Norwood	L. H. Plympton, M. D.	62.
23	Gloucester	Philip Mooney, M. D.	47.
24	Randolph, Brockton	Benedict Donovan, M. D., Brockton	29, 43.
25	Bridgewater	G. H. Watson, M. D.	45.
26	North Attleborough	T. F. McDonough, M. D.	48.
27	Worcester	H. P. Kelly, M. D.	59.
28	Holyoke	F. P. Donoghue, M. D.	63.
29	Springfield	A. J. Dunne, M. D.	64.

MEDICAL EXAMINERS — *Continued.*

30 Franklin	.	.	.	.	.	J. C. GALLISON, M. D.	. 66.
31 Canton .	.	.	.	.	.	THOS. D. LONERGAN, M. D.	67.
32 Stoughton	.	.	.	.	.	MICHAEL GLENNON, M. D.	69.
33 Newburyport	.	.	.	.	.	J. J. HEALY, M. D.	. 71.
34 Haverhill	.	.	.	.	.	JOHN F. CROSTON, M. D.	. 72.
35 Taunton	.	.	.	.	.	J. B. MURPHY, M. D.	. 73.
36 N. Easton	.	.	.	.	.	T. H. McCARTHY, M. D.	. 74.
37 Amesbury	.	.	.	.	.	J. H. O'TOOLE, M. D.	. 75.
38 Quincy .	.	.	.	.	.	S. M. DONOVAN, M. D.	. 76.
39 Medford	.	.	.	.	.	C. H. WINN, M. D.	. 77.
40 Lawrence	.	.	.	.	.	D. J. O'SULLIVAN, M. D.	. 78.

REPRESENTATIVES.

	Representatives.	Court.	Proxy Representatives.
1	A. M. Lanigan	Cathedral 1	N. M. Williams.
2	Thomas J. Dunn	" 1	Jeremiah Sullivan.
3	M. J. Mahoney	" 1	John M. Singler.
4	Thos. P. Burke	Fenwick.......3	Patrick J. O'Connell.
5	W. E. Shay	St. Francis 4	T. F. Crosby.
6	J. J. O'Brien	" 4	John E. Heslan.
7	John Brant	Leo 5	Daniel Hayes.
8	George F. Lowe	" 5	D. T. McCallion.
9	Owen A. Galvin	Cheverus 6	William T. Rich.
10	James Cashin	" 6	Andrew Golding.
11	Augustus F. Caldwell ...	St. Patrick.........7	Henry P. Muldoon.
12	Dennis A. Flynn	Sherwood 8	R. Farrenkopf.
13	D. F. Sullivan	" 8	M. J. Fitzgerald.
14	Hugh Montague	" 8	C. E. Colbert.
15	James F. Supple	Columbus 9	Wm. H. Bodfish.
16	James B. Buckley	Iona.............10	Thos. Powell.
17	P. H. Desmond	" 10	John M. Neville.
18	Charles F. Dolan	St. Joseph 11	John P. Magee.
19	Daniel A. Cronin	" 11	Edw. Riley.
20	Patrick M. Keating	" 11	Patrick O'Loughlin.
21	Henry F. Scanlan	Fulton 12	Denis Shea.
22	Chas. J. Jordan	Fitzpatrick.........13	John Feeney.
23	Dr. C. A. Ahearne	Lafayette.........14	John Hayes.
24	Gregory Lemasney	" 14	M. B. Mooney.
25	Patrick A. Donovan	SS. Peter & Paul ...15	Edw. J. Leary.
26	Jas. J. Murphy	Essex............16	D. J. O'Brien.
27	M. A. Dodd	" 16	W. J. McGee.
28	L. J. Lyons	Hamilton.........17	P. E. Neagle.
29	E. F. Chamberlain	St. Peter.........18	T. J. Lane.
30	F. S. Maloney	Williams 19	Philip Smith.
31	John J. Gately	Mt. Pleasant......20	Frank J. McGrath.
32	Wm. J. Downing	" 20	G. H. Keefe.
33	Francis A. Mahan	St. Alphonsus......21	Charles Mahan.
34	Charles F. Morrison	St. John.........23	Thomas Murray.
35	Michael Dunican	St. Gregory........24	Stephen A. Meagher.
36	J. C. Pendis	St. Francis 25	
37	John Vogel	" 25	John Cole.
38	Charles H. Riley	St. Raphael........26	John F. Riley.
39	John T. Daly	Erin 28	Jeremiah O'Mara.
40	Daniel Shannon	" 28	C. J. Lynch.
41	John E. Saxton	St. Thomas 29	Daniel Connelly.
42	Thomas F. Sullivan	" 29	Timothy F. Roach.
43	Patrick Guinevan	Bass River........30	D. H. Guinevan.
44	John Bowler	Qualey 32	Thomas D. Hevey.
45	D. J. Donovan	St. John.........33	John S. Kenney.
46	John W. Brown	Americus 34	Jas. J. McLaughlin.
47	Michael Leonard	" 34	P. A. Sullivan.
48	John C. Carson	Sheil............35	J. P. J. Ward
49	J. W. Keenan	Friendship........37	T. H. Duggan.
50	Peter Morris	St. Joseph.........38	John P. Ego.
51	Joseph D. Couch	Benedict.........39	William A. Flaherty.
52	Nicholas Fairclough	Star of the Sea 41	W. R. Fairclough.

REPRESENTATIVES — *Continued.*

	REPRESENTATIVES.	COURT.	No.	PROXY REPRESENTATIVE.
53	M. P. O'Connor	St. Mary	43	Wm. W. Hurley.
54	B. D. Farrell............	St. Bernard	44	Michael Taafe.
55	William Condon	Unity.............	45	Patrick A. Reynolds.
56	Francis M. Hughes	St. Augustine	46	F. M. McCarthy.
57	William F. Moore	St. Anne...........	47	John F. Curran.
58	John J. Flaherty........	"	47	Chas. O'Brien.
59	Thomas Kelly	Sarsfield	48	Patrick Ryan.
60	Edw. A. Irvine	"	48	Wm. H. Rogers,
61	William Daughan	Constantine	49	James A. Berrill.
62	David Leahy	"	49	William T. Maloney.
63	Joseph Tondorf, Jr.......	Holy Trinity	51	Gerhard Kranefuss.
64	Fred Schwaab	"	51	Mark Hasenfuss.
65	H. H. Collins...........	Highland	52	J. J. Corbett.
66	John J. Bartlett	Emerald	53	Jas. B. Carbrey.
67	Thomas F. Lyons	"	53	W. J. McCarthy.
68	Jeremiah G. Fennessey...	St. James	54	Thomas W. O'Rourke.
69	J. A. Burns	Charles River	55	Peter McGrath.
70	E. J. Burke	"	55	M. E. Conroy.
71	J. D. Fallon............	Carroll	57	J. H. Morton.
72	M. J. Boland...........	Prospect..........	58	William F. Rooney.
73	T. H. Murphy	Worcester	59	John B. Ratigan.
74	P. A. Murray	Middlesex	60	J. E. Bristen.
75	P. A. Mulligan	"	60	R. J. Morrisey.
76	F. F. Muldowney	St. Lawrence......	61	Michael Driscoll.
77	John T. Brady..........	St. Catherine......	62	M. E. Hayden.
78	J. J. Callanan..........	Shields	63	F. F. O'Neill.
79	J. J. Leonard	Gallagher.........	64	John J. Toomey.
80	William Mackin	St. Columbkille.....	65	Geo. F. Mitchell.
81	Albert F. Staples	Griffin............	66	Matthew F. Conroy.
82	Patrick F. Brady........	Canton	67	Edw. C. Murphy.
83	Laurence J. Watson.....	St. Margaret......	68	Wm. J. Graham.
84	Archibald H. McDonald.	Stoughton	69	John S. Madden.
85	Jas. P. Duffy...........	St. Michael........	70	T. J. Giblin.
86	James F. Carens........	Phil Sheridan	71	J. W. Buckley.
87	R. Dwyer...............	Merrimack	72	D. S. Maguire.
88	G. F. Brammer.........	Taunton	73	B. Morris.
89		"	73	
90	Daniel F. Buckley	Hendricken	74	Francis Jackson, Sr.
91	T. F. Lynes	St. Jarlath........	75	Jas. W. Higgins.
92	Dr. J. H. O'Toole	"	75	Jno. E. McGrath.
93	John H. Dinegan	Quincy	76	Jno. Neagle.
94	John Crowley	Mystic	77	Jno. W. Lynch.
95	John F. McQueeny......	St. Monica	76	Maurice Dwyer.

57

DIRECTORY.

NAMES OF COURTS, TIME AND PLACE OF MEETING, OFFICERS AND THEIR ADDRESSES.

NO. AND COURT NAME.		OFFICERS.	ADDRESS.	
1. Cathedral, Boston. Instituted Sept. 3, 1879. Meets 1st and 3d Wednesday, Greystone Hall, 1125 Washington St., Boston.	C. R. R. S. F. S. T.	C. H. Tighe, W. P. Walsh, John W. Sweeney, Michael Edmonds,	26 W. Dedham St., 84 E. Brookline St., 92 Mercer St., 7 Elmwood Pl.,	Boston " So. Boston Roxbury
3. Fenwick, Boston. Inst. Nov. 14, 1879. Meets 1st and 3d Wednesday, Tremont Hall, 1435 Tremont St., Boston.	C. R. R. S. F. S. T.	Thos. P. Burke, Jeremiah J. Crane, John Keenan, John J. Irving,	27 Beacon St., 9 N. Bennett St., Rear, 7 N. Hanover Ct., 193 Salem St., Rear,	Chelsea Boston " "
4. St. Francis, Roxbury. Inst. Dec. 18, 1879. Meets 1st and 3d Wednesday, Tremont Hall, Tremont St., Roxbury.	C. R. R. S. F. S. T.	Thos. J. Finneran, Thos. F. Crosby, John M. Lehan, J. J. O'Brien,	780 Parker St., 44 Bickford St., 106 Conant St., 4 Vernon Pl.,	Roxbury " " "
5. Leo, E. Boston. Inst. Jan. 16, 1880. Meets 2d and 4th Wednesday, Knights of Honor Hall, 144 Meridian St., East Boston.	C. R. R. S. F. S. T.	George F. Lowe, John W. Heenan, James H. Donovan, Michael Killilea,	271 Sumner St., 142 Arlington St., 202 Paris St., 163 Webster St.,	E. Boston Chelsea E. Boston "
6. Cheverus, Boston. Inst. Feb. 11, 1880. Meets 1st and 3d Monday, Foresters' Hall, 9 Elm St.	C. R. R. S. F. S. T.	James W. Maguire, James Casbin, James O. Kane. Edward O'Hara,	143 Cabot St., 52 Nashua St., 90 Bunker Hill St., 59 Chestnut St.,	Roxbury Boston Charlestown "
7. St. Patrick, So. Boston. Inst. Feb. 16, 1880. Meets 2d and 4th Monday, Crystal Wave Hall, 376 Broadway.	C. R. R. S. F. S. T.	Joseph F. Carroll, J. H. Pentoney, J. J. Mahoney, James Cahill,	263 Fifth St., 225 E St., 47 Gates St., 317 Silver St.,	So. Boston " " "
8. Sherwood, Boston. Inst. March 4, 1890. Meets 2d and 4th Tuesday, Eagle Hall, 616 Washington St.	C. R. R. S. F. S. T.	Rudolph Farrenkopf, John J. McDonald, A. J. Lill, Thomas J. Lane,	108 Kneeland St., 14 Knapp St., 3 Champney Pl., 121 Centre St.,	Boston " " Roxbury
9. Columbus No. 9. Meets 2d and 4th Monday, Carroll Hall, 375 Harrison Ave.	C. R. R. S. F. S. T.	James F. Fleming, Wm. H. Murphy, M. T. Gleason, M. T. Milliken,	Prentiss Pl., 62 Allen St., 53 Harvard St., 282 E St.,	Roxbury Boston " So. Boston
10. Iona, Malden. Inst. March 15, 1880. Meets 1st and 3d Thursday, Deliberative Hall, Pleasant St., Malden.	C. R. R. S. F. S. T.	Paul J. McMahon, Dennis Kelliher, M. A. Divver, David M. Cosgrove,	14 Main St., 1 Willow Ct., 192 Kneeland St., 91 West St.,	Malden " Boston Malden
11. St. Joseph, Boston. Inst. March 22, 1880. Meets 2d and 4th Wednesday, Y. M. L. Hall, 60½ Leverett St.	C. R. R. S. F. S. T.	Henry Griffin, John P. McGee, Chas. W. Mullen, Daniel Carney,	8 Eaton St., 19 Parkman St., 17 Parkman St., 5 Revere St. Pl.,	Boston " " "
12. Fulton, Boston. Inst. March 18, 1880. Meets 2d and 4th Saturday, Carroll Hall, 375 Harrison Avenue, Boston.	C. R. R. S. F. S. T.	James Finnegan, Michael O'Brien, Henry F. Scanlan, Daniel O'Brien,	36 Hanson St., 108 E. Canton St., 117 Union Park St., 14 Village St.,	Boston " " "
13. Fitzpatrick, Boston. Inst. May 5, 1880. Meets 2d and 4th Tuesday, 9 Elm St.	C. R. R. S. F. S. T.	John M. Jordan, Patrick F. Reynolds, Frank J. McFarland, Antonio Thompson,	North Hanover Ct., 14 N. Bennett St., 425 Hanover St., 5 Vernon Pl.,	Boston " " "
14. Lafayette, Lynn. Inst. June 8, 1880. Meets 1st and 3d Wednesday, Emmett Hall, 65 Munroe St.	C. R. R. S. F. S. T.	James O'Neal, Geo. E. Monroe, G. A. Lemasny, Timothy Donovan,	102 Jefferson St., 149 Broad St., 37 Robinson St., 105 Adams St.,	Lynn " " "

No. and Court Name.		Officers.	Address.
15. SS. Peter & Paul, So. Boston. Inst. June 25, 1880. Meets 1st and 3d Friday, Crystal Wave Hall, 376 Broadway.	C. R. R. S. F. S. T.	John S. Concannon, John A. Francis, John B. White, Thomas Sullivan,	697 Huntington Ave., Bosto 134 C St., So. Bosto 83 Baxter St., " 13 Mercer St., "
16. Essex, Salem. Inst. June 23, 1880. Meets 1st and 3d Wednesday, 199 Essex St.	C. H. R. S. F. S. T.	John J. Hartigan, Michael A. Finnegan, Arthur Hennessey, Dennis F. Hallohan	Sale " 31 Ocean Ave., " 328 Essex St., "
17. Hamilton, Charlestown. Inst. July 8, 1880. Meets 2d and 4th Friday, 162 Main St.	. R. . S. C S. R.	John Hurley, Patrick Quinlan, S. J. Cochrane, Jas. Crowley,	28 Mt. Vernon St., Charlestow 8 First St., " 22 Soley St., " 70 Ferrin St., "
18. St. Peter, Dorchester. Inst. July 22, 1880. Meets 1st and 3d Thursday, Blake's Hall, Field's Corner.	C. R. R. S. F. S. T.	John J. Curran, Edward F. Shields, Patrick Reddington, Thos. J. Lane,	Davidson Pl., Dorcheste 196 Bowdoin St., " Highland St., " 59 Richfield St., "
19. Williams, E. Boston. Inst. Sept. 16, 1880. Meets 1st and 3d Monday, O.F. Hall, Maverick Sq.	R. . S. C S R.	James Douglas, M. J. Kelley, D. J. O'Regan, Thomas Arthur,	377 Sumner St., E. Bosto 7 Paris St., " 537 Sumner St., " 72 Marginal St., "
20. Mt. Pleasant, Roxbury. Inst. Oct. 20, 1880. Meets 2d and 4th Monday, 2319 Washington St.	C. R. R. S. F. S. T.	Edward A. Dever, Wm. E. Walsh, John J. Gately, David O'Brien,	120 Eustis St., Roxbur 15½ Taber St., " 5 Clarence St., " 30 Mall St., "
21. St. Alphonsus, Roxbury. Inst. Oct. 13, 1880. Meets 2d and 4th Wednesday, Gurney Hall, Gurney St.	C. R. R. S. F. S. T.	James J. Morgan, Francis A. Mahan, John Killion, Cornelius McCarthy,	Roxbur 85 Longwood Ave., " 8 Oscar St., " 12 Cottage Pl., "
23. St. John, Hyde Park. Inst. Dec. 14, 1880. Meets 2d and 4th Monday, Lyric Hall.	C. R. R. S. F. S. T.	Thos. Mulcahy, John Owen Dunn, Michael Faby, F. S. Sullivan,	West St., Hyde Par 18 Allen St., " 5 Oak St., " 35 Garfield St., "
24. St. Gregory, Milton. Inst. Dec. 20, 1880. Meets 1st Tuesday, Associates' Hall.	C. R. R. S. F. S. T.	Thos. P. Lockney, Michael Dunican, Wm. A. Chamberlain, Patrick Fallon,	Cor. Codman St. and Dor. Ave., Bosto Box 87, E. Milto 121 River St., Mattapa " "
25. St. Francis, W. Quincy. Inst. Dec. 21, 1880. Meets 2d and 4th Tuesday, Old Engine House.	C. R. R. S. F. S. T.	John Vogel, James L. Fennessey, Charles C. Hearn, James Doyle,	W. Quinc " " "
26. St. Raphael, Dedham. Inst. Dec. 31, 1880. Meets 1st and 3d Sunday, Parochial Hall.	C. R. R. S. F. S. T.	John F. Rilley, John F. Barrett, Thos. F. Lawton, P. O'Sullivan,	Dedha " Walnut Hill, " Walnut Hill,
28. Erin, Boston. Inst. Feb. 3, 1881. Meets 2d and 4th Tuesday, 1125 Washington St., Greystone Hall.	C. R. R. S. F. S. T.	Wm. A. Daly, C. J. Lynch, peter D. O'Meally, J. O'Mara,	10 Vinton St., So. Bost 10 Shelburn St., Dorchest 278 D St., So. Bost 93 Pembroke St., Bost
29. St. Thomas, Brockton. Inst. Feb. 17, 1881. Meets 2d and 4th Thursday, Hibernian Hall, E. Elm St.	C. R. R. S. F. S. T.	Fred L. Smith, Thos. J. O'Rourke, John Shea, Chas. Wakeling,	12 Bryant St., Brockt 29 Emmet St., " 68 Eliot St., " 8 Hamilton St., "
30. Bass River, Beverly. Inst. Feb. 24, 1881. Meets 1st Thursday, Bell's Hall, Cabot St.	. . R C S. R.	Wm. J. Brown, P. M. Riordan, Philip Fitzgibbons, Jeremiah Murphy,	Bever " " "
32. Qualey, Woburn. Inst. March 2, 1881. Meets 1st and 3d Wednesday, Hibernian Hall, Main St.	C. R. R. S. F. S. T.	James Dolan, John Maguire, Frank E. Tracey, Wm. O'Brien,	64 Fowle St., Wobu 32 Highland St., " 50 Prospect St., " 20 Church Ave., "

DIRECTORY—Continued.

No. and Court Name.	Officers.		Address.	
33. St. John, E. Cambridge. Inst. March 3, 1881. Meets 1st and 3d Friday, 115½ Cambridge St.	C. R. R. S. F. S. T.	D. J. Donovan, J. S. Kenney, John O'Connell, Jos. J. Kelly,	31 East St., 39 7th St., 143 Gore St., 110 Otis St.,	E. Cambridge " " "
34. Americus, Boston. Inst. March 15, 1881. Meets 1st and 3d Thursday, Greystone Hall, 1125 Washington St.	C. R. R. S. F. S. T.	R. T. Purcell, C. A. Donohue, P. P. Sullivan, Michael McCarthy,	19 Wareham St., 99 E. Dedham St., 13 Waltham St., 52 Stoughton St.,	Boston " " "
35. Sheil, Boston. Inst. March 18, 1881. Meets 1st Friday.	C. R. R. S. F. S. T.	Wm. H. Pierce, C. J. Kelly, Thos. Jacobs, Wm. Connolly,	148 Chambers St., 26 Hull St., 89 Chelsea St. (rear), 5 Fleet St.,	Boston " B. H. D. Boston
37. Friendship, Roxbury. Inst. March 25, 1881. Meets 2d and 4th Tuesday. Old School-House, Weston St.	C. R. R. S. F. S. T.	John W. Riley, Edward N. Lee, W. F. Arkinson, Jeremiah J. Hurley,	28 Berlin St., 3 Reims Pl., 141 Dartmouth St., 957 Tremont St.,	Roxbury " Boston "
38. St. Joseph, Roxbury. Inst. March 29, 1881. Meets 1st and 3d Wednesday, Foresters' Hall, Washington St., near Dudley.	C. R. R. S. F. S. T.	Peter Morris, Wm. B. Reardon, John P. Ego, M. Lennon,	Geneva Ave., Grove Hall, 380 Warren St., 411 " " Grove Hall,	Dor. Roxbury " Dorchester
39. Benedict, Somerville. Inst. March 31, 1881. Meets 1st and 3d Thursday, Temperance Hall, Hawkins St.	C. R. R. S. F. S. T.	Joseph D. Couch, Michael Harrington, Wm. A. Flaherty, Cornelius McGonagle,	42 Bow St., Greenville St., 261 Washington St., Linden St.,	Somerville " " "
41. Star of the East, E. Boston. Inst. Dec. 13, 1881. Meets 2d and 4th Tuesday, Good Templars' Hall, 23 Meridian St.	C. R. R. S. F. S. T.	Wm. R. Fairclough, J. A. Turcotte, Chas. H. Cragin, N. Fairclough,	617 Bennington St., 4 Homer St., 610 Bennington St., 617 " "	E. Boston " " "
43. St. Mary, Randolph. Inst. Sept. 4, 1882. Meets 1st Sunday, Hibernian Hall, North St.	C. R. R. S. F. S. T.	Wm. W. Hurley, R. P. Barrett, John B. Walsh, Patrick Brady,		Randolph " " "
44. St. Bernard, W. Newton. Inst. Sept. 23, 1882. Meets 1st and 3d Monday, Foresters' Hall, Waltham St.	C. R. R. S. F. S. T.	Bernard Farrell, Thos. C. Donovan, John W. Gaw, Martin Nagle,		W. Newton " " "
45. Unity, Bridgewater. Inst. Nov. 12, 1882. Meets 2d and 4th Tuesday, Y. M. Ben. Hall, Centre St.	C. R. R. S. F. S. T.	David Cashon, Michael Cashon, Jas. Devine, Thos. Danther,	Box 42,	Bridgewater " " "
46. St. Augustine, So. Boston. Inst. Nov. 14, 1882. Meets 2d and 4th Thursday, 376 Broadway.	C. R. R. S. F. S. T.	Francis Hughes, Jas. J. Hughes, Chas. H. Doolin, J. F. McNulty,	31 Utica St., 251 Fourth St., 211 W. Third St., 12 Woodward St.,	So. Boston " " "
47. St. Anne's, Gloucester. Inst. Dec. 22, 1882. Meets 1st and 3d Tuesday, G. A. R. Hall, 171 Main St.	C. R. R. S. F. S. T.	John F. Riley, Daniel J. Galvin, Morris F. Foley, Daniel Carroll,	4 Sadler St., 14 Maplewood Ave., 67 Perkins St., 5 Shepherd St.,	Gloucester " " "
48. Sarsfield, No. Attleboro. Inst. March 6, 1883. Meets every Tuesday, cor. East and Elm Sts.	C. R. R. S. F. S. T.	James F. O'Brien, John J. Ford, John P. Zilch, James B. Smith,	Box 360,	N. Attleboro " " "
49. Constantine, Boston. Inst. April 5, 1883. Meets 2d and 4th Thursday, Greystone Hall, 1125 Washington St.	C. R. R. S. F. S. T.	John J. Kilroy, John J. Dolan, M. J. Dunshy, Wm. Daughan,	29 Marcella St., 8 Oxford Pl., 345 Third St., 14 Bennet St.,	Roxbury Boston So. Boston "

51. Holy Trinity, Boston.	C. R.	Frederick Schwaab,	31 Avon Pl.,	Rox
Inst. April 13, 1883.	R. S.	Joseph Fandel,	113 W. Canton St.,	B
Meets 2d Sunday, Casino, 133	F. S.	Leopold Kohler,	15 Whitney St.,	Rox
Shawmut Ave.	T.	Jos. Spang,	31 Warwick St.,	Rox
52. Highland, Roxbury.	C. R.	Mark E. Gallagher,	221 Cabot St., (	Rox
Inst. April 16, 1883.	R. S.	John Scannell,	11 Prentiss St.,	
Meets 2d Monday, Vernon	F. S.	John J. Corbett,	300 Ruggles St.,	
Hall, Tremont St., corner	T.	Thos. O'Flynn,	Cabot cor. Linden Park St.,	
Culvert.				
53. Emerald, Peabody.	C. R.	John J. Sweeney,		Pea
Inst. July 2, 1883.	R. S.	James J. McCann,		
Meets every Wednesday,	F. S.	James B. Carbrey,		
Thomas Hall, Peabody Sq.	T.	Daniel J. Sweeney,		
54. St. James, Boston.	C. R.	Michael J. Collins,	10 G St.,	So. B
Inst. July 2, 1883.	R. S.	Michael J. Noonan,	214 South St.,	B
Meets 1st and 3d Tuesday, Car-	F. S.	J. J. Desmond,	286 Third St.,	So. B
roll Hall, 375 Washington St.	T.	Cornelius Desmond,	466 E. Sixth St.,	"
55. Charles River, Watertown.	C. R.	J. J. Barnes,		Water
Ins. Oct. 8, 1883.	R. S.	J. J. Herlihy,		'
Meets 2d and 4th Monday,	F. S.	M. E. Conroy,		'
Main, cor. Mt. Auburn St.	T.	J. A. Burns,		'
57. Carroll, Jamaica Plain.	C. R.	John H. Laughan,	Walk Hill St.,	Roslii
Inst. June 30, 1885.	R. S.	J. H. Lennon,	3 Hyde Park Ave.	Jamaica
Meets 1st and 3d Monday,	F. S.	J. J. Carty,	Washington St.,	"
Association Hall, Bur-	T.	J. H. Moy,	Child St.,	"
roughs St.				
58. Prospect, Waltham.	C. R.	Patrick F. Hennelly,	32 Cross St.,	Wal
Inst. Aug. 25, 1885.	R. S.	Michael Bergin,	14 Common St.,	.
Meets 1st and 3d Sunday,	F. S.	John E. Burke,	Grant St.,	
A. O. H. Hall, Main St.	T.	Timothy F. Buckley,	41 Moody St.,	
59. Worcester, Worcester.	C. R.	Jas. H. Fitzgerald,	7 Gold St.,	Worc
Inst. Dec. 17, 1885.	R. S.	Mich'el J. Madden,	61 Eastern Ave.,	'
Meets 1st and 3d Thursday,	F. S.	Geo. B. Chandley,	20 Washington St.,	'
I. C. B. S. Hall, 98 Front St.	T.	James Eaton,	22 Ingalls St.,	'
60. Middlesex, Newton.	C. R.	M. J. Joyce,	Green St.,	Ne
Inst. Feb. 19, 1886.	R. S.	Michael Morrisey,	Cross St.,	Water
Meets 2d and 4th Tuesday,	F. S.	P. R. Mullen,	Avon Pl.,	Ne
Forester Hall, Prackett's	T.	P. A. Mulligan,	Adams St.,	
Block.				
61. St. Lawrence, Brookline.	C. R.	Jeremiah T. Crotty,	Morse Ave.,	Broo
Meets 1st and 3d Tuesday,	R. S.	Daniel Frawley,	Chestnut St.,	'
Lyceum Hall, Wash'ton St.	F. S.	Thomas F. McMahon,	Kerrigan Pl.,	'
	T.	Michael O'Day,	Boylston St.,	'
62. St. Catherine, Norwood.	C. R.	John F. Riley,		Nor
Inst. Dec. 21, 1886.	R. S.	R. B. Oldham,		'
Meets 1st and 3d Wednesday,	F. S.	John H. Williams,		'
Casey Hall.	T.	George A. O'Brine,		'
63. Shields, Holyoke.	C. R.	F. F. O'Niell,	441 High St.,	Ho
Inst. Jan. 14, 1887.	R. S.	M. J. Conway,	124 Cabot St.,	'
Meets 2d Sunday & 4th Tues-	F. S.	Odilon Moreau,	571 Bridge St.,	'
day, O'Niell Hall, High St.	T.	M. J. Laporte,	448 High St.,	'
64. Gallagher, Springfield.	C. R.	Patrick J. Murray,	356 Chestnut St.,	Sprin
Inst. April 17, 1887.	R. S.	John T. Lovett,	105 Tenth St.,	"
Meets 2d and 4th Friday, C.	F. S.	John J. Leonard,	City Hall,	"
M. Hall, cor. Main and State	T.	Peter Burke,	308 Chestnut St.,	"
Sts.				
65. St. Columbkille, Brighton.	C. R.	Charles E. Sanderson,	Parsons St.,	Bri
Inst. May 26, 1887.	R. S.	John Comerford,	Eastburn St.,	
Meets 1st and 3d Tuesday,	F. S.	John H. Greenleaf,	Winship St.,	
O. F. Hall, Brighton.	T.	John J. O'Keefe,	" "	

DIRECTORY—Continued.

No. and Court Name.	Officers.		Address.
66. Griffin, Franklin. Inst. Sept. 12, 1887. Meets 1st and 3d Tuesday, Basement of Church.	C. R. R. S. F. S. T.	M. F. Conroy, John F. Cody, Philip Doherty. Jeremiah McCarthy,	Franklin " " "
67. Canton, Canton. Inst. Jan. 26 1888. Meets 2d and 4th Friday. Washington Street Hall.	C. R. R. S. F. S. T.	Patrick F. Brady, Matthew A. Skelton, James E. Grimes, James H. Murphy,	Canton " " "
68. St. Margaret, Beverly Farms. Inst. April 14, 1888. Meets 1st and 3d Wednesday, Marshall's Hall, cor. Hale and West Sts.	C. R. R. S. F. S. T.	Wm. M. Moriarty, Thos. M. Dix, Samuel A. Fogg, Michael J. Riordan,	Hale St., "	Pride's Crossing " Beverly Farms "
69. Stoughton, Stoughton. Inst. June 7, 1888. Meets 1st and 3d Thursday, Foresters' Hall.	C. R. R. S. F. S. T.	Daniel E. Lane, James F. Cotter, P. Henry Burns, W. A. Welsh,	Stoughton " " "
70. St. Michael, So. Boston. Inst. Sept. 14, 1888. Meets 1st and 3d Tuesday, Gray's Hall.	C. R. R. S. F. S. T.	Jas. T. Costello, Robert Dwyer, John J. Barry, Timothy F. Shea,	681 Second St., 187 Bowen St., 144 K St.,	Randolph ,Mass. So. Boston " "
71. Phil Sheridan, Newburyport. Inst. Sept. 18, 1888. Meets 1st and 3d Tuesday, G. A. R. Hall, State St.	C. R. R. S. F. S. T.	Wm. J. Jordan, Albert E. Moylan, Jeremiah Healy, Wm. C. Cuseck,	337 Merrimack St., 33 Olive St., 16 Dove St., 25 Merrimack St.,	Newburyport " " ",
72. Merrimack, Haverhill. Inst. Dec. 20, 1888. Meets 2d and 4th Thursday, Foresters' Hall, 78 Merri- mack St.	C. R. R. S. F. S. T.	Richard Dwyer, Thos. L. Lennox, John J. Murphy, M. P. Fitzgerald,	Blossom St., 6 Bartlett St., 277 River St., 31 Charles St.,	Bradford Haverhill " "
73. Taunton, Taunton. Inst. March 12, 1889. Meets 1st and 3d Monday, G. A. R. Hall.	C. R. R. S. F. S T.	Benjamin Morris, John J. McGinty, P. J. Edgar, James P. Galligan,	38 No. Pleasant St., 77 Broadway, 3 Pearl St., 47 Park St.,	Taunton " " "
74. Hendricken, No. Easton. Inst. March 29, 1889. Meets 1st Monday and 3d Thursday, Foresters' Hall.	C. R. R. S. F. S. T.	A. A. Clarke, Wm. J. Heelan, Dennis Sweeney. James Dermody,	No. Easton " " "
75. St. Jarlath, Amesbury Inst. June 12, 1889. Meets every Wednesday, Pa- rochial Hall.	C. R. R. S. F. S. T.	T. F. Lynes, P. J. Cummings, James Shorten, John Armitage,	School St., " Sparhawk St., Church St.,	Amesbury " " "
76. Quincy, Quincy. Inst. Oct. 24, 1889. Meets 1st and 3d Thursday, Red Men's Hall, Hancock St.	C. R. R. S. F. S. T.	John H. Dinegan, H. A. Talbot, John W. McAnarney, John A. McDonnell,	16 Hancock St., 7 Newcomb Pl., " "	Quincy " " "
77. Mystic, Medford. Inst. Dec. 12, 1889. Meets ——	C. R. R. S. P. S. T.	John Crowley, John J. O'Brien, John A. Gaffey, Peter Dohahoe,	Medford " " "
78. St. Monica, Lawrence. Inst. March 26, 1890. Meets ——	C. R. R. S. F. S. T.	J. F. McQueeny, J. J. Greene, H. McGoldrick, F. J. Murphy,	116 Hancock St., 85 Willow St.,	Lawrence " " "

During the past year new forms of account books were made for the use of the Subordinate Courts. One book is for the use of the Vice Chief Ranger, and that officer is required to keep the financial standing of each member, so that he can tell at any time which members are financial. The Constitution has called for such a book for many years, and many enquiries have been made by Vice Chief Rangers for the book.

The Recording Secretary is to keep one roll of members, and the Financial Secretary the other. The Financial Secretary also has the book for receipts of meetings, and in that book he is expected to keep each meeting separate and distinct. All money received after a meeting closes is to be entered with, and counted in, the receipts of the following meeting. The ledger is also kept by the Financial Secretary, and in it he keeps the individual accounts by posting the various items from the receipts of the meeting book. The book for the Treasurer needs no explanation.

Nearly all the Courts have taken hold of the new books with a will, and if their use develops some imperfections, or demonstrates that improvement can be made, experience will probably show just what is needed; but, at present, the new forms tend to remedy some of the defects of the old.

ASSESSMENT CALLS.

During the year 1889 twelve assessment calls were issued, viz.: 54, 55, 56, 57, 58, 59, 60, 61, 62, 63, 64, and 65. This was considered sufficient at the time; but the epidemic which since visited us was not foreseen and, of course, could not be provided for.

The total deaths in 1889 were fifty-four, and occurred in the following months:

January	 4	July	 5
February	 2	August	 4
March	 3	September	 2
April	 9	October .	 4
May	 5	November	 7
June	 1	December	 8

Thirty in the last six months, and fifteen in the last two months of the year.

We also take pleasure in noting, that although many additions have been made to the Order, our present membership being about 4,450, our average age has remained nearly the same as last year. This is remarkable, and shows that the new blood coming into the Order is young blood, and will keep the organization still in the foremost rank.

During the year one Court became so careless in making payments, that the High Standing Committee felt that something should be done to make the members realize their obligations, and accordingly on March 21, 1890, Highland Court, No. 52, was suspended. This had the desired effect, and payment of arrears immediately followed, and the Court was reinstated March 28, 1890.

Of the officers of the various Subordinate Courts the High Secretary-Treasurer desires to say, that in the main they have endeavored to do their duty, and when occasion required any communication with the head-quarters, it was marked by an uniform spirit of courtesy which was extremely gratifying to your humble servant, and for which he returns his most sincere thanks.

Respectfully submitted,

JAMES F. SUPPLE,
High Secretary-Treasurer

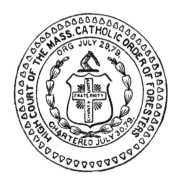

ELEVENTH ANNUAL CONVENTION

OF THE

Massachusetts Catholic Order of Foresters

HELD AT THE

UNIVERSITY HALL, 1371 WASHINGTON STREET, BOSTON,

APRIL 23, 1890.

In compliance with the following call, the representatives of the various Courts assembled at University Hall, Wednesday, April 23, 1890.

MASSACHUSETTS CATHOLIC ORDER OF FORESTERS.

HIGH STANDING COMMITTEE,

(SEAL,)   597 Washington Street,

Boston, April 2, 1890.

To the Officers and Members of the Massachusetts Catholic Order of Foresters:

BROTHERS,— In accordance with the powers vested in the High Standing Committee of the Massachusetts Catholic Order of Foresters (under Art. IV., Constitution of High Court, Page 11), a call is hereby issued for the assembling of the Representatives of the Subordinate Courts of the Massachusetts Catholic Order of Foresters in annual session of the High Court of the Order, to be held at University Hall, No. 1371 Washington Street, Boston, to be opened in regular form at 9.30 o'clock A. M., on Wednesday the twenty-third day of April, A. D. 1890, as provided for in the High Court Constitution.

The basis of Representation shall be as laid down in Art. II., Sect. 3, Constitution of High Court, page 8.

Forms of Credential to the Annual Session of the High Court accompany this Call, one to be retained and held by the Representative for use at the Convention. If the Credential be transferred for cause, this should be stated on the back of Credential under the endorsements of Chief Ranger and Recording Secretary of the Court.

By order of the High Standing Committee,

JEREMIAH G. FENNESSEY,   JAMES F. SUPPLE,

High Chief Ranger.   *High Secretary-Treasurer.*

The hour having arrived, High Chief Ranger, Jeremiah G. Fennessey, called the Convention to order.

High Senior Conductor, Edward Riley, reported following officers absent: High Junior Conductor Murray, High Inside Sentinel Dunn, and High Outside Sentinel Farrenkopf.

High Chief Ranger Fennessey appointed,

Bro. J. C. Pendis, of No. 25, to act as Junior Conductor.

Bro. L. J. Watson, of No. 68, to act as Inside Sentinel.

Bro. E. F. Chamberlain, No. 18, to act as Outside Sentinel.

High Chief Ranger Fennessey then opened the convention in due form and appointed the following

COMMITTEE ON CREDENTIALS:

Bros.	J. J. Leonard	of Gallagher	No.	64
	J. P. Duffy	" St. Michael	"	70
	T. F. Lynes	" St. Ja:lath	"	75
	J. Dinegan	" Quincy	"	76
	P. A. Mulligan	" Middlesex	"	60
	J. Crowley	" Mystic	"	77
	J. F. McQueeny	" St. Monica	"	78

Pending report of the Committee, High Chief Ranger Fennessey declared a recess.

At 11.50 High Chief Ranger Fennessey called the Convention to order, and announced as first business the report of Committee on Credentials.

Bro. Leonard, chairman of Committee on Credentials, reported following present and credentials all right:

Cathedral, No. 1	A. M. Lanigan.
" "	Thos. J. Dunn.
" "	M. J. Mahoney.
Fenwick, No. 3	Thos. P. Burke.
St. Francis, No. 4	W. E. Shay.
Leo, No. 5	Geo. F. Lowe.
Cheverus, No. 6	Andrew Golding.
St. Patrick's, No. 7	A. F. Caldwell.
Sherwood, No. 8	R. Farrenkopf.
" "	D. F. Sullivan.
" "	Hugh Montague.
" "	M. J. Fitzgerald.
Columbus, No. 9	James F. Supple.
Iona, No. 10	James B. Buckley.
" "	P. H. Desmond.

St. Joseph, No. 11	. . .	Chas. F. Dolan.
" "	. . .	Daniel A. Cronin.
" "	. . .	P. M. Keating.
" "	. . .	Edw. Riley.
Fulton, No. 12	. . .	H. F. Scanlan.
Fitzpatrick, No. 13	. . .	Chas. J. Jordan.
Lafayette, No. 14	. . .	Dr. C. A. Ahearne.
" "	. . .	John Hayes.
Essex, No. 16	. . . .	James J. Murphy.
" "	. . . .	M. A. Dodd.
Hamilton, No. 17	. . .	L. J. Lyons.
St. Peter, No. 18	. . .	E. F. Chamberlain.
Williams, No. 19	. . .	F. S. Maloney.
Mt. Pleasant, No. 20 .	. .	J. J. Gately.
" "	. . .	F. J. McGrath.
St. John, No. 23	. . .	Chas. F. Morrison.
St. Gregory, No. 24	. . .	M. Dunican.
St. Francis, No. 25	. . .	J. C. Pendis.
" "	. . .	John Vogle.
Erin, No. 28	. . .	John T. Daly.
" "	. . .	Daniel Shannon.
St. Thomas, No. 29	. . .	John E. Saxton.
" "	. . .	T. F. Sullivan.
Bass River, No. 30	. . .	P. Guinevan.
Qualey, No. 32	. . .	John Bowler.
Americus, No. 34	. . .	John W. Brown.
" "	. . .	M. Leonard.
Sheil, No. 35	. . .	John C. Carson.
Friendship, No. 37	. . .	J. W. Keenan.
" "	. . .	T. H. Duggan.
Benedict, No. 39	. . .	J. D. Couch.
Star of the Sea, No. 41	. .	N. Fairclough.
St. Bernard, No. 44	. . .	B. O'Farrell.
Unity, No. 45	. . .	Wm. Condon.
St. Augustine, No. 46 .	. .	F. M. Hughes.
" "	. . .	F. McCarty.
Sarsfield, No. 48	. . .	E. A. Irvine.
" "	. . .	Wm. H. Rogers.
Holy Trinity, No. 51 .	. .	Jos. Tondorf, Jr.
" "	. . .	Fred Schwaab.
Emerald, No. 53	. . .	Jas. B. Carbrey.
" "	. . .	Thos. F. Lyons.
St. James, No. 54	. . .	J. G. Fennessey.
Charles River, No. 55 .	. .	J. A. Burns.
" "	. . .	E. J. Burke.
Carroll, No. 57	. . .	J. H. Morton.
Worcester, No. 59	. . .	T. H. Murphy.
Middlesex, No. 60	. . .	P. A. Murray.

Middlesex, No. 60,	. . .	P. A. Mulligan.
St. Lawrence, No. 61 .	. .	Michael Driscoll.
St. Catharine, No. 62 .	. .	M. E. Hayden.
Shields, No. 63	. . .	J. J. Callanan.
Gallagher, No. 64	. . .	J. J. Leonard.
St. Columbkille, No. 65	. .	Wm. Mackin.
Canton, No. 67	. . .	P. F. Brady.
St. Margaret, No. 68 .	. .	L. J. Watson.
" "	. . .	Wm. J. Graham.
Stoughton, No. 69	. . .	A. H. McDonald.
" "	. . .	John S. Madden.
St. Michael, No. 70 .	. .	Jas. P Duffy.
Phil Sheridan, No. 71	. .	Jas. F. Carens.
Merrimack, No. 72	. . .	R. Dwyer.
Taunton, No. 73	. . .	B. Morris.
St. Jarlath, No. 75	. . .	J. W. Higgins.
Quincy, No. 76	. . .	John H. Dinegan.
Mystic, No. 77	. . .	John W. Lynch.
St. Monica, No. 78	. . .	J. F. McQueeny.

Eighty-two Representatives present, representing fifty-eight Courts.

Voted to accept report of Committee on Credentials.

On motion of Bro. Daly, of Erin No. 28, voted to dispense with reading of roll call.

High Chief Ranger Fennessey announced reading records of last session in order.

Bro. Carson, of Sheil No. 35, moved to dispense with reading records of last session.

Bro. Daly, of Erin No. 28, claimed that the last convention ratified its own acts, adjourned *sine die*, and that this convention had nothing to do with its records.

Bro. Shay, of St. Francis No. 4, asked for a ruling.

High Chief Ranger Fennessey ruled that each Convention is a separate and distinct body; and after the records have been read and approved the business of that Convention is finished, and no subsequent Convention has anything to do with it or its records.

High Chief Ranger Fennessey then announced the next business report of the High Chief Ranger, High Standing Committee, and High Secretary-Treasurer, and then read his address to the Convention.

During the reading of High Chief Ranger Fennessey's address, Rev. Hugh Roe O'Donnell, High Court Chaplain, entered, and was escorted to the platform by High Senior Conductor Riley and High Junior Conductor Murray.

At the conclusion of the address the representatives applauded heartily.

High Chief Ranger Fennessey then introduced Father O'Donnell, who spoke briefly on the Order, and said he just came from burying a member, and stated that the death was occasioned by an accident, and exhorted all to pray that they may not have a sudden and unprovided death, and that it impressed him very much with the necessity of all Catholics joining the order.

That the Order was being perfected, and he was pleased to hear of its success.

That the Church is the only perfect organization because it is the work of God, and all else is the work of man, and necessarily imperfect.

He was proud to be with the Order, and be present at the Convention; but he was here because of his interest in the Order, and not because he looked for any honors in the Order. He then spoke of the proposal to celebrate the Annual Mass for the Order under the auspices of the Knights of St. Rose at his church, and said he would be glad to have the members come to the Star of the Sea Church, and he would do the best he could. He was glad the Mass was celebrated every year, and hoped it would continue.

Concluding, he hoped the Order would increase, and wished the Organization long life and prosperity.

Father O'Donnell's remarks were warmly received, and the representatives evidently appreciated every word.

Bro. Rogers, of Sarsfield No. 48, moved the adoption of report of High Chief Ranger and High Standing Committee and that it be printed.

Voted to adopt and print.

Bro. Shay, of St. Francis No. 4, moved to refer such portion as necessary to a committee of five to report to-day.

Motion was carried, and the following were appointed:

COMMITTEE ON HIGH CHIEF RANGER'S ADDRESS AND REPORT OF HIGH STANDING COMMITTEE.

Bro. W. E. Shay	of St. Francis No.	4
Bro. W. H. Rogers	" Sarsfield "	48
Bro. A. M. Lanigan	" Cathedral "	1
Bro. Dr. C. A. Ahearne	" Lafayette "	14
Bro. J. J. Callanan	" Shields "	63

High Chief Ranger Fennessey then appointed the following Committees:

On Constitution

Bro. Hon. O. A. Galvin . . .	of Cheverus	No. 6
Bro. J. J. Flaherty	" St. Anne	" 47
Bro. P. M. Keating . . .	" St. Joseph	" 11
Bro. J. J. Callanan . . .	" Shields	" 63
Bro. J. Torndorf, Jr. . . .	" Holy Trinity	" 51
Bro. J. F. Carens	" Phil. Sheridan	71
Bro. J. T. Daly	" Erin	28

On Secret Work.

Bro. T. H. Murphy	of Worcester	No. 59
Bro. J. T. Daly	" Erin	" 28
Bro. T. F. Sullivan	" St. Thomas	" 29
Bro. M. Leonard	" Americus	" 34
Bro. M. Dunican	" St. Gregory	" 24
Bro. D. F. Sullivan . . .	" Sherwood	" 8
Bro. G. F. Brammer . . .	" Taunton	" 73

On Petitions.

Bro. C. H. Riley	of St. Raphael	No. 26
Bro. E. A. Irvine	" Sarsfield	" 48
Bro. J. B. Buckley	" Iona	" 10
Bro. J. J. Gately	" Mt. Pleasant	" 20
Bro. A. H. McDonald . . .	" Stoughton	" 69
Bro. T. P. Burke	" Fenwick	" 3
Bro. C. F. Morrison	" St. John	" 23

On Appeals.

Bro. A. F. Caldwell	of St. Patrick	No. 7
Bro. J. T. Brady	" St. Catharine	No. 62
Bro. W. T. Maloney . . .	" Constantine	" 49
Bro. L. J. Watson	" St. Margaret	" 68
Bro. A. M. Lanigan	" Cathedral	" 1
Bro. J. C. Pendis	" St. Francis	" 25
Bro. Dr. C. A. Ahearne . . .	" Lafayette	" 14

On State of the Order.

Bro. W. E. Shay . . .	of St. Francis	No. 4
Bro. W. Mackin . . .	" Columbkille	" 65
Bro. H. F. Scanlan . . .	" Fulton	" 12
Bro. E. F. Chamberlain . .	" St. Peter	" 18
Bro. P. A. Donovan . .	" SS. Peter & Paul	" 15
Bro. T. F. Lyons . . .	" Emerald	" 53
Bro. J. A. Burns . . .	" Charles River	" 55

Bro. Daly, of Erin No. 28, declined service on Committee on Secret Work.

High Chief Ranger Fennessey appointed in Bro. Daly's place Bro. G. F. Lowe, of Leo No. 5.

High Chief Ranger announced reception of petitions, etc., and read amendments to Constitution offered by Bros. J. Tondorf, Jr., of Holy Trinity No. 51, John Vogle, of St. Francis No. 25, P. A. Mulligan, of Middlesex No. 60.

Bro. Daly, of Erin No. 28, objected to reading by High Chief Ranger.

Bro. Callanan, of Shields No. 63, wanted them read.

Bro. Daly, of Erin No. 28, withdrew objection, and High Chief Ranger Fennessey continued to read.

Bro. Pendis, of St. Francis No. 25, moved to refer to Committee on Constitution.

The question was stated by the High Chief Ranger.

Bro. Callanan, of Shields No. 63, took the floor, but High Chief Ranger Fennessey soon rapped him to order and stated that Bro. Callanan must speak to the question.

Bro. Daly, of Erin No. 28, moved that the privilege of the floor be given to Bro. Callanan, of Shields No. 63.

Motion was carried.

Bro. Callanan then said he came here to do business and wanted to hear everything read.

High Chief Ranger Fennessey then explained his position and said he merely wished to follow the example of the last ten years by referring all amendments to Committee on Constitution without debate. His only purpose was to be the servant of the Order and treat all fairly.

High Chief Ranger Fennessey again stated the question.

Bro. Murphy, of Worcester No. 59, hoped they would be read.

Bro. Pendis, of St. Francis No. 25, hoped all would be referred without debate, and there would be time enough for arguing when the report of the Committee came in.

Bro. Rogers, of Sarsfield No. 48, moved the previous question.

Motion was carried and previous question was ordered.

High Chief Ranger Fennessey stated the question and declared it not a vote and the motion to refer without reading was lost.

High Chief Ranger Fennessey read amendments offered by Bro. J. P. Duffy, of St. Michael No. 70. " That this convention take into consideration the advisability of extending the Order in the New England States."

By Bro. T. F. Sullivan, of St. Thomas No. 29, to strike out "Past Chief Rangers, of the Courts in his district," in third line, page 26, and insert "twelve members in good standing, from each Court in his district," also to strike out all of Sect. 2, page 27.

By Bro. J. A. Burns, of Charles River No. 55, strike out on page 47, line four, Sect. 3, "producing a certificate of health from District Medical Examiner," also strike out on page 48, line four, Sect. 4, "and shall pay for such re-examination one dollar," also on page 47, Sect. 2, strike out all after "committee" in line four, and insert "shall be allowed until the next regular meeting to pay his assessment, provided that said meeting occurs within fifteen days from the expiration of the call, and, if not paid in that time, shall, by his failure to pay, stand suspended from the Order, and shall forfeit all claims to the Endowment Fund."

By Bro. J. J. Gately, of Mount Pleasant No. 20, to repeal on page 43, Sect. 4, all after "fund" line six; also add to Sect. 2, page 22, " This fund is for the purpose of making more secure the Endowment of every member in the Order, also for the purpose of offering an additional inducement to others to join the Order, and it shall be allowed to accumulate, but may be drawn upon as provided for in Sect. 1, Art. VIII., for the payment of endowments, where very many deaths occur from accidents, contagious diseases, or other calamities. The laws applicable to the payment of Endowment and Per Capita calls shall apply to Reserve calls.

Offered by Bro. John J. Gately, of Mount Pleasant Court, No. 20.

Resolution. That the Committee on Secret Work consider the feasibility of including, in the initiation ceremony, the obligation of members, as to the promptness of the payments of assessments when calls are issued, and the penalties attached for neglect of same.

Resolution. That the Committee on State of the Order consider as to whether any additional legislation is necessary in order that the High Standing Committee may enforce the constitution as to payments of the endowment by Subordinate Courts.

That the Committee on State of the Order consider the feasibility of having but three officers of Subordinate Courts (viz. Chief Ranger, Recording Secretary and Financial Secretary) sign death certificates, so as to avoid delay in forwarding the same.

By Bro. C. F. Dolan, of St. Joseph No. 11, to insert after the word "of," in line four, page 46, the words "five hundred and."

By Bro. Vogle, of St. Francis No. 25, to change Sect. 2, page 63, so as to read "Any member who shall be guilty of any scandalous conduct, drunkenness, or practices unbecoming a member of this Order, shall, upon conviction thereof, for the first offence, be fined not less than one dollar nor more than five dollars; and for the second, be suspended or expelled as the District Arbitration Court, by its vote, shall determine;" also to strike out all after "cents," in line eight, Sect. 10, page 51, as far as "shall" in line ten, and insert "for the first time, and fifteen cents for the second time, such neglect is provided for but no more than two calls."

By Bro. T. H. Murphy, of Worcester No. 59, add to Art. XIII., page 68, new Sect. No. 5, "all moneys received from entertainments, or from such sources not provided by the Constitution, may be used by the Court for the employment of a doctor or weekly benefit, or both as the Court may so vote."

By Bro. P. A. Mulligan, of Middlesex No. 60, "a Court may assess each member a sum not exceeding one dollar a year for the purpose of creating a fund for the payment of sick benefits, but no member shall receive more than five dollars a week nor more than twenty dollars in any one year from said fund. A member shall be entitled to sick benefits only, when his sickness is such as to prevent him from following his usual occupation, and no member shall receive said benefits except by vote of the Court after an investigation has been made by the Chief Ranger, Recording Secretary and Treasurer."

By Bro. T. P. Burke, of Fenwick No. 3, to strike out in line two, Sect. 1, page 51, the word "twice" and insert the word "once."

By Bro. J. Tondorf, Jr., of Holy Trinity No. 51, to strike out in line two, Sect. 2, page 22, "fifty cents" and insert "one dollar."

High Chief Ranger Fennessey then referred the various matters to the proper Committees.

Bro. Callanan, of Shields No. 63, asked about laws governing Fraternal Organizations and High Chief Ranger Fennessey explained them.

High Chief Ranger Fennessey announced recess for dinner.

Bro. McGrath, of Mt. Pleasant No. 20, moved recess to 2.30.

Bro. Callanan, of Shields No. 63, moved to amend to take a recess till 2 P. M.

High Chief Ranger Fennessey put question on the amendment. Amendment was carried.

High Chief Ranger Fennessey put question on the amended motion.

Motion as amended was carried, and at 12.35 recess was taken until 2 P. M.

High Chief Ranger Fennessey called the Convention to order at 2 P. M.

High Conductors Riley and Murray took up password.

High Chief Ranger Fennessey announced reports of Committees in order.

Bro. Shay, of St. Francis No. 4, for Committee on State of the Order, gave way to Bro. Cronin, of Trustees of Reserve Fund, who said he was gratified to be able to present his report of the condition of the fund.

Bro. Cronin said two of the Trustees had qualified; Bro. O'Boyle not having qualified, and that over $2,000 were now in the Fund.

BOSTON, April 23, 1890.

To the Officers and Brothers of the Massachusetts Catholic Order of Foresters in Meeting assembled.

BROTHERS,— The Trustees respectfully submit their first annual report for your consideration — Art. VIII., Sect. 2, which reads as follows: An assessment of fifty cents shall be levied on all members in good standing, on first day of October in each year. Said assessment to be known as Reserve Fund Assessment, and each new member admitted after said date shall also be assessed fifty cents for said fund.

Amount received to date, $2,056.49.

Respectfully submitted,

JOSEPH TONDORF, JR.,
DANIEL A. CRONIN.

Bro. Cronin spoke at length, and hoped the Fund would be allowed to remain intact until it amounted to a much larger sum.

Bro. Sullivan, of St. Thomas No. 29, moved that names of Courts not paying be not read.

Motion to amend to accept report of Trustees.

Voted to accept and adopt report.

Bro. Shay for Committee on State of the Order, reported on amendment offered by Bro. Duffy, of St. Michael No. 70, not wholly inexpedient, but would recommend such part as expedient as complied with the Constitution.

Bro. Lanigan, of Cathedral No. 1, moved to accept and adopt.

Voted to accept and adopt.

Bro. Shay, for Committee on High Chief Ranger's Address, recommended printing the address, and the payment of the Hanson claim, and the adoption of the decision of High Chief Ranger Fennessey about legitimate expenses.

Voted to accept the report.

High Chief Ranger Fennessey asked the pleasure of the Convention.

Dr. Ahearne, of Lafayette No. 14, moved to pay the Hanson claim.

Seconded by Dr. Couch, of Benedict No. 39.

High Chief Ranger Fennessey put the question.

Voted to pay unanimously.

High Chief Ranger Fennessey then read his decision about legitimate expenses of which the Committee recommended the adoption.

" What are the legitimate expenses of a Court?

This question has been often asked, but I am not aware that any official decision has been rendered in relation to the matter.

The provisions of the Constitution that relate to it, are Sect. 3 and 4, Art. IV., Subordinate Court Constitution, page 43; and Sect. 1 and 2, Art. XIII., Subordinate Court Constitution, page 67.

Article XIII., Sect. 1, provides that " The funds provided for shall be accounted for respectively, as Endowment, General, Per Capita, and Reserve Funds." The Endowment, Reserve, and Per Capita, are funds that must be paid to the High Standing Committee or Trustees, to hold in trust for the purposes provided in the Constitution. These funds are absolutely beyond the control of the Subordinate Courts, except through their representatives in Annual Convention, and then only in accordance with the provisions of the Constitution.

Section 3, of Art. IV., provides that " All revenues (except Endowment and Reserve Fund assessments) received from the initiation of new members and fines shall be placed by the Treasurer of each Court in the General Fund. Section 4, same Article, provides that " each Court shall have power to assess its members at a monthly rate, for the expenses of the Court, said rate shall be decided by a two-thirds' vote of the members present, at a regular meeting. The revenue from this assessment shall be known as a General Fund, and shall not be used for any purpose other than the legitimate expenses of the Court."

In addition to the money specified as above, at times large sums of money are raised by the Courts under the name of the Court, in various ways that I need not mention here. The funds thus raised are in many instances placed in the General Fund because there is no other place to put them, unless they are kept entirely separate from the affairs of the Court, and managed by members of the Court who cannot be amenable to any legislation of the Order, because they are practically members of another society, and yet the money has been raised in the name of, and for a Court of the Massachusetts Catholic Order of Foresters.

If the Article is to be construed as some would have it, money could not be appropriated for the purpose of paying for a carriage for Pall Bearers notwithstanding that the Constitution provides it shall be secured. Members cannot pay for anything except for mere routine work, and then it is safe to assume that some member would object.

Other Courts provide that the Assessments shall be quite large in order that a sick benefit may be paid, and others that a doctor and medicines may be secured for members who may be sick, and yet some have held that this cannot be done. It to me at least seems unreasonable to take this view of it.

I therefore decide that all money raised in the name of the Order shall be the property of the Order. That the Endowment, Reserve, and Per Capita Tax Funds, are for the general purposes of the Order, to be used as defined in the Constitution, that the General Fund of each Court is for the purposes of the Court to be expended by it, for the members of the Court, under the provisions of such By-Laws as may be approved by the High Standing Committee, and that such By-Laws may provide for the payment of ordinary expenses, such as are incurred by societies of a similar nature; that is to say, the payment of sick benefits, the payment of a Court Physician, and for the advancement of the Order, but that the giving away, or donating the funds of the Court, cannot be done.

I also rule that the funds or property of a Court in the event of its dissolution, cannot be used by, or divided amongst, its members, but must be turned over to the representatives of the High Standing Committee for the general purposes of the Order."

Decision was received with applause.

Bro. Callanan, of Shields No. 63, asked if a Court dissolved, would a Contingent Fund revert to the Order.

High Chief Ranger Fennessey answered yes!

Bro. Sullivan, of St. Thomas No. 29, said a member of his Court was sick and the Court paid a nurse to care for him, and asked the opinion of High Chief Ranger Fennessey if it was proper to take the money out of the Court Fund.

High Chief Ranger Fennessey said that an article in the Constitution explained the matter.

Bro. Rogers, of Sarsfield No. 48, commended the decision.

High Chief Ranger Fennessey said it was necessary for every Court to have By-Laws.

Bro. Daly, of Erin No. 28, for Committee on Constitution, reported an amendment offered by Bro. Mulligan inexpedient.

High Chief Ranger Fennessey stated question.

Bro. Mulligan asked to speak on the amendment now.

Bro. Lanigan moved that each be acted on as presented.

Motion was carried.

Bro. Rogers moved to accept report of the Committee.

Bro. Mulligan spoke in favor of the amendment.

Bro. Daly, of Erin No. 28, called attention to the abuses which crept in when the Order had a sick benefit, and the difficulty of preventing them again.

Bro. Sullivan, of St. Thomas No. 29, spoke against the adoption of the sick benefit.

Bro. Rogers, of Sarsfield No. 48, agreed with Bro. Sullivan, and said his Court had a Relief Fund they used for the purpose.

The question was stated by the High Chief Ranger.

Voted to accept and adopt the report.

The Committee reported on amendment offered by Bro. Dolan, of St. Joseph No. 11, and recommended its adoption.

High Chief Ranger stated the question.

Bro. McGrath, of Mt. Pleasant No. 20, spoke against it.

Bro. Callanan, of Shields No. 63, spoke in favor of it.

Bro. Tondorf, of Holy Trinity No. 51, spoke in favor of it.

Bro. Callanan, of Shields No. 63, asked if a man who had five hundred dollars, and wished a thousand dollars, must be examined again.

Bro. Desmond, of Iona No. 10, spoke against.

Dr. Couch asked for an explanation.

Bro. Fairclough, of Star of the Sea No. 41, spoke in favor.

Bro. Carson, of Sheil No. 35, moved previous question.

Bro. Keating, of St. Joseph No. 11, asked privilege of speaking.

Bro. Riley, of St. Joseph No. 11, objected.

High Chief Ranger Fennessey put question on the previous question, and the previous question was not ordered.

Bro. Golding doubted vote, and High Chief Ranger ordered a count, and declared the previous question not ordered.

Bro. Keating, of St. Joseph No. 11, spoke in favor, and explained why the amendment was reported.

Dr. Ahearne, of Lafayette No. 14, spoke against any tinkering of the Constitution.

Bro. Morrison, of St. John No. 23, spoke against.

Bro. Dinegan, of Quincy No. 76, spoke in favor.

Bro. Irvine, of Sarsfield No. 48, spoke against.

Bro. Hayes, of Lafayette No. 14, spoke against the amendment, and said it would look as if the Order was getting poor and not able to pay $1,000.

Bro. Riley, High Senior Conductor, said it was a vital question, and moved referring to next Convention.

Bro. Rogers said referring it would give Courts a chance to discuss.

High Chief Ranger Fennessey stated question.

Bro. Duffy, of St. Michael No. 70, wanted it settled now.

High Chief Ranger Fennessey stated the question on reference to the next Convention.

Bro. Dolan, of St. Joseph No. 11, spoke in favor of the amendment and against reference.

Bro. Guinevan, of Bass River No. 30, spoke against.

Bro. Shay moved previous question.

Voted.

High Chief Ranger Fennessey stated the question.

Voted to refer.

Vote was doubted, and a count showed 47 yes, 26 no; and the High Chief Ranger declared it a vote.

The Committee reported, on amendment offered by Bro. Burke, of Fenwick No. 3, inexpedient.

Vice High Chief Ranger Smith (in the chair) put the question.

Bro. Lowe, of Leo 5' moved to accept and adopt.

Voted to accept and adopt.

Committee reported on amendment offered by Bro. Burns, of Charles River, No 55, inexpedient.

Bro. Sullivan, of St. Thomas No. 29, moved to accept and adopt.

Voted to accept and adopt.

The Committee reported on amendment offered by J. J. Gately, of Mount Pleasant No. 20, inexpedient.

High Chief Ranger Fennessey stated the question.

Bro. Fairclough moved to accept and adopt.

Bro. McGrath, of Mt. Pleasant No. 20, wanted the amendment adopted.

Voted to accept and adopt report.

Committee reported on amendment offered by Bro. Burns, of Charles River No. 55, inexpedient.

Bro. Lanigan moved to accept and adopt.

Voted to accept and adopt.

Committee reported on amendment offered by Bro. Murphy, of Worcester No. 59, inexpedient.

Bro. Murphy asked to withdraw the article.

No objection being made it was withdrawn.

Committee reported on amendment offered by Bro. Sullivan, of St. Thomas No. 29, inexpedient.

Bro. Sullivan, of St. Thomas No. 29, said that was his amendment and he wished to speak on it.

Bro. Callanan, of Shields No. 63, said if a man was tried, he would have a better trial if tried by men not in his Court.

High Chief Ranger Fennessey stated the question.

Voted to accept and adopt report.

The Committee reported on amendment offered by Bro. Gately, of Mount Pleasant No. 20, inexpedient.

High Chief Ranger Fennessey stated the question.

Voted to accept and adopt.

Committee reported on amendment offered by Bro. Gately, of Mount Pleasant No. 20, to amend the present form of death certificate, expedient.

, Voted to accept and adopt.

Committee reported on both amendments offered by Bro. Vogle, of St. Francis No. 25, inexpedient.

High Chief Ranger Fennessey stated the question.

Voted to accept and adopt.

Committee reported on amendment offered by Bro. Tondorf, of Holy Trinity No. 51, inexpedient.

Minority report was offered by Bro. J. Tondorf, Jr.

High Chief Ranger Fennessey stated the question.

Bro. Fairclough moved to accept majority report.

Bro. Tondorf moved to amend to accept the minority report instead of the majority report.

Bro. Callanan, of Shields No. 63, spoke against increasing the assessment for Reserve Fund.

High Senior Conductor Riley spoke on the question, and said we were weak without a Reserve Fund, and said we ought to adopt the minority report.

Dr. Ahearne, of Lafayette No. 14, was always in favor of a Reserve Fund, but would vote against any change now.

Bro. Shay, of St. Francis No. 4, spoke on the question, and said he wanted no sacrifice in order to increase the Reserve Fund, and was against the change.

Bro. Hayes, of Lafayette No. 14, was in favor of increase.

Bro. Callanan, of Shields No. 63, explained some matters referred to by Dr. Ahearne.

Bro. Pendis moved previous question.

Voted.

High Chief Ranger Fennessey stated the question on Bro. Tondorf's amendment and declared it not a vote.

Voted to accept and adopt report of the Committee.

Bro. Daly asked that the Committee on Constitution be discharged.

Bro. Shay, for the Committee on Finance, reported books of High Secretary-Treasurer well kept and in good condition. Also, that eleven Courts did not send blanks filled out, as should be done, and recommended a per capita of seventy-five cents.

Bro. Golding, of Cheverus No. 6, said that he found that the oldest Courts in the Order were the ones most derelict in the matter of forwarding statements.

Bro. Lanigan, of Cathedral No. 1, said if anything was wrong in his Court it would be remedied at the next meeting.

Bro. Pendis moved to accept and adopt the report of the Committee on Finance.

Voted unanimously.

Bro. Rogers, of Sarsfield No. 48, moved to proceed to election of officers.

Bro. Murphy, of Worcester No. 59, raised point of order, that there was another Committtee to report.

Bro. Riley, of St. Raphael No. 26, for the Committee on Secret Work, reported on petition from Sarsfield Court No. 48, to furnish a duplicate application to each member, expedient.

Bro. Irvine, of Sarsfield No. 48, said he was sent by his Court to urge the matter; and said some of the members of No. 48 wanted duplicate applications.

Bro. Fairclough moved to reject the report of Committee.

Bro. Callanan, of Shields No. 63, thought a certificate of some kind should be issued.

High Chief Ranger Fennessey stated the question, viz:

Committee report of, which was in favor of issuing a duplicate application.

Amended to reject report of the Committee.

Bro. Callanan, of Shields No. 63, moved to substitute.

Bro. Duffy, of St. Michael No. 70, was not in favor of a duplicate.

Bro. Rogers, of Sarsfield No. 48, was in favor of a duplicate, because, if the original was lost and there was no duplicate, there would be delay, because of the difficulty of determining who were the heirs.

Bro. Leonard, of Gallagher No. 64, spoke on the question, and said the record book was good.

High Chief Ranger Fennessey stated that the book was only a copy of the original paper, and was of no value unless sworn to.

Bro. Carson, of Sheil No. 35, said the course of the High Standing Committee was the proper one.

Bro. Lowe, of Leo No. 5, was in favor of a duplicate application.

High Chief Ranger Fennessey stated that in 1884 all the applications were returned to the Courts in order to have the members fix the Endowment; since that time efforts were made to get them back, but some are still out. Even to-day nineteen papers were sent in of members initiated in 1880, and he hoped unnecessary obstacles would not be placed in the way.

Bro. Callanan, of Shields No. 63, spoke in favor.

Bro. Hayes, of Lafayette No. 14, moved previous question.

Bro. Leonard, raised point of order, that motion was not in order because not seconded.

High Chief Ranger decided point well taken.

Dr. Ahearne, of Lafayette No. 14, wanted more information.

Bro. Sullivan, of St. Thomas No. 29, said if a certificate was issued payable to a wife, a member might marry again, and then a question would arise.

High Chief Ranger Fennessey said that receipts of payment were the best evidence of membership.

Bro. Rogers, of Sarsfield No. 48, moved to refer to the next convention.

Bro. Callanan, of Shields No. 63, objected to postponement.

Bro. Fairclough moved previous question.

Seconded.

Vote taken and previous question was ordered.

High Chief Ranger Fennessey stated question first on Bro. Callanan's substitute.

Bro. Daly, of Erin No. 28, thought proper way was to act on report of Committee.

High Chief Ranger Fennessey again stated question.

Bro. Golding said the matter was not properly before the Convention.

High Chief Ranger Fennessey decided that the report of the Committee must be acted on.

Bro. Daly moved to accept the report of the Committee.

Bro. Callanan moved to substitute a certificate cf membership instead of application.

Voted to not accept report.

The vote was doubted and a count showed yes, 18; no, 40; and High Chief Ranger declared it was not a vote.

Bro. Callanan moved a substitute, but Bro. Shay raised a point of order, and High Chief Ranger Fennessey ruled point well taken.

Bro. Murphy, of Worcester No. 59, reported for the Committee on Secret Work on resolution offered by Bro. Gately, of Mt. Pleasant No. 20, inexpedient.

Voted to accept and adopt.

Bro. Lanigan, for Committee on Appeals reported no business.

High Chief Ranger Fennessey called for

Unfinished business.

New business.

Bro. Callanan moved that the High Standing Committee issue a certificate with the name of the beneficiary.

Bro. Daly, of Erin No. 28, said the Committee was not discharged, and moved to reconsider the vote rejecting report of Committee on Secret Work.

Bro. Fitzgerald, of Sherwood No. 8, moved to refer to next Convention.

Motion to lay on the table.

Voted to lay on table.

Bro. Rogers, of Sarsfield No. 48, moved to proceed to elect officers.

Voted.

Bro. Lanigan moved that a Committee of three be appointed to distribute, collect, and count votes.

High Chief Ranger Fennessey stated the question.

Voted, and Bro. A. M. Lanigan, of Cathedral No. 1, Bro. J. J. Murphy, of Essex No. 16, and Bro. J. J. Callanan, of Shields No. 63, were appointed on the Committee.

Bro. Shay, of St. Francis No. 4, took the floor and nominated Jeremiah G. Fennessey, for High Chief Ranger.

Vice High Chief Ranger Smith in the chair.

Bro. Leonard, of Gallagher No. 64, and Rogers, of Sarsfield No. 48, seconded the nomination, and moved that the High Secretary-Treasurer cast one ballot for Jeremiah G. Fennessey, for High Chief Ranger.

Past High Chief Ranger John H. Watson also seconded; great applause followed Bro. Watson's remarks.

Vice High Chief Ranger Smith put the question.

Voted that the ballot be cast.

High Secretary-Treasurer Supple cast ballot, and Bro. Lanigan for the Committee reported accordingly, that Jeremiah G. Fennessey was elected, and Vice High Chief Ranger Smith announced the result and declared Jeremiah G. Fennessey elected unanimously to the honorable office of High Chief Ranger of the Massachusetts Catholic Order of Foresters.

Bro. Fennessey then took the chair and addressed the Convention, thanking the Convention for its confidence in him, and hoped the members would give him the same support in the coming year that was given him the past two years.

Bro. Callanan, of Shields No. 63, moved that the High Secretary-Treasurer cast one ballot for Philip Smith for Vice High Chief Ranger.

Seconded by Bros. Dolan, of St. Joseph No. 11, Morris, of Taunton No. 73, Rogers, of Sarsfield No. 48.

High Chief Ranger stated the question.

Voted.

The High Secretary-Treasurer cast the ballot, and Bro. Lanigan reported accordingly, and High Chief Ranger declared Philip Smith elected unanimously.

Bro. Morrison, of St. John No. 23, nominated Bro. Supple for High Secretary-Treasurer, and moved that High Chief Ranger cast one ballot for James F. Supple, for High Secretary-Treasurer.

Bro. Shay seconded.

High Chief Ranger cast ballot.

Bro. Lanigan reported accordingly, and the High Chief Ranger declared James F. Supple elected High Secretary-Treasurer for the coming year.

Bro. Dolan, of St. Joseph No. 11, nominated Bro. Riley for High Senior Conductor, and moved that High Secretary-Treasurer Supple cast one ballot for Edward Riley for High Senior Conductor.

High Secretary-Treasurer cast one ballot for Bro. Riley.

The Committee reported accordingly, and the High Chief Ranger declared Edward Riley elected unanimously.

Bro. Lanigan nominated P. A. Murray for High Junior Conductor, and moved that one ballot be cast by High Secretary-Treasurer Supple for P. A. Murray for High Junior Conductor.

Seconded by Bro. Fairclough, of Star of the Sea No. 41.

Voted that High Secretary-Treasurer cast one ballot for P. A. Murray for High Junior Conductor.

High Secretary-Treasurer Supple cast the ballot. The Committee reported accordingly, and High Chief Ranger declared Bro. P. A. Murray elected.

Bro. Sullivan, of St. Thomas No. 29, nominated Thomas J. Dunn for High Inside Sentinel.

Bro. Dunn declined to serve because of family afflictions.

Bro. Shay sympathized with Bro. Dunn, and thought it was a wise move, and nominated Bro. John T. Daly, of Erin No. 28.

Seconded by Bros. Fitzgerald, of Sherwood No. 8, and Leonard, of Gallagher No. 64, who moved that High Secretary-Treasurer cast one ballot for John T. Daly for High Inside Sentinel.

Bro. Rogers knew Bro. J. T. Daly since 1884, and seconded the nomination.

Voted.

High Secretary-Treasurer cast ballot. The Committee reported accordingly, and the High Chief Ranger declared John T. Daly elected High Inside Sentinel.

Bro. Carson, of Sheil No. 35, nominated Bro. John Hayes for High Outside Sentinel.

Bro. Carens, of Phil Sheridan No. 71, seconded.

Bro. Tondorf nominated Bro. R. Farrenkopf.

Bro. Shay seconded.

Bro. Callanan hoped the name of Bro. Hayes would be withdrawn.

Bro. Carson objected, and would not withdraw.

Bro. Murphy, of Worcester No. 59, seconded the nomination of Bro. Farrenkopf.

Bro. Dolan, of St. Joseph No. 11, moved to proceed to ballot.

Voted.

The Committee distributed ballots, and High Chief Ranger ordered roll of Courts called.

The roll being called and ballots collected, the Committee reported

Whole number of votes cast	67
Necessary for choice	34
Bro. Farrenkopf	48
Bro. Hayes	19

and High Chief Ranger declared Rudolph Farrenkopf elected High Outside Sentinel.

Bro. Hayes moved to make the vote unanimous.

Seconded.

Voted.

Dr. Ahearne nominated Dr. Couch for High Medical Examiner.

High Chief Ranger Fennessey took the floor and seconded the nomination.

Moved that High Secretary-Treasurer cast one ballot for Dr. J. D. Couch for High Medical Examiner.

Voted, and the ballot was cast, and the Committee reported accordingly, and High Chief Ranger declared Joseph D. Couch, M. D., elected High Medical Examiner.

Past High Chief Ranger Watson, in fitting terms, nominated Rev. Hugh Roe O'Donnell for High Court Chaplain.

One ballot was ordered and cast; the Committee reported accordingly, and the High Chief Ranger declared Rev. Hugh Roe O'Donnell unanimously elected High Court Chaplain.

High Chief Ranger nominated J. J. Callanan as Trustee; seconded by Bros. Shay, Riley, and Fitzgerald.

High Chief Ranger stated the question.

Vice High Chief Ranger Smith, in the chair, put question.

Voted, that High Secretary-Treasurer cast one ballot for J. J. Callanan.

The Committee reported that ballot was cast, and High Chief Ranger declared J. J. Callanan elected Trustee of Reserve Fund.

High Chief Ranger announced the election of Committee on Finance.

Bro. Daly moved that High Secretary-Treasurer cast one ballot for

Bros. W. E. Shay	.	.	.	.	of St. Francis No. 4
Hon. J. P. Dore	.	.	.	"	Sherwood " 8
J. J. Lanigan	.	.	.	"	Cathedral " 1
A. Golding	.	.	.	"	Cheverus " 6
W. F. Rooney	.	.	.	"	Prospect " 58

Voted.

Committee reported ballot cast; and High Chief Ranger declared them elected.

High Chief Ranger Fennessey announced recess for supper, at 6.15.

Reassembled at 7 P. M.

High Chief Ranger announced installation of officers, and invited Past High Chief Ranger John H. Watson to act as installing officer.

Past High Chief Ranger Watson then took the chair and requested officers to vacate stations.

Past High Chief Ranger Watson appointed Bro. Shay, of St. Francis No. 4, to act as High Senior Conductor; Bro. Fitzgerald, of Sherwood No. 8, to act as High Junior Conductor; Bro. Rogers, of Sarsfield No. 48, to act as High Inside Sentinel; Bro. Duffy, of St. Michael No. 70, to act as High Outside Sentinel, and then installed the officers, viz.:

High Chief Ranger,
JEREMIAH G. FENNESSEY . . . St. James Court No. 54

High Vice-Chief Ranger,
PHILIP SMITH . . . . . Williams Court No. 19

High Secretary-Treasurer,
JAMES F. SUPPLE . . . . Columbus Court No. 9

High Senior Conductor,
EDWARD RILEY . . . . St. Joseph Court No. 11

High Junior Conductor,
P. A. MURRAY . . . . . Middlesex Court No. 60

High Inside Sentinel,

JOHN T. DALY . . . . . Erin Court No. 28

High Outside Sentinel,

R. FARRENKOPF . . . . . Sherwood Court No. 8

High Medical Examiner,

JOSEPH D. COUCH, M. D. . . . Benedict Court No. 39

High Chaplain.

REV. HUGH ROE O'DONNELL . Star of the Sea Court No. 41

High Chief Ranger Fennessey on taking the chair addressed the Convention briefly, and expressed his gratitude for the honor conferred.

That in the future as in the past, he would do what he could to advance the Order, and he asked the representatives to continue to be zealous in the work for the Order.

High Chief Ranger then asked for names of Past Chief Rangers.

PAST CHIEF RANGERS.

Jeremiah McSweeney	of No. 1
Thomas Finneran	" " 4
John Vogle	" " 25
J. W. Keenan	" " 37
P. F. Brady	" 67
John Brady	" 23
H. Montague	" 8
M. E. Hayden	" 62
J. J. Leonard	" " 64
John O'Callaghan	" " 24
E. A. Irvine	" " 48
A. F. Staples	" 66
J. P. H. Duffy	" 70
T. H. Murphy	" " 59
J. D. Casey	" " 14
J. J. Callanan	" " 63
D. J. Gallagher	" 3
E. J. Burke	" 55
F. M. Hughes	" 46
John Bowler	" " 32
John E. Briston	" " 60
John Dinegan	" " 76
L. J. Watson	" " 68
G. F. Mitchell	" " 65
John E. Saxton	" 29
M. F. Muldowney	" " 61
D. J. Murphy	" 16

John F. Riley	of No. 26
F. S. Maloney	" " 19
F. Schwaab	" " 51
C. H. Riley	" " 26
J. D. Fallon	" " 57
C. J. Fay	" " 11
C. F. Morrison	" " 23

High Chief Ranger Fennessey announced reading of records.

Bro. Callanan, of Shields No. 63, said he hoped the next Convention would be held outside of Boston.

Bro. Murphy, of Worcester No. 59, invited the Convention to meet in Worcester next year.

Bro. Shay, of St. Francis No. 4, said it was in the power of the Convention to name the place.

Vice High-Chief Ranger Smith, in the chair, said the Convention could name the place, unless such action conflicted with the Constitution.

Bro. Mackin moved, as sense of this Convention, that next Convention be held in Worcester.

Past High Chief Ranger Watson said Essex County had done what was not done elsewhere : it had a parade five hundred strong, which gave Essex County prior claim ; and he hoped the Convention would be held in Salem, and so moved.

Bro. Murphy, of Worcester, withdrew his suggestion.

High Chief Ranger Fennessey said that the High Standing Committee came to the conclusion that Boston was the best place.

Bro. Callanan suggested that Salem be the next place.

High Chief Ranger Fennessey stated the question, viz : That it is the sense of this Convention that next Convention be held in Salem.

Voted.

Bro. Duffy, of St. Michael No. 70, said he was instructed to ask decision about Reserve Fund. Men now initiated pay fifty cents ; will they pay next October again ?

High Chief Ranger decided yes.

High Senior Conductor Riley suggested a parade when the Convention met in Salem.

Bro. Shay, of St. Francis No. 4, said the Knights of St. Rose would parade on Decoration Day, this year, in East Boston, and he hoped all would attend the Mass.

Bro. Golding, of Cheverus No. 6, moved to close.

Bro. Daly moved to read records.

Voted.

High Secretary-Treasurer Supple proceeded to read records.

Bro. Daly moved to consider the records read; and moved to approve the records.

Voted to approve the records; and High Chief Ranger Fennessey declared the records read and approved.

Dr. Couch moved a vote of thanks to Thomas J. Dunn, for his long service.

Seconded by Vice High Chief Ranger Philip Smith.

High Chief Ranger stated the question.

Bro. Murphy, of Worcester No. 59, moved standing vote.

Carried.

Vote was taken and was carried unanimously.

High Chief Ranger Fennessey then presented the thanks of the Convention to Bro. Dunn.

Bro. Dunn returned thanks, and said he would not stop work because he was off the High Standing Committee, and would still work to advance the Order.

Bro. Leonard moved vote of thanks to the High Standing Committee.

Voted.

On motion, voted to adjourn *sine die.*

High Chief Ranger Fennessey then closed, in due form, at 8.15 P. M., and declared the Eleventh Annual Convention of the Massachusetts Catholic Order of Foresters closed.

TWELFTH ANNUAL REPORT

OF THE

HIGH SECRETARY-TREASURER

OF THE

Massachusetts Catholic Order of Foresters

To the High Court, April 22, 1891.

WITH

REPORT OF PROCEEDINGS

OF THE

TWELFTH ANNUAL CONVENTION

AND

A List of Medical Examiners and D. H. C. R's, and Meetings and List of Officers.

BOSTON:
THE EASTBURN PRESS,
165 Devonshire Street.

TWELFTH ANNUAL REPORT

OF THE

HIGH SECRETARY-TREASURER

OF THE

Massachusetts Catholic Order of Foresters

To the High Court, April 22, 1891.

WITH

REPORT OF PROCEEDINGS

OF THE

TWELFTH ANNUAL CONVENTION

AND

A List of Medical Examiners and D. H. C. R's, and

Meetings and List of Officers.

BOSTON:

THE EASTBURN PRESS,

165 Devonshire Street.

HIGH COURT OFFICERS

For Term Ending April, 1892.

HIGH CHIEF RANGER,

Hon. Owen A. Galvin . . . Cheverus Court No. 6

HIGH VICE CHIEF RANGER,

J. J. McLaughlin . . . . Americus Court No. 34

HIGH SECRETARY-TREASURER,

James F. Supple . . . . Columbus Court No. 9

HIGH SENIOR CONDUCTOR,

P. A. Murray . . . . . Middlesex Court No. 60

HIGH JUNIOR CONDUCTOR,

John P. Dore . . . . . Sherwood Court No. 8

HIGH INSIDE SENTINEL,

John T. Daly . . . . . . Erin Court No. 28

HIGH OUTSIDE SENTINEL,

John Hayes . . . . . Lafayette Court No. 14

HIGH MEDICAL EXAMINER,

Joseph D. Couch, M. D. . . . Benedict Court No. 39

HIGH CHAPLAIN,

Rev. Hugh Roe O'Donnell . Star of the Sea Court No. 41

ANNUAL REPORT

HIGH STANDING COMMITTEE

FOR THE TERM ENDING APRIL 21, 1891.

Representatives to the Annual Convention of the High Court of the Massachusetts Catholic Order of Foresters.

BROTHERS,—Annually, we come together for advice, consultation and improvement; advice from each other; consultation in order that the advice may become useful; improvement in our laws and methods when necessary. We meet in a new location, not new in incorporation, because it was the second oldest town to be founded in our old Commonwealth, not new in the sisterhood of cities because it also was the second town in the Commonwealth to receive a charter, and we are sure that the spirit of religion that permeated the founders in 1629, the desire for growth that actuated the good citizens in 1836, the slow but steady progress that has governed the City of Witches from the beginning down to the present day, will in some degree tend to make us desire to take all that is beneficial in old Essex's oldest seat and all that we would wish to avoid have well forgotten. We are sure then of a generous share of the hospitality of the new Pilgrims in this ancient town, and we are also assured that no alarms false or otherwise, will place any of us in any danger on account of any opinions about race, religion, witchcraft or free speech—when in order.

We meet to render to the members who sent us here, an account of our stewardship, to report what has been done to advance the interests of the Order, to again pledge anew our devotion and fealty to our cause, to remember our duties and be zealous in doing good.

We also meet to hear good news, in this the largest convention that has yet been held, the first one in which it could be said our society is ready to pay on demand, all legal claims that can be made against it, with sufficient money on hand to meet every claim that may be made. We meet with an increased membership, we meet with a larger number of courts, with abundant faith in the present and future, and with a renewed desire to continue the work commenced twelve years ago.

We meet some of us to lay down the badge of honor, trust and responsibility that was placed in our custody three years ago, and with the hope and prayer that it may be placed in better and nobler hands to be cared for, used and made useful in carrying out the principles of our Order, Fraternity, Unity and True Christian Charity.

MEETINGS OF HIGH STANDING COMMITTEE.

Since the last Convention the High Standing Committee has held forty-seven regular meetings all of which were well attended by the members of the Committee. In addition numerous visits were made to various Courts and the members who attended must feel grateful for the kind welcome with which they were uniformly received.

APPLICATIONS FOR MEMBERSHIP.

Since the last Convention six hundred and eighty-six applications were made for membership in the order, of this number six hundred and thirty were approved and fifty-six were rejected. It is unnecessary here to say any thing in relation to the method of acting on the applications; it is the same as was reported to the convention last year, and yet men will come thoughtlessly perhaps, not only to the rooms of the High Standing Committee, or worse still, to the places of business of the members of the Committee for information, when if they would only read the reports they would save much valuable time and patience.

Members should also remember that it is the desire of the High Standing Committee to make as good a showing for its work as possible, and that it will not needlessly delay action on a paper that comes properly before it.

Members should also understand that when a man is rejected that it is neither right nor wise to try and find out the cause. If the medical examiners reject, the members of the Committee are in honor bound to keep that knowledge to themselves; a man must be protected in his profession else there would be no protection for the Order from the men who would only be pleased to make out of it a graveyard for their bodies and our hopes. The members of the Committee cannot give the information because they are in honor bound to act for the best interests of the entire Order, and if members of the Order knew how they were voting it would be neither beneficial to the Committee or the honest opinions of the members of it. All desire to have. the Order grow, but it must be a healthy growth and a moral one as well, and sometimes a little honest investigation will accomplish much more than a superficial one.

NEW COURTS.

During the year but two new Courts were formed, John Boyle O'Reilly No. 79 of New Bedford and Court Gen. Sherman No. 80 of Plymouth. Attempts have been made in many other localities but with indifferent success. We are reasonably sure of having Courts in Arlington where already fourteen have been examined and Rockland where good men have the proposed Court in charge and will bring it to a successful issue.

SUSPENSIONS.

We have not had occasion to suspend any Court this past year, although in more than one instance it would have saved some trouble and anxiety.

We regret to say that something like 250 members have suspended themselves, either intentionally or through neglect. This could have been avoided if the Court officers had interested themselves in the welfare of the Court and the members at the time of danger. No man should be. compelled to leave ·on account of poverty when caused through no fault of his own, and no leech should be allowed to remain any longer than the time actually required to get rid of him. Have charity toward the needy, and the Committee on the welfare of the members could often assist a needy and yet a worthy member with the right hand without the left hand knowing it.

MORTALITY.

From the date of the last Convention, April 23, of last year, we had 41 deaths, being 14 less than the year previous, and occurring in the following months:

April	. 1	November	. 5
May	. 4	December	. 5
June	. 4	January	. 6
July	. 3	February	. 2
September	. 3	March	. 3
October	. 4	April	. 1
			41

is made.

We find that the deceased brothers became members of the Order during the following years;

1 was initiated in	. . . . .	1879
6 were initiated in	. . . . .	1880
12 were initiated in	. . . . .	1881
6 were initiated in	. . . . .	1883
2 were initiated in	. . . . .	1884
1 was initiated in	. . . . .	1885
2 were initiated in	. . . . .	1886
2 were initiated in	. . . . .	1887
3 were initiated in	. . . . .	1888
5 were initiated in	. . . . .	1889
1 was initiated in	. . . . .	1890

41

These figures show again the remarkable loss due to the early years of the organization, but the death rate is rapidly diminishing and with the percentage of the past year taken as a fair standard during a very trying period, we can feel assured that the normal death rate within the next two years will not be more than eight to the thousand. This of course will lessen the cost to the insured and will make the Massachusetts Catholic Order of Foresters the cheapest in price for the amount paid of any of the honest and well managed fraternal associations.

Endowment Calls.

Since the last Convention eleven (11) calls for the Endowment Fund have been issued, Call No. 81, the last issued, not coming due until May 5th, 1891. This is one below the average and during the coming year less will be issued in all probability than the average for the last three years.

Finance.

The most important question that comes before any convention is that of Finance.

What is our financial condition to-day?

We have paid every death claim that we can pay; we do not mean by this, that all claims are paid, but every claim where proper papers have been presented, and where no legal objection exists as to payment, have been paid.

We have in Treasurer's hands on account of
Endowment Fund, . . .	$10,100.00
General Fund, ...	113.00
Trustees on account of Reserve Fund, .	4,448.50

Total Cash on hand, ...	$14,661.50
Due on Calls expired and not yet paid about, . .	1,000.00
Due by Courts for Supplies, about	400.00

Making a Total of	$16,061.50
From this deduct for all claims pending, one of which will not be paid, ...	6,000.00

Would leave a balance on hand of	$10,061.50

This would leave the Order in a better condition than it has been at any time since its formation.

Call No. 81 has been issued and is due on May 5th, amount about $4,500, and when that is paid, and if no deaths occur until that date, we will have a balance on hand of $14,561.50, with every copper of indebtedness paid and a good surplus that might safely be laid by to meet any emergency that may arise.

Unsettled Claims.

One of the most disagreeable features that any executive board has to contend with and report on is in relation to Unsettled Claims, or to report on claims where papers are not properly made out. We have to report to the Convention the largest number yet reported to any Convention of the Massachusetts Catholic Order of Foresters; they are six in number.

We, have three claims that there is no question about as soon as the proper papers are prepared. Michael McCready of Canton Court, No. 67, was initiated January 26, 1888, died of phthisis October 29, 1890, on his decease it was ascertained that his endowment should be paid to his wife. She died before him. They left a boy and a suit is now pending in the Probate Court of Norfolk County as to who the guardian shall be. When the guardian is appointed the endowment will be immediately paid him.

Frederick McGroary of Griffin Court No. 66, initiated September 12, 1887, killed on N. Y. & N. E. R. R., March 5, 1891, left his endowment payable to his father, James McGroary, residing in Ireland. When the proofs arrive the money will be paid as directed.

Daniel Cronin of Cheverus Court No. 6, was initiated in Lyndon Court originally, January 3, 1881, and transferred to Cheverus Court March 19, 1886, died March 21, 1891, of pericarditis. The endowment was made payable to his wife and children. As soon as the proper papers are ready this money will be paid.

James H. Fox of Constantine Court No. 49, was initiated October 11, 1888, died August 20, 1890, at the House of Industry in the City of Boston. The facts in this case briefly stated are, that Fox was arrested for drunkenness a few days before his death and committed to the House of Industry for that offence, that while there he died and the attending physician gave the cause of death as delirium tremens. The Constitution forbids the payment of the endowment to any man dying of suicide or delirium tremens, and this case is submitted to you for your consideration.

William F. Hastings of St. Anne Court No. 47, was initiated July 2, 1889, and is supposed to have been drowned November 10, 1890. The facts seem to be that he was fishing with two other men, the boat was upset in the surf, and the other men were drowned and the bodies recovered, Hastings has not been. The matter is referred to the Convention for its consideration.

Henry Chambers was initiated in St. Francis Court No. 4, July 8, 1880, and made his endowment payable to his wife, Mary Chambers; he died January 24, 1891, his wife died before him. He made a will by which he left all his property, real and personal, to the Boston Society of Redemptorist Fathers. Under the law governing fraternal organizations Endowment money cannot be devised by will, and it is well settled that the money cannot be paid for this purpose, such has been the decree of the courts in numerous instances.

Membership.

We reported to you last year that we had in the Order a membership of something less than 4,500. To-day we have a membership of about 4,800. While the increase has not been what we would like to have had it, and perhaps not what we expected, yet taking every thing into consideration, the bids made by other societies and organizations good and bad, the inducements held out without any pretense on the part of the parties who made them to keep them, we should indeed be gratified that we have been able to hold our own, and add to our ranks. And while we are discussing this question, it seems proper to enter an earnest protest against the projects of individuals whose only purpose is to get a number of men into schemes of all kinds, for to-day, get their money, pay a fair interest or a large part of the premium collected from a multitude, to a few, in order that the few may speak its praises, irrespective of the impoverishment it may create in many families, and the wild-cat speculation it may engage thousands upon thousands of people in. If such combinations have been formed, and are pursuing practices detrimental to the interests of the artisan, the mechanic and the laborer; if honest toil is to be deprived of its hard earnings, and the money that should go into the home, the provision and grocery stores, be diverted from its proper channel, it is time to invoke legislative action and compel all societies to show that they are able to perform what they promise, or at least make some preparation for the future, to enable them when their schemes mature to have something more than broken promises and prettily printed paper left to the honest but trusting dupe, who parted with his hard earned money.

We believe that all societies doing an insurance business in fact, if not in name, should be under proper supervison, not so much for the purpose of giving them legislative sanction, but for the security and protection they may give the public, who may be deluded into the belief that any thing that bears the imprint of the great seal of some Commonwealth, is a parchment that gives unlimited power to do things that were never intended and that are widely foreign to the purpose for which it was received. It has been said that it is not wise to have legislative interference, because it will be against the poorer societies, and in favor of the great companies. To that we would say, "it is impossible that any principle of law or government, useful to the community, should be established without an advantage to those who have the greatest stake in the country. The same laws which secure property, encourage avarice; and the fences made about honest acquisitions, are the strong-bars which secure the hoards of the miser."

Death Certificates.

Prompt payment will be in the future as well as it has been in the past one of the surest ways to help increase our ranks. Nothing should be done to retard the prompt payment of any claim that should be paid. Take away from the Deputy High Chief Ranger the power of approving the Death Certificate and examining the books after death. It will in many cases advance the payment materially. The Officers of the Court, and the Certificate of the attending physician is all that is required, and more than that is unnecessary.

Reserve Fund.

The Trustees will report to you, the condition of the Reserve Fund; it now amounts to $4,448.50 and at the present rate it will increase at the rate of $2,500.00 a year. Why not make it $1.00, instead of 50 cents? Sooner or later we will be compelled to, and we should not wait for that. It is paid cheerfully, and when the members realize that what they are paying is for the benefit of their families, they will not hesitate to pay, and will continue to do it cheerfully.

Under the present Article in the Constitution, the Trustees are powerless to do anything with this money. They should be given the right to invest, either with the approval of the High Chief Ranger and the High Standing Committee, or the High Chief Ranger and the Corporation Council. Saving Banks will not take more than $1000 in each one, and that must be in the name of only one member. National Banks will not pay interest; good and safe investments will, and there are plenty of them, at all times. Loan the money in Town or City Bonds; good mortgages here at home; not in some Western Quarry or Southern Swamp, and it will earn something. Give these matters your serious consideration, it demands that; there is a necessity for it, and it should receive more than ordinary thought from you.

Knights of St. Rose.

The Second Degree is in a prosperous condition and during the year was incorporated and purchased a building under the name of the Knights of St. Rose. The stock of the Corporation is held and must be held by the members of the Massachusetts Catholic Order of Foresters, and it is within the means of each to be a part owner in the building. The same interest paid by savings banks will be paid by the Corporation and all of the stock should be owned by members of the Order. A large mortgage is now on the building that could easily be taken by the members and without any danger of loss. Far better for the members to invest here than in wildcat speculative bond companies that are sure to soon come to a timely and well merited death, that will leave many mourners after them. The building would also be a safe place for the investment of the Reserve Fund of the Order.

By-Laws.

We would recommend a uniform system of By-Laws in all courts in the Order. Now each court has the right to draft such by-laws as it may see fit and they are then submitted to the High Standing Committee for approval. If they do not conflict with the provisions of the Constitution the Committee must in the minds of many approve them. The Convention should pass uniform rules for the government of all alike and then no fault can be found.

What is good for one court is good for all and the united wisdom of the delegates assembled is much better than the isolated action of subordinate courts. It will also relieve the High Standing Committee from much needless outside work.

Per Capita Tax.

We would recommend that the Per Capita Tax be increased to $1.00. Last year it was 75 cents. This will be necessitated by the changes that will be made if the recommendations of this report are adopted.

New Courts.

The great objection raised by men who are desirous of joining new courts in localities where none now exist is, that it will cost more to come in as a charter member than after the court is formed. This should not be so. It is desirable to have a court connected with every parish, but it is not always possible to get a sufficient number of men to assist in the organization, and have the court when formed out of debt. Either the charter fee should be made lower, or when the court is formed it should be allowed to increase the amount to be paid by the applicants after the charter is granted, at least until the amount of the charter fee is realized. This is not an organization conducted for profit and all should have an opportunity to join it. We believe in cheap insurance, but it must be good, we want all to join who possess the requisite qualifications and with as little cost as possible.

INVESTIGATING COMMITTEE.

We again call the attention of the delegates to the duties of the Investigating Committee. The success of the Order depends in a great measure on the faithful performance of the duty assigned this committee. Every man who seeks admission should be willing to have his antecedents inquired into in the closest manner, not for the purpose of ascertaining evil about him, but with the idea that by his becoming a member it will strengthen the Order as well as benefit him.

The investigation should not apply solely to his physical condition. His employment, whether hazardous or not. His social standing in the community wherein he resides. His habits of life, and whether he is temperate or not, also whether he is a Catholic in fact or in name only. He should be up to the standard in all things, have a healthy and safe occupation, be a temperate man, have a good family history and be a practical Catholic. He should then, after passing the requisite examination, be admitted to membership, and no personal reason should allow a blackball to be cast against him.

Examine thoroughly and fearlessly, keep your counsel and report the facts honestly and then we will have a society that we will indeed be proud of, and that will be an ornament to our country and our religion. You are in duty bound to impress on your court and its members this duty, and it will add to its welfare and prosperity and assist in reducing materially the death-rate of our Order.

REPORTS.

The Constitution provides that each subordinate court shall before the 15th day of February present its report for the previous year. The penalty for not complying is, that any court not so reporting shall not be allowed representation at the Annual Convention. This section has never been enforced, we believe it ought to be.

Unless the reports are presented in due season it will be impossible to give to the Convention a correct statement of the condition of the Order, and the other provisions of the Constitution in relation to printing and distributing the reports cannot be carried out. The Deputy High Chief Ranger should never install the officers of a court until the reports are ready, and then the members will see to it that they will be.

MEDICAL EXAMINATIONS.

The Medical Examiners of the Order have in the main done their duty thoroughly and well. Only one trouble exists, viz.: after examinations are made, the applicant's papers should be forwarded by the Medical Examiner to the High Secretary-Treasurer without delay. This will allay criticism, both on the part of the applicant, who is entitled to know as soon as possible whether he is eligible or not and the officers of the courts, who seem to think that the delay is caused at the headquarters. We would also remind some of the Medical Examiners that they are not to give any information to any person about the examinations, except in the regular way, and never to the applicant or court officers. The examiners are appointed by the High Standing Committee to look after the physical condition of applicants and they should report only to the High Standing Committee and to no one else.

Ritual.

For some time, fault has been found with the Ritual of the Order, many say that it is not as impressive as the occasion warrants and that it does not meet the requirements of the Order. If this is so, and the feeling appears to be universal, a new one should be adopted. Appoint a permanent Committee on Ritual, who shall not revise the old one but write a new one, have this committee confer with the High Court Chaplain, and then the Order will have what it has been asking for for some time, a Ritual that will be simple yet expressive of the purposes of our Order.

Deputy High Chief Rangers.

The Deputy High Chief Rangers have well performed the duties assigned to them by the Constitution. They are the representatives of the High Standing Committee, to look after the discipline and welfare of the Courts.

The duties they have to perform are at times arduous and disagreeable and at a loss of time and money to themselves. They are the eyes and ears of the committee to see and hear, and act for it. They should rigidly adhere to the provisions of the Constitution and all instructions issued by the High Standing Committee. If a disagreeable duty is to be performed it should be done fearlessly and yet in a gentlemanly manner, decisions should never be made except as provided for in the Constitution and when made they should be enforced. The Order is indeed fortunate in having so many men who are willing, without compensation, to give so much of their time to its service. We are sure that it is appreciated by all. The High Standing Committee, in the name of the Order, returns its thanks to the gentlemen who have served the past year.

In Memoriam.

Brother Thomas F. Sullivan of St. Thomas Court No. 29, departed this life March 17, 1891. Brother Sullivan was a member of the Order since September 8, 1881, and as a member of St. Thomas Court did his work well. In the last three years he was Deputy High Chief Ranger of Stoughton, North Easton and Taunton, and performed his duty in a manner unsurpassed by any in the Order.

His time, labor and money were always at the service of the Order, and on his death it met with a severe loss. The sympathy of this Convention will be given to his sorrowing widow and children, and while they mourn for a husband and father, we mourn for a loyal brother, a true Forester, a good friend, and the community an honest man. May his soul rest in peace!

High Secretary-Treasurer.

The office of the High Standing Committee and the High Secretary-Treasurer has been open every working day in the year, and the High Secretary-Treasurer and an assistant have been present.

The work on the books and records has been continued and we hope soon to be able to announce that the end is in view. The time devoted to the work of the Order by the High Secretary-Treasurer has not been appreciated by some of the members, because it has not been seen by them. We who have been in constant and daily communication with him can speak of his unswerving attention to the duties of his office, in season and out. We can appreciate the labor he is doing, and a labor not made lighter by some of the carping critics who have neither the inclination or ability to assist in doing the work, often unnecessary, only for some men who do not perform their duty. Hours of every day and every night have been given to the service of the Order, an assistant is in constant attendance and paid by the High Secretary-Treasurer. We believe the time has come to make the office a permanent one, and give proper compensation for the labor performed. By this we do not mean to say how little it may be done for and then fill it with a man who will work for the price set. We do not believe in letting the place out by contract. First decide to make it a permanent office, then have the whole time of the officer given to the Order, make the compensation sufficient for a first-class man and hold him strictly accountable for the manner in which the work is performed. A uniform system of accounts should prevail throughout the Order, this cannot be had unless by the supervision of a competent man. A system of auditing should be had and the books of the courts should show at all times their exact condition.

Once a year at least the books of each court should be examined, and the proper person to make that examination is the High Secretary-Treasurer. The Deputies perform that duty now and necessarily it must be done in an indifferent manner. No matter how good the intention or inclination, all are not bookkeepers or accountants, and the systems while supposed to be alike are entirely different. We must have an organizer in connection with the Order who can devote his time, when wanted, to that work. Volunteers may assist, but you cannot always rely on them. Men who have business to attend to cannot at all times leave it and give their time to the Order. If the High Secretary's office is made permanent he can perform the work of an organizer and will at all times be at the service of the organization.

Treat the matter fairly, act intelligently, as you will, and for the best interests of our society.

WOMEN.

Some years ago an application was made to the High Standing Committee, by a number of women in the City of Boston, for permission to form a Court of the Massachusetts Catholic Order of Foresters. Under the law then, as well as to-day, a charter could not be granted even if the proposition had been seriously entertained. It seems to us it would be well to consider whether it would be desirable to have women branches of our Order, or whether it would be best to have them admitted to full membership in the Courts now existing. Their influence would undoubtedly be salutary, and they would bring new interest into the organization. Woman has assisted in many movements for the reclamation of man. She has been an important auxiliary in the effort to benefit the people of Ireland in the struggle for freedom, that they have been making. She was a tireless worker in the anti-slavery movement. She is to-day a prominent factor in the temperance movement of all denominations.

In this country she is entering into all the trades and professions, and is successful in all she undertakes. The highest branches of education are open to her. She is the teacher of the youth, the protector of the children, and the center of home life.

Why not give our mothers, our wives and sisters, an opportunity to provide for those they hold dear. They are considered good risks in the Old Line Companies. They actively participate in and strengthen other Fraternal Societies not of our Faith. They are interested in our welfare, we are doubly so in theirs, and we can help each other. It is a serious question. We commend it to you for your serious consideration.

EXTEND THE ORDER.

The Organization was formed 12 years ago. It was then confined to Massachusetts. The time has arrived when in our judgment it should be extended. Rhode Island, Connecticut. New Hampshire and Maine have sent requests, asking that courts be formed within their borders. Form a New England District. The localities are all healthy, and while it may not be of any material benefit to us, it will confer a benefit on those who want to join. The expense will not be any greater, the cost of administration will not be any more burdensome, and with proper supervision, we can add a new class of equally good risks as there are in our ranks at the present time. It will give men, at present in our Order, an opportunity to change from place to place, and continue in membership, whether in search of employment, or for pleasure, and to make friends where they may be very desirable.

Enlarging the jurisdiction of the Order would involve a change of name. This should not be done without great thought on your part. It may not be done at this Convention, but it will give you and the members of the Order a chance to think over the matter, if action is not to be taken at present.

CONSTITUTION.

The Constitution will again receive your attention. Changes have been suggested in this report and others will undoubtedly be proposed by some of the representatives. It should be changed in some of its provisions and that at once. Strike out the approval of death certificates by the Deputies, it leads only to delay. Appoint a permanent Committee on Constitution, to whom all amendments shall be referred, and then have them report to the Convention in a form that will not conflict. If the changes cannot be made to-day, have the committee report at some future session of the Convention, or at a special session called for the purpose of acting on the Constitution. This change has been heretofore recommended by us. We hope that it will be adopted now. While we do not deem it advisable to constantly change the Constitution, yet experience in working under it would suggest some changes that to the inexperienced would not be thought of.

We return thanks to the various courts and gentlemen in them for courtesies received. Also to the *Boston Democrat* for the notices of our Order published by it.

High Medical Examiner Joseph D. Couch, is entitled to the thanks of the Order and its members, for the unwearying work performed by him. He has ever been ready with his advice and suggestions whenever he could help, and the High Standing Committee are under unbounded thanks to him for his kindness in at all times giving his services to the Order.

Past High Chief Ranger John H. Watson, has generously responded whenever asked, and his advice was never asked for in vain.

Brothers—In presenting this report, we do so with a feeling that our work has been of some benefit to the Order, that it was a labor of love done for our own people and in our own way. All have assisted in furthering their interests, and none have felt the cost. Race or nationality has not been taken into consideration. The principles of our Order are as broad as prudence will allow. Fraternity has governed us in our dealings with each other. Unity has taught us, that good can be accomplished where dissension has caused bitterness and want. Charity has enabled us to pay in twelve years $500,000, and time alone can determine the good accomplished. Be true to your society, to your country—your devotion is unquestioned— and let the term Forester be synonymous for, I am an American! I am a Catholic!

Brothers—All that I have said was in connection with, and as far as my judgment would allow me, for the benefit of our grand organization ; Allow me to say a few words personal to myself.

On the 2nd day of July, 1883, I became a member of our beloved Order, nearly eight years have elapsed since then, from that date I have been its servant, ready to do its bidding and its work ; from the night of initiation to this moment I have been an officer in some capacity and sometimes holding more than one office, my voice was never silent when any court or prospective court wanted me. The time has come when I must lay down the insignia of office, when I must go back to the ranks to do my labor as a private, equally as well, if not better than as an officer. I am not a candidate for any other preferment at your hands, but I assure you that the pleasantest recollections of not a very long life at the best, will always be of the last three years, wondering as I have if the friends I won are satisfied, if they are, for the little labor I have done, my reward is full and complete. For the support I have received, the organization and all its members have my sincere thanks, and if you are satisfied that my duty, though at times hard, was faithfully performed, remember that it was made lighter for me by the many kind hands who were willing to assist me over the rough places.

I cannot help thanking one or two personally while I would like to mention all. To our beloved Secretary I now return my sincere thanks and assure him that only for his consideration and forethought many blunders would have been committed. To High Medical Examiner Couch I would say, keep on in the course you have started, doing justice to all, fearing none, and you will have the love of all fair-minded men.

To the members I would say, you have a great society, actuated by good motives, higher or better were never planted in the mind of man. Remember you are Catholic in fact, in working remember you are American, and don't forget Fatherland wherever you were born or reared, and if you do that you will indeed leave to your families, perhaps not wealth in lands or goods, but you will leave a priceless heritage to an endless posterity.

JEREMIAH G. FENNESSEY,

HIGH CHIEF RANGER.

Boston, April 22, 1891.

REPORT OF HIGH SECRETARY-TREASURER.

To the Representatives of the Massachusetts Catholic Order of Foresters:

BROTHERS, — The Massachusetts Catholic Order of Foresters has again had the good fortune to add another year to the increasing number, which it has presented already so full of charity and good works.

The year just passed has not differed materially from the others immediately preceding and shows that the Order is to-day the best organization of the kind in the State. This statement is easily borne out by the facts as a perusal of the reports from the various Courts will show and an examination of the increase in membership, which has been so general. There seems to have been a general desire on the part of the members to make this a good year and applications have been many and varied. In many districts where little or no life seemed to exist, there sprang up a desire to get new members, and as a consequence new applications poured in to the High Standing Committee in such number as to cause that body a considerable degree of unexpected work. It was congenial work, however, and was a source of great gratification to the High Chief Ranger and his associates. In some districts a smart rivalry sprang up between two or three neighboring Courts to see which could secure the greatest number of new applicants. This in itself was productive of much good, because it awakened an interest in the work of the Order, which benefited those already in the ranks and caused them to look into themselves as it were, and note, how golden an opportunity for doing good to themselves and their fellow man, had been presented to them all those years and they had allowed it to pass by without a thought. Seeing then the chance to help themselves by helping others, they took hold and endeavored to make up for lost time. It is notable too that the class of applications was of a superior order and there was evidence from all sides of a desire to get only the best possible risks. Good men were wanted and only those seem to have been solicited who presented no evidence of disease, or whose surroundings were suggestive of long life. This significant fact is worthy of much consideration, in that it indicates that the members no longer looked on the Organization as a refuge for invalids, and were beginning to realize that the possibilities of the Order for doing good were to be measured by the good that was put into it. That, being in the Order themselves they should naturally desire to prolong and propagate the Order, as in the natural order of things, the time might come when they would look for the benefits of the Order themselves. It may have been a selfish motive which prompted them, but stripping it of all possible selfishness, we still find a desire to help others which must have existed, or we would not have the results, which we now with so much pleasure contemplate.

Of the Courts which have sent in new applications during the year ending March 31, 1891, the largest number is again credited to St. Thomas Court No. 29, which received 38; Holy Trinity Court No. 51 and Canton Court No. 67 have 29 each, Sherwood No. 8 has 28, Qualey Court No. 32 has 24, Merrimack No. 72 has 23, Cathedral Court No. 1 has 17, Cheverus Court No. 6, Erin Court No. 28 and Emerald Court No. 53 have 16 each, Essex Court No. 16 and Phil Sheridan Court No. 71 have 15 each, Iona No. 10 and St. Gregory No. 24 have 14 each, St. John 33 has 13, St. Francis No. 4 and Star of the Sea No. 41 have 12 each, St. Peter No. 18, St. Francis No. 25, St. Catherine No. 62 and Taunton No. 73 have 11 each, Charles River Court No. 55 has 10. Five Courts only had no new applications.

New Courts.

During the year efforts have been made to establish new Courts in various towns in the State and the following were instituted :

John Boyle O'Reilly No. 79, in New Bedford, 24 Charter members. Instituted Jan. 24, 1891.

Gen. Sherman Court No. 80, in Plymouth, 25 Charter members. Instituted March 7, 1891.

The following table gives the number applying to each Court :

New applications received from April 23, 1890, to March 31, 1891 :

No.	Court.		No.	Court.	
1	Cathedral . . .	17	45	Unity . . .	1
3	Feuwick . .	1	46	St. Augustine .	3
4	St. Francis . .	12	47	St. Anne . . .	9
5	Leo . . .	2	48	Sarsfield . .	2
6	Cheverus . . .	16	49	Constantine . .	2
7	St. Patrick . .	2	51	Holy Trinity .	29
8	Sherwood . . .	28	52	Highland . . .	1
9	Columbus . .	3	53	Emerald . .	16
10	Iona	14	54	St. James . . .	5
11	St. Joseph . .	4	55	Charles River .	10
12	Fulton . . .	4	59	Worcester . .	4
14	Lafayette . .	5	60	Middlesex . . .	5
15	SS. Peter and Paul .	1	61	St. Lawrence .	8
16	Essex . . .	15	62	St. Catherine . .	11
17	Hamilton . . .	3	63	Shields . . .	9
18	St. Peter . .	11	64	Gallagher . . .	9
19	Williams . . .	6	65	St. Columbkille .	2
20	Mt. Pleasant .	4	66	Griffin . . .	4
21	St. Alphonsus . .	3	67	Canton . . .	29
23	St. Jonn . .	4	69	Stoughton . .	11
24	St. Gregory . .	14	70	St. Michael . .	4
25	St. Francis .	11	71	Phil Sheridan . .	15
26	St. Raphael . .	3	72	Merrimack . .	23
28	Erin . . .	16	73	Taunton . .	11
29	St. Thomas . .	38	74	Hendricken . .	4
30	Bass River . .	6	75	St. Jarlath . .	3
32	Qualey . . .	24	76	Quincy . . .	9
33	St. John . .	13	77	Mystic . . .	7
34	Americus . . .	4	78	St. Monica . .	5
37	Friendship . .	3	79	John Boyle O'Reilly,	30
38	St. Joseph . .	1	80	Gen. Sherman, . .	25
39	Benedict . . .	3			
41	Star of the Sea .	12			618
43	St. Mary	9			

The percentage of increase is shown by the following table : —

No. of Court.	NAME OF COURT.		No. of Court.	NAME OF COURT.	
1	Cathedral	.08	43	St. Mary	.347
4	St. Francis	.083	45	Unity	.045
6	Cheverus	.047	46	St. Augustine	.035
8	Sherwood	.027	47	St. Anne	.217
9	Columbus	.24	51	Holy Trinity	.118
10	Iona	.044	52	Highland	.043
11	St. Joseph	.125	53	Emerald	.151
14	Lafayette	.013	55	Charles River	.133
15	SS. Peter and Paul,	.045	57	Carroll	.022
16	Essex	.125	59	Worcester	.027
18	St. Peter	.144	61	St. Lawrence	.061
19	Williams	.128	62	St. Catherine	.296
21	St. Alphonsus	.02	64	Gallagher	.037
23	St. John	.021	65	St. Columbkille	.037
24	St. Gregory	.125	66	Griffin	.363
25	St. Francis	.046	67	Canton	.558
26	St. Raphael	.022	68	St. Margaret	.035
28	Erin	.128	69	Stoughton	.422
29	St. Thomas	.277	71	Phil Sheridan	.108
30	Bass River	.024	72	Merrimack	.307
32	Qualey	.314	74	Hendricken	.172
37	Friendship	.045	76	Quincy	.437
41	Star of the Sea	.06	77	Mystic	.481

The average age of the Order, January 1, 1891, was 38.2 years, which is a very good indication of the condition of the membership.

The applications received by the High Standing Committee since the last Convention to April 1, 1891, number 618 — of this number 48 were rejected, which is less than 8 per cent. of the whole number.

Of the rejections, some were by the Medical Examiners and some by the High Standing Committee.

OCCUPATIONS OF APPLICATIONS APPROVED

FROM JANUARY 1, 1890, TO JANUARY 1, 1891.

Agent	1	Florist	3
Builder	1	Foreman	3
Bill-poster	1	Fireman	5
Blacksmith	6	Furniture dealer	4
" helper	2	Fresco painter	1
Baker	7	Farmer	5
Barber	9	Fruit dealer	3
Book-keeper	4	Fish pressman	1
Butcher	7	" cutter	2
Boiler maker	1	Grocer	13
Britannia smith	1	" clerk	1
Bartender	1	Glass painter	1
Brass finisher	2	Gate tender	2
Butter dealer	1	Gardener	5
Bleacher	1	Granite polisher	1
Brush maker	2	" dealer	1
Boot maker	1	Hatter	3
Bricklayer	1	Hackman	13
Clerk	12	Hostler	3
Can maker	4	Hair dresser	1
Contractor	4	Horse car conductor	2
Cabinet maker	1	Horse shoer	1
Currier	15	Iron worker	2
Cook	1	" moulder	4
Clergyman	7	Inspector (Tool Works)	1
Coachman	5	Ice dealer	2
Coal dealer	2	Janitor	3
Cigar maker	2	Junk dealer	3
Carpenter	11	Jeweller	3
Carriage washer	1	Laborer	82
" blacksmith	1	Livery stable keeper	1
" driver	1	Last maker	1
" trimmer	1	Lamp lighter	1
Collector	1	Lawyer	2
Collar finisher	1	Liquor dealer	2
Copper worker	2	" clerk	1
Clothing cutter	1	Laster	4
Carpet maker	3	Loom fixer	1
Comber	1	Manufacturer	1
Case maker	1	Mason	2
Car driver	1	Millman	1
Dentist	1	Machinist	5
Draw tender	1	Manager	1
Druggist	3	Mill hand	2
Express driver	3	Miller	1
Engineer (Sta.)	5	Moulder	2

Morocco shaver	3	Shoemaker	27
" dresser	5	" finisher	1
" finisher	1	" cutter	1
Marble worker	3	" laster	7
" cutter	1	" stitcher	1
Meat cutter	1	Store-keeper	1
Mattress maker	2	Stone cutter	6
Merchant	3	Stone mason	5
Nail maker	1	Station agent	1
Night watchman	4	Stock fitter	1
Nailer	1	Shipping clerk	4
Photographer	1	Sole leather cutter	2
Printer	2	Silversmith	2
Piano varnisher	1	Stair builder	1
" polisher	2	School teacher	1
" maker	1	Superintendent	1
Provision dealer	3	Safe maker	1
Plasterer	3	Section hand	3
Paper cutter	2	Spinner	1
Puddler	1	Teamster	25
Pattern maker	1	Tinsmith	1
Policeman	1	Tinman	1
Paver	1	Tanner	5
Plumber	7	Teacher	2
Packer	2	Tailor	5
Paper maker	8	Telegraph operator	1
Painter	7	Undertaker	4
Physician	5	Wheelwright	1
Pharmacist	3	Whitener	1
Periodicals	1	Wool grader	1
Quarryman	1	Watchman	3
Rubber worker	2	Wool spinner	1
" coat maker	2	Waiter	1
Rope maker	2	Winder	1
Real estate dealer	1	Weaver	1
Salesman	8	Wine clerk	1
Saddler	1		
Stahle-keeper	2		557
Stable-man	1		

The average age of applications approved from April 23, 1890, to March 31, 1891, is 32 1-10 years.

OCCUPATIONS OF APPLICANTS REJECTED

FROM JANUARY 1, 1890, TO JANUARY 1, 1891.

Bricklayer	1	Milkman	1
Blacksmith	1	Mariner	1
Bartender	1	Nail-maker	2
Butcher	1	Plasterer	1
Barber	1	Painter	1
Cigar maker	1	Porter	1
Clerk	1	Rope-maker	1
Carpenter	1	Restaurant keeper	1
Currier	2	Shipping agent	1
Cooper	1	Stock broker	1
Confectioner	1	Salesman	1
Coal dealer	1	Stationer	1
Conductor	1	Shoe maker	2
Dry goods dealer	1	Tailor	1
Furniture finisher	1	Teamster	3
Laborer	5	Varnish maker	1
Liquor dealer	2	Watch maker	1

Our pace for several years has been as follows: —

January 1, 1888	3,230	members.
" 1, 1889	3,644	"
" 1, 1890	4,270	"
" 1, 1891	4,556	"

Our suspensions have been large as the table shows, 262 having been dropped from the rolls. This of course was a positive gain to the members remaining, although some of those dropping out probably supposed the Order would go to pieces immediately on their leaving. It must be remembered, however, that the number given as suspended, does not reduce the figure against January 1, 1891 — 4,556 being the number on the Roll independent of deaths, suspensions and expulsions — a detailed statement of the membership is given in the following table: — This is made up from the reports as sent in by the Courts and if any variations occur it is because the figures could not be made to agree.

MEMBERSHIP.

No. of Court.	NAME OF COURT.	Membership Dec. 31, 1889.	Membership Dec. 31, 1890.	Initiated in 1890.	Admitted on W. Card in 1890.	Reinstated in 1890.	Average age of Court Dec. 31, 1890.	Average age of Court Dec. 31, 1889.	Withdrawn on Card in 1890.	Resigned Membership in 1890.	Suspended for Non-payment in 1890.	Expelled in 1890.	Died in 1890.	Rejected by ballot in 1890.	Rejected by H. S. C. in 1890.
1	Cathedral	149	161	15	1		38.9	40.1		1	1	1	1		
3	Fenwick	68	64		3		35.4	43.2	2		2		2		2
4	St. Francis	108	117	9			42.6	43	2	1	1		1		1
5	Leo	102	101				43.4	42.1	2		1				
6	Cheverus	84	88	15	2		43.2	43.8		1	1		4		4
7	St. Patrick	48	43	2			42.4	42	1		7		2		1
8	Sherwood	148	152	19	1	1	39.2	38.6			5				
9	Columbus	33	41	10			33.07				13				
10	Iona	89	93	16	1		39.9	39.1	1		2		1		
11	St. Joseph	133	132	5			42.4	41.2			9		2		
12	Fulton	28	28				45.2	44.2	2		5		1		
13	Fitzpatrick	52	51	5			45.3	45					2		
14	Lafayette	75	76	6			41.1	41.1			4		1		
15	SS. Peter and Paul	66	69	16			40.6	41.5		1	2		1		
16	Essex	104	117	5			38.6	38.1	1		1		1		
17	Hamilton	67	66	12	1		46.3	47.1		1	3		2		
18	St. Peter	69	79	10	3	1	39.8	39.8	1	1	3		1		
19	Williams	70	79	9	1	1	40.1	40.8	2				1		
20	Mt. Pleasant	83	83	4			38.3	38.2	1		6		1		2
21	St. Alphonsus	50	51	5	1		45.3	43.9	2		3		1		2
23	St. John	46	47	9	1		36.6	34.5	1		2				
24	St. Gregory	64	72	8			36.9	37.1			5				1
25	St. Francis	108	113	3	1		37.7	37.6					1		
26	St. Raphael	45	46	15			39.3	39.08	1				3		
28	Erin	78	88	33			34.08	42.7			1				
29	St. Thomas	119	152	2		2	34.08	34.4			1	2	2		1
30	Bass River	41	42	16			39.4	38.9					1		
32	Qualey	35	46	1			37.4	38.7	1		1				
33	St. John	59	52	5			44.8	42			3		1	1	
34	Americus	86	83	1			37.3	36.1	1	2	8				
35	Sheil	24	24	2			40.04	39.4	1		6				1
37	Friendship	44	46	4				38.3							
38	St. Joseph	41	41	2			46.2	46.8	1		3		1		
39	Benedict	33	32	3			40	39	1		2		1		1

MEMBERSHIP — *Continued.*

No. of Court	NAME OF COURT	Membership Dec. 31, 1889	Membership Dec. 31, 1890	Initiated in 1890	Admitted on W. Card in 1890	Reinstated in 1890	Average age of Court Dec. 31, 1890	Average age of Court Dec. 31, 1889	Withdrawn on Card in 1890	Resigned Membership in 1890	Suspended for Non-payment in 1890	Expelled in 1890	Died in 1890	Rejected by ballot in 1890	Rejected by H. S. C. in 1890
41	Star of the Sea	83	85	6			39.05	38.3		1	2		1		3
42	St. Mary	23	31	8			39.8	42.4			4				1
43	St. Bernard	50	46				36.9	36	3		1				
44	Unity	44	46	6			40.06	39.5			1				
45	St. Augustine	28	29	2			42.4	42.1			6				
46	St. Anne	85	95	6			37.4	31.4			6		4		
47	Sarsfield	85	85	8			37.4	38.4			13		1		
48	Constantine	81	64	14	1	1	39.2	37.7	1	3	2		1		
49	Holy Trinity	93	104	2			36.5	38		1	7		1		3
50	Highland	23	24	21			33.7	38.7			6				2
51	Emerald	79	91	6	2	1	37.2	34.8		3	4	6	1		
52	St. James	62	60	15			31.7	30.4	1		4				1
53	Charles River	75	85	1	1		35.02	35.3		1	2				5
54	Carroll	41	45				37.7	37.7	1		5		1		2
55	Prospect	37	36	5		1	40.5	37.7	1		7				
56	Worcester	72	74	3	1		38.5	37.4							
57	Middlesex	81	71	6	1		36	34.6			10		2		
58	St. Lawrence	65	69	21		1	33.9	35.1			3				
59	St. Catherine	54	70	6	1	3	36.6	30.2							
60	Shields	33	31	9		1	39.05	35.6		2					2
61	Gallagher	54	56	8			33.8	38.6			5				
62	St. Columbkille	54	56	12			33.3	32.9			7				
63	Griffin	33	45				33.4	34.4							
64	Canton	28	67	19		1	33.5	35.4	2						1
65	St. Margaret	28	29	4			30.9	33.4		2	3				3
66	Stoughton	45	64	13	1		31.3	30.8			2				
67	St. Michael	43	40	14			32.08	31.5			4			1	
68	Phil Sheridan	74	82	10		2	32.6	30.5		7	15				
69	Merrimack	39	51	7	1	1	35.4	31.7	1		3			1	
70	Taunton	105	105	6			34.1	34.1		8	4		1		1
71	Hendricken	9	34	18	3		27.8	27.6		1	4				3
72	St. Jarlath	71	55	14			33.1	30.6							
73	Quincy	32	46				32.9	30.6		1					
74	Mystic	27	40	14			36.3	33.3							
75	St. Monica		20	25			35.3	28.4		1					3
	Total	4,237	4,556	559	26	17			29	37	230	10	45	2	45

MEDICAL EXAMINERS.

During the year very slight changes have been made in the Medical districts, because it was found that the districts as arranged were in good working shape. The changes made were: The appointment of Dr. O. M. Sheridan of Randolph, to be examiner for St. Mary Court No. 43, who were formerly obliged to send applicants to Brockton for examination; and the appointment of Dr. J. P. Lumbard of Dorchester, to be examiner for St. Peter Court No. 18, and St. Gregory Court No. 24. These Courts were obliged to send applicants to Roxbury for examination and the distance was too great. Much satisfaction is expressed over the changes, and the members of the Courts thus provided for promise immediate and large increase of membership. The Medical Examiner for John Boyle O'Reilly Court No. 79 is Dr. J. F. Sullivan of New Bedford, and is spoken of as a conscientious gentleman who will give the Order good service. Gen. Sherman Court No. 80 is still under the supervision of the High Medical Examiner, but a local Examiner will no doubt soon be selected. The work of the Medical Examiners has been performed the past year with apparent satisfaction to all concerned and, with one or two exceptions, to the satisfaction of the High Standing Committee. When fault has been found by the High Standing Committee, the matter in dispute has always been amicably settled, and the Medical Examiners now pretty well understand the kind of work required and seem disposed to meet all the requirements.

The High Standing Committee appreciates the fact that the Medical Examiners mean to give the Order the best service possible, and there is no doubt professional pride will insure its continuance.

Since the organization of the Massachusetts Catholic Order of Foresters, the number deceased each year is as follows:

1880	3
1881	17
1882	25
1883	40
1884	41
1885	48
1886	32
1887	34
1888	46
1889	54
1890	47
Total	387

ENDOWMENTS PAID.

Names of Deceased Members. Date and Cause of Death, Court of which the Deceased was a Member, and Beneficiaries, Age, Length of Memberships.

No.	NAME.	URT.	AGE.	INITIATED.	Yrs.	Mos.	Dys.	DATE OF DEATH.	CAUSE.	Endowment.	NUMBER OF BENEFICIARIES.	TO WHOM PAID.
1	... Cronin,	Iona, No. 10,	Malden	49	Mar. 14, 1880		7		Oct. 5, 1880	Typho-Malaria	$1,000	1, Widow	Administratrix
2	Dennis McCarthy,	... 5,	Boston	31	Nov. 14, 1879	1		6	Nov. 20, "	Phthisis	"	1, "	Widow
3	M. J. ...,	Fenwick, 3,	"	29	Mar. 14, 1880		9	19	Dec. 3, 1881	... Consumption	"		Executor
4	D. J. Desmond,	Iona, 10,	Men	48	Sept. 3, 1879	1	3	8	Jan. 11, "	Typhoid	"	1,	Administrator
5	P. H. ...,	...1,	Boston	33	Oct. 15, "		3	12	Jan. 27, "	...	"	1,	Widow
6	Jeremiah Lawton,	...1,	"	38	Feb. 11, 1880	1	0	24	Mar. 5, "	Typhoid ...	"	1,	"
7	Edward A. Burbank,	... 6,	"	42	May 26, "		11	0	April 26, "	... in Groin	"	1,	"
8	John ...,	Fitzpatrick, 13,	"	43	Aug. 3, "	10	14		June 17, "	Phthisis Pulmonalis	"	1,	"
9	Jack Kelley,	..., 17,	"	46	April 21, "		1	27	June 18, "	Typhoid ...	"	1,	"
10	Patrick Murray,	..., 10,	Boston	26	Mar. 15, 1881	6	1		Aug. 29, "	... Peritonitis	"	1,	"
11	Patk C. Dailey,	..., 5,	"	27	Aug. 13, 1880	1	0	8	Aug. 23, "	...	"	1,	"
12	James L. Meagher,	Leo, 5,	"	24	Aug. 10, 1881		1	27	Sept. 3, "	Bright's ...	"	3, ... & children	" ... & guardian
13	Thomas F. ...,	Leo, 5,	"	47	July 6, 1880	1	2	14	Sept. 3, "	Chronic Catarrhal Pneumonia	"	4,	"
14	Archibald Morrison,	Hamilton, 17,	"	36	Aug. 16, "	1	8	5	Oct. 30, "	Chronic Gastritis & Pneumonia	"	1,	" ... & children
15	... McCarthy,	..., 5,	"	40	April 12, "		7	1	Nov. 17, "	Cancerous Dis. of Æsophagus	"	1,	"
16	William Whitley,	St. Patrick, 7,	"	31	April 21, 1881		9	14	Nov. 22, "	Lobular Pneumonia, sec'd ...	"	1,	"
17	Daniel J. McDonald,	Hamilton, 17,	"	49	Feb. 13, 1880		8	26	Nov. 27, "	Pneumonia, ...	"	1,	"
18	Henry Steele,	Fenwick, 3,	"	23	Mch. 4, "	11	9		Nov. 30, "	Bronchitis and Cong. of Brain	"		"
19	David O'Callaghan,	Sherwood, 8,	"	26	Dec. 27, "		7	26	Dec. 9, "	Inflammation of ...	"	1, Children,	Guardian
20	Michael O'Brien,	..., 11,	"	23	May 10, "	1	9	17	Dec. 6, 1882	...	"	1, Widow,	Widow
21	John M. ...,	St. ..., 11,	"	31	Mar. 22, "	3	10		Jan. 3, "	Heart ...	"	1,	"
22	Thos. T. McDonough,	St. Joseph, 11,	"	28	Oct. 15, "	2	3	16	Jan. 9, "	... a Potu	"	1,	"
23	James McNulty,	St. Alphonsus, 21,	"	25	Oct. 15, 1879	1		10	Jan. 25, "	Colloid ... of ...	"	1,	"
24	... Condon,	Cathedral, 1,	"	46	Mar. 29, 1881		1	18	Feb. 1, "	Cancer of ...	"	1,	"
25	Mark B. ...,	... Joseph, 38,	"	36	Jan. 18, "	1	10	26	Feb. 18, "	...	"	1,	"
26	John Boles,	Sullivan, 27,	"	36	June 25, 1880	1	11	4	Mar. 25, "	...	"	1,	"
27	Thos. Moore Bayley,	St. Patrick, 7,	Somerville	35	June 24, 1881		10	17	Mar. 28, "	Cirrhosis of Liver	"	1,	"
28	Ths. Clark,	... 5,	Boston	39	May 12, "	1	11		May 28, "	...	"	1,	"
29	Jas Purcell,	Benedict, 39,	"	40	June 23, 1880	1	11	17	May 29, "	...	"	1,	"
30	Patrick ...,	Essex, 16,	Salem	33	June 1, 1882			26	June 10, "		"	1,	"
31	John ...,	... Francis, 4,	Boston						June 27, "		"		"

ENDOWMENTS PAID—Cont'd.

No.	NAME.	COURT.	AGE.	INITIATED.	Membership Yrs.	Membership Mos.	Membership Dys.	DATE OF DEATH.	CAUSE.	Endow- ment.	NUMBER OF HEIRS.	TO WHOM PAID.
33	Wm Miller,	Wm 3,	25	Sept. 3, 1880	1	8	21	May 24, 1882	Phs	$1,000	1, Father	Fr
34	John Bentley,	Fitzpatrick, 13,	32	April 13, 1881	1	9	14	Jan. 27, "	Ws	"	1, Ww	Widow
35	Wm By,	SS. Peter & Paul, 15,	34	Nov. 17, 1880	1	8	24	Aug. 11, "	Phth. of Heart [Brain	"	1, Fr	Fr
36	Thomas Devenny,	Fenwick, 3,	28	Mar. 12, "	2	5	6	Aug. 18, "	Wm. and Congr. of the	"	1, "	"
37	Jno. B. Foley, M.D.,	Wal, 1,	37	Aug. 3, 1879	2	4	24	July 27, "	Td Fever	"	5, "	Hs
38	Hugh McDade,	Wmk, 3,	24	April 29, 1880	2	1	8	Sept. 7, "	Wy	"	1, "	"
39	Wm W. Wm,	Wm 3,	38	Dec. 2, 1881	0	9	25	Sept. 27, "	Wm	"	1, Ww	Wi dow
40	Wm Diver,	Ws, 6,	40	Mar. 23, 1880	2	7	5	Oct. 28, "	Wm n of Brain	"	1, "	"
41	Wm Oe,	St. Ws, 25, W. Quincy	50	Jan. 8, "	2	1	1	Nov. 21, "	Wd by stone fal hig	"	1, Fr	Fr
42	Henry Conroy,	St. Wk, 4,	48	Feb. 11, "	0	13	0	Nov. 14, "	Wm	"	1, Widow	Son
43	Patrick Carroll,	Leo, 5, 6,	22	April 26, 1882	2	8	3	Oct. 14, "	Phia	"	1, Mr	"
44	Wm F. Decker,	Cheverus, 6, 13,	68	Feb. 15, "	3	10	28	Jan. 6, 1883	Piaa	"	1, Son	Son
45	Ed. I. Burns,	Wm & Peter, 8,	34	Nov. 17, "	1	1	5	Jan. 22, 1882	Wt Disease	"	1, Ww	Wmw
46	Wm Halloran,	St. Ws, 4,	23	Jan. 4, 1883	1	10	1	Oct. 14, 1883	Aa, Hp	"	1, Father	Fr
47	James Ws,	St. Wm, 4,	28	May 26, 1881	1	8	18	Feb. 14, "	Ws of Wm	"	1, Ww	Ww
48	Wm. A. Breen,	Wm 35,	32	Dec. 21, 1882	1	2	28	Feb. 19, "	See	"	2, Wm	Wm
49	James Wm,		32	June 24, 1881	8	1	10	Mar. 4, "	Wm	"	1, "	"
50	Wm Horan,	Sherwood, 8, 8,	35	Mar. 4, 1880	3	14	14	Mar. 18, "	Wm	"	1, Ww	Ww
51	Wm Neville,	St. Wm, 3,	51	Mar. 29, 1881	1	18	10	April 16, "	Wm	"	1, Sr	Sr
52	Richard Collins,	Wm, 6, 3,	64	Mar. 30, "	1	4	23	April 22, "	Heart of Wm	"	1, Ww	Widow
53	Ws Carey,	Salem Wm, 6,	35	May 4, "	3	6	1	May 5, "	Cyst of Wm	"	1, Wm	Wm
54	P. I. McDevitt,	St. Francis, 4,	38	Aug. 18, 1879	3	9	18	May 6, "	Die of the Brain	"	1, Ww	Ww
55	Ws Doherty,	Wm 8,	41	July 8, 1880	3	7	9	May 30, "	Wmy	"	4, Wm	Wmw
56	Wm Kerrigan,	St. Peter, 18,	42	Oct. 21, "	2	0	6	June 28, "	Wm	"	1, "	"
57	Wm Wm,	Wm 7,	33	Dec. 22, 1882	2	7	6	June 3, "	Wc	"	4, "	"
58	James Wm,	Wm 3,	21	April 2, 1880	2	9	1	Jan. 3, "	Wy	"	1, Fr	Fr
59	James F. Bly,	Wm 6,	24	Mar. 1, "	2	2	5	May 17, "	Wm	"	3, Children	Wmw
60	William B. I Wm,	Fenwick, 3,	26	Nov. 14, 1879	3	6	3	June 13, "	Wm	"	1, Ww	"
61	C. J. S Wm,	Wm & the Sea, 41,	37	Nov. 14, "	2	6	7	June 28, "	Ws	"	1, "	"
62	John Rickard,	Wm 7,	45	Dec. 1, 1880	2	6	20	June 28, "	Whc	"	1, "	Wm
63	Wm Murphy,	Cheverus, 6,	48	Feb. 10, "	3	4	18	June 30, "	Wm	"	1, "	"
64	Thomas G. Ryan,	Lyndon, 50,	37	April 8, 1883	2	2	17	July 2, "	Wme	"	1, "	"
65	Wm O'Brien, Wmr,	Wm n, 3,	49	May 27, 1882	1	1	24	July 12, 1883	Heart	"	1, Widow	Ww
66	Ws T.	Wm of the Sea,41,	50	Dec. 5, "	3	7	15	July 23, "	Wm	"	1, "	"
67	J. A.	Fenwick, 3,	51	Nov. 14, "	3	28	8	Aug. 30, "	Tid Fever	"	3, Heirs	Ww
68	Wm J. Wy,	Williams, 19,	27	Sept. 16, 1880	3	10	11	Sept. 30, "	Wl Fever	"	3, "	Wmr

No.	Name	Residence (Parish, No.)	Place	Date	Cause of Death	Year	Amount	Beneficiaries
73	M. H. Byrne	..., 39	Somerville	Mar. 31, 1881	Pulmonary Hemorrhage	1883	$1,000	1, Wdw ... Widow
74	Bart. Whalen	Essex, 16	Salem	Aug. 1, 1883	Uremic	"	"	1, Mer ... Mer
75	E. F. Dever	Fenwick, 3	Boston	Feb. 16, 1881	Phthisis	"	"	1, Widow ... Widow
76	John O'Brien	..., 11	"	Sept. 15, 1881	Heart Disease	"	"	4, " ... Widow
77	Patrick Monaghan	St. Joseph, 11	Boston	June 14, 1880	Injury to Brain by fall	"	"	1, " ... Heirs
78	John Sweeney	Benedict, 39	Somerville	Mar. 31, 1881	Pulmonary Consumption	"	"	
79	Michael H. Murray	Mt. Pleasant, 20	Boston	Oct. 20, 1880	Catarrhal Pneumonia, C'nsum'p.	"	"	
80	Michael Donahue	Fenwick, 3	"	Jan. 30, "	Pleurisy	"	"	
81	John Murray	Cathedral, 1	"	Oct. 8, 1879	Pulmonary Phthisis	"	"	1, Sister ... Sister
82	T. H. O'Rourke	St. ..., 54	"	July 2, 1883	Cerebral Paralysis	1884	"	1, Widow ... Widow
83	Philip McDonald	St. ..., 29	Brockton	Feb. 17, 1881	...	"	"	1, Mer ... Mother
84	John B. Reagan	Charles Riv. 55	...	Nov. 28, 1883	...	"	"	1, Widow ... Mw
85	Thomas McDonough	Qualey, 32	Woburn	Nov. 28, 1881	Cong. of Lungs and Peritonitis	"	"	1, " ... "
86	Thomas Welsh	Americus, 34	Boston	July 31, 1883	Quick Consumption	"	"	1, " ... "
87	...	St. Patrick, 7	So.	May 10, 1880	Bright's Disease	"	"	4, " ... "
88	Frank A. Spitz	St. Alphonsus, 21	"	Oct. 13, 1881	Phthisis Pulmonalis	"	"	4, 3 child'n
89	...	..., 6	"	Feb. 25, "	Pulmonary Consumption	"	"	3, 3
90	John A. ...	..., 13	...	Oct. 12, 1882	Pulmonary Consumption	"	"	1, 2
91	John F. Cunningham	Iona, 10	...	Mar. 14, 1880	Pneumonia	1883	"	1, "
92	Stephen T. Sliney	SS. Pet. & Paul, 15	S. Bos'n	May 20, 1881	Bright's Disease of Kidneys	"	"	9, 2 Parents ... 8
93	Thomas Garvey	Fenwick, 3	Boston	April 7, "	..., falling off staging	1884	"	2, "
94	John H. Matthews	Essex, 16	Salem	April 26, 1880	Phthisis	"	"	1, Sister ... Sister
95	John W. Lynch	St. ..., 11	Boston	Feb. 8, 1880	Phthisis Pulmonalis	1883	"	5, 4 child'n
96	John P. Diffin	Erin, 28	"	Jan. 8, "	Heart Disease	1884	"	5, 4
97	Wm Meagher	St. Francis, 4	"	April 26, "	Acid'nt, bl. sugar fell on him	"	"	1, " ... "
98	Mel McCarthy	Fitzpatrick, 13	"	April 22, 1881	Diabetes Melletus	"	"	3, 2 ... 2
99	Charles Lyons	Cathedral, 1	"	Sept. 8, "	Pneumonia. r. lung & ... pr lt	"	"	4, 3
100	Daniel Bailey	Sherwood, 8	"	Mar. 24, 1881	Phthisis	"	"	3, "
101	Patrick A. ...	Iona, 10	Malden	April 11, "	Phthisis	"	"	3, 2 ... 2
102	Edward W. Wright	St. Francis, 4	Boston	April 22, 1880	Hemplegia of Larynx	"	"	1, Daughter ... Daughter
103	John J. Donovan	Sherwood, 8	"	April 22, 1881	Shock, ..., crushing of leg	"	"	1, Mr ... Mr
104	Michael Maguire	Williams, 19	"	April 23, "	Phthisis Pulmonalis	"	"	4, 9 child'n ... Wid. and child'n
105	Phil A. Cunningham	Liberty, 40	"	June 23, "	Chronic Bronchitis	"	"	1, " ... Widow
106	Jnes F. Lynch	Americus, 34	"	Mar. 11, "	Pulmonary Consumption	"	"	1, " ... "
107	Patrick Donohue	Americus, 34	"	Nov. 21, 1882	Pulmonary Consumption	1883	"	1, Sister ... Sister
108	Rev. Wm. J. Daly	St. Joseph, 11	"	Mar. 22, 1880	Cancer of Stomach	"	"	1, Brother ... Brother
109	Rev. J. B. ...	Star of Sea, 41	E. Boston	Dec. 13, 1881	Carcinoma of liver	1884	"	1, Widow, 3 child'n ... Mw
110	Thomas ...	St. Alphonsus, 21	Boston	April 26, 1883	Alcoholism	"	"	4, " ... Mother
111	M. J. Devine	Fitzpatrick, 13	"	Mar. 29, 1882	Cirrhosis	"	"	2, " ... Wid. and child'n
112	M. C. Boles	Cheverus, 6	"	Feb. 11, 1880	Phthisis	"	"	1, " ... "
113	Thomas Gaill	SS. Pet. & Paul, 15	S'ds'n	Mar. 7, 1882	Hemorrhage of Lungs	"	"	2, 4 child'n ... "
114	P. H. Smith	St. Thomas, 29	Brockton	Mar. 31, 1881	Consumption	"	"	1, 1 child
115	J. S. Tompkins	Shiel, 35	"	Jan. 13, 1882	Cholera-Morbus	"	"	3, "
116	B. A. ...	St. Peter, 18	Dorchester	July ..., "	Killed by ...	"	"	4, 3 child'n
117	Martin McDonnell	St. ..., 4	Boston	Nov. 11, "	Consumption	"	"	1, "
118	John Drury	Shiel, 35	Boston	Mar. 30, 1881	Consumption	"	"	1, Sister ... Sister
119	T. H. ...	Hamilton, 17	Charlest'wn	Mar. 2, 1882	Concussion of Brain	"	"	3, Mw ... Widow
120	E. W. Bergen	St. Francis, 4	Boston	May 13, 1880	Phthisis	"	"	1, Sister ... Sister

ENDOWMENTS PAID—Continued.

No.	NAME.	URT.	AGE.	INITIATED.	Yrs.	Mos.	Dys.	DATE OF DEATH.	CAUSE.	Endowment.	NUMBER OF BENEFICIARIES.	TO WHOM PAID
121	Thomas Lynch,	St. Joseph, 11, Boston	35	June 27, 1881	3	4	7	Nov. 4, 1884	Pneumonia	$1,000	3, Children	Guardian
122	Matthew	St. Alphonsus, 21,	43	Oct. 13, 1880	4	2	2	Dec. 17, "	Consumption	"	5, Widow, 4 child'n	Wid. & children
123	J. M. Tirrell,	St. Patrick, 7, So. Boston	25	Jan. 24, 1882	2	11	27	Jan. 21, 1885	Phthisis	"	3, "	"
124	John Delaney,	Leo, 5, E. Boston	24	Jan. 16, 1880	5	11	26	Feb. 9, "	Consumption	"	2, 2	Guardian
125	Patrick O'Gorman,	St. Joseph, 11, Boston	32	Jan. 12, 1882	3	11	26	Jan. 8, "	Phthisis	"	3, Broth., wid., ch.	Broth., wid. & g.
126	J. W.,	McGlew, 36, Bea	35	Oct. 3, 1881	3	11	27	Jan. 30, "	Phthisis	"	1, Widow	Widow
127	W. J. Barry,	Essex, 16, Salem	35	Oct. 23, 1880	3	3	15	Feb. 8, 1885	Phthisis Pulmonalis	"	1, Sister	Sister
128	P. F. Welsh,	Friendship, 37, Boston	35	Feb. 6, 1882	3	1	1	Mar. 7, "	Injis	"	5, Widow, 4 child'n	Widow
129	Michael Ferrin,	Qualey, 32,	44	Jan. 15, 1883	1	10	27	Dec. 12, 1884	Enteritis	"	4, "	Wid. & guardian
130	Edward Doherty,	6, Boston	30	May 7, 1880	4	5	20	Oct. 27, "	Phthisis	"	3, "	Brothers
131	John Sullivan,	St. Patrick, 7, So. Boston	48	Mar. 4, "	4	7	21	Mar. 17, 1885	Phthisis Pulmonalis,	"	1, Widow, 5 child'n	Wid. & guardian
132	T. J. Flynn,	SS.Pet.&Paul,15, "	26	Aug. 18, "	4	4	23	April 9, "	Phthisis Pulmonalis	"	1, "	"
133	Bel Holland,	O'Connell, 22, Winchester	31	Feb. 15, "	5	1	20	April 10, "	bria	"	1, "	"
134	James Rice,	Erin, 28,	32		2	0	13	April 15, "	Accident, crushing h'd & shl'd'r	"	1, "	"
135	John M. Perkins,	Bass, 30, Beverly	42	June 5, 1882	5		3	April 18, 1885	Pneumonia	"	1, Father	Father
136	Daniel M. Gillis,	Fenwick, 3, Boston	25	Feb. 9, 1885		3	1	May 10, "	Pneumonia	"	2, Father & Mother	& mother
137	Joseph A. Devenny,	Holy Trinity,	22	Mar. 19, 1880	5		28	April 17, "	Consumption	"	3, Widow	Widow
138	John Schultz,	Mar. 36,	39	April 21, 1881	3		29	May 16, "	Accident	"	1, "	"
139	W. O'Neil,	Glea 44	44	Mar. 2, 1882	3	1	25	May 25, "	Pneumonia	"	1, 1 child	"
140	J. S. MacCorry,	Friendship, 37, Boston	28	April 2, 1882	3	1	23	May 13, "	Heart Disease	"	1, Brother	Brother
141	J. S. MacCorry,	Columbus, 9,	35	Dec. 13, 1881	3	5	24	June 7, "	Drowned	"	3, 3 child'n	Widow
142	Edward Gallagher,	Star of the Sea, 41, E.	29	May 12, 1881	3	10	27	April 9, 1882	Phthisis	"	4, "	Brother
143	Daniel R. McDonald,	Lyndon, 50, Boston	48	Mar. 30, 1880	4	2	26	June 14, "	Inflammation of Bowels	"	6, Uncles & aunts	Uncles & aunts
144	Dr. W. P. Kelley,	Liberty, 40,	39	Oct. 11, "	3	3	14	June 11, 1885	Congestion of Brain	"	5, 4 child'n	Widow & child'n
145	Peter ...,	St. Pleasant, 20,	32	Feb. 24, "	5	5	13	July 14, "	Bright's Disease	"	4, "	"
146	O'Hearn,	St. Patrick, 7, So.	22	April 6, "	5	5	13	July 12, "	Pneumonia	"	5, 4	"
147	Timothy Long,	6,	47	April 22, "	5		22	July 24, "	Phthisis	"	5, Mother	Mother
148	David Lane,	Sherwood, 6,	43	Dec. 13, 1881	3	2	19	Aug. 14, "	Apoplexy	"	1, Widow	Widow
149	Joseph F. Murphy,	Star of the Sea, 41, E.	25	Sept. 25, 1882	2	10	27	Mar. 2, 1884	Pneumonia	"	4, "	Widow
150	Michael Reardon,	St.Bernard,44,W.Newton	39	Dec. 21, 1881	2	8	18	Aug. 22, 1885	Phthisis	"	4, Father, 3 sisters	Brothers
151	Peter Hawkins,	Leo, 5, E.	32	Mar. 21, "	4	5	10	Sept. 15, "	Pyæmia	"	6, Children	Father & sister
152	P. W. ...	Cathedral, 1, Boston	40	Sept. 3, 1879	6	16		Sept. 1, "	Phthisis	"	7, "	Guardian
153	Thomas Daly,	Fenwick, 3,	37	Mar. 12, 1880	5	6	9	Sept. 19, "	Typhoid Pneumonia	"	7, 3	Widow
154	B. F. Harrington,	Hamilton, 17,	38	July 6, 1882	2	11	7	Sept. 21, "	bis	"	7, 8	"
155	Owen Murphy,	Unity, 45, Bridgewater	44	Nov. 2, 1882	2	11	7	Sept. 30, "	Neuralgia of Stomach	"	6, 5	"
156	Timothy Leary,	Emerald, 53, Peabody	42	Jn'y 1, 1883	2	3	24	Oct. 19, 1885	Pneumonia	"	6, 5	"
157	James H. Phalan,	Cheverus, 6, Boston	29	Feb. 11, 1880	4	7	26	Oct. 26, "	bis Pulmonalis	"	2, 1 child	"
158	Timothy Dwyer,							Oct. 17, "	Consumption	"	2, Sisters	Guardian
159	John Sheehan,											
160	Hugh A. Carr,											

No.	Name	Parish / Residence		Date		Cause of Death	Date		Amount		Beneficiary		
161	D. M. ...	... Boston	31	Feb. 3, 1881	9 28	His and ...	Feb. 1, 1885		$1,000	6,	Widow, 5	...	New Att'y for wid., g.
162	Michael Sullivan,	Essex, 16, Salem	40	May 14, 1880	3 29	Uremia	Nov. 3, "			3,	" 2	"	Widow & gnar.
163	John Carney,	St. John, 23, Hyde Park	40	Dec. 21, 1879	4 11	1 Phthisis	Nov. 4, "			3,	" 8	"	"
164	Patrick Prendergast,	Americus, 34, Boston	39	Nov. 18, 1879	6 14	...	Dec. 5, "			6,	" 5	"	"
165	J. R. ...	St. Francis, 4,	36	Dec. 2, 1881	5	Phthisis	Dec. 20, "			3,	" 4	"	"
166	John O'Day,	..., 28,	38	April 6, 1881	8 15	Killed by ...	Dec. 21, "			3,	" 1	child	held
167	Jas J. Quinn,	St. John,	44	Dec. 8, "	4 9 22	Pulmonary Phthisis	Dec. 60.			3,	" 2	child'n	held
168	John H. Shea,	(St. Francis, 4,	56	Dec. 18, 1879	6 4	Valvular Disease of Heart	60.			3,	"		"
169	Peter Daly,	Erin, 28,	48	Feb. 3, 1881	4 10 24	Pyæmia	Dec. 26.			4,	" 3		"
170	John Handran,	St. Anne, 47,	33	July 6, 1885	11 20	Blood Poisoning	loc. 22,		177.50	3,	Widow		N'se, und'r la w y
171	Edward Brennan,	Cathedral, 1,	35	Oct. 15, 1879	5 11 22	Pneumonia	Sept. 22,		$1,000	2,	Widow, 9	child'n	N
172	Michael Harvey,	St. Joseph, 11,	31	Oct. 11, 1885	6 2 18	Heart Disease	Jan. 2, 1886			1,	Bros. and sister		Brother & sister
173	W. H. Fitzgerald,	Mt. Pleasant, 20,	49	April 14, 1882	8 18	... of Lungs	Jan. 9, "			3,	Widow, 9	child'n	Widow
174	C. J. Hurley,	St. ..., 7,	31	Feb. 16, 1880	10 21	Heart Disease	Jan. 7, "			4,	" 3	"	" & child'n
175	James J. McNealy,	St. ..., 25,	41	Dec. 18, "	5	...	Jan. 18, "			5,	" 4	"	"
176	John Donovaro,	Williams, 19,	45	April 4, 1881	4 10 20	Phthisis	June 25, 1886			8,	" 5	"	"
177	Francis P. Paten,	Fulton, 12,	41	July 5, 1883	5 20	Phthisis	Jan. 10, 1886			5,	" 4	"	"
178	Patrick W. Sullivan,	Leo, 5,	48	Nov. 26, 1880	7	Pulmonary Pneumonia	Feb. 17, "			4,	Mother & wido		Guardian
179	Edward J. Kenney,	St. Joseph, 11,	35	Mar. 22, "	5 11	Paralysis	Feb. 19, "			4,	Widow, 3	child'n	Mother & wid.
180	Jas W. Norris,	Quaoley, 32,	33	Jan. 2, 1882	5 8	... Pneumonia	Feb. 28, "			1,	Parents		Wid. and child'n
181	William Fay,	Hamilton, 17,	33	July 24, "	2	... Pulmonary	Mar. 4, "			3,	Widow, 2	child'n	Father
182	Michael Devine,	Essex, 16,	41	June 23, "	5 9 13	Loss of Lung from Injury	Mar. 30, "			3,	" 2	child'n	Wid. and child'n
183	Patrick Bellen,	St. Peter, 18,	37	Dec. 22, 1882	5 2	...	April 6, "			3,	" 1	child	"
184	Michael McNeil,	Iona, 10,	47	Mar. 3, 1881	3 7 1	Chronic Catarrhal	April 4, "			2,	" 5	child'n	"
185	...	Mt. Pleasant, 20,	40	Feb. 10, "	5 11	Drowning	May 1, "			2,	" 3	"	"
186	Luke Kelley,	Williams, 19,	52	July 13, 1883	9 17	...	May 21, "			6,	Niece		Niece
187	C. G. Kullburg,	Sarsfield, 48,	28	Mar. 27, 1882	2	... Fever	April 30, "			4,	Widow, 3	child'n	Widow
188	A. J. McGivney,	St. Bernard, 44,	38	Mar. 26, 1883	4 2	Pulmonary Phthisis	May 29, "			7,	" 8	"	"
189	Rev. C. ...,	Mt. ..., 20,	40	Feb. 26, 1882	3 29	... of Liver	April 13, "			4,	" 2	"	"
190	Richard A. ...,	Fulton, 12,	30	April 10, 1884	3 18	Cerebral Apoplexy	June 28, "			2,	Wid. o w & child		Widow
191	William Sullivan,	Americus, 34,	37	Dec. 9, 1880	6 2	... of Lungs	July 1, "			2,	"		"
192	William H. Bay,	Sherwood, 8,	26	Mar. 15, 1881	5 13	Inflam. of Brain from sunstroke	July 21, "			3,	" 2	child'n	Widow & ...
193	John McClure,	Leo, 5,	25	Jan. 16, "	6 11	Typhoid Fever and Lung Dis.	July 27, "			3,	"		"
194	Joseph B. Fenelon,	Sherwood, 8,	31	June 22, 1881	5 1 7	Laryngitis (Infl. of the spinal mar.)	July 29, "			3,	Wid. fath.		Fath, moth, wid.
195	William ...,	Sherwood, 8,	40	May 12, "	3 1	Myelitis	Sept. 29, "			6,	Heirs		Heirs
196	Hugh Harkins,	Fitzpatrick, 13,	36	Mar. 16, "	5 6 13	Hæmorrhage (from thor. aneur.)	Dec. 16, "			7,	Widow, 3	"	Widow
197	John ...,	St. Patrick, 7,	45	Jan. 1, 1884	5 11 15	Phthisis	Dec. 24, "			5,	" 4	"	"
198	Daniel Gallivan,	SS. Peter & Paul, 15,	35	Mar. 28, 1881	5 8 26	...	Aug. 26, "			6,	" 4	"	"
199	John F. Daly,	SS. Peter & Paul, 15,	36	Sept. 15, 1880	4 27	...	Jan. 11, 1887			7,	Widow, ...		Widow
200	William Pierce,	Shiel, 35,	30	April 22, 1880	6 10 12	... Bronchitis	Mar. 4, "			5,	" 4		"
201	Edmund C Green,	St. Francis, 4,	42	April 31, 1881	1 26	...	Mar. 27, "			5,	Father & sister		Father & sister
202	James O'Toole,	Benedict, 39,	21	Mar. 31, 1881	2 1 16	Phthisis	Aug. 22, 1886			2,	Father & sister		Widow
203	...	Emerald, 53,		Sept. 6, 1883	6	...	April 12, 1887			5,	Widow, 5	child'n	Children
204	Timothy Hurley,	St. John, 33,	44	Mar. 8, 1881	6 0 3	... of Brain	Mar. 11, "			5,	Children		Widow
205	Dennis ...,	Williams, 19,	23	Oct. 3, "	5 6 26	...	April 29, "			3,	Widow, 2	child'n	

ENDOWMENTS PAID—Continued.

No.	NAME.	COURT.	AGE.	INITIATED.	Yrs.	Mos.	Dys.	DATE OF DEATH.	CAUSE.	Endowment.	NUMBER OF BENEFICIARIES.	TO	[Sum] PAID.
209	Wm. F. Kean	Erin, 28,	39	Feb. 17, 1881	6	2	17	May 4, 1887	Pneumonia	$1,000	6, Widow, 5 child'n	Ww	Ww & [rd]
210	Michael Connell	Leo, 5,	35	Nov. 19, 1886		2	7	May 30, 1885	Acute Meningitis'	"	4, " " 3 "	Widow	Ww &
211	Joseph McGilvray	Hamilton, 17,	23	July 23, 1885	1	10	2	Jan. 26, 1887	Phthisis Pulmonalis	"	4, " " 3 "	Widow	
212	J. J. [illegible]	[illegible] 49,	33	Sept. 8, 1881	5	8	6	May 14, "	Progressive Paralysis	"	3, " " 5 "	Wd. & guardian	
213	Philip [illegible]	Bass River, 30,	30	Sept. 9, "	5	9	12	June 21, "	Haemoptysis	"	6, " " 5 "	"	
214	[illegible]	St. Joseph, 38,	35	April 6, 1882	5	2	18	June 29, "	Phthisis	"	2, " 1 child	"	
215	John Broderick	[illegible] 17,	50	Mar. 4, 1880	7	3	25	July 23, "	Liver, Kid., & Lung Dis., Dropsy	"	6, " 5 child'n	"	
216	[illegible] Fahey	Sherwood, 8,	40	Jan. 21, 1881	6	6	2	July 27, "	Inflammation of Liver	"	5, " 5 "	"	
217	Cornelius Driscoll	Fenwick, 3,	28	Jan. 14, 1887		6	13	July 19, "	[illegible]	"	5, " 4 "	after	
218	Joseph [illegible]	Shields 63,	38	Dec. 24, 1880	6	6	10	July 31, "	Typhoid-Pneumonia	"	2, Ffler & Wdw	Mother &	
219	Wm Brooks	Leo, 5,	34	Mar. 20, 1881	6	2	10	May 19, "	Consumption of Lungs	"	2, Vdw & hdd	Ww	
220	Thaddeus J. [illegible]	Leo, 5,	34	May 20, 1881	6	2	25	May 31, "	Pulmonalis Phthisis	"	1, Widow	Guardian	
221	Michael J. Fennessy	St. John, 33,	44	Aug. 14, 1884	2	11	22	Sept. 23, "	Drowned	"	6, Children	Widow	
222	J. J. [illegible]	Essex, 16,	39	Nov. 14, 1884	2	8	11	Aug. 25, "	Senile Marasmus	"	3, Father, 2 sirs	F. & At'y for 2s.	
223	[illegible] O'Keefe	St. Augustine, 46,	44	Dec. 27, 1882	1	9	6	July 3, "	Phthisis Pulm otis	"	6, Widow, 5 child'n	G. of C. A. for W.	
224	John F. Rahl	St. Joseph, 11,	27	Mar. 8, "	5	7	12	Oct. 20, "	Pneumonia	"	2, " 1 hild	Guard. of child'n	
225	B. H. Holthaus	Columbus, 9,	39	April 23, 1883	4	5	27	Oct. 20, "	Dropsy, Heart Disease	"	4, " 3 child'n	Widow	
226	G. W. [illegible]	Iona, 10,	49	Mar. 14, 1880	7	8	5	Nov. 19, "	Pneumonia	"	1, Father	after	
227	B. J. [illegible]	Erin, 28,	42	Feb. 3, 1881	6	9	25	Nov. 28, "	Degeneration of Lungs	"	7, Widow, 6 child'n	Widow	
228	Thos Sweeney	Unity, 45,	49	Nov. 17, 1882	4	10	24	Oct. 6, "	Pneumonia	"	4, Children	Son & guardian	
229	John F. Reavy	Gallagher, 64,	25	April 17, 1887		7	17	Dec. 4, "	Railroad Accident	"	2, Father	Guardian	
230	M. J. Reagan	Cheverus, 6,	28	Oct. 15, 1886	1	1	15	Nov. 21, "	Railroad [kit]	"	2, Father & mother	Mother	
231	D. F. McGilvray	[illegible]	35	Dec. 1, 1880	7		7	Dec. 8, "	Pneumonia	"	5, Widow, 4 child'n	Widow	& held
232	Walter [illegible]	St. Colum[bkill], 65,	27	May 26, 1887		7	21	Jan. 17, 1888	Fract. of Skull, Blasting Accident	"	2, 1 child	Father	
233	John [illegible]	Columbus, 9,	36	May 12, 1881	6	6	27	Dec. 9, 1887	[ter] of Jaw	"	1, Widow, 5	Widow	
234	[illegible]	Fulton, 12,	45	April 27, 1880	7	8	14	Dec. 14, 1887	Chronic Interst. Pnmia	"	1, " 10	"	
235	[illegible]	Benedict, 39,	49	Mar. 31, 1881	1	10	11	Jan. 14, 1887	Paraplegia	"	11, " 7	"	& child'n
236	A. J. Harrington	Sherwood, 8,	55	Mar. 4, 1880		10	1	Dec. 24, 1886	Cerebral Paresis	"	8,	"	"
237	J. J. Callahan	St. James, 54,	29	July 2, 1883	3	7	2	Feb. 15, 1887	Phthisis Pulmonalis	"	1, Mother	Mother	
238	T. J. Dacey	Americus, 34,	38	Jan. 21, 1886	2	1	24	Feb. 22, 1888	Peritonitis	"	1, Brother	Brother	
239	M. Brahenny	St. Joseph, 11,	38	Mar. 13, 1882	5	11	9	Feb. 13, "	Dropsy	"	1, Widow	Widow	
240	H. H. Sullivan	Cathedral, 1,	56	Sept. 3, 1879	8	4	10	Jan. 13, "	Heart Disease	"	6, Children	Children	
241	John Murray	St. Joseph, 11,	38	Feb. 13, 1884	3	10	22	Jan. 5, "	Bright's Disease	"	5, Widow, 4	Widow	
242	[illegible] Ward	St. Alphonsus, 21,	34	May 4, 1881	6	9	27	Mar. 7, "	Consumption	"	1, Mother	Mother	
243	Wm. J. McAleer	[illegible] 13,	31	June 2, 1881	6	9	15	Mar. 1, "	Phthisis	"	4, Widow, 3	Widow	
244	John J. Craig	Leo, 5,	32	Feb. 7, 1880	8	1	17	Mar. 14, "	Hemorrhage of Lungs	"	1, Mother,	Mother	
245	Peter Kelliher	Leo, 5,	41	Mar. 21, 1881	6	11	11	Nov. 2, 1887	Phthisis Pulmonalis	"	10, Relatives	Relatives	
246	Peter Kilroy	St. Francis, 4,	56	Dec. 18, 1879	8	3	16	April 4, 1888	Chronic Bronchitis	"	2, Widow, 1 child	Widow	
247	John Collins	St. Thomas, 23,	28	Nov. 8, 1883	4	5	16	April 24, "	Typhoid Fever	"	1,	"	Ww

No.	Name	Society, No.	Age	Admitted	Died	Cause of Death	Amount	Beneficiaries	Relationship
249	James [Mw],	[Gus], 6,	45	April 28, 1882	5 May 3, 1888	Erysipelas	$1,000	4, Wdw, 3 child'n	Widow
250	M. A. Fox,	Essex, 16,	33	Feb. 10, 1881	24 May 4, 1887	Laryngeal Tumor	"	2, Mther and unt	Mher and unt
251	M. H. Kerrigan,	St. [Ags], 21,	53	Oct. 15, 1880	7 April 22, 1887	Pneumonia [Mia]	"	8, Children	Guardian
252	John J. Sullivan,	Leo, 5,	46	Feb. 9, 1887	1 May 10, 1888	Cardiac [Mia]	"	1,	Wdw
253	T. F. Powel,	[Gus], 6,	40	May 26, 1882	8 June 4, "	Val. Disease of Heart	"	5,	"
254	John Hines,	Essex, 16,	49	Oct. 4, 1883	7 May 21, "	Catarrhal Pneumonia	"	4, Widow	Sister-in-law
255	J. J. Callaghan,	Lafayette, 14,	55	April 29, 1881	11 April 3, "	Septicemia	"	6, Bro. and sistert	Wdw
256	Joseph Carley,	[Gus], 6,	36	May 27, "	2 June 29, "	Peritonitis	"	5, Wdw, 5 chil'n	"
257	[udes] Gorman,	Williams, 19,	33	My 2, "	28 June 30, "	Pleuritis	"	3,	"
258	Patrick Dowd,	St. Francis, 25,	42	July 12, "	1 July 12, "	Phthisis Pulmonalis	"	2, Children	Guardian
259	A. A. Vogel,	Holy [Ag], 51,	34	April 13, 1883	3 July 13, 1883	Bright's Disease	"	5, Wdw, 4 chil'n	Guardian & widow
260	James J. Whalen,	St. Anne, 41,	28	[do] 22, 1882	4 July 2, 1882	Phthisis Pulmonalis	"	3, moth., wid. & ch.	Moth., wid. & ch.
261	J. J. McKernan,	Iona, 10,	27	March 17, 1887	11 May 2, 1887	Phthisis Pulmonalis	"	3, Mther	Mother
262	Ines H. Hurley,	[Said], 48,	52	March 15, 1883	12 July 29, 1883	Cancer of Liver	"	3, Wdw, 2 child'n	Widow and child'n
263	Michael Maguire,	Fenwick, 3,	46	Jan. 16, 1880	5 August 6, "	Ascites	"	1, Son	Guardian
264	John Kelley,	St. Francis 4,	64	[do] 18, 1879	6 July 30, "	[Scid] Fever	"	3, Wdw, 3 chil'n	Widow and chil'n
265	P. Doherty,	Sherwood 8,	28	[do] 23, 1884	9 Aug. 14, "	Apoplexy	"	3, 2	Widow and
266	P. C. Fennelly,	St. Patrick, 7,	38	May 18, 1879	22 Aug. 15, "	Phthisis Pulmonalis	"	1, 3	i Wdw and child'n
267	J. L. Hennessey,	O'Connell, 22,	26	[do] 26, 1882	13 Jan. 23, "	Consumption	"	1, Mother	Mother
268	J. [Se],	Sherwood, 8,	35	Aug. 10, "	6 Aug. 26, 1886	Consumption	"	2, Children	Guardian
269	T. R. Fallon,	Essex, 16,	50	June 12, 1883	16 Sept. 17, 1888	Fracture of Skull	"	1, Widow	i Wdw
270	Wm. Lynch,	Cheverus, 6,	46	April 6, 1883	25 Oct. 1, "	Scelerosis	"	3, Wdw, 9 child'n	Widow and child'n
271	Ines Smith,	[Sul], 35,	45	June 18, "	5 Oct. 9, "	Pleurisy	"	3, 3	Widow and daugh.
272	James Fay,	St. Francis, 4,	53	Dec. 18, 1879	9 Oct. 15, "	Phthisis	"	3, 8	Widow
273	James Connell,	[Ma], 10,	48	Sept. 8, 1880	7 Oct. 7, "	Bright's Disease	"	9, iWdw	"
274	W. Manning,	Cathedral, 1,	68	Sept 3, 1879	11 Oct. 11, "	Paralysis	"	4, 3	Widow and child'n
275	John Burke,	Cathedral, 1,	39	Sept 12, 1883	1 Oct. 13, "	Phthisis	"	5, 4	Father
276	A. M. [uffe],	St. [Ja], 39,	35	June 12, 1883	4 Oct. 12, "	Pneumonia	"	1, Mother	Widow and child'n
277	M. Hogan,	SS. Peter and Paul, 15,	31	Oct. 5, 1886	21 Oct. 26, "	Chr. Catar. [Bnia]	"	1, Father	Father
278	M. H. Ryan,	SS. Peter and Paul, 15,	32	[Fb.] 5, 1884	9 Nov. 6, "	Pneumonia	"	9, Children	Child'n and guard.
279	J. F. Bradley,	Sheil, 35,	54	March 26, 1888	18 Nov. 20, "	Typhoid Pneumonia	"	5, Wdw, 4 child'n	Widow and child'n
280	Bartley Feeney,	Fitzpatrick, 13,	56	May 26, 1880	15 Nov. 11, "	Peritonitis	"	1, Wdw	Widow
281	[Mel] McDonough,	[Puk], 13,	44	Aug. 18, "	7 Nov. 25, "	Drowning	"	3, Wdw, 2 child'n	i Wdw and child'n
282	[Thas] L. Silk,	Mt. Pleasant, 20,	47	Aug. 10, 1883	20 Dec. 30, 1888	[Aplexy]	"	2, Widow, 1 son	Widow and son
283	Coleman O'Melia,	Leo, 5,	48	Jan. 16, 1880	19 Dec. 25, "	[Mfor] of Bowels	"	1, Widow, 1 son	Sister
284	Maurice Neville, [Mal],	Iona, 10,	53	Oct. 20, "	27 Jan. 17, 1889	Heart Disease	"	1, Sister	Wdw
285	Ines H.,	St. Joseph, 11,	35	Jan. 10, 1881	21 Dec. 31, 1888	Consumption	"	1, Widow	Mther
286	[Thas] F. Kelly,	Highland, 52,	40	April 16, 1883	2 Jan. 25, 1889	Phthisis Pulmonalis	"	1, Mother	Wer
287	Patrick Magee,	Erin, 28,	38	May 23, 1883	20 Feb. 7, "	Consumption	"	1,	Mw
288	James Dorgan,	St. [Ths], 29,	50	Feb. 17, 1881	8 Feb. 21, "	Phthisis	"	1,	Mther
289	Edward Millin,	Alphonsus, 21,	30	May 15, 1880	4 March 23, "	Consumption	"	2,	Mw
290	Michael D. Sullivan,	Sherwood, 8,	36	[do] 7, 1856	2 Jan. 31, "	Phthisis Pulmonalis	"	1, Wdw and daugh.	Widow and guard.
291	P. H. Kerrigan,	St. Augustine, 46,	45	Nov. 14, 1882	8 Jan. 17, "	Hemorrhage from Lung	"	1, Wdw	Widow
292	[Thy san],	Iona, 10,	51	[do] 23, 1880	24 March 17, "	Phthisis	"	1, Wdw	Widow
293	James Shortell,	Essex, 16,	...	June 23, "	... Phthisis	Phthisis	"	...	...
294	John F. Carroll,	St. John, 33,	54	[Mrch] 8, 1881	11 ...	Heart Disease	"	2, Wdw and daugh.	Widow and daugh.

ENDOWMENTS PAID — Cd.

No.	NAME.	COURT.	Age.	INITIATED.	Mem-bership. Yrs.	Mos.	Dys.	DATE OF DEATH.	CAUSE.	En-dow-ment.	NUMBER OF BENEFICIARIES.	TO WHOM PAID.
295	Alexander Mahoney,	St. 37,	40	March 25, 1881	8	9	22	Apl 17, 1889		$1,000	1, Widow	Widow
296	Peter H. Curley,	St. Francis, 4,	52	ed. 18, 1879	9	3	22	April 10, "		"	1, "	"
297	Jas.	na 10,	58	March 14, 1880	9	6	29	April 13, "		"	1, "	"
298	Wm Lynch,	k, 13,	35	May 5, "	8	11	11	April 16, "		"	7, sisters & 2 bros.	Sisters and bros.
299	Patrick L. ee,	St. rds. 4,	52	June 29, 1882	6	10	27	April "		"	1, Daughter	Dgr
300	John L. Sullivan,	Williams, 19,	50	une 1, 1882	5	5	16	May "		"	1, Ch	Ch
301	Corn us,	St. Gregory, 24,	46	Feb. 26, 1884	5	3	16	May 12, "	Uremia	"	4, Widow	Widow
302	L. Olny,	Leo, 5,	32	Feb. 26, "	5	1	1	May 27, "	Cerebral Hemorrhage	"	1, "	"
303	Maurice Sheehan,	St. Peter, 18,	53	Jan. 16, 1880	8	2	16	April 2, "		"	1, "	"
304	E. C. Bullard,	Sl 8,	52	July 22, "	9	1	9	May "	Cho.	"	1, Uncle	Attorney
305	Francis J. Daly,	6,	34	March 2, "	9	1	19	April 13, "	dis of	"	1, "	Attorney
306	Denis Od,	Jo, 5,	45	Feb. "	9	3	14	April 21, "	dis of r	"	1, Widow and child'n	Widow and chil ch
307	John Curley,	SS. Peter Paul 8, 15,	47	March 1, 1881	8	4	1	May 27, "	Toxaemia	"	7, Widow and child'n	Widow and guard.
308		St.	52	March 15, 1887	1	7	16	July 3, "	al Hemorrhage	"	7, Widow and child'n	Widow
309	George B. Duffy,	St.		N. 15, "	1	3	16	ly 1, "	Exhaustion att. leg	"	1, Mer	Mer
310	John L. O'Dea,	t 61, 67,	45	ch 14, 1888	6	4	6	July 8, "	ly c de	"	1, Widow	Widow
311	R. J. es,	Cheverus, 8,	29	Sept. 17, 1882	7	10	14	ug. 20, "	Cholera Morbus	400	1, Sister	Sister
312		Cheverus, 6,	26	Jan. 27, 1882	3	1	27	Mch 24, 1885		1,000		Hrs
314	Edward J. Franey,	Williams, 19,	44	March 9, 1880	8	4	18	ly 27, 1889	Heart Disease md by Chl. Morb.			
315	Martin L. Ford,	St. 19,	25	Jan. 20, 1888	4	1	5	Aug. 25, "	Hrt		1, Father	r
316	John L. O'Brien,	St. Peter, 18,	43	March 29, 1881	8	4	4	Aug. 5, "			8, Widow and child'n	Widow and guard.
37	Henry Seis,	St. Francis, 4,	51	ly 22, 1880	8	13		Aug. 5, "	es		2, Daughters	Ch
318	Charles Haney,	32,	40	an. 13, 1881	8	3	27	May 10, "	ly		1, Ch	Widow
320	Ts.	hs, 9,	42	March 4, "	8	4	4	Oct. 15, "	Ph		2, Ch	Ch
321	Andrew	o a, 10,	45	May 12, "	8	9	7	Set. 16, "	el		1, Widow	Guardian
322	Jas. McEnaney,	ns, 19,	57	Sept. 4, 1880	8	7	12	Ot 16, "	Phis dis		3, Widow	Widow
323	John J. y Driscoll,	a 3,	36	Sept. 16, 1883	4	1	22	Nov. 8, "	Phis and Heart		6, Widow and child'n	Widow and guard.
324	Thos. H. ny,	Americus, 34,	42	June 24, Oct. "	6	4	24	Dv. 13, "	Pa re		1, Widow	Widow
325	Hy J. Duggan,	St. 32,	42	March 15, 1881	8	7	28	Nov. 20, "	a causing Septicaemia		1, Widow	To 1dr
326		St. 3,	33	Sept. 18, 1883	5	2	5	Nov. 20, "			1, Mother	Widow
327	Martin Phelan,		39	l, 1883	4	1	16	Nov. "	Phthisis		1, Widow	Widow
328	John T.	Iona, 10,	48	ch 19, 1880	8	8	24	ec. 16, "	Phis		1, Widow	Widow
329	Edw'd F. ld	ona, 10,	51	March 4, "	9	1	27	ec. 8, "	els		1, Sister	Sister
330	Patrick L. sy,	St. Peter, 18,	32	April 16, 1883	6	2	4	Nov. 29, "	Phthisis		1, Mr	r
331		Shields, 63,	39	Jan. 4, 1887	2	7	22	Ot 20, "	Phthisis		10, Mr, Ww & Ch	Widow and Attorney
332								Sept. 6, "	r		1, Ww	

No.	Name	Branch, No.	Age	Date admitted		Date of death		Cause of death	Amount	Beneficiary	Relation
333	Hhs (Ein),	Benedict, 39,	47	da	27, 1883	16 Dec.	13, 1889	Heart Disease	$1,000	1, Hhw	Hhw
334	John (Hin),	St. Joseph, 11,	51	Dec.	22, 1882	23 da	15, "	Phthisis	"	1, i Hhw	"
335	Lawrence Andrews,	St. (Eis, 23),	39	da	12, 1885	7 Dec.	19, "	Phthisis	"	1, Hhw	"
336	Jeremiah Daly,	Iona, 10,	33	Aug.	18, 1887	2 Dec.	20, "	Phthisis	"	2, Hhw and hald	"
337	Ines (Ty),	Constantine, 49,	44	June	14, 1888	4 Jan.	2, 1890	Phthisis	"	1, Hhw	Hhw as guardian
338	James P. (My),	St. Francis, 4,	31	June	9, 1881	23 Jan.	10, "	Phthisis	"	1, Mother	Mother
339	John J. Sheely,	St. Joseph, 11,	37	Dec.	27, 1883	13 Jan.	10, "	Phthisis	"	1, Wl. and 2 ifn	Widow
340	Michael Keyes,	Sherwood, 8,	42	da	22, 1881	5 da	27, 1889	Insanity and drowning	"	3, Children	Guardian
341	F. P. Hansen,	Sarsfield, 48,	49	Feb.	8, 1884	16 Nov.	8, "	Pneumonia	"	2, Hhw and child	i Hhw
342	James McGinn,	Sarsfield, 48,	40	April	17, 1883	30 Jan.	3, "	Osteo-myelitis	"	4, Children	Guardian & child'n
343	John J. McCarthy,	St. Peter, 18,	29	June	7, 1883	20 Jan.	6, 1890	Phthisis Pulmonalis	"	1, Wow	i Hhw
344	Daniel (Mg),	St. Francis, 25,	35	da	18, 1882	5 Jan.	8, "	Phthisis	"	1, Sister	Sister
345	Michael B. Murphy,	Hamilton, 17, 20,	45	Ot.	7, 1880	2 Jan.	12, "	Phthisis	"	1, Sister	Sister
346	Patrick T. (Gk),	Mt. east,	52	June	8, 1885	19 Jan.	13, "	Cancer of stomach	"	8, Wid. and 7 child'n	Widow
347	John Breslin,	Qualey, 32,	31	July	17, 1882	2 Jan.	19, "	Phthisis	"	3, Wid. and 9 ifn	"
348	Bernard McLaughlin,	Cathedral, 1,	50	Sept.	9, 1879	19 Jan.	22, "	da	"	4, Wid. and 3 child'n	ad child'n
349	Hhs Deegan,	Benedict, 1,	46	Dec.	8, 1887	25 Feb.	4, "	Angina Pectoris	"	1, Widow	"
350	Edmund Boylan,	Constantine, 19,	33	Aug.	8, 1880	9 Feb.	17, "	Hd Fever	"	1, Sister-in-law	Sister-in-law
351	C. Morrissey,	St. Francis, 25,	55	My	10, 1881	9 Feb.	13, "	Phthisis Pulmonalis	"	5, Hhw and child'n	Hhw
352	W. H. O'Connor,	Erin, 28,	38	June	25, 1889	28 Feb.	23, "	Drowning	"	2, Hhw and hald	Hhw
353	Lawrence Forrest,	Constantine, 49,	26	Oct.	27, 1887	24 March	20, "	Pneumonia	"	1, Mother	Mother
354	James E. Doherty,	St. Joseph, 38,	40	Oct.	26, 1883	27 March	22, "	Ate Phthisis	"	9, Hhw and child'n	Hhw as guard.
355	Ihel G. Ryan,	Middlesex, 60,	26	Sept.	13, 1887	18 da	31, "	Pneumonia	"	3, Mother and child'n	as ther
356	W. C. J. Horsley,	St. da, 29,	31	Aug.	9, 1881	27 Apil	6, "	Spinal Neuritis	"	5, Hhw and child'n	"
357	Patrick F. Loxy,	St. Francis, 25,	45	Dec.	21, 1880	2 April	13, "	Phthisis	"	5, "	"
358	John B. Flynn,	Star of the Sea, 41,	39	May	5, 1887	11 April	21, "	Fra-ture of still	"	5, "	"
359	Maurice Walsh,	St. Columbkille, 65,	29	Aug.	16, 1888	16 April	23, "	Exhaust on from cdent	"	4, "	"
360	Michael Sull' ran,	Highland, 52,	31	Jan.	13, 1881	18 May	3, "	Phthisis	"	2, "	as guard.
361	M. J. Connolly,	Iona, 10,	33	July	2, 1883	23 May	5, "	Phthisis	"	3, "	"
362	M. J. Dris:oll,	St. ins 54,	45	da	2, 1884	9 May	13, "	Phthisis Pulmonalis	"	5, "	"
363	William Dunn,	SS. Peter and Paul, 15,	26	May	23, 1887	24 May	26, "	Ghc Bronchitis	"	6, "	"
364	Bryan Norton,	St. ins, 54,	38	Mar.	23, 1880	20 June	7, "	Spinal Meningitis	"	2, "	"
365	James C. Harkins,	Cheverus, 6,	51	July	21, 1883	14 June	17, "	Phthisis	"	6, "	"
366	John J. Bartlett,	Emerald, 53,	52	da	10, 1881	15 June	19, "	der	"	2, "	"
367	John Russell,	St. Per, 18,	52	Jan.	21, 1884	9 June	10, "	Accident	"	4, "	"
368	Adis Martin,	Holy Thnity, 51,	42	June	14, 1883	21 July	11, "	Meningitis	"	4, "	"
369	Jeremiah Horgan,	St. Alphonsus, 21,	43	April	5, 1883	25 July	31, "	Broncho Pneumonia	"	6, "	as guard.
370	John Morley,	Ide, 9,	38	June	11, 1889	26 July	19, "	Sunstroke	"	2, "	"
371	Timothy J. Soy,	Erin, 28,	36	Feb.	8, 1888	3 Sept.	6, "	Typhoid Fever	"	6, "	"
372	Diel P. Shn,	Sherwood, 8,	26	Mar.	4, 1890	16 Sept.	20, "	Uraemic poisoning	"	2, "	"
373	Edward Fitzgerald,	St. Kolumbkille, 65,	26	Feb.	5, 1889	8 Oct.	10, "	Typhoid Fever	"	4, "	"
374	My Callahan,	Phil Sheridan, 71,	37	Aug.	17, 1881	27 Oct.	14, "	Hem. from amputation of arm	"	1, "	"
375	Ines O'Hagan,	Essex, 16,	46	Jan.	28, 1881	8 Oct.	25, "	Consumption	"	6, "	Guardian
376	D. J. McCarthy,	Cheverus, 6,	38	da	7, 1881	20 Oct.	27, "	Phthisis Pulmonalis	"	4, "	"
377	John J. Ryan,	Mis, 19,	39	June	23, 1880	12 Nov.	5, "	Heart Failure	"	7, "	Hhw
378		Essex, 16,									

ENDOWMENTS PAID — Cont'd

No.	NAME.	CERT.	Age.	INITIATED.	Yrs.	Mos.	Dys.	DATE OF DEATH.	CAUSE.	Endow-ment.	NUMBER OF BENEFICIARIES.	TO WHOM PAID.
379	Michael Cadagan,	Fenwick, 3,	54	Jan. 21, 1881	9	9	15	Nov. 6, 1890	Typhoid fever	$1,000	4,	Widow and child'n
380	Patrick Sheerin,	St. Joseph, 11,	58	Sept. 12, 1881	9	2	3	Nov. 15, "	Meningitis	"	1,	Widow and
381	Hugh Canny,	... 6,	66	Feb. 11, 1880	10	9	25	Dec. 6, "	Heart Disease	"	6,	"
382	Michael ...,	St. Joseph, 11,	49	July 11, 1881	4	4	29	Dec. 10, "	Hernia	"	2,	"
383	William Richmond,	... 6,	49	March 2, 1880	10	9	17	Dec. 19, "	Consumption	"	4,	Daughter
384	...d Barry,	Fenwick, 3,	53	Feb. 18, 1881	9	10	4	Dec. 22, "	Fracture of skull	"	4,	Widow and child
385	Stephen Gay,	Williams, 19,	47	Dec. 19, 1881	9		14	Jan. 3, 1891	Heart Failure	"	4,	"
386	Al... Lausmann,	Holy Trinity, 51,	33	Aug. 9, 1886	4	4	26	Aug. 5, "	Pneumonia	"	6,	"
387	James H. Millerick,	St. ...ath, 75,	39	June 13, 1889	1	7	1	Jan. 14, "	Phthisis	"	7,	"
388	James Sweeney,	Sherwood, 8,	40	Jan. 11, 1883	8		4	Jan. 15, "	Intestinal obstruction after accident	"	7,	"
389	James Kenney,	... 19,	46	Jan. 3, 1881	10		21	Jan. 24, "	Phthisis	"	2,	"
390	Patrick ...,	Charles River, 55,	50	Oct. 6, 1885	5	3	26	Feb. 2, "	Tuberculosis Pulmonalis	"	7,	"
391	Jeremiah ...haney,	...al, 1,	46	Oct. 19, 1879	11	3	18	Feb. 2, "	Double Hernia	"	3,	"
392	Thos. F. Sullivan,	St. Thos, 29,	36	Sept. 8, 1881	9	6	9	Mch 17, "	Phthisis	"	5,	"
393	Michael Killilea,	Leo, 5,	58	May 14, 1880	10	10	4	Mch 18, "	Fatty Degeneration of heart	"	1,	"

Of the 54 deaths added to the Endowments paid since the last report there were initiated in

1879	2	1885	2
1880	7	1886	1
1881	14	1887	5
1882	2	1888	3
1883	9	1889	5
1884	3	1890	1

The member initiated in 1890 died of Typhoid fever. Of those initiated in 1889, 3 were Typhoid fever, 1 was accident, 1 was Phthisis.

The following deaths are also reported :

NAME.	COURT.	DIED.	CAUSE.
James H. Fox...	Constantine No. 49	Aug. 20, 1890.	Delirium Tremens...
M. McCready....	Canton No. 67...	Oct. 29, 1890..	Phthisis............
W. F. Hastings..	St. Anne No. 47...	Nov. 10, 1890.	(Supposed) Drowning
Henry Chambers.	St. Francis No. 4.	Jan. 24, 1891.	Cardiac Hypertrophia
F. M. McGroary ..	Griffin, No.66	March 5, 1891.	Accident............
Daniel Cronin....	Cheverus No. 6...	March 21, 1891	Pericarditis.........

These are held over for the reasons given below which are, of course, well understood in the Courts particularly interested.

James H. Fox who was a member of Constantine Court No. 49, died at Deer Island August 20, 1890, and the cause of death was returned by Dr. Thomas F. Roche, as Delirium Tremens.

Michael McCready was a member of Canton Court No. 67, and his Endowment was payable to his wife. His wife died first and the relatives are unable to agree upon a person for guardian.

W. F. Hastings was a member of St. Anne Court No. 47, and when initiated was a laborer on shore, the information is that being out of work, he with others engaged in a fishing venture, and at the time he was lost, Nov. 10, 1890, were fishing in Ipswich Bay, and while away from their vessel in a dory, he and two of his partners were drowned. The bodies of the other two were found, but Hastings was not found — proof of death was not considered sufficient.

Henry Chambers was a member of St. Francis Court No. 4, and is reported to have left no family or relatives. It is said that he made a will leaving the Endowment to the " Boston Society of Redemptorist Fathers." No claim has been made for the money.

Frederick McGroary was a member of Canton Court No. 67, and died from the consequences of an accident. His Endowment is payable to his father who is in Ireland and will be paid as soon as matters concerning the death and burial are settled.

Daniel Cronin was a member of Cheverus Court No. 6, and was before joining that Court, a member of Lyndon Court No. 50. Previous to joining Lyndon Court, he was a member of Sullivan Court No. 27. His application has not been found and as soon as a guardian is appointed the Endowment will be paid.

FINANCIAL CONDITION OF COURTS.

AMOUNTS RECEIVED FOR INITIATION FEES, COURT DUES AND ASSESSMENTS.

No. of Court.	NAME OF COURT.	Received for Initiation Fees 1890.	Received for Court Dues 1890.	Received for Endowment Fund 1890.	Per Capita for High Court Received 1890.	Received for Withdrawal Cards 1890.	Received from Other Sources 1890.	Received for Reserve Fund 1890.
1	Cathedral.	$15.00	$475.00	$ 2,034.25	$117.75	....	$57.70	$88.50
3	Fenwick.	3.00	69.45	921.60	49.50	....		33.00
4	St. Francis	33.00	316.50	1,592.60	83.25	....	55.66	109.50
5	Leo.	....	291.60	1,260.90	....	....	195 35	101.50
6	Cheverus.	45.00	123.00	1,085.10	57.00	....	2.00	88.50
7	St. Patrick.	10.00	130.00	639.55	....	.25	21.90	46.00
8	Sherwood.	....	....	2,051.80	....	....	536.75	71.00
9	Columbus.	33.00	115.50	506.00	30.00	....	14.05	38.50
10	Iona.	46.00	248.00	1,150.90	66.00	....	89.23	52.00
11	St. Joseph.	15.00	301.52	1,811.30	99.00	.25	....	75.38
12	Fulton.	2.00	75.50	371.80	21.00	....	....	28.00
13	Fitzpatrick.	....	153.75	735.90	38.25	.25	....	51.50
14	Lafayette.	15.00	201.75	1,024.00	53.75	....	46.13	72.50
15	SS. Peter and Paul.	18.00	206.64	796.10	50 25	....	36.00	3.00
16	Essex.	48.00	269.60	1,325.90	81.75	....	....	104.50
17	Hamilton.	12.00	184.75	904.20	50.25	50	....	66.50
18	St. Peter.	12.00	201.75	929.40	56.25	....	18.10	75.00
19	Williams.	30.00	438.50	954.10	.75	....	54 50	75.00
20	Mt. Pleasant.	23.00	237.00	1,075.10	63.00	.50	89.47	85.00
21	St. Alphonsus.	10.00	138.25	682 50	37.50	....	3.00	51.00
23	St. John	13.00	115.75	578.90	33.00	....	76 80	41.00
24	St. Gregory.	9.00	167.25	778.60	44.25	.25	31.60	60.50
25	St. Francis	24.00	332.25	1,349.70	....	....	290.00	56.00
26	St. Raphael.	12.00	101.85	595.65	34.50	....	46.25	....
28	Erin.	15.00	255.00	1,224.00	63.75	....	....	88.50
29	St. Thomas.	....	284.80	1,470.60	98 25	....	108 06	132.00
30	Bass River.	6.00	124.00	590.00	....	.25	....	19.00
32	*Qualey.	48.00	144.20	499.60	27.75	.25	27.60	38.00
33	St. John	5.00	201.40	808.70	32 25	....	125.70	47.50
34	*Americus.	15.00	215.55	1,053 00	49.50	....	.10	67.10
35	Sheil.	3.00	67.05	316.25	18.00	.25	....	24.00
37	Friendship	8.00	121.00	509.30	33.00	....	....	44.00
38	St. Joseph.	4 00	131.70	570.50	32.25	....	....	42.00
39	St. Benedict.	9.00	45.70	378.30	18.00	.25	5.10	26.00
41	Star of the Sea	28.00	104.55	477 40	25.50	....	....	32.00
43	St. Mary.	28.00	43.05	345.10	19.50	....	8 50	29.00
44	St. Bernard.	....	18.00	662.10	35.25	....	69.75	44.50
45	Unity	18.00	131.75	514.50	32.25	.50	67.75	47.50
46	St. Augustine.	6.00	78.00	369.80	21.00	....	....	14.50
47	St. Anne.	72.00	245.50	967.30	69.75	....	154.88	94 50
48	Sarsfield	12.00	256.75	1,064.90	63.75	....	263.85	87.50
49	Constantine.	9.00	176.25	888.90	47.25	.25	....	67.50
51	Holy Trinity.	42.00	171.15	1,388.50	75.00	....	77.79	51.00
52	Highland.	3.00	60.75	265.90	16.50	....	....	22.50
53	Emerald.	63.00	241.25	1,136 60	8.25	.25	313.88	49.50
54	St. James.	18.00	168.75	582.40	45 00	....	165.50	57.00
55	Charles River.	35.00	144.45	1,046.80	60.00	....	1.75	82.00
57	*Carroll.	3.00	42.05	519.45	27.75	....	131.85	33.50
58	Prospect.	....	83.10	465 65	19.25	....	26.20	20.00
59	Worcester.	12.00	158.00	843.30	57.50	....	34.87	37.00
60	Middlesex.	11 00	115.25	908.10	51.75	....	108.00	66.00
61	St. Lawrence.	15.00	182.25	823.80	49.50	.25	294.00	67.50
62	St. Catherine.	55.00	252.83	731.50	48.00	....	2 00	72.50
63	*Shields.	29.00	146.00	340.40	....	....	....	10.00
64	Gallagher.	33.00	159.80	703.80	39.75	....	107.72	56.45
65	St. Columbkille.	24.00	150.50	650.30	42.00	....	140.97	58.00
66	Griffin.	43.00	44.00	541.50	33 75	....	59 37	45.00
67	Canton.	25.00	79.75	634.10	43.50	....	306.48	63.00
68	St. Margaret.	....	119.60	397.85	20.25	.50	47.00	28.00
69	Stoughton.	28 00	130.00	655.80	45.75	....	387.84	....
70	St Michael.	14 00	114.00	476.10	30.00	....	82.05	21.50
71	Phil Sheridan.	13.00	208.25	935.90	55.25	.50	160.78	76.50
72	Merrimack.	48.00	128.25	447.70	34.50	....	518.85	50.00
73	Taunton.	30.00	109.30	1,268.55	82.50	....	143.98	107.00
74	Hendricken.	11.00	96.25	350.50	24.00	....	63.87	33.50
75	St. Jarlath.	6.00	91.90	786.70	48.00	.25	320 20	64.00
76	Quincy.	54.00	119.00	387.00	33.75	....	....	38 00
77	Mystic.	123.00	95.60	426.00	28.50	....	149.00	18.00
78	St. Monica.	75.00	34.75	167.65	15.00	....	....	10.00
	Total.	1,527.00	10,557.19	53,836 70	2,665.75	5.00	5,979 75	3,478.93

*Errors in returns.

FINANCIAL CONDITION OF COURTS.

AMOUNTS [PAID FOR ASSESSMENTS PER CAPITA, RESERVE AND DETAILED EXPENSES.

No. of Court.	NAME OF COURT.	Paid Endowment Calls 1890.	Paid H. C. Per Capita 1890.	Paid for Rent 1890	Paid for Salaries of Officers 1890.	Paid Medical Examiner 1890.	Paid H.C.P. 1890.	Paid for Sick Benefits 1890.	Paid Court Physician for Attendance on Members 1890.	Paid for Other Expenses 1890.	Paid Reserve Fund 1890.
1	Cathedral	$2,128.90	$117.75	$87.75	$87.25			$92.05	$113.00	$113.00	$158.50
3	Fenwick	921.60	49.50	30.00	49.00	$ 1.75	$ .25		34.00	40.13	33.00
4	St. Francis	1,937.30	83.25	100.25	100.00	21.00	3.00		96.43	129.19	109.50
5	Leo	1,328.50	76.50	57.00	16.50			95.00	102.00	34.65	101.50
6	Cheverus	1,085.10	57.00	57.50	50.60	28.00	4.00			46.30	88.50
7	St. Patrick	640.90	33.75	54.50	40.00	5.25	.75		45.00	61.33	46.50
8	Sherwood	1,990.70	104.25	96.00	125.00				141.75	98.83	149.50
9	Columbus	494.00	30.00	47.85	27.00	19.25	2.75			49.60	36.50
10	Iona	1,171.65	70.50	48.00	40.00	17.50	2.50	10.00	96.00	44.82	93.50
11	St. Joseph	1,977.60	99.00	48.00	62.00		.50		132.75	113.99	133.50
12	Fulton	371.80	21.00	52.00	15.00	1.75	.25		28.25	17.25	28.00
13	Fitzpatrick	735.90	39.00	38.00	41.00				26.00	46.98	51.50
14	Lafayette	1,125.10	55.50	36.00	64.00	12.25	1.75		81.00	32.25	75.00
15	SS. Peter and Paul	872.80	50.25	54.50	40.00	10.50	1.50			66.20	36.50
16	Essex	1,202.00	84.00	156.00	25.00	28.00	7.50			143.49	108.00
17	Hamilton	901.80	50.25	60.00	75.00	7.00	1.00		66.00	25.90	67.00
18	St. Peter	940.20	56.25	63.00					110.50	55.97	76.00
19	Williams	1,018.80	57.75	78.00	27.00	17.50	2.50	90.00	75.75	156.12	75.50
20	Mt. Pleasant	1,092.20	63.00	82.00	54.00	8.75	2.00	2.45	76.91	131.97	85.00
21	St. Alphonsus	682.50	37.50	70.00	51.00	5.25	.75	5.15		49.30	51.00
23	St. John	578.90	33.00	72.00		7.00	1.25			40.14	41.00
24	St. Gregory	781.70	45.00	75.00	20.90					106.45	68.00
25	St Francis	1,349.70	83.25	100.00	94.00	14.00			107.50	133.33	109.50
26	St. Raphael	617.30	34.50	25.00					44.00	71.44	
28	Erin	1,209.90	58.50	72.25	36.00				83.75	36.13	86.50
29	*St. Thomas	1,470.60	98.25	49.00	12.00		5.50	14.60	115.40	135.90	132.00
30	Bass River	624.00	25.50	53.08		5.50	.50		50.00		37.50
32	*Qualey	448.70	25.50	34.50	24.00	28.00	4.00		42.45	29.84	43.50
33	St. John	777.40	32.25	57.50	18.00	3.50	.50	105.00	58.00	42.20	47.50
34	*Americus	1,016.80	44.25	72.25	71.70	8.75	1.25		81.00	34.95	67.00
35	Sheil	328.50	18.00	20.00	15.55	1.75	.25			18.00	24.00
37	Friendship	440.30	33.00	48.00	30.00	4.25			57.50	15.00	22.00
38	St. Joseph	567.50	32.25	55.50					21.00	42.90	42.00
39	St. Benedict	378.80	18.00	25.00		5.25	.75			25.05	26.00
41	Star of the Sea	477.40	25.50	60.00		19.25	1.50		49.50	17.74	32.00
43	St. Mary	345.10	19.50	20.50		21.00	3.00			28.00	29.00
44	St. Bernard	674.00	35.25	128.75	15.00					5.27	49.00
45	Unity	614.80	32.25	35.00		10.50	1.50			59.87	45.50
46	St. Augustine	369.30	21.00	52.00		3.50	.50		15.25	12.75	29.50
47	St, Anne	950.30	69.75	51.50		47.25	5.25	115.00	182.25	212.02	85.50
48	Sarsfield	1,064.90	63.75	143.75	32.50	5.25	.75		135.50	185.49	87.50
49	Constantine	432.20	51.00	74.50	15.60	5.25	2.25			97.47	72.50
51	Holy Trinity	1,326.00	75.00	60.00	30.00	24.50	3.50	175.86		206.03	97.50
52	Highland	278.80	17.25	37.50		1.75	.25			5.05	23.00
53	Emerald	1,162.80	58.50	150.00		45.50	6.50	21.00	88.00	257.31	49.50
54	St. James	687.80	45.00	62.00	27.50	10.50	1.50	15.95	2.00	75.00	61.50
55	Charles River	1,042.90	61.50	75.00	25.00	17.50	2.50			17.65	86.00
57	Carroll	566.40	33.75	80.50	36.90	1.75	.25			66.65	45.00
58	*Prospect	472.40		24.00						30.40	39.95
59	Worcester	1,008.60	57.50	62.50	40.55	8.75	1.25			58.75	73.00
60	Middlesex	856.80	53.25	99.96	62.05	7.00	1.00			138.32	76.50
61	St. Lawrence	819.20	49.50	64.00	33.10	14.00	2.00		64.81	251.63	68.00
62	St. Catherine	737.50	49.50	47.00	3.00	26.25	4.00	82.00	75.00	108.18	69.00
63	*Shields	372.20	18.75	48.00		30.00	.50			168.02	30.50
64	Gallagher	737.30	39.75	46.00	60.00	23.00	1.00			120.63	56.00
65	St. Columbkille	650.30	42.00	68.50	33.20		1.75			218.05	58.00
66	Griffin	541.50	33.75	30.00		24.50	3.50			6.15	45.00
67	Canton	716.90	43.50	60.00						138.33	62.00
68	St. Margaret	420.10	21.00	40.00			.25		60.00	39.47	29.50
69	Stoughton	661.30	45.75	137.50		24.50	3.50		61.50	183.27	60.50
70	St. Michael	466.40	30.00	96.00		8.75	1.25			27.10	40.00
71	Phil Sheridan	935.90	55.25	72.00	15.00			95.00		123.60	76.50
72	Merrimack	526.40	34.50	65.00		31.50	3.50			395.53	48.50
73	Taunton	1,348.40	52.50	83.10	33.00	17.50	2.50	147.90	44.50	26.56	107.00
74	Hendricken	350.50	24.00			12.25	1.75		28.50	89.70	33.50
75	St. Jarlath	786.70	48.00	18.75	25.80	3.50	.50	70.00		263.34	63.50
76	Quincy	375.80	33.75	46.00		33.25				31.38	38.00
77	Mystic	426.00	28.50	26.00		71.75	10.25	25.00	27.00	55.25	18.00
78	St. Monica	167.65	15.00	18.00		43.75	6.25			29.60	10.00
	Total	54,543.60	3,109.00	4,124.74	1,784.20	799.50	104.00	1,046.96	2,532.50	5,678.04	4,088.95

*Error in returns.

FINANCIAL CONDITION OF COURTS.

No. of Court.	NAME OF COURT.	Balance on Hand Dec. 31, 1889.	Total Receipts 1890.	Total Expenditures 1890.	Total Balance on Hand Dec. 31, 1890.	Deficit from Business of 1890.	Bal. from Business of 1890.	Endowment Fund on Hand Dec. 31, 1890.	General Fund on Hand Dec. 31, 1890.	Contingent Fund on Hand Dec. 31, 1890.	Special Fund on Hand Dec. 31, 1890.	Court Reserve Fund on Hand Dec. 31, 1890.
1	Gabriel	$519.86	$2,788.20	$2,898.20	$409.86	$110.00		$ 33.55	$373.81			$ 2.50
3	Fenwick	89.96	1,076.56	1,159.13	7.28	82.68			7.28			
4	St. Francis	523.49	2,190.51	2,579.92	1808	389.41		18.70	115.38	81.35	$188.00	
5	Leo	337.87	1,849.35	1,811.30	3792		$ 38.05	53.30	53.27			
6	Cheverus	49.33	1,400.60	1,417.00	640	640		15.10	32.93			
7	St. Thick	203.93	847.70	927.98	8265	8028		61.10	33.90	74.65		17.25
8	Sherwood	785.42	2,659.55	2,706.03	738.94	46.48		14.90	677.84	4.05		32.00
9	Columbus	42.29	737.05	1,594.41	72.39		30.10		36.19	64.13		
10	Iona	122.14	1,652.13	2,567.84	9130	264.89	57.66		83.17	37.70	54.75	
11	St. Joseph	392.48	2,302.45	535.80	127.59	37.00		31.35	3.79			
12	Fulton	93.89	498.31	978.38	56.89		1.27		56.89			
13	Peck	81.95	979.65	83.22	88.22	69.72			75.27	7.95		
14	Lafayette	228.50	1,472.85	1,413.13	158.75	22.26		13.70	158.78			
15	SS. Peter and Paul	205.48	1,109.99	1,182.25	188.22		75.76		169.52		2.25	
16	Essex	304.13	K?9.15	1,753.99	379.89	35.75		2.40	379.89			
17	Hilton	44.57	1,218.20	1,283.95	1588	9.42			6.42			
18	St. Peter	205.30	1,292.50	1,301.92	882	46.07		15.30	195.88	67.00		2.00
19	Williams	427.19	1,552.85	1,598.92	8).1.12	25.21		9.10	365.82	332.60		87.08
20	Mt. Saint	201.24	1,573.07	1,598.28	8103	30.20			166.93			
21	St. Alphonsus	106.59	922.25	952.45	76.39		85.16	16.30	76.39			
22	St. John	27.50	858.45	773.29	112.66	5.60			112.66			
23	St. Gregory	106.75	1,091.45	1,097.05	101.15	1.99	60.67		84.85	63.96		
24	St. Francis	124.73	2,051.95	1,991.28	185.40				118.40	332.60		
25	St. Raphael	426.55	790.25	792.24	424.56	56.83	63.22	28.00	128.80	58.96		
26	Erin	88.58	1,583.03	1,583.03	1180		60.46	21.00	99.96	69.52		
28	*St. Thomas	336.35	2,098.71	2,033.25	396.81			81.23	57.20			
29	Bass River	114.03	739.25	796.08	57.20		104.91		74.27		2.25	
30	*Qualey	97.08	785.40	630.49	201.99		78.70	500	78.70	80.07		
32	St. John		1,220.55	1,141.85	78.70		2.30	10.50	44.65			
33	*Americus	138.97	1,100.25	1,397.95	141.27	56.07	2.50	39.52	54.77	36.60		
34	Sheil	52.27	428.55	426.05	54.77		65.25	43.25	22.00			
35	Friendship		715.30	650.05	65.25		19.30	3.00	18.00	31.00	28.00	
37	St. Joseph	60.70	780.45	711.15	80.00	15.44	4.00					
39	Benedict		476.35	472.35	4.00							
41	Star of the Sea	100.70	667.45	682.89	85.26		85.26		85.26			
43	St. Mary	11.22	473.15	466.10	187		7.05		18.27			

*Error in returns.

FINANCIAL CONDITION OF COURTS—*Continued*

No. of Court.	NAME OF COURT.	Balance on Hand Dec. 31, 1889.	Total Receipts 1890.	Total Expenditures 1890.	Total Balance on hand Dec. 31, 1890.	Deficit from Business of 1890.	Bal. from Business of 1890.	Endowment Fund on Hand Dec. 31, 1890.	General Fund on Hand Dec. 31, 1890.	Contingent Fund on Hand Dec. 31, 1890.	Special Fund on Hand Dec. 31, 1890.	Court Reserve Fund on Hand Dec. 31, 1890.
44	St. Bernard	$91.01	$829.60	$907.27	$13.34	$77.67		$13.34	$214.55			$3.00
45	Unity	257.02	813.25	742.42	1685		$13.83	58.30	40.94	41.40		6.00
46	St. Augustine	103.34	488.80	503.80	88.34	15.00			2.62	139.12		4.50
47	St. Anne	261.13	1,603.93	1,718.82	1424	11489			99.61			
48	Sarsfield	70.25	1,748.75	1,719.39	99.61		29.36		140.08			
49	Holy Trinity	227.56	1,189.15	750.77	154.58			14.50	50.76		$34.25	
51	Highland	340.46	1,805.44	1,998.39	147.51		192.95	62.50	45.63			
52	Emerald	40.58	368.65	363.60	45.63	21.38	5.05		148.50			
54	St. James	172.38	1,812.73	1,834.11	151.00		46.40	2.50	43.10			
55	Giles River	144.35	1,036.65	990.25	190.75		41.95	147.63	120.72			
57	*Carroll	155.77	1,370.00	1,328.05	197.72	73.60		77.00	49.28	121.97		
58	*Prospect	248.65	757.60	831.20	175.05	168.23			60.79		3.80	24.50
59	Worcester	308.77	614.20	566.75	9.08	34.78			18.07	55.25		
60	Middlesex	104.15	1,142.67	1,310.90	140.54		66.06	51.30	129.96			
61	St. Lawrence	71.80	1,260.10	1,294.88	69.37	39.60		7.90	194.93			
62	St. Catherine	234.53	1,432.30	1,366.24	187.86				50.17			
63	*Shields	150.34	1,161.83	1,201.43	194.93	142.07		24.00	38.88			
64	Gallagher	50.39	525.40	667.47	74.17		16.84	27.90	158.15	86.58		.45
65	St. Columbkille	250.76	1,100.52	1,083.68	67.23	6.03			17.32		50.67	64.32
66	Griffin	50.09	766.62	1,071.80	244.73		82.22		6.76	188.12	220.76	1.00
67	Canton	299.94	1,151.83	684.40	132.31		131.10	14.40	84.61	4.00		
68	St. Margaret	85.73	613.20	1,020.73	431.04		2.88		287.51			
69	Stoughton	236.94	1,247.89	610.32	88.61		9.57		94.88			19.00
70	St. Michael	32.03	737.65	1,177.82	306.51		68.15	5.30	30.40			
71	Phil Sheridan	164.16	1,450.18	669.50	100.18		76.93		260.69		166.69	44.00
72	Taunton	203.22	1,227.30	1,373.25	241.09		122.37	26.10	84.97		36.30	2.50
73	Hendricken	332.96	1,741.83	1,104.93	325.59	151.63		96.86	58.92			
74	St. Jarlath		1,892.96	1,280.09	181.83		38.92	29.02	64.32	123.13	40.89	.50
75	Quincy	191.88	579.12	558.18	38.92		36.96		15.00			
76	Mystic	29.55	1,317.05	687.75	228.84		73.57		162.35			
77	St. Monica		631.75	290.25	44.02		12.15		12.15			
	St. Monica		840.10		152.35							
			302.40		12.15							
	Total	$11,206.80	$77,908.32	$77,909.69	$10,712.60	$2,075.62	$1,872.07	$1,175.75	$6,720.74	$1,499.93	$996.44	$306.10

*Error in returns.

ENDOWMENT FUND.

Dr.

Assessment Call No. 62		$3 10
" " " 63		5 20
" " " 64		5 20
" " " 65		6 20
" " " 66		91 60
" " " 67		554 75
" " " 68		1,393 50
" " " 69		4,728 35
" " " 70		4,789 13
" " " 71		4,795 70
" " " 72		4,974 70
" " " 73		4,963 60
" " " 74		4,890 00
" " " 75		5,015 25
" " " 76		4,999 10
" " " 77		4,936 90
" " " 78		5,038 50
" " " 79		5,221 95
" " " 80		140 90
		$56,553 70
Balance, April, 1890		7,803 29
		$64,356 99

Cr

Patrick T. Clark,	of Mt. Pleasant,	No. 20	$1,000 00
Thomas Deegan,	" Benedict,	" 39	1,000 00
Daniel Manning,	" St. Francis,	" 25	1,000 00
Bernard McLaughlin,	" Cathedral,	" 1	1,000 00
Michael Keyes,	" Sherwood,	" 8	1,000 00
Frank P. Hansen,	" Sarsfield,	" 48	1,000 00
Edmund Boylen,	" Constantine,	" 49	1,000 00
Michael B. Murphy,	" Hamilton,	" 17	1,000 00
John J. McCarthy,	" St. Peter,	" 18	1,000 00
John Breslin,	" Qualey,	" 32	1,000 00
Christopher Morrissey,	" St. Francis,	" 25	1,000 00
W. H. O'Connor,	" Erin,	" 28	1,000 00

W. C. J. Horsley,	of St. Thomas,	No. 29....	1,000 00
Maurice Walsh,	" St. Columbkille,	" 65....	1,000 00
John B. Flynn,	" Star of the Sea,	" 41....	1,000 00
Michael G. Ryan,	" Middlesex,	" 60....	1,000 00
James E. Doherty,	" St. Joseph,	" 38....	1,000 00
Matthew J. Driscoll,	" St. James,	" 54....	1,000 00
Michael J. Connolly,	" Iona,	, " 10....	1,000 00
Patrick F. Lacy,	" St. Francis,	" 25....	1,000 00
Michael Sullivan,	" Highland,	" 52....	1,000 00
Bryan Norton,	" St. James,	" 54....	1,000 00
John Russell,	" St. Peter,	" 18....	1,000 00
James J. Harkins,	" Cheverus,	" 6....	1,000 00
John J. Bartlett,	" Emerald,	" 53....	1,000 00
Alois Martin,	" Holy Trinity,	" 51....	1,000 00
Michael McTigne,	" Erin,	" 28....	1,000 00
Jeremiah Horgan,	" St. Alphonsus,	" 21....	1,000 00
William Dunn,	" SS. Peter and Paul,	" 15....	1,000 00
John Morley,	" Constantine,	" 49....	1,000 00
Timothy J. Sweeney,	" Sherwood,	" 8....	1,000 00
Lawrence Forrest,	" Constantine,	" 49....	1,000 00
Daniel P. Sullivan,	" St. Columbkille,	" 65....	1,000 00
Edward Fitzgerald,	" Phil Sheridan,	" 71....	1,000 00
Timothy Callahan,	" Essex,	" 16....	1,000 00
James O'Hagan,	" Williams,	" 19....	1,000 00
John J. Ryan,	" Essex,	" 16....	1,000 00
Patrick Sheerin,	" St. Joseph,	" 11....	1,000 00
Michael Cadagan,	" Fenwick,	" 3....	1,000 00
William Richmond,	" Cheverus,	" 6....	1,000 00
Michael Walsh,	" St. Joseph,	" 11....	1,000 00
James McGinn,	" Sarsfield,	" 48....	1.000 00
Hugh Canney,	" Cheverus,	" 6....	1,000 00
Daniel J. McCarthy,	" Cheverus,	" 6....	1,000 00
David Barry,	" Fenwick,	" 3....	1,000 00
Stephen Gray,	" Williams,	" 19....	1,000 00
Alphonse Lausman,	" Holy Trinity,	" 51....	1,000 00
James H. Millerick,	" St. Jarlath,	" 75....	1,000 00
James Sweeney,	" Sherwood,	" 8....	1,000 00
James Kenney,	" Williams,	" 19....	1,000 00
Jeremiah McSweeney,	" Cathedral,	" 1....	1,000 00
Patrick McCarthy,	" Charles River,	" 55....	1,000 00
Thomas F. Sullivan,	" St. Thomas,	" 29....	1,000 00
Michael Killilea,	" Leo,	" 5....	1,000 00

$54,000 00

Balance on hand 10,356 99

$64,356 99

GENERAL FUND.

Dr.

Balance, April, 1890.....................	$30 91	
Sale of Postal Cards, Books, &c.....................	877 10	
Per Capita, 1890	3,266 75	
Charter to Court No. 80, on account	35 00	
Benefit Certificates..............................	69 50	
		$4,279 26

Cr.

RENT.

Cashman, Keating & Co. :
    Office of High, Standing Committee to March 1891....... $300 00

PRINTING.

Eustis Towle :

6 Lots Postal Cards	$4 20	
1,000 Envelopes (addressed).................	2 50	
3,000 Re-instatement Blanks	12 75	
Assessment Call	4 00	
10 Lots Postal Cards	7 00	
1,000 Envelopes (addressed).................	2 25	
6 Lots Postal Cards .....:...................	4 20	
Assessment Call	4 00	
Financial Statements	4 00	
Report of Membership	4 00	
Roll of Officers	2 50	
Reports of D. H. C. R......................	3 50	
Roll of Membership........................	4 50	
16 Lots Postal Cards .:.....................	11 50	
Assessment Call	4 00	
200 Cards	75	
Assessment Call	4 00	
14 Lots Postal Cards	9 80	
		$89 45

Cashman, Keating & Co. :

200 Annual Reports........................	$143 15	
3,500 Annual Reports	274 32	
100 Circulars .....:........................	4 75	
		422 22

W. F. & P. B. Dunham :

4 Lots Postal Cards	$3 20
500 Bill Heads..............................	4 00
18 Lots Postal Cards	14 40
Assessment Call	4 00
" "	4 00
500 Notice of Meeting Cards H. S. C.	1 75
1,000 Cards	2 00
3,000 Medical Examiner Slips	3 50
List of D. H. C. R...........................	5 50
Assessment Call	4 00
2 Lots Postal Cards	1 60
Assessment Call	4 00
17 Lots Postal Cards	13 60
1,000 Letter Heads blocked	4 00
1,000 Receipts	2 50
Assessment Call	4 00
500 Notices to C. R.........................	1 50
500 Notices to Treasurer.....................	1 50
Assessment Call	4 00
" "	4 00
2 Lots Postal Cards	1 60
Electrotype Plate	1 45
1,000 Envelopes.............................	3 00
1 Lot Postal Cards	80

93 90

Eastburn Press :

1,000 Envelopes..........	$4 00
300 D. H. C. R..............................	9 25

13 25

9.?3.47

TRAVELLING EXPENSES.

High Standing Committee :

To Newburyport	$2 00
780 Mile Ticket Boston & Albany Railroad	15 60
In Boston	90
To Haverhill	12 35
1,000 Mile Ticket Boston & Maine Railroad....	20 00
To Randolph	4 95
In Boston..................................	45
327 Mile Ticket Boston & Albany Railroad	6 54
In Boston	3 70
556 Mile Ticket Boston & Albany Railroad	11 12
To Norwood...............................	14 80
In Boston	2 25
To Taunton	16 95
1,000 Mile Ticket Old Colony Railroad........	20 00

9×3.47

To Brighton, Newburyport, and Brockton	$ 4	10
1,000 Mile Ticket Boston & Maine Railroad....	20	00
To New Bedford (4 Trips)	37	65
1,000 Mile Ticket Old Colony Railroad	20	00
To Taunton and New Bedford	25	55
To Amesbury............................	1	50
To New Bedford	7	79
1,000 Mile Ticket Old Colony Railroad........	20	00
To Lynn and Worcester	7	25
To Plymouth (2 Trips)	32	08
In Boston	1	50
To Ipswich.............................	11	30
1,000 Mile Ticket Boston & Maine Railroad ...	20	00
565 Mile Ticket N. Y. & New England R. R. ..	11	30
To Taunton		65
917 Mile Ticket Boston & Albany Railroad	18	34
To Salem, Quincy, and Newburyport..........	8	25

$378 87

Deputy High Chief Rangers :

Peter A. Sullivan	$17	25
George A. O'Bryan	26	00
Andrew M. Lanigan	21	50
Thomas J. Dunn	24	50
Thomas F. Sullivan	5	00
" "	14	00
" "	16	50
" "	8	00
Archibald McDonald......................	13	00
John C. Pendis	5	30
Henry P. Muldoon.	3	25
N. Fairclough	12	00
" "	8	00
P. A. Donovan	2	50
John Hayes	5	00
William T. Maloney	6	00
P. Smith D. H. C. R......................	2	50

190 30

REGALIA.

Frederick Alford :

1 Set	$8	50
4 "	34	00
2 "	17	00

155Y.1Y

SEALS.

S. M. Spencer :

Repairs	$2 00	
Repairs	1 20	
1 Seal	5 00	
Repairs	1 25	
1 Seal	5 00	
		$14 45

BOSTON POST OFFICE.

Postal Cards	$645 00	
Stamped Envelopes and Stamps	134 40	
		779 40

MISCELLANEOUS.

John Carter, Paper	$2 83	
H. M. Temple, Catering for Convention	118 50	
Thomas A. Jackson, Insurance, Office Furniture and Stationery	18 00	
Town Clerk of Tilton, N. H., Certificate of death	25	
Boston Gas Light Company	12 09	
H. W. Upham, Binder, on account	50 00	
H. Dodd, for the " Dial "	3 85	
J. J. Banta, Halls for Convention	20 00	
W. E. Fitzgerald, Labor	5 00	
Boston Regalia Company, 2 Ballot boxes	2 50	
M. R. Warren, 3 Record books	2 10	
T. J. Murphy, Preliminary Expenses forming Court	27 60	
Samuel Hobbs, Stationery	8 35	
C. Bowen, moving Safe	8 00	
Cleaning Office, 14 times	17 00	
Telegrams, Messengers and Expressing	10 92	
Expenses of Convention	30 65	
Cashman, Keating & Co., Gas	8 24	
Hon. O. A. Galvin, Professional Services	125 00	
		470 88
Salary High Secretary-Treasurer to April, 1890		150 00
to April, 1891		1,200 00
Balance on hand		113 03

4.279.
113.
4.166

RESERVE FUND.

Dr.

Assessment No. 1	$2,191 48	
" " 2	2,248 50	
		$4,439 98

Cr.

Paid Trustees		$4,439 98
Due from Courts for Books and Cards		396 83

DEPUTY HIGH CHIEF RANGERS.

FOR TERM OF 1891-'92.

DIS-TRICT.	COURTS.	No.	NAME AND RESIDENCE OF D. H. C. R.	COURT OF WHICH D. H C.R IS A MEMBER.
1	Cathedral	1	Geo. A. O'Bryan, Norwood	St. Catherine....62
	St. James	54		
2	Fenwick	3	George F. Low, 271 Summer Street, E. Boston...	Leo..... 5
	Cheverus	6		
3	St. Francis	4	James O'Kane, Charlestown	Cheverus.........6
	LaFayette	14		
	St. Michael	70		
4	Leo	5	Garret H. Keefe, No. 63 Palmer Street, Roxbury...	Mt. Pleasant.....20
	Williams	19		
	Star of the Sea	41		
5	St. Patrick	7	John E. Heslin, 33 Arklow Street, Roxbury	St. Francis.......4
	SS. Peter and Paul.	15		
6	Sherwood	8	Thomas W. O'Rourke, No. 108 Boston St., Dorchester...	St. James....... 54
	Holy Trinity	51		
	Quincy	76		
7	Columbus	9	E. F. Chamberlain, Mattapan	St. Peter.........18
	St. Francis	25		
	Erin	28		
8	Iona	10	D. F. Sullivan, No. 25 Hudson Street, Boston....	Sherwood.... 8
	Canton	67		
9	St. Joseph	11	J. B. Buckley, Malden	Iona 10
	Fitzpatrick	13		
10	Fulton	12	R. Farrenkopf, No. 108 Kneeland Street, Boston.	Sherwood.........8
	St. Peter	18		
	St. John	23		
11	Essex	16	Lawrence J. Watson, Beverly Farms	St. Margaret.... 68
12	Hamilton	17	H. C. Griffin, No. 8 Eaton Street	St. Joseph....No 11
13	Mt. Pleasant	20	F. L Smith, Brockton	St. Thomas......29
	St. Alphonsus	21		
14	St. Gregory	24	Michael Edmonds, 13 Gay Head Street, Roxbury...	Cathedral.........1
	Sarsfield	48		
15	St. Raphael	26	A. M. Lanigan, No. 644 Harrison Avenue, Boston.	Cathedral.........1
	St. Catharine	62		
16	St. Thomas	29	A. H. McDonald, Stoughton	Stoughton 69
	Hendricken	74		
17	Bass River	30	G. A. Lomasney, Lynn	Lafayette....... 14
	St. Margaret	68		
18	Qualey	32	J. H Watson, P. H. C. R., Beverley Farms	Essex............16
19	St. John	33	T. F. Crosby, Parker Hill Avenue, Roxbury....	St. Francis.......4
	St. Joseph	38		
20	Americus	34	J. F. Riley, Dedham	St. Raphael......26
	Constantine	49		
21	Sheil	35	P. A. Sullivan, No. 19 Wareham Street, Boston..	Americus....... 34
	St. Mary	43		
22	Friendship	37	John Vogel, West Quincy	St. Francis......25
23	St. Benedict	39	Wm. A. Flaherty, Somerville	St. Benedict......39
	Mystic	77		

DEPUTY HIGH CHIEF RANGER — *Continued.*

DIS-TRICT.	COURTS.	No.	NAME AND RESIDENCE OF D. H. C. R.	COURT OF WHICH D. H. C. R. IS A MEMBER.
24	St. Bernard........ 33 Middlesex 60		Wm. F. Rooney, Waltham	Prospect.........58
25	Unity 45		Willam Condon, Bridgewater	Unity.......... 45
26	St. Augustine...... 46		Edward J. Leary, South Boston..................	SS. Peter & Paul..15
27	St. Anne........... 47		John J. Flaherty, Gloucester......................	St. Anne........ 47
28	Highland.......... 52 Carroll............. 57		J. F. Fleming, 1 Prentiss Street, Roxbury.......	Columbus 9
29	Emerald............53		F. E. Hines, M. D., Salem	Essex.......... 16
30	Charles River...... 55		Dr. Jas. R. McLaughlin, Newton....	Charles River....55
31	Prospect........... 58		T. F. Gallagher, Watertown	Charles River....55
32	Worcester 59		J. H. Fitzgerald, Worcester	Worcester 59
33	Shields............. 63		P. J. Murray, Springfield.....................	Gallagher....... 64
34	Gallagher.......... 64		J. J. Callanan, Holyoke.......................	Shields......... 63
35	St. Columbkille.... 65 St. Lawrence...... 61		P. O'Loughlin, Brookline ....:........	St. Joseph.......11
36	Griffin............. 66		William H. Rogers, North Attleborough.............	Sarsfield........ 48
37	Stoughton.......... 69		D. F. Buckley, North Easton...................	Hendricken......74
38	Phil Sheridan...... 71 St. Monica......... 78		D. H. Maguire, Haverhill......................	Merrimac........72
39	Merrimack......... 72 St. Jarlath......... 75		James F. Carens, Newburyport...................	Phil Sheridan... 71
40	Taunton........... 73 J. B. O'Reilly...... 79 Gen. Sherman..... 80		J. G. Fennessey, P. H. C. R. Court House, Boston............	St. James....... 54
	AT LARGE.....		Philip Smith, P. V. H. C. R., East Boston. John H. Watson, P.H. C. R., Beverly Farms. Thos. Sproules, P.V.H.C.R., Roxbury. E. A. Irvine, North Attleborough. George F. Brammer, Taunton.	

MEDICAL EXAMINERS.

For Term Ending April, 1891.

Dist.	Place.	Examiner.	Courts.
1	Boston	S. A. Callanan, M. D., Warren St., cor. Warren Place	1, 12, 34.
2	Boston	J. A. Coogan, M. D.	3, 6, 13, 35.
3	Boston, Brookline	Joseph P. Murphy, M. D., 1607 Tremont St., Rox., also at Brookline	4, 61, 52.
4	Boston, East Boston	James F. Ferry, M. D., 10 Chelsea St., E. B.	5, 19, 41.
5	South Boston	Wm. H. Devine, M. D., 599 Broadway, S. B.	7, 15, 46, 70.
6	Boston	Wm. G. McDonald, M. D., 221 Shawmut Av	8, 11, 28, 49, 51.
7	Boston	F. T. Mara, M. D., 93 Broadway, S. B.	9, 54,
8	Malden	C. D. McCarthy, M. D.	10.
9	Lynn	C. A. Ahearne, M. D.	14.
10	Salem	Francis E. Hines, M. D.	16, 30, 68.
11	Somerville	J. A. Gregg, M. D.	17, 33, 39.
12	Dorchester	J. P. Lumbard, M. D.	18, 24.
13	Boston	E. T. Galligan, M. D., 88 Warren St., Roxbury,	20, 21, 37, 38.
14	Hyde Park	John C. Lincoln, M. D.	23.
15	Quincy	Jos. M. Sheahan, M. D.	25.
16	Dedham	A. H. Hodgdon, M. D.	26.
17	Brockton	Benedict Donovan, M. D.	29.
18	Woburn	J. H. Conway, M. D.	32.
19	Randolph	O. M. Sheridan, M. D.	43.
20	West Newton, Waltham	C. J. McCormick, M. D.	44, 58.
21	Bridgewater	G. H. Watson, M. D.	45.
22	Gloucester	Philip Mooney, M. D.	47.
23	North Attleborough	T. F. McDonough, M. D.	48.

MEDICAL EXAMINERS — *Continued.*

24 Peabody.......................JOHN SHANNAHAN, M. D.....53.

25 Watertown, Brighton.............M. J. KELLEY, M. D.,
Watertown.............55, 65.

26 Jamaica Plain...................J. P. BROIDRICK, M. D ....57.

27 Worcester.......................J. H. KELLY, M. D........59.

28 Newton.........................F. M. O'DONNELL, M. D....60.

29 Norwood........................L. N. PLYMPTON, M. D....62.

30 Holyoke........................F. P. DONOGHUE, M. D.....63.

31 Springfield.....................A. J. DUNNE, M. D....... 64.

32 Franklin........................J. C. GALLISON, M. D.......66.

33 Canton.........................THOS. D. LONERGAN, M. D..67.

34 Stoughton......................MICHAEL GLENNON, M. D...69.

35 Newburyport....................J. J. HEALY, M. D........71.

36 Haverhill.......................JOHN F. CROSTON, M. D....72.

37 Taunton........................J. B. MURPHY, M. D........73

38 North Easton...................T. H. McCARTHY, M. D.....74.

39 Amesbury.......................J. H. O'TOOLE, M. D.......75.

40 Quincy.........................S. M. DONOVAN, M. D......76.

41 Medford........................C. H. WINN, M. D........77.

42 Lawrence.......................D. J. O'SULLIVAN, M. D. ...78.

43 New Bedford....................J. F. SULLIVAN, M. D.....79.

44 Plymouth.......................EDGAR D. HILL, M. D.....80.

REPRESENTATIVES.

	Representatives.	Court.	No.	Proxy Representatives.
1	J. J. Lanigan	Cathedral	1	D. F. O'Sullivan.
2	M. Edmonds....... .	"	"	Jeremiah Sullivan.
3	J. M. Singler	"	"	M. McBarron.
4	Thos. P. Burke	Fenwick	3	Patrick F. Mahoney.
5	W. E. Shay..........	St. Francis	4	T. F. Crosby.
6	T. Sproules..........	"	"	Jere. J. O'Brien.
7	John Brant	Leo	5	Daniel Hayes.
8	George F. Lowe......	"	"	Thomas F. Doherty.
9	Owen A. Galvin......	Cheverus	6	William T. Rich.
10	James Cashin.......	"	"	D. J. Harkins.
11	H. P. Muldoon.......	St. Patrick	7	Edward Tracy.
12	John P. Dore.......	Sherwood...........	8	A. J. Lill.
13	D. F. Sullivan	"	"	M. J. Fitzgerald.
14	Hugh Montague.....	"	"	J. J. Stephan.
15	James F. Supple	Columbus...........	9	James F. Fleming.
16	P. J. McMahon.......	Iona................	10	J. B. Buckley.
17	P. H. Desmond	"	"	M. A. Divver.
18	H. C. Griffin	St. Joseph...........	11	P. F. McGarrigle.
19	Daniel A. Cronin.....	"	"	Edw. Riley.
20	Patrick M. Keating...	"	"	Patrick O'Loughlin.
21	Michael O'Brien	Fulton..............	12	James Finegan.
22	J. M. Jordan........	Fitzpatrick	13	P. F. Reynolds.
23	Dr. C. A. Ahearne ...	Lafayette	14	John Hayes.
24	James O'Neill.......	"	"	G. A. Lomasney.
25	Patrick A. Donovan..	SS. Peter & Paul	15	J. B. White.
26	D. J. O'Brien....	Essex	16	W. J. McGee.
27	J. J. Hartigan........	"	"	Dr. F. E. Hines.
28	John Hurley.........	Hamilton	17	L. J. Lyons.
29	T. J. Lane...........	St. Peter	18	E. F. Chamberlain.
30	John H. Donovan	"	"	John J. Curran.
31	F. S. Maloney	Williams............	19	M. J. Kelly.
32	Philip Smith.........	"	"	James Douglass.
33	J. J. Gately..........	Mt. Pleasant........	20	Frank J. McGrath.
34	G. H. Keefe	"	"	J. F. Dever.
35	J. T. Brickley........	St. Alphonsus	21	Francis A. Mahan.
36	F. S. Sullivan........	St. John	23	John Brady.
37	Michael Dunican	St. Gregory	24	John O'Callaghan.
38	John Cole	St. Francis...........	25	M. F. O'Brien.
39	John Vogel..........	"	"	J. C. Pendis.
40	John F. Riley........	St. Raphael	26	Patrick A. Nolan.
41	John T. Daly	Erin	28	Daniel Shannon.
42	Jeremiah O'Mara.....	"	"	C. J. Lynch.
43	John E. Saxton	St. Thomas	29	P. McCarthy.
44	Thomas F. Sullivan ..	"	"	Timothy F. Roach.
45	F. L. Smith.........	"	"	P. Gilmore.
46	W. J. Brown.........	Bass River..........	30	D. H. Guinivan.
47	James Dolan.........	Qualey	32	Thomas D. Hevey.
48	B. J. Brogan	St. John	33	Thomas Cawley.
49	J. J. McLaughlin.....	Americus.............	34	J. W. Brown.
50	Michael Leonard	"	"	J. J. King.
51	John C. Carson	Sheil	35	J. P. J. Ward.
52	T. H. Duggan........	Friendship...........	37	J. W. Keenan.

REPRESENTATIVES— *Continued.*

	Representatives.	Court.	No.	Proxy Representatives.
53	Peter Morris	St. Joseph............ 38		John P. Ego.
54	Joseph D. Couch, M.D.	Benedict............. 39		William A. Flaherty.
55	Nicholas Fairclough ..	Star of the Sea...... 41		W. F. O'Donnell.
56	W. W. Hurley.......	St. Mary.............. 43		M. P. O'Connor.
57	D. B. Farrell........	St. Bernard.......... 44		
58	William Condon	Unity 45		Patrick A. Reynolds.
59	Francis M. McCarthy.	St. Augustine........ 46		John Doolin.
60	Thomas F. Burns	St. Anne 47		Thomas Golden.
61	John F. Riley........	" .... "		Chas. O'Brien.
62	James O'Brien.......	Sarsfield 48		Patrick Ryan.
63	Edw. A. Irvine.......	" .... "		Thomas Kelly.
64	James A. Berrill	Constantine.......... 49		William T. Maloney.
65	J. Torndorf, Jr.	Holy Trinity 51		Gerhard Kranefuss.
66	G. Kranefuss.........	" .... "		M. Hasenfuss.
67	M. E. Gallagher......	Highland............. 52		J. J. Corbett.
68	John J. Sweeney	Emerald 53		Thos. F. Lyons.
69	James B. Carbrey	" .... "		W. J. McCarthy.
70	Jeremiah G. Fennessey,	St. James............ 54		Thomas W. O'Rourke.
71	J. J. Barnes..........	Charles River 55		E. J. Burke.
72	Thos. J. Gallagher....	" ,....... "		M. E. Conroy.
73	J. D. Fallon	Carroll............... 57		J. H. Morton.
74	M. J. Boland.........	Prospect 58		William F. Rooney.
75	T. H. Murphy	Worcester........... 59		John B. Ratigan.
76	R. J. Morrissey	Middlesex............ 60		J. E. Bristen.
77	J. T. Crotty.........	St. Lawrence........ 61		F. F. Muldowney.
78	M. E. Hayden	St. Catherine 62		G. A. O'Bryan.
79	J. J. Callanan........	Shields 63		F. F. O'Neill.
80	J. J. Leonard	Gallagher 64		P. J. Murray.
81	William Mackin......	St. Columbkille 65		Geo. F. Mitchell.
82	M. F. Conroy	Griffin 66		A. F. Staples.
83	Patrick F. Brady....	Canton............... 67		Edw. C. Murphy.
84	Lawrence J. Watson..	St. Margaret 68		E. H. Higgins.
85	Daniel E. Lane.......	Stoughton............ 69		A. H. McDonald.
86	J. T. Costello	St. Michael 70		J. P. Duffy.
87	James F. Carens......	Phil Sheridan 71		J. W. Buckley.
88	W. J. Jordan	" .... "		J. J. McGlew.
89	R. Dwyer............	Merrimack........... 72		D. H. Maguire.
90	Benj. Morris.........	Taunton.............. 73		P. Coyle.
91	F. P. Conaty.........	" .... "		J. H. Cosgrove.
92	Daniel F. Buckley....	Hendricken.......... 74		A. A. Clarke.
93	T. F. Lynes..........	Q. Jarlath 75		J. H. O'Toole, M. D.
94	John H. Dinegan	uincy 76		S. M. Donovan, M. D.
95	John Crowley...... ..	Mystic............... 77		Luke Coyne.
96	John F. McQueeney ..	St. Monica........... 78		
97	John N. O'Brien......	John Boyle O'Reilly, 79		T. E. Day.
98		Gen. Sherman....... 80		

DIRECTORY.

Names of Courts, Time and Place of Meeting, Officers and Their Addresses.

No. and Court Name.		Officers.	Address.	
1. Cathedral, Boston.	C. R.	John T. Mahoney	10 Rand Street,	Roxbur;
Instituted Sept. 3, 1879.	R. S.	W. P. Walsh.............	38 Worcester Square,	Bostoi
Meets 1st and 3rd Wednesday;	F. S.	R. S. Bowman...........	18 W. Second Street,	South Bostoi
Greystone Hall, 1125 Washington St., Boston.	T.	Thos. J. Dunn...........	521 Harrison Avenue,	Bostoi
3. Fenwick, Boston.	C R.	P. J. McIntire...........	12 Prince Street,	Bostoi
Inst. Nov. 14, 1879.	R. S.	Jeremiah J. Crane.......	9 Hill Street,	Charlestowi
Meets 1st and 3rd Thursday,	F. S.	John Keenan.............	7 N. Hanover Court,	Bostoi
Lusitana Hall, Hanover St., Boston.	T.	John J. Irving...........	193 Salem Street, Rear,	Bostoi
4. St. Francis, Roxbury.	C. R.	Michael.J. O'Brien.......	818 Parker Street,	Roxbur;
Inst. Dec. 18, 1879.	R. S.	Thos. F. Crosby........	Parker Hill Avenue,	Roxbur;
Meets 1st and 3rd Wednesday,	F. S.	T. J. Finneran...........	780 Parker Street,	Roxbur;
Tremont Hall, 1435 Tremont St., Roxbury.	T.	J. J. O'Brien...........	4 Vernon Place,	Roxbur;
5. Leo, E. Boston.	C. R.	John Brant..............	315 Paris Street,	East Bostoi
Inst. Jan. 16, 1880.	R. |S.	Daniel A. Glavin........	439 Bennington Street,	East Bostoi
Meets 2nd and 4th Wednesday,	F. S.	James H. Donovan.......	202 Paris Street,	East Bostoi
Knights of Honor Hall, 144 Meridian St., East Boston.	T.			
6. Cheverus, Boston.	C. R.	James W. Maguire........	17 Cordis Street,	Charlestowi
Inst. Feb. 11, 1880.	R. S.	James Cashin...........	52 Nashua Street,	Bostoi
Meets 1st and 3rd Monday, Foresters' Hall, 9 Elm St.	F S.	Wm. T. Rich.............	44 Cooper Street,	Bostoi
	T.	Edward O'Hara..........	59 Chestnut Street,	Charlestowi
7. St. Patrick, So. Boston.	C. R.	Thos. F. Toomey........	321 Fourth Street,	South Bostoi
Inst. Feb. 16, 1880.	R. S.	A. F. Caldwell...	317 Broadway,	South Bostoi
Meets 2nd and 4th Monday, Tonta Hall, 327 E St.	F. S.	T. F. Toomey...........	321 Fourth Street,	South Bosto:
	T.	James Cahill.............	317 Silver Street,	South Bosto:
8. Sherwood, Boston.	C. R.	James Delury............	50 Oak Street,	Bosto:
Inst. March 4, 1890.	R. S.	John J. McDonald........	1 Holland Place,	Bosto:
Meets 2nd and 4th Thursday,	F. S	A. J. Lill.................	3 Champney Place,	Bosto'
St. Rose Hall, 17 Worcester St.	T.	Thomas J. Lane..........	21 Centre Street,	Roxbur
9. Columbus, Boston.	C. R.	Chas. E Stumcke........	2 Rand Street,	Roxbur
Inst. March 9, 1880.	R. S.	Wm. H. Murphy.........	62 Allen Street,	Bosto
Meets 2nd Monday, 19 Essex St.	F. S.	M. T. Gleason............	433 Milton Avenue,	Dorcheste
	T.	M. T. Milliken......	282 E Street,	South Bosto
10. Iona, Malden.	C. R.	John M Neville..........	55 Hubbard Street,	Malde
Inst. March 15, 1880.	R. S.	Dennis Kelliher..........	39 Sherman Street,	Malde
Meets 1st and 3rd Thursday,	F. S.	Edmund Flavin....	130 Commercial Street,	Malde
Deliberative Hall, Pleasant St., Malden.	T.	Paul J. McMahon	238 Main Street,	Maldc
11. St. Joseph, Boston.	C. R.	Daniel A. Cronin.........	8 Allen Street,	Bostc
Inst March 22, 1880.	R. S.	John P. McGee...........	19 Parkman Street,	Bostc
Meets 2nd and 4th Wednesday,	F. S.	Chas. W. Mullen.........	17 Parkman Street,	Bostc
Y. M. L. Hall, 70½ Leverett St.	T.	Daniel Carney...........	5 Revere Street Place,	Bostc
12. Fulton, Boston.	C. R.	Michael Nolan............	38 Hampden Street,	Rostc
Inst. March 18, 1880.	R. S.	H. F. Scanlan............	117 Union Park Street,	Bostc
Meets 1st and 3rd Friday,	F. S.	James B. Quinn..........	78 Sawyer Street,	Bostc
Carroll Hall, 375 Harrison Avenue, Boston.	T.	Daniel O'Brien..........	14 Village Street,	Bostc
13. Fitzpatrick, Boston.	C. R.	James Cullinane..........	1 Foster Street,	Bostc
Inst. May 5, 1880.	R. S.	Michael Cleary...........	Rear 43 Carter Place,	Bostc
......d 4th Tuesday,	F. S	Frank J McFarland	28 Cottage Street.	Bostc

No. and Court Name.	Officers.		Address.	
15. S.S. Peter & Paul, So. Boston.	C. R.	Thos. F. Gallagher.......	27 Colony Street,	South Bo
Inst. June 25, 1880.	R. S.	John S. McGann.........	70 Tudor Street,	South Bo
Meets 1st and 3rd Tuesday, Tonta	F. S.	John B. White..........	83 Baxter Street,	South Bo
Hall, 327 E St.	T.	Thomas Sullivan.........	13 Mercer Street,	South Bo
16. Essex, Salem.	C. R.	P. F. J. Carney..........	Hancock Street,	Sa
Inst. June 23, 1880.	R. S.	James Murphy...........	169 Federal Street,	Sa
Meets 1st and 3rd Wednesday,	F. S.	Arthur Hennessey.......	31 Ocean Avenue,	Sa
Mansfield B'ldn'g, 199 Essex St.	T.	Dennis F. Hallohan......	328 Essex Street,	Sa
17. Hamilton, Charlestown.	C. R.	John Hurley.............	28 Mt. Vernon Street,	Charlest
Inst. July 8, 1880.	R. S.	Wm. Middlestadt........	Wilton Street,	Somer
Meets 2nd and 4th Friday, 162	F. S.	Patrick A. Quinlan.......	8 First Street,	Charlest
Main St.	T.	Jas. Crowley.............	70 Ferrin Street,	Charlest
18. St. Peter, Dorchester.	C. R.	John J. Curran..........	Davidson Avenue,	Dorche
Inst. July 22, 1880.	R. S.	Edward T. Shields	196 Bowdoin Street,	Dorche
Meets 1st and 3rd Thursday,	F. S.	Dennis J. Coleman.......	1385 Dorchester Avenue,	Dorch
Blake's Hall, Field's Corner.	T.	Thos. J. Lane...........	61 Richfield Street,	Dorch
19. Williams, E. Boston,	C. R.	James Douglass	377 Sumner Street,	East Bo
Inst. Sept. 16, 1880.	R. S.	M. J Kelly.............	107 Paris Street,	East Bo
Meets 1st and 3rd Monday, O.F.	F. S.	F. S. Maloney	123 Maverick Street,	East Bo
Hall, Maverick Sq.	T.	Thomas Arthur..........	Maverick Square,	East Bo
20. Mt. Pleasant, Roxbury.	C. R.	Edward A. Dever........	120 Eustis Street,	Rox
Inst. Oct 20, 1880.	R. S.	Wm. E. Walsh..........	15½ Taber Street.	Rox
Meets 2nd and 4th Monday, K. of	F S.	John J. Gately	5 Clarence Street,	Rox
H. Hall, 2319 Washington St.	T.	David O'Brien..........	30 Mall Street,	Rox
21. St. Alphonsus, Roxbury.	C. R.	James P. Lennon........	1445 Tremont Street,	Rox
Inst. Oct. 13, 1880.	R. S.	Francis A. Mahan	85 Longwood Avenue,	Rox
Meets 2nd and 4th Wednesday,	F. S.	John Killiou........	8 Oscar Street,	Rox
Gurney Hall, Gurney St.	T.	Cornelius McCarthy......	36 Carey Street,	Rox
23. St. John, Hyde Park.	C. R.	R. J. Sullivan...........	Water Street,	Hyde
Inst. Dec. 14, 1880	R. S.	Mark B. Gill...........	Central Park Avenue,	Hyde
Meets 1st and 3rd Tuesday, Lyric	F. S.	Michael Fahy...........	5 Oak Street,	Hyde
Hall.	T.	F. S. Sullivan..........	35 Garfield Street,	Hyde
24. St. Gregory, Milton.	C. R.	Thos. P. Lockney........	Cor. Codman St. and Dor. Ave.,	Bo
Inst. Dec. 20, 1880.	R. S.	Michael Dunican.........	Box 87,	East M
Meets 1st and 3rd Tuesday, Asso-	F. S.	Frank A. Duffy		Matt
ciate's Hall.	T.	Patrick Falon...........	River Street,	Matt
25. St. Francis, W. Quincy.	C. R.	John Vogel.............		West Qu
Inst. Dec. 21, 1880.	R. S.	James L. Fennessey......		West Qu
Meets 2nd and 4th Tuesday, Old	F. S.	Charles C Hearn........		West Qu
Engine House.	T.	James Doyle............		West Qu
26. St. Raphael, Dedham.	C. R.	Thomas P. Murray.......	Walnut Hill,	Ded
Inst. Dec. 31, 1880.	R. S.	C. H. Riley.............		Ded
Meets 1st and 3rd Sunday, St.	F. S.	Peter Gallagher..........	Walnut Hill,	Ded
Mary's Hall.	T.	P. O'Sullivan...........	Walnut Hill,	Ded
28. Erin, Boston.	C. R.	Wm. A. Daly...........	824 Dorchester Avenue,	South B
Inst. Feb. 3, 1881.	R. S.	C. J. Lynch.............	10 Shelburn Street,	Dorch
Meets 2nd and 4th Tuesay, St	F. S.	Peter D. O'Meally.......	272 D Street,	South Bo
Rose Hall, 17 Worcester St.	T.	J. O'Mara...............	93 Pembroke Street,	B
29. St. Thomas, Brockton.	C. R.	Wm Linnehan	156 Mt Warren Avenue,	Broc
Inst. Feb. 17, 1881.	R. S.	Thos. J. O'Rourke.......	29 Emmet Street,	Broc
Meets 2nd and 4th Thursday,	F. S	John Shea..............	68 Eliot Street,	Broc
Hibernian Hall, E. Elm St.	T.	Chas. Wakeling.........	8 Hamilton Place.	Broc
30. Bass River, Beverly.	C. R.	Philip Fitzgibbons........	Abbott Street,	Be
Inst. Feb. 24, 1881.	R. S.	P M Riordan.·········...	16 Rantoul Street,	Be
Meets 1st and 3rd Thursday, O F.	F. S	John Geary.............	School Street,	Be
Hall, Cabot St.	T.	Jeremiah Murphy........	16 Pleasant Street,	Be
32. Qualey, Woburn.	C. R.	James Dolan............	64 Fowle Street,	Wo
Inst. March 2, 1881.	R. S.	John Maguire...........	121 Main Street,	Wo
Meets 1st and 3rd Wednesday,	F. S.	Frank E. Tracey........	50 Prospect Street,	Wo
Hibernian Hall, Main St.	T.	Wm. O'Brien............	20 Church Avenue,	Wo

No. and Court Name.	Officers.		Address.	
33. St. John, E. Cambridge. Inst. March 3, 1881. Meets 1st and 3rd Friday, G. A. R. Hall, 95 Cambridge St.	C. R. R. S. F. S. T.	D. J. Donovan........... J. S. Kenney............. John O'Connell.......... Jos. J. Kelly.............	31 East Street, 39 Seventh Street, 143 Gore Street, 110 Otis Street,	East Cambr East Cambr East Cambr East Cambr
34. Americus, Boston. Inst. March 15, 1881. Meets 1st and 3rd Thursday, Greystone Hall, 1125 Washington St.	C. R. R. S. F. S. T.	P. J. Gorman .... C. A. Donohue.......... P. P. Sullivan.......... Michael McCarthy.......	49 Brook Avenue, 99 East Dedham Street, 13 Waltham Street, 52 Stoughton Street,	Dorche Bo: Bo: Bo:
35. Shell, Boston. Inst. March 18, 1881. Meets 1st Friday.	C. R. R. S. F. S. T.	Wm. H. Peirce........... C J. Kelly.............. Thos. Jacobs..... .... Wm. Connolly	148 Chambers Street, 26 Hull Street, 3 Lexington Avenue, 5 Fleet Street,	Bo: Bo: Charlest Bo.
37. Friendship, Roxbury. Inst. March 25, 1881. Meets 2nd and 4th Tuesday, St. Rose Hall, 17 Worcester St.	C. R. R. S. F. S. T.	John W. Riley .... Edward N. Lee .. .. John F. Dolan .... T. H. Duggan............	28 Berlin Street, 3 Reims Place, 99 Hampshire Street, 130 Camden Street,	Roxl Roxl Roxl Bo:
38. St. Joseph, Roxbury. Inst. March 29, 1881. Meets 1st and 3rd Wednesday, Foresters' Hall, Washington St., near Dudley.	C. R. R. S. F. S. T.	John J. Fox............. Wm. B. Reardon......... John P. Ego .... M. Lennon...............	Grove Hall, 384 Warren Street, 411 Warren Street, Grove Hall,	Dorche Roxl Roxl Dorche
39. Benedict, Somerville. Inst. March 31st, 1881. Meets 1st and 3rd Thursday, Temperance Hall, Hawkins St.	C. R. R. S. F. S. T.	John J. McGonagle....... Michael Harrington ..... Wm. A. Flaherty......... Cornelius McGonagle.....	Linden Street, Greenville Street, 261 Washington Street, Linden Street,	Somer' Somer' Somer' Somer'
41. Star of the East, E. Boston. Inst. Dec. 13, 1881. Meets 2nd and 4th Tuesday, Good Templars' Hall, 23 Meridian St.	C. R. R. S. F. S. T.	Chas. H. Cragin......... Thos. E. Cragin......... Jas. W. Prest .... N. Fairclough...........	Gladstone Street, 157 Havre Street, 617 Bennington Street, 617 Bennington Street,	Orient Hei East Bo East Bo East Bo
43. St. Mary, Randolph. Inst. Sept. 4, 1882. Meets 1st Monday, Hibernian Hall, North St.	C. R. R. S. F. S. T.	Wm. W. Hurley......... R. P. Barrett............. John B. Walsh .... Patrick Brady...........		Rand Rand Rand Rand
44. St. Bernard, W. Newton. Inst. Sept 23. 1882. Meets 1st and 3rd Monday, Forester's Hall, Waltham St.	C. R. R. S. F. S. T.	Bernard Farrell .... Thos. C. Donovan........ John W. Gaw .... Martin Nagle............		West Ne' West Ne' West Ne' West Ne'
45. Unity, Bridgewater. Inst. Sept. 12, 1882. Meets 2nd and 4th Tuesday, Y. M. Ben. Hall, Centre St.	C. R. R. S. F. S. T.	David Cashon........... Michael Cashon.......... William Condon.......... Thos. Daniher...........	Box 42, Box 42,	Bridgev Bridgev Bridgev Bridgev
46. St. Augustine, So. Boston. Inst. Nov. 14, 1882. Meets 2nd and 4th Thursday, Tonta Hall, 327 E St.	C. R. R. S. F. S. T.	John Doolin .... John W. Rigby .... Bernard Flanagan........ J. F. McNulty	211 Third Street, 44 Fifth Street, 732 East Second Street, 12 Woodward Street,	South B South B South B South B
47. St. Anne's, Gloucester. Inst. Dec. 22, 1882. Meets 1st and 3rd Tuesday, G. A. R. Hall, 171 Main St.	C. R. R. S. F. S. T.	Chas. O'Brien........... Eben C. Carroll.......... John H. Gourville....... Daniel Carroll	56 Warner Street, 32 Commercial Street, 8 Middle Street, 5 Shepherd Street,	Glouc Glouc Glouc Glouc
48. Sarsfield, No. Attleborough. Inst. March 6, 1883. Meets every Tuesday, cor. East and Elm Streets.	C. R. R. S. F. S. T.	John P. Zilch............ James I. McGowen....... John B. Altermath .... James B. Smith........		North Attlebo North Attlebo North Attlebo North Attlebo
49. Constantine, Boston. Inst. April 5, 1883. Meets 2nd and 4th Friday, Carroll Hall, 375 Harrison Ave.	C. R. R. S. F. S. T.	James T. Riley........... John J. Dolan............ James A. Berrill .... John Carroll.............	2 Pearl Place, 8 Oxford Place, Hotel Gloucester, 375 Harrison Avenue,	Some B B B

DIRECTORY—Continued.

No. and Court Name.	Officers.		Address.	
51. Holy Trinity, Boston. Inst. April 13, 1883. Meets 2nd and 4th Wednesday, 987 Washington St.	C. R. R. S. F. S. T.	Frederick Schwaab....... J. H. Hampe............. Leopold Kohler.......... Jos. Spang..............	31 Avon Place, 117 West Canton Street, 15 Whitney Street, 31 Warwick Street,	Roxbury Boston Roxbury Roxbnry
52. Highland, Roxbury. Inst. April 16, 1883. Meets 2nd Monday, Vernon Hall, Tremont St., corner Culvert.	C. R. R. S. F. S. T.	Mark E Gallager........ Jere. Sullivan............ John J. Corbett.......... Thomas O'Flynn.........	221 Cabot Street, 29 Davenport Street, 14 Halleck Street, Cabot, cor. Linden Park St.,	Roxbury Roxbury Roxbury Roxbury
53. Emerald, Peabody, Inst. July 2, 1883. Meets every Thursday, Thomas Hall, Peabody Sq.	C. R. R. S. F. S. T.	James M. Regan.......... James J. McCann........ James B. Carbrey........ Daniel J. Sweeney.......	Midway Street, Lowell Street, Shillaber Street, Central Street,	Peabody Peabody Peabody Peabody
54. St. James, Boston. Inst. July 2, 1883. Meets 1st and 3rd Tuesday, Carroll Hall, Harrison Av. nr. Dover St.	C. R. R. S. F. S. T.	Michael J. Collins....... Michael J. Noonan....... J. J. Desmond.......... Cornelius Desmond......	10 G Street, 214 South Street, 286 Third Street, 466 East Sixth Street,	South Boston Boston South Boston South Boston
55. Charles River, Watertown. Inst. Oct. 8, 1883. Meets 1st and 3rd Monday, G.A.R. Hall.	C. R. R. S. F. S. T.	John J. Herlihy.......... C. H. Keefe............. M. E. Conroy............ D. J. Mahoney...........	227 Watertown Street,	Watertown Watertown Watertown Newton
57. Carroll, Jamaica Plain. Inst. June 30, 1885. Meets 1st and 3rd Monday, Association Hall, Burroughs St.	C. R. R. S. F. S. T.	John H. Laughan .... J. H. Lennon............. J. J. Carty.............. J. H. Moy...............	Walk Hill Street, Cor. Smith and Child Sts. Washington Street, Child Street,	Roslindale Jamaica Plain Jamaica Plain Jamaica Plain
58. Prospect, Waltham. Inst. Aug. 25, 1885. Meets 1st and 3rd Sunday, A O.H. Hall, Main St.	C. R. R. S. F. S. T.	David Walsh............ Michael Bergin.......... John E. Burke.......... Timothy F. Buckley......	205 River Street, 14 Middle Street, Francis Street, 105 Cushing Street,	Waltham Waltham Waltham Waltham
59. Worcester, Worcester. Inst. Dec. 17, 1885. Meets 1st and 3rd Thursday, I. C. B. S. Hall, 98 Front St.	C. R. R. S. F. S. T.	Patrick J. Quinn..... ... Michael J. Madden....... Geo. B Chandley........ John W. Delehanty.....	26 Spruce Street, 61 Eastern Avenue 20 Washington Street, 5 Preston Street,	Worcester Worcester Worcester Worcester
60. Middlesex, Newton. Inst. Feb. 19, 1886 Meets 2nd and 4th Tuesday, Arcanum Hall.	C. R. R. S. F. S. T.	M. J. Joyce.............. Michael Morrissey....... P. R. Mullen............. P. A. Mulligan...........	Green Street, 14 Cross Street, 18 Avon Place, Adams Street,	Newton Watertown Newton Newtonville
61. St. Lawrence, Brookline. Meets 1st and 3rd Tuesday, Good Fellows Hall, Guild Block.	C. R. R. S. F. S. T.	James F. Donovan....... Daniel Frawley.......... Thomas F. McMahon..... Timothy Driscoll.........	Walnut Street, Chestnut Street, Kerrigan Place, Morse Avenue,	Brookline Brookline Brookline Brookline
62. St. Catherine, Norwood. Inst. Dec. 31, 1886. Meets 1st and 3rd Wednesday, Casey Hall.	C. R. R. S. F. S. T.	John B. Rooney......... Daniel Murray.......... John H. Williams....... George A. O'Bryan		Walpole Norwood Norwood Norwood
63. Shields, Holyoke. Inst. Jan. 14, 1887. Meets 2nd Sunday and 4th Tuesday, O'Neil Hall, 438 High St.	C. R. R. S. F. S. T.	John Riley.............. M. J. Conway........... Odilon Moreau.......... M. J. Laporte............	159 Elm Street, 124 Cabot Street, 571 Bridge Street, 448 High Street,	Holyoke Holyoke Holyoke Holyoke
64. Gallagher, Springfield. Inst. April 17, 1887. Meets 2nd and 4th Friday, Harrigan Hall, cor. Main and State Sts	C. R. R. S. F. S. T.	Patrick J. Murray....... John T. Lovett.......... John J. Leonard........ Peter Burke............	856 Chestnut Street, 100 Franklin Street, 118 Greenwood Street, 308 Chestnut Street,	Springfield Springfield Springfield Springfield
65. St. Columbkille, Brighton. Inst. May 26, 1887. Meets 1st and 3rd Tuesday, O. F. Hall, Brighton.	C. R. R. S. F. S. T.	James Muldoon.......... Wm. J. Van Etten....... Michael Featherstone.... John J. Greenleaf........	Lincoln Street, Market Street, Market Street, Market Street.	Brighton Brighton Brighton Brighton

DIRECTORY — Concluded.

No. and Court Name.	Officers.		Address.	
66. Griffin, Franklin. Inst Sept. 12, 1887. Meets 1st and 3rd Tuesday, Basement of Church.	C. R. R. S. F. S. T.	A. F. Staples .... John W. Bradley......... B. W. McCabe .... Wm. F. Buckley.	Unionville,	Franklin Franklin Franklin Franklin
67. Canton. Canton. Inst. Jan. 26, 1888. Meets 2nd and 4th Friday, Washington Street Hall.	C. R. R. S. F. S. T.	Owen F. Sullivan .... James Quinn............. James C. Grimes .... James H. Murphy........		Canton Canton Canton Canton
68. St. Margaret, Beverly Farms. Inst. April 14, 1888. Meets 1st and 3rd Wednesday, Marshall's Hall, cor. Hale and West Sts.	C. R. R. S. F. S. T.	Thos. M. Dix............. John C. McCarthy....... Michael J. Cadigan....... Michael J. Riordan.......	Box 107, Box 105,	Pride's Crossing Beverly Farms Beverly Farms Beverly Farms
69. Stoughton, Stoughton. Inst. June 7, 1888. Meets 2nd and 4th Thursday, Foresters' Hall.	C. R. R. S. F. S. T.	John S. Madden.......... Wm. J. Cronin...... .... John Baird............... Wm. J. Power...........	Box 649,	Stoughton Stoughton Stoughton Stoughton
70. St. Michael, So. Boston. Inst. Sept. 14, 1888. Meets 1st and 3rd Tuesday, Gray's Hall.	C. R. R. S. F. S. T.	Jas. H. Coughlin........ Jas. P. Duffy .... John J. Barry........... Timothy F. Shea........	901 Broadway, 508 Sixth Street, 187 Bowen Street, 144 K Street,	South Boston South Boston South Boston South Boston
71. Phil Sheridan, Newburyport. Inst. Sept. 18, 1889. Meets 1st and 3rd Tuesday, G. A. R. Hall, Charter St.	C. R. R. S. F. S. T.	Robert E. Burke......... Albert E. Moylan........ Hugh Hart.............. David Collins......... ..	76 State Street, 81 Merrimack Street, 16 Salem Street, 79 Water Street.	Newburyport Newburyport Newburyport Newburyport
72. Merrimack, Haverhill. Inst. Dec. 20, 1888. Meets 2nd and 4th Thursday, Foresters' Hall, 78 Merrimack St.	C. R. R. S. F. S. T.	Daniel H. Maguire. ...... Jeremiah J. Ring.... .... John J. Murphy......... John A. Burns...........	5 Lewis Street, 277 River Street, 26 Emerson Street,	Haverhill Haverhill Haverhill Haverhill
73. Taunton, Taunton. Inst. March 12, 1889. Meets 2nd and 4th Monday, Forester's Hall, Union Block.	C. R. R. S. F. S. T.	Geo. F. Brammer........ Wm. P. Crowley .... Edwin F. Goodwin....... Patrick Coyle···········	11 Second Street, 47 North Pleasant Street, 12 Prospect Street, 58 Court Street,	Taunton Taunton Taunton Taunton
74. Hendricken, No. Easton. Inst. March 29, 1889. Meets 1st Monday and 3rd Thursday, Foresters' Hall.	C. R. R. S. F. S. T.	W. J. Heslan............. John F. Lyons........... Edward E. Ready.... ... Joseph J. Reed		North Easton North Easton North Easton North Easton
75. St. Jarlath, Amesbury. Inst. June 13, 1889. Meets every Wednesday, St. Jarlaths Rooms, Main St.	C. R. R. S. F. S. T.	T. F. Lynes.............. Hugh Kellett, Jr........ John Kellett............. John Armitage...........	School Street, Arlington Street, Church Street,	Amesbury Amesbury Amesbury Amesbury
76. Quincy, Quincy. Inst. Oct. 24, 1889. Meets 1st and 3rd Thursday, Red Men's Hall, Hancock St.	C. R. R. S. F. S. T.	John H. Dinegan........ H. A. Talbot.............. Joseph A. Dasha........ John A. McDonnell	16 Hancock Street, 7 Newcomb Place, 10 Summer Street, 16 Jackson Street,	Quincy Quincy Quincy Quincy
77. Mystic, Medford. Inst. Dec. 12, 1889. Meets 2nd and 4th Thursday, Phillips Hall, High St.	C. R. R. S. F. S. T.	John Crowley··········· John J. O'Brien........... John A. Gaffey.......... Peter Donahoe...		Medford Medford Medford Medford
78. St. Monica, Lawrence. Inst. March 26, 1890. Meets 1st and 3rd Monday, St. Mary's Hall, Haverhill St.	C. R. R. S. F. S. T.	J. F. McQueeny.......... J. J. Greene. .... H. McGoldrick.......... F. J. Murphy	116 Hancock Street, 85 Wiliow Street,	Lawrence Lawrence Lawrence Lawrence
79. John Boyle O'Reilly, New Bedford. Inst. Jan. 24, 1891. Meets 1st and 3rd Friday, Bank Building, Purchase St.	C. R. R. S. F. S. T.	James H. Miskell .... Thos. E. Day .... John N. O'Brien .... Joseph P. Kennedy......	96 South Sixth Street, 8 Wing Street, 60 Rivet Street, 139 Acushnet Avenue,	New Bedford New Bedford New Bedford New Bedford
80. Gen. Sherman, Plymouth. Inst. March 7, 1891. Meets	C. R. R. S. F. S. P.	Thos. Marron............ J. A. Tracey............ James J. Noble.......... John W. Hallinan........	18 South Russell Street, Lothrop Street, Main Street, 53 Alerton Street,	Plymouth Plymouth Plymouth Plymouth

Assessment Calls.

During the year 1890 the following calls were issued, viz. 66, 67, 68, 69, 70, 71, 72, 73, 74, 75, 76, 77, the last No. 77, expiring Jan. 9, 1891.

The total deaths in 1890 were 45, of which

8 were accidental.
15 " from Consumption (various forms.)
4 " " Pneumonia.
3 " " Heart Disease.
5 " " Typhoid Fever.
3 " " Cancer.
5 " " Spinal Disease.
1 " " Delirium Tremens.
1 " " Uræmic Poisoning.

The High Standing Committee has held nearly 50 meetings during the past year and the attendance has been good at each meeting, Some of them were held at a distance from Boston, and at all such a good representation of the Committee was present. Each one seemed desirous of contributing his share of labor, and whenever service of any kind was needed for the benefit of the Order, personal comfort was thrown aside and the work was accomplished. Although only two new Courts have been formed this year, we have every reason to believe that a large number can be formed the coming year, as many visits have been made to different localities and a foundation laid which must result in increased membership. Many of these visits and journeys were made in the day-time as much better and more effective work can then be done than in the evening, which is of necessity short. Many times it was necessary to remain away from Boston over night, when if the pleasure of the individual members could be consulted they would prefer to remain at home. As the work was needed for the Order, however much of a hardship it may have been, the work was done. Although success did not crown every effort of the High Standing Committee, yet there is no doubt that good results will follow and successive High Standing Committees will reap the benefit of much of the labor put into the Organization the past year and which does not appear on the surface. It may not perhaps be out of place to speak here of the labor of the High Medical Examiner Dr. Joseph D. Couch, who deserves more than passing mention for his services to the Order and his kindly advice to the High Standing Committee. Always having in mind the rights of those who are now in the Order, he has also given exact justice to every paper laid before him. This he has done without fear or favor and the Order cannot too highly value his services.

The reports as sent in by the Courts have been very defective and have apparently received very little thought from those through whose hands they passed. This matter can be remedied in course of time, but while Financial Officers of subordinate Courts are changed as frequently as sometimes happens much confusion must result.

Generally it appears that all mean to get matters right if possible, and in all cases where the returns could be corrected it has been done. In the others the figures are given as they occur and an effort will be made to set them right when opportunity occurs.

The year 1890 has been one of prosperity for our organization and this in the face of an avalanche of money making (for their founders) schemes for insuring every one who had enough money to pay the charter fees required. Our present membership adding those applications, approved since Jan. 1, 1891, is now 4,775, and there is no doubt, but that within the next year a large number will be added to the membership, and the record of the Massachusetts Catholic Order of Foresters, so brilliant in the past will continue and show to all our people an organization of which they should be proud and to which they will be attracted for all time.

Respectfully submitted,

JAMES F. SUPPLE,
High Secretary Treasurer.

PROCEEDINGS OF THE TWELFTH ANNUAL CONVENTION

OF THE

Massachusetts Catholic Order of Foresters

HELD AT

Hamilton Hall, Corner of Chestnut and Cambridge Streets, Salem, Mass.

APRIL 22, 1891.

In compliance with the following call, the representatives of the Courts assembled at Hamilton Hall, Salem, Wednesday, April 22, 1891.

MASSACHUSETTS CATHOLIC ORDER OF FORESTERS.

HIGH STANDING COMMITTEE.

[SEAL.]   611 Washington Street,

Boston, April 1, 1891.

To the Officers and Members of the Massachusetts Catholic Order of Foresters:—

BROTHERS,—In accordance with the powers vested in the High Standing Committee of the Massachusetts Catholic Order of Foresters (under Art. IV, Constitution of High Court, Page 11,) a call is hereby issued for the assembling of the Representatives of the Subordinate Courts of the Massachusetts Catholic Order of Foresters in Annual Session of the High Court of the Order, to be held at Hamilton Hall, corner of Chestnut and Cambridge Streets, Salem, to be opened in regular form at 9.30 o'clock, A. M., on Wednesday the twenty-second day of April, A. D., 1891, as provided for in the High Court Constitution.

The Basis of Representation shall be as laid down in Art. II, Sec. 3, Constitution of High Court, page 8.

Forms of Credential to the Annual Session of the High Court accompany this Call, one to be retained and held by the Representative for use at the Convention. If the Credential be transferred for cause, this should be stated on the back of Credential under the endorsements of Chief Ranger and Recording Secretary of the Court.

By Order of the High Standing Committee,

JAMES F. SUPPLE,   JEREMIAH G. FENNESSEY,
  High Secretary-Treasurer.   *High Chief Ranger,*

High Chief Ranger Jeremiah G. Fennessey called the convention to order when the hour arrived and instructed the High Conductors to take up the Pass Word.

The High Conductors reported the High Court Officers all present and everything correct.

High Chief Ranger Fennessey then opened the convention in due form and prayer was offered by Rev. Father McManus of Salem.

High Chief Ranger Fennessey appointed the following

COMMITTEE ON CREDENTIALS.

Bros. J. J. Leonard....................of Gallagher No. 64
James F. Carens.............of Phil Sheridan No. 71
Daniel O'Brien . ...of Essex No. 16
T. H. Murphy.....................of Worcester No. 59
W. F. Rooney.....................of Prospect No. 58
T. F. Lynes.....................of St. Jarlath No. 75
J. N. O'Brien.........of John Boyle O'Reilly No. 79

While the Committee on Credentials was out, Rev. Father Masterson of Emerald Court No. 53, Peabody, arrived and was escorted to the platform by High Outside Sentinel, R. Farrenkopf. The High Chief Ranger welcomed the Reverend gentleman and then presented him to the Convention as a member of the Order and one who wished to see the Order prosper.

Father Masterson was pleased to say he expected to meet a large body of men but found a larger gathering than he anticipated. He was glad to meet men like them from every portion of the State, and was pleased to see the movement to bring young catholics together, who were not afraid to stand together as catholics and hoped the feeling would spread that when one of our creed became prominent if he was a good catholic, he must be a good citizen.

We should have confidence in each other, stand by each other, and help one another, and if we did all this, and had harmony we could accomplish all we desired.

Capt. Leonard for the Committee on Credentials reported —

Whole number of Courts represented...............57
Whole number of Credentials.....................85

High Chief Ranger said the regular representatives could vote for each Court and the proxies only in their absence.

Past High Chief Ranger McLaughlin moved to accept report, seconded by Bro. Brickley of No. 21.

Voted to accept.

High Chief Ranger announced next business in order, reading of records of last convention, and said it was not necessary under his former decision.

High Chief Ranger announced next business in order, calling of the roll, which was done by the High Secretary-Treasurer. 87 representatives were present, representing 64 courts.

Cathedral No. 1 .... J. J. Lanigan.
"   " .... M. Edmonds.
"   " .... J. M. Singler.
Fenwick No. 3 .... Thos. P. Burke.
St. Francis No. 4 .... W. E. Shay.
"   " .... T. Sproules.
Leo No. 5 .... John Brant.
"   " .... Geo. F. Lowe.
Cheverus No. 6 .... Hon. Owen A. Galvin.
"   " .... James Cashin.
Sherwood No. 8 .... John P. Dore.
"   " .... D. F. Sullivan.
"   " .... Hugh Montague.
Columbus No. 9 .... James F. Supple.
St. Joseph No. 11 .... H. C. Griffin.
"   " .... Daniel A. Cronin.
"   " .... P. F. McGaragle.
Fulton No. 12 .... Michael O'Brien.
Fitzpatrick No. 13 .... J. M. Jordan.
Lafayette No. 14 .... Dr. C. A. Ahearne.
"   " .... G. A. Lomasney.
SS. Peter and Paul No. 15 .... Patrick A. Donovan.
Essex No. 16 .... D. J. O'Brien.
"   " .... J. J. Hartigan.
St. Peter No. 18 .... T. J. Lane.
"   " .... John H. Donovan.
Williams No. 19 .... F. S. Maloney.
"   " .... Philip Smith.
Mt. Pleasant No 20 .... G. H. Keefe.
"   " .... Frank J. McGrath.
St Alphonsus No. 21 .... J. T. Brickley.
St. John No. 23 .... F. S. Sullivan.
St. Gregory No. 24 .... Michael Dunican.
St. Francis No. 25 .... John Vogel.
St. Raphael No. 26 .... John F. Riley.

Erin No. 28........................John T. Daly.
"   "   ....Jeremiah O'Mara.
St. Thomas No. 29.................John E. Saxton.
"   "   ....P. Gilmore.
"   "   ....F. L. Smith.
Bass River No. 30.................W. J. Brown.
Qualey No. 32.....................James Dolan.
St. John No. 33 ....B. J. Brogan.
Americus No. 34 ....J. J. McLaughlin.
"   "   ....Michael Leonard.
Friendship No. 37.................T. H. Duggan.
Benedict No. 39...................Joseph D. Couch, M. D.
Star of the Sea No. 41.............N. Fairclough.
St. Bernard No. 44 ....B. Farrell.
Unity No. 45......................William Condon.
St. Augustine No. 46...... ....John Doolin.
St. Anne No. 47...................Thomas F. Burns.
"   "   ....John F. Riley.
Sarsfield No. 48...................James O'Brien.
"   "   ....Edw. A. Irvine.
Constantine No. 49................James A Berrill.
Holy Trinity No. 51...............J. Torndorf, Jr.
"   "   ....G. Kranefuss.
Highland No. 52...................J. J. Corbet.
Emerald No. 53 ....John J. Sweeney.
"   "   ....James B. Carbrey.
St. James No. 54..................Capt. Jeremiah G. Fennessey.
Charles River No. 55..............J. J. Barnes.
"   "   ....P. F. Gallagher.
Carroll No. 57 . ...J. H. Morton.
Prospect No. 58...................William F. Rooney.
Worcester No. 59..................T. H. Murphy.
Middlesex No. 60................ ..R. J. Morrissey.
St. Lawrence No. 61...............J. T. Crotty.
St. Catherine No. 62..............M. E. Hayden.
Shields No. 63.....................J. J. Callanan.
Gallagher No. 64..................Capt. J. J. Leonard.
Griffin No. 66 ....A. F. Staples.
Canton No. 67.....................Patrick F. Brady.
St. Margaret No. 68...............Lawrence J. Watson.
Stoughton No. 69 ....Daniel E. Lane.
St. Michael No. 70 ....J. P. Duffy.
Phil Sheridan No. 71...............James F. Carens.
"   "   ....J. W. Buckley.
Merrimack No. 72.................R. Dwyer.
Taunton No. 73...................Benj. Morris.
"   "   ....F. P. Conaty.
Hendricken No. 74.. ....A. A. Clarke.
St. Jarlath No. 75.................T. F. Lynes.
Mystic No. 77.....................John Crowley.
St. Monica No. 78.................John F. McQueeney.
John Boyle O'Reilly No. 79.........J. N. O'Brien.

High Chief Ranger then read his address to the Convention, giving the report of the work of the High Standing Committee the past year. The address of the High Chief Ranger occupied a full hour, and was listened to with great interest, and frequently the Representatives interrupted to applaud.

Bro. H. C. Griffin, of St. Joseph Court No. 11, made a motion to accept report, and print and distribute the same.

Motion was seconded by Bro. D. F. Sullivan, of Sherwood Court No. 8.

Bro. Callanan, of Shields Court No. 63, said he hoped it would be referred to a committee and certain portions, relating to other organizations be stricken out.

High Chief Ranger ruled it was his address, the recommendations were his, and nobody could strike out anything.

Bro. Rogers, of Sarsfield Court No. 48, hoped motion to accept and print would be adopted, as it was one of the best addresses he had ever heard.

Past High Chief Ranger McLaughlin said there was no Committee on Address, and raised that point of order against motion of Bro. Callanan to refer.

High Chief Ranger ruled the point of order well taken.

High Chief Ranger ruled debate out of order, except on the motion to accept report, and put the motion of Bro. Griffin.

Voted to accept report and print.

Bro. Sproules, of St. Francis Court No. 4, moved the appointment of a Committee of Three, to consist of High Chief Ranger and two others, to consider matters spoken of in address of High Chief Ranger.

Past High Chief Ranger McLaughlin moved to refer such portions as could be referred to proper Committees.

Bro. Brickley, of St. Alphonsus Court No. 21, moved to take recess for dinner.

High Chief Ranger put motion on recess, and decided it was not a vote.

High Chief Ranger Fennessey then appointed the following Committees :—

COMMITTEE ON CONSTITUTION.

Bros. Hon. Owen A. Galvin............of Cheverus No. 6
J. J. Callanan....................of Shields No. 63
J. F. Carens................of Phil Sheridan No. 71
W. E. Shay...................of St. Francis No. 4
T. J. Lane....................of St. Peter No. 18
J. P. Duffy...................of St. Michael No. 70
Richard Dwyer................of Merrimack No. 72

70

Committee on Petitions.

Bros. J. J. Leonard....................of Gallagher No. 64
Dr. C. A. Ahearne..............of Lafayette No. 14
John Brant..........................of Leo No. 5
P. F. McGaragle...............of St. Joseph No. 11
L. J. Watson ....of St. Margaret No. 68
D. J. O'Brien..... ....of Essex No. 16
T. F. Lynes....................of St. Jarlath No. 75

Committee on State of the Order.

Bros. Joseph Torndorf ....of Holy Trinity No. 51
Hon. J. P. Dore.................of Sherwood No. 8
F. P. Conaty....................of Taunton No. 73
F. L. Smith..................of St. Thomas No. 29
P. A. Donovan.........of SS. Peter and Paul No. 15
P. J. Sweeney....................of Emerald No. 53
J. F. Riley....................of St. Raphael No. 26

Committee on Secret Work.

Bros. J. J. McLaughlin, P. H. C. R.....of Americus No. 34
Charles O'Brien..................of St. Anne No. 47
T. H. Duggan..................of Friendship No. 37
P. F. Gallagher..............of Charles River No. 55
Hon. Benjamin Morris.............of Taunton No. 73
Hon. J. F. McQueeney..........of St. Monica No. 78
M. Edmonds....................of Cathedral No. 1

Committee on Appeals.

Bros. James J. Lanigan................of Cathedral No. 1
H. C. Griffin....................of St. Joseph No. 11
T. H. Murphy..................of Worcester No. 59
H. Montague....................of Sherwood No. 8
J. H. Morton......................of Carroll No. 57
J. Cashin ....of Cheverus No. 6
G. A. Lomasney...............of La Fayette No. 14

On motion the Convention
Voted to take recess for dinner until 2.30 P. M.
High Chief Ranger declared recess at 1.15 P. M.
Convention reassembled at 2.30 P. M., and were called to order by
the High Chief Ranger at 2.40 P. M.

Bro. J. J. Lanigan, of Cathedral Court No. 1, moved to extend the courtesies of the Convention to Past High Chief Ranger D. F. O'Sullivan, of Cathedral Court No. 1, and Past High Chief Ranger John H. Watson, of Essex Court No. 16, who were present but not as Representatives.

High Chief Ranger put the question, remarking that Bro. O'Sullivan was the first High Chief Ranger of the Order, having held the office until April, 1882.

Voted unanimously.

High Chief Ranger appointed Bro. Lanigan to escort Past High Chief Ranger O'Sullivan to the platform.

High Chief Ranger Fennessey then introduced Bro. O'Sullivan to the Convention, calling attention to the noble work he had performed in the early days of the Order.

Bro. O'Sullivan briefly addressed the Representatives, saying he was proud to meet such a good looking and intelligent body of men, and glad of the opportunity to give them a word of encouragement, and, if possible, incite them to greater zeal in the work of charity in which they were engaged. [Applause.]

High Chief Ranger called for report of Committee on Constitution.

Hon. Owen A. Galvin, Chairman of the Committee, said the Committee was ready to report, and that Bro. Shay, Secretary of the Committee, had the papers and would read them.

Bro. Shay read—"The Committee recommend ; following out the suggestion of the High Chief Ranger, that a Committee on Constitution be appointed, to consist of the High Chief Ranger and six other delegates, to sit during recess to receive and consider proposed amendments to the Constitution, that all amendments proposed to the Committee shall be printed, and one copy sent to each Court ten days prior to the next Convention, and by the Committee submitted to the Convention. No proposed amendment to the Constitution to be considered unless received by the Committee thirty days before the Convention."

The Committee on Constitution recommend its adoption.

High Chief Ranger said question was on accepting report of Committee on Constitution.

Bro. Mackin, of St. Columbkille No. 65, moved to amend—time should be made sixty for the Committee and thirty for the Courts instead of ten days.

Bro. W. E. Shay, of St. Francis No. 4, raised the point of order that the Convention was not proceeding in order.

High Chief Ranger said point of order was well taken, as password has not been taken up.

High Chief Ranger appointed as additional High Conductors to take up the password :—

    Bros. N. Fairclough..............of Star of the Sea No. 41
           G. F. Low...........................of Leo No. 5
           M. Edmonds...................of Cathedral No. 1

The High Conductors reported all correct, and High Chief Ranger said Convention was now in order and could proceed.

High Chief Ranger put the question 'as amended, and declared it Voted unanimously.

Bro. Shay, reported for Committee on Constitution :—

Amend Constitution Subordinate Courts, so as to provide that the time allowed for reinstatement of a suspended member, for failure to pay dues, assessments and fines, be changed from fifteen days to thirty days.

Committee recommended its adoption.

Voted to accept and adopt.

Bro. Shay, reported for Committee on Constitution :—

The Committee on Constitution be requested to consider and report on the feasibility of petitioning the Legislature of Massachusetts for permission to amend the charter of this Order, by changing the name from the Massachusetts Catholic Order of Foresters to the name Catholic Widows and Orphans Benefit Society.

Committee recommended leave to withdraw.

Voted to accept and adopt report of Committee.

Bro. Shay, reported for Committee on Constitutions :—

The Committee on Constitution be requested to consider and report whether any additional legislation is necessary in order that the Records of the High Court may be read in full, for correction and approval, before final adjournment.

Committee reported inexpedient.

Voted to accept and adopt report of Committee.

Bro. Shay, reported for Committee on Constitution :—

Amend Constitution so that the offices of Financial Secretary and Treasurer of Subordinate Courts be consolidated, and the new office be known by the title of Secretary-Treasurer.

Committee reported inexpedient.

Voted to accept and adopt report of Committee.

Bro. Shay, reported for Committee on Constitution :—

Amend Constitution of High Court, page 19, sec. 3, by substituting in the first line of section the word " twenty " in the place of the word " forty."

Committee reported inexpedient.

Voted to accept and adopt the report of the Committee.

Bro. Shay reported on amendment relative to Social Members. Committee reported inexpedient.

Voted to accept and adopt report of Committee.·

Bro. Shay reported :—

Amend by adding on page 9, Constitution of High Court, new section of Art. II, to be known as:—Section 5. Recording and Financial Secretaries and Treasurers of subordinate Courts, who have served in either office five consecutive years, are eligible to membership, and to hold office in the High Court.

Committee recommended adoption.

Bro. Low, of Leo No. 5, moved to refer to permanent Committee on Constitution.

Vice High Chief Ranger Smith moved the previous question.

The main question was ordered.

Voted to refer to the permanent Committee on Constitution.

Bro. McQueeney, of St. Monica No. 78, moved to suspend the order of business and proceed to the election of officers.

High Chief Ranger stated the question, and declared it was a vote.

The vote was doubted and a count was ordered which showed Yes 57, No 15, and High Chief Ranger Fennessey declared it was a vote, and that the next business was the election of officers.

On motion of Bro. Lomasney, of Lafayette No. 14, voted to appoint a Committee of three to distribute, sort and count votes.

High Chief Ranger appointed Bros. Lomasney, of Lafayette No. 14, Lanigan, of Cathedral No. 1, Crotty, of St. Lawrence No. 61.

Bro. Callanan, of Shields No. 63, moved to proceed to ballot for High Chief Ranger.

Voted.

Past High Chief Ranger James J. McLaughlin rose and nominated Past High Chief Ranger, Hon. Owen A. Galvin for the position of High Chief Ranger.

The nomination was seconded by Bro. Callanan, of Shields No. 63.

Bro. O'Brien, of Essex No. 16, nominated Vice High Chief Ranger Philip Smith.

Bro. Carbrey, of Emerald No. 53, seconded the nomination.

High Chief Ranger announced the polls open and that all Representatives should come forward and deposit their votes as their names were called by the Secretary-Treasurer.

Roll was called and High Chief Ranger declared polls closed.

Bro. Sproules, of St. Francis No. 4, nominated Past High Chief Ranger James J. McLaughlin, for the position of Vice High Chief Ranger.

Nomination was seconded by Bro. Irvine, of Sarsfield No. 48.

Bro. McGaragle, of St. Joseph No. 11, nominated Bro. Sproules, of St. Francis No. 4, for Vice High Chief Ranger.

Past High Chief Ranger J. J. McLaughlin, seconded the nomination.

Bro. Sproules declined the nomination.

Bro. Maloney, of Williams No. 19, moved that High Secretary-Treasurer cast one ballot for James J. McLaughlin, for the office of Vice High Chief Ranger and it was so

Voted.

The Committee to Count Ballots, for High Chief Ranger reported

Whole number of ballots cast......................91

Necessary for choice...............................46

Philip Smith.......................................22

Owen A. Galvin.....................................67

Blank.. 2

and High Chief Ranger announced Owen A. Galvin elected High Chief Ranger for the ensuing term.

Vice High Chief Ranger Smith moved to make the ballot unanimous and it was so

Voted.

High Chief Ranger announced that the ballot had been cast for Vice High Chief Ranger, and James J. McLaughlin received that ballot, and was elected Vice High Chief Ranger.

Bro. Berrill, of Constantine No. 49, moved to postpone election of High Secretary-Treasurer, until he had a chance to present some grievances he had against the present High Secretary-Treasurer.

Bro. Callanan, of Shields No. 63, moved to lay election of High Secretary-Treasurer on the table.

Voted.

Bro. Galvin said he hoped Bro. Berrill would present his grievances, and had no doubt the High Secretary-Treasurer was as desirous of having Bro. Berrill make his statement as any one present.

Bro. Berrill then stated his case, that the Treasurer of Constantine Court No. 49, had embezzled the funds of Constantine Court, and that the Secretary-Treasurer had neglected to advise the Court of the non-payment of the calls.

Several rose to speak, when

Bro. Callanan, of Shields No. 63, raised a point of order that the High Secretary-Treasurer was entitled to make his statement of the matter.

Vice High Chief Ranger Smith ruled the point of order well taken and

The High Secretary-Treasurer then stated that the Treasurer of No. 49 represented to him that he had not received the money because of the removal of the Financial Secretary; that he had seen the Treasurer a number of times, and having no reason to suspect him, supposed the statements he made were true.

Bro. Berrill again addressed the Convention repeating his former statement. (High Chief Ranger Fennessey in the chair.)

Bro. Condon, of Unity No. 45, wished to know why the time of the Convention was taken up by this matter; that it seemed to him it was the business of Constantine Court to settle with the bondsmen of the Treasurer of the Court.

Bro. Carson, of Sheil Court No. 35, said he supposed the matter was now sufficiently ventilated, and moved to take the election of officers from the table, and

It was so voted.

Bro. Galvin, of Cheverus No. 6, nominated James F. Supple for High Secretary-Treasurer.

Bros. Callanan, of Shields No. 63, and Lowe, of No. 5, seconded the nomination.

Bro. Griffin, of St. Joseph No. 11, moved that High Chief Ranger Fennessey cast one ballot for James F. Supple for High Secretary-Treasurer.

Bro. Dolan, of Qualey No. 32, seconded the motion, and said he would like to have Bro. Supple hold the office as long as he wanted it.

Past High Chief Ranger John H. Watson said he was glad to hear the endorsement of Bro. Supple from Berkshire to Suffolk, and was happy to say that Essex County would give its vote to James F. Supple.

High Chief Ranger ruled that under the Rules the motion of Bro. Griffin could not be put, as there was one or more other candidates.

Bro. McGrath, of Mt. Pleasant Court No. 20, nominated J. P. J. Ward for the office of High Secretary-Treasurer.

Some debate ensued, and

Bro. Daly, of Erin No. 20, raised a point of order, that the question before the Convention was not a controversy between Bro. McGrath and some one else, but on a motion that we elect a High Secretary-Treasurer.

The High Chief Ranger ruled the point of order well taken, and that Bro. McGrath was out of order, because the High Chief Ranger was the proper one to decide points of law.

High Chief Ranger said the question was to proceed to ballot for High Secretary-Treasurer.

Voted to take the ballot.

High Chief Ranger ordered the roll called, and after all had voted declared the polls closed.

High Chief Ranger said the next business was the election of a High Senior Conductor.

Bro. McLaughlin nominated Bro. P. A. Murray, of Middlesex Court No. 60, for High Senior Conductor.

Bro. Edward Riley, the present High Senior Conductor, declined a nomination.

Bro. Rooney, of Prospect No. 58, seconded the nomination of Bro. Murray.

Bro. Sullivan, of Sherwood No. 8, moved that High Secretary-Treasurer cast one ballot for Bro. P. A. Murray for High Senior Conductor.

Voted.

High Chief Ranger announced ballot cast as directed, and declared Bro. P. A. Murray, of Middlesex No. 60, elected High Senior Conductor.

Bro. Carson, of Sheil No. 35, nominated Hon. J. P. Dore for High Junior Conductor.

Bro. Lowe, of Leo No. 5, nominated Bro. John Brant for the place.

Bro. Brant declined

Bro. Duggan, of Friendship No. 37, moved that High Chief Ranger Fennessey cast the ballot of the Convention for Bro. Dore.

The High Chief Ranger did so, and declared Bro. Dore elected High Junior Conductor.

Bro. Lomasney, for Committee to Count Ballots for High Secretary-Treasurer, reported :—

```
Whole number of ballots cast......................87
Necessary for a choice............................44
H. C. Byrne.......................................  1
J. P. J. Ward....................................11
M. Leonard........................................  1
James F. Supple..................................74
```

High Chief Ranger declared James F. Supple elected High Secretary-Treasurer.

Bro. Lane, of St. Peter No. 18, nominated Bro. John T. Daly for High Inside Sentinel.

Bro. Cashin, of Cheverus, seconded the nomination.

High Chief Ranger stated question on choice of High Inside Sentinel.

Bro. Dunnican, of St. Gregory No. 24, nominated Bro. Farrenkopf.

Voted unanimously that Bro. John T. Daly be the choice of the Convention for High Inside Sentinel, and that High Chief Ranger so ballot.

High Chief Ranger declared ballot cast, and Bro. John T. Daly elected High Inside Sentinel.

Bro. Callanan, of Shields No. 63, nominated Bro. Farrenkopf, as Outside Sentinel.

Several delegates nominated Capt. Jeremiah G. Fennessey, for Outside Sentinel.

Bro. Hartigan, of Essex No. 16, nominated John Hayes, of Lafayette No. 14.

Bro. Sweeney, of Emerald No. 53, and Lomasney, of Lafayette No. 14, seconded the nomination of Bro. Hayes.

Bro. Irvine, of Sarsfield No. 48, seconded the nomination of Bro. Fennessey.

A motion was made to cast one ballot for John Hayes.

Bro. Farrenkopf withdrew his own name.

Bro. Brown, of Bass River No. 30, seconded the nomination of Bro. Hayes.

Bro. Sullivan moved the previous question—which was—

Voted.

High Chief Ranger stated the question, and added that if a single member objected to his candidacy he would not be a candidate.

High Chief Ranger stated the question again that one ballot be cast for Bro. John Hayes, for High Outside Sentinel.

Voted.

High Chief Ranger declared John Hayes elected High Outside Sentinel.

High Chief Ranger Fennessey announced next business, the election of High Medical Examiner.

Dr. Joseph D. Couch was nominated by half a dozen representatives.

Vice High Chief Ranger Philip Smith said it gave him great pleasure to second the nomination of so worthy and hard working an officer, and moved that one ballot be cast for him.

Dr. Hines also seconded the nomination.

High Chief Ranger stated the question to cast one ballot for Dr. Joseph D. Couch, for High Medical Examiner and declared it was a Vote.

And declared the ballot cast, and Dr. Joseph D. Couch elected High Medical Examiner.

High Chief Ranger announced next business election of High Chaplain.

Bro. John Brant, of Leo, No. 5, nominated Rev. Hugh Roe O'Donnell, and moved that High Secretary-Treasurer, cast one ballot for him.

Voted.

High Chief Ranger declared the ballot cast, and Rev. Hugh Roe O'Donnell elected High Chaplain.

Bro. McGaragle nominated Bro. D. A. Cronin, of St. Joseph No. 11, for Trustee of Reserve Fund, for three years, and that High Secretary-Treasurer cast one ballot.

Voted.

High Chief Ranger declared the ballot cast, and Bro. D. A. Cronin was elected.

Bro. Callanan, of Shields No. 63, declined election as Trustee, and High Chief Ranger announced the election of another Trustee in order.

Bro. Sproules, of St. Francis No. 4, was nominated by Bro. McLaughlin, of Americus No. 34, who moved that High Secretary-Treasurer cast one ballot.

Voted.

Ballot was cast, and High Chief Ranger declared Bro. Sproules elected as Trustee.

Vice High Chief Ranger, moved to elect by one ballot the present Finance Committee, Bros. Shay, Golding. Doré, Lanigan and Rooney.

Bro. Shay declined.

Bro. D. A. Cronin, of St. Joseph No. 11, nominated Bro. McGaragle, of St. Joseph No. 11.

High Chief Ranger announced that another vacancy existed, caused by the election of Bro. Dore on the High Standing Committee.

Bro. Hartigan, of Essex No. 16 was nominated.

High Chief Ranger stated question, to elect on one ballot for Finance Committee,

Bros. Golding	of Cheverus No. 6
Lanigan	" Cathedral " 1
Rooney	" Prospect " 58
McGaragle	" St. Joseph " 11
Hartigan	" Essex " 16

and declared the ballot cast as directed, and announced them elected.

Voted to take a recess of 45 minutes for supper.

Recess at 6.35 P. M.

Reassembled at 7.45 P. M.

Vice High Chief Ranger Smith, moved to suspend order of business, and install the officers.

Seconded by Bro. Callanan, of 63.

Dr. Ahearne, of Lafayette No. 14, objected.

Bro. Sullivan, of St. John No. 23, objected.

Dr. Ahearne, of No. 14, moved, to amend, to proceed in regular order.

High Chief Ranger stated the question on amendment.

Voted.

High Chief Ranger announced report of Committee on Constitution.

Bro. Shay, for the Committee, read amendment to page 9, to add new Section, to be Section 3.—

Amend by adding on page 9, High Court Constitution, Art. III. (Officers of High Court,) a new section, to be known as,— Section 3. No member of the Order shall be eligible to hold office in the High Court or High Standing Committee, for more than five consecutive terms; provided however that should the occupant of the office of High Chief Ranger be serving his fifth year of consecutive service, and in the first year as High Chief Ranger, he shall be eligible for service, an additional year, as High Chief Ranger if elected.

The Committee recommend adoption.

Bro. Duggan, of Friendship No. 37, moved to refer to permanent Committee on Constitution, when appointed.

Voted to refer.

Bro. Shay reported on amendment, changing limit of age for admission to the Order, 50 to 55 years,—
Inexpedient.

Voted to accept and adopt report of Committee.

Bro. Riley, of St. Joseph No. 11, moved to refer to Committee on Constitution, when appointed.

Voted to refer.

Bro. McLaughlin, of Americus No. 34, moved that all amendments now in hands of Committee on Constitution, be referred to the permanent Committee, when appointed.

Bro. Galvin, of Cheverus Court No. 6, asked to except one relating to Trustees, and moved previous question.

Bro. Callanan objected.

High Chief Ranger asked the Secretary of the Committee on Constitution, to read the article in question.

Bro. Shay read:—

Amendment to Article VIII, Section 1:— The Trustees shall hold the bonds of all High Court Officers, who are required to give bonds, said bonds shall be approved by the Corporation Counsel. They shall deposit any funds received by them, in some bank or banks, to be selected by the Trustees, and they shall also have power to invest sums of money, received for the Reserve Fund, in mortgages on real estate, not exceeding 60 per cent. of tax valuation; or in city or county bonds, as are approved by High Chief Ranger, Secretary-Treasurer and Corporation Counsel. They shall report to the High Standing Committee, every six months, namely on the first Wednesdays of April and October, of each year, a full statement of all their investments and such other information in regard to the Reserve Fund, as may be required of them by the High Standing Committee, and they shall make a full report to the Convention in annual session. No portion of the Reserve Fund shall be drawn upon, except by vote of the convention.

Bro. Torndorf of Holy Trinity No. 51, moved to amend, that no other investment be made than mortgages on real estate.

High Chief Ranger stated the question, which was on the amendment of Bro. Torndorf, which included the amendment of Bro. McLaughlin to strike out.

Vote was taken and High Chief Ranger declared it was not a vote.

Bro. Callanan moved to amend by inserting Massachusetts Bonds.

Bro. Cronin accepted the amendment offered by Bro. Callanan.

High Chief stated question as amended with a further amendment to add, in banks to be selected by the Trustees.

Vote was taken and High Chief Ranger declared it was a vote.

High Chief Ranger stated question on adoption of article as amended, and the Convention voted to adopt as amended.

Bro. Shay for Committee on Finance made the following report—

To the Officers and Members of the High Court Massachusetts Catholic Order of Foresters:

Your committee appointed to audit the books of the High Secretary-Treasurer, would report that they have attended to their duty and that the books and vouchers of money received and expended by the Secretary-Treasurer, as presented to us are all right, but the duty of an Auditing Committee is, as we understand it, in presenting a true account of the liabilities and assets of the Order.

This is impossible to do in the time allowed the committee, and from the present system of receiving the reports and moneys due the High Court, it is impossible for any committee to do the work.

The Secretary-Treasurer is the only one who can tell anything about the condition of the Order financially, and we think some better system should be adopted.

Upon asking the Secretary-Treasurer who made up the amount that the courts pay on each endowment call, we find that the work is done by the Secretaries of the courts and that the Secretary-Treasurer relies upon their reports and has no means of verifying it. Now this should not be.

We think that the accounts of the High Court and subordinates should be so kept that the Secretary-Treasurer should at a glance, be able to tell the number of members, and the amount which each court pays on an endowment call. We have no way by which we can find any information but from the report made annually by the Secretary-Treasurer and that report in printed form, is in the hands of all the members of the High Court.

The members of the High Court are as well informed as we are in reading the reports and if any information is required we can but refer them to the High Court Secretary-Treasurer.

All of which is respectfully submitted,

W. E. SHAY,
JAMES J. LANIGAN,
JOHN P. DORE.

Moved to accept report and refer to next High Standing Committee.

High Chief Ranger stated question on acceptance and reference and declared it was a vote.

High Chief Ranger asked for the report of any committee.

Bro. O'Brien for Committee on Petitions reported —

SALEM, APRIL 22, 1891.

The committee appointed for the purpose of considering the petitions referred to them have attended to the subject matter and would submit the following report for the consideration of the convention, and would recommend their adoption,

First. To pay the death claim of James H. Fox, of Constantine No. 49.

Second. That the Order supply all members with certificates of membership.

Third. That the death claim of the heirs of Wm. F. Hastings, of St. Anne No. 47, of Gloucester, be paid, provided, that they furnish a sufficient bond for the protection of the Order for one year.

For the Committee,

D. J. O'BRIEN, Secretary.

High Chief Ranger stated the question on accepting report of the committee.

Voted to accept report.

High Chief Ranger then stated question on adoption of first part of report, recommending payment of endowment to the heirs of James H. Fox, who died of "Delirium Tremens."

Bro. Daly of Erin No. 28, inquired if Fox did not sign an agreement to forfeit all rights if he used alcoholic liquors to excess, and inquiring if the law of the Order at that time was different from now.

High Chief Ranger stated that members were governed by the laws of the Order whether adopted after admission or not.

High Medical Examiner Couch stated that as an autopsy had been performed and said to show no evidence of the abuse of liquor, there was a reasonable doubt as to the correctness of the Death Certificate. Dr. Francis M. Hines of Essex No. 16, took the same ground as did also Dr. Ahearne of Lafayette No 14.

On motion the previous question was ordered, and the High Chief Ranger stated the question, to pay the endowment to the heirs of James H. Fox.

Voted to pay.

Bro. O'Brien of Essex No. 16, moved that Hastings' claim be paid.

High Chief Ranger stated the question to pay the endowment to the heirs of W. F. Hastings of St. Anne No. 47, provided a sufficient bond was given to protect the Order.

The Chief Ranger of St. Anne No. 47, Bro. Charles O'Brien, then stated the facts in the case, which were as reported and published.

An amendment was offered to strike out the giving of a bond.

Bros. Torndorf, J. H. Watson and others advocated payment.

High Chief Ranger said the High Standing Committee felt satisfied Hasting was dead but thought a reasonable time should elapse before payment.

High Chief Ranger stated the question to pay without requiring bond. Voted to pay.

High Chief Ranger in answer to a question, ruled that Chambers' case could not be paid as there was no person under the law who could claim it.

High Chief Ranger read recommendation for a Benefit Certificate to be issued to the members of the Order.

Voted to refer to High Standing Committee.

Voted to adjourn subject to call of the High Standing Committee. Adjourned 9.15, P. M.

JAMES F. SUPPLE,
High Secretary-Treasurer.

SECOND SESSION.

UNIVERSITY HALL, 1371 WASHINGTON STREET,

BOSTON, MAY 5, 1891.

The Convention was called to order at 2.30 P. M. by High Chief Ranger Capt. Fennessey.

The High Conductors reported all present, but High Inside Sentinel and High Outside Sentinel. High Chief Ranger Fennessey appointed Bro. F. P. Conaty, of Taunton No. 73, as High Inside Sentinel, Bro. J. C. Carson, of Shéil Court No. 35, as High Outside Sentinel.

The Convention was opened in due form by the High Chief Ranger, who also offered prayer.

High Chief Ranger Fennessey announced as the first business in order, the reception of credentials.

High Chief Ranger announced as next business, the reading of records of the last session.

The records were read, and Bro. McGrath, of Mt. Pleasant No. 20, objected to a term entered in the record as used by him.

The High Chief Ranger ruled that the record was correct.

Bro. McGrath appealed from the decision of the High Chief Ranger.

The previous question was ordered, the High Chief Ranger put the question, "Shall the decision of the chair stand?"

Voted to sustain the decision of the chair.

Bro. Duggan, of Friendship No. 37, moved that the part of the record referring to the language used by Bro. McGrath be stricken out.

The High Chief Ranger said the question was on accepting the records, and put the question on approving the records as read.

Voted to approve the records.

Bro. Lomasney, of Lafayette No. 14, moved to suspend the regular order of business, and proceed to installation of officers.

And it was voted.

High Chief Ranger appointed Bro. Farrenkopf, High Inside Sentinel ; Bro. Carson, High Outside Sentinel ; and then invited Past High Chief Ranger John H. Watson to install the officers.

Bro. Watson suggested that Bro. Fennessey install the High Chief Ranger elect, Bro. Owen A. Galvin, and he would act as High Conductor.

High Chief Ranger Fennessey said it would give him great pleasure to do so.

High Chief Ranger announced that credentials had been received from the following delegates :—

E. F. Chamberlin, St. Peters, No. 18 ; Jeremiah Crotty, St. Lawrence, No. 61 ; Michael Edmonds, Cathedral No. 1 ; P. F. McGaragle, St. Joseph No. 11 ; Owen A. Galvin, Cheverus No. 6 ; R. Farrenkopf, Sherwood No. 8 ; J. H. Coughlin, St. Michael No. 70.

High Chief Ranger instructed the High Conductors to prepare for installation. High Chief Ranger Fennessey then installed the following officers :—

High Chief Ranger—OWEN A. GALVIN, Cheverus Court No. 6.

High Secretary-Treasurer—JAS. F. SUPPLE, Columbus Court No. 9.

High Senior Conductor—P. A. MURRAY, Middlesex Court No. 60.

High Junior Conductor—JOHN P. DORE, Sherwood Court No. 8.

High Inside Sentinel—JOHN T. DALY, Erin Court No. 28.

High Outside Sentinel—JOHN HAYES, Lafayette Court No. 14.

Bro. Fennessey then introduced Bro. Galvin as High Chief Ranger of the Massachusetts Catholic Order of Foresters for the ensuing term.

The Convention received Bro. Galvin with great and continued applause.

Bro. Galvin made a speech, thanking the delegates for their confidence in him, and predicting continued success for the Order.

Bro. Fennessey then proclaimed the officers duly installed, and Bro. Galvin was conducted to his seat as High Chief Ranger.

Bro. Griffin, of St. Joseph No. 11, asked the privilege of discharging a duty which was very agreeable to him. He said three years ago he had opposed Bro. Fennessey's election; but he now acknowledged he was wrong then, and moved a standing vote of thanks to Capt. Jeremiah G. Fennessey, Past High Chief Ranger of the Massachusetts Catholic Order of Foresters.

High Chief Ranger Galvin put the question, and it was

Voted unanimously.

Bro. Riley, of St. Raphael No. 26, moved a vote of thanks to all the members of the High Standing Committee.

Voted.

High Chief Ranger Galvin announced the next business, reception of reports and petitions.

Bro. Torndorf, for the Committee on State of the Order, reported as follows :—

To the High Court of the Massachusetts Catholic Order of Foresters, in Annual Convention.

The Committee on State of the Order, find the Order in a very satisfactory condition. The Committee recommend :—

First. That steps be taken by this Convention, which will lead to the extension of the Order throughout the New England States.

Second. That the High Standing Committee be empowered to employ the services of an organizer, for the purpose of organizing new courts, whenever in their judgment they find it necessary to employ such services.

Third That the High Standing Committee be instructed to notify delinquent courts, on or before the first day of February in every year, that the representatives of such courts will not be admitted to the annual convention, unless the financial report of such courts is sent to the High Secretary-Treasurer, within a specified time.

Fourth. That more commodious headquarters be provided, to include a document room, in addition to the office of the High Standing Committee, and further recommend that said headquarters shall be established in the Knights of St. Rose Building.

Fifth. That the High Standing Committee be requested to explain why the provision in the High Court Constitution, which calls for the distribution of the Secretary-Treasurer's annual report, two weeks previous to the annual convention, is not carried out.

Sixth. That a permanent Committee on Constitution be elected, to which the above recommendations be referred, with power to report at the next special or regular session of the High Court.

JOSEPH TORNDORF, *Chairman.*

Bro. McGaragle, of St. Joseph No. 11, moved to accept the report.

Voted to accept report.

Bro. Shay, of St. Francis No. 4, inquired if the convention adopted the report.

High Chief Ranger said no, and then read the first section for the action of the convention.

Bro. McGaragle moved to have that section printed and forwarded to all the Courts.

High Chief Ranger Galvin said he thought it would be well to read the remainder of the report and did so.

Bro. Cronin, of St. Joseph No. 11, moved to adopt the report.

Bro. Shay, of St. Francis No. 4, asked that action be deferred until the Finance Committee report, and moved to lay the report of the Committee on State of the Order on the table.

Voted.

Bro. Shay, of St. Francis No. 4, for Committee on Finance reported that a per capita tax of one dollar be levied, and in explanation said that the organization should be supported and some man should give all his time to it, and he for the committee, favored the payment of a sufficient sum to the High Secretary-Treasurer, to enable this to be done, and recommended payment of $ 2,000 to the High Secretary-Treasurer.

High Chief Ranger put the question.

Voted to accept the report.

High Chief Ranger Galvin said the question now was on the adoption of the recommendation of the Committee on Finance, to pay $2,000 to the High Secretary-Treasurer, for him to attend to the organization of new courts, and making per capita tax one dollar.

Bro. Shay and Bro. Carson spoke in favor of the motion.

Vice High Chief Ranger Smith said he was not in favor of increasing the expenses, and wanted the report adopted by sections.

Bro. Brady said he believed the time had come when we should have a larger membership.

Bro. Dore also favored the motion, and thought we could not expect a man to give his whole time to the organization unless he was paid a proper amount, and he thought $2,000 was not enough.

Bro. Conaty of 73, Sullivan of No. 8, Chamberlin of No. 18, all spoke in favor of the motion.

Bros. Carbery of No. 53, and Murphy of No. 59, were opposed to increasing the expenses.

Bros. Carson of No. 6, Farrenkopf of No. 8, Riley of 26, were in favor of the motion.

Bro. Ervine of 48, suggested that every member in the order should act as organizer.

Bro. Fennessey said he was in a peculiar position, as he had been previously referred to ; he said he believed in sentiment in connection with everything in the Order for this reason that every death certificate shows the existence of orphans, for whose benefit the Order was carried on. He asked how long the Order could continue, and depend on the gratuitous exertions of the High Standing Committee. He said the standard to go by, was the work worth the money ; if it was, pay it ; other organizations paid larger salaries than we propose to pay. We do not pay enough.

Bro. McGaragle, of St. Joseph No. 11, announced supper.

Bro. Carson moved a recess for supper.

Bro. O'Brien, of Essex No. 16, wanted the vote taken by yeas and nays.

On motion, a recess was voted at 6.30 P. M. until 7.15 P. M.

After supper, High Chief Ranger Galvin called the convention to order at 7.20, P. M.

Bro. McGrath of Mt. Pleasant No. 20, asked if we were establishing a new office. High Chief Ranger Galvin explained that we were not.

On motion of Bro. Daly of Erin No. 28, the previous question was ordered.

High Chief Ranger Galvin stated the question on adopting the recommendation of the finance committee to levy a per capita tax of $1.00, and that the salary of the High Secretary-Treasurer be $2,000, and an amendment to divide the question.

Bro. McGrath of Mt. Pleasant No. 20, moved that power be given to any member to act as organizer with suitable pay ; seconded by Bro. Berrill. Bro. Cronin of St. Joseph No. 11, said it was a very important matter and now is the time to do what is proposed. Bro. Lowe of Leo No. 5, objected to the motion of Bro. McGrath and said that so many interfering would spoil all.

Bros. Griffin and Lanigan were in favor of the recommendation of the committee on finance. Bro. Hartigan of Essex No. 16, said he wished to be conscientious in the matter and moved to amend by referring the matter to the courts.

High Chief Ranger Galvin said there was an amendment to the amendment ; Bro. Hartigan moved to substitute his motion. Bros.

Dunnican of No. 24, and Lomasney of No. 14 were against the substituting of the motion.

Bro. Clark of No. 74 moved the previous question.

High Medical Examiner Couch spoke in favor of the report of the committee on finance, and called attention to the fact that no organization in the state could show the report of the Massachusetts Catholic Order of Foresters; our physical condition was the best of any.

High Chief Ranger Galvin stated the question.

The previous question was ordered.

High Chief Ranger then stated that the main question was on the substitute motion of Bro. Hartigan of Essex No. 16, to refer to the courts, and declared it was not a vote.

The High Chief Ranger stated the question on the motion of Bro. McGrath of Mt. Pleasant No. 20, that every man act as organizer and declared it was not a vote.

The High Chief Ranger stated the question to be on division of the report; first, to levy a per capita tax of $1.00; second, to pay $2,000 to the High Secretary-Treasurer. The question was on division.

Voted.

The High Chief Ranger stated the question on the motion to call the roll, and to take the vote by yeas and nays, and declared it was a vote. The vote was doubted and a count was ordered and showed yeas, 47, nays, not taken. High Chief Ranger declared it was a vote.

The High Chief Ranger stated the question to be on the report of the committee on finance; the roll was called, the result was 50 yeas, 11 nays, and the High Chief Ranger declared it was a vote.

High Chief Ranger stated the question to be on second part of the recommendation of finance committee, and declared it was a vote.

Bro. Carson of Cheverus No. 6, moved that the per capita tax be levied in two parts. Past High Chief Ranger Fennessey moved to amend, to refer to the High Standing Committee. Bro. Carson accepted the amendment.

Voted to refer.

High Chief Ranger said he had a suggestion to make, which came to him from a very honest worker in the organization, that a proposal was on foot to form a society called the Catholic Order of Odd Fellows and that we should take some action on the matter. Past High Chief Ranger Fennessey moved that the matter be referred to a committee of two, to consist of the High Chief Ranger and High Chaplain, be appointed, and take action in the matter.

And it was so voted.

Bro. Shay moved to take from the table the report of committee on state of the Order, and it was so

Voted.

Vice High Chief Ranger Smith moved to adopt the report as presented. Past High Chief Ranger Fennessey said that the rules provided that each article be acted on singly. High Chief Ranger Galvin read the report of the committee, and said the first question was on the article relating to the extension of the Order.

Bro. Torndorf asked to take the last section first and refer all to the permanent committee on constitution. Voted to so refer.

The High Chief Ranger stated the question on second article to employ an organizer. Bro. Torndorf moved to amend to strike it out. High Chief Ranger stated the question and declared it was a vote.

The High Chief Ranger stated the question on the third recommendation that delinquent courts should not be represented at the convention. Bro. Torndorf moved to adopt as an instruction to the High Standing Committee and said that if the constitution was enforced he could not represent his court. The High Chief Ranger stated the question and declared it was a vote.

The High Chief Ranger read the fourth recommendation to provide a document room in addition to the office of the High Standing Committee. Bro. Shay of St. Francis No. 4, moved to refer to the High Standing Committee. High Chief Ranger stated the question on reference and declared it was a vote.

The High Chief Ranger read section 5, viz.: why the annual report was not published two weeks before the convention, as required by the Constitution.

Bro. Fennessey explained that it was owing to the negligence of the courts in not forwarding the reports in the proper time, and that without the reports from the courts, the annual report could not be published.

Bro. Torndorf moved to adopt the sixth recommendation; namely, to appoint a permanent Committee on Constitution.

The High Chief Ranger corrected the section, and suggested that it be stricken out.

The High Chief Ranger stated the question on adoption.

Voted to adopt.

Bro. D. A. Cronin, of St. Joseph No. 11, presented the report of the Trustee Fund.

Boston, April 22, 1891.

To the Honorable the Massachusetts Catholic Order of Foresters, in High Court assembled.

GENTLEMEN,—The Trustees beg leave to present for your consideration their Second Annual Report.

Total amount received to April 22, 1891 :—

From Calls Nos. 1 and 2	$4,439.90
Union Bank Interest to May, 1890	8.52
Total	$4,441.50

Invested as follows :—

Union Savings Bank Principal	$2,056.49
" " Interest to May, 1890	8.52
Franklin Savings Bank	1,000.00
Cash on hand	1,383.49
Total	$4,448.50

Respectfully submitted,

DANIEL CRONIN, } *Trustees.*
JOSEPH TORNDORF, }

Bro. Daly, of Erin No. 28, moved to accept and adopt the report of the Trustees.

High Chief Ranger stated the question and declared it was a vote.

The High Chief Ranger appointed the following as the Permanent Committee on Constitution :—

Bros. Jeremiah G. Fennessey	of St. James	No.	54
James Cashon	" Cheverus	"	6
D. F. Sullivan	" Sherwood	"	8
G. F. Low	" Leo	"	5
A. A. Clark	" Hendricken	"	74
D. J. O'Brien	" Essex	"	16

Bro. Fennessey called attention to delay of the Deputy High Chief Rangers in looking after and certifying death claims, and suggested a change, and then moved to strike out on page 25, of the of the Constitution, "from the receipt thereof," in the 11th line to the end of the section on page 26.

The High Chief Ranger stated the question, and declared it a vote.

Bro. Hartigan of Essex No. 16, said he considered it a great compliment to Essex Court that the Convention was held in Salem, and thanked the High Standing Committee on behalf of his court.

The High Chief Ranger announced that the Annual Mass for the souls of deceased members of the Order, under the auspices of the Knights of St. Rose, would take place on May 30, at St. Mary's Church.

The following resolutions were offered and read by the High Secretary-Treasurer.

Resolutions on death of Bro. Thomas F. Sullivan, of St. Thomas Court No. 29.

WHEREAS:—As it has .pleased Almighty God in his infinite wisdom, to remove from our midst, our esteemed brother Thomas F. Sullivan, who was an exemplary Christian, a devoted husband and father, a true friend and brother, and one who never spared himself in any case where he could do good to others.

Be it therefor resolved that while we bow with humble submission to the Divine will we cannot but mourn our loss.

Resolved, that in the death of Bro. Sullivan, the Order has lost a true brother, the community a good citizen, and the widow and orphans have suffered a loss which is to them a loss indeed.

Resolved, that we tender the family of our deceased and beloved brother our heartfelt sympathy in this their time of need, and that we sincerely mourn with them for the loss they have sustained.

Resolved, that these resolutions be spread upon the records of this Convention and that a copy of the same be forwarded to the bereaved widow and family.

Signed,

FRED R. SMITH, of St. Thomas No 29,
A. A. CLARKE, of Hendricken No. 74,
E. E. LANE, of St. Thomas No. 29.

Vice High Chief Ranger Smith moved that the resolutions be adopted by a rising vote.

Bro. Fennessey spoke feelingly of the loss the Order sustained in the death of Bro. Sullivan, and extolled his character as a man and Forester.

The High Chief Ranger stated the question.

The Convention voted to adopt by rising unanimously.

Bro. Daly, of Erin 28, said that as nothing had been heard from the Committee on Secret Work, he would like to see a Committee on Secret Work appointed.

Bro. Duggan, of Friendship No. 37, reported for the Committee on Secret Work.

The Committee recommended offering a prize of $ 50 for the best ritual.

Bro. Gallagher recommended that the prize be given by October next.

High Chief Ranger Galvin stated the question on accepting and adopting the report of the committee.

Voted to accept and adopt.

Bro. Daly, of Erin No. 28, moved reference to a Permanent Committee of seven to be appointed by the High Chief Ranger.

The High Chief Ranger stated the question, and declared it was a vote.

The High Chief Ranger appointed the following Committee on Secret Work:—

Bros. John T. Daly.......................of Erin No. 28
T. H. Duggan..................of Friendship No. 37
P. A. Donovan..........of SS. Peter and Paul No. 15
Philip Smith....................of Williams No. 19
P. F. McGaragle............... of St. Joseph No. 11
Garret H. Keefe ....of Mt. Pleasant No. 20

High Chief Ranger announced new business now in order.

Bro. Riley, of St. Raphael No. 26, asked if a list of extra hazardous risks was kept.

Bro. Fennessey said there was not, and that each application was acted upon on its own merits.

High Chief Ranger announced next business, a Committee of Three on the address of the High Chief Ranger.

Bro. Smith moved to reconsider.

Voted.

Bro. Smith then moved to refer the address of the High Chief Ranger to the Permanent Committee on Constitution.

Voted.

Bro. Berrill, of Constantine No. 49, said he wished to bring the defalcation of the late Treasurer of his Court before the Convention, and moved that the amount of one call be received from Court 49, and that the bondsman be excused from paying the balance.

Bro. Torndorf objected, saying he thought it would be a bad precedent.

Bro. Sproules moved to refer to the High Standing Committee with full power.

Bro. Fennessey moved as a substitute reference to the High Standing Committee.

The High Chief Ranger stated the question on the substitute motion, and declared it was a vote.

Bro. Berrill asked the privilege of the floor.

The High Chief Ranger declared Bro. Berrill out of order.

High Chief Ranger Galvin called for the names of Past High Chief Rangers.

J. W. Maguire.................of Cheverus No. 6
F. M. Hughes.................of St. Augustine No. 46
E. A. Dever..................of Mt. Pleasant No. 20
M. J. Collins................of St. James No. 54
James Douglass...............of Williams No. 19
P. J. McKenna...............of SS. Peter and Paul No. 15
J. W. Riley..................of Friendship No. 37
M. O'Brien...................of Fulton No. 12
J. Costello..................of St. Michael No. 70
A. A. Clark..................of Hendricken No. 74
J. F. O'Brien................of Sarsfield No. 48
M. F. Conroy.................of Griffin No. 66
T. F. Fineran................of St. James No. 54
H. Montague..................of Sherwood No. 8

The High Chief Ranger announced the next business, the reading of the records of the Convention for approval.

The High Secretary-Treasurer proceeded to read.

Bro. Fennessey moved to dispense with further reading of the records, and that the records be considered read and approved.

The High Chief Ranger stated the question on the approval of the records.

Voted to approve the records.

On motion voted to adjourn, and the High Chief Ranger adjourned the Convention *sine die.*

The High Chief Ranger closed in due form at 10.55 P. M.

JAMES F. SUPPLE,

High Secretary-Treasurer.

ERRATA.

Sherwood, No. 8, instituted March 4, 1880.

St. Lawrence, No. 61, instituted October 26, 1886.

Stoughton, No. 69, meets 1st and 3rd Thursday.

THIRTEENTH ANNUAL REPORT

OF THE,

HIGH SECRETARY-TREASURER

OF THE

𝕸𝖆𝖘𝖘𝖆𝖈𝖍𝖚𝖘𝖊𝖙𝖙𝖘 𝕮𝖆𝖙𝖍𝖔𝖑𝖎𝖈 𝕺𝖗𝖉𝖊𝖗 𝖔𝖋 𝕱𝖔𝖗𝖊𝖘𝖙𝖊𝖗𝖘

AND ADDRESS OF HIGH CHIEF RANGER

To the High Court, April 27, 1892.

WITH

REPORT OF PROCEEDINGS

OF THE

THIRTEENTH ANNUAL CONVENTION

AND

A List of Medical Examiners and D. H. C. R's, and

Meetings and List of Officers.

BOSTON:

THE EASTBURN PRESS,

165 Devonshire Street.

THIRTEENTH ANNUAL REPORT

OF THE

HIGH SECRETARY-TREASURER

OF THE

Massachusetts Catholic Order of Foresters

AND ADDRESS OF HIGH CHIEF RANGER

To the High Court, April 27, 1892.

WITH

REPORT OF PROCEEDINGS

OF THE

THIRTEENTH ANNUAL CONVENTION

AND

A List of Medical Examiners and D. H. C. R's, and

Meetings and List of Officers.

BOSTON:

THE EASTBURN PRESS,

165 Devonshire Street.

HIGH COURT OFFICERS,

For Term Ending April, 1893.

HIGH CHIEF RANGER,

Hon. Owen A. Galvin . . . Cheverus Court No. 6

HIGH VICE CHIEF RANGER,

J. J. McLaughlin . . . . Americus Court No. 34

HIGH SECRETARY-TREASURER,

James F. Supple . . . . Columbus Court No. 9

HIGH SENIOR CONDUCTOR,

P. A. Murray . . . . . Middlesex Court No. 60

HIGH JUNIOR CONDUCTOR,

John P. Dore . . . . . Sherwood Court No. 8

HIGH INSIDE SENTINEL,

John T. Daly . . . . . . Erin Court No. 28

HIGH OUTSIDE SENTINEL,

John Hayes . . .. . . Lafayette Court No. 14

HIGH MEDICAL EXAMINER,

Joseph D. Couch, M. D. . . . Benedict Court No. 39

HIGH CHAPLAIN,

Rev. Hugh Roe O'Donnell . Star of the Sea Court No. 41

ADDRESS OF HIGH CHIEF RANGER

AND

ANNUAL REPORT OF HIGH STANDING COMMITTEE

For the Term ending April 26, 1892.

Representatives to the Annual Convention of the High Court of the Massachusetes Catholic Order of Foresters.

BROTHERS,—To-day begins the Thirteenth Annual Convention of the Massachusetts Catholic Order of Foresters. We have great cause to congratulate ourselves on the progress we have made during the past year, for reasons which are apparent to you as representatives of the membership of the Order, you are all active workers in the various Courts, and cognizant of the detail work of the Order. You are, it seems to me, fully able to appreciate how much is meant when I say we have great cause for congratulation. Entering upon a resume of the work of the year, let me congratulate the members of the Organization that to-day we are, without doubt, the strongest Order financially among the people of our faith in the State of Massachusetts. Our membership has increased rapidly and steadily, and at the same time the average death rate has been reduced, and the average age of membership has also been reduced.

Since the last Convention the High Standing Committee has held 63 meetings. Some of these have been held at the office of the Order, 611 Washington Street. Many of them have been held away from home, and right here, it seems to me, I ought to call your attention to the spirit of disinterestedness and willingness to sacrifice personal comfort on the part of my associates on the High Standing Committee. Trips have been made away from home from which we have received no apparent results, but, whenever I have said to them I think you should go to a certain place and see what you can do either in the way of encouragement of a Court already in existence or in taking steps towards the formation of a new Court, they have invariably responded, and in many instances not reaching their homes until very late at night. This self-sacrifice shows that my associates are very much interested in the success of the Organization.

From April 22, 1891, to April 22, 1892, the High Standing Committee has received 1,023 applications, and of this number 98 were rejected. The High Standing Committee considers that it is its duty to act upon applications for membership in the same manner as a Board of Directors of an insurance company act on application for insurance. The matter of friendship and personal popularity never enters into the question of examination, the only test is whether or not the candidate is a good risk. From time to time complaints are made against the High Standing Committee, and against the supervision of medical examinations made by the High Court Physician by members in the Order who believe that friends of theirs ought to be admitted, when they have been rejected; but to all these complaints our invariable reply has been that the reports on the application blank is our only guide, and that the examination of the examining physician justifies our refusal to admit the applicant to membership. While this work is sometimes very unpleasant indeed the High Standing Committee believe that it is their duty to perform it, and perform it without reference to the position of the applicant, or their own private desires in the matter.

I take great pleasure in reporting that seven new Courts have been added during the year, as follows :—

St. Malachi Court, No. 81, in Arlington, 20 charter members. Instituted September 3, 1891.

Brockton Court, No. 82, in Brockton, 61 charter members. Instituted December 11, 1891.

John Henry Newman Court, No. 83, in Everett, 27 charter members. Instituted December 12, 1891.

Danvers Court, No. 84, in Danvers, 33 charter members. Instituted February 10, 1892.

George Washington Court, No. 85, in West Lynn, 44 charter members. Instituted February 22, 1892.

Avon Court, No. 86, in Avon, 38 charter members. Instituted March 19, 1822.

Robert Emmett Court, No. 87, in Walpole, 22 charter members. Institued April 1, 1892.

We have now on our roll 77 Courts with a membership of 5,400.

January 1, 1887, we had 2,800; January 1, 1888, we had 3,230; January 1, 1889, we had 3,644; January 1, 1890, we had 4,270; January 1, 1891, we had 4,550.

You will see by this our gain has been steady, and, except in 1884, we have never made a net loss in any year since organization.

One Court, Star of the Sea, 41, surrendered its charter and was dissolved. Some of the members took withdrawal cards intending to go into the neighboring Courts, Leo Court, No. 5, and Williams Court, No. 19. About one-third of the members of Star of the Sea Court, 41, left the Order. Although this reduced the number of Courts on our roll by one, yet the loss in membership was very slight.

It seems to me that the Order was a gainer in reality by the loss of this Court. It had a number of indifferent members on its roll, and where such a feeling of indifference exists it is almost impossible to keep the membership up to the proper standard. It is needless for me to say that in any Court where the members are indifferent to the welfare of the Court, where all are not willing to take hold and help on the good work, where no proper spirit exists among the members, it is only a question of a short time when that Court will go to pieces. This has been the case in Star of the Sea Court, No. 41, for a long time, and, while we may regret the existence of such a state of affairs, there seemed to be no remedy for it. The Deputy High Chief Ranger who had charge of that Court was willing, and did put himself out a great deal, to try and infuse a little life into the members, but it was only time and money thrown away, and while as I have said we have one Court less on our roll, the Order is really a gainer by the loss.

From the last Convention to the 1st of April, 1892, we had 52 deaths, occurring as follows :—

April	.	.	.	.	2	October	. . . .	8
May	.	.	.	.	5	November	. . . .	4
June	.	.	.	.	2	December	. . . .	6
July	.	.	.	.	4	January	. . . .	4
August	.	.	.	.	1	February	. . . .	8
September	.	.	.	.	4	March	. . . .	4

The unsettled claims are Patrick Flynn of St. Thomas Court, No. 29, where a portion of the money was left to the mother of the deceased to pay certain bills, and the balance unequally divided between two children of different mothers. When the parties who have made counter-claim have settled matters between themselves, the Order stands ready to pay over the death benefit. The other is the case of John F. Kerrigan, of the same Court, said to have been killed while walking upon a railroad track. This claim cannot be settled until we receive the report of the inquest and legal identification.

The Reserve Fund now amounts to about $7,000. A portion of this, as you will see by the report of the Trustees, is in the Savings Bank, and a portion placed on mortgage at 5 per cent. Under the rule applied in other organizations like ours, the test of success is the possession of a Reserve Fund. It may be that the Reserve Fund will never be called upon, but in case of an epidemic the Reserve Fund held under our Constitution, would be the means of providing for the increased death rate we might then be called upon to meet.

Originally in favor of the organization of the Reserve Fund, I again give it my approbation, and trust that means will be had in the future to increase it far more rapidly.

During the year 1891, nine assessment calls were issued, and from the last Convention to April 1, only eight calls have been issued, 82, 83, 84, 85, 86, 87, 88 and 89.

The per capita tax was placed at $1 last year and brought in $4,700. It seems to me that a per capita tax of 75 cents would be enough for the ensuing year.

Very slight changes were made in the list of Medical Examiners, the new additions to the list being Dr. P. J. Conroy of Everett, Dr. Thomas J. Hayes of Beverly, Dr. J. A. McGuigan of Lynn, Dr. H. V. McLaughlin of Brighton, Dr. P. T. Conlon of Brockton, Dr. John Duff of Charlestown, and Dr. F. J. McQueeney of Boston Slight changes were made in three districts to better accommodate the members of the Order. The total number of Medical Examiners now on the roll is 51.

In relation to the disposition of applications after approval by the High Standing Committee, a word or two ought to be said. Some Recording Secretaries have been extremely careless about forwarding applications after applicants have been initiated, and in some cases, even this past year, applications have been lost. In order to obviate this difficulty which has been extremely annoying to the High Standing Committee, your Committee has now under consideration a plan which will prevent further trouble in this direction by retaining the applications after they are received from the Medical Examiner. This plan as soon as perfected will be put in force at once.

At the last Convention a Committee on Secret Work was appointed. The Chairman of that Committee has asked from time to time for suggestions, recommendations and amendments to the present ritual. He informs me that up to the present time he has not received a single line. I am anxious that something may be done to improve our ritual. I think I am safe in saying that it was very crude originally, and that no improvement has been made in it. No other organization, with a membership such as we have, has so incomplete a ritual. It seems originally to have been copied in part from two or three secret societies, and it is incongruous, difficult to learn, and entirely out of keeping with an organization such as we have grown to be. A member of the Organization who will frame and submit to the High Standing Committee a ritual will deserve well of the Order.

I desire to praise the work of the Deputy High Chief Rangers. During the past year they have made 210 visits. With a very few exceptions the Deputies have fully performed their duty, and have given to Subordinate Courts the benefit of their wisdom and experience.

The average age of applicants approved this year was 31.4, the average age of applicants rejected was 33.6, the average age of members of the Order is 38.3.

I desire to suggest that each Court shall form a Society within its ranks to pay assessments for members who for good reason are unable to pay assessments. This has been done in some of the Courts and has proved most beneficial.

Brother Representatives:—We are assembled here to-day for a good purpose. It is not that I should praise you, or praise the High Standing Committee, or that we should compliment ourselves on the work which has been accomplished, We are here in our annual meeting with one end in view, and that is the advancement of the Massachusetts Catholic Order of Foresters. Your High Standing Committee has endeavored to do its duty during the past year; it has aimed to place the Organization where it should be. You here to-day coming as you do from the various Courts of the Order, know the needs of the Order, and also know whether the efforts put forth by your High Chief Ranger and your High Standing Committee have been seconded by the rank and file of the Order. The amount of good which has been accomplished could not have been done without your co-operation, and the co-operation of your brothers in the various Courts. If the High Standing Committee of this year, or any succeeding year ask your assistance, it will be well for you to remember that they have the interests of the Order just as much at heart as you have, and that they as well as you are working with one purpose in view—the advancement of the Massachusetts Catholic Order of Foresters.

OWEN A. GALVIN,
HIGH CHIEF RANGER.

Report of High Secretary-Treasurer.

To the Representatives of the Massachusetts Catholic Order of
Foresters:

BROTHERS,—With this reassembling we open the Thirteenth
Annual Convention of the Order. The reports from the Courts of
the organization are given here, and show their condition to be, with
very few exceptions, excellent. Many of the Courts have made
large gains in membership and funds, which shows that the feeling
of fraternity is taking a deep hold on our hearts, and teaching us to
do something to help our brother while living, as well as to provide
a death benefit.

The reports as presented by the Courts are in fairly good shape,
and they are here presented in as good condition as was possible to
make them. Some of them do not agree in some particulars with
reports as submitted last year, and an effort has been made to
straighten them out. It was apparent, however, that it was more of
a task than could be accomplished in the time, and consequently the
work in that direction was of necessity abandoned, and only errors
in computation or misplacements corrected. This in itself was an
item of considerable amount, as in many cases the reports were
accepted by Deputy High Chief Rangers as rendered to them by
officers of Courts. It may be said that Deputy High Chief Rangers
should not accept reports in this way, but this cannot be avoided
under the present arrangement. The work of the Deputy High
Chief Rangers is a labor of love, purely and solely, and we should
congratulate ourselves that we are able to select so good a body of
men who are willing to perform the duties of the office. Of course
it is understood that Deputy High Chief Rangers are reimbursed
for expenses of travel in the discharge of duty, but this is not
sufficient, and some provision should be made for paying a Deputy
High Chief Ranger a stated sum for each official visit. This should
come out of the treasury of the Subordinate Court, and would in the
very nature of things bind the relations between the Subordinate
Court and the Deputy High Chief Ranger more closely than could
otherwise be done,

In 1891 the High Standing Committee approved **726** applications for membership, and rejected **75**.

OCCUPATIONS OF APPLICANTS APPROVED
FROM JANUARY 1, 1891, TO JANUARY 1, 1892.

Armorer	1	Fireman	2
Baker	5	Fish cutter	1
Barber	5	Fish dealer	1
Bartender	3	Florist	1
Blacksmith	18	Foreman	6
Book-keeper	5	Freight handler	5
Boot maker	2	Furniture dealer	1
Bottler	1	Furniture finisher	1
Brass finisher	3	Furniture polisher	1
Brewer	1	Gardener	14
Bricklayer	3	Gas fitter	1
Brushmaker	1	Gents furnishing dealer	1
Butcher	7	Glass cutter	4
Carder	2	Granite cutter	1
Carpenter	9	Granite polisher	2
Carriage body maker	1	Grocer	21
Case maker	1	Hack driver	3
Chocolate maker	1	Harness maker	2
Cigar dealer	1	Hatter	5
Clergyman	6	Horsecar conductor	1
Clerk	36	Hostler	5
Clothing cutter	2	Household goods dealer	1
Clothing trimmer	1	Inspector (U. S.)	1
Coachman	5	Insurance agent & collector,	6
Coal dealer	3	Iron worker	3
Conductor	1	Janitor	2
Contractor	2	Jeweller	3
Cooper	2	Junk dealer	4
Copper roller	1	Laborer	106
Cornice maker	1	Laundryman	1
Currier	12	Lawyer	5
Cutter	1	Leather worker	3
Decorator	1	Lighthouse keeper	1
Dentist	1	Liquor dealer	7
Draughtsman	1	Locksmith	1
Druggist	1	Loom fixer	1
Dry goods dealer	1	Machine adjuster	1
Dyer	1	Machinist	12
Easel maker	1	Manufacturer	2
Editor	1	Marble worker	2
Electro plater	1	Marketman	1
Engineer	7	Messenger	1
Engraver	1	Milkman	3
Expressman	2	Mill hand	1
Factory hand	1	Morocco dresser	5
Farmer	8	Moulder	5

Musician .	.	.	2	Shoe dealer	. .	3
Nail feeder	.	.	1	Shoemaker .	. .	80
News agent	.	.	1	Shovel maker .	. .	1
Officer .	.	.	1	Slater .	. .	1
Overseer .	.	.	1	Soap maker	. .	1
Painter	.	.	4	Sole leather cutter	.	5
Paper dealer	.	.	1	Stable keeper .	. .	3
Paper maker	.	.	1	Stitcher	. .	1
Pedler .	.	.	1	Stone cutter	. .	9
Pharmacist .	.	.	1	Stone dealer .	. .	1
Physician	.	.	12	Stone mason	. .	15
Piano finisher	.	.	1	Stove dealer .	. .	1
Piano maker	.	.	2	Tailor	. .	9
Piano polisher	.	.	2	Tanner	. .	3
Plasterer .	.	.	1	Tea dealer	. .	3
Plumber	.	.	3	Terra Cotta maker	.	2
Policeman	.	.	6	Teamster .	. .	37
Porter .	.	.	3	Tinsmith	. .	3
Potter .	.	.	1	Twine dealer .	. .	1
Pressman	.	.	1	Twine maker	. .	1
Printer .	.	.	4	Undertaker	. .	3
Produce dealer	.	.	1	Upholsterer .	. .	5
Provision dealer	.	.	8	Varnish polisher	. .	1
Publisher	.	.	1	Vocal music teacher	.	1
Puddler .	.	.	1	Waiter .	. .	1
Paver .	.	.	2	Wall paper stainer	.	1
Restaurant keeper	.	.	3	Watchman	. .	8
Roofer .	.	.	1	Weaver	. .	6
Rope maker	.	.	1	Wheelwright .	. .	2
Rubber cutter	.	.	1	Wire dresser	. .	1
Rubber worker	.	.	1	Woolen shearer	. .	1
Salesman	.	.	14	Wool sorter .	. .	1
School teacher .	.	.	1			
Shipper	.	.	1	Total	. .	725

Since the last Convention to April 1, 1892, the High Standing Committee received 928 applications, of this number 89 were rejected, about 9½ per cent. of the whole number received. The average age of applications approved was $31\frac{4}{10}$ years, and the average age of applications rejected was $33\frac{6}{10}$ years.

The membership of the Order, January 1, 1892, was, according to reports now in, 4,782. This does not include St. Francis No. 4, Middlesex No. 60, and Quincy No. 76. If we add their probable membership we have as total membership, January 1, 1892, 5,025 members; add 350 approved between January 1, 1892, and April 1, 1892 (if all were initiated), and we have as our present membership 5,383.

OCCUPATION OF APPLICANTS REJECTED

JANUARY 1, 1891, TO JANUARY 1, 1892.

Occupation	No.	Occupation	No.
Baker	1	Laborer	8
Blacksmith	1	Manufacturer	1
Bottler	1	Marble worker	1
Brakeman	1	Mason	1
Brewer	1	Morocco dresser	1
Bricklayer	2	Moulder	2
Brush maker	1	Painter	3
Carpenter	1	Policeman	1
Clerk	3	Publisher	1
Clothing cutter	1	Salesman	1
Collector	1	Saloon keeper	1
Commercial traveller	1	Section hand	2
Cook	1	Shoe maker	10
Crockery packer	1	Shovel maker	1
Currier	2	Shoe machine operator	1
Farmer	1	Steam fitter	1
Flour inspector	1	Tailor	1
Glazier	1	Teamster	3
Granite cutter	1	Tennis player	1
Granite dealer	1	Terra Cotta maker	1
Grain dealer	1	Track layer	1
Gardener	1	Trader	1
Hack driver	2	Waiter	1
Hair dresser	1	Wood polisher	1
Horse car conductor	2		

The average age of the Order on January 1, 1892, was 38.3 years. This is correct; as nearly so as it can be arrived at. In order to be sure, we have taken the roll of members of each Court and figured out from time of initiation of each member, and corrected the returns on report of membership from each. It involved a great deal of labor, but it was necessary, and has been done. This average age is needed to show us the condition of our membership in regard to expectancy of life, and also to help us in our provision for deaths, as we may base our calculations very nearly on that figure just as if it were only one man. In fact we can come nearer to certainty in a run of 15 or 20 years than we can in the consideration of a single life. If we take the American Table of Mortality as a guide we may look for an expectation of life of $29\frac{1}{2}$ years for the Order at 38 years of age. The average age of the Order,

January 1, 1888, was a fraction over 39 years,—4 years have elapsed, and we now can show an average age of 38 years. Our admissions during these years have been at an average age of 31, 32 and 33 years, and it is this fact which now enables us to show figures we have never seen in any report of a similar organization.

The following table gives the number applying to each Court:

New applications received from April 22, 1891, to March 31, 1892

No.	Court.		No.	Court.	
1	Cathedral . . .	25	49	Constantine . .	8
3	Fenwick . .	1	51	Holy Trinity . .	12
4	St. Francis . .	6	52	Highland . . .	66
5	Leo . . .	7	53	Emerald . .	8
6	Cheverus . . .	23	54	St. James . . .	8
7	St. Patrick . .	1	55	Charles River .	13
8	Sherwood . .	12	57	Carroll . . .	11
9	Columbus . .	3	58	Prospect . .	5
10	Iona	10	59	Worcester .	73
11	St. Joseph . .	12	60	Middlesex . .	5
12	Fulton . . .	10	61	St. Lawrence . .	11
13	Fitzpatrick . .	4	62	St. Catherine . .	6
14	Lafayette . . .	19	63	Shields . . .	96
15	SS. Peter and Paul	6	64	Gallagher : .	25
16	Essex . . .	21	65	St. Columbkille . .	1
17	Hamilton . .	2	66	Griffin . . .	7
18	St. Peter . . .	10	67	Canton . . .	1
19	Williams . .	12	68	St. Margaret . .	93
20	Mt. Pleasant . .	4	69	Stoughton . .	44
21	St. Alphonsus .	1	70	St. Michael . .	63
23	St. John . . .	13	71	Phil Sheridan . .	8
24	St. Gregory . .	9	72	Merrimack . .	9
25	St. Francis . .	5	73	Taunton . . .	23
26	St. Raphael . .	3	74	Hendricken . .	5
28	Erin	5	75	St. Jarlath . .	6
29	St. Thomas . .	34	76	Quincy . . .	4
30	Bass River . .	6	77	Mystic . . .	4
32	Qualey . . .	12	78	St. Monica . .	6
33	St. John . . .	10	79	John Boyle O'Reily .	1
34	Americus . .	7	80	Gen. Sherman .	12
37	Friendship . .	2	81	St. Malachi . .	36
38	St. Joseph . .	1	82	Brockton . .	65
39	Benedict . : .	5	83	John Henry Newman	36
43	St. Mary . .	5	84	Danvers . .	46
45	Unity . . .	7	85	Geo. Washington .	62
46	St. Augustine .	7	86	Avon . . .	41
47	St. Anne . . .	13			
48	Sarsfield . .	5			894

MEMBERSHIP.

No. of Court.	NAME OF COURT.	Membership Dec. 31, 1890.	Membership Dec. 31, 1891.	Initiated in 1891.	Admitted on W. Card in 1891.	Reinstated in 1891.	Average age of Court Dec. 31, 1891.	Average age of Court Dec. 31, 1890.	Withdrawn on Card in 1891.	Resigned Membership in 1891.	Suspended for Non-payment in 1891.	Expelled in 1891.	Died in 1891.	Rejected by ballot in 1891.	Rejected by H. S. C. in 1891.
1	Cathedral	161	175	19	2		40.1	38.9		1	3		3		6
3	Fenwick	64	63	1			43.9	35.4	1		1		1		1
4	St. Francis	117	103	5				4.26		1	2				5
5	Leo	101	100	16	1		42.7	43.4	1	1	1		1		1
6	Cheverus	88	44	2			42.6	43.2		1	1		3		2
7	St. Patrick	43	154	15	1		14.	42.4	2		8				
8	Sherwood	152	43	5			38.5	39.2			3				
9	Hins	41	94	7			37.8	33.07			3		2		1
10	Iona	93	134	6			40.6	39.9			1				
11	St.	132	39	12			42.1	42.4	2	1		2	2		1
12	Fulton	28	49				41.2	45.2		1	1		1		1
13	Fitzpatrick	51	86	13			46.2	45.3			1				
14	Lafayette	76	71	3			41.2	41.1			2		3		
15	SS. Peter and Paul	69	126	15		1	41.5	40.6					1		
16	Essex	117	66		2		38.01	38.6		1	1		1		1
17	Hamilton	66	94	11	6		47.07	46.3	3	1	1				2
18	St. Peter	79	88	14			39.9	39.8	1		2		1		1
19	Williams	79	81	4	1		39.6	40.1		1	1		1		1
20	Mt. Pleasant	83	49	1			40.5	38.3			1		3		3
21	St. Alphonsus	51	51	6			34	45.5	2		4		1		4
24	St. John	47	73	7	1		36.9	36.6		1	3				2
25	St. Gregory	72	118	10			37.1	36.9			4		1		3
26	St. Francis	113	44	3	1		38.1	37.7	2	1	2		4		1
28	St. Raphael	46	98	9			41.04	39.3	1		3		1		
29	Erin	88	174	28	1	4	41.5	34.08							
30	St.	152	44	3			34.5	34.08		1	8		1		2
32	Bass River	42	55	12	1		39.5	39.4			7		1		3
33	Qualey	46	56	10			39.01	37.4							1
34	St. John	52	80				45.1	44.8			9				
35	Americus	83	21	2	1		39.3	37.3	1	1	1		1		2
37	Sheil	24	45	1			42.3	40.04							3
38	Friendship	46	43	3			37.4		3	1			2		1
39	St. Joseph	41	32				45.6	46.2			3		1		
	St. Benedict	32					41.3	40.							

MEMBERSHIP — *Continued.*

41	*Star of the Sea	35	32				39.4	39.8			2 1			1		1
43	St. Mary	31	35				8.4	36.9			1	1				
44	St. Bernard	46	44				40.				1					3 1
45	Unity	46	48	6			41.	40.06		1	1			1		
46	St. Augustine	29	31				32.7	42.4		1						
47	St. Anne	95	103	3			38.4	37.4	1	1	1					3
48	Sarsfield	85	98	7			39.2	37.4		1						
49	...ane	64	70	9			39.8	39.2								3
51	Holy Trinity	104	136	2			38.9	36.5			5					1
52	Highland	24	25	8	1		38.9	39.7			5					
53	...eld	91	101	32			375	37.2	3		5					1
54	St. James	60	62	2	1		32.9	31.7		1	2			2		3
55	Charles River	85	92	17			36.05	35.02		1	1			1		1
57	...oll	45	48	1	4		38.7	37.7								
58	Prospect	36	38	1			40.9	40.5	1	1	2			1		1 3
59	Worcester	71	86	1			39.1	38.5								
60	Middlesex	74	77	3				36.								3 1
61	St. Lawrence	69	69	14			36.	33.9			12			1		1
62	St. Catherine	70	83	10	1		34.9	366	2							
63	Shields	31	63	2	1		36.8	39.05		1						
64	In...	56	57	14			39.4	33.8								1
65	St. ...lle	56	49	7			35.03	33.3						1		2
66	Griffin	45	70	3	1		34.	38.4	3	1	3	1				1
67	Canton	67	27	5	1		36.8	38.5			1			1		4
68	St. Margaret	29	73	10			37.1	30.9			4					1
69	Stoughton	64	39				31.9	31.3			2	2				1
70	St. Michael	40	83	18	1		32.6	32.8	3	2	2	1				4
71	Phil Sheridan	82	83	2	2		29.9	32.6		1	1					1
72	Merrimack	51	70	5	1		33.07	35.4			6					1
73	...on	105	113	19			35.1	27.8								
74	...in	34	34	14			29.2	33.1						1		1
75	St. Jarlath	55	55	1			35.05				6			1		1
76	Quincy	46	39	1			37.5	36.3								
77	Mystic	40	26	7	1		36.2	35.3		1	2			1		1
78	St. Monica	20	31	1			36.4									1
80	J. B. O'Reilly		31	6	6		33.7									
81	Gen. Sherman		25	31	2		34.4				1 2			1		2
82	St. Malachi		27	25			29.5									4
83	Brockton	61	61	27			31.07									2
79	J. H. Newman	28	28	61												
	Total	**4,556**	**4,777**	**662**	**34**	**12**			**35**	**24**	**142**	**3**	**49**	**3**		**77**

*Dissolved—charter surrendered.

The percentage of increase is shown by the following table:—

No. of Court.	NAME OF COURT.		No. of Court.	NAME OF COURT.	
1	Cathedral	.086	45	Unity	.043
5	Leo	.019	46	St. Augustine	.172
6	Cheverus	.136	47	St. Anne	084
7	St. Patrick	.023	48	Sarsfield	.011
8	Sherwood	.013	49	Constantine	.093
9	Columbus	.023	51	Holy Trinity	.307
10	Iona	.01	52	Highland	.041
11	St. Joseph	.015	53	Emerald	.109
12	Fulton	.392	55	Charles River	.082
14	Lafayette	.13	57	Carroll	.066
15	SS. Peter and Paul	.028	58	Prospect	.055
16	Essex	.076	59	Worcester	.162
18	St. Peter	.189	61	St. Lawrence	.115
19	Williams	.113	63	Shields	.064
23	St. John	.108	64	Gallagher	.125
24	St. Gregory	.013	65	St. Columbkille	.017
25	St. Francis	.044	66	Griffin	.088
28	Erin	.056	67	Canton	.044
29	St. Thomas	.144	69	Stoughton	.140
30	Bass River	.047	72	Merrimack	.372
32	Qualey	.195	73	Taunton	.076
33	St. John	.076	78	St. Monica	30
38	St. Joseph	.023	80	Gen. Sherman	.12
43	St. Mary	.129	81	St. Malachi	.074

COURT DISSOLVED.

During the past year one Court has been dropped from membership, although the members were not lost to the Order. Star of the Sea Court, No. 41, was in such bad shape, that the Deputy for that District, Brother G. H. Keefe, thought it was advisable for the Court to either consolidate with another Court or surrender its Charter. The members finally decided to surrender the Charter, and 19 members took withdrawal cards with the intention of joining either Williams Court No. 19 or Leo Court No. 5. Some of them have done so and the others (12) have left the Order.

The property of the Court has been delivered to the High Standing Committee and the Treasurer has paid over to the High Standing Committee the funds remaining (about $10) in the treasury of No. 41.

While it reduces the number of Courts in the Order the loss of membership was very small.

New Courts.

During the past year the following new Courts have been formed :

St. Malachi Court No. 81, Arlington, with 20 Charter members. Instituted September 3, 1891.

Brockton Court No. 82, Brockton, with 61 Charter members. Instituted December 11, 1891.

John Henry Newman Court No. 83, Everett, with 27 Charter members. Instituted December 12, 1891.

Danvers Court No. 84, Danvers, with 33 Charter members. Instituted February 10, 1891.

George Washington Court No. 85, Lynn, with 44 Charter members. Instituted February 22, 1892.

Avon Court No. 86, Avon, with 38 Charter members. Instituted March 16, 1892.

Robert Emmett Court No. 87, Walpole, with 22 Charter members. Instituted April 1, 1892.

Efforts have been made in many other directions, which we confidently expect will bear fruit in the coming year. 25 names have been taken for a Court in Pittsfield and about 30 for a new Court in Charlestown. Examinations are progressing for the Charlestown Court, under the supervision of Past High Senior Conductor Edward Riley, who lives in that section.

The total number of Courts on the roll April 1, 1892, is 77.

Assessment Calls.

During the year 1891 the following calls were issued, viz. :

78, 79, 80, 81, 82, 83, 84, 85, 86—the last, No. 86, expiring January 1, 1892.

In addition to above a call was sent out for Reserve Fund, and it added quite materially to that Fund. The report of the Trustees is given elsewhere.

The initiations of those names addded to the endowments paid occurred as follows —

1879	1	
1880	10	
1881	11	
1882	3	
1883	3	
1884	3	
1885	1	
1886	4	
1887	2	
1888	4	
1889	6	
1890	2	
1891	2	

A little analysis of this list will be of service and we find the single death of 1879 to be caused by Empyæma. In 1880 initiations, there were ten deaths from the following causes — Heart Disease 3, Pneumonia 4, Bronchitis 2, Typhoid Fever 1. These indicate that they must have been perfectly good risks at time of admission.

In 1881 initiations, there were 11 deaths, from — Heart Disease 1, Cerebral Hemorrhage 1, Bright's Disease 2, Phthisis 7. These may also be considered as good risks at time of admission, as all were in the Order over ten years.

In 1882 initiations, there were 3 deaths, from Phthisis 2, Pneumonia 1. Tnese, in view of length of membership, were undoubtedly good risks.

In 1883 initiations, there were 3 deaths, from Pneumonia, Orchitis caused by accident, Bright's Disease. There is nothing about these to indicate them other than good risks at time of admission.

In 1884 initiations, there were 3 deaths. from Pneumonia, Cerebral Hemorrhage, Spinal Inflammation.

In 1885 initiations, there was 1 death from Pneumonia.

In 1886 initiations, there were 4 deaths, from Cerebral Hemorrhage 1, Bright's Disease 1, Paralysis 1, Bowel Disease 1.

In 1887 initiations there were 2 deaths, from Phthisis 1, Accident 1.

The small number of deaths from initiations in these years, is due to the fact that not many were admitted.

We have nothing which will show, positively, just what our gain or loss was in those years.

In 1888 initiations, (there were about 450) there were 4 deaths— Phthisis 2, Delirium Tremens (?) 1, Jaundice 1.

In 1889 initiations, (about 600) there were 6 deaths—Phthisis 3, Drowning 1, Peritonitis 1, Paralysis 1.

Investigation of these showed that all were good risks at the time of admission, provided, of course, that statements made about family history were true.

In 1890 initiations, there were 2 deaths, from Typhoid Fever 1, Accident 1.

In 1891 initiations, there were 2 deaths, from Heart Disease 1, Peritonitis 1.

32 of the number occurred from initiations prior to the order giving supervision of applications to the High Standing Committee. In the 20 remaining, 6 were from Phthisis, 1 Delirium Tremens,(?) 1 Drowning, 1 Bowel Disease, 1 Heart Disease, 2 Peritonitis, 1 Typhoid Fever, 2 Accidents, 1 Cerebral Hemorrhage. 1 Bright's Disease, 2 Paralysis, 1 Jaundice.

Of the 6 initiated since 1886, who died from Phthisis in 1891, we find the following :—

No. 1—age, 31 ; occupation, jeweler ; initiated March 26, 1889 ; good family history and nothing to show hereditary disease.

No. 2—age, 26 ; occupation, laborer in abattoir ; initiated March 20, 1888 ; good family history ; disease probably brought on by poisoning at his work.

No. 3—age, 34 ; occupation, iron-worker ; initiated January 26, 1888 ; very poor family history.

No. 4—age, 29 ; occupation, teamster ; initiated May 1, 1889 ; very poor family history.

No. 5—age, 41 ; occupation, sexton ; initiated December 7, 1887 ; poor family history.

No. 6—age, 40 ; occupation, boot-maker, initiated June 21, 1889 ; poor family history.

Here we have 6 deaths from Consumption, and in only 2 do we find a good family history. Comment is hardly necessary, except to say that, some fault having been found with the High Standing Committee for holding applications in cases of doubtful family history until clear and straightforwad answers were received about the family history of applicants, the above is a sufficient answer and demonstrates that too much care cannot be used in consideration of applications.

In 1891 we had 53 deaths, occurring as follows :—

January, 1891, 6 ; February, 2 ; March, 5 ; April, 6 ; May, 5 ; June, 2 ; July, 4 ; August, 1 ; September, 4 ; October, 8 ; November, 4 ; December, 6. The average length of membership of those who died in 1891 was 7 years, 1 month, 24 days.

April, 1888, the length of membership of those deceased in 1887, is shown to be $3\frac{1}{3}$ years. The comparison speaks volumes for our organization.

The following deaths are also reported :

NAME.	COURT.	CAUSE OF DEATH.
Patrick Flynn,	St. Thomas, No. 29,	Phthisis.
John F. Kerrigan,	St. Thomas, No. 29,	Killed by the Cars.
P. F. McBride,	Emerald, No. 53,	Pneumonia.
M. W. Byrnes,	Griffin, No. 66,	Pneumonia.
Thomas A. Byrnes,	Griffin, No. 66,	Pneumonia.
P. A. Morrissay,	Cathedral, No. 1,	Typhoid Pneumonia.
M. Brennan,	St. Alphonsus, No. 21,	Typhoid Pneumonia.
William Garrity,	Iona, No. 10,	Acute Bronchitis.
Michael Sheehan,	Mystic, No, 77,	Bronchitis.
Jeremiah Chamberlain.	St. Peter, No. 18,	Cancer of Rectum.

In the case of Patrick Flynn, he left part of the Endowment to his mother to pay his bills, and the balance to his two children unequally divided. The money can not be paid to the mother, and the case is delayed until she voluntarily withdraws any claim she has.

In the case of John F. Kerrigan, it is reported that he was killed by the cars, and some sort of identification was made of the remains, which were badly mangled. The High Standing Committee declined to pay until a report of the inquest is made, and identification legally established.

No objection is made to the others which will be paid in their order, when proper papers are filed. In McBride's case, guardianship papers, and in the case of one of the Byrnes' of No. 66, the Endowment is made payable to his mother; but he married since joining the Order, and neglected to make the necessary change. As soon as an agreement is arrived at between the parties the claim will be paid.

In the case of P. A. Morrissey of Cathedral Court No. 1, a similar state of affairs exists; he married after joining the Order, and never changed the Endowment from his mother to whom he made it payable on joining. As soon as the parties agree, it will be adjusted.

DEPUTY HIGH CHIEF RANGERS.

The present corps of Deputy High Chief Rangers is a good body of men, and have endeavored to perform the duties required during the past year. In cases where there has been an apparent neglect of duties it can be traced to carelessness or indifference on the part of the subordinate Court. It is safe to say that there is not a man at present on the list, who has not the welfare of the Order at heart, and would do all in his power to further the interests of the Courts in his district, if he received the co-operation which is absolutely necessary for success. Compulsion is at best, a very disagreeable business, and some would prefer to let a matter slip by, than by exercise of power to compel obedience.

In order to ascertain how much the Courts were visited by Deputy High Chief Rangers, the High Standing Committee sent out a duplicate blank stating date of Deputy's visit to be filled, and one art given to the Deputy the other fowarded to the High Standing Committee. Eighty-five of these have been received here between August 3, 1891, and March 25, 1892. The reports of the Deputy High Chief Rongers show 210 visits made in 1891.

MEDICAL EXAMINERS.

The list of Medical Examiners selected by High Chief Ranger Galvin does not differ much from the previous list. A few changes have been made as follows:—Dr. T. J. Hayes of Beverly, was appointed examiner for Bass River Court No. 30, and St. Margaret Court No. 68. Dr. F. J. McQueeney was appointed examiner for Fenwick Court No. 3, Cheverus Court No. 6, Fitzpatrick Court No. 13, and Sheil Court No. 35. Dr. H. V. McLaughlin was appointed examiner for St. Columbkille Court No. 65.

The following assignments were made for new Courts ;—St. Malachi No. 81, Dr. J. D. Couch ; Brockton No. 82, Dr. T. P. Conlan ; John Henry Newman Court No. 83, Dr. P. J. Conroy ; Danvers No. 84, Dr. F. E. Hines ; George Washington No. 85, Dr. J. A. McGuigan ; Avon No. 86, Dr. O. M. Sheridan ; Robert Emmett No. 87, Dr. L. H. Plympton ; Dr. John Duff has also been appointed to make examinations for new Court in Charlestown.

It is hardly necessary to say anything in praise of these gentlemen as we think they are all conscientious, and take a professional pride in giving us good work. A comparison between the work now done by our Medical Examiners and that given us in the early days of the Order, shows in a remarkable degree the progress made by the Massachusetts Catholic Order of Foresters in the minds of the community ; and it is no detriment to the medical profession to say that our corps of Examiners fully realize the importance of the work given them to do, and while it may bring to them only a small fraction of their income, they welcome it, as an acknowledgment from a body of people whose presence is being felt in the Commonwealth more and more every year.

MEETINGS OF HIGH STANDING COMMITTEE.

The High Standing Committee has held sixty meetings since the last Convention (to April 1), and the attendance of the Committee has averaged as well as any recent years.

A great deal of travelling has been done by the High Standing Committee, and many times it was necessary to divide the committee for work in different places on the same day or night ; many trips were made which cannot be given in detail as no special result could be pointed out.

A great deal of work was planned by the High Chief Ranger at the beginning of the year, and the High Standing Committee has endeavored to follow the lines as laid out by him. Much of the valuable time of the High Chief Ranger has been given to the organization both by day and night, and he has visited and addressed many meetings, not only in the interest of forming new Courts, but to help along Courts already formed, which had sufficient spirit to get up a public meeting. The work he has done the past year has been of incalculable benefit to the Order.

The High Medical Examiner has been a constant attendant at meetings of the High Standing Committee, and has carefully looked after the interests of the Order by the careful examination he has given each paper presented to him. He has not spared himself in looking after new Courts, and has accompanied the High Standing Committee in its various journeys in order to give the Committee the benefit of his judgment, so that the work might not be delayed. His counsel has been of great benefit to the High Standing Committee in determination of risks presented, and the Order has in him a gentleman who possesses the confidence of the High Standing Committee and the Medical Examiners.

In 1891, there were 53 deaths from the following causes — Heart Disease 8, Pneumonia 6, Phthisis 17, Intestinal Obstruction 2, Empyæmia 1, Peritonitis 2, Bronchitis 2, Typhoid Fever 2, Cerebral Hemorrhage 1, Accident 3, Bright's Disease 4, Paralysis 2, Pleurisy 1, Cerebral Embolism 1, Spinal Inflammation 1.

Since the organization of the Massachusetts Catholic Order of Foresters, the number deceased each year is as follows:

Year	Number
1880	3
1881	17
1882	25
1883	40
1884	41
1885	48
1886	32
1887	34
1888	46
1889	54
1890	47
1891	53
Total	440

ENDOWMENTS PAID.

NAMES OF DECEASED MEMBERS, DATE AND CAUSE OF DEATH, COURT OF WHICH HE DECEASED WAS A MEMBER, AND BENEFICIARIES, AGE, LENGTH OF MEMBERSHIPS.

No.	NAME	COURT	AGE	INITIATED	Membership Yrs.	Mos.	Dys.	DATE OF DEATH	CAUSE	Endowment	NUMBER OF BENEFICIARIES	TO WHOM PAID
1	Cornelius Cronin,	Iona, No. 0,	Malden 49	Mar. 14, 1880		7	5	Oct. 19, 1880	Typho-Malaria	$1,000	1, Wife &	Administ'x
2	Dennis McCarthy,	B, 5,	Boston		Nov. 14, 1879	1	1	6	Nov. 20, "	his	"	1,	Widow
3	M. J. Kiley,	Bk, 3,	31	Mar. 14, 1880		9	19	Dec. 3, 1881	Pulmonary Consumption	"		Ex'tor
4	D. J. Desmond,	ah, 10,	Malden 29	Mar. 14, 1880		9	11	Jan. 11, "	Typhoid Pneumonia	"	1,	Administrator
5	P. H. ah,	ell, 1,	Boston 48	Sept. 3, 1879	1	3	8	Jan. 27, "	Pay	"	1,	Widow
6	Jeremiah Lawton,	Cathedral, 1,	33	Oct. 15, "		3	12	Jan. "	Pneumonia	"		"
7	Edward A. Bk,	Cheverus, 6,	38	Feb. 11, 1880	1	0	24	Mar. 5, "	Typhoid Pneumonia	"	1,	"
8	hn. Bn,	Fitzpatrick, 13,	43	May 26, "		0	11	April 26, "	Pneumonia	"	1,	
9	Prick Kelley,	Hamilton, 17,	46	Aug. 3, "	1	10	14	June 17, "	Cancer in Groin	"	1,	
10	Patrick Murray,	Iona, 0,	Malden 26	April 21, "			0	June 18, "	Phthisis & his	"	1,	
11	Patrick C. y,	Americus, 34,	Boston	Mar. 15, 1881	1	6	14	Aug. 29, "	Typhoid Pneumonia	"	1,	
12	James L.	B, 5,	27	Aug. 13, 1880		0		Aug. 23, "	Phthisis Pulmonalis	"	1,	& guardian
13	Thomas F. n,	A, 5,	24	Aug. 13, 1881				Sept. "	ms & Perito'itis	"	3,	& children
14	hal al Morrison,	Mn, 17,	47	July 6, 1880	1	24	27	Sept. 3, "	Acute Phthisis	"	1,	
15	Mel McCarthy,	Leo, 5,	36	Aug. "	1	2	14	Oct. 30, "	his Mse	"	4,	
16	William Whitley,	St. Patrick, 7,	40	April 12, "		8	5	Nov. 17, "	Chronic Catarrhal Ammonia	"	1,	
17	Daniel J. McDonald,	Hamil'on, 17,	31	April 21, 1881		7	1	Nov. 22, "	Chronic his & Pneumonia	"	1,	
18	Henry Steele,	Ak, 3,	49	Feb. 13, 1880		9	14	Nov. 30, "	Cancerous Dis. of Æsophagus	"	1,	
19	David O'Callaghan,	Sherwood, 8,	23	Mch. 4, "		8	26	Nov. 30, "	hn hr Pneumonia, sec'd stage	"	1,	
20	Mel Bn,	St. Fph, 11,	26	Dec. 27, "		11	9	Dec. 6, "	hnia,	"	1,	
21	John M. Galvin,	St. Joseph, 11,	23	May 10, "	1	7	26	Jan. 6, 1882	Bronchitis and Cong. of Brain	"	2, hn,	Guardian
22	Thos. T. McDonough,	St. hi, 11,	31	Mar. 22, "		9	17	Jan. 9, "	his & of Bowels	"	1, hw,	Widow
23	James McNulty,	St. Alphonsus, 21,	28	Oct. 15, "	2	3	16	Jan. 25, "	his	"		
24	hal Condon,	Cathedral, 1,	25	Oct. 15, 1879	1	10	19	Feb. 1, "	Pneumonia	"	1,	
25	Mark B. Mulvey,	St. Joseph, 38,	46	Mar. 29, 1881		1	18	Feb. 6, "	Heart Mse	"	1,	
26	hn hs,	Sullivan, 27,	36					Mar. "	Mania a Btu	"		
27	Thos. Moore Bayley,	St. Patrick, 7,	36	Jan. 18, "	1	10	26	Mar. 25, "	Colloid Ca'ner of the tines	"	1,	
28	Thos. Clark,	A, 5,	36	June 25, 1880	1	11	4	May 21, "	Cancer of Stomach	"	1,	
29	James Purcell,	Benedict, 39, Somerville 35		June 24, 1881		0	17	May 28, "	Phthisis	"	1,	
30	Patrick Cashman,	hly, 0,	Boston 39	May 12, "	1	0	17	May 29, "	Pneumonia	"	1,	
31	hn Chambers,	Essex, 0,	Salem 40	June 23, 1880	1	11	17	June 10, "	Cirrhosis of Liver	"	1,	
32	John Hayes,	St. hs, 4,	Boston 33	June 1, 1882			26	June 27, "	Pneumonia	"	1,	

ENDOWMENTS PAID—Continued.

No.	NAME.	COURT.	AGE.	INITIATED.	Yrs.	Mos.	Dys.	DATE OF DEATH.	CAUSE.	Endowment.	NUMBER OF BENEFICIARIES.	TO WHOM PAID.
33	...	Fenwick, 3,	25	Sept. 3, 1880	1	8	21	May 24, 1882	Delirium ...	$1,000	1, Father	Father
34	John Bentley,		32	April 13, 1881	1	9	14	Jan. 27, "	...	"	1, Widow	Widow
35	Michael Leahey,	SS. Peter &..., 15,	34	Nov. 17, 1880	1	8	24	Aug. 11, "	Rheumatism of Hrt [Brain	"	1, ...	Father
36	Thomas Devenny,	..., 3,	28	Mar. 12, "	2	5	6	Aug. 18, "	Rheumatism and Cong. of the	"	...	
37	Jno. B. ... M.D.,	Cathedral, 1,	37	Aug. 3, 1879	2	11	24	July 27, "	Typhoid ever	"	5,	Heirs
38	Wm. ...,	Fitzpatrick, 12,	24	April 29, 1880	2	4	8	Sept. 7, "	Pulmonary...	"	1,	Wi dw
39	...	Cheverus, 6,	38	Dec. 23, 1881	0	9	25	Sept. 27, "	Pulmonary...	"	1, Widow	"
40	John Diver,		40	Mar. 23, 1880	2	7	5	Oct. 28, "	Crushed by...	"	1,	"
41	John Joyce,	St. ..., 25, W. Quincy	40	Dec. 21, "	1	1	1	Nov. 21, "	Pyæmia	"	1, Daughter	Mother
42	Henry Conroy,	St. Francis, 4,	50	Jan. 8, "	2	10	13	Nov. 14, "	Typhoid Pneumonia	"	1, Widow	Son
43	Patrick Carroll,	Cheverus, 6, Boston	48	Feb. 11, "	2	8	3	Oct. 14, "	Pulmonary...	"	1, Mother	"
44	... F. ...,	..., 5,	22	April 26, 1882	0	10	28	Jan. 9, 1883	Hrt Disease	"	1, Son	Ww
45	R. J. Burns,	..., 6, 13,	68	Feb. 11, 1880	2	11	5	Oct. 22, 1882	..., Hip Disease	"	1, ...	Father
46	Florence ...,	St. ..., 18,	34	Nov. 17, "	2	11	0	Feb. 14, 1883	...	"	1, Father	"
47	... Canney,	St. Francis, 4,	23	Jan. 4, 1883	0	1	18	Feb. 14, "	... of ...	"	1, Widow	
48	... McCormick,	St. ..., 4,	29	May 26, 1881	1	8	18	Feb. 19, "	...	"	2, Children	Guardian
49	...,	Bil, 35,	32	Dec. 24, 1882	0	1	28	Mr. 4, "	Obstruction from Gall Stone	"	1, Widow	Widow
50	Thos. A. Breen,	Sherwood, 8,	35	June 24, 1881	0	8	10	Ar. ..., "	Catarrhal...	"		"
51	... ...,	St. ..., 13,	51	Mar. 4, 1880	3	1	18	April 16, "	Hrt Dis	"	1, Sister	Sister
52	John ...,	Essex, 16,	64	Mar. 30, "	3	0	23	April 22, "	St. of ...	"	1, Widow	Widow
53	... Neville,	..., 6,	38	Nov. 4, 1880	2	6	1	May 5, "	Phthisis	"	1, Sister	...
54	Richard Collins,	St. Francis, 4,	32	Aug. 4, "	2	9	1	My 6, "	Tuberculosis	"	1, Child	...
55	... Carey,	St. Peter, 18,	41	July 18, 1879	3	4	18	My 6, "	Disease of the Brain	"	1, Widow	Ww
56	P. H. ...,	St. ..., 47, Gloucester	21	Oct. 21, 1880	2	10	9	My 30, "	... Phthisis	"	4,	Heirs
57	Charles Doherty,	Fenwick, 3, Boston	33	Dec. 2, 1882	0	6	1	June 30, "	Drowning	"	1, Father	Father
58	John Kerrigan,	..., 6,	26	Mar. 2, 1880	2	9	2	Jan. 3, "	Mc Pyæmia	"	...	...
59	John J. ...,	Fenwick, 3,	24	Nov. 14, 1879	3	6	3	My 4, "	...	"	3, Children	Guardian
60	... Callahan,	St. Patrick, 7,	37	Dec. 14, 1880	2	6	20	My 17, "	...	"	1,	"
61	... F. Daly,	Cheverus, 6,	45	Feb. 10, "	4	18	...	June 13, "	Carditis	"	1,	"
62	William B. Smith,	..., 13,	43	April 8, 1883	3	17	...	June 28, "	Chronic Bronchitis	"	1,	Ww
63	C. J. ...,	St. John, & Hyde Park	48	May 27, 1882	3	24	...	June 30, "	Consumption	"		
64	John ...,	Star of the Sea, 41, Boston	27	Dec. 5, "	1	15	...	July 2, 1883	Heart Disease	"	1, Widow	1, Ex'r
65	Daniel Murphy,	..., 3,	49	Dec. 12, 1879	7	28	...	July 12, "	General Debility	"	3,	Widow
66	Michael ...,	..., 3,	50	Nov. 14, 1881	8	11	...	Aug. 3, "	Septicæmia	"	3,	Heirs
67	John O'Brien,	..., 19,	30	Dec. 16, 1880	3	16	...	Sept. 23, "	Typhoid ever	"	3,	"
68	... G. Ryan,				3	1	1	... 17, "	Scarlet Fever	"	1,	Mr
69	... T. Walker,								Pulmonary Phthisis			
70	... Maguire,											
71	J. A. ..., M.D.,											
72	John J. Duffey,											

No.	Name	Society	Residence	Date of Admission	Date of Death	Cause of Death	Amount	Beneficiary
73	A. H. Byrne.	Essex, 39,	Somerville		Mar. 31, 1881	Hemorrhage	$1,000	
74	Pat. Whalen.	Fenwick,	Salem		Aug. 1, 1883		"	1, Widow
75	E. F. Dever,	Hamilton, 17,	Boston		Feb. 16,		"	1, Widow
76	Jno. O'Brien,	St.Joseph, 11,	"		June 14, 1880	Injury to Brain by	"	4,
77	J. Meghan,	Benedict, 39,	Somerville		Mar. 31, 1881		"	
78	John Sweeney,	Mt. Pleasant, 20,	Boston		Oct. 20, 1880	Pneumonia, C'nsum'n	"	
79	Mt H.				Jan. 30,	Pleurisy	"	
80	John Murray,				Oct. 8, 1879	Phthisis	"	1,
82	T. H. O	St.			July 2, 1883	Cerebral	"	1, Sister
83	Jno. B.	St.	Brockton		Feb. 17, 1881		"	1, Widow
84		Charles	Watert'n		Nov. 5, 1883		"	1,
85	Thos Welsh,	Qualey, 3,	Woburn		Nov. 28, 1881		"	1,
86	Thos Ahearn,	Americus, 34,	Boston		July 31, 1883	Bright's Disease	"	4, 3 child'n
87	K. A.	St. Alphonsus, 21,	"		May 10, 1880	Phthisis	"	4, 3
89	Alfred Green,	Cheverus, 6, 13,	"		Feb. 25,		"	3, 2
	John A.		Malden		Oct. 14, 1882	Bright's	"	4,
92	Stephen I. Sliney,	SS.Pet.&	Ill.15,S.Bos'n		May 20, 1881		"	9,
93	Thos Garry		Boston		Mar. 29,		"	2,
94	John W.	Essex,	"		April 26, 1880	Phthisis Pulmonalis	"	5, 4 child'n
95	John W.	St.	"		Feb. 3, 1881	Heart Disease	"	5, 4
96	John W.	St. Francis, 4,	"		Jan. 8, 1880		"	5,
97	John H		"		April 26,		"	3,
99	Geo.		"		Sept. 8,	Phthisis	"	4, 3
	John H.	Iona, 10,	Malden		April 11,		"	1,
102	John W. Wright,	St. Francis, 4,	Boston		April 22, 1880		"	3, 2
103	John J.		"		April 22,		"	3,
104	Michael		"		April 4, 1881	Phthisis	"	1,
105	John W.		"		Mar. 23,	Bronchitis	"	1,
106	James F. Ly		"		Mar. 21,		"	4,
107	E. Donohue,	St.	"		Nov. 21, 1882		"	1, Sister
108	Rev. Wm. J. Daly,	Star of Sea. 41,	E. Boston		Dec. 22, 1880		"	4,
109	Rev. J. J. O'Donnell,	St.	Boston		Dec. 26, 1881		"	4, 3 child'n
110	John Chas	St.	"		April 29, 1882		"	1,
111	M. L.				Feb. 11, 1880	Cirrhosis	"	4, 4 child'n
112	M. C.				Mar. 7, 1882	Phthisis	"	2, 1 child
113	Thos Gill,	SS.Pet.&Paul,15,	S.Bos'n		Mar. 31, 1881	Hemorrhage of lungs	"	1,
114	I. J. Smith,	St. Thomas, 29,	Brockton		Jan. 13, 1880		"	3, 3 child'n
115	L. L. Whins,	St. Peter, 18,	Do		July 3, 1880	Cholera-Morbus	"	2,
116	R. A. Brown,	St. Louis, 4,			Nov. 11,	Killed by	"	1,
118	John Drury,	Hamilton,17,			Mar. 30, 1881		"	3, 1 Sister
119	T. H. Martin,	St. Louis, 4,			Mar. 2, 1882		"	1, Sister
	E. W.				May 13, 1880	Phthisis	"	1, Sister

ENDOWMENTS PAID—Cont'd.

No.	NAME.	COURT.	AOF.	INITIATED.	Yrs.	Mos.	Dys.	DATE OF DEATH.	CAUSE.	Endowment.	NUMBER OF BENEFICIARIES.	TO WHOM PAID.
121	Hs Lynch,	St. , 11,	35	June 27, 1881	3	4	7	Nov. 4, 1 84	Pneumonia	$1,000	3, Children	Guardian
122	w Cusack,	St. , 21, "	43	Oct. 15, 1880	4	2	2	Dec. 17, "	Consump tin	"	5, w, 4 child'n	Wid. & children
123	J. M. Tirrell,	St. Patrick, 7, So. Boston	23	Jan. 24, 1882	2	11	27	Jn. 21, 1 85	hs	"	3, 2 "	Guardian
124	hn Delaney,	Bo, 5, E.	24	Jan. 16, 1880	5	1	23	Feb. 9, "	Consump tin	"	2, 2 "	Broth., wid. & g.
125	Patrick O'Gorman,	St. , oth, 11,	32	Jan. 12, 1882	2	11	26	Jan. 8, "	Phthisis	"	3, Broth, wid., ch.	Widow
126	J. W.	Boston	a	Oct. 3, 1881	3	3	27	Jn. 20, "	ut	"	1, w	Sister
127	W. J. Barry,	Em,	n	June 23, 1880	4	7	15	Feb. 1, 85	Phthisis Pulmonalis	"	5, Sister	Widow
128	P. F. Welsh,	Friendship, 37,	35	Feb. 6, 1882	2	3	1	Mar. 7, "	hs	"	5, Widow, 4 child'n	Wid. &
129	Michael Ferrin,	y, 3,	n	Jan. 15, 1883	1	10	27	Dec. 12, 1 84	Enteritis	"	4, 3 "	Wid. &
130	rd Doherty,	s, 6,	30	May 7, 1880	4	5	20	r. 27, "	Phthisis	"	3, Brothers	Brothers
131	John Sullivan,	St. Patrick, 7, So.	48	Mar. 16, "	4	8	16	Mr. 17, 1 85	hthisis Pulmonalis	"	6, w, 5 child'n	Wid. & guardian
132	T. J. Flynn,	SS.Pet.&Paul,15, " "	26	Aug. 18, "	4	7	21	April 15, "	hsis Prlm ns	"	1, "	"
133	Daniel Holland,	O'Connell,22,Winchester	39	Nov. 22, "	4	1	20	April 15, "	ha	"	1, "	"
134	James Rice,	ity, 32,	39	June 5, 1882	2	10	13	April 18, 1 85	ha	"	1, "	"
135	John M. Perkins,	Erin, 28,	42	Feb. 9, 1885			3	May 1, "	accident, crushing h'd & shl'd'r	"	1, Father	Father
136	Daniel M. Gillis,	Bass River,	25	Mar. 19, 1880	5	1	28	May 10, "	Consumption	"	2, Father	" " &
137	A. Dev ny,	Fenwick, 3,	44	April 13, 1883	1	10	29	May 12, "	nt	"	3, Widow, 2 child'n	Widow
138	W. O'Neil,	Holy		Mar. 21, 1881	4	1	23	May 16, "	ha	"	1, "	"
139	J.S.	McGlew, 36,	28	April 2, 1882	3	1	23	May 25, "	Consumption	"	2, 1 child	Brother
140	John Donovan,	hn, 37,	35	Mar. 9, 1880	5	2	4	May 13, "	Heart se	"	1, Brother	"
141	Edward Gallagher,	Star of the Sea,41, E. "	29	Dec. 13, 1881	3	5	24	June 7, "	Drowned	"	4, w, 3 child'n	Widow
142	Hn R. McDonald,	Lyndon, b, Boston	26	Feb. 14, 1882	3	3	18	June 9, 1882	1 hts	"	1, "	"
143	Dr. W. P. ky,	lty, 40, "	48	May 12, 1881	4	1	27	pril 2, 1882	Inflammation of Bowels	"	6, s & aunts	Uncles & aunts
144	Peter ry, n,	Mt. Pleasant, 20, "	39	Mar. 11, "	4	2	26	June 7, 1 85	Congestion of Brain	"	5, Widow, 4 child'n	w & child'n
145	e O', hn,	, 7, So.	32	Oct. 11, "	4	8	1	June 14, "	Bright's Disease	"	1, "	"
146	hy Long,	Cheverus, 6, Boston	49	April 6, "	4	1	13	June 12, "	Pneumonia	"	4, 3 "	"
147	d Lane,	Cheverus, 6, "	22	Feb. 24, "	5	5	21	J ly 19, "	Phthisis	"	5, Mother	Mother
148	Michael	Sherwood, 8, "	47	April 22, "	4	2	22	Aug. 14, "	ky	"	1, Widow	Widow
149	Peter Hawkins,	St.Bernard,44,W.Newton	43	Dec. 13, 1881	3	10	27	Feb. 2, 1 84	Pneumonia	"	3, Brothers	Brothers
150	P. W. Sweeney,	Bo, 5, E. Boston	39	Sept. 25, 1882	2	5	24	July 22, 1 85	Phthisis	"	3, Father, 3 sisters	Father & sister
151	s Daly,	My, 5,	32	Mar. 21, "	5	5	10	Sept. 15, "	hs	"	6, Children	Guardian
152	B. F.	Cathedral, 1,	40	Sept. 3, 1879	6	9	16	Sept. 1, "	Typhoid Pneumonia	"	7, Widow, 6 child'n	Widow
153	n McCarthy,	Fenwick, 3, "	37	Mar. 12, 1880	5	6	7	Sept. 19, "	Pneumonia	"	4, 3 "	"
154	s H n,	Hamilton, 1, "	38	July 6, "	5	2	24	Mar. 21, "	Pyæmia	"	6, 5 "	"
155	hy Dwyer,	My, 4, Bridgewater	44	Nov. 2, 1882	2	11	7	t. 30, "	Neuralgia of Stomach	"	6, 5 "	"
156	John Sheehan,	Emerald, 53, Peal dly	42	July 12, 1883	3	3	24	t. 26, "	Phthisis Pu	"	6, 1 hild	"
157	Hugh A. Carr,	Cheverus, 6, Boston	29	Feb. 11, 1880	4	7	26	t. 17, "	Consumption	"	2, Sisters	Sisters

No.	Name		Date		Cause	Amount	Paid to	
161	D. M. Lynch,	Erin, 8,	Feb. 3, 1881	Dec. 1, 1885		$1,000	Widow, 5 child'n	Widow
162	Carney,	Essex,	May 4,	Nov. 3,		"	2 "	Att'y of wid., g.
163	Carney,		Dec. 14, 1880	Nov. 4,		"	3 "	Widow & gr.
164						"	8 "	"
165	J. R.	St. Francis, 4,	Dec. 18, 1879	Dec. 20,		"	5 "	"
166	John O'Day,	Erin, 28,	April 6, 1881	Dec. 15,		"	1 child	"
167	J.		Mar. 18, 1879	Dec. 22,		"	2 child'n	"
168	H. Shea,	St. Anne, 47,	Dec. 18, 1879	Dec. 4,		"		"
169		Erin, 8,	July 6, 1885	Dec. 24,	Blood	177.50		
170		St. Anne, 47,	Oct. 15, 1879	Dec. 26,		$1,000	Widow, 2 child'n	N'se, und'r lawy
171			July 1,	Sept. 22,				Widow
172	Michael Harvey,	St. Patrick, 7,	Feb. 11, 1880	Jan. 2, 1886		1,		
173	W. H.	Mt. Pleasant, 20,	April 14, 1882	Jan. 7,		4,	Widow & sister	
174	C. J.	St. Patrick, 7,	Dec. 21, 1880	Jan. 9,		3,	Widow, 2 child'n	Widow
175	J.	St. Francis, 8,	April 4, 1881	Jan. 10,		4,	4 "	& child'n
176	Donovaro,	Williams, 19,	July 14, 1883	Feb. 6,		5,	7 "	"
177	Francis P. Paten,	Fulton, 12,	Nov. 26, 1880	Feb. 17,		6,	5 "	Guardian
178	W.	Leo, 5,	July 6,	Feb. 19,	Phthisis	4,	4 "	Guardian
179	J. Kenney,	St. Joseph, 11,	July 22,	Feb. 28,		4,		Widow, 2 child'n
180	James W. Norris,	Oakley, 32,	Jan. 2, 1882	Mar. 3,		1,	3 child'n	Wid. & child'n
181	William Logue,	Milton, 17,	July 6, 1880	Mar. 4,		3,	Parents	
182	William,	Essex, 47,	June 22, 1882	April 6,		2,	2 child'n	Wd. and child'n
183	Devine,	Ina, 10,	Mar. 3, 1881	My 21,		4,	1 kid	
184	Bellen,	Mt.	Feb. 10,	My 6,	Chronic	8,	5 child'n	
185	Cahill,		July 13, 1883	April 9,	Drowning		7 "	
186		St. Bernard, 44,	Mar. 27, 1882	Jne 3,	Gastric Fever	4,		Me
187	Luke Kelley,	Mt.	Mar. 6, 1883	Jne 18,	Phthisis	4,	Widow, 3 child'n	Widow
188	C. G.	Fulton, 12,	Feb. 26, 1882	Jne 18,		4,	6 "	"
189	A. J.		Dec. 9, 1880	July 1,		3,	4 "	"
190	C.	Leo, 5,	May 13, 1880	July 26,	of Lungs	2,		Me
191	Richard A. Carroll,		Jan. 16,	July 27,		2,	Gw & kid	Nw
192	William		June 22, 1881	July 29,		3,		
193	William H.		May 12,	Ag. 3,	Typhoid	2,	2 child'n	Widow & gar.
194	Pierce,		Oct.	Oct. 4,	of Brain from	3,	Wid. fath. moth.	Fath, moth, wid.
195	B.	SS. Peter & Paul, 15,	Jan. 1, 1884	Dec. 15,		3,		
196	William	SS.	Mar. 28, 1881	April 26,		6,	Widow, 6 child'n	Heirs
197	Hugh	Shiel, 35,	Sept. 15, 1880	April 27, 1887	Chronic Bronchitis	7,	2 "	Widow
198		St. Francis, 4,	April 14, 1882	Jan. 11,		5,	4 "	
199	Connors,	Benedict, 39,	Mar. 31, 1881	Mar. 27,		5,		Mr & sister
200	Daniel		Sept. 1, 1883	Ag. 22, 1886		6,	Father &	Widow
201	John F. Daly,	SS.	Sept. 12, 1881	April 12, 1887		6,	Widow, 5 child'n	Widow
202	William Pierce,	St. Paul, 15,	Mar. 8, 1881	Mar. 11,		5,		
203			Oct. 3,	April 9,		3,	2 child'n	

ENDOWMENTS PAID—Continued.

NO.	NAME.	COURT.	AGE.	INITIATED.	Yrs.	Mos.	Dys.	DATE OF DEATH.	CAUSE.	Endowment.	NUMBER OF BENEFICIARIES.	TO WHOM PAID.
209	Terence ?an,	Erin, 28,	39	Feb. 17, 1881	6	2	17	May 4, 1887	Pneumonia	$1,000	6, Widow, 5 chil'n	?dw
210	Wm. F. Kean,	Leo, 5,	35	Nov. 19, 1886	2	7		May 30, 1885	Acute Meningitis'	"	4, " 3 "	1 ?dian & wid.
211	Michael Connell,	Hamilton, 17,	23	July 23, 1885	1	10	2	Jan. 26, 1887	Phthisis Pulm ?lis	"	3, " 3 "	Widow
212	Joseph McGilvray,	Cons ?tine, 49,	33	Sept. 8, 1881	8	6		May 25, "	Progressive Paralysis	"	3, " 5 "	Wid. & guardian
213	Patrick Murphy,	Bass River, 30,	30	Sept. 9, "	5	9	12	May 14, "	Haemoptysis	"	6, " 1 child	"
214	Philip Carney,	St. ?ph, 38,	35	April 6, 1882	5	2	18	June 21, "	Phthisis	"	2, " 5 child'n	"
215	John Broderick,	Ham ?on, 17,	50	Mar. 4, 1880	7	3	25	June 28, "	?br. Kid., & Lung Dis., Dropsy	"	6, " 5 "	"
216	David Fahey,	Sherwood, 8,	40	Jan. 21, 1881	6	3		June 29, "	Inflammation of ?ver	"	5, " 4	"
217	Cornelius Driscoll,	Fenwick, 3,	28	Jan. 21, 1887	6	6	13	July 23, "	Malarial Causes	"	2, Mother & ?	Mother & widow
218	? ?ah,	Shields, 63,	38	Dec. 24, 1880	6	6	25	July 27, "	Typhoid-Pneumonia	"	2, ?dw & ?ild	Widow
219	William Brooks,	Leo, 5,	34	Mar. 20, 1881	6	2	10	July 19, "	Consumption of Lungs	"	6, Children	Guardian
220	?s J. Walsh,	?h, 5,	44	May 14, 1880	6	4	3	May 31, "	Pulmonalis Phthisis	"	1, Widow	?dw
221	?el J. Fennessy,	St. John, 33,	39	Aug. 14, 1884	4	11	22	Sept. 23, "	Drowned	"	3, ?br,	F. & ?ty for 2s.
222	J. J. Cunningham,	Essex, 16,	44	Nov. 14, 1884	6	2	8	Aug. 6, "	Senile Marasmus	"	6, Widow, 5	G. of C. A. for W.
223	Michael O'Keefe,	St. Augustine, 46,	27	Dec. 27, 1882	7	8	11	July 25, "	Pneumonia	"	2, " ?ild	Guard. of child'n
224	John F. Rahl,	St. Joseph, 11,	39	Mar. 8, "	4	7	6	Oct. 3, "	Phthisis Pulmonalis	"	2, " 3 child'n	Widow
225	B. H. Holthaus,	Cathedral, 12,	23	April 23, 1883	7	5	12	Oct. 20, "	Dropsy, Heart Disease	"	1, Father	Father
226	G. W. ?ey,	Columbus, 9,	49	Mar. 4, 1880	8	5	27	Oct. 20, "	Pneumonia	"	7, Widow, 6 child'n	Father
227	Patrick Connell,	Iona, 10,	42	Feb. 3, 1881	7	9	25	Nov. 19, "	Degeneration of Lungs	"	4, Children	Son & guardian
228	B. J. ?ly,	Erin, 28,	49	Nov. 17, 1887	10	10	24	Nov. 28, "	Pneumonia	"	2, Father & ?	Guardian
229	?as Sweeney,	?ty, 45,	25	April 15, 1886	1	7	15	Oct. 6, "	Railroad ?t	"	5, Widow, 4 child'n	?dw
230	John F. Reavy,	Gallagher, 64,	35	Oct. 7, 1880	7	1	1	Dec. 4, "	?nia	"	2, Father & ?	? & child
231	M. J. Reagan,	Cheverus, 6,	27	May 26, 1887	1	7	15	Nov. 21, "	?nd Accident	"	1, " 1 child	Father
232	D. F. McGilvray,	Cheverus, 6,	36	May 12, 1881	7	1	1	Dec. 8, "	Fract. of Skull, Blasting Accident	"	6, Widow, 5 child'n	?dw
233	?? ?ee,	St. Columbkill, 65,	45	April 31, 1880	7	6	27	Jan. 17, 1888	?er of Jaw	"	11, " 10	"
234	John Martin,	?is, 9,	49	Mar. 4, 1880	8	8	14	Dec. 9, 1887	Chronic Interst. Pneumonia	"	1, Mother	? & child'n
235	Timothy Collins,	?un, 12,	55	July 2, 1883	7	10	1	Jan. 7, 1888	Paraplegia	"	1, Brother	Brother
236	Michael Durant,	?t, 39,	29	Jan. 21, 1886	2	7	22	Dec. 14, 1887	?ral Paresis	"	1, Widow	?dw
237	A. J. Harrington,	Sherwood, 8,	38	Mar. 13, 1882	10	1	24	Jan. 5, 1888	Phthisis Pulmonalis	"	5, Children	Children
238	J. J. Callahan,	St. James, 54,	56	Sept. 3, 1879	5	10	11	Feb. 24, 1886	Peritonitis	"	1, Mother	?er
239	T. J. Dacey,	Americus, 34,	38	Oct. 22, 1884	4	3	10	Feb. 15, 1887	Dropsy	"	1, Widow	?dw
240	M. Brahenny,	St. Joseph, 11,	34	May 4, 1882	10	3	22	Feb. 22, 1888	Heart Disease	"	5, ?dw, 4 child'n	Children
241	H. H. Sullivan,	?al, 1,	56	Jan. 13, 1882	9	4	10	Jan. 13, "	Bright's Disease	"	1, Mother	Mother
242	John Murray,	St. Joseph, 11,	38	Feb. 7, 1880	3	10	22	Jan. 5, "	Consumption	"	5, Widow, 4 child'n	Widow
243	Edw. Ward,	St. ? ?s, 21,	34	May 4, 1882	9	15		Mar. 7, "	Phthisis	"	1, Mother	Mother
244	Wm. J. McAleer,	Fitzpatrick, 13,	31	June 22, 1881	1	17		Mar. 14, "	Hemorrhage of Lungs	"	4, ?dw, 3 child'n	Widow
245	John J. Craig,	Leo, 5,	32	Feb. 7, 1880	8	1	11	Nov. 1, 1887	Phthisis Pulmonalis	"	1, Mother,	?er
246	Peter Kilroy,	Leo, 5,	41	Mar. 18, 1881	8	3	16	April 2, 1888	Chronic Bronchitis	"	19, Relatives	Relatives
247	?ter Collins,	St. Francis, 4,	56	Dec. 18, 1879	8	4	11	April 24, "	Typhoid Fever	"	2, Widow, 1 child	Widow
248	John Collins,	St. Thomas, 29,	28	Nov. 8, 1883	4	5	16			"	1,	

No.	Name	Society	Age	Admitted	Died	Cause of Death	Amount	Beneficiaries
249	Ias Widow,	Cheverus, 6,	45	April 28, 1882	May 3, 1888	Ms	$1,000	4, Widow, 3 child'n — Widow
250	M. A. Fox,	Essex, 16,	33	Eb. 15, 1881	May 4,		"	2, Ser and aunt — Mother and
251	B. Kerrigan,	St. Alphonsus, 21,	53	Oct. 15, 1880	April 22, 1887	Fn gl Tumor	"	8, Children — Guardian
252	John J. Sullivan,	Leo, 5,	40	Feb. 9, 1887	May 10, 1888	Pneumonia	"	5, Widow, 7 child'n — Widow
253	T. F. Powel,	Ms, 6,	46	Oct. 4, 1883	June	ec Neuralgia	"	1, Widow — "
254	John Hines,	Essex, 16,	49	April 20, 1881	May 25,	Wl. Disease of Heart	"	4,
255	J. J. Gllaghan,	Lafayette, 14,	56	May 27,	April 3,	Catarrhal Pneumonia	"	3, Bro. and sistert — Sister-in-law
256	Gn Carley,	Cheverus, 6,	36	My 12,	June 29,	Septicæmia	"	6, Widow, 5 child'n — Widow
257	ms Gnn,	Ms, B,	33	July 13, 1883	June 30,	Peritonitis	"	5, Widow, 5 — "
258	Mk Dowd,	Gnn,	42	April 23, 1883	July 12,	Ms	"	2, Children
259	A. A. Vogel,	St. Francis, 25,	34	Dec. 17, 1887	July 15,	Ms Pulmonalis	"	5, Widow, — Guardian
260	James J. Whalen,	Holy Trinity, 51,	28	March 16, 1883	July 2,	Bright's Disease	"	5, sth., Md. & ch. — Guardian &, wid. & ch.
261	J. J. McKernan,	St. Anne, 47,	27	Jan. 18, 1880	July 29,	Phthisis Pulmonalis	"	1, Mother — Mother
262	James H. Hurley,	Iona, 10,	52	March 23, 1879	August 6,	Cancer of Liver	"	3, Widow, 2 child'n — Widow and
263	Michael Maguire,	Sarsfield, 48,	46	Dec. 10, 1880	July 30,	Ascites	"	3, Son Ms, 3 — Guardian
264	John Kelley,	Fenwick, 3,	64	May 10, 1882	Aug. 14,	Typhoid Fever	"	4, 2 — W idw and child'n
265	P. Doherty,	St. Francis, 4,	28	Aug. 6, 1880	Aug. 15,	Apoplexy	"	1, 3 — Widow
266	P. C. Fennelly,	Sherwood, 8,	38	Ot. 18, 1883	Jan. 23,	Phthisis Pulmonalis	"	1, Mother — Ser
267	J. L. Hennessey,	St. Patrick 7,	26	June 6, 1880	May 2, 1886	Consumption	"	2, Children — Guardian
268	J. Keohane,	O'Connell, 22,	35	Dec. 3, 1879	Aug. 26, 1888	Consumption	"	3, Widow — Widow
269	T. R. Fallon,	Sherwood, 8,	50	Et. 12, 1883	Sept. 17,	Fracture of Skull	"	4, Widow, 2 c — W idw and
270	Wm. Lynch,	Es, 16,	46	Ot. 5, 1886	Oct. 9,	Sel reis	"	4, 3 — W dw and daugh.
271	ms Smith,	Sheil, 35,	45	Feb. 26, 1884	Aug. 13,	Pleurisy	"	9, 8 — Widow
272	J ms Fay,	St. Francis, 4,	53	March 18, 1888	Nov. 2,	Phthisis	"	4, Widow
273	ms Connell,	Iona, 10,	48	May 10, 1880	Oct. 13,	Bright's	"	5, 3
274	W. Manning,	Cathedral, 1,	68	Aug. 16, 1880	Oct. 14,	Ms	"	1, 4 — W idw and
275	John Burke,	Cathedral, 1,	39	Jan. 20, 1881	Oct. 16,	Paralysis	"	1, Mer — Father
276	A. M. Cuffe,	SS. Peter and Paul, 15,	66	June 10, 1883	Oct. 24,	Phthisis	"	1, all ur
277	M. Hogan,	St. Joseph, 38,	35	Oct. 16, 1883	Oct. 26,	Chr. Catar. Pneumonia	"	9, Children — Children
278	M. H. W,	SS. Peter and Rnl, 15,	31	April 23, 1881	Nov. 6,	Ms	"	5, Widow, 4 child'n — Widow and child'n
279	J. F. Bradley,	Sheil, 35,	32	Feb. 17, 1881	Nov. 20,	Md Pneumonia	"	1, Widow — W idw
280	Bartley My,	Fitzpatrick, 13,	54	May 7, 1886	Nov. 11,	Peritonitis	"	3, Widow, 2 child'n — Widow and child'n
281	Michael McDonough,	Fitzpatrick, 13,	56	Aug. 14, 1882	Nov. 25,	Apoplexy	"	2, 1 son — i Widow
282	Mrs L. Silk,	Mt. Pleasant, 0,	44	Nov. 23,	Nov.	Drowning	"	1, ister — W idw and son
283	Coleman O'Melia,	Leo, 5,	47	Jan. 16, 1880	Dec. 25,	Tumor of Bowels	"	1, Ser — Sister
284	Maurice Neville,	Iona, 10,	48	Oct. 20, 1881	Jan. 17, 1889	Heart Disease	"	1, Widow — W iw
285	James H. McDowell,	St. Gph, 11,	53	April 10, 1881	Jan. 31,	Consumption	"	1, Widow — Ser
286	Thomas F. Kelly,	Highland, 32,	35	April 16, 1883	Dec. 24,	Phthisis Pulmonalis	"	1, — Widow
287	Patrick Magee,	Erin, 28,	40	Feb. 17, 1881	Nov. 24,	Consumption	"	2, i Widow and — W idw and guard.
288	J ms Dorgan,	St. Ms, 29,	38	Feb. 15, 1880	Feb. 25, 1889	Ms	"	1, Widow — Widow
289	Edward Millin,	Alphonsus, 21,	50	Ot. 7, 1886	Feb. 7,	Consumption	"	1, Widow — "
290	Michael D. Sullivan,	Sherwood, 8,	30	May 14, 1882	ab. 23,	Phthisis Pulmonalis	"	2, i Widow and — W idw and guard.
291	P. H. Kerrigan,	St. Augustine, 46,	36	Nv. 23,	Feb. 21,	Hemorrhage from Lung	"	1, Widow — Widow
292	Timothy Sheehan,	Iona, 10,	45	Nov. 1880	March 18,	Ms	"	
293	James Shortell,	Ex, 16,	51	June 23,	March 17,	Phtl Ms	"	2, Widow and daugh. — W idw and daugh.
294	An F. Carroll,	St. John, 33,	54	March 8, 1881	March 91,	Heart Disease	"	

ENDOWMENTS PAID— Continued.

No.	NAME.	HT.	Age.	INITIATED.	Mem-bership. Yrs.	Mos.	Dys.	DATE OF [death].	CAUSE.	En-dow-ment.	NUMBER OF BENEFICIARIES.	TO WHOM PAID.
295	Alexander ...	Friendship, 37,	40	March 25, 1881	8		22	April 17, 1889	...	$1,000	1, Wdw	Wdw
296	Peter H. ...	St. ... 4,	52	Dec. 18, 1879	9	3	22	April 10, "	Cancer of the Stomach	"	1,	"
297	Jas. Cunningham,	Iona 10,	58	March 14, 1880	8	11	29	April 29, "	...	"	7,	Sisters and bros.
298	William Lynch,	Fitzpatrick, 13,	35	May 5, "	8	11	11	April 16, "	Pernicious ...	"	5 sisters & 2 bros.	Sisters.
299	Patrick H. ...	Essex, 16,	52	June 9, "	8	10	10	April 9, "	Cirrhosis of ...	"	1, Daughter	Daughter
300	John Mullen,	St. Francis. 4,	50	June 1, 1882	6	10	27	April ...	...	"	1, Widow	Widow
301	Eugene Sul...	Wills, 19,	46	Feb. 26, 1884	5	3	16	May 12, "	Uraemia	"	4, Children	Guardian
302	... Lyons,	St. Gregory, 24,	32	June ...	5	5	1	May 27, "	Cerebral Hæmorrhage	"	1, Wdw	Wdw
303	J. McCarthy,	Leo, 5,	53	Jan. 16, 1880	9	2	16	April 2, "	... Pulmonalis	"	1,	"
304	...	St. Peter, 18,	52	July 22, "	10	5	5	May 27, "	Chronic ...	"	1,	"
305	E. C. Bullard,	...	49	May 4, "	9	1	9	April 13, "	...	"	1, Wfe	Wfe
306	Francis J. ...	Cheverus, 6,	34	March 2, "	9	1	19	April 21, "	Phthisis	"	1, Wdw	Wdw
307	Thos. E. Atherton,	Leo, 5,	45	Feb. 13, "	9	3	14	April 27, "	Cirrhosis of ...	"	1, Wdw	i Wdw
308	Denis ...	SS. Peter and Paul, 15,	47	March 2, 1881	8	4	1	July 3, "	Toxæmia	"	1, Wdw	Wdw
309	John ...	St. ..., 8,	52	March 11, 1880	9	3	15	June 26, "	Cerebral ...	"	7, Wdw and child'n	Wdw and child'n
310	John ...	St. ..., 61,	41	Nov. 15, 1887	1	7	16	July 1, "	...	"	7, Wdw and child'n	Wdw and guard.
311	... B. Duffy,	...	24	April 5, "	1	2	3	July 8, "	...	"	1, Wfer	Wfr
312	...	St. Alphonsus, 21,	45	March 11, 1888	1	4	6	July 20, "	...	"	1, Wdw	Wdw
313	John H. ...	St. ..., 67,	29	Sept. 17, "	10	14		Aug. 1, "	Acquired ...	400	1, Sir	Sister
314	R. J. ...	...	26	Jan. 27, 1882	3	1	27	Mch. 24, 1885	... failure	1,000	1, Mrs	Mrs
315	James Cavenaugh,	Cheverus, 6,	44	March 9, 1880	9	4	18	July 27, 1889	...	"	1, Fffr	Guardian
316	Edward J. ...	Williams, 19,	25	Jan. 20, 1881	8	7	5	Aug. 3, "	...	"	1, Father	Ffer
317	... J. ...	St. ..., 38,	43	March 29, 1881	8	4	4	Aug. 4, "	...	"	8, Wdw and child'n	i Wdw and guard.
318	John J. O'Brien,	St. ..., 88,	51	July 22, 1880	8	13		Aug. 5, "	...	"	2, Daughters	Guardian
319	Henry ...,	St. Francis. 4,	40	Jan. 13, 1881	8	3	27	Oct. 10, "	Phthisis ...	"	2, Wdn	Guardian
320	Charles ...,	..., 32,	45	May 6, "	8	7	9	Oct. 15, "	Chronic Pneumonia	"	1, Wdw	Wdw
321	Thos. McFarland,	Iona, 10,	12	March 14, 1880	8	4	4	Oct. 16, "	Railroad ...	"	3, Children	Guardian
322	Andrew ...,	..., 9,	57	Sept. 16, "	9	7	12	Oct. 16, "	... Pulmonalis	"	1, Wdw	Wdw
323	Jas. P. ...,	Iona, 10,	36	June 5, 1883	6	4	22	Oct. 8, "	Paralysis and ... Failure	"	6, Wdw and child'n	Wdw and guard.
324	Timothy ...,	Americus, 34,	42	March 15, 1881	8	4	24	Oct. 29, "	...	"	1, Wdw	Wdw
325	John J. ...,	Americus, 34,	42	Sept. 18, 1883	6	2	5	Oct. 13, "	... ing Septicæmia	"	1, Widow	Widow
326	Thos. H. Brennan,	St. ..., 54,	33	April 4, 1888	1	7	16	Oct. 23, "	...	"	1, Mother	Mo. thr
327	Henry J. Duggan,	..., 3,	39	March 19, 1880	9	8	27	Dec. 16, "	Typhoid Fever and Pernicious Anæmia	"	1, Wdw	Wdw
328	...	...,	48	April 7, "	9	8	24	Dec. 16, "	...	"	1, Wdw	Wdw
329	John ...,	Iona, 10,	57	...	14	7	22	Nov. 29, "	Phthisis	"	1, Sister	Sister
330	... T. Coleman,	Iona, 10,	32	April 7, "	9	6	24	Oct. 29, "	Phthisis	"	1, Mfer	Mfer
331	... F. Hallahan,	St. ..., 18,	50	Aug. 16, 1883	6	2	4	Oct. 6, "	Phthisis	"	10, Wdw & child'n	Wdw and child'n
332	Patrick J. ...,	..., 6,	39	Jan. 14, 1887	2	7	22	St. "	Typhoid Fever	"	1, Wdw	Wdw

No.	Name	Council	Cause of Death	Date of Death	Date Admitted	Amt.	Beneficiary		Beneficiary 2
333	Thomas Griffin,	Benedict, 39,	Heart Disease	Dec. 16, 13, 1889	Dec. 47, 27, 1883	$1,000	1, Wdw		Wdw
334	John Sheenan,	St. Joseph, 11,	Phthisis	Dec. 23, 15,	dn. 51, 22, 1882	"	1, Wdw		"
335	Lawrence Andrews,	St. Chas, 29,	Phthisis	Dec. 7, 19,	Mr. 39, 12, 1885	"	1, Widow		Widow
336	Jeremiah Daly,	Iona,	Phthisis	Dec. 2, 20,	Aug. 33, 18, 1887	"	2, Wdw and child		Wdw and child
337	...s Wholly,		Phthisis	Dec. 18, 2, 1890	...e 44, 14, 1888	"	1, Son		Mother
338	...s P. Mulvey,	St. Francis, 4,	Phthisis	Jan. 23, 10,	June 31, 9, 1881	"	1, Mother		Wdw
339	John J. Sheely,	St. Joseph, 11,	Phthisis	Jan. 13, 1,	Dec. 37, 27, 1883	"	3, Wd. and 2 child'n		Wdw
340	Michael Keyes,	Sherwood, 8,	Phthisis	Dec. 5, 27, 1889	Nov. 42, 22, 1881	"	2, Children		Guardian
341	F. P. Hansen,	...d, 8,	J...nity and drowning	Nov. 9, 8,	Feb. 49, 2, 1884	"	2, Wdw and child		Wdw
342	...s McGinn,	...d, 8,	Pneumonia	April 6, 7,	J...ne 40, 7, 1883	"	4, Children		Wdw
343	John J. McCarthy,	St. ...r, 18,	Osteo-myelitis	April 16, 1,	June 29, 7, 1883	"	1, Widow		Sister
344	Daniel Manning,	St. Francis, 25,	Phthisis	Jan. 20, 8,	Nov. 35, 18, 1880	"	1, Sister		Sister
345	Michael B. Murphy,	Hamilton, 17,	Phthisis Pulmonalis	Jan. 5, 2,	...a 45, 7, 1885	"	1, Sister		Wdw
346	Patrick T. G...,	Mt. Pleasant,	...th or of ...l	Jan. 7, 13,	June 52, 8, 1885	"	8, Wd. and 7 child'n		"
347	John Breslin,	Qualey, 32,	Phthisis	Jan. 2, 19,	July 31, 17, 1882	"	3, Wd. and 2 child'n		"
348	Bernard McLaughlin,	...a, 1,		Jan. 19, 22,	Sept. 50, 9, 1879	"	4, Wd. and 3 child'n		"
349	...s Deegan,			Jan. 25, 4,	July 46, 9, 1887	"	1, ...Wdw		"
350	Edmund Boylan,	Benedict, 9,	...s	Feb. 9, 17,	Aug. 33, 8, 1889	"	1, Sister-in-law		Sw
351	C. Morrissey,	Constantine, 49,	Phthisis Pulmonalis	Feb. 7, 19,	My 55, 10, 1881	"	5, Wdw and child'n		Wdw
352	Wm. H. ...nnor,	St. ...is, 25,	Drowning	Feb. 28, 23,	June 38, 25, 1880	"	3, dw and child		Wdw
353	Lawrence Forrest,	Erin, 8,	Pneumonia	March 24, 0,	Oct. 26, 27, 1887	"	1, Mother		Mother
354	James E. Doherty,	Constantine, 49,	...e Phthisis	March 4, 22,	...t. 40, 26, 1883	"	9, Wdw and child'n		Widow as guard.
355	Michael G. Ryan,	...i Alex, 60,	Pneumonia	March 18, 31,	...t. 26, 13, 1887	"	3, Mother and child'n		as ...ther
356	W. C. J. ...,		Spinal	April 27, 3,	Aug. 31, 9, 1888	"	5, Widow and child'n		"
357	...k F. Lacey,	St. Francis, 25,	Phthisis	April 22, 6,	...s 45, 21, 1888	"	5, "		"
358	John B. Flynn,	Star of the Sea, 41,	Fracture of skull	May 16, 21,	May 39, 5, 1887	"	5, "		as guard.
359	Maurice Walsh,	S. Columbkille, 65,	Exhaustion f'm accident	Aug. 16, 23,	Aug. 29, 2, 1887	"	2, "		"
360	Michael Sullivan,	Highland, 52,	Phthisis	April 18, 3,	April 44, 16, 1883	"	5, "		"
361	M. J. Connolly,	Iona, 10,	Phthisis Pulmonalis	May 23, 5,	Jan. 31, 13, 1881	"	5, "		"
362	M. J. Driscoll,	St. James, 54,	Chronic Bronchitis	May 10, 9,	July 33, 13, 1883	"	2, "		"
363	William Dunn,	St. James, 54,	Spinal M ...g	May 24, 13,	Sept. 45, 2, 1884	"	5, "		Guardian
364	Bryan ...,	Cheverus, 6,	Phthisis	June 20, 7,	May 26, 17, 1887	"	2, "		Widow
365	J...ns C. ...kins,	Emerald, 53,	Cancer	June 14, 17,	Mar. 38, 23, 1880	"	2, "		as guard.
366	John J. Bartlett,	St. ...r, 8,	Accident	June 15, 19,	July 51, 21, 1883	"	6, "		Guardian
367	John ...,	...t, 8,	Meningitis	June 7, 10,	Nov. 52, 10, 1881	"	4, "		Widow
368	...is Martin,	Holy Trinity, 51,	Broncho Pneumonia	July 21, 11,	Jan. 52, 21, 1884	"	4, "		"
369	Jeremiah Horgan,	St. Alphonsus, 21,	Sunstroke	July 27, 31,	June 42, 14, 1883	"	7, "		as guard.
370	John Morley,	Constantine, 40,	Typhoid Fever	July 26, 6,	April 43, 5, 1883	"	4, "		"
371	...el ...,	Erin, 28,	Uremic poisoning	August 3, 20,	June 38, 11, 1889	"	6, "		and broth'r
372	Timothy J. Sweeney,	Sherwood, 8,	Typhoid Fever	7, 3,	...b. 36, 3, 1888	"	2, "		"
373	Daniel P. Sullivan,	St. Koltmbkille, 65,	Typhoid Fever	6, 16,	Mar. 26, 4, 1890	"	4, "		"
374	Edward Fitzgerald,	Phil Sheri dn., 71,	Hem. from amputation of arm	8, 18,	...t. 26, 5, 1889	"	6, "		"
375	Tim ...ly Callahan,	Essex, 16,	Consmption	Oct. 27, 14,	Aug. 37, 17, 1881	"	6, "		Guardian
376	D. J. McCarthy,	Cheverus, 6,	Phthisis Pulmonalis	Oct. 27, 25,	Jan. 46, 28, 1881	"	4, "		i Wdw
377	James O'Hagan,	Williams, 19,	Heart Failure	Nov. 12, 5,	...he 39, 23, 1880	"	7, "		
378	John J. ...n,	Essex, 16,					1,		

ENDOWMENTS PAID — Continued.

No.	NAME.	COURT.	Age.	INITIATED.	Membership. Yrs.	Mos.	Dys.	DATE OF DEATH.	CAUSE.	Endowment.	NUMBER OF BENEFICIARIES.	TO WHOM PAID.
379	Michael Cadagan,	Fenwick, 3,	54	Jan. 21 1881,	9		15	Nov. 6, 1890,	Typhoid Fever	$1,000	4, New and child'n	Widow and child'n
380	Patrick Sheerin,	St. Joseph, 11,	58	Sept. 12, 1881,	9	2	3	Nov. 15, "	Meningtis	"	1, "	"
381	Hugh Canny,	Cheverus, 6,	66	Feb. 11, 1880,	10	9	25	Dec. 6, "	Heart Disease	"	6, "	"
382	Michael Walsh,	St. Joseph, 11,	49	July 11, 1881,	9	4	29	Dec. 10, "	Pneumonia	"	6, "	"
383	William Richmond,	Fenwick, 6,	49	March 2, 1880,	9		17	Dec. 19, "	Fere of skull	"	2, "	Dau'ter
384	David Barry,	Fenwick, 3,	53	Feb. 18, 1881,	9		10	Dec. 22, "	Heart Failure	"	4, "	Widow and child
385	Stephen Gray,	Williams, 19,	47	Dec. 19, 1881,	9			Jan. 4, 1891,	Heart Failure	"	4, "	"
386	Jesse Lansmann,	Holy Trinity, 51,	33	Aug. 9, 1886,	4		26	Jan. 5, "	Pneumonia	"	4, "	"
387	James H. Millerick,	St. John, 75,	39	June 13, 1889,	1	7	1	Jan. 14, "	Phthisis	"	4, "	"
388	James Sweeney,	Sherwood, 8,	46	Jan. 11, 1883,	8			Jan. 17, "	Intestinal obstruction after accident	"	7, "	"
389	James Kenney,	Williams, 19,	40	Jan. 3, 1883,	8		10	Jan. 24, "	Phthisis Pulmonalis	"	4, "	"
390	Patrick McCarthy,	Charles River, 55,	50	Oct. 8, 1885,	5	3	26	Feb. 2, "	Tuberculosis Pulmonalis	"	2, "	"
391	Jeremiah McSweeney,	Cathedral, 1,	46	Oct. 19, 1879,	11	3	13	Feb. 2, "	Double Pneumonia	"	3, "	"
392	Thomas F.	St. Thomas, 29,	36	Sept. 8, 1881,	9		6	March 17, "	Phthisis	"	5, "	"
393	Michael Killilea,	La, 5,	58	May 14, 1880,	10		4	March 18, "	Fatty Degeneration of heart	"	5, "	"
394	Daniel	Cheverus, 6,	52	Jan. 16, 1881,	10		2	March 21, "	Pericarditis	"	7, "	Widow
395	Martin Havey,	St. Francis, 4,	50	Dec. 1811,	3		14	April 2, "	Empyema	"	7, Mother	Mother
346	McGowan,	Sarsfield, 48,	31	March 26, 1889,	2		1	April 13, "	Phthisis	"	1, Mother	Mother
397	James H.	Constantine, 49,	35	Oct. 11, 1888,	2	1	10	Aug. 20, 1890,		"	6, Widow and child'n	Widow
398	Patrick Quinn,	St. 11,	32	June 14, 1880,	10		10	April 22, 1891,	Pneumonia	"	8, "	"
399	William F. Hastings,	St. Anne, 47,	53	July 8, 1889,	1	4	8	Nov. 8, 1890,	Drowning	"	6, "	"
400	William Clancy,	St. Joseph, 11,	43	Feb. 14, 1881,	10	2	13	April 27, 1891,	Phthisis Pulmonalis	"	6, "	"
401	John Ray,	Erin, 28,	48	Nov. 12, 1889,	1	5		April 9, "	Peritonitis	"	6, "	"
402	Michael Dunphy,	St. 25,	48	Jan. 15, 1881,	10	3		April 24, "	Phthisis Pulmonalis	"	4, "	"
403	Francis Keniy,	Charles River, 55,	35	Jan. 23, 1884,	7	8		May 3, "	Pneumonia	"	3, Widow	Widow
404	Hugh Foley,	St. John, 13,	60	June 20, 1889,	1	10	23	May 23, "	Nic Bronclitis	"	9, "	Sister
405	Jeremiah Lane,	St. Columbkille, 65,	26	March 17, 1888,	3	2		May 16, "	Acute Tuberculosis	"	7, Moth., sis's & bros.	Son
406	Thomas F. Meagher,	St. 6,	60	Jan. 23, 1811,	3		29	May 29, 1890,	Heart Disease	"	1, Son	Son
407	Michael McCready,	Cathedral, 1,	34	Jan. 26, 1888,	3	3		Oct. 3, "	Phthisis	"	1, Child	Guardian
408	John J. Claxton,	St. 1,	35	Feb. 8, 1882,	9	4		June 10, 1891,	Tuberculosis	"	2, Uncles	Uncles
409	Daniel H. Drew,	Hamilton, 17,	57	May 27, 1881,	10	0	24	June 24, "	Phthisis	"	4, Widow and child'n	Widow
410	Patrick Flynn,	Sol, 35,	48	July 6, 1880,	11		29	July 5, "	Typhoid Fever	"	4, "	"
411	Thomas O'Flynn,	Highland, 52,	45	April 16, 1883,	8		22	July 13, "	Tuberculosis following accident	"	1, "	"
412	Daniel Keohane,	Cathedral, 1,	29	May 1889,	2	1	12	July 13, "	Tuberculosis	"	1, Gin	Gin
413	Daniel Sullivan,	La Fayette, 14,	54	Aug. 4, 1886,	5		0	Aug. 3, "	Cerebral Hemorrhage	"	3, Daughters	Daughters
414	John Goggins,	Fenwick, 3,	57	Oct. 1810,	5		16	March 30, "	Heart Disease	"	3, Widow and child'n	New and child'n
415	Jeremiah Barry,	St. 67,	44	Sept. 25, 1890,		11	9	Sept. 5, "	Railroad Accident	"	5, "	"
416	Jeremiah Murphy,	Bass River, 30,	54	Feb. 24, 1881,	10	6	15	Sept. 9, "	Brights Disease	"	4, "	"

No.	Name	Post, Age		Date of Admission			Date of Death	Cause of Death	Amount	Dependents	Relationship
417	Jeremiah Grady,	Williams, 19,	37	Jan. 3, 1881	10 8 3	Sept. 6, 1891		Bright's Disease	$1,000	3, Children	Guardian
418	Frederick McGreary,	[m], 66,	23	Sept. 12, 1887	3 5 23	March 5,		Accidental blow on head	"	1, Father	Father
419	William St. Croix,	Americus, 84,	48	[h] 16, 1886	4 9 2	Sept. 18,		Bright's Disease	"	4, Wdw and child'n	Widow
420	[Jhs Bre]nan,	St. Thomas, 29, 71,	46	June 14, 1883	8 8 18	Oct. 10,		Bright's Disease	"	6, "	"
421	John [My],	Phil Sheridan, 71,	42	Feb. 5, 1880	2 8 5	Oct. 17,		Paralysis	"	10, "	"
422	James B.	Cheverus, 6,	51	Feb. 11, 1880	11 6 11	Oct. 18,		Bronchitis	"	7, "	"
423	Lawrence [Ghell],	[Rex], 16,	45	April 5, 1886	5 6 19	Oct. 24,		Paralysis	"	5, Brothers & sisters	Sister
424	James H. Neagle,	Hamilton, 17,	48	Aug. 1, 1881	2 5 27	Oct. 28,		Heart Disease	"	3, Widow and child'n	[Wdw]
425	Wm. P. McCarthy,	Americus, 84,	28	May 1, 1881	10 0 28	Nov. 24,		Consumption	"	3, "	"
426	Thomas F. [Giley],	St. Lawrence, 61,	44	Oct. [h], 1886	3 11 11	Nov. 18,		Intestinal [obstruction]	"	2, "	"
427	Benj. J. Shorten,	La Fayette, 14,	41	[h] 7, 1887	10 8 7	Nov. 16,		Pleurisy	"	10, "	"
428	Thomas Murphy,	St. John, 33,	56	March 8, 1881	8 2 7	Nov. 20,		Cerebral Embolism	"	1, Sister	Sister
429	James Mahoney,	Sherwood, 8,	46	Sept. 22, 1881	6 3 23	Dec. 9,		Consumption	"	4, Widow and child'n	Widow
430	Thomas O'Neil,	Prospect, 58,	49	Aug. 16, 1885	1 7	Dec. 22,		Pneumonia	"	1, Father	Father
431	Michael J. Downey,	Gen. Sherman, 80,	35	March 7, 1891	7 8 8	Dec. 25,		Heart Disease	"	2, Mother & brother	Mother
432	J. J. Ryan,	[m], 67,	25	March 17, 1890	13 14	Dec. 19,		Typhoid Fever	"	2, Widow and child	[Wdw]
433	P. R. Quinlan,	[Scht], 20,	30	March 31, 1884	7 13	Dec. 29,		Spinal Inflammation	"	6, Widow and child'n	"
434	Patrick Killion,	St. Alphonsus, 21,	60	Oct. 15, 1880	11 2	Dec.		Pneumonia	"	4, "	"
435	John Moore,	[m], 73,	32	[Mh] 9, 1891	11 9 20	Jan. 8, 1892		Peritonitis	"	8, "	"
436	Hugh McConnell,	St. Francis, 4,	60	[April] 8, 1880	8 2 0	Jan. 6,		Congestion of Lungs	"	7, Children	Guardian
437	Thomas F. English,	St. Mary, 43,	40	June 7, 1889	2 9 4	Jan. 24,		Phthisis Pulmonalis	"	6, Wdw and child'n	Widow
438	Jnes Foley,	Williams, 19,	37	[Mh] 18, 1881	10 17	Jan. 19, 1881		Phthisis	"	7, "	"
439	Matthew Hanley,	St. Mary, 43,	44	May 18, 1882	9 11	Jan. 22, 1882		Tuberculosis Pulmonalis	"	6, "	"
440	James M. Holland,	St. Francis, 4,	29	Feb. 12, 1888	3 11 20	Jan. 2,		Acute Jaundice	"	1, [Mer]	Mother
441	William F. Dugan,	Gallagher, 64,	48	Feb. [2], 1884	2 11	Feb. 18,		Paralysis and Phthisis	"	1, Mother	Mother
442	William Nolan,	St. Gregory, 24,	41	Oct. 2, 1882	9 11 16	Feb. 20,		[dn]	"	6, Wdw and child'n	Widow
443	John Flanigan,	St. Peter, 18,	51	Oct. 8, 1883	8 4 12	Feb. 1,		[dn]	"	6, "	"
444	William Woods,	Charles River, 55,		Nov. 23, 1880	3 1	Feb. 24, 1880		Pneumonia	"	10, "	"
445	George Burns,	Fitzpatrick, 13,	46	Aug. 10, 1881	9 11	July 21, 1891		Hemorrhage of Lungs	7,	1, Dependent	Dependent

FINANCIAL CONDITION OF COURTS.

AMOUNTS RECEIVED FOR INITIATION FEES, COURT DUES AND ASSESSMENTS.

No. of Court.	NAME OF COURT.	Received for Initiation Fees 1891.	Received for Court Dues	Received for Endowment Fund	Per Capita for High Court Received 1891.	Received for Withdrawal Cards 1891.	Received from Other Sources 1891.	Received for Reserve Fund 1891.
1	Cathedral	$19.00	$446.75	$1,719.80	$162.00	....	$55.12	$81.00
3	Fenwick	....	86.67	700.40	66.00	....	....	33.00
4	St. Francis	27.00	471.75	1,249.80	117.00	....	44.40	63.00
5	Leo	13.00	305.75	1,067.20	....	....	121.90	54.00
6	Cheverus	45.00	183.05	1,103.35	95.00	.25	....	57.50
7	St. Patrick	6.00	131.75	501.60	45.00	....	38.83	22.50
8	Sherwood	47.00	424 00	1,632.80	....	....	142.75	78.00
9	Columbus	12.00	152.14	418.40	44.00	....	6.80	25·00
10	Iona	21.00	293.75	1,066.00	92.00	.25	226.70	51 50
11	St. Joseph	20.00	354.25	1,365.10	125.25	....	....	....
12	Fulton	42.00	99.75	353.10	34.00	....	.50	24.00
13	Fitzpatrick	....	138 00	481.10	50.00	....	2.94	24.50
14	Lafayette	41.00	231.90	825.40	80.00	....	7. 0	42.00
15	SS. Peter and Paul	9.00	202.00	711.50	68 00	....	27.08	36.00
16	Essex	41.00	315.45	1,113.75	101 55	....	7.65	55.45
17	Hamilton	....	212.00	810.00	65.00	....	....	32.50
18	St. Peter	33.00	261.45	865.40	86.00	....	5 5	46.50
19	Williams	42.00	482.00	797.60	83.00	....	0.50	47.50
20	Mt. Pleasant	12.00	242.25	814.20	79.00	1.00	13.98	41.00
21	St. Alphonsus	–3.00	151.35	561.90	50.00	....	....	24.50
23	St. John	21.00	103 35	466.40	46.25	....	9.00	20.00
24	St. Gregory	21.00	201.00	679.10	67.00	.50	....	38.00
25	St. Francis	30.00	321.00	1,161.60	....	....	116.16	58.50
26	St. Raphael	8.00	141.75	457.15	....	....	2.25	....
28	Erin	27.00	270.75	1,009 30	93.00	.25	....	50.50
29	St. Thomas	84.00	413.80	1,536 30	176.00	.50	59 50	88.50
30	Bass River	9.00	132.00	495 80	....	....	156.74	22.00
32	Qualey	36.00	184.25	499.20	43.50	....	8.25	28.00
33	St. John	12.25	214.10	615.00	59 90	....	78.70	32 60
34	Americus	30.00	210.35	804.20	66.00	.25	2.30	37.50
35	Sheil	....	61.30	213.85	21.00	....	....	10.50
37	Friendship	3.00	138.00	429.10	46.00	.25	....	23.00
38	St. Joseph	3.00	123.60	521 85	42.00	....	....	22 00
39	Benedict	9 00	38.70	344.50	28.00	....	....	15.00
41	Star of the Sea	....	71.25	337.30	29.00	....	....	15.50
43	St. Mary	15.00	54.00	350 00	33.00	....	....	20.50
44	St. Bernard	....	93.00	440.10	44.00	.25	30.00	23.00
45	Unity	11.00	138 00	485.00	45.00	.25	44.82	24 50
46	St. Augustine	21.00	86.25	312.10	28.00	....	....	17.00
47	St. Anne	....	....	....	....	....	....	....
48	Sarsfield	6.00	256.00	965.60	85.00	....	227.00	43.50
49	Constantine	24.00	196.45	749.40	67.75	.25	5.00	41.00
51	Holy Trinity	96.00	251.55	1,275.40	131.00	....	134.14	67.50
52	Highland	6.00	61.25	246.30	22.00	....	....	11.00
53	Emerald	51.00	280.00	978.40	95.75	.75	98.91	59.50
54	St. James	3.00	182.50	575.10	53 75	....	139.09	29.50
55	Charles River	37.00	119.05	860.30	85.00	....	137.89	47.00
57	Carroll	11.00	52.90	444.75	36.25	....	172.94	21.00
58	Prospect	13.00	100.55	405.70	30.25	....	....	16.00
59	Worcester	35.00	187.00	794.80	80.00	....	35.15	41.00
60	Middlesex	....	....	....	....	....	....	....
61	St. Lawrence	66.00	205.50	731.30	71.00	....	31.20	39.50
62	St. Catherine	6.00	205.50	653.90	69.00	....	92.30	35.00
63	Shields	46.00	169.20	334.50	32.00	....	10.75	15.00
64	Gallagher	25.00	183 95	665.50	61.75	....	115.54	33.05
65	St. Columbkille	13.00	180 75	609.05	54.00	....	189.80	28.00
66	Griffin	21.00	57.10	477.30	49.00	....	....	24.50
67	Canton	10.00	212.00	723.90	74.00	....	212.30	41.00
68	St. Margaret	....	68.50	283.35	27.00	....	26.25	12.00
69	Stoughton	39 00	165.60	681.50	72.00	....	322.93	42.50
70	St. Michael	2.00	106.25	357.30	36.00	....	28.73	15.50
71	Phil Sheridan	5.00	119.47	749.40	77.75	.25	318.40	40.50
72	Merrimack	63.00	173.50	570.10	63.00	....	299.20	39.50
73	Taunton	22.00	140.40	1,227.05	109.00	....	1,235.47	63.00
74	Hendricken	5.00	78.25	317.10	35.00	....	217 65	17.50
75	St. Jarlath	21.00	407.57	540.90	55.00	....	327.40	29.50
76	Quincy	....	....	....	....	....	....	....
77	Mystic	12.00	124.25	453.20	41.00	.25	33.65	20.00
78	St. Monica	18.00	67.50	236.30	23.00	....	48.00	13.00
79	J. B. O'Reilly	93.00	57.90	191.20	20.00	.25	22.21	10.00
80	Gen. Sherman	95.00	90.30	175.50	26.00	....	102.50	27.00
81	St. Malachi	81.00	21 35	80.20	....	....	11.00	13 00
82	Brockton	....	....	....	....	....	....	....
83	J. H. Newman	90.00	....	18.90	....	....	10.00	6.50
	Total	1,788.25	11,704.55	46,689.45	3,990.70	5.50	5,964.12	2,332.60

FINANCIAL CONDITION OF COURTS.
Amounts Paid for Assessments Per Capita, Reserve and Detailed Expenses.

NAME OF COURT.	Paid Endowment Calls 1891.	Paid H. C. Per Capita 1891.	Paid for Rent 1891.	Paid for Salaries of Officers 1891.	Paid Medical Examiner 1891.	Paid H. C. P. 1891.	Paid for Sick Benefits 1891.	Paid Court Physician for Attendance on Members 1891.	Paid for Other Expenses 1891.	Paid Reserve Fund 81.
hedral	$1,706.80	$167.00	$70.00	$90.00			$94.45	$121.50	$219.06	$87.50
wick	700.40	66.00	24.00	49.00					4.93	33.00
Francis	1,230 30	117.00	99.50	100.00	$15.75	$2.25		115.50	184.37	65.00
	1,079.60	99.00	64.00	62.50	7.00	.75	105.00	101.00	32.63	51.50
verus	1,103.35	95.00	60.00	43.10	26.25	3.75			42.40	57.50
Patrick	515.40	45.00	60.00	50.00	3.50	.50		45.00	32.03	22.50
rwood	1,632.80	152.00	68.00	125.00	28.00	4.00		153.00	98.50	78.00
umbus	415.70	44.00	84.00	27.00	7.00	1.00			69.20	22.00
a	1,066.00	92.00	50.00	40.00	12.25	4.75		92.50	252.20	46.50
Joseph	1,355.20	132.50	60.00	62.00	7.00			132.00	77.56	65.50
tou	343.00	34.00	52.00	10.00	26.25	3.75		53.75	12.40	21.50
patrick	481.10	50.00	40.50	32.00					53.75	24.50
ayette	826 60	80.00	36.00	32.00	24.50	3.50	11.10	88.00	38.95	42.00
Peter and Paul.	711.50	68.00	60.00	40.00	5.25	.75			100.55	36.00
ex	1,324.10	120.00	156.00	25.00	22.75	3.25			168.81	60.00
ilton	812 40	65.00	60.00	67.00				50.00	34.20	32.50
eter	881.75	86.00	61.50	45.00	19.25	2.75	5.00	86.00	18.47	48.50
liams	810.80	83.00	66.00	15.05	24.50	4.00	235.00	85.00	103.30	47.50
Pleasant	817.60	79.00	72.00	54.38	7.00	1.00	10.25	60.00	55.49	41.00
p onsus	561.90	50.00	69.00	44.10	1.75	.25			19.70	24.50
John	466.40	46.25	62.50		10.50	1.25			55.44	20.00
Gregory	702.00	68.00	78.00	52.00	12.25	1.75		46.00	120.80	36.00
anc s	1,161.60	116.00	90.00	97.25	21.00	3.50		108.00	121.02	58.50
Raphael	463.70	45.00	50.00			1.00		46.00	8.50	23.50
a	980.60	93.00	66.00	75.00	15.75	2.25		92.25	14.75	47.00
Thomas	1,536.30	176.00	158.00	82.50	57.75	5.00	60.40	104.50	403.43	86.50
s River	492.40	45.00	36.00	12.00	10.50	1.25	80.00	50.00	57.70	22.00
ley	502.00	46.00	45.00	18.00	21.00	3.00	60.00	14.70	31.23	28.00
John	615.00	59.90	60.00	16.75		.25	130.00	56.25	19.75	32.10
ericus	777.20	80.00	60.00	37.50	17.50	2.50	11.60	84.00	21.55	12.00
il	221.50	21.00	24.00	13.50					5.25	10.50
endship	429.10	46.00	72.00	30.00	1.75	.25		11.50	10.77	23.00
oseph	527.00	43.00	60.00		1.75	.25		52.50	2.70	22.00
ene c	344.50	28.00	25.00		5.25	.75			10.50	15.00
r of the Sea	337.30	29.00	25.00					48.00	11.80	15.50
Mary	350.00	33.00	20.75		10.50	.75			4.82	20.50
Bernard	447.20	45.00	40.00	22.50					36.65	22.00
ty	481.40	45.00	35.00		7.00	1.00		93.00	27.19	24.00
Augustine	312.10	28.00	60.00		12.25	1.75		8.00	12.60	16.00
Anne.										
field	966.20	85.00	150.00	25.00	3.50	.50	12.00	133.50	145.50	42.50
stantine	679.15	69.00	46.00	32.00	14.00	2.00			26.61	38.50
y Trinity	1,217.70	131.00	79.50	45.00	61.25	8.75			233.72	67.50
hland	263.50	23.00	27.00		3.50	.75			9.55	11.50
erald	947.20	95.75	150.00	25.00	31.50	4.50	15.00	94.50	102.59	59.50
James	598.30	60.00	66.00	29.50	1.75	.25	15.75		113.43	27.50
rles River	875.20	89.00	75.00	18.75	22.75	3.25	1.75		42.05	47.00
roll	462.10	45.00	84.00	12.60	8.75	1.25			8.60	23.00
pect	426.10	63.00	33.00		8.75	1.25			9.50	18.00
cester	794.80	80.00	47.50	36.90	5.25	3.25		74.50	81.44	41.00
dlesex										
Lawrence	722.30	71.00	70.00	43.20	47.25	6.75		70.76	116.75	37.50
Catherine	728.00	69.00	69.50	15.00	3.50	.50	100.00	77.50	105.38	34.00
lds	335.80	32.00	48.00		36.75		60.00		77.35	13.50
agher	633.35	62.75	67.25	60.00	10.50	1.75			130.07	32.00
Columbkille	609.05	54.00	103.50	47.45					136.91	28.00
n	477.30	49.50	30.00		8.75	1.25			88.79	24.50
on	719.40	74.00	30.00				57.00		135.22	42.00
argaret	294.10	29.00	40.00					58.00	9.75	14.00
ghton	659.00	74.00	157.00	27.00	22.75	3.25	27.15	35.50	245.98	42.00
Michael	415.40	38.00	104.00						57.75	19.50
Sheridan	749.40	77.75	72.00	31.10			171.31		106.53	40.50
rimack	539.70	63.00	60.00	9.95	35.00	5.75	25.00		245.65	41.00
nton	1,227.05	109.00	500.00	50.00	14.00				333.02	55.00
dricken	317.10	35.00	90.00		3.50	.50		33.50	172.90	17.50
arlath	542.30	55.00	231.62	26.65	14.00	2.00	130.00		164.38	29.50
ncy										
tic	453.20	41.00	60.00	30.00	7.00	1.00		39.75	92.81	20.00
Monica	236.30	23.00	51.25		10.50	1.50			26.75	13.00
. O'Reilly	91.20	20.00	41.50		54.25	7.75			24.99	10.00
. Sherman	146.40	28.00	49.50		54.25	7.75			74.40	27.00
Malachi	79.20		17.50		47.25	6.75			37.65	12.00
ekton										
I. Newman					52.50	7.50			30.00	
	46,829.40	4,663.40	5,030.37	2,035.23	1,025.50	142.50	1,417.76	2,615.46	5,780.97	2,369.60

FINANCIAL CONDITION OF COURTS.

No. of Court.	NAME OF COURT.	Balance on Hand Dec. 31, 1890.	Total Receipts 1891.	Total Expenditures 1891.	Total Balance on Hand Dec. 31, 1891.	Deficit from Business of 1891.	Bal. from Business of 1891.	Endowment Fund on Hand Dec. 31, 1891.	General Fund on Hand Dec. 31, 1891.	Contingent Fund on Hand Dec. 31, 1891.	Special Fund on Hand Dec. 31, 1891.	Court Reserve Fund on Hand Dec. 31, 1891.
1	Cathedral	$409.86	$2,483.67	$2,556.31	$337.22	$72.64			$269.32			
3	Fenwick	7.28	886.07	877.33	16.02		$8.74		16.02			
4	St. Francis	136.08	1,895.95	1,929.67	179.36	41.18	43.28	38.20	141.16	85.50	$83.00	
5	Leo	375.92	1,561.85	1,602.98	334.79			40.90	122.89			2.50
6	Cheverus	32.80	1,484.15	1,431.35	85.60		52.80		85.60			
7	St. Patrick	123.65	768.68	773.93	95.40	28.25			76.40		19.00	
8	Sherwood	67.84	2,324.55	2,339.80	663.09	14.75			663.09			
9	Ros	72.39	658.34	669.90	60.83	11.56		17.60	12.93	6.05		24.25
10	Iona	179.80	1,751.20	1,656.20	274.80	27.16	95.00		156.27	74.53	68.75	44.00
11	St. Joseph	129.59	1,864.60	1,891.76	102.43	3.30		41.25	37	18.10		
12	Fulton	57.39	553.35	556.65	54.09			10.10	41.49			2.50
13	Fitzpatrick	83.97	696.51	681.85	98.66		14.69		87.77	10.89		
14	Lafayette	158.78	1,227.30	1,182.65	203.43		44.65		203.43			
15	SS. Peter and Paul	169.51	1,054.18	1,022.05	201.64		32.13		201.64			
16	Essex	379.79	1,635.05	1,879.41	43	244.36			43			
17	Hamilton	8.82	1,119.50	1,121.10	7.22	1.60			7.22			
18	St. Peter	205.43	1,342.90	22	294.11		88.68		243.56		50.55	
19	Lee	381.62	1,456.10	1,474.15	363.57	18.05		3.20	37		46.00	3.50
20	Mt. Pleasant	176.03	1,203.43	1,197.72	674		5.71	11.75	166.49			
21	St. Alphonsus	76.39	790.75	771.20	95.94		19.55		95.94			
23	St. John	112.66	666.00	634	116.32		3.66		56.32		60.00	
24	St. Gregory	101.15	1,060	1,116.30	60	109.70			28.79	67.00		
25	St. Francis	185.40	1,687.26	1,776.87	95.79	89.61		49.70	63.41	352.73		3.50
26	St. Raphael	91.96	609.15	637.70	63.41	28.55		16.10	162.80			2.00
28	Erin	151.80	1,450.80	1,386.60	216.00		64.20		162.80			
29	St. Thomas	396.81	2,358.60	2,730.38	25.03	371.78		48.10	6.33			
30	Bass River	65.79	806.85	768.93	48		8.69		74.48			
32	Bay	201.74	1,020	900	232.01		30.27		106.49	77.42		
33	St. John	78.70	655	275	101.25		22.55		101.25			
34	Americus	158.09	1,150.60	1,103.85	204.84		46.75	37.50	40.84	49.52	51.48	25.50
35	Sheil	58.37	306.65	624.37	69.27	10.90		23.50	45.77			
36	Friendship	65.25	639.35	709.20	85.23	14.98		43.25	36.98	5.00		
38	St. Joseph	80.00	124.5	429.00	83.25	3.25		3.00	21.25	31.00	28.00	
39	Benedict	4.00	435.20	429.00	10.20		6.20		10.20			
41	Star of the Sea	85.26	453.05	466.60	71.71				71.71			
43	St. Mary	18.27	472.50	440.32	50.45	18.55	32.18		50.45			

FINANCIAL CONDITION OF COURTS—Continued.

44	St. Bernard	$13.34	$630.35	$618.35	$30.34		$17.00	$56.90	$30.34			$3.50
45	Unity	219.66	748.57	713.59	314.64		34.98		254.24			7.00
46	St. Augustine	88.34	464.35	450.70	101.99		13.65		53.59	$11.40		
47	St. Anne											
48	Sarsfield	41.36	1,583.10	1,563.70	60.76		19.40		60.76			
49	Constantine	154.58	1,083.85	907.26	231.17		176.59	84.75	241.42	5.00		
51	Holy Trinity	147.51	1,955.59	1,844.42	258.68		111.17	120.20	88.55		49.98	
52	Highland	45.63	346.55	338.80	53.38		7.75		53.38			
53	Emerald	151.00	1,564.81	1,525.54	189.77		38.77	30.40	159.37			
54	St. James	190.75	982.94	912.48	261.21		70.46		261.21			
55	Charles River	197.72	1,286.24	1,174.75	309.21		111.49	101.30	209.91			
57	Carroll	203.55	738.84	645.30	297.09		93.54			292.29	4.80	
58	Prospect	9.08	565.50	559.60	14.98		5.90		14.98			
59	Worcester	140.54	1,313.49	1,164.64	148.85		8.31		28.56	89.79		30.50
60	Middlesex											
61	St. Lawrence	137.86	1,144.50	1,185.51	96.85	41.01		16.90	77.95			2.00
62	St. Catherine	94.93	1,061.70	1,202.38	54.25	140.68			54.25			
63	Shields	71.17	607.45	603.40	75.22		4.05	27.70	45.00		1.00	1.50
64	Gallagher	67.23	1,084.79	997.67	154.35		87.12	60.05	93.80			1.50
65	St. Columbkille	244.73	1,074.60	978.91	340.42		95.69		122.69	217.73		
66	Griffin	132.31	629.40	680.09	81.62	50.69			2.30			79.32
67	Canton	431.04	1,273.20	1,057.62	646.62		215.58	18.90	7.84	364.48	255.40	
68	St. Margaret	88.61	417.10	444.85	60.86	27.75			56.86	4.00		
69	Stoughton	306.51	1,323.53	1,293.r8	336.41		29.90	21.80	314.61			
70	St. Michael	100.18	545.78	634.65	11.31	88.87			11.31			
71	Phil Sheridan	275.00	1,310.77	1,254.59	331.18		56.18		67.04		264.14	
72	Merrimack	325.59	1,208.30	1,025.05	508.84		183.25	46.40	181.47		279.97	1.00
73	Taunton	181.33	2,796.92	2,288.07	630.18		508.85		500.85		181.33	8.00
74	Hendricken	39.42	670.50	670.00	39.42		.50		39.42			
75	St. Jarlath	228.84	1,381.87	1,196.85	413.36		184.52	18.90	125.93	213.16	73.77	
76	Quincy											
77	Mystic	152.35	684.85	744.76	70.50		43.50		22.50			
78	St. Monica	27.00	405.80	862.30	44.87		44.87		44.87		48.00	
79	J. B. O'Reilly		394.56	349.69								
80	Gen. Sherman		516.80	387.30	129.00		129.00	29.10	19.90	80.00		1.00
81	St. Malachi		206.55	200.35	6.20		6.20	1.00	4.20			
82	Brockton											
83	J. H. Newman		125.40	90.00	35.40		35.40	18.90			10.00	6.50
	Total	$10,031.94	$73,614.21	$71,876.59	$11,683.54	$1,324.39	$2,982.48	$1,086.95	$7,107.19	$2,065.59	$945.12	$250.07

ENDOWMENT FUND.

Dr.

Assessment Call No. 71	$29 30	
" " " 74	1 30	
" " " 75	1 30	
" " " 76	65 10	
" " " 77	105 90	
" " " 78	155 30	
" " " 79	935 60	
" " " 80	5,083 00	
" " " 81	5,166 65	
" " " 82	5,346 60	
" " " 83	5,378 90	
" " " 84	5,356 20	
" " " 85	5,460 60	
" " " 86	5,594 70	
" " " 87	5,567 20	
" " " 88	5,160 10	
" " " 89	49 30	
		$49,457 05
Balance, April 22, 1891		10,172 24
		$59,629 29

Cr.

Daniel Cronin,	of St. Joseph,	No. 11	$1,000 00
Martin Havey.	" St. Francis,	" 4	1,000 00
Terence McGowan,	" Sarsfield,	" 48	1,000 00
James H. Fox,	" Constantine,	" 49	1,000 00
Patrick Quinn,	" St. Joseph,	" 11	1,000 00
W. F. Hastings,	" St. Anne,	" 47	1,000 00
William Clancy,	" St. Joseph,	" 11	1,000 00
John Ready,	" Erin,	" 28	1,000 00
Michael Dunphy,	" St. Francis,	" 25	1,000 00
Francis Kenney,	" Charles River,	" 55	1,000 00
Hugh Foley,	" Fitzpatrick,	" 13	1,000 00
Jeremiah Lane,	" St. Columbkill,	" 65	1,000 00
J. F. Meagher,	" Cheverus,	" 6	1,000 00
Michael McCready,	" Canton,	" 67	1,000 00
J. J. Claxton,	" Cathedral,	" 1 ...	1,000 00
D. H. Drew,	" Sheil,	" 35	1,000 00
Patrick Flynn,	" Hamilton,	" 17	1,000 00
Thomas O'Flynn,	" Highland	" 52 ...	1,000 00

Daniel Keohan,	of Cathedral,	No. 1....$1,000 00	
Daniel Sullivan,	" Lafayette,	" 14.... 1,000 00	
John Goggins,	" Fenwick,	" 3.... 1,000 00	
Jeremiah Barry,	" Canton,	" 67.... 1,000 00	
Jeremiah Murphy,	" Bass River,	" 30.... 1,000 00	
Jeremiah Grady,	" Williams,	" 19.... 1,000 00	
Frederick McGroary,	" Griffin,	" 66.... 1,000 00	
William St. Croix,	" Americus,	" 34.... 1,000 00	
Thomas Brennan,	" St. Thomas.	" 29.... 1,000 00	
John Crowley,	" Phil. Sheridan,	" 71.... 1,000 00	
James B. Shannon,	" Cheverus,	" 6.... 1,000 00	
Lawrence Campbell,	" Essex,	" 16.... 1,000 00	
J. H. Neagle,	" Hamilton,	" 17.... 1,000 00	
W. P. McCarthy,	" Americus,	" 34.... 1,000 00	
Thomas F. Gooley,	" St. Lawrence,	" 61.... 1,000 00	
Benjamin Shorten,	" Lafayette,	" 14.... 1,000 00	
Thomas Murphy,	" St. John,	" 33.... 1,000 00	
James Mahoney,	" Sherwood,	" 8.... 1,000 00	
Thomas O'Neil,	" Prospect,	" 58.... 1,000 00	
M. J. Downey,	" Gen. Sherman,	" 80.... 1,000 00	
J. J. Ryan,	" Canton,	" 67.... 1,000 00	
P. R. Quinlan,	" Mt. Pleasant,	" 20.... 1,000 00	
Patrick Killion,	" St. Alphonsus,	" 21.... 1,000 00	
John Moore,	" Taunton,	" 73.... 1,000 00	
H. McConnell,	" St. Francis,	" 4.... 1,000 00	
Thomas F. English,	" St. Mary,	" 43.... 1,000 00	
James Foley,	" Williams,	" 19.... 1,000 00	
Matthew Hanley,	" St, Francis,	" 4.... 1,000 00	
James M. Holland,	" Gallagher,	" 64.... 1,000 00	
William F. Dugan,	" St. Gregory,	" 24.... 1,000 00	
William Nolan,	" St. Peter,	" 18.... 1,000 00	
John Flanigan,	" Charles River,	" 55.... 1,000 00	
William Woods,	" Iona,	" 10.... 1,000 00	
George Burns,	" Fitzpatrick,	" 13.... 1,000 00	

$52,000 00

7,629 29

GENERAL FUND.

Dr.

Balance, April, 1891.............................	$119 78	
Sale of Postal Cards, Books, &c	800 57	
Per Capita, 1890..................................	1 75	
" " 1891..................................	4,747 65	
Charters...	215 00	
Benefit Certificates...............................	67 50	
		$5,952 25

Cr.

RENT.

Estate of James Parker :

Rent of office at 611 Washington St., to April 1, 1892....	$400 00

POSTAGE.

Boston Post Office :

Stamped Envelopes and Stamps................	$172 55	
Postal Cards................................	495 50	
		$668 05

REGALIA.

Frederick Alford :

2 Sets Badges.............................	$17 00	
1 " 2 extra........	10 06	
. "	8 50	
1 " repaired	5 00	
1 "	0 78	
1 " repaired	5 00	
2	17 00	

W. J. Dinsmore :

1 Ballot Box................................	1 50	

Boston Regalia Co. :

2 Ballot Boxes.............................	2 20	
12 Gavels..................................	3 50	
2 Ballot Boxes.............................	2 20	
2 "	2 20	
15 Dozen Ballots...........................	1 80	
		76 74

1144.79

STATIONERY.

S. Hobbs & Co.:

6 Document Boxes...........................	$3 50	
Blotting Paper and Pens....................	2 35	
1 Blank Book...............................	5 75	
1 "	3 00	
1 Quart Mucilage...........................	0 75	
1 Blank Book...............................	3 75	
6 Document Boxes...........................	3 75	
1 Gross Pencils.............................	1 00	
1 Dozen Blank Books........................	b 0U	
3 Stylographic Pens........................	3 75	
1 Fountain Pen.............................	2 00	
Rubber and Seals...........................	0 30	
	———	$35 90

SEALS.

S. M. Spencer:

1 Seal.....................................	$5 00	
1 Rubber Stamp............................	1 60	
Repairs on Stamp..........................	2 11	
2 Seals....................................	10 00	
1 Rubber Stamp............................	0 25	
1 Seal.....................................	5 00	
1 "	5 00	
2 "	10 00	
	———	38 96

TRAVELLING EXPENSES.

Deputy High Chief Rangers:

A. H. McDonald. Brockton, North Eaton ..	$8 80	
" " "	4 50	
" " "	8 70	
A. M. Lanigan, Dedham, Norwood............	6 50	
W. H. Rogers, Franklin....................	7 00	
" "	15 00	
John F. Reilly, No. 34, No. 49..............	3 30	
F. L. Smith, No. 21, No. 20.................	4 00	
" No. 21, No. 20.................	3 00	
R. Farrenkopf, Dorchester, Hyde Park........	5 00	
James Cashin, No. 4, No. 70	10 00	
James F. Fleming, No. 52, No. 57............	1 25	
D. F. Buckley, Stoughton...................	5 00	
J. J. Crean, Chicopee......................	1 50	
J. F. Carens, Haverhill, Amesbury...........	9 50	
James P. Duffy, Watertown, Quincy.........	5 28	
John Hayes, Boston, Beverly, Beverly Farms..	5 15	
Richard Dwyer, Newburyport, Lawrence......	5 56	
D. F. Sullivan, Malden, Canton..............	11 20	
	———	120 24

226.89

High Standing Committee:

1,000 Mile Ticket Boston & Maine Railroad....	$20 00
In Boston...............................	2 50
In Boston...............................	0 95
To Gloucester.	2 00
In Boston...............................	5 15
In Boston...............................	7 50
To Haverhill............................	5 40
In Boston...............................	2 50
To Salem and Quincy......................	0 95
To Plymouth............................	7 50
To Framingham..........................	3 50
To Dedham	0 50
1,000 Mile Ticket Old Colony Railroad........	20 00
1,000 Mile Ticket Boston & Maine Railroad....	20 00
To Salem and Beverly.....................	4 32
To Amesbury and South Framingham.........	14 91
To Neponset.............................	4 83
In Boston...............................	1 60
To Arlington............................	4 24
"	0 75
" (3 trips)......................	10 83
1,000 Mile Ticket Old Colony Railroad........	20 00
To Middleboro'..........................	7 25
To Beverly..............................	2 50
In Boston...............................	3 00
To Everett..............................	0 77
To Newburyport.........................	1 60
To Beverly	2 50
To Brookline............................	5 00
To East Boston..........................	5 00
To Brockton, Roxbury....................	12 25
To Everett..............................	8 70
To Gloucester...........................	0 50
In Boston...............................	0 75
In Boston...............................	0 75
To Canton and Stoughton..................	2 20
To Everett..............................	10 00
To Beverly Farms........................	1 31
To Brockton............................	13 20
To Everett..............................	10 75
To Arlington............................	9 10
To New Bedford.........................	1 40
1,000 Mile Ticket Boston & Maine Railroad....	20 00
To Gloucester...........................	2 50
To Lynn................................	2 10
To Taunton.............................	5 20
To Plymouth............................	4 90
In Boston...............................	5 00
To Medford and Boston...................	6 60

1339.89

In Boston...................................	$4 00	
To Danvers.................................	3 39	
To Hyde Park, Brighton.....................	8 95	
To Lynn	1 85	
To Danvers.................................	4 55	
To Arlington...............................	2 25	
To Taunton	2 75	
To Danvers.................................	10 10	
To Fall River..............................	3 10	
To Brockton................................	2 30	
In Boston...................................	1 60	
To East Cambridge.........................	9 05	
To Lynn....................................	12 39	
To Avon....................................	2 60	
To Danvers.................................	1 05	
To Lynn....................................	6 14	
To Danvers.................................	0 60	
1,000 Mile Ticket Old Colony Railroad........	20 00	
To Malden	0 85	
To New Bedford............................	15 95	
To Walpole.................................	18 10	
"	2 70	
To Avon....................................	3 05	
In Boston...................................	0 75	
To Springfield.............................	1 50	
To Walpole.................................	5 95	
In Boston...................................	1 20	
1,000 Mile Ticket Boston & Albany Railroad...	20 00	
	———	$471 48

PRINTING.

Cashman, Keating & Co.:		
1,000 Constitutions.......................	$28 50	
500 Note Circulars........................	3 00	
	———	
	$31 50	
Less Allowance..........	13 45	
	———	18 05
The Eastburn Press:		
3,500 Annual Reports......................	$260 80	
2,000 Constitutions.......................	53 00	
1,000 "	28 00	
300 Annual Reports.......................	173 00	
Engraving, Seal and Electro................	8 00	
	———	522 80
Eustis Towle:		
Assessment Call...........................	$4 00	
1,000 D. H. C. R. Visits (duplicates)...... ...	2 50	
500 Notices (Application Missing).............	1 50	
7 Lots Postal Cards.......................	4 90	
List D. H. C. Rangers.....................	3 00	

√352. 22

500 Letter Heads.............	$1	75
Benefit Certificates.............	16	00
1,000 Application for Charter.................	5	00
5 Lots Postal Cards.........................	3	50
Assessment Call.............................	4	00
7 Lots Postal Cards.................	4	90
1,000 Circulars (half-letter)..................	4	50
Assessment Call $1.50.......................	4	00
Credentials (Rep. and proxy).................	7	00
Call for Convention..........................	2	00
1,000 Envelopes.............................	2	50
Ballots	6	75
1,000 Envelopes.............................	3	75
1,000 Key to Certificate......................	4	50
5 Lots Postal Cards..................	3	50
250 Half-Note Circulars	1	75
Assessment Call.............................	4	00
1,000 Duplicate Receipts.....................	3	00
Treasurer and Financial Secretary Bonds......	5	00
500 Notices of Meetings.....................	2	00
5 Lots Postal Cards..........................	3	50
Assessment Call.............................	4	00
19 Lots Financial Statements.................	16	15
9 Lots Postal Cards..........................	6	30
Assessment Call.............................	4	00
5 Lots Financial Statements.................	4	25
2,250 Envelopes.............................	8	50
List of Medical Examiners....................	3	50
List of D. H. C. Rangers....	4	50
7 Lots Postal Cards..........................	4	90
	$164	90

L. F. Clarke:

Financial Statements........................	$5	70
Assessment Call.............................	4	00
D. H. C. R. Reports	3	50
Report of Members..........................	4	00
Financial Statements........................	4	00
Roll of Officers.............................	2	50
Roll of Members............................	4	00
Assessment Call.............................	4	00
20 Lots Postal Cards.........................	14	00
1,000 Envelopes.............................	2	10
15 Lots Postal Cards.........................	10	50
2,000 Withdrawal Cards......................	6	00
Assessment Call.............................	4	00
11 Lots Financial Statements.................	9	35
6 Lots Postal Cards.........................	4	20
50 Stub Receipt Books.......................	21	00
2,000 Envelopes.............................	5	50

2517.1

250 Circulars	$ 1 75	
Assessment Call	4 09	
2,000 Letter Heads	7 00	
8 Lots Postal Cards	5 60	
2,000 Envelopes	3 00	
38 Lots Financial Statements	32 30	
Assessment Call (Reserve)	4 00	
Letter Heads	3 50	
Assessment Call	4 00	
7 Lots Postal Cards	4 90	
Benefit Certificates	25 75	
4 Lots Postal Cards	2 80	
		$207 15

MISCELLANEOUS.

John M. Foster, Salem, Hall for Convention	$ 20 00	
McCrillis & Co., Salem, Catering for Convention	174 00	
C. Bowen, Moving Safe	5 00	
H. M. Temple, Catering for Convention	37 00	
J. J. Banta, Halls for Convention	20 00	
N. E. R. Pub. Co., for A B C Pathfinder to Mar. 14, '92	5 00	
Expenses of Convention	14 00	
Sampson, Murdock & Co., Boston Directory	5 00	
J. A. Blaisdell, Lettering Office Door	2 95	
Samuel Hano Co., 24 Receipt Books	29 00	
J. E. Duffy, Arlington, Rent of Hall	4 00	
Div. 23, A.O.H., " "	2 50	
W. M. Belcher & Co., 1 Caligraph	85 00	
M. O'Brien, Repairs on Book Case	5 00	
H. W. Upham, Binding Constitutions and Reports	56 10	
James Green, Lynn, Rent of Hall	3 00	
W. M. Belcher, Ribbon for Typewriter	1 00	
S. M. Spencer, Numbering Stamp	26 04	
Boston Gas Light Co	15 86	
Cleaning Office	8 75	
Convention Expenses	27 95	
"	16 50	
1 Gross Pencils	1 00	
N. E. Medical Register	2 50	
Preliminary Expenses in Brockton	20 50	
" in Lynn	3 00	
" in Avon	12 40	
Telegrams, Messengers and Expressing	14 80	
		$617 85

| Salary High Secretary-Treasurer to April, 1892 | 2,000 00 | |
| Balance on hand | 704 81 | 60 |

| Due from Courts for Books and Cards | 323 60 | |

93.

DEPUTY HIGH CHIEF RANGERS.

For Term of 1892-93.

DIS-TRICT.	COURTS. No.	NAME AND RESIDENCE OF D. H. C. R.	COURT OF WHICH D. H. C. R. IS A MEMBER.
1	Cathedral............ 1 ⎱ Fitzpatrick.........13 ⎰	J. B. Rooney, Walpole....................	Robert Emmett..87
2	Fenwick............. 3 ⎱ Cheverus........... 6 ⎰ St. Joseph.........11	George F. Low, 271 Summer Street, E. Boston...	Leo 5
3	St. Francis......... 4 ⎱ Carroll.............57 ⎰	P. M. Keating, 83 Pemberton Square, Boston....	St. Joseph.......11
4	Leo .... 5 ⎱ Lafayette...........14 ⎰ Williams 19	Garret H. Keefe, 63 Palmer Street, Roxbury.......	Mt. Pleasant.....20
5	St. Patrick.......... 7 ⎱ SS. Peter and Paul..15 ⎰ Qualey 32	Michael J. Collins, 10 G Street, South Boston.. ...	St. James....... 54
6	Sherwood........... 8 ⎰	Thomas W. O'Rourke, 108 Boston St., Dorchester.......	St. James.......,54
7	Columbus........... 9 ⎱ St. Francis.........25 ⎰ Erin 28	E. F. Chamberlain, Mattapan.....................	St. Peter.........18
8	Iona................10 ⎱ Mystic..............77 ⎰ John Henry Newman.83	J. B. Buckley, Malden.......................	Iona 10
9	Fulton..............12 ⎰	E. A. Dever, 120 Eustis Street, Roxbury......	Mt. Pleasant.....20
10	Essex...............16 ⎱ St. Augustine.......46 ⎰ St. Michael.........70	J. T. Mahoney, 10 Rand St., Boston Highlands..	Cathedral........ 1
11	Hamilton...........17 ⎰	H. C. Griffin, No. 8 Eaton Street, Boston	St. Joseph.......11
12	St. Peter...........18 ⎰	John Vogel, West Quincy...................	St. Francis.......25
13	Mt. Pleasant........20 ⎱ Quincy.............76 ⎰	F. L Smith, 12 Bryant Street, Brockton......	St. Thomas......29
14	St. Alphonsus.......21 ⎱ Highland...........52 ⎰ St. James...........54	J. F. Fleming, 1 Prentiss Place, Roxbury........	Columbus 9
15	St. John...........23 ⎱ Friendship ....37 ⎰	R. Farrenkopf, 108 Kneeland Street, Boston.....	Sherwood.... ... 8
16	St. Gregory.........24 ⎱ Sarsfield............48 ⎰	Michael Edmonds, 18 Gay Head Street, Roxbury...	Cathedral........ 1
17	St. Raphael.........26 ⎱ St. Catharine.......62 ⎰	A. M. Lanigan, 664 Harrison Avenue, Boston.....	Cathedral... ... 1
18	St. Thomas.........29 ⎱ Hendricken.........74 ⎰	A. H. McDonald, Stoughton	Stoughton 69
19	Bass River.........30 ⎱ St. Margaret........68 ⎰ George Washington..85	Timothy Donovan, Adams Street, Lynn.............	Lafayette 14
20	St. John............33 ⎱ St. Joseph..........38 ⎰	T. F. Crosby, Parker Hill Avenue, Roxbury....	St. Francis....... 4
21	Americus...........34 ⎱ Constantine ....49 ⎰	J. F. Riley, Dedham.....................	St. Raphael......26
22	Sheil...............35 ⎱ Danvers............84 ⎰	P. A. Sullivan, 19 Wareham Street, Boston......	Americus........84

DEPUTY HIGH CHIEF RANGERS—*Continued.*

DIS-TRICT.	COURTS.	No.	NAME AND RESIDENCE OF D. H. C. R.	COURT OF WHICH D. H C. R. IS A MEMBER.
23	Benedict .... 39 St. Malachi. 81		**Wm. A. Flaherty,** 261 Washington St., Somerville..	Benedict......... 39
24	St. Mary.......... 43		**A. A. Clarke,** North Easton..................	Hendricken......74
25	St. Bernard......... 44 Middlesex 60		**J. A. Burns,** Watertown....................	Charles River. ...55
26	Unity 45		**Willam Condon,** High Street, Bridgewater........	Unity.......... 45
27	St. Anne............ 47		**D. J. Horrigan,** 133 Boston Street, Salem........	Emerald..... ...53
28	Holy Trinity........ 51		**D. A. Cronin,** 8 Allen Street, Boston...........	St. Joseph.......11
29	Emerald............ 53		**P. F. J. Carney,** 42 Buffom Street, Salem.........	Essex........... 16
30	Charles River....... 55		**John E. Briston,** Newton......................	Middlesex 60
31	Prospect........... 58		**T. F. Gallagher,** Bemis........................	Charles River....55
32	Worcester 59		**J. H. Fitzgerald,** 21 Spruce Street, Worcester	Worcester.......59
33	St. Lawrence....... 61 St. Columbkille..... 65		**P. O'Loughlin,** 23 Court Street, Boston..........	St. Joseph.......11
34	Shields............. 63		**P. J. Murray,** 356 Chestnut Street, Springfield..	Gallagher........64
35	Gallagher.......... 64		**J. J. Callanan,** 107 Dwight Street, Holyoke......	Shields.......... 63
36	Griffin............. 66		**William H. Rogers,** Washington St., North Attleboro.	Sarsfield......... 48
37	Canton............. 67		**P. F. Brady,** Canton.......................	Canton 67
38	Stoughton.......... 69		**D. F. Buckley,** North Easton.................	Hendricken......74
39	Phil Sheridan....... 71 St. Monica.......... 78 Enterprise.......... 88		**D. H. Maguire,** Bradford.....................	Merrimac........72
40	Merrimack.......... 72 St Jarlath.......... 75		**James F. Carens,** 20 Fair Street, Newburyport.....	Phil Sheridan 71
41	Taunton........... 73 J. B. O'Reilly....... 79 Gen. Sherman...... 80		**J. G. Fennessey, P. H. C. R.** New Court House, Boston.......	St. James........54
42	Brockton......... 82 Avon.............. 86		**W. H. Linnehan,** 156 N. Warren Ave., Brockton...	St. Thomas......29
43	Robert Emmett..... 87		**F. S. Sullivan,** 35 Garfield Street, Hyde Park....	St. John........ 23
	AT LARGE.....		**P. Smith, P.V.H.C.R.,** E.Boston **J. H. Watson, P.H.C.R.,** Bev. F's **T. Sproules, P.V.H.C.R.,** Rox. **E. A. Irvine,** North Attleboro. **G. F. Brammer,** Taunton. **J. H. Donovan,** 50 Broad St. Boston	

MEDICAL EXAMINERS.

For Term Ending April, 1893.

| Dist. | Place. | Examiner. | Courts. |

1 Boston.........................S. A. CALLANAN, M. D.,
Warren St., cor. Warren
Place, Roxbury..........1, 12, 34.

2 Roxbury........................F. J. McQUEENEY, M. D.,
35 W. Dedham Street.....3, 6, 13.

3 Roxbury, Brookline..............Joseph P. MURPHY, M, D.,
1607 Tremont St., Rox.,
also at Brookline.... .....4, 61, 52.

4 East Boston.....................JAMES F. FERRY, M. D.,
10 Chelsea St., E. B.........5, 19.

5 South Boston....................WM. H. DEVINE, M. D.,
599 Broadway, S. B., 7, 15, 46, 54, 70.

6 Roxbury.........................THOMAS M. SHAY, M. D.,
88 Warren Street, Rox...8, 35, 37.

7 Boston ....WM. G. McDONALD, M. D.,
221 Shawmut Avenue...11, 28, 51.

8 Boston..........................F. T. MARA, M. D.,
93 Broadway, S. B..........9, 49.

9 Malden..........................C. D. McCARTHY, M. D.....10.

10 Lynn............... ....C. A. AHEARNE, M. D......14.

11 Salem.......... ....FRANCIS E. HINES, M. D....16, 84.

12 Somerville........ ....J. A. GREGG, M. D........17, 33, 39.

13 Dorchester......................J. P. LUMBARD, M. D.........18, 24.

14 Boston..........................E. T. GALLIGAN, M. D.,
88 Warren St., Rox.....20, 21, 38.

15 Hyde Park.......................JOHN C. LINCOLN, M. D....23.

16 Quincy..........................JOSEPH M. SHEAHAN, M. D. 25.

17 Dedham..........................A. H. HODGDEN, M. D...... 26.

18 Brockton........................BENEDICT DONOVAN, M. D..29.

19 Beverly ....T. J. HAYES, M. D.........30, 68.

MEDICAL EXAMINERS — *Continued.*

20 Woburn ....J. H. Conway, M. D........32.
21 Randolph......................O. M. Sheridan, M. D .....43, 86.
22 West Newton....................C. J. McCormick, M. D....44, 58.
23 Bridgewater ....:G. H. Watson, M. D.......45.
24 Gloucester......................Philip Mooney, M. D.....47.
25 North Attleborough. ....T. P. McDonough, M. D....48.
26 Peabody......................John Shannahan. M. D.....53.
27 Watertown.....................M. J. Kelley, M. D........55.
28 Jamaica Plain...................J. P. Broidrick, M. D.....57.
29 Worcester.....................J. H. Kelly, M. D.........59.
30 Newton.........................F. M. O'Donnell, M. D.....60.
31 Norwood......................:.L. N. Plympton, M. D.....62, 87.
32 Holyoke.......................F. P. Donoghue, M. D......63.
33 Springfield ....A. J. Dunne, M. D.........64.
34 Franklin.......................J. C. Gallison, M. D.......66.
35 Brighton......................H. V. McLaughlin, M. D..65.
36 Canton ....Thos. D. Lonergan, M. D..67.
37 Stoughton.....................Michael Glennon, M. D...69.
38 Newburyport....................J. J. Healy, M. D.........71.
39 Haverhill ....John F. Croston, M. D....72.
40 Taunton.......................J. B. Murphy, M. D.......73.
41 North Easton...................T. H. McCarthy, M. D....74.
42 Amesbury......................J. H. O'Toole, M. D.......75.
43 Quincy......................S. M. Donovan, M. D......76.
44 Medford.......................J. B. Mahoney, M. D.......77.
45 Lawrence......................D. J. O'Sullivan, M. D....78.
46 New Bedford...................J. F. Sullivan, M. D......79.
47 Plymouth......................Edgar D. Hill, M. D......80.
48 Cambridge ....Joseph D. Couch, M. D.....81.
49 Brockton......................T. P. Conlan, M. D..82, 89, Rockland
50 Everett........................P. J. Conroy. M. D........83
51 West Lynn.....................J. A. McGuigan, M. D.....85.
52 West Newbury, also Amesbury.....D. D. Murphy, M. D.......88,
53 Winchester....................C. H. Winn, M. D.......Winchester.
54 Portland.......................J. B. O'Neil, M. D........

REPRESENTATIVES.

	REPRESENTATIVES.	COURT.	No.	PROXY REPRESENTATIVES.
1	J. J. Lanigan.......	Cathedral...........	1	N. M. Williams.
2	M. Edmonds.......	"	"	Jeremiah Sullivan
3	M. J. Mahoney. .	"	"	A. M. Lanigan.
4	Daniel J. Gallagher.	Fenwick...........	3	Patrick J. O'Connell.
5	W. E. Shay........	St. Francis........	4	T. F. Crosby.
6	Michael J. O'Brien..	"	"	James P. Cleary.
7	John Brant........	Leo..............	5	Daniel Hayes.
8	George F. Lowe.....	"	"	D. F. McCallion.
9	Owen A. Galvin.....	Cheverus...........	6	William T. Rich.
10	James Cashin.......	"	"	James W. Maguire.
11	Joseph F. Carroll...	St. Patrick.........	7	Henry P. Muldoon.
12	John P. Dore......	Sherwood..........	8	Rudolph Farrenkopf.
13	D. F. Sullivan.....	"	"	Hugh Montague.
14	Alfred J. Lill.......	"	"	Charles E. Colbert.
15	James F. Supple....	Columbus..........	9	Charles E. Stumcke.
16	John M. Neville.....	Iona..............	10	M. C. Desmond.
17	P. H. Desmond.....	"	"	Thomas Tracy.
18	P. F. McGaragle....	St. Joseph.........	11	Henry C. Griffin.
19	Daniel A. Cronin...	"	"	M. Dolan.
20	Patrick M. Keating..	"	"	Patrick O'Loughlin.
21	James Finegan......	Fulton.............	12	Henry F. Scanlan.
22	James Cullinane....	Fitzpatrick........	13	John Feeney.
23	Michael J. Malone...	Lafayette..........	14	John Hayes.
24	James O'Neil.......	"	"	Timothy Donovan.
25	Peter J. McKenna..	SS. Peter & Paul...	15	Patrick A. Donovan.
26	P. F. J. Carney.....	Essex..............	16	John J. Hartigan.
27	Daniel J. O'Brien...	"	"	John B. Harding.
28	Dr. F. E. Hines.....	"	"	James J. Murphy.
29	John Hurley.......	Hamilton..........	17	John A. Finnegan.
30	John J. Curran.....	St. Peter..........	18	E. F. Chamberlain.
31	John H. Donovan...	"	"	Hugh J. McNabb.
32	F. S. Maloney.....	Williams..........	19	M. J. Kelly.
33	Philip Smith.......	"	"	James Douglass.
34	John F. Dever......	Mt. Pleasant.......	20	Edward A. Dever.
35	Frank J. McGrath...	"	"	Wm. J. Downing.
36	Francis A. Mahan...	St. Alphonsus......	21	Patrick Hurley.
37	Thomas Murray....	St. John...........	23	Thomas Mulcahy.
38	Thomas P. Lockney.	St. Gregory........	24	John O'Callaghan.
39	John Cole.........	St. Francis.........	25	M. F. O'Brien.
40	John Vogel........	"	"	T. J. Foley.
41	T. P. Murray......	St. Raphael........	26	Bernard J. McCaffrey.
42	John T. Daly......	Erin..............	28	Daniel Shannon.
43	Jeremiah O'Mara...	"	"	C. J. Lynch.
44	John E. Saxton.....	St. Thomas........	29	James P. Conley.
45	Wm. Linnehan.....	"	"	Timoth F. Roach.
46	F. L. Smith.......	"	"	Daniel Connolly.
47	Philip Fitzgibbon ..	Bass River.........	30	Patrick Stanton.
48	James Dolan.......	Qualey............	32	Thomas D. Hevey.
49	Daniel J. Donovan..	St. John..........	33	Bernard J. Brogan.
50	J. J. McLaughlin....	Americus..........	34	J. W. Brown.
51	Richard T. Purcell..	"	"	Michael Leonard.
52		Sheil..............	35	

REPRESENTATIVES.—*Continued.*

	REPRESENTATIVES.	COURT.	No.	PROXY REPRESENTATIVES.
53	John W. Riley......	Friendship...........	37	J. W. Keenan.
54	Peter Morris........	St. Joseph...	38	John P. Ego.
55	JosephD.Couch,M.D.	Benedict	39	William A. Flaherty.
56	M. P. O'Connor.....	St. Mary.............	43	W. W. Hurley.
57	B. D. Farrell.......	St. Bernard.........	44	M. J. Duane.
58	William Condon....	Unity	45	Patrick A. Reynolds.
59	John Doolin........	St. Augustine.......	46	Francis M. Hughes.
60	John J. Flaherty....	St. Anne.............	47	John F. Riley.
61	William Moore.....	''	''	Thomas J. Carroll.
62	John P. Zilch.......	Sarsfield.............	48	Patrick Ryan.
63	Wm. H. Rogers.....	''	''	Thomas E. Kiely.
64	John J. Kilroy......	Constantine..........	49	William T. Maloney.
65	J. Torndorf, Jr.....	Holy Trinity........	51	Martin Hasenfuss.
66	G. Kranefuss.......	''	''	Henry Wesling.
67	F. Schwaab........	''	''	C. Reiser.
68	J. J. Corbett........	Highland.............	52	Hugh H. Collins.
69	John J. Sweeney....	Emerald.............	53	Thos. F. Lyons.
70	James M. Regan....	''	''	David J. Horrigan.
71	Jere. G. Fennessey..	St. James	54	Michael J. Collins.
72	John J. Herlihy.....	Charles River.....,..	55	E. J. Burke.
73	M. E. Conroy.......	''	''	Peter McGrath.
74	J. H. Loughan......	Carroll	57	J. D. Fallon.
75	David Walsh.......	Prospect..............	58	William F. Rooney.
76	James H. Fitzgerald.	Worcester	59	Timothy H. Murphy.
77	....	Middlesex............	60	
78	Michael Driscoll ...	St. Lawrence........	61	Patrick Johnson.
79	James T. Donovan..	''	''	Jere. T. Crotty.
80	John B. Rooney.....	St. Catherine.........	62	G. A. O'Bryan.
81	F. F. O'Neil........	Shields...............	63	John Riley.
82	John J. Toomey.....	Gallagher............	64	John J. Leonard.
83	William Mackin....	St. Columbkille......	65	Geo. F. Mitchell.
84	M. F. Conroy.......	Griffin	66	A. F. Staples.
85	Owen F. Sullivan...	Canton...............	67	Edw. C. Murphy.
86	Lawrence J. Watson.	St. Margaret.........	68	Thomas M. Dix.
87	John S. Madden....	Stoughton............	69	A. H. McDonald.
88	J. H. Coughlin.....	St. Michael..........	70	J. T. Costello.
89	James F. Carens....	Phil Sheridan........	71	J. J. Dunn.
90	Robert E. Burke....	''	''	A. E, Moylan.
91	R. Dwyer..........	Merrimack............	72	D. H. Maguire.
92	Benj. Morris........	Taunton	73	Francis P. Conaty.
93	George F. Brammer.	''	''	J. H. Cosgrove.
94	Daniel F. Buckley...	Hendricken..........	74	William J. Heelan.
95	T. F. Lynes........	St. Jarlath	75	J. H. O'Toole, M. D.
96	....	Quincy...............	76	
97	John Crowley.......	Mystic...............	77	John W. Lynch.
98	John H. Cronin.....	St. Monica...........	78	Andrew Caffrey.
99	....	John Boyle O'Reilly,	79	
100	Henry S. Healy. ...	Gen. Sherman........	80	James J. Noble.
101	Patrick A. McCarthy.	St. Malachi..........	81	Daniel C. Kelleher.
102	John Kent..........	Brockton.............	82	
103	F. Frederick Driscoll.	JohnHenryNewman	83	Thomas F. Hickey.
104	....	Danvers..............	84	
105	J. B. McCarthy.....	Geo. Washington ...	85	Richard Nagle.......
106	P. E. McGonnigle...	Avon..................	86	J. F. Sheehan........
107	....	Robert Emmett.....	87	

DIRECTORY.
NAMES OF COURTS, TIME AND PLACE OF MEETING, OFFICERS AND THEIR ADDRESSES.

NO. AND COURT NAME.	OFFICERS.		ADDRESS.	
1. Cathedral, Boston. Instituted Sept. 8, 1879. Meets 1st and 3rd Wednesday, St. Rose Hall, 17 Worcester St., Boston.	C. R. R. S. F. S. T.	John T. Mahoney..... W. P. Walsh .... Joseph A. Barry...... Thos. J. Dunn........	10 Rand Street, 38 Worcester Square, 99 E. Lenox Street, 521 Harrison Avenue,	Roxbury Boston Boston Boston
3. Fenwick, Boston. Inst. Nov. 14, 1879. Meets 2nd Thursday, Lusitana Hall, 164 Hanover St., Boston.	C. R. R. S. F. S. T.	P. J. Heasley......... Jeremiah J. Crane.... John Keenan......... John J. Irving........	184 Salem Street, 9 Hill Street. 7 North Hanover Court, 6 Hichborn Street,	Boston Charlestown Boston Revere
4. St. Francis, Roxbury. Inst. Dec. 18, 1879. Meets 1st and 3rd Wednesday, Tremont Hall, 1435 Tremont St., Roxbury.	C. R. R S. F. S. T.	William F. Finneran.. Thos. F. Crosby ...... Thomas J. Finneran.. J. J. O'Brien........	74 Smith Street, Parker Hill Avenue, 780 Parker Street, 4 Vernon Place,	Roxbury Roxbury Roxbury Roxbury
5. Leo, East Boston. Inst. Jan. 16, 1880. Meets 2nd and 4th Wednesday, Knights of Honor Hall, 144 Meridian St , East Boston.	C. R. R. S. F. S. T.	John Brant.......... Daniel A. Galvin .... James H. Donovan.... Michael Galligan	315 Paris Street, 439 Bennington Street, 110 Porter Street, 81 Webster Street,	East Boston East Boston East Boston East Boston
6. Cheverus, Boston. Inst. Feb. Feb. 11, 1880. Meets 1st and 3rd Monday, Foresters' Hall, 9 Elm St.	C. R. R. S. F. S. T.	James W. Maguire.... James Cashin........ Wiliam T. Rich .... Edward O'Hara.......	461 Main Street, 52 Nashua Street, 44 Cooper Street, 59 Chestnut Street,	Charlestown Boston Boston Charlestown
7. St. Patrick, South Boston. Inst. Feb 16, 1880. Meets 2nd and 4th Monday, Tonta Hall, 327 E St.	C. R. R. S. F. S. T.	Thos. F. Toomey ..... Wm. J. Broderick..... J. J. Mahoney........ James Cahill	321 Fourth Street, 237 Dorchester Street, 282 Bowen Street, 317 Silver Street,	South Boston South Boston South Boston South Boston
8. Sherwood, Boston. Inst. March 4, 1880. Meets 2nd and 4th Thursday, St. Rose Hall, 17 Worcester St.	C. R. R. S. F. S. T.	James Delury......... John J. McDonald.... A. J. Lill .... Thomas J. Lane......	50 Oak Street, 1147 Dorchester Avenue, 3 Champney Place, 121 Centre Street,	Boston Dorchester Boston Roxbury
9. Columbus, Boston. Inst. March 9, 1880. Meets 2nd Monday, Lincoln Hall, 19 Essex St., Boston.	C. R. R. S. F. S. T.	R. J. Brooks .... Richard D. Cleary.... M. T. Gleason........ M. T. Milliken	11 Gardiner Avenue, 778 Parker Street, 43 Milton Avenue, 282 E Street,	Roxbury Roxbury Dorchester South Boston
10. Iona, Malden. Inst. March 15, 1880. Meets 1st and 3rd Thursday, Deliberative Hall, Pleasant St., Malden	C. R. R. S. F. S. T.	John M. Neville...... Dennis Kelliher....... Edmund Flavin ...... Paul J. McMahon....	55 Hubbard Street, 39 Sherman Street, 130 Commercial Street, 288 Main Street,	Malden Malden Malden Malden
11. St. Joseph, Boston. Inst. March 22, 1880. Meets 2nd and 4th Wednesday, Y. M. L. Hall, 60½ Leverett St.	C. R. R. S F. S. T.	Daniel A. Cronin ..... John P. McGee ..... Chas. W. Mullen .... Daniel Carney.......	8 Allen Street, 19 Parkman Street, 17 Parkman Street, 5 Revere Street Place,	Boston Boston Boston Boston
12. Fulton, Boston. Inst. March 18, 1880. Meets 1st and 3rd Friday, Carroll Hall, 375 Harrison Avenue, Boston.	C. R. R. S. F. S. T.	Michael Nolan........ James T. Kilroy...... Henry F. Scanlan .... Daniel O'Brien.......	38 Hampden Street, 1 Lovedeed Court, 117 Union Park Street, 14 Village Street,	Boston Roxbury Boston Boston
13. Fitzpatrick, Boston. Inst. May 5, 1880. Meets 2nd and 4th Tuesday, Sawainmote Hall, 164 Hanover St.	C. R. R. S. F. S. T.	James Cullinane...... Michael Cleary .... Antonio Thompson.... Charles J. Jordan	43 Charter Street, Rear 43 Charter Street, 5 Vernon Place, 3 Vernon Place,	Boston Boston Boston Boston
14. Lafayette, Lynn. Inst. June 8, 1880. Meets 1st and 3rd Wednesday, Emmett Hall, 65 Munroe St.	C. R. R. S. F. S. T.	Michael S. Keenan ... Geo. E. Monroe....... John Driscoll......... Timothy Donovan.....	149 Broad Street, 54 Linden Street, Adams Street,	Lynn Lynn Lynn Lynn

53

DIRECTORY — Continued.

No. and Court Name.	Officers.		Address.	
15. S.S. Peter & Paul, So. Boston.	C. R.	Thomas Desmond	250 W. Fourth Street,	South Boston
Inst. June 25, 1880.	R. S.	Patrick R. Reardon...	144 Athens Street,	South Boston
Meets 1st and 3rd Tuesday, Tonta	F. S.	John S. McGann......	70 Tudor Street,	South Boston
Hall, 327 E St.	T.	Thomas Sullivan......	13 Mercer Street,	South Boston
16. Essex, Salem.	C. R.	James J. Murphy.....	8½ Allen Street,	Salem
Inst. June 23, 1880.	R. S.	John B. Tirnan.......	Howard Street,	Salem
Meets 1st and 3rd Wednesday,	F. S.	Arthur Hennessey....	31 Ocean Avenue,	Salem
Mansfield Hall, 199 Essex St.	T.	Michael A. Dodd.....	6 High Street,	Salem
17. Hamilton, Charlestown.	C. R.	John Hurley.........	28 Mt. Vernon Street,	Charlestown
Inst. July 8, 1880.	R. S.	William Mittlestadt...	11 Berwick Street, North	Somerville
Meets 2nd and 4th Friday, Lin-	F. S.	Patrick A. Quinlan...	119 Medford Street,	Somerville
coln Hall, Warren St.	T.	James Crowley.......	70 Ferrin Street,	Charlestown
18. St. Peter, Dorchester.	C. R.	James H. Dixon......	Davidson Avenue,	Dorchester
Inst. July 22, 1880.	R. S	Edward T. Shields....	196 Bowdoin Street,	Dorchester
Meets 1st and 3rd Thursday,	F. S.	Dennis J. Coleman....	1385 Dorchester Avenue,	Dorchester
Blake's Hall, Field's Corner.	T.	James J. Kelly.......	14 Bowdoin Street,	Dorchester
19. Williams, E. Boston.	C. R.	James Douglass	377 Sumner Street,	East Boston
Inst. Sept. 16, 1880.	R. S.	M. J. Kelly..........	107 Paris Street,	East Boston
Meets 1st and 3rd Monday, O. F.	F. S.	Francis M. Kievenaar.	306 Sumner Street,	East Boston
Hall, Maverick Sq.	T.	Thomas Arthur	69 Maverick Square,	East Boston
20. Mt. Pleasant, Roxbury.	C. R.	John W. Bogue.......	20 Copeland Street,	Roxbury
Inst. Oct. 20, 1880.	R. S.	M. W. Kelly..........	37 Woodward Avenue,	Roxbury
Meets 2nd and 4th Monday, K. of	F. S.	Edward A. Dever.....	120 Eustis Street,	Roxbury
H. Hall, 2319 Washington St.	T.	David O'Brien	30 Mall Street,	Roxbury
21. St. Alphonsus, Roxbury.	C. R.	Patrick F. Shea	62 Whitney Street,	Roxbury
Inst. Oct 13, 1880.	R. S.	Francis A. Mahan....	36 Delle Avenue,	Roxbury
Meets 2nd and 4th Wednesday,	F. S.	John Killion	8 Oscar Street,	Roxbury
Gurney Hall, Gurney St.	T.	Cornelius McCarthy..	36 Carey Street,	Roxbury
23. St. John, Hyde Park.	C R.	R. J. Sullivan........	77 Water Street,	Hyde Park
Inst. Dec. 14, 1880.	R. S.	Mark B Gill	Central Park Ave.,	Hyde Park
Meets 2nd and 4th Monday, Odd	F. S.	George James	68 Pierce Street,	Hyde Park
Fellows Hall, Everett Sq., H. P.	T.	F. S. Sullivan	35 Garfield Street,	Hyde Park
24. St Gregory, Milton.	C. R.	Thomas P. Lockney...	Cor.Codman St.and Dor. Ave.,	Boston
Inst. Dec. 20, 1880.	R. S.	Michael Dunican	Box 87,	East Milton
Meets 3rd and 3rd Tuesday, Asso-	F. S.	Frank A. Duffy.......		Mattapan
ciate's Hall.	T.	Patrick Fallon........	River Street,	Mattapan
25. St. Francis, W. Quincy.	C. R.	J. L. Fennessey		West Quincy
Inst. Sept. 21, 1880.	R. S.	Patrick Hughes......		West Quincy
Meets 2nd and 4th Tuesday, For-	F. S.	T. J. Lamb..........		West Quincy
esters' Hall, W. Quincy.	T.	Michael Dineen.......		West Quincy
26. St. Raphael, Dedham.	C. R.	John F. Barrett	Walnut Hill,	Dedham
Inst. Dec. 31, 1880.	R. S.	John F. Riley		Dedham
Meets 1st and 3rd Sunday, Me-	F. S.	Charles J. Hurley.....		Ashcroft
chanics Hall, Dedham.	T.	P. O'Sullivan........	Walnut Hill,	Dedham
28. Erin, Boston.	C. R.	John J. Madden......	190 Athens Street,	South Boston
Inst. Feb. 3, 1881.	R. S.	C. J. Lynch	10 Shelburn Street,	Dorchester
Meets 2nd and 4th Tuesday, St.	F. S.	Peter D. O'Meally	278 D Street,	South Boston
Rose Hall, 17 Worcester St.	T.	J. O'Mara...........	93 Pembroke Street,	Boston
29. St. Thomas, Brockton.	C R	Patrick McCarthy	30 Packard Street,	Brockton
Inst. Feb 17, 1881.	R. S.	Thos. J. O'Rourke....	29 Emmet Street,	Brockton
Meets 1st and 4th Thursday, For-	F. S.	John Shay...	68 Eliot Street,	Brockton
esters' Hall, Centre St.	T.	Daniel Connolly.. ...	33 Packard Street,	Brockton
30. Bass River, Beverly.	C. R.	P M. Riordan........	16 Rantoul Street,	Beverly
Inst. Feb. 24, 1881.	R. S.	Philip Fitzgibbon.....	42 Abbott Street,	Beverly
Meets 1st and 3rd Thursday,	F. S.	John Geary	20 Rantoul Street,	Beverly
Y. M. C. T. Hall, 87 Cabot St.	T.	Timothy Hennessey...	16 Pleasant Street,	Beverly
32. Qualey, Woburn.	C. R.	James Dolan	64 Fowle Street,	Woburn
Inst. March 2, 1881.	R. S.	John Maguire	121 Main Street,	Woburn
Meets 1st and 3rd Wednesday,	F. S.	Frank E. Tracey......	59 Prospect Street,	Woburn
Hibernian Hall, Main St.	T.	Wm. O'Brien	20 Church Avenue,	Woburn

No. and Court Name.	Officers.		Address.
33. St. John, E. Cambridge. Inst. March 3, 1881. Meets 1st and 3rd Friday, G. A. R. Hall, Cambridge St.	C. R. R. S. F. S. T.	Bernard J. Brogan .... Peter Gardner .... John O'Connell ..... Jos. J. Kelly	Cor. Otis and Sixth Sts., E. Cambridge 29 Warren Street, Cambridgeport 143 Gore Street, E. Cambridge 110 Otis Street, E. Cambridge
34. Americus, Boston. Inst. March 15, 1881. Meets 2nd and 4th Wednesday. St. Rose Hall, 17 Worcester St.	C. R. R. S. F. S. T.	John T. Whyte ...... John J. Griffin .... Michael Leonard ..... J. Henry Gramer	1 Andrews Place, Boston 141 Beach Street, Boston 98 E. Canton Street, Boston 32 Thornton Street, Boston
35. Sheil, Boston. Inst. March 18, 1881. Meets 1st Friday, Y. M. L. Hall, 70½ Leverett Street.	C. R. R. S. F. S. T.	Cornelius J. Kelly.... John C. Carson....... Thos. Jacobs .... Thos. Jacobs..........	27 Courtland Street, Everett 6 Charter Street, Boston 3 Lexington Avenue, Charlestown 3 Lexington Avenue, Charlestown
37. Friendship, Roxbury. Inst. March 25, 1881. Meets 1st and 3rd Monday, St. Rose Hall, 17 Worcester St.	C. R R. S. F. S. T.	Jeremiah J. Buckley.. Edward N. Lee ...... John F. Dolan........ Thomas H Duggan...	2 Rogers Court, Roxbury 3 Reins Place, Roxbury 1335 Tremont Street, Roxbury 130 Camden Street, Roxbury
38. St. Joseph, Roxbury. Inst. March 29, 1881. Meets 2nd and 4th Thursday, K. of Honor Hall, 2319 Washington St.	C. R. R. S. F. S. T.	John J. Fox.......... Wm. B. Reardon .... John P. Ego .... M. Lennon..........	Grove Hall, Dorchester 384 Warren Street, Boxbury 411 Warren Street, Roxbury Grove Hall, Dorchester
39. Benedict, Somerville. Inst. March 31, 1881. Meets 3rd Thursday, Temperance Hall, Hawkins St.	C. R. R S. F. S T.	John J. McGonagle... Michael Harrington .. William A. Flaherty... Cornelius McGonagle.	Linden Street, Somerville Greenville Street, Somerville 261 Washington Street. Somerville Linden Street, Somerville
43. St. Mary, Randolph. Inst. Sept. 4, 1882. Meets 1st Monday, Hibernian Hall, Porter's Block.	C. R. R. S. F. S. T.	Charles S. Dolan .... M. F. Cunningham ... John P. Brady....... Patrick Brady.......	Randolph Randolph Randolph Randolph
44. St. Bernard, West Newton. Inst. Sept. 23, 1882. Meets 1st and 3rd Monday, For- ester's Hall, Waltham St.	C. R. R. S. F. S. T.	M. J. Duane......... Thos. C. Donovan .... John W. Gaw........ James Dolan	River Street, West Newton Sharon Avenue, West Newton Auburndale Avenue, West Newton Auburndale Avenue, West Newton
45. Unity, Bridgewater. Inst. Sept. 12, 1882. Meets 2nd and 4th Tuesday, Benevolent Hall, Centre St.	C. R. R. S. F. S. T.	Patrick A. Reynolds.. Michael Cashon ...... William Condon...... Thos. Daniher........	Oak Street, Bridgewater Box 42, Bridgewater High Street, Bridgewater Bedford Street, Bridgewater
46. St. Augustine, So. Boston, Inst. Nov. 14, 1882. Meets 2nd and 4th Thursday, Tonta Hall, 327 E St.	C. R. R. S. F. S. T.	John Doolin .... John M. Rigby....... Bernard Flanagan ... J. F. McNulty.......	211 Third Street, South Boston 42 W. Fifth Street, South Boston 730 E. Second Street, South Boston 12 Woodward Street, South Boston
47. St. Anne's, Gloucester. Inst. Dec. 22, 1882. Meets 1st and 3rd Tuesday, G. A. R. Hall, 171 Main St.	C. R. R. S. F. S. T.	Chas. O'Brien .... Edw. J Downey..... John Kincade........ Daniel Carroll........	56 Warner Street, Gloucester 10 Fort Square, Gloucester 22 Sadler Street, Gloucester 5 Shepherd Street, Gloucester
48. Sarsfield, No. Attleborough. Inst. March 6, 1883. Meets every Tuesday, cor. East and Elm Streets.	C. R. R. S. F. S. T.	James H. Carley...... Wm. Doyle.......... John B. Alternath... James B. Smith	36 West Street, N Attleborough N. Attleborough Mt. Hope Street, N. Attleborough Chestnut Street, N. Attleborough
49. Constantine, Boston. Inst. April 5, 1883. Meets 2nd and 4th Friday, Carroll Hall, 375 Harrison Ave.	C. R. R. S. F. S. T.	James T. Riley....... John J. Dolan........ James A. Berrill...... John Carroll.........	2 Pearl Place, Somverille 8 Oxford Place, Boston Hotel Gloucester, Boston 375 Harrison Avenue, Boston

DIRECTORY — Continued.

No. and Court Name.	Officers.	Address.	
51. Holy Trinity, Boston.	C. R.	Henry Wesling.......	135 Thornton Street,	Roxbury
Inst. April 13, 1883.	R. S.	George Wirth	170 W. Fifth Street,	South Boston
Meets 2nd and 4th Wednesday,	F. S.	Leopold Kohler	15 Whitney Street,	Roxbury
987 Washington St.	T.	Jos Spang, Sr........	Fulda Street,	Boston
52. Highland, Roxbury.	C. R.	Hugh H. Collins	1471 Tremont Street,	Roxbury
Inst. April 16, 1883.	R. S.	Jeremiah Sullivan	29 Davenport Street,	Roxbury
Meets 2nd Monday, Kossuth	F. S.	Mark E. Gallagher...	221 Cabot Street,	Roxbury
Hall, 1083 Tremont St.	T.	John J. Corbett	14 Hallock Street,	Roxbury
53. Emerald, Peabody.	C. R	Thos. F. Lyons.......	Washington Street,	Peabody
Inst. July 2, 1883.	R. S.	John L. McManus....	5 Highland Park,	Peabody
Meets every Thursday, Thomas	F. S.	James B. Carbrey	10 Shillaber Street,	Peabody
Block, Central St.	T.	Daniel J. Sweeney....	Peabody Square,	Peabody
54. St. James, Boston.	C. R.	James F. Gleason	6 Dorchester Street,	South Boston
Inst. July 2, 1883.	R. S.	John J. Desmond....	286 Third Street,	South Boston
Meets 3rd Tuesday, Carroll	F. S.	Theodore J. Mignault.	86 Emerson Street,	Boston
Hall, 375 Harrison Ave.	T.	Michael J. Noonan ...	214 South Street,	Boston
55. Charles River, Watertown.	C. R.	James D. Monahan...		Watertown
Inst. Oct. 8, 1883.	R. S.	M. T. Holland........	Box 28,	Bemis
Meets 1st and 3rd Monday,G.A.R.	F. S.	M. E. Conroy		Watertown
Hall, Mt. Auburn St.	T.	James J. Barnes.....		Watertown
57. Carroll, Jamaica Plain.	C. R.	Wm. Rooney	Spring Park Ave.,	Jamaica Plain
Inst. June 30, 1885.	R. S.	J. H. Lennon	Cor. South & Child Sts.,	Jamaica Plain
Meets 1st and 3rd Wednesday	F. S.	Charles Mahan	Boylston Ave.,	Jamaica Plain
Association Hall, Burroughs St.	T.	J. H. Moy	Child Street,	Jamaica Plain
58. Prospect, Waltham.	C. R.	David Walsh	205 River Street,	Waltham
Inst. Aug. 25, 1885.	R. S.	Michael Bergin.......	13 Middle Street,	Waltham
Meets 1st and 3rd Sunday, A.O.H.	F. S.	John E. Burke.......	12 Hall Street,	Waltham
Hall, Main St. and Common St.	T.	Timothy F. Buckley..	105 Cushing Street.	Waltham
59. Worcester, Worcester.	C. R.	Patrick J. Quinn	26 Spruce Street,	Worcester
Inst. Dec. 17, 1885.	R. S.	Michael J Madden	61 Eastern Avenue,	Worcester
Meets 1st and 3rd Thursday,	F. S.	John McCullough	22 Arlington Street,	Worcester
I. C. B. Hall, 93 Front St.	T.	John W. Delehanty..	530 Main Street,	Worcester
60. Middlesex, Newton.	C. R.	James Cannon........		Newton
Inst. Feb. 19, 1886.	R. S.	Wm. E. McDonald....	95 Gardner Street,	Newton
Meets 2nd and 4th Tuesday,	F. S.	P. R. Mullen.........	12 Waban Street,	Newton
Arcanum Hall.	T.			
61. St. Lawrence, Brookline.	C. R.	John Cook	Morse Avenue,	Brookline
Meets 1st and 3rd Tuesday, Good	R. S.	Daniel Feeney	White Place,	Brookline
Fellows Hall, Washington st.	F. S.	Thos. F. McMahon....	Kerrigan Place,	Brookline
	T.	Timothy Driscoll.....	6 Morse Avenue,	Brookline
62. St. Catherine, Norwood.	C. R.	R. E. Oldham........		Norwood
Inst. Dec. 31, 1886.	R. S.	F. E. Nagle		Norwood
Meets 1st and 3rd Wednesday,	F. S.	John H. Williams ..		Norwood
Union Hall.	T.	George A O'Bryan...		Norwood
63. Shields, Holyoke.	C. R.	James Bartley	643 High Street,	Holyoke
Inst. Jan. 14, 1887.	R. S.	M. J. Conway	80 Hamilton Street,	Holyoke
Meets 2nd Sunday and 4th Tues-	F. S.	Odilon Moreau..	69 High Street,	Holyoke
day, Redmen's Hall, 441 High	T.	Dr. Geo. H. Clarke ...	441 High Street,	Holyoke
St.				
64. Gallagher, Springfield.	C. R.	John J. Cruse........	93 St. James Avenue	Springfield
Inst. April 17, 1887.	R. S.	John T. Lovett	100 Franklin Street,	Springfield
Meets 2nd and 4th Friday, Foot's	F. S.	John Lawler	Morris Street,	Springfield
Block, Main St.	T.	Peter Burke..........	308 Chestnut Street,	Springfield
65. St. Columbkille, Brighton.	C. R.	John J. O'Keefe......	Winship Street,	Brighton
Inst. May 26, 1887.	R. S.	Michael Featherstone.	249 Market Street,	Brighton
Meets 1st and 3rd Tuesday, K. of	F. S.	Robert Naghten......	247 Market Street,	Brighton
Honor Hall, cor. Washington	T.	John J. Greenleaf ...	Winship Street,	Brighton
and Chestnut Hill Ave.				

DIRECTORY — Continued.

No. and Court Name.	Officers.		Address.
66. Griffin, Franklin. Inst. Sept. 12, 1887. Meets 1st and 3rd Tuesday, Morse's New Block, Central St.	C. R. R. S. F. S. T.	D. F. O'Sulliuan . ... M. F. Conroy......... J. E. O'Donnell...... William F. Buckley ..	Franklin Franklin Franklin Franklin
67. Canton, Canton. Inst Jan. 26, 1888. Meets 2nd and 4th Friday, G.A.R. Hall, Church St.	C. R. R. S. F. S. T.	Matthew A. Skelton.. James J. Quinn...... James E. Grimes ..... Edward C. Murphy...	Canton Canton Canton Canton
68. St. Margaret, Beverly Farms. Inst. April, 14, 1888. Meets 1st and 3rd Wednesday, Marshall's Hall.	C. R. R. S. F. S. T.	Edward H. Higgins... John C. McCarthy.... Michael J. Cadigan... Lawrence J. Watson..	Beverly Farms Box 105, Beverly Farms Beverly Farms Beverly Farms
69. Stoughton, Stoughton. Inst. June 7, 1888. Meets 1st and 3rd Thursday, Foresters' Hall, Main st.	C. R. R. S. F. S. T	John E. Tighe........ Wm. J. Cronin...... Edward O. Cox...... Timothy Cronin .:....	Stoughton Stoughton Stoughton Stoughton
70. St. Michael, South Boston. Inst. Sept. 14, 1888. Meets 1st and 3rd Tuesday, Gray's Hall.	C. R. R. S. F. S. T.	Robert Dwyer........ W. G. Cunningham... J. J. Barry........... T. F. Shea...........	681 Second Street, South Boston K and Third Street, South Boston 187 Bowen Street, South Boston 144 K Street, South Boston
71. Phil. Sheridan, Newburyport. Inst. Sept. 18, 1888. Meets 1st and 3rd Tuesday, G. A. R. Hall, Charter St.	C. R. R. S. F. S. T.	John J. Dunn........ Albert E. Moylan.... Hugh Hart........... George W. Hussy.....	14 Peck Street, Newburyport 33 Olive Street, Newburyport 16 Salem Street, Newburyport 31 Monroe Street, Newburyport
72. Merrimack, Haverhill. Inst. Dec. 20, 1880. Meets 2nd and 4th Thursday, Foresters' Hall, 78 Merrimack St.	C. R. R. S. F. S. T.	Daniel H. Maguire.... Edward P. Ryan...... John J. Murphy...... John A. Burns	Bradford 26 Howard Street, Haverhill 277 River Street, Haverhill 26 Emerson Street, Haverhill
73. Taunton, Taunton. Inst. March 12, 1889. Meets 2nd and 4th Tuesday, Foresters' Hall, Union Block, Main St.	C. R. R. S. F. S. T.	Geo. F. Brammer..... John Kenely .... Wm. P. Crowley...... Thos. G. Hankard	11 Second Street, Taunton 5 Hope Street, Taunton 47 No. Pleasant Street, Taunton 114 Weir Street, Taunton
74. Hendricken, No. Easton. Inst. March 29, 1889. Meets 1st Monday and 2nd Thursday, Foresters' Hall, Centre St.	C. R. R. S. F. S. T.	W. J. Heelan......... John F. Long ... ... Anthony A. Clarke... Dennis H. Sweeney...	North Easton North Easton North Easton North Easton
75. St. Jarlath, Amesbury. Inst. June 12, 1889. Meets every Tuesday, Bohan's Hall, Main St.	C. R. R. S. F. S. T.	John McGrath....... Andrew J. Carr....... Albert A. Gallagher... John J. Joyce........	Orchard Street, Amesbury 13 Powow Street, Amesbury School Street, Amesbury East Haverhill Street, Amesbury
76. Quincy, Quincy. Inst Oct. 24, 1889. Meets 1st and 3rd Thursday, Red Men's Hall, Hancock St.	C. R. R. S. F. S. T.	Conrad Mischler...... Henry A. Talbot...... Jos. A. Dasha .... John A. McDonnell...	Braintree 7 Newcomb Place, Quincy 10 Sumner Street, Quincy 16 Jackson Street, Quincy
77. Mystic, Medford. Inst. Dec. 12, 1889. Meets 2nd and 4th Thursday, Tufts Hall, Main St.	C. R. R. S. F. S. T.	John W. Lynch ...... John J. O'Brien ...... John A. Gaffey... ... Wm. B. Hellen.......	14 Tufts Street, Medford 26 Fountain Street, Medford 7 Curtis Street, Medford Medford
78. St. Monica, Lawrence. Inst. March 26, 1890. Meets 1st and 3rd Monday, Unity Hall, cor. Essex and Appleton Sts.	C. R. R. S. F. S. T.	John H. Cronin ...... Terrence J. Kelly.... Patrick Hogan........ John J. Doody.......	13 Wyman Street, Lawrence 116 Hancock Street, Lawrence 16 Acton Street, Lawrence 218 Oak Street, Lawrence

DIRECTORY — Continued.

No. and Court Name.	Officers.		Address.
79. John Boyle O'Reilly, New Bedford. Inst. Jan. 24, 1891. Meets 2nd and 4th Wednesday, Young Men's T. A. B. Hall, Purchase St.	C. R.	James II. Miskell....	96 South Sixth Street, New Bedford
	R. S.	James Doyle	New County Street, New Bedford
	F. S.	John N. O'Brien.....	Cottage St., near Robeson N. Bedford
	T.	Lawrence J. Durant...	405 County Street, New Bedford
80. Gen. Sherman, Plymouth. Inst. March 7, 1891. Meets 2nd and last Tuesday, Good Templars' Hall, Main St.	C. R.	Henry S. Healy.......	27 Main Street, Plymouth
	R. S.	James H. Bagnell.....	Water Street, Plymouth
	F. S.	Joseph J. Reddy......	155 Court Street, Plymouth
	T.	John W. Hallinan	53 Alerton Street, Plymouth
81. St. Malachi. Arlington. Inst. Sept 3, 1891. Meets 1st and 3rd Thursdays, G. A. R. Hall, Arlington Ave.	C. R.	Patrick A. McCarthy..	Medford Street, Arlington
	R. S.	John F. McBride	Franklin Street. Arlington
	F. S.	Thomas H. Scannell..	Moore's Court, Arlington
	T.	Donald P. McNeil	Broadway, Arlington
82. Brockton, Brockton. Inst. Dec. 11, 1892. Meets 1st and 3rd Thursday, Foresters' Hall, Bay State Block, Centre Street.	C. R.	John Kent	39 Winthrop Street, Brockton
	R. S.	J. H. Mahoney.......	68 North Warren Avenue, Brockton
	F. S.	J. C. Kelly..........	20 Foster Street, Brockton
	T.	J. J. Hickey	152 North Warren Avenue, Brockton
83. John Henry Newman, Everett. Inst. Dec. 12, 1891. Meets 1st and 3rd Weduesday, G. A. R. Hall, Everett.	C. R.	Thomas F. Hickey...	74 Chestnut Street, Everett
	R. S.	Francis J. McBride..	146 Main Street, Everett
	F. S.	T. B. Brogan......	8 Oakland Avenue, Everett
	T.	Thomas Kirwan......	52 Vine Street. Everett
84. Danvers, Danvers. Inst. Feb. 10, 1892. Meets 2nd and 4th Wednesday.	C. R.	T. J. Lynch..........	32 Putnam Street, Danvers
	R. S.	P. H. Kirby..........	Locust Street, Danvers
	F. S.	J. F. McCarthy......	Wenham Street, Danvers
	T.	D. McCarthy	
85. George Washington, W. Lynn. Inst. Feb. 22, 1892. Meets every Thursday.	C. R.	John B. McCarthy....	42 Robinson Street, Lynn
	R. S.	Daniel Dunn.........	72 Essex Street, W .Lynn
	F. S.	James F. Kelly.......	2 Mace Street, Lynn
	T.	James S. Barry........	896 Western Avenue, Lynn
86. Avon, Avon. Inst. March 16, 1892.	C. R.	P. E. McGonnigle.....	Avon
	R. S.	W. F. Feeney........	Avon
	F. S.	J. J. Collins..........	Avon
	T.	J. F. Sheehan	Avon
87. Robert Emmett, Walpole. Inst. April 1, 1892.	C. R.	J. F. Kiley...........	Norwood
	R. S.	John M. Smith.......	E. Walpole
	F. S.	Thomas F. Gookin....	Walpole
	T.	Wm. Mahoney........	Walpole
88. Enterprise, W. Newbury. Inst. June 2, 1892.	C. R.	Daniel Cooney.......	Post Office Square, W. Newbury
	R. S.	Daniel McCauliffe ...:	Maple Street, W. Newbury
	F. S.	Frederick E. Condon..	W. Newbury
	T.	Thomas J. Murphy....	Main Street, E. Haverhill
89. Union, Whitman. Inst. August 24, 1892.	C. R.	Montague McKinnon..	Stetson Street, Whitman
	R. S.	John F. Murphy......	30 Stetson Street, Whitman
	F. S.	Thomas S. Tobin.....	Crescent Street, Whitman
	T.	Thomas Cody........	10 Crescent Street, Whitman

As the year 1890 was a prosperous one for our organization, we may say without fear of contradiction, that 1891 was prosperous, since our net gain in membership was so large. A year ago we had 71 courts with a membership of 4,775 ; now, we have 77 courts with a membership of nearly or quite 5,400. With a realization of one-half the prospects we have in view, there is no reason to believe that 1892 will not show a still greater gain and enable us to point with pride to the growing record of the Massachusetts Catholic Order of Foresters as one worthy of our best efforts to uphold. As one commending the Order to the consideration of the community at large and particularly to those of our people who are eligible for membership and have not availed themselves of the opportunity to join in the good work. With the large amount of material available we should have a membership in this State alone of 20,000 : Can we get them ? The answer remains with ourselves and our people.

Respectfully submitted,

JAMES F. SUPPLE,
High Secretary-Treasurer.

THIRTEENTH ANNUAL CONVENTION

OF THE

Massachusetts Catholic Order of Foresters

HELD AT

Encampment Hall, 724 Washington Street, Boston.

APRIL 27, 1892.

Opened in regular form by High Chief Ranger Hon. Owen A. Galvin, at 9.30, A. M. High Chief Ranger read the call for the Convention, which was as follows:—

MASSACHUSETTS CATHOLIC ORDER OF FORESTERS.

HIGH STANDING COMMITTEE.

611 Washington Street,

Boston, April 1, 1892.

To the Officers and Members of the Massachusetts Catholic Order of Foresters:—

BROTHERS,—In accordance with the powers vested in the High Standing Committee of the Massachusetts Catholic Order of Foresters (under Art. IV, Constitution of High Court, Page 11,) a call is hereby issued for the assembling of the Representatives of the Subordinate Courts of the Massachusetts Catholic Order of Foresters in Annual Session of the High Court of the Order, to be held in Encampment Hall, 724 Washington Street, Boston, to be opened in regular form at 9.30 o'clock, A. M., on Wednesday the twenty-seventh day of April, A. D. 1892, as provided for in the High Court Constitution.

The Basis of Representation shall be as laid down in Art. II, Sec. 3, Constitution of High Court, page 8.

Forms of Credential to the Annual Session of High Court accompany this Call, one to be retained and held by the Representative for use at the Convention. If the Credential be transferred for cause, this should be stated on the back of Credential under the endorsements of Chief Ranger and Recording Secretary of the Court.

By Order of the High Standing Committee,

OWEN A. GALVIN,
High Chief Ranger.

JAMES F. SUPPLE,
High Secretary-Treasurer.

High Chief Ranger appointed the following—

COMMITTEE ON CREDENTIALS.

Bros. J. J. Leonard................of Gallagher No. 64
    J. B. Rooney..............of St. Catherine No. 62
    W. H. Rogers..................of Sarsfield No 48
    J. C. Carson.....................of Sheil No. 35
    P. M. Keating...............of St. Joseph No. 11
    G. F. Lowe.......................of Leo No. 5

While Committee was out High Secretary-Treasurer Supple read letter from High Inside Sentinel J. T. Daly, stating that illness of his oldest son would prevent his attendance.

High Chief Ranger Galvin also appointed the following Committees :—

COMMITTEE ON SECRET WORK.

Bros. J. J. Lanigan................of Cathedral No. 1
    John T. Daly.....................of Erin No. 28
    J. G. Fennessey..............of St. James No. 54
    J. Cashin.....................of Cheverus No. 6
    G. F. Lowe.......................of Leo No. 5

COMMITTEE ON PETITIONS.

COMMITTEE ON APPEAL.

Bros. J. Torndorf................of Holy Trinity No. 51
    P. Morris...................of St. Joseph No. 38
    P. Smith.....................of Williams No. 19
    F. F. O'Neil..... ....of Shields No. 63
    W. E. Shay.................of St. Francis No. 4
    J. G. Fennessey.............of St. James No. 54
    John Doolin...............of St. Augustine No. 46

COMMITTEE ON STATE OF THE ORDER.

Bros. John Vogel.................of St. Francis No. 25
    J. B. McCarthy......of George Washington No. 85
    P. McKenna........of SS. Peter and Paul No. 15
    M. J. Zilch....................of Sarsfield No. 48
    T. F. Lynes.................of St. Jarlath No. 75
    J. O'Mara.......................of Erin No. 28
    L. Lyons... ....of Hamilton No. 17

Committee on Credentials reported—
58 Courts represented.
74 Representatives present.
21 Proxies present.

Voted to accept report.

Past High Chief Ranger Fennessey arrived and was escorted to the platform, where he received numerous congratulations.

High Chief Ranger Galvin then delivered his address, which was listened to closely and warmly applauded.

High Chief Ranger Galvin asked if any petitions were to be presented.

Bro. Lyons presented petition for payment of James Mitchell claim. Referred to Committee on Appeals.

Amendment to Constitution from Sherwood Court No. 8 was presented.

High Chief Ranger ruled it could not come in.

Bro. D. F. Sullivan of No. 8 said he presented it at request of Sherwood Court No. 8 ; but he understood it could not come in.

Amendment by W. E. Shay to change time of holding Convention from April to January was presented.

High Chief Ranger ruled it out.

By request referred to Permanent Committee on Constitution.

High Chief Ranger asked for any reports ready.

Bro. Cronin, of Trustees of Reserve Fund, reported—

To the High Standing Committee of the Massachusetts Catholic Order of Foresters :

Gentlemen : —

The Trustees of your Order respectfully present the following report for the fiscal year ending April 20, 1892 : —

Cash deposited in the Union Institution for Savings, - -	$2,056.49
Interest on the same to May, 1890, - - - - - - - -	8.52
Cash deposited in Franklin Institution for Savings, - -·	1,000.00
Mortgage on Estate No. 40–42 Market Street, Cambridgeport, Mass., at 5 per cent., - - - - - - - - -	2,800.00
Cash on hand, - - - - - - - - - - - - - -	939.39
Total, - - - - - - - - - - - - -	$6,804.50

Respectfully submitted,
DANIEL A. CRONIN,
JOSEPH TORNDORF, Jr.,
Trustees.

Voted to accept report.

High Chief Ranger asked for report of Committees.

Bro. Fennessey reported in print for Committee on Constitution as follows :—

The following proposed amendments to the Constitution have been considered by the Committee on Constitution, and their report is appended to each.

1. Amend Constitution of the High Court, Sec. 3 of Article IV, on page 19. So that the charter fee shall be twenty-five dollars instead of forty-five dollars.
The Committee on Constitution voted inexpedient.

2. Amend by adding on page 9, Constitution of High Court, new section of Article II, to be known as :—Section 5. Recording and Financial Secretaries and Treasurers of Subordinate Courts, who have served in either office five consecutive years are eligible to membership, and to hold office in the High Court.
The Committee on Constitution voted inexpedient.

3. Amendment to Article III, Section 1, on page 37. After "fifty" in line 3 insert "five." (The intention being to admit persons up to 55 years of age.)
The Committee on Constitution voted inexpedient.

4. Amend by adding on page 9, High Court Constitution, Article III. (Officers of High Court,) a new section, to be known as,—Section 3. No member of the Order shall be eligible to hold office in the High Court or High Standing Committee, for more than five consecutive terms; provided however that should the occupant of the office of High Chief Ranger be serving his fifth year of consecutive service, and in the first year as High Chief Ranger, he shall be eligible for service, an additional year, as High Chief Ranger if elected.
The Committee on Constitution voted inexpedient.

5. Amendment to Article III, Section 1, on page 37. Strike out the word " male " in line 1, and make any other changes in the Constitution necessary to agree with this so that women may be entitled to all the rights and privileges of membership in the Order.
The Committee on Constitution voted to adopt.

6. Amendment to Object, page 6. Strike out " widows " in line 6, and insert " families."
The Committee on Constitution voted to adopt.

7. Amendment to Sec. 3, Article III, on page 41. Insert after "join" in line 6 "within 60 days."
The Committee on Constitution voted to adopt.

JEREMIAH G. FENNESSEY, of St. James No. 54,
JAMES CASHIN,   " Cheverus   "   6,
D. F. SULLIVAN,   " Sherwood "   8,
G. F. LOW,   " Leo   "   5,
A. A. CLARK,   " Hendricken " 74,
Committee on Constitution.

Voted to accept as progressive.

Recess for dinner at 12.30 P. M.

Called to order at 2.30 P. M.

Bro. Lanigan, for Finance Committee, reported—"The Finance Committee of this year having examined the books, accounts and vouchers of High Secretary-Treasurer, James F. Supple, report them correct, and the finances of the Order in good condition. Your Committee would recommend a reduction of the per capita to 75 cents. as in their opinion this amount, together with the balance in the hands of the Secretary-Treasurer, will be sufficient for the ensuing year."

Voted to accept and adopt.

Bro. Torndorf, reported for Committee on Appeals :—

That Mitchell case should not be paid.

High Chief Ranger stated question.

Bro. Torndorf explained how the Committee reached its conclusion.

Voted to accept and adopt.

Bro. Keating moved to pay back to heirs of Mitchell the money he paid in.

High Chief Ranger stated question.

Dr. Hines spoke against such payment.

Bro. Keating spoke in favor of payment.

Bro. Bergin also spoke in favor of payment.

Bro. J. Cashin was against payment.

High Chief Ranger put the question, and declared it was not a vote.

Bro. Fennessey, for Committee on Constitution, reported :—

On Amendment No. 1, inexpedient.

Bro. Fennessey explained about cost.

Voted to accept report.

Bro. Fennessey reported :—

On Amendment No. 2, inexpedient.

Motion was made to accept and adopt.

Amendment by Bro. McGrath to adopt as expedient.

Bro. Cashin moved to amend the amendment to allow any member in good financial standing for one year to be eligible to membership, and hold office in High Court.

Bro. Crosby spoke against the amendment to amend, and in favor of amendment.

Bro. Shay raised point of order that Bro. Cashin's amendment was out of order.

High Chief Ranger ruled point of order not well taken.

Bro. Fennessey was against changing the Constitution so much, and spoke in favor of report of Committee.

Bro. Low moved previous question.

Vice High Chief Ranger McLaughlin, in the chair, stated the question on amendment of Bro. Cashin, and declared it was not a vote; on amendment of Bro. McGrath, and declared it was not a vote; on report of Committee, voted to accept.

Bro. Fennessey, on Amendment No. 3, reported inexpedient.

Bro. P. Smith moved to accept report.

Voted to accept.

Bro. Fennessey reported on Amendment No. 4, inexpedient.

Bro. P. Smith moved to accept and adopt report of Committee.

Bro. McGrath moved to amend to adopt the article proposed.

Bro. Cashin thought Bro. McGrath was aiming at one officer he did not wish to name.

Bro. Carson said he served on High Standing Committee two years, and had enough of it.

Vice High Chief Ranger McLaughlin stated question on Bro. McGrath's amendment, and declared it was not a vote.

Vice High Chief Ranger McLaughlin stated question on accepting the report of Committee on Constitution.

Voted to accept report of Committee.

Bro. Fennessey reported on Amendment No. 7, and explained purpose of it as absolutely necessary.

Vice High Chief Ranger McLaughlin stated question.

Voted to accept and adopt.

Bro. Fennessey reported on Amendment No. 5, ought to be adopted.

Motion to accept report.

Bro. O'Brien, of 16, moved to amend, inexpedient.

Bro. Fennessey spoke at length in favor of the report, that we should give to our sisters, wives, mothers and relatives an opportunity to join.

Bro. Torndorf spoke against the report because women were poor risks in his opinion.

Bro. Keating thought it would create uneasiness in the Order.

Bro. Cronin, of 11, was against it.

Bro. Smith, of 19, reported that his Court was in favor of admitting women, that the list of deaths in an organization he belonged to showed more men dying than women; and it was a move in the right direction.

Bro. Gallagher, of 3, was opposed to the admission of women.

Bro. Donovan, of 14, was in favor of admission of women, because if a woman wanted insurance she ought to get it here.

Bro. Dolan, of 32, was against admission of women, and said his Court so voted.

Bro. McLaughlin, Vice High Chief Ranger, moved as a substitute motion, a Committee of Seven to formulate a system, and report at next Convention.

Bro. Driscoll, of 61, wanted High Standing Committee to get opinion of Courts during year.

High Chief Ranger Galvin stated question on substitute, and declared it a vote.

Bro. Fennessey wanted a chance to speak on the question.

Bro. O'Brien withdrew his amendment.

Bro. Fennessey reported on No. 6, and moved to refer No. 6 to same Committee.

Voted to refer.

Bro. Fennessey moved that it is the sense of the Convention that High Standing Committee extend this Order throughout the New England States.

Bro. Keating amended that High Standing Committee inquire into the feasibility, obtain information from Courts about the matter, and report at next Convention.

Bro. Fennessey said this was before the Courts several years, and it was time for the Order to spread out.

Bro. Rogers, of 48, was in favor.

Bro. Leonard, of 64, was in favor of extension.

Bro. Healy, of 80, was in favor.

Bro. Cashin, of 6, was in favor of extension in New England.

Bro. Dore, of Sherwood No. 8, said he was instructed to vote for extension.

Bro. Torndorf, of 51, was in favor.

Bro. Sullivan, of 8, was instructed by his Court to vote for extension.

Bro. Keating would like to see the Order extended, but unless we could take care of the ground covered it was no use.

Bro. Fennessey wanted extension, and we should have it now.

Bro. McGrath was opposed to extension.

High Chief Ranger stated question on amendment of Bro. Keating, and declared it was not a vote.

High Chief Ranger stated question on motion of Bro. Fennessey to extend the Order throughout New England.

Voted to so extend.

Bro. Vogel, for Committee on State of the Order, reported :—

Judging from the reports of the High Chief Ranger and High Secretary-Treasurer the Order is in a prosperous condition, and recommend as follows:—

First. That the members of the Order have a uniform emblem or badge.

Second. That a public parade take place in Boston at some time, to be decided by the Convention.

Third. That each Court hold a public rally each year, for the advancement of the Court.

Fourth. That the Committee on Constitution consider whether it would be advisable for each member to hold an exact copy of the conditions specified in his application ; the same to be sent to each member by the High Standing Committee.

Bro. Fennessey moved to refer to High Standing Cammittee with full power to act.

Voted to refer.

Bro. Lanigan, for Committee on Secret Work, reported :—

The adoption of the recommendation of the High Chief Ranger.—the appointment of a Special Committee of five to revise the secret work of the Order.

Also that a prize in amount not exceeding $100 be given for the best secret work presented, the High Standing Committee to decide.

The Committee would also recommend the adoption of a membership badge, to be used at Court meetings.

(Signed)   J. J. LANIGAN,
For Committee.

Bro. Fennessey moved to accept and adopt.

Voted.

On motion, voted to proceed to election of officers.

On motion, High Chief Ranger Galvin appointed following Committee to receive and count votes :—

> Bros. Cashin.........................of Cheverus No. 6
> Lill.............................of Sherwood No. 8
> Lyons.......................of Hamilton No. 17

Bro. Cronin moved that High Secretary-Treasurer cast one ballot for Bro. Owen A. Galvin for High Chief Rarger.

Voted.

The ballot was cast and Hon. Owen A. Galvin was elected High Chief Ranger.

On motion, voted that High Secretary-Treasurer cast one ballot for J. J. McLaughlin for Vice High Chief Ranger.

The ballot was cast and J. J. McLaughlin was declared elected.

Bro. Torndorf moved that the Committee cast one ballot for J. F. Supple for High Secretary-Treasurer.

Ballot was cast and J. F. Supple was declared elected.

Bro. Cronin moved that Committee cast one ballot for P. A. Murray for High Senior Conductor.

The ballot was cast and Bro. Murray was declared elected.

Bro. Shay nominated for High Junior Conductor Hon. John P. Dore, and moved to cast one ballot for him for High Junior Conductor.

The ballot was cast and Bro. Dore was declared elected.

Bro. Smith moved to elect J. T. Daly as High Inside Sentinel on one ballot.

The ballot was cast and Bro. Daly was declared elected.

On motion, Bro. John Hayes was nominated for High Outside Sentinel, and the Committee was instructed to cast one ballot for Bro. Hayes.

The ballot was cast and Bro. Hayes was declared elected.

On motion of Dr. Hines, the Committee cast one ballot for Dr. J. D. Couch for High Medical Examiner, and Dr. Couch was declared elected.

On motion of Bro. Lowe, Rev. H. R. O'Donnell was elected on one ballot as High Court Chaplain.

Bro. Fennessey moved that salary of High Secretary-Treasurer be same as last year.

Voted.

Bro. Shay moved to elect Bro. J. Torndorf on one ballot as Trustee of Reserve Fund.

Elected.

Bro. Galvin said next business was to elect a Committee on Finance.

Bro. Smith moved to elect old Committee on one ballot.

Bro. Lanigan objected.

Bro. Smith withdrew his motion.

Bro. Sullivan, of Sherwood No. 8, moved to elect Bro. J. J. Lanigan on Finance Committee.

Voted.

Bro. Lowe moved to elect Bro. John Brant.

Voted.

Bro. Shay moved to elect T. F. Crosby.

Voted.

Bro. Smith moved to elect Bro. Frank J. McGrath.

Voted.

Bro. Cronin moved to elect Bro. P. F. McGaragle.

Voted.

High Chief Ranger Galvin declared those Brothers elected.

Bro. Fennessey moved to proceed to installation of officers.

Bro. McCarthy of 85, moved to elect Bro. T. Donovan as Trustee of Reserve Fund on one ballot to be cast by High Secretary-Treasurer.

Voted.

Ballot was cast and Bro. Donovan was declared elected.

High Chief Ranger appointed following Committees :—

On Secret Work.

Bros. J. T. Daly........ ....of Erin No. 28

J. F. Roche..................of Cathedral No. 1

A. J. Lill.... ....of Sherwood No. 8

G. F. Lowe........................of Leo No. 5

J. J. McLaughlin.............of Americus No. 34

On Admission of Women.

Bros. Dr. F. E. Hines................·.......of Essex No. 16

P. M. Keating...............of St. Joseph No. 11

P. Smith....................of Williams No. 19

J. B. McCarthy......of George Washington No. 85

J. J. Leonard................·of Gallagher No. 64

Fred L. Smith.............of St. Thomas No. 29

J. B. Rooney.............of St. Catherine No. 62

On Constitution.

Bros. J. G. Fennessey.............of St. James No. 54

James Cashin..................of Cheverus No. 6

D. F. Sullivan ....of Sherwood No. 8

G. F. Low........................of Leo No. 5

A. A. Clarke............:.,of Hendricken No. 74

W. E. Shay........ ....of St. Francis No. 4

J. Vogel...................of St. Francis No. 25

By invitation of High Chief Ranger Galvin, Past High Chief Ranger J. G. Fennessey took the chair, and installed the officers for the ensuing year.

High Chief Ranger Galvin addressed the Convention, and thanked the delegates for their kindness and consideration, as well as for their confidence in him,—that, as the head of 5,400 Catholics, he was proud of the organization, and was sure of the success of the Order. He was sure the extension of the Order could be accomplished, although many times it would mean days and nights away from home and business. [Applause.]

The High Secretary-Treasurer proceeded to read records, and

On motion, it was voted to consider the records read and approved.

High Chief Ranger Galvin then closed in due form at 6.50 P. M.

Bro. Fennessey then asked permission for Bro. T. B. Fitz to say a few words.

Bro. Fitz spoke at some length on the duties of Catholics toward each other, and said the Order was a good means of teaching us what we owed to each other in a social and fraternal way, and he hoped the day was not far distant when all the Catholics of the country would be as united in the fraternal spirit as they now were in the Church. [Applause.]

The Convention then, on motion, adjourned *sine die* at 7.05 P. M.

JAMES F. SUPPLE,

High Secretary-Treasurer.

FOURTEENTH ANNUAL REPORT

OF THE

HIGH SECRETARY-TREASURER

OF THE

Mass. Catholic Order of Foresters

AND ADDRESS OF HIGH CHIEF RANGER

To the High Court April 26, 1893.

WITH

REPORT OF PROCEEDINGS

OF THE

FOURTEENTH ANNUAL CONVENTION

AND

A LIST OF MEDICAL EXAMINERS AND D. H. C. R's, AND

MEETINGS AND LIST OF OFFICERS.

BOSTON:
THE EASTBURN PRESS,
165 DEVONSHIRE STREET.

FOURTEENTH ANNUAL REPORT

OF THE

HIGH SECRETARY-TREASURER

OF THE

Mass. Catholic Order of Foresters

AND ADDRESS OF HIGH CHIEF RANGER

To the High Court April 26, 1893.

WITH

REPORT OF PROCEEDINGS

OF THE

FOURTEENTH ANNUAL CONVENTION

AND

A List of Medical Examiners and D. H. C. R's, and Meetings and List of Officers.

BOSTON:

THE EASTBURN PRESS,

165 Devonshire Street.

HIGH COURT OFFICERS,

For Term Ending April, 1894.

HIGH CHIEF RANGER,

J. J. McLaughlin . . . . Americus Court No. 34

HIGH VICE CHIEF RANGER,

Hon. John P. Dore . . . . Sherwood Court No. 8

HIGH SECRETARY-TREASURER,

James F. Supple . . . . . Columbus Court No. 9

HIGH SENIOR CONDUCTOR,

P. A. Murray . . . . . Middlesex Court No. 60

HIGH JUNIOR CONDUCTOR.

John Hayes . . . . . Lafayette Court No. 14

HIGH INSIDE SENTINEL.

Fred. L. Smith . . . . . St. Thomas Court No. 29

HIGH OUTSIDE SENTINEL.

Jeremiah G. Fennessey . . . St. James Court No. 54

HIGH MEDICAL EXAMINER.

Joseph D. Couch, M. D. . . . Benedict Court No. 39

HIGH CHAPLAIN.

Rev. Hugh Roe O'Donnell . . . Williams Court No. 19

ADDRESS OF HIGH CHIEF RANGER

AND

ANNUAL REPORT OF HIGH STANDING COMMITTEE

FOR THE TERM ENDING APRIL 25, 1893.

Representatives to the Annual Convention of the High Court of the Massachusetts Catholic Order of Foresters.

BROTHERS : — To-day it is my duty as High Chief Ranger of the Massachusetts Catholic Order of Foresters to report to you in a general way on the work of the Organization for the past year. It has been the best and the most prosperous year of the Organization since it was established. Our membership has largely increased during the past year, in fact for the last five years we have had a steady and constant growth. Since the last Convention over 1,200 applications have been received, and while this includes new Courts formed, yet a steady and healthy increase has taken place in the old Courts.

During the past year eight new Courts have been formed, namely :—

Enterprise Court, No. 88, in West Newbury.
Union Court, No. 89, in Whitman.
Rockland Court, No. 90, in Rockland.
St. Vincent Court, No. 91, in Holliston.
Harmony Court, No. 92, in East Bridgewater.
Germania Court, No. 93, in Roxbury.
Loyola Court, No. 94, in Boston.
Columbia Court, No. 95, in Roxbury.

In addition to these we have a number examined for a new Court in Middleboro, and there is every prospect that Courts will soon be formed in Medway and Pittsfield.

We can safely say that this year the character of the new applications is much better than ever. We have had, in nearly every instance where new Courts were formed, the ready and willing assistance of the Clergy, and wherever the purposes of the Organization were made known, there came a desire from the people to join. Where the Clergy has such confidence, the people soon become imbued with the same spirit of confidence. While the fraternal and brotherly feeling underlies all our actions we must not forget that business principles must run all through our movements. All proper claims against the Organization have been met, and all our promises have been kept. In saying this I wish to call your attention to the fact that many claims have been paid, from payment of which we might possibly have been relieved if the cases went to a Court of Law. Our policy has been, however, to avoid litigation. The exceeding care used in the admission of new members has given us a result very much to our advantage. That this care will continue to be exercised by successive High Standing Committees, there is not in my mind the slightest doubt. One result of this care is the reducing of the average age of the membership of the Order.

The average age of applications approved during the past year was 32 years, and the average age of the entire membership of the Order on January 1, 1893, was 39 years. This is a remarkable showing when we consider the ages of those admitted in the early days of the Order. By this you will see that the age of the Organization has not increased as the membership increased, and the continuance of such a policy, a continuance of the same care in the scrutiny of the applications of those who apply for membership, will give us life for an indefinite period.

From the last Convention to the 1st of April, 1893, we had 64 deaths, occurring as follows:—

May	. . . .	6	October .	. . .	3
June	. . . .	3	November	. . .	6
July	. . . .	3	December	. . .	4
August	. . . .	5	January .	. . .	16
September	. . .	4	February	. . .	8
			March	. . . .	6

During the year 1892, ten assessment calls were issued, the last one, however, not expiring until late in January. In passing, while it has no special place here, I call your attention to the large number of deaths occurring in January, 1893 — sixteen in all. Most of them were probably due to the effects of the "grip," and in my judgment no extra assessments will be necessary, as the close of the year 1893 will amply demonstrate, and our death rate for the year will be found to be only normal.

The per capita tax last year was found to be sufficient, and I would recommend that this year it be placed at the same figure, namely, 75 cents.

A matter of great interest to the Order is the report of the Trustees of the Reserve Fund. The fund has been judiciously invested according to law, and the thanks of the Order should be extended to the Trustees. This fund now amounts to over $10,000 and has been accumulated without any hardship to the members. I would advise that it be allowed to grow.

In the consideration of applications for membership, all doubts as to the advisability of accepting risks are decided in favor of the Order. We can now afford to be somewhat exclusive, and accept only those who are unmistakably good risks. This we should do because the older members of the Order, who have stood by it in all its trials and vicissitudes are entitled to the constant consideration of the managers of the Order, and to all the protection and all the safeguards which can be thrown around them.

The High Standing Committee of last year endeavored to do this as well as its knowledge and experience went. There is no doubt in my mind but that the future High Standing Committees will also do it. In this connection it seems proper to me to speak of the amount of labor performed by the High Medical Examiner, Dr. Joseph D. Couch. He has always given his time freely to the High Standing Committee, and day after day, and night after night, has always been found at his post of duty. Every application passes through his hands, and receives all the consideration necessary. Since the last Convention he has examined over 1,200 applications. Of this number about 150 have been rejected. We cannot too highly appreciate the services of so faithful and conscientious an officer.

It seems to me proper at this time to call your attention to the work of the High Standing Committee which has increased gradually each year of the existence of the Organization. This work consists in the examination of papers, consideration of letters, hearing of complaints, settlement of difficulties between members of Subordinate Courts, travel in various directions throughout the State for the purpose of extending the Order, and attention to calls of various kinds for meetings and visits. No person, not a member the High Standing Committee, can understand just what that means; but the High Standing Committee has been glad to do it for the satisfaction it gave them to be engaged in a good work, and for the sake of the fruit realized. The High Standing Committee of the past year has held 75 meetings in addition to attending to other business and calls made upon it.

Unsettled Claim.

In the case of Ferdinand Shields of St. John Court No. 33, the High Standing Committee have decided not to pay.

Medical Examiners and Deputy High Chief Rangers.

Not many changes were made in the list of Medical Examiners. New additions to the list are Dr. J. D. McIntosh of Rockland, Dr. F. G. Atkins of Holliston, Dr. A. L. Shirley of East Bridgewater, Dr. C. W. MacDonald of Roxbury, and Dr. C. F. McCarthy of Franklin. The total number of Medical Examiners now on the roll is 56, and we think we have a very efficient corps. We have now 49 Deputy High Chief Rangers, and while some may not be as zealous as others, we think that all have tried to do their full duty. These men·are the eyes and hands of the High Standing Committee, and we have no words but of praise for these men who have many times been placed in trying positions. According to reports received from them they have made 262 visits during the past year. The majority of them are good workers, and have endeavored to give the Subordinate Courts the full benefit of their wisdom and experience.

Reviewing the work of the Organization, not only for last year but for several years past, not only during my term, just closing, but those of my predecessors, covering a period of six or seven years, I have only to say that the Order has constantly and conservatively grown, the average age has decreased, all claims have been paid, no defalcations have occurred, and a large reserve fund has been accumulated. These are the essentials of fraternal assessment insurance, and the Massachusetts Catholic Order of Foresters possesses all of them and possesses also the confidence of the people.

Now if you wish to aid the High Standing Committee in carrying forward the good work which is surely, year by year, building up a monument to forever stand to our credit as exponents of the truths of Unity, Fraternity, Charity and Catholicity. Then, as our Organization has shown itself to be grounded on sound principles, able to keep all its promises, that it is useful to us and our people as a Catholic, fraternal and business Organization. Then advertise it, speak of it and advance its claims among the people with whom you come in contact, among the people we want. *Get new members.* Every new member means additional security for the payment of the endowment of the present membership. Let every man in the Organization go out from here with this purpose in view, to bring in one good member. We should get a membership of 25,000.

Brother Representatives :—I have been four times elected to the highest position in this Organization, it is an honor of which I am deeply sensible. If I have been, in my humble way, in the least instrumental in bringing the Organization to its present advanced position, that is sufficient recompense for all the work done. If we work as we should, the day will come when we shall be the strongest Catholic Organization in the country.

Gentlemen of the Convention :—I return thanks to you for the honors you have given me, and I assure you I appreciate them highly. I only ask each one within the sound of my voice to 'labor on and soon our membership in this State alone will reach the round 25,000.

OWEN A. GALVIN,

HIGH CHIEF RANGER.

REPORT OF HIGH SECRETARY-TREASURER.

To the Representatives of the Massachusetts Catholic Order of Foresters :

BROTHERS,—On April 5, 1880, the Massachusetts Catholic Order of Foresters held its first Convention. Twelve Courts had been formed at that time, and the total membership was 659. No restriction had been placed on age, and many were admitted who were pretty well advanced in years. At that first Convention the folly of such a course was seen, and the limit of fifty years was placed in the Constitution. Since that time, no person has been admitted who was over fifty years of age, unless applicants have made untrue statements, and the line then drawn has been observed by every Convention of the Order since.

To-day we hold the Fourteenth Convention of the Organization, and we find ourselves a band of eighty-five Courts, spread over the whole State of Massachusetts, with a membership of about 6,400 Catholic men, who are beginning to see some of the fruits of fraternal organization and who desire to profit by the experience gained. They do not desire to use this experience for themselves, but with the same unselfish motives which have characterized every movement in the Order since its formation, they wish to apply the full benefit of this experience to those associated with them and their successors. It need not be said that this statement is not easy of proof; witness the proceedings of every yearly gathering of the Delegates from the Subordinate Courts, and in each will be seen, no matter how warm the argument—no matter how varied the views put forth, an earnest desire to get only the best measures adopted. That this will be the case this year we do not doubt. We have a larger representation this year than ever before. Many of the Representatives are new to the Convention work of the Order but have had a training in the Subordinate Courts which peculiarly fits them for carrying forward the work of the Organization through the Annual Session, in a manner which shall reflect credit on themselves and redound to the lasting benefit of the Organization.

1892 was commenced with a roll of seventy-three Courts and a membership of 5,000.

The following new Courts have since been added :—

NEW COURTS.

During the past year the following new Courts have been formed :

Enterprise Court No. 88, West Newbury, with 20 Charter members. Instituted June 2, 1892.

Union Court No. 89, Whitman, with 21 Charter members. Instituted August 24, 1892.

Rockland Court No. 90, Rockland, with 22 Charter members. Instituted November 21, 1892.

St. Vincent Court No. 91, Holliston, with 26 Charter members Instituted December 8, 1892.

Harmony Court No. 92, East Bridgewater, with 23 Charter members. Instituted February 20, 1893.

Germania Court No. 93, Roxbury, with 21 Charter members. Instituted February 26, 1893.

Loyola Court No. 94, Boston, with 32 Charter members. Instituted March 6, 1893.

Columbia Court No. 95, Roxbury, with 37 Charter members. Instituted March 28, 1893.

From April 27, 1892, to April 1, 1893, the High Standing Committee has received 1,119 applications. Of this number 956 were approved and 152 were rejected. From January 1, 1892, to January 1, 1893, 1,204 applications were received, and of this number 1,058 were approved and 144 were rejected.

The following table gives the number applying to each Court :

New applications received from April 27, 1892, to March 31, 1893.

No.	Court.				No.	Court.			
1	Cathedral	-	-	11	55	Charles River	-	-	8
3	Fenwick	-	-	11	57	Carroll	-	-	13
4	St. Francis	-	-	10	58	Prospect -	-	-	1
5	Leo	-	-	14	59	Worcester	-	-	17
6	Cheverus -	-	-	13	60	Middlesex	-	-	8
8	Sherwood	-	-	24	61	St. Lawrence	-	-	16
9	Columbus	-	-	3	62	St. Catherine	-	-	4
10	Iona	-	-	8	63	Shields	-	-	5
11	St. Joseph	-	-	4	64	Gallagher	-	-	9
12	Fulton -	-	-	4	65	St. Columbkille	-		6
13	Fitzpatrick	-	-	1	66	Griffin	-	-	28
14	Lafayette	-	-	24	67	Canton	-	-	2
15	SS. Peter and Paul	-		9	68	St. Margaret	-	-	3
16	Essex -	-	-	29	69	Stoughton	-	-	12
17	Hamilton	-	-	9	70	St. Michael	-	-	9
18	St. Peter	-	-	14	71	Phil Sheridan	-		6
19	Williams -	-	-		72	Merrimack	-	-	17
20	Mt. Pleasant	-			73	Taunton	-	-	20
21	St. Alphonsus	-			74	Hendricken	-	-	8
23	St. John	-	-	16	75	St. Jarlath	-	-	2
24	St. Gregory	-	-	17	76	Quincy	-	-	8
25	St. Francis	-	-	16	77	Mystic -	-	-	12
26	St. Raphael	-	-	7	78	St. Monica	-	-	5
28	Erin	-	-	10	79	John Boyle O'Reilly			2
29	St. Thomas	-	-	26	80	Gen. Sherman	-	-	2
30	Bass River	-	-	14	81	St. Malachi	-	-	4
32	Qualey	-	-	7	82	Brockton -	-	-	14
33	St. John	-	-	16	83	John Henry Newman			29
34	Americus -	-	-	11	84	Danvers -	-	-	14
37	Friendship	-	-	2	85	Geo. Washington	-		60
38	St. Joseph	-	-	5	86	Avon	-	-	4
39	Benedict	-	-	4	87	Robert Emmett	-		9
43	St. Mary -	-	-	8	88	Enterprise	-	-	25
45	Unity -	-	-	5	89	Union -	-	-	27
46	St. Augustine	-	-	14	90	Rockland -	-	-	42
47	St. Anne	-	-	15	91	St. Vincent	-	-	31
48	Sarsfield -	-	-	5	92	Harmony -	-	-	28
49	Constantine -	-		7	93	Germania	-	-	26
51	Holy Trinity	-	-	20	94	Loyola	-	-	36
52	Highland	-	-	6	95	Columbia	-	-	54
53	Emerald -	-	-	39					
54	St. James	-	-	20		Total	-	-	1119

The class of occupations does not vary much from previous years.

In 1892 the High Standing Committee approved 1,058 applications for membership, and rejected 144.

OCCUPATIONS OF APPLICATIONS APPROVED
FROM JANUARY 1, 1892, TO JANUARY 1, 1893.

Agent	4	Dresser's tender	2	
Apothecary	1	Dyer	2	
Attendant	1	Electrician	1	
Baker	4	Engineer	11	
Barber	9	Expressman	7	
Blacksmith	17	Engraver	1	
Bottler	1	Electro plater	1	
Broker	1	Editor	1	
Brushmaker	1	Electrical inst'm't maker	1	
Builder	2	Farmer	18	
Butcher	6	Fireman	8	
Book-keeper	6	Fish Cutter	2	
Book-binder	1	Foreman	7	
Beamster	1	Furnace man	1	
Bricklayer	5	Gardener	8	
Brickmaker	1	Glass polisher	2	
Boiler maker	4	Glass Cutter	1	
Back tender on machine	1	Glass finisher	1	
Brass finisher	1	Glue maker	1	
Boot and shoe dealer	2	Grocer	14	
Carriage spring maker	1	Granite cutter	1	
Cabinet maker	2	Granite dealer	1	
Clerk	30	Grease renderer	1	
Clergyman	6	Gas fitter	1	
Coachman	16	Grocery & provision dealer	1	
Chocolate maker	1	Horse shoer	2	
Carder	1	Hostler	11	
Carpenter	10	Hatter	7	
Cooper	1	Hotel-keeper	1	
Confectioner	2	Harness maker	1	
Collector	2	Hair dresser	3	
Currier	20	Hackman	1	
Cigar manufacturer	2	Hardware dealer	1	
Comb maker	5	Iron dresser	1	
Cracker dealer	1	Iron fitter	1	
Conductor	4	Inspector	1	
Core maker	3	Iron worker	1	
Coal and wood dealer	1	Janitor	4	
Chair maker	1	Jeweller	5	
Carriage smith	1	Junk dealer	3	
Cook	2	Journalist	1	
Contractor	4	Knitter	3	
Clothing Cutter	1	Laborer	16	
Driver	7	Leather worker	6	
Druggist	2	Longshoreman	1	
Dining room keeper	1	Leather manufacturer	3	

Liquor dealer	.	.	.	7
Lawyer	.	.	.	2
Landlord .	.	.	.	1
Letter carrier	.	.	.	3
Leather cutter .	.	.	.	3
Lithographer	.	.	.	1
Lamp lighter .	.	.	.	1
Mailer .	.	.	.	1
Mason	.	.	.	11
Moulder	.	.	.	8
Merchant	.	.	.	7
Marketman .	.	.	.	3
Morocco dresser	.	.	.	27
Marble worker	.	.	.	4
Machinist	.	.	.	22
Machine operator .	.	.	.	1
Mechanic .	.	.	.	4
Mill hand	.	.	.	6
Motorman	.	.	.	1
Meat cutter .	.	.	.	2
Magnet winder	.	.	.	1
Morocco manufacturer .	.	.	.	1
Mill operator .	.	.	.	2
Overseer	.	.	.	1
Operator .	.	.	.	2
Officer .	.	.	.	3
Packer	.	.	.	4
Proprietor .	.	.	.	1
Printers' supplies	.	.	.	1
Paper maker	.	.	.	3
Picture dealer .	.	.	.	1
Porter .	.	.	.	3
Printer	.	.	.	5
Painter	.	.	.	11
Provision dealer	.	.	.	5
Plumber	.	.	.	12
Pedler	.	.	.	2
Plasterer	.	.	.	8
Policeman	.	.	.	4
Piano polisher	.	.	.	1
Pressman	.	.	.	1
Piano maker	.	.	.	2
Piano stainer .	.	.	.	1
Physician	.	.	.	11
Paver	.	.	.	2
Paper hanger	.	.	.	2
Restaurant keeper	.	.	.	1

Rubber grinder	.	.	.	5
Refiner	.	.	.	1
Real estate dealer	.	.	.	2
Receiver .	.	.	.	1
Salesman	.	.	.	14
Shipper .	.	.	.	3
Stove mounter	.	.	.	1
Steam fitter	.	.	.	3
Ship rigger	.	.	.	1
Stable keeper .	.	.	.	2
Store keeper	.	.	.	2
Shoe manufacturer .	.	.	.	3
Silk finisher .	.	.	.	2
Silver maker .	.	.	.	1
Shoemaker .	.	.	.	176
Stain glass worker .	.	.	.	1
Shoe dealer .	.	.	.	1
Stevedore	.	.	.	1
Stone cutter .	.	.	.	3
Starch maker .	.	.	.	1
Superintendent	.	.	.	1
Shovel maker .	.	.	.	1
Stock fitter .	.	.	.	1
Student .	.	.	.	3
Spinner	.	.	.	2
Stone layer	.	.	.	1
Shoe shop	.	.	.	1
Tailor	.	.	.	8
Tanner	.	.	.	6
Teamster .	.	.	.	57
Time keeper	.	.	.	1
Tinsmith .	.	.	.	1
Track repairer	.	.	.	1
Telegraph operator .	.	.	.	1
Tallyman	.	.	.	2
Trader	.	.	.	1
Undertaker .	.	.	.	7
Upholsterer	.	.	.	4
Wire drawer	.	.	.	2
Weaver .	.	.	.	4
Wool sorter .	.	.	.	2
Waiter	.	.	.	2
Watchman .	.	.	.	3
Wheelwright .	.	.	.	1
Whitener .	.	.	.	1
Total	.	.	.	1058

OCCUPATION OF APPLICANTS REJECTED

January 1. 1892, to January 1, 1893.

Baker	2	Leather worker	1
Barber	1	Machinist	3
Bar tender	2	Marble worker	1
Blacksmith	1	Merchant	1
Book-keeper	1	Marble polisher	2
Blue stone dealer	1	Milkman	1
Bricklayer	1	Morocco dresser	1
Brushmaker	1	Painter	1
Butcher	1	Pedler	1
Carpenter	7	Plater	1
Cigar maker	1	Plumber	1
Cigar manufacturer	1	Provision dealer	1
Carder	1	Quarryman	2
Clerk	6	Roofer	2
Conductor	2	Rubber boot maker	1
Cooper	1	Salesman	3
Currier	2	Saloon keeper	1
Diver	1	Section hand	1
Draughtsman	1	Sheet iron worker	1
Driver	1	Shoemaker	19
Engineer	1	Slate and metal worker	1
Expressman	1	Selectman	1
Foreman	6	Steam fitter	1
Gardener	2	Stone cutter	2
Glass blower	1	Steward	1
Granite manufacturer	1	Tanner	2
Grocer	1	Teamster	4
Hotel keeper	1	Tailor	1
Hostler	1	Undertaker	1
Horseshoer	1	Upholsterer	2
Jig sawyer	1	Watchman	1
Laborer	27		
Liquor dealer	2	Total	144
Lamp lighter	1		

The average age of applicants approved was 32.8 years. The average age of applicants rejected was 33.5 years.

Our membership January 1, 1893, was 5,932. If we add the number approved since that time 387 to April 1, we have a total membership of 6,319. The average age of the Order January 1, 1893, was 39.3 years.

MEMBERSHIP.

No. of Court	NAME OF COURT	Membership Dec. 31, 1891	Membership Dec. 31, 1892	Initiated in 1892	Admitted on W. Card in 1892	Reinstated in 1892	Average age of Court Dec. 31, 1892	Average age of Court Dec. 31, 1891	Withdrawn on Card in 1892	Resigned Membership in 1892	Suspended for Non-payment in 1892	Expelled in 1892	Died in 1892	Rejected by ballot in 1892	Rejected by H. S. C. in 1892
1	Cathedral	175	181	15	8	1	39.	40	2	1	5		1		3
3	Fenwick	63	67	3	2		45.5	43.9	1		3		2		8
4	St. Francis	118	130	9			42.5	43.5	1		4		4		8
5	Leo	103	133	17	1		43.2	42.7	1		1		1		1
6	...	100	106	8			44.1	42.6			2				4
7	St. Patrick	44	41	2	1		43.1	44.	4		7		1		3
8	Sherwood	154	162	15	1		39.	38.5							1
9	...	43	40	3	2		40.25	37.8		1			5		
10	Iona	94	100	13			40.	40.6	6		3		1	1	
11	St. Joseph	131	141	8	1		41	42.1	1		1				1
12	Fulton	39	41	6	1		41.2	41.2	1		3				2
13	Fitzpatrick	49	54	1	2		43.3	46.2	2				2		6
14	Lafayette	86	99	18			40.1	41.2					1		4
15	SS. Peter and Paul	71	79	12			47.3	41.5	1		2		2		4
16	Essex	126	149	23			37.	38.01	1		2		1		1
17	Hamilton	66	69	5	3		39.3	47.07	1		1		2		3
18	St. Peter	94	101	7			41.	39.9			3		1		1
19	...	88	90	1			39.6	39.6					2		2
20	Mt. ...	81	84	3		1	41.5	40.5	1	1					
21	St. ...	49	49	7			45.2	45.4	3				1		
23	St. John	51	63	14	2		36.4	36.9					2		7
24	St. Gregory	73	88	17	4		36.3	37.1					1		2
25	St. Francis	118	118	6			38.06	38.1	1		2				5
26	St. Raphael	44	45	1	1		41.8	41.04			1		1		3
28	Erin	98	90	5			42.2	415	1		2		3		
29	St. ...	174		12		2	37.	34.5	1						
30	Bass River	44	55	15	1		39.1	39.5	1						7
32	Qualey	56	66	19			45.5	39.01	1		6		1		2
33	St. John	80	72	6			39.9	45.1	1		2		1		
34	Americus	21	80				13.5	39.3			1		1		5
35	Sheil	45	20	1			40.6	42.3			2		3		3
37	Friendship	43	42	4			46.	B4							
38	St. Joseph	32	47	5				45.6	1			1			
39	St. Benedict	35						41.3							
43	St. Mary	44	36	8			39.08	39.4					1		
44	...	48	44		1		38.	38.4	2						
45	Unity	34	56	11			40.2	40.							3
46	St. Augustine		45	11			38.5	41.							5
47	St. Anne	103	110				33.2	32.7			2		1		

MEMBERSHIP — *Continued.*

No.	Court							Avg. age	Avg. age							
48	Sarsfield	86	90	9				38.5	38.4					1		1
49	Constantine	70	66	4	1			39.2	39.2	4				2		2
51	Holy Trinity	136	145	11				37.8	39.8							2
52	Highland	25	29	4				37.8	38.8							5
53	Innit	101	130	31	1			33.1	38.9							2
54	St. James	56	76	24				32.4	37.5							
55	Charles River	92	102	12				37.1	32.9							
57	Carroll	48	57	9	1			39.2	36.05					1	1	3
58	Prospect	38	43	5	1			43.2	38.7							
59	Worcester	86	96	11				40.1	40.9							5
60	Middlesex	71	81	10	1			35.7	39.1	20	1	6		1		1
61	St. Lawrence	77	103	27				36.	36.							
62	St. Columbkille	69	55	8	1			35.6	34.		2	2				2
63	Shields	33	28	2	1			39.	36.8			6				1
64	Gallagher	63	67	7	1			40.4	39.4			8		2		1
65	St. Columbkille	57	64	8	3			35.2	35.03			2		1		
66	Griffin	49	69	24				36.04	34.			1		2		
67	Canton	70	73	5				36.4	36.8	1						1
68	St. Margaret	27	32	5	1			35.75	37.1							2
69	Stoughton	73	33	11	5			32.7	31.9			1				1
70	St. Michael	39	47	6				35.	32.6	1		2				2
71	Phil Sheridan	83	82	9	3			30.1	29.9	3		6	1	1		1
72	Merrimack	83	83	17				34.4	33.07	1		3		1		4
73	Taunton	113	129	18				35.	35.1	1		2				1
74	Hendricken	34	44	10				29.2	29.2		1	1		1		1
75	St. Jarlath	55	52	3	1			30.5	35.05		1	6				
76	Quincy	51	47	2	1			30.6	34.8	2	1	3		1		1
77	Mystic	39	50	16	1			37.4	37.5	2		2		1		1
78	St. Monica	26	24	5				36.2	36.2							
79	John Boyle O'Reilly	20	33	4				38.4	36.4	1		5				1
80	Gen. Shea	28	34	9	1			35.3	33.7		2					1
81	St. Mal	29	73	7				34.02	34.4							
82	Isen	61	40	15				30.	29.5	1	1			1		
83	John Henry Shea	28	53	11	3			33.2	31.07		1	3		1		1
84	Danvers		83	53	1			32.5		1		1		1		
85	George Washington		44	6				82.6								4
86	Avon		45	40	1			31.2								10
87	Robert Emmett		45	29	19			28.								2
88	Enterprise		22	23				82.1				3				6
89	Union		25	25				32.9				1				
90	Rockland		24	23	1			28.4								4
91	St. Vincent		26	26				0.1								
	Total	**4,913**	**5,572**	**903**	**98**	**10**				**74**	**17**	**132**	**1**	**57**	**10**	**144**

* The average age given for each Court is taken from the reports sent in by the officers.

The percentage of increase is shown by the following table :—

No. of Court	NAME OF COURT.				No. of Court.	NAME OF COURT.			
1	Cathedral	.	.	.034	52	Highland	.	.	.16
3	Fenwick	.	.	.015	53	Emerald	.	.	.28
4	St. Francis	.	.	.111	54	St. James	.	.	.35
5	Leo	.	.	.291	55	Charles River	.		.108
6	Cheverus	.	.	.06	57	Carroll	.	.	.21
8	Sherwood	.	.	.051	58	Prospect	.	.	.13
10	Iona	.	.	.063	59	Worcester	.	.	.116
11	St. Joseph	.	.	.052	60	Middlesex	.	.	.14
12	Fulton	.	.	.05	61	St. Lawrence	.	.	.33
13	Fitzpatrick	.	.	.102	64	Gallagher	.	.	.063
14	Lafayette	.	.	.137	65	St. Columbkille	.	.	.12
15	SS. Peter and Paul			.112	66	Griffin	.	.	.40
16	Essex	.	.	.182	67	Canton	.	.	.042
17	Hamilton	.	.	.045	68	St. Margaret	.		.185
18	St. Peter	.	.	.074	69	Stoughton	.	.	.136
19	Williams	.	.	.022	70	St. Michael	.	.	.205
20	Mount Pleasant	.	.	.024	72	Merrimack	.	.	.185
23	St. John	.	.	.235	73	Taunton	.	.	.141
24	St. Gregory	.	.	.205	74	Hendricken	.	.	.294
26	St. Raphael	.	.	.022	77	Mystic	.	.	.28
30	Bass River	.	.	.25	78	St. Monica	.	.	.19
32	Qualey	.	.	.20	79	J. B. O'Reilly	.		.20
33	St. John	.	.	.28	80	Gen. Sherman	.	.	.178
38	St. Joseph	.	.	.105	81	St. Malachi	.	.	.17
43	St. Mary	.	.	.028	82	Brockton	.	.	.216
45	Unity	.	.	.166	83	J. H. Newman	.		.50
46	St. Augustine	.	.	.32	85	Geo. Washington	.		.064
47	St. Anne	.	.	.111	87	Robert Emmett	.		1.045
48	Sarsfield	.	.	.046	30	Rockland	.	.	.043
51	Holy Trinity	.	.	.066					

ASSESSMENT CALLS.

During the year 1892 the following Assessment Calls were issued : 87, 88, 89, 90, 91, 92, 93, 94, 95, 96. No. 96 did not expire until January 21, 1893.

The Reserve Fund Assessment Call was also sent out as required by the constitution, and was turned over to the Trustees, whose report will be found elsewhere. The Reserve Fund now amounts to over $10,000.00.

The initiation of those whose names were added to the endowments paid occurred as follows.

1880	-	-	-	6	1887	-	-	-	6
1881	-	-	-	9	1888	-	-	-	6
1882	-	-	-	1	1189	-	-	-	6
1883	-	-	-	4	1890	-	-	-	3
1884	-	-	-	2	1891	-	-	-	9
1885	-	-	-	2	1892	-	-	-	2
1886	-	-	-	3					

In this list the only item of special interest is that of the initiations In 1891 there were 9 deaths. That year there were 726 applications approved. The deaths, then, are a fraction over 12 per cent. of the members admitted.

The deaths were distributed as follows:

Leo, No. 5, - - - - - - 1	St. Thomas, No. 29, - - - 1
Cheverus, No. 6, - - - - 1	Stoughton, No. 69, - - - 1
Lafayette, No. 14, - - - 2	Brockton No. 82, - - - 1
Erin, No. 28, - - - - - 1	John Henry Newman, No. 83, 1

The causes of death are, Consumption, 1 ; Pneumonia, 3 ; Heart Disease, 3 ; Typhoid Fever, 1 ; Bright's Disease, 1.

The Medical Examiners, who examined the above for admission, are all careful men who have the interest of the Order at heart. In the single case of Bright's Disease, the Medical Examiner was careful to say, on the application blank, that he found all the organs of the applicant sound. In view of all this, we can only say we have done the best we could to keep poor risks out of the Order, and if some have succeeded in getting in, it can only serve to make us more careful in our selections of those we solicit to join.

In 1892 we had 56 deaths, which occurred as follows :

January	-	-	4	July	-	-	-	3
February	-	-	9	August	-	-	-	5
March	-	-	5	September -	-	-	4
April	-	-	4	October	-	-	-	3
May	-	-	6	November -	-	-	6
June	-	-	3	December -	-	-	4

The average length of membership of those who died in 1892 was 6 years 6 months 20 days.

The following deaths are also reported :

NAME.	COURT.	CAUSE OF DEATH.
P. Mulvey,	St. Joseph, No. 38,	Pul. Tuberculosis.
J. A. Harrington,	Bass River, No. 30,	Chr. Int. Nephritis.
J. F. Reddy,	St. Columbkille, No. 65,	Paralysis.
J. Tobin,	St. Joseph, No. 38,	Consumption. [Kidneys.
W. Syms,	St. Anne, No. 47,	Tuberc. of Bladder and
J. Torndorf,	Holy Trinity, No. 51,	Gastritis.
W. H. Sullivan,	Stoughton, No. 69,	Consumption.
M. J. Glynn,	Prospect, No. 58,	Pneumonia,
E. J. Kerrigan,	St. Francis, No. 4,	Drowning.
J. J. Driscoll,	Merrimack, No. 72,	Typhoid Fever.
T. Hennessey,	Sherwood, No. 8,	Catarrhal Infl. of Lungs.
T. McKeague,	St. Margaret, No 68,	Pneumonia.
Jere. Callahan,	St. Francis, No. 25,	Phthisis Pul.
Robert Colbert,	Leo, No. 5,	Crushed by Elevator.
James Delury,	Sherwood, No. 8,	Pneumonia.
J. F. Hunt,	Taunton, No. 73,	Bronchitis.
J. J. Murphy,	Sherwood, No. 8,	Nephritis.
J. A. Gill,	Leo, No. 5,	Nephritis.
J. H. Lennon,	Carroll, No. 57,	Strangulated Hernia.

The deaths in January were extraordinary, numbering 16, which is unprecedented in our experience. It may be said that extra calls should have been sent out to meet these, but it seems better to make our calculations on the death rate for the year, which is not likely to be more than one per cent. above the normal rate, than to cause alarm by raising a cry that an extra call must be met by the members.

With all the unfortunate admissions of the early years of the Order to take care of, since the manner of assessment was changed, we can say that, in the last 9 years or 108 months, only 99 calls were issued, and these were all that were necessary.

The only cases calling for special mention are that of William Syms, of St. Anne Court, No. 47, who made his endowment payable to his mother, then married and neglected to change the beneficiary. He left a wife in poor health, who makes claim for the endowment and will ask the law courts to give it to her. M. J. Glynn, of Prospect Court, No, 58, whose name on the roll of members of that Court is the only evidence we have that he was a member.

Another case not placed on the list, is that of Ferdinand Shields, of St. John Court, No. 33, East Cambridge. Shields died October 10, 1892, at the Massachusetts General Hospital. The Death Certificate was received by the High Standing Committee February 14, 1893. The Deputy High Chief Ranger wrote that the delay was caused by the illness of Shields' wife, the absence of the attending physician and the neglect of the officers of the Court

The facts of the case appear to be that Mrs. Shields was sick and about to have an operation performed. Shields visited her at the Carney Hospital, went home under the influence of liquor and was found, in a few minutes after entering the house, vomiting. Dr. P. J. Finnegan was sent for and responded at once. The doctor asked Shields if he had taken Paris Green, and he answered he had. The doctor, at once, sent Shields to the hospital, after doing what he could for him. At the hospital all was done for him that could be done, but he died in three hours.

The High Standing Committee considered it a case of suicide and refused to pay the claim.

MEETINGS OF HIGH STANDING COMMITTEE.

The High Standing Committee has held seventy-two meetings since the last Convention, and has endeavored to hold itself in readiness at all times to meet the various wants arising from the Subordinate Courts. In this respect, it has not differed much from preceding High Standing Committees, except that each year the work increases and the demands on the time of the Committee become greater.

In response to the feeling that Courts should be formed outside of Massachusetts, an effort was made to form, in Portland, Maine, but without success. The seed sown there may bear fruit some time, but, at present, the High Standing Committee does not feel warranted in proceeding further in that direction.

A member of the Order, who lives in Eastport, Maine, is endeavoring to form a Court, and authority has been given him to collect names, only, and report to the High Standing Committee the number he can get.

An invitation was received from a sufficient number to form a Court in Richmond, Virginia, but the High Standing Committee declined to accept them.

Arrangements are now progressing for meetings in Medway and Pittsfield, in this State, and with a reasonable prospect of success.

DEPUTY HIGH CHIEF RANGERS.

We have now 49 Deputy High Chief Rangers, who have made 262 visits to the various Courts, during the year 1892. The report sent in by the Deputy High Chief Rangers, do not contain any comments worthy of mention. The usual report is, the "Court is in good condition." This is sufficient to show that matters in the Subordinate Courts are harmonious. Only 3 District Arbitration trials have taken place, so far as reported. No official report has been made here about them, and it is safe to assume that a settlement was reached of benefit to the order.

MEDICAL EXAMINERS.

The corps of Medical Examiners is constituted about as it was for 1891. The additions made necessary by formation of new Courts are—Dr. J. D. McIntosh, of Rockland, for Rockland Court No. 90 ; Dr. F. G. Atkins, of Holliston, for St. Vincent Court No. 91 ; Dr. A. L. Shirley, of East Bridgewater, for Harmony Court No. 92 ; Dr. C. W. McDonald, of Roxbury, for Columbia Court No. 95 ; Dr. P. F. McCarthy, of Franklin, was appointed for Griffin Court No. 66.

As is usual with him, the High Medical Examiner, Dr. Joseph D. Couch, 684 Main Street, Cambridge, has attended to the duties of the office with the greatest care and in a most conscientious manner. He has been present at nearly every meeting of the High Standing Committee, and all the applications have passed through his hands. he fully merits the high confidence reposed in him by the Order.

The deaths in 1892 were from the following causes—Phthisis 10 Jaundice 1, Paralysis 1, Pneumonia 13, Cancer 2, Typhoid Pneumonia 2, Accident 1, Heart Disease 5, Erysipelas 1, Bright's Disease 7, Concussion of Brain 1, Paresis 1, Cerebral Hemorrhage 3, Sunstroke 1, Apoplexy 1, Typhoid Fever 2, Cirrhosis of Liver 1, Meningitis 1, Asphyxia 1, Gangrene 1—56 in all.

Since the organization of the Massachusetts Catholic Order of Foresters, the number deceased each year is as follows :

1880	3	1887	34
1881	17	1888	46
1882	25	1889	54
1883	40	1890	47
1884	41	1891	53
1885	48	1892	56
1886	32		
		Total	496

ENDOWMENTS PAID.

NAMES OF ... AND ... Ms. DATE AND ... OF DEATH, ... OF ... WH HE DECEASED WAS A MEMBER, AND BEN... FEES, ... LENGTH OF MEMBERSHIPS.

No.	NAME.	BY.	AGE.	INITIATED.	Yrs.	Mos.	Dys.	DATE OF DEATH.	CAUSE.	Endowment.	MR. OF MS.	TO WHOM PAID.
1	...	... No. 0,	49	Mar. 14, 1880		7	5	Oct. 19, 1880	Typho-Malaria.	$1,000	1, Widow	...
2	...	... 5,	...	Nov. 14, 1879	1	1	6	Nov. 20, "	...	"	1,	...
3	M. J. ...	... 3,	31	Mar. 14, 1880		9	19	Dec. 3, 1881	...	"		...
4	D. I. ...	... 10,	29	Sept. 3, 1879	1	3	8	Jan. 11, "	...	"	1,	...
5	P. H. McGrath,	... 1,	48	Feb. 11, 1880	1	3	12	Jan. 27, "	...	"		Widow
6	...	... 6,	38	May 26, "	0	11	0	Mar. 5, "	...	"	"	"
7	Edward A. Burbank,	... 17,	42	Aug. 3, "		10	14	April 26, "	... in Groin	"	1,	"
8	J ...	...	...	April 21, "	1	1	27	June 17, "	...	"	1,	"
9	... Kelley,	... 0,	...	Mar. 15, 1881		6	14	June 18, "	...	"	1,	"
10	Patrick ...	... 34,	...	April 13, 1880	1	0	8	Aug. 29, "	...	"	1,	"
11	... C. Dailey,	... 5,	26	Aug. 10, 1881		1	27	Aug. 23, "	...	"	1,	"
12	... L. ...	... 5,	...	July 6, 1880	1	2	14	Sept. 3, "	...	"	3, ... & chil ...	... &
13	... F. ...	... 17,	24	Aug. 16, "	1	1	8	Sept. 27, "	...	"	3,	... & children
14	... Morrison,	... 5,	47	April 12, "	1	5	5	Oct. 30, "	Bright's ...	"	1,	"
15	William Whitley,	... Patrick, 7,	36	April 21, 1881	1	7	1	Nov. 17, "	...	"	4,	"
16	Daniel J. ...	Hamilton, 17,	40	Feb. 13, 1880	1	8	26	Nov. 22, "	...	"	1,	"
17	...	... 3,	31	Mch. 4, "	1	11	9	Nov. 27, "	... Gastritis & ... Dis. of ...	"	1,	"
18	...	... 8,	23	Dec. 27, "	1	9	17	Nov. 30, "	...	"	1,	"
19	...	St. Joseph, 11,	26	Mar. 10, "	1	3	10	Dec. 6, 1882	... al Cong. of ...	"	1,	Guardian
20	... O'Brien,	... 11,	23	Mar. 22, "	2	3	16	Jan. 9, "	...	"	2, ...	Widow
21	... M. Galvin,	... 11,	31	Oct. 15, 1879		1	18	Jan. 25, "	...	"	1,	"
22	... T.	St. ... 21,	28	Oct. 15, "	1	10	26	Feb. 1, "	...	"	1,	"
23	...	... 33,	25	Mar. 29, 1881	1	11	4	Feb. 18, "	Phthisis	"	1,	"
24	... B. Mulvey,	Sullivan, 27,	46	Jan. 18, "		10	17	Mar. 25, "	...	"	1,	"
25	...	St. Patrick, 7,	36	June 25, 1880	1	11	11	May 21, "	...	"	1,	"
26	... Clark,	... 5,	35	June 24, 1881		11		May 28, "	...	"	1,	"
27	... Purcell,	... 39, Somerville	40	May 12, "		11		June 10, "	...	"	1,	"
28	...	... 40,	39	May 10, "				June 27, "	...	"	1,	"
29	J ...	St. Francis, 4,	Salem 40	June 23, 1880								
30	J ...		33	June 1, 1882								

ENDOWMENTS PAID — Ont' [...].

NO.	NAME	COURT	AGE	INITIATED.	Yrs.	Mos.	Dys.	DATE OF DEATH	CAUSE	Endow-ment.	N OF BENEFICIARIES	TO WHOM PAID
33			25	Sept. 3, 1880	1	8	21	May 24, 1882		$1,000	1,	Widow
34			3	April 13, 1881	9	1	4	Jan. 27, "		"	1,	Widow
35			34	Nov. 17, 1880	1	2	24	Aug. 11, "	1st at Sea	"	1,	
36		S.	31	Mar. 12, "	2	5	6	Aug. 18, "	Rheumatism and Cong. of the	"	1,	Father
37			27	Aug. 3, 1879	2	11	24	July 27, "	Scarlet Fever [Brain	"		"
38			24	April 29, 1880	2	4	8	Sept. 7, "		"	5,	"
39			24	Dec. 2, 1881		9	25	Sept. 27, "		"	1,	Widow
40			38	Mar. 23, 1880	2	7	5	Oct. 24, "	of Brain	"	1,	Wi dow
41	J			Dec. 8, "	1	11		Nov. 3, "	the falling	"		"
42	Henry Conroy,	St. Quincy		Jan. 11, "	2	10	13	Nov. 3, "		"	1,	"
43	Patrick	St. Francis, 4,		Feb. 11, "	4		8	Oct. 3, "		"	1,	Widow
44		5,	22	April 26, 1882	2	10		Jan. 6, 1883		"	8,	8n
45	R. L.	6,	68	Feb. 11, 1880	2	10	28	Jan. 9, "	Heart	"	1,	Widow
46		6,	34	Oct. 4, 1883	1	1	10	Feb. 22, 1882		"	1,	
47		St. Francis, 4,	23	Jan. 4, 1883	1		10	Feb. 14, 1883	Typhoid	"	1,	
48	J	Sheil, 35,	29	May 26, 1881	1	8	18	Feb. 19, "	from	"	1,	
49	J	Sherwood, 8,	32	Dec. 21, 1882	1		28	Mar. 4, "		"	2,	Children
50	M. A. Breen,		35	June 24, 1881	3	1	14	Mar. 18, "		"	1,	Widow
51	Horan,	St. John, 8,	51	Mar. 29, 1880	3		3	April 16, "	of Heart	"	1,	"
52	Hanney,		64	Mar. 30, "	2	1	18	April 16, "		"	1,	Sister
53		Ex, 6,	38	Nov. 4, 1880	2	6	23	April 22, "		"	1,	Widow
54	Collins,	Ex, 16,	35	Aug. 4, "	2	9	1	May 3, "	of the Brain	"	1,	"
55			32	Dec. 18, 1879	3	4	18	May 5, "	Pulmonary	"	1,	Widow
56	P. L.		41	July 21, 1880	2	7	9	May 8, "	Drowning	"	4,	Widow
57	Charles	St. Peter, 8,	33	Oct. 22, 1882	6	1	6	May 30, "		"	1,	
58	Kerrigan,	A, 47,	27	Dec. 22, 1880	2	2	6	June 28, "		"	1,	
59			33	Mar. 2, "	2	9	1	May 4, "		"	1,	
60		6,	26	Nov. 14, 1879	3	7	3	May 17, "		"	3,	Children
61	F.	St. 3,	37	Nov. 1, "	3	6	20	June 13, "		"	1,	"
62		3,	45	Dec. 1, 1880	2	6	18	June 21, "		"	1,	"
63	C. L.		43	Feb. 10, "	3	4	18	June 28, "		"	1,	"
64	Murphy,	7,	48	April 13, 1883	1	2	17	June 30, "		"	1,	"
65	Brown,	St. 6,	37	April 27, 1882		2	24	July 2, "	Heart	"	1,	Widow
66	G.		27	May 5, "	1	1	15	July 12, 1883	General	"	1,	"
67	O'Brien,	St. Ann, 2,	50	Dec. 8, 1883	3		28	Aug. 3, "		"	1,	
68	T.	Star of the Sea, 41,	49	Nov. 14, "	3	8	11	Aug. 23, "	Fever	"	1,	Widow
69	Maguire,	Fenwick, 3,	31	Sept. 16, 1880	3	10	16	Sept. 30, "	Fever	"	3,	Heirs
70	J. A.,	Williams, 19,	27		3	1	1	Oct. 17, "		"	3,	
71	J. A. M.D.,										1,	
72	John J. Duffey,											

No.	Name	Church, Residence	Town	Age	Date Admitted				Date of Death	Cause of Death	Amount	Beneficiaries	
73	M. H. Byrne,	Benedict, 39,	Somerville	28	Mar. 31, 1881	2	5	17	Sept. 28, 1883	Pulmonary Hemorrhage	$1,000	1, Widow	New
74	Bart. Wien,	Essex, 16,	Salem	35	Aug. 1, 1883	2	8		Oct. 4, "	Uremic	"	1, "	"
75	E. F. Dever,	Hamilton, 17,	Boston	22	Sept. 16, "	3	3	18	Nov. 21, "	Phthisis	"	1, Mother	Mother
76	John O'Brien,	St. Joseph, 11,	"	47	Sept. 15, 1881	3	7	6	Nov. 25, "	Heart Disease	"	1, Widow	Widow
77	Patrick Monaghan,	Benedict, 39,	Somerville	32	June 14, 1880	1	7	24	Nov. 14, "	Injury to Brain by fall	"	4, "	Heirs
78	John Sweeney,	Mt. Pleasant, 20,	Boston	46	Mar. 31, 1881	2	10	1	Dec. 1, "	Pulmonary Consumption	"	1, "	
79	Michael H. Murray,	Fenwick, 3,	"	42	Oct. 20, 1880	2	2	11	Dec. 11, "	Catarrhal Pneumonia,C'nsum'p.	"	1, "	
80	Michael Donahue,	Cathedral, 1,	"	40	Jan. 30, "	2	10	22	Dec. 22, "	Pleurisy	"	1, "	
81	John Murray,	St. James, 54,	"	39	Oct. 8, 1879	5	2	17	Dec. 25, "	Phthisis	"	1, Sister	Sister
82	T. H. O'Rourke,	St. Thomas, 29,	Brockton	25	July 2, 1883	3	5	25	Dec. 27, "	Pulmonary Phthisis	"	1, New	Widow
83	Philip McDonald,	St. Thomas, 29,	Brockton	39	Feb. 17, 1881	3	4	4	Feb. 21, 1884	Cerebral Paralysis	"	1, Mother	Mother
84	John B. Reagan,	Charles Riv.55,	Waterr'n	23	Nov. 5, 1883	3	23		Feb. 28, "	Pneumonia	"	1, Widow	New
85	Thomas McDonough	Bay, 32,	Woburn,	33	Nov. 28, 1881	2	23		Feb. 23, "	Cong. of Lungs and Peritonitis	"	1, "	
86	Thomas Welsh,	Americus, 34,	Boston	40	July 31, 1883	5	28		Jan. 28, "	Quick Consumption	"	1, "	
87	ehis Ahearn,	St. Patrick, 7, So.		31	May 31, 1880	3	9	25	Mar. 25, "	Bright's Disease	"	1, "	
88	Frank A. Shez,	St. Alphonsus, 21,		31	Oct. 13, 1881	2	4	27	Mar. 10, "	Phthisis Pulmonalis	"	4, " 3 child'n	& child'n
89	Alfred Green,	ras, 6,		31	Feb. 25, "	3	10	17	Jan. 12, "	Pulmonary Consumption	"	4, " 3 "	
90	John A. McCarthy,	Fitzpatrick, 13,	Malden	41	Oct. 12, 1882	1	11		Feb. 6, "	Pulmonary Consumption	"	3, " 2 "	
91	John F. Cunningham	Iona, 10,		32	Mar. 14, 1880	3	10	21	April 21, 1883	Pneumonia	"	1, "	
92	Stephen T. Sliney,	SS.Pet.& Paul,15,	S.B son	26	April 7, "	3	11	12	Jan. 23, 1884	Bright's Disease of Kidneys	"	9, Parents 8	Father & mother
93	Thomas Gay,	Fenwick, 3,	Boston	50	April 26, 1880	3	8	2	Mar. 19, "	Accident, falling off staging	"	2, Sister	Guardian
94	John H. Matthews,	Essex, 16,	Salem	32	Feb. 3, 1881	3	4	16	May 2, "	Phthisis	"	1, Sister	Widow
95	John W. Lynch,	St. Joseph, 11,		28	Jan. 8, 1880	4	1	18	May 14, "	Phthisis Pulmonalis	"	5, Widow, 4 child'n	"
96	John P. Duffin,	Erin, 28,		45	Mar. 24, 1881	3	7	25	May 18, "	Heart Disease	"	5, " 4 "	
97	William Meagher,	St. Francis, 4,		43	April 11, "	4	1	8	May 24, "	Accid'nt, hhd. sugar fell on him	"	1, "	
98	Mel McCarthy,	Fitzpatrick, 13,		49	Sept. 8, "	3	18		May 3, "	Diabetes Melletus	"	1, " 2 "	
99	Charles Lyons,	Cathedral, 1,		30	Mar. 24, 1881	4	2	17	May 2, "	Pneumonia. r. lung & upper lt.	"	4, " 3 "	
100	Daniel Bailey,	Sherwood, 8,	Malden	31	April 11, "	3	11	29	April 29, 1883	Phthisis	"	3, "	
101	Patrick A. Finn,	Fula, 10,	Boston	30	April 22, 1880	4	2	9	June 9, "	Hemphlegia of Larynx	"	3, " 2 "	
102	Edward W. Wright,	St. Francis, 4,		40	April 22, "	3	1	1	May 17, "	Shock, accident, crushing of leg	"	1, Daughter	Daughter
103	John J. Donovan,	Sherwood, 8,		23	April 4, 1881	3	11	15	June 23, "	Phthisis Pulmonalis	"	1, Mother	Mother
104	Mel Maguire,	Williams, 19,		40	June 23, "	3	24		June 15, "	Chronic Bronchitis	"	4, Widow, 3 child'n	Wid. and child'n
105	Phil A. Cunningham,	Liberty, 40,		34	Mar. 11, "	1	3		June 24, "	Pulmonary Consumption	"	1, Widow	Widow
106	James F. Lynch,	Americus, 34,		33	Nov. 21, 1882	1	9	19	July 3, "	Pulmonary Consumption	"	1, "	
107	Patrick Donohue,	St. Joseph, 11,		40	Mar. 22, 1880	2	9	22	June 24, 1883	Cancer of Stomach	"	1, Sister	Sister
108	Rev. Wm. J. Daly,	Star of Sea, 41,	E. Boston	37	Dec. 13, 1881	2	8	9	July 3, "	Carcinoma of Liver	"	1, Brother	Brother
109	Rev. J. B. O'Donnell,	St. Alphonsus,21,	Boston	36	April 26, 1883	1	22		Aug. 10, 1884	Alcoholism	"	4, Widow, 3 child'n	Widow
110	Thomas Toohey,	Fitzpatrick, 13,			Mar. 29, 1882	1	15		June 18, "	Cirrhosis	"	1, Mother	Mother
111	M. J. Devine,	Cheverus, 6,		46	Feb. 11, 1880	4	5	29	Aug. 10, "	Phthisis	"	4, Widow, 4 child'n	Wid. and child'n
112	M. C. Boles,	SS.Pet.&Paul,15,	Bos'n	29	Mar. 7, 1882	2	5	13	Sept. 5, "	Hemorrhage of Lungs	"	2, " 1 child	"
113	Thos Cahill,	St.Thomas,29,	Brockton	34	Mar. 31, 1881	3	5	14	Sept. 14, "	Consumption	"		
114	P. H. Smith,	Shiel, 35,		43	Jan. 13, 1882	4	28		Oct. 1, "	Cholera-Morbus	"	3, " 3 child'n	3 child'n
115	J. S. Tompkins,	St. Peter, 18,	Dorchester	34	July 3, 1880	3	1	23	Oct. 4, "	Killed by locomotive	"	1, "	
116	B. A. Brown,	St. Francis, 4,	Boston	30	Nov. 11, "	3	6	10	Oct. 21, "	Consumption	"		
117	aMin McDonnell,	Shiel, 35,	Boston	34	Mar. 30, 1881	3	6	21	Oct. 27, "	Consumption	"	1, Sister	Sister
118	John Drury,	Hamilton,17,	Charles'wn	24	Mar. 2, 1882	2	8	25	Nov. 4, "	Concussion of Brain	"	1, Widow	Widow
119	T. H. Martin,	St. Francis, 4,	Boston	48	May 13, 1880	4	6	24	Dec. 21, "	Phthisis	"	1, Sister	Sister

ENDOWMENTS PAID — Continued.

No.	NAME.	COURT.	AGE.	INITIATED.	Membership Yrs.	Mos.	Dys.	DATE OF DEATH.	CAUSE.	Endowment.	NUMBER OF BENEFICIARIES.	TO WHOM PAID.
121	Thos Lynh	St. Joseph, 11, Boston	35	June 27, 1881	3	4	7	Nov. 4, 1884	Pneumonia	$1,000	3, Children	Guardian
122	Matthew Cusack	St. Alphonsus, 21, "	43	Oct. 15, 1880	2	11	2	Dec. 17, "	Consumption	"	5, Widow, 4 child'n	Wid. & children
123	J. M. Tirrell	St. Patrick, 7, So. Boston	23	Jan. 24, 1882	2	11	27	Jan. 21, 1885	Phthisis	"	2, "	Guardian
124	John Delaney	Leo, 5, E. Boston	24	Jan. 16, 1880	5		23	Feb. 9, "	Consumption	"	2, "	"
125	Patrick O'Gorman	St. Joseph, 11, Boston	32	Jan. 12, 1882	2	11	26	Jan. 8, "	Phthisis	"	3, Broth., wid., ch.	Broth., wid. & ch.
126	J. W. McClellan	Hea Mw, 36,	35	Oct. 3, 1881	3	3	27	Jan. 30, "	Heart Disease	"	1, Widow	Widow
127	W. J. Barry	Essex, 16, Salem	25	June 23, 1880	4	7	15	Feb. 8, 1885	Phthisis Pulmonalis	"	5, Sister	Sister
128	P. F. Welsh	Friendship, 37, Boston	35	Feb. 6, 1882	3	1	1	Feb. 7, "	Paralysis	"	1, Mw	Mw
129	Michael Perrin	ay, 32,	44	Jan. 15, 1883	1	10	27	Dec. 12, 1884	Enteritis	"	4, " 3	Wid. & guardian
130	Edward Doherty	s, 6, Boston	30	May 7, 1880	4	5	5	Oct. 15, "	Phthisis	"	3, Brothers	Brothers
131	John Sullivan	St. Patrick, 7, So. Boston	48	Mar. 1, "	4	5	16	Mar. 17, 1885	Phthisis Pulmonalis	"	6, W, 5 child'n	Wid. & guardian
132	T. J. Flynn	SS.Pet.&Paul,15, " "	26	Aug. 18, "	4	7	21	April 9, "	Phthisis Pulmonalis	"	1, "	"
133	Daniel Holland	O'Connell,22,Winchester	32	Nov. 9, "	4	4	23	April 15, "	Pneumonia	"	1, "	"
134	James Rae	Qualey, 32, Woburn	39	Feb. 15, "	4	1	20	April 10, "	Accident, crushing h'd & sh'l'd'r	"	1, "	"
135	John M. Perkins	Erin, 28, Boston	42	June 9, 1882	2	10	13	April 18, 1885	Pneumonia	"	1, "	"
136	Daniel M. Gillis	Bass River, 30, Beverly	25	Feb. 9, 1885			3	May 10, "	Pneumonia	"	2, Father	Father
137	Joseph A. Devenny	Fenwick, 3, Boston	25	Mar. 19, 1880	5		29	April 17, "	Consumption	"	2, Father& Mother	Father & ther
138	John Schultz	Holy Trinity, "	39	April 13, 1883	2	1	4	May 25, "	Accident	"	3, Widow,2 child'n	Widow
139	W. O'Neil	v Mw,	44	Mar. 21, 1881	4	1	25	N Ma 16, "	Pneumonia	"	1, "	"
140	John Donovan	Friendship, 37, Boston	35	Mar. 9, 1880	5	2	4	N Ma 13, "	Consumption	"	1, 1 child	"
141	J. S. MacCorry	Hns, 9,	25	Dec. 13, 1881	3	5	18	uhe 2, "	Heart Disease	"	1, Brother	Brother
142	Edward Gallagher	Star of the Sea,41, E. "	26	Feb. 14, 1882	3	3	18	uhe 7, "	Drowned	"	4, Widow, 3 child'n	Widow
143	Daniel R. Mid	Lyndon, 50, Boston	35	May 12, 1881	3	10	27	April 9, 1882	Inflammation of Mis	"	6, es & aunts	Uncles & ants
144	Dr. W. P. Kelley	Liberty, 40, "	48	Mar. 11, "	4	2	26	uhe 7, 1 85	Congestion of Brain	"	5, Widow, 4 child'n	Widow & chil.d'n
145	Peter Tracy	Mt. Pleasant, 20, "	39	Mar. 30, 1880	5	3	14	July 14, "	Bright's Disease	"	4, " 3	"
146	Maurice O'Hearn	Cheverus, 6, "	11	Oct. 11, "	4	8	1	June 12, "	Pneumonia	"	1, "	"
147	Timothy Long	St. Patrick, 7, So. "	39	April 6, "	5	3	13	July 19, "	Phthisis	"	4, "	"
148	David Lane	Cheverus, 6, Boston	49	Feb. 24, "	5	5		July 24, "	Apoplexy	"	5, Mother	Mother
149	Joseph F. Murphy	Cheverus, 6, "	47	April 22, "	5	3	2	July 14, "	Phthisis	"	1, Mw	Widow
150	Michael Reardon	Star of the Sea,41.E. "	43	Dec. 13, 1881	3	2	19	Mar. 2, 1884	Pneumonia	"	3, Brothers	Brothers
151	Peter Hawkins	St.Bernard,44, E. Boston	25	Sept. 25, 1882	2	10	22	Aug. 15, "	Phthisis	"	4, Father, 3 sisters	Father & sister
152	P. W. Sweeney	Leo, 5, "	39	Dec. 27, 1881	2	8	18	Sept. 15, "	Pyæmia	"	6, Children	Guardian
153	Thomas Daly	McGlew, 36, Chelsea	32	Mar. 21, 1879	6	5	16	Sept. 1, "	Phthisis	"	7, Widow, 6 child'n	Mw
154	B. F. Harrington	Cathedral, 1, Boston	40	Sept. 3, 1880	4	6		Sept. 19, "	Typhoid Pneumonia	"	4, " 3	"
155	Owen McCarthy	Fenwick, 3, "	37	Mar. 12, 1880	6	6	9	Sept. 21, "	Phthisis	"	5, "	"
156	Timothy Leary	Hamilton, 17, "	38	July 6, "	5	2	24	Sept. 30, "	Neuralgia of Stomach	"	5, "	"
157	James H. Phalan	Unity, 45, Bridgewater	44	Nov. 12, 1882	2	11	7	d. 19, 1885	Pneumonia	"	6, " 1	"
158	Timothy Dwyer	Emerald, 53, Peabody	32	July 2, 1883	1	8	24	d. 26, "	Phthisis Pulmonalis	"	2, " hild	"
159	John Sheehan	Cheverus, 6, Boston	29	Feb. 11, 1880	4	7	26	d. 17, "	Consumption	"	2, Sisters	Guardian

No.	Name	Court	Residence	Age	Date admitted	Date of death	Cause of death	Amount	Benef.	Beneficiaries	Relation
161	D. M. Lynch	Erin, 28	Boston	31	Feb. 3, 1881	Dec. 1, 1885	Phthisis and Gen'l tuberculosis	$1,000	6	Widow, 5 child'n	Widow.
162	Michael Sullivan	Essex, 16	Salem	40	May 4, 1880	Nov. 3, "	Uremia	"	3	" 3	Att'y for wid., g.
163	John Carney	St. John, 23	Hyde Park	40	Dec. 14, 1880	Nov. 20, "	Consumption	"	9	" 8	Widow & guar.
164	Patrick Prendergast	Americus, 34	Boston	39	Nov. 21, 1882	Nov. 14, "	Phthisis	"	6	" 5	"
165	J. R. Yendley	St. Francis, 4	"	36	Dec. 18, 1879	Dec. 2, "	Chronic Interstitial Cirrhosis	"	5	" 4	"
166	John O'Day	Erin, 28	"	38	Mar. 8, 1881	Dec. 21, "	Killed by ...	"	2	" 1 child	"
167	...es J. Quinn	St. John, 23	E. Cambridge	33	Mar. 18, 1879	Dec. 30, "	Pulmonary Phthisis	"	3	" 2 child'n	"
168	John H. ...	St. Francis, 4	Boston	56	Dec. 3, 1881	Dec. 22, "	Valvular Disease of Heart	"	1	"	"
169	Peter Daly	Erin, 28		48	Feb. 3, 1885	Dec. ..., "	Pyaemia		1	3*	"
170	John Handran	St. Anne, 47	Gloucester	33	July 6, 1885	Dec. 26, "	Drowned	177.50	4	3*	N'se, und'r la wy
171	Edward Brennan	Cathedral, 1		35	Oct. 15, 1879	Dec. 27, "	Blood Poisoning	$1,000	None		Widow
172	Michael Harvey	St. Joseph, 11		31	Oct. 11, 1880	Sept. 22, 1886	Pneumonia	"	3	Widow, 2 child'n	Widow
173	W. H. Fitzgerald	Mt. Pleasant, 20		49	April 14, 1882	Dec. 29, "	Heart Disease	"	4	Bros. and sister	Brother & sister
174	C. J. Hurley	St. Patrick, 7		31	Feb. 16, 1880	Jan. 18, "	Congestion of Lungs	"	3	Widow, 2 child'n	Widow
175	James J. McNealy	St. Francis, 25		41	Dec. 21, 1880	Jan. 7, "	Heart Disease	"	3	Widow, 9 child'n	& child'n
176	Joseph Donovaro	Williams, 19		45	April 21, 1881	Jan. 9, "	Consumption	"	5	" 4	"
177	Francis P. Paten	Fulton, 12		41	July 14, 1883	Jan. 10, 1886	Pneumonia	"	5	" 7	"
178	Patrick W. Sullivan	Leo, 5		48	Nov. 26, 1880	Feb. 17, "	Pleuro-Pneumonia	"	6	" 4	"
179	Edward J. Kenney	Hamilton, 17		40	July 6, "	Feb. 19, "	Phthisis	"	4	" 4	Guardian
180	James W. Norris	St. Joseph, 11		35	Mar. 22, "	Feb. 28, "	Phthisis	"	2	...er & widow	Mother & widow
181	William Logue	Qualey, 32		33	Jan. 2, 1882	Mar. 4, "	Pulmonary Pneumonia	"	2	...w, 3 child'n	Wid. and child'n
182	William Fay	Hamilton, 17		41	July 6, 1880	Mar. 30, "	Paralysis	"	4	Parents	Father
183	Michael Devine	Essex, 16		41	June 21, "	April 2, "	Catarrhal Pneumonia	"	1	Parents	Father
184	Patrick Bellen	St. Anne, 47		37	Dec. 22, 1882	April 6, "	Acute Pulmonary Tuberculosis	"	3	Widow, 2 child'n	Wid. and child'n
185	Michael McNeil	St. Peter, 18		47	Mar. 10, 1881	May 4, "	Loss of Lung from injury	"	3	" 2	"
186	Jeremiah Cahill	Iona, 10		52	Feb. 13, "	May 1, "	Consumption	"	2	" 1 child	"
187	Luke Kelley	Mt. Pleasant, 20		52	July 13, 1883	April 30, "	Chronic Catarrhal Pneumonia	"	4	" 5 child'n	"
188	C. G. Kullburg	Williams, 19		28	May 27, 1882	May 2, "	Drowning	"	4	" 5	"
189	A. J. McGivney	Sarsfield, 48		38	Mar. 6, 1883	April 5, "	Pneumonitis	"	8	" 7	"
190	Rev. C. McGrath	St. Bernard, 44		40	Feb. 26, 1882	June 13, "	Chronic Bronchitis	"		Nce	Nce
191	Richard A. Carroll	Mt. Pleasant, 20		30	April 10, 1884	June 18, "	Gastric Fever	"	4	Widow, 3 child'n	Widow
192	William Sullivan	Fulton, 12		37	Dec. 9, 1880	June 1, "	Pulmonary Phthisis	"	7	" 6	"
193	William H. Sliney	...es, 34		26	Mar. 15, 1881	July 26, "	Inflammation of ...	"	4	" 3	"
194	John McClure	Sherwood, 8		45	May 13, 1880	July 13, "	Cerebral ...	"	3	" 2	"
195	Joseph B. Fenelon	Leo, 5		25	Jan. 16, "	July 11, "	Consumption of Lungs	"	3	Widow & child	Widow
196	William Musler	Cathedral, 1		31	June 22, 1881	July 1, "	Phthisis	"	2	"	"
197	Hugh Harkins	Sherwood, 8		40	May 12, "	Aug. 29, 1887	Inflam. of Brain from sunstroke	"	3	2 child'n	Widow & guar.
198	Thomas ...	Fitzpatrick, 13		36	Mar. 16, "	Sept. 13, "	Typhoid Fever and Lung Dis.	"	2	" 2	"
199	John ...	SS. Peter & Paul, 15		34	Jan. 1, 1884	Aug. 1, "	Laryngitis	"	3	Wid. fath. moth.	Fath., moth., wid.
200	Daniel Gallvan	St. Patrick, 7		45	Jan. 28, 1881	Aug. 26, "	Myelitis (Infl. of the spinal mar.)	6		Heirs	Heirs
201	John F. Daly	SS. Peter & Paul, 15		35	Sept. 15, 1880	Aug. 24, "	Phthisis Pulmonalis	"	7	Widow, 6 child'n	Widow
202	William Pierce	Shiel, 35		36	April 14, 1882	Aug. 27, "	Pneumonia	"	4	" 3	"
203	Edmund C. Green	St. Francis, 4		30	April 12, 1880	M. ... 11, 1887	Chronic Bronchitis	"	2	" 1	"
204	John J. Fenelon	Benedict, 53		42	Mar. 31, 1881	Mar. 4, "	Haemorrhage (from thor. aneur.)	"	5	" 2	"
205	...es O'Toole	Emerald, 53		21	Sept. 1, 1883	Aug. 27, "	Unknown	"	2	Father & sister	Father & sister
206	Michael Ledwith	SS. Peter and Paul, 15		34	Sept. 1, 1880	April 22, 1886	Phthisis	"	2	Widow, 5 child'n	Widow, 5 child'n
207	Timothy Hurley	St. John, 33		34	Mar. 8, 1881	Mar. 11, 1887	Inflammation of Brain	"	5	Children	Children
208	Dennis Crawford	Williams, 19		23	Oct. 3, "	April 29, "	Consumption	"	3	Widow, 2 child'n	Widow

ENDOWMENTS PAID— Continued.

No.	Name	Court	Age	Initiated	Mem. Yrs.	Mos.	Dys.	Date of Death	Cause	Endowment	Number of Beneficiaries	To Whom Paid
209	Terence Griffin,	Erin, 28,	39	Feb. 17, 1881	6	2	17	May 4, 1887	Pneumonia	$1,000	6, Widow, 5 child'n	Widow
210	Wm. F. Kean,	Leo, 5,	35	Nov. 19, 1886		2	10	May 30, 1885	Acute Meningitis'	"	4, " 3 "	Guardian & wid.
211	Michael Connell,	Hamilton, 17,	23	July 23, 1885		10	2	Jan. 26, 1887	Phthisis Pulmonalis	"	4, " 3 "	Wid.
212	Joseph McGilvray,	Constantine, 49,	33	Sept. 8, 1881		8	6	May 25, "	Nerve Paralysis	"	3, " 5 "	Wid. & guardian
213	Patrick Murphy,	Bass River, 30,	30	Sept. 9, "		9	12	May 14, "	Haemoptysis	"	2, " 1 child	"
214	Philip Carney,	St. Joseph, 38,	28	April 6, 1882		3	18	June 21, "	Phthisis	"	2, " 1 child'n	"
215	John Broderick,	Ham tln, 17,	50	Mar. 4, 1880		3	25	June 29, "	Liver, Kid., & Lung Dis., Dropsy	"	6, " 5 "	"
216	David Fahey,	Sherwood, 8,	40	Jan. 21, 1881		6	13	July 23, "	Inflammation of liver	"	5, " 5 "	"
217	Cornelius Driscoll,	Fenwick, 3,	28	Jan. 21, 1887		6	13	July 27, "	Malarial Causes	"	2, Mother & widow	Mother & widow
218	Joseph Welsh,	Shields, 63,	34	Dec. 24, 1880		6	25	July 19, "	Typhoid-Pneumonia	"	2, Mw & hild	Widow
219	William Brooks,	Leo, 5,	38	Jan. 21, 1881		6	25	July 31, "	Consumption of Lungs	"	6, Children	Guardian
220	Thaddeus J. Walsh,	St. John, 33,	34	Mar. 20, 1881		6	10	May 23, "	Pulmonalis Phthisis .	"	1, Widow	Widow
221	Michael H. Fennessy,	Essex, 16,	44	May 14, 1880		4	3	Sept. 6, "		"	3, Father, 2 sisters	F. & At'y for 2s.
222	J. J. Cunningham,	St. Augu. tine, 46,	44	Aug. 14, 1880		11	22	Aug. 3, "	Senile Marasmus	"	6, Widow, 5 child'n	G. of C. A. for W.
223	Michael O'Keefe,	St. Joseph, 11,	27	Nov. 14, 1884		8	11	Oct. 20, "	Pneumonia	"	2, " 1 child	Guard. of child'n
224	John F. Rahl,	Cathedral, 1,	39	Dec. 27, 1882		7	12	Oct. 3, "	Phthisis Pulmonalis	"	4, " 3 child'n	Widow
225	B. H. Holthaus,	Columbus, 9,	23	Mar. 4, "		5	27	Oct. 20, "	Dropsy, Heart Disease	"	1, Father	Father
226	G. W. Cleary,	Iona, 10,	23	April 23, 1883		4	5	Nov. 19, "	Pneumonia	"	7, Widow, 6 child'n	Widow
227	Patrick Connell,	Erin, 28,	42	Mar. 14, 1880		6	9	Nov. 28, "	Degeneration of Lungs	"	4, Children	Son & guardian
228	B. J. O'Daly,	Unity, 45,	49	Nov. 12, 1886		10	24	Oct. 6, "	Pneumonia	"	2, Father & mother	Guardian
229	Thomas Sweeney,	Gallagher, 64,	25	April 17, 1887		7	17	Dec. 4, "	Railroad Accident	"	5, Widow, 4 child'n	Mother
230	John F. Reavy,	Cheverus, 6,	28	Oct. 15, 1886		1	15	Nov. 21, "	Railroad Accident	"	1, Widow, 1 hild	Widow
231	M. J. Reagan,	Cheverus, 6,	35	May 26, 1887		7	1	Dec. 8, "	Pneumonia	"	1, Father	Father
232	D. F. McGilvray,	St. Columbkill, 65,	27	May 26, 1887		7	1	Jan. 17, 1888	Fract. of Sk ull, Blasting Accident	"	6, Widow, 5 child'n	Widow
233	Walter Grace,	Columbus, 9,	36	May 12, 1881		6	27	Dec. 9, 1887	Cancer of Jaw	"	1, " "	"
234	John Martin,	Fulton, 12,	45	April 17, 1880		8	10	Jan. 7, 1888	Chronic Interst. Pneumonia	"	11, " 10 "	"
235	Timothy Collins,	Benedict, 39,	49	Mar. 31, 1881		8	14	Dec. 14, 1887	Paraplegia	"	1, Mother	Mother
236	Michael Durant,	Sherwood, 8,	55	Mar. 4, 1880		7	10	Jan. 1, 1888	Cerebral Paresis	"	8, " 7	"
237	A. J. Harrington,	St. ... 54,	29	July 2, 1883		1	22	Feb. 5, 1886	Phthisis Pulmonalis	"	1, Mother	Mother
238	J. J. Callahan,	Americus, 3,	38	Jan. 13, 1886		10	11	Feb. 24, 1886	Peritonitis	"	1, Brother	Brother
239	T. J. Dacey,	St. Joseph, 11,	38	Mar. 13, 1882		9	5	Dec. 15, 1887	Dropsy	"	1, Widow	Widow
240	M. Brahenny,	Cathedral, 1,	56	Sept. 13, 1879		4	10	Jan. 13, "	Heart Disease	"	6, Children	Children
241	H. H. Sullivan,	St. Joseph, 11,	38	Feb. 13, 1884		10	22	Jan. "	Bright's Disease	"	5, Widow, 4 child'n	Widow
242	John Murray,	St. Alphonsus, 21,	34	May 22, 1882		9	27	Mar. 1, "	Consumption	"	1, Mother	Mother
243	Edw. Ward,	Fitzpatrick, 13,	31	June 22, 1881		9	15	Mar. "	Phthisis	"	4, Widow, 3 child'n	Widow
244	Wm. J. ..,	Leo, 5,	32	Feb. 7, 1880		1	17	Mar. 14, "	Hemorrhage of Lungs	"	1, Mother	Mother
245	John J. Craig,	Leo, 5,	33	Mar. 18, 1881		8	16	Nov. 2, 1887	Phthisis Pulmonalis	"	19, Relatives	Relatives
246	Peter Kelliher,	St. Francis, 4,	56	Dec. 21, 1879		3	16	April 4, 1888	Chronic Bronchitis	"	2, Widow, 1 child	Widow
247	Peter Kilroy,	St. Francis, 4,	56	Dec. 21, 1879		3	16	April 4, "	Chronic Bronchitis	"	2, Widow, 1 child	"
248	John Collins,	St. Thomas, 29,	28	Nov. 8, 1883		4	16	April 24, "	Typhoid Fever .	"	1, "	"

No.	Name	Branch	Cause of Death	Year	Beneficiary	Amount	Relationship
249	James Goodfellow,	Cheverus, 6,	Erysipelas	1888	4, Widow, 3 child'n	$1,000	Widow
250	M. A. Fox,	Essex, 16,	Laryngeal Tumor	1887	2, Mother and aunt	"	Mother and aunt
251	M. H. Kerrigan,	St. Alphonsus, 21,	...	1888	8, Children	"	Guardian
252	John J. Sull...an,	Leo, 5,	Cardiac ...	"	4, " "	"	...
253	T. F. Powel,	Cheverus, 6,	Val. Disease of Heart	"	1, Widow	"	...
254	John Hines,	Essex, 16,	Catarrhal Pneumonia	"	4, Bro. and sister†	"	Sister-in-law
255	J. J. Callaghan,	Lafayette, 14,	Septicæmia	"	6, Widow, 5 child'n	"	...
256	Joseph Carkey,	Cheverus, 6,	Peritonitis	"	2, " 5 "	"	...
257	James Gorman,	Williams, 19.	Pleuritis	"	2, Children	"	Guardian
258	Patrick Dowd,	St. Francis, 25,	Phthisis Pulmonalis	"	5, " 4 child'n	"	...an & ...
259	A. A. Vogel,	Holy Trinity, 51,	Bright's Disease	"	3, moth., wid. & ch.	"	Moth., wid. & ch.
260	James J. Whalen,	St. Anne, 47,	Phthisis Pulmonalis	"	1, ...er	"	Mo...er
261	J. J. McKernan,	Iona, 10,	...er of Liver	"	3, Widow, 2 child'n	"	Guardian
262	James H. Hurley,	Sarsfield, 48,	Ascites	"	1, Son	"	...
263	Michael Maguire,	Fenwick, 3,	Typhoid Fever	"	4, Widow, 3 child'n	"	Widow and child'n
264	John Kelley,	St. Francis, 4,	Phthisis Pulmonalis	"	4, " 3 "	"	" and child'n
265	P. Doherty,	Sherwood, 8.	Consumption	1886	1, Mother	"	Mother
266	P. C. Fennelly,	St. Patrick, 7,	Consumption	1888	2, Children	"	Guardian
267	J. L. Hennessey,	O'Connell, 22,	Fracture of Skull	"	1, Widow	"	Widow
268	J. ...,	Sherwood, 8,	Scelerosis	"	3, Widow, 2 child'n	"	"
269	T. R. Fallon,	Essex, 16,	Pleurisy	"	4, " 3 "	"	Widow and daugh.
270	Wm. Lynch,	Cheverus, 6,	Phthisis	"	9, " 8 "	"	Widow and daugh.
271	James Smith,	Sheil, 35,	Bright's Disease	"	4, Widow	"	Widow
272	...es Fay,	St. Francis, 4,	Phthisis	"	3, " 3 "	"	"
273	James Connell,	Iona, 10,	Phthisis	"	2, " 4 "	"	"
274	W. Manning,	Cathedral, 1,	Paralysis	"	5, ...	"	...
275	John Burke,	Cathedral, 1,	Phthisis	"	1, Mother	"	Father
276	A. M. Cuffe,	SS. Joseph and Paul, 15,	...	"	1, Father	"	Child'n and guard.
277	M. Hogan,	St. Joseph, 33,	Chr. Catar. Pneumonia	"	9, Children	"	Widow and child'n
278	M. H. Ryan,	SS. Peter and Paul, 15,	Pneumonia	"	5, Widow, 4 child'n	"	Widow
279	J. F. Bradley,	Sheil, 35,	Typhoid Pneumonia	"	3, " 2 "	"	Widow and son
280	Bartley Feeney,	Fitzpatrick, 13,	Peritonitis	"	2, Widow, 1 son	"	"
281	Michael McDonough,	Fitzpatrick, 13,	Drowning	"	1, Widow, 1 son	"	"
282	Thomas L. Silk,	Mt. ..., 20,	...	"	1, Sister	"	Sister
283	...an O'Melia,	Leo, 5,	Tumor of Bowels	1888	1, Widow	"	"
284	Maurice Neville,	St. ...eph, 11,	Heart Disease	1889	1, Mother	"	Mother
285	James H. McDowell,	Highland, 52,	Consumption	1888	1, Widow	"	Widow
286	Thomas F. Kelly,	Erin, 28,	Phthisis Pulmonalis	"	1, Mother	"	...
287	Patrick Magee,	St. Thomas, 29,	Consumption	1889	1, Widow	"	... and daugh.
288	James Dorgan,	Alphonsus, 21,	Phthisis	"	1, "	"	...
289	Edward Millin,	...,	Phthisis Pulmonalis	"	1, "	"	... and daugh.
290	Michael D. Sullivan,	St. Augustine, 46,	Consumption	"	2, ... and daugh.	"	Widow and guard.
291	P. H. Kerrigan,	Iona, 10,	Hemorrhage from Lung	"	1, Widow	"	Widow
292	...hy Sheehan,	Essex, 16,	Phthisis	"	1, "	"	"
293	James Shortell,	Essex, 16,	Phthisis	"	2, ... and daugh.	"	Widow
294	John F. Carroll,	St. John, 33,	Heart Disease	"	2, ... and daugh.	"	Widow and daugh.

ENDOWMENTS PAID — Continued.

No.	N. E.	COURT.	Age.	INITIATED.	Membership Yrs.	Membership Mos.	Membership Dys.	DE OF DEATH.	CAUSE.	En- dw- mt.	NUMBER OF BENEFICIARIES.	TO WM PAID.
295		St. Paul, 37,	40	Mch 25, 1881	8	9	22	April 17, 1889	Iofic of the Stomach	$1,000	1, Widow	Widow
296	Mr H.	Iona 10, 4,	52	Dec. 18, 1879	9	3	22	April 10, "	Or of the Stomach	"	1, "	"
297	Jas. Cunningham,	Fitzpatrick, 3,	58	March 14, 1880	9	1	29	April 13, "	Age of Stomach	"	1, "	"
298	William Lynch,	Essex, B,	35	My 5, "	8	11	11	April 16, "	Jas hia	"	7, 5 sisters & 2 b.	Sisters nd bros.
299	Patrick H.	S. Francis. 4,	52	June 29, 1882	8	10	27	April 9, "	Cirrhosis of Lir	"	1, Daughter	Daughter
300	John Mullen,	Williams, 19,	50	Die 1, 1884	8	10	27	April 28, "	Iffia	"	1, Wow	Wow
301	Die Sullivan,	St. Gregory, 24,	46	Feb. 26, 1881	6	1	16	May 12, "	Uremia	"	4, Children	Wow
302	Cornelius Jos,	Leo, 5,	32	" 1, "	5	3	1	May 27, "	Cerebral Age	"	1, W Iow	iWow
303	J. McCarthy,	St. Dr, 18,	53	Jan. 16, 1880	9	2	16	April 2, "	Phthisis this	"	1, "	"
304	Maurice Sheehan,	Sherwood, 8,	52	July 22, "	5	0	5	May 27, "	Chronic Nephritis	"	1, "	"
305	E. C. Bullard,	Cheverus, 6,	49	Mch 4, "	9	1	9	April 13, "	Rheumatic Iffis	"	1, Uncle	Attorney
306	Francis J. Dia,	Bo, 5,	34	March 2, "	9	1	19	April 21, "	Phthisis Iffis	"	1, Widow	Attorney
307	Thos. E. Atherton,	SS. Peter nd Paul, 15,	45	May 18, "	9	3	14	May 27, "	Iffis of Lir	"	1, Widow	Widow
308	Denis Gr,	Sherwood, 8,	47	March 2, 1881	8	4	1	July 3, "	Iffia	"	1, Widow	dWow
309	John Donohue,	St. Columbkille, 65,	52	March 15, 1880	9	3	15	die 26, "	Gel Hemerrhage	"	7, Widow and hel'n	Wow and child'n
310	John Curley,	St. Lawrence, 61,	41	Nov. 15, 1887	1	7	16	July 1, "	Can ol. m fract. leg	"	7, Widow and child'n	Wow nd
311	Age B. Ely,	St. Alphonsus, 21,	34	April 5, 1888	1	2	3	July 8, "	dry Iffis	"	1, Mr	Widow
312	Die Downey,	G 67,	45	July 4, "	1	0	6	July 20, "	Cholera Morbus cardiac failure	"	1, Widow	Widow
313	John H. J. ol,	Cheverus, 6,	29	Sept. 17, "	7	10	14	Aug. 1, "	nl Ion	"	1, er	Sister
314	R. J. Downey,	Cheverus, 6,	26	March 9, 1882	3	1	27	March 24, 1885	Het Ice nd By	400		Heirs
315	Jas Cavenaugh,	Ms, 129,	44	March 9, 1880	9	4	18	May 27, 1889	Heart failure this	1,000	1, Daughter	Guardian
316	Ird J. Franey,	St. eph, 38,	25	Jan. 29, 1888	1	7	1	Aug. 5, "	Iffis	"	1, Father	Father
317	Nun J. Ford,	St. 4,	43	Nov 29, 1881	7	8	4	Aug. 3, "		"	8, Widow nd	Widow ad guard.
318	John J. O'Brien,	St. 4,	51	July 22, 1880	4	0	13	Aug. 5, "	Diabetes	"	2, Daughters	Wow
319	Dey Setts,	St. 4,	40	Jan. 13, 1881	3	1	27	May 10, "		"	2, Children	Children
320	Charles Key,	Iona, 32,	45	March 12, "	8	4	9	Oct. 15, "	Phthisis this	"	1, Wow	Wow
321	Thos.	Columbus, 9,	45	May 16, "	8	4	4	St. 16, "	Chronic Bent	"	3, Chfldren.	Cdin
322	Andrew McKinney,	Iona, 10, 19,	57	March 14, 1880	9	7	12	Oct. 8, "	Phthisis Iffis	"	1, Wow	Wow
323	Jas. P. McEnaney,	Williams, 19,	36	St. 16, "	9	1	22	Oct. 29, "	Paralysis ad Ile	"	6, Wow and child'n	iWow nd guard.
324	Dy Driscoll,	Americus, 34,	42	Die 16, "	4	0	24	Oct. "	Iffia	"	1, Wow	Wow
325	John J. Nfhy,	St. Janes, 54,	42	March 15, 1881	7	2	28	Oct. 13, "	Inig Sept	"	1, Wow	Wow
326	Thos. H.	Fay, 32,	38	May 18, 1883	6	2	5	Nov. 23, "	Phthisis	"	1, Mother	Mother
327	Henry J. Jam,	Fenwick, 3,	39	April 4, 1888	1	7	16	Oct. 20, "	Typhoid Fever nd	"	1, iWow	iWow
328	Nan Phelan,	Iona, 10,	48	March 9, 1880	8	8	21	Oct. 20, "	Iffis	"	1, dWow	dWow
329	John J.	Iona, 10,	57	March 14, "	9	7	22	Nov. 16, "	Myelitis	"	1, Sister	Sister
330	John T.	Idin,	32	April 7, "	9	2	14	Nov. 29, "	Phthisis	"	1, Mother	Mother
331	Edw'd F. Hallisey,	Ms, 18, 63,	50	Die 16, 1883	6	0	6	Oct. 20, "	Phthisis	"	10, dWow & child'n	dWow nd hel'n
332	Patrick J. Hallisey,	Ms, 63,	39	Jan. 14, 1887	2	7	22	Oct. 6, "	Typhoid Ier	"	1, Wow	Attorney

No.	Name	Parish		Date of Death	Cause of Death	Year	Amount	Beneficiary		
333	Thos ___	Benedict, 39,	47	Dec. 27, 1883	5 11 16 Dec. 13, 1889	Heart Disease	$1,000	1,	Ww	Ww	Ww as guardian
334	John Hahn,	St. ___ 11,	51	Dec. 22, 1882	6 11 23 Dec. 15, "	Phthisis	"	1,	Ww	Ww	"
335	Lawrence Andrews,	St. ___ 29,	39	Mar. 12, 1885	4 9 7 Dec. 19, "	Phthisis	"	2,	Ww	Ww	"
336	Jeremiah Daly,	Ina, 10,	33	Aug. 18, 1887	2 4 2 Dec. 20, "	Phthisis	"	1,	Ww	Ww and child	Ww as guardian
337	James ___	Constantine, 49,	44	June 14, 1888	1 5 18 ___ "	Phthisis	"	1,	Son		Widow
338	James P. ___	St. Francis, 4,	31	June 9, 1881	8 6 23 Jan. "	Phthisis	1890	3,	Wid. and 2 child'n	Wid. and child'n	___
339	Jno J. ___	St. Joseph, 11,	37	Dec. 27, 1883	8 1 13 Jan. "	Phthisis	"	2,	Children		Children
340	Michael ___	Sherwood, 8,	42	Nov. 22, 1881	5 1 5 ___ "	Phthisis	1889	2,	Widow and ___	Widow and ___	Widow
341	F. P. Hansen,	Sarsfield, 48,	49	Feb. 8, 1884	5 9 5 Nov. 3, "	Injury and drowning	"	4,	Children		i Ww
342	Ines McGinn,	Sarsfield, 48,	40	April 7, 1883	6 7 9 Nov. 3, "	___	"	1,	i Ww		Guardian & child'n
343	John J. ___	St. Peter, 18,	29	June 18, 1880	6 6 16 Nov. 3, 1890	Osteo-myelitis	"	1,	Sir		Sister
344	Daniel Manning,	St. Francis, 25,	35	Nov. 18, 1883	7 9 30 ___ "	Phthisis	"	1,	Sier		Sister
345	Michael B. Murphy,	Hamilton, 17,	45	___ 7, 1880	9 1 20 ___ "	Phthisis Pulmonalis	"	8,	Wid. and 7		Ww
346	Patrick T. ___	Mt. ___ 20,	52	July 8, 1885	7 4 5 Jan. 13, "	Cancer of stomach	"	4,	Wid. and 2		___ and child'n
347	John Breslin,	___ 32,	31	July 17, 1882	5 2 1 Jan. 19, "	Gr ___	"	4,	Wid. and 3		"
348	Bernard McLaughlin,	Cathedral, 1,	50	Sept. 8, 1879	10 4 19 Jan. 22, "	___	"	1,	Widow		"
349	Thos Deegan,	___ 39,	46	___ 8, 1887	2 1 25 ___ 4, "	Angina Pectoris	"	1,	Sister-in-law		Sister-in-law
350	Edmund Boylan,	___ 19,	33	May 10, 1881	8 9 9 Feb. 17, "	Typhoid Fer ___	"	3,	Ww and child'n		Ww
351	C. ___	St. ___ 25,	55	June 25, 1880	7 28 Feb. 19, "	Phth isis Pulmonalis	"	5,	Ww ad child		i Ww
352	Wm. H. O'Connor,	Erin, 28,	38	Oct. 27, 1887	2 4 24 March 20, "	Drowning	"	1,	Sir		Sier
353	Lawrence Forrest,	St. ___ 49,	40	Oct. 26, 1883	6 4 27 ___ 22, "	___	"	9,	Ww and child'n		Ww as guard.
354	Ines E. Doherty,	___ 6,	26	Sept. 13, 1887	2 6 18 March 31, "	Phthisis	"	3,	Ww and ___		as ___
355	Thel G. Ryan,	St. ___ 29,	31	Aug. 9, 1888	1 7 27 April 6, "	Spal Neuritis	"	5,	Widow and		i Ww
356	W. C. J. Horsley,	St. ___	45	Dec. 21, 1890	3 22 April 13, "	Phthisis	"	5,	"		"
357	Patrick F. Lacey,	Star of the Sea, 41,	39	May 5, 1887	2 11 16 April 21, "	Fracture of skull-	"	5,	"		"
358	John B. ___	Highland, 3,	29	Aug. 7, 1888	1 8 16 April 23, "	Exhaustion from	"	2,	"		as guard.
359	Maurice Walsh,	Iona, 10,	31	April 16, 1883	7 3 May 3, "	Phthisis	"	5,	"		"
360	Thel Sullivan,	St. ___ 54,	33	July 13, 1881	6 10 9 May 5, "	Phthisis	"	2,	"		"
361	M. J. Connolly,	St. Peter and Paul, 15,	45	Sept. 2, 1884	5 5 24 May 13, "	Phthisis Pulmonalis	"	5,	"		"
362	M. J. Bell,	St. Ines, 54,	26	May 17, 1887	3 20 May 26, "	Chronic Bronchitis	"	2,	"		"
363	Wm Dunn,	___ 6,	38	Mar. 23, 1880	10 2 14 June 7, "	Spinal Meningitis	"	6,	"		"
364	Bryan Norton,	Emerald, 53,	51	July 21, 1883	8 1 15 ___ 17, "	___	"	2,	"		"
365	James C. Harkins,	St. Peter, 18,	52	Nov. 10, 1881	7 1 9 ___ 19, "	___	"	6,	"		Guardian
366	John J. Butt,	Holy Trinity, 51,	42	___ 21, 1884	6 5 21 July 10, "	Meningitis	"	7,	"		Ww
367	th Ball,	St. Alphonsus, 21,	14	June 14, 1883	6 1 27 July 11, "	Broncho Pneumonia	"	4,	"		"
368	Adis Martin,	Constantine, 19,	43	___ April 5, 1883	7 3 26 July 31, "	Sunstroke	"	4,	"		"
369	Jeremiah Horgan,	Erin, 28,	38	June 11, 1889	1 1 25 ___ 6, "	___ Fever	"	6,	"		as guard.
370	John Morley,	Sherwood, 8,	36	Feb. 3, 1888	2 1 7 Sept. "	Uraemic poisoning	"	4,	"		"
371	Michael McTigue,	St. ___ 71,	26	Mar. 4, 1890	2 7 13 Sept. 20, "	Typhoid Fever	"	1,	"		"
372	Timothy J. Sweeney,	___ sheridan, 71,	26	___ "	1 6 16 Oct. 10, "	Typhoid Fever	"	4,	"		"
373	Daniel P. Sullivan,	Essex, 16,	37	Aug. 17, 1881	9 3 27 Oct. 14, "	___ from ___	"	6,	"		Guardian
374	Edward Fitzgerald,	Cheverus, 6,	46	___ 28, 1881	9 8 27 Oct. 25, "	___	"	4,	"		Ww
375	Timothy Callahan,	Williams, 19,	38	Mar. 7, 1881	9 7 20 Oct. 27, "	___ Pulmonalis	"	7,	"		"
376	D. J. McCarthy,	Essex, 16,	39	June 23, 1880	10 4 12 ___ 5, "	Heart Failure	"	1,	"		"

ENDOWMENTS PAID — Continued.

No.	NAME.	COURT.	Age.	INITIATED.	Mem. Yrs.	Mos.	Dys.	DATE OF DEATH.	CAUSE.	Endowment.	NUMBER OF BENEFICIARIES.	TO WHOM PAID.
379	Michael Cadagan,	Fenwick, 3,	54	Jan. 21, 1881,	9	9	15	Nov. 6, 1890,	Typhoid Fever	$1,000	4, Widow and child'n	Widow and child'n
380	Patrick Sheerin,	St. Joseph, 11,	58	Sept. 12, 1881,	9	2	3	Nov. 15, "	Meningitis	"	1, "	"
381	Hugh Canny,	Cheverus, 6,	66	Feb. 11, 1880,	10	9	25	Dec. 6, "	Heart Disease	"	6, "	"
382	Michael Walsh,	St. Joseph, 11,	49	July 11, 1881,	9	4	29	Dec. 10, "	Pneumonia	"	6, "	"
383	William Richmond,	Cheverus, 6,	49	March 2, 1880,	10	9	17	Dec. 19, "	Consumption	"	2, "	Daughter
384	David Barry,	Fenwick, 3,	53	Feb. 18, 1881,	9	10	4	Dec. 22, "	Fracture of skull	"	4, "	Wdw and child
385	Stephen Gray,	Williams, 19,	47	do. 19, 1881,	9	4	14	Jan. 4, 1891,	Heart Failure	"	4, "	"
386	Alphonse Lausmann,	Holy Trinity, 51,	33	Aug. 9, 1886,	4		26	Jan. 3, "	Pneumonia	"	5, "	"
387	James H. Millerick,	St. Jarlath, 75,	39	June 13, 1889,	1	7		Jan. 1, "	Phthisis	"	6, "	"
388	James Sweeney,	Sherwood, 8,	40	Jan. 11, 1883,	8		4	Jan. 4, "	Intestinal obstruction after accident	"	7, "	"
389	James Kenney,	Williams, 19,	40	Jan. 3, 1881,	10		21	Jan. 15, "	Phthisis Pulmonalis	"	2, "	"
390	Patrick McCarthy,	Charles River, 55,	50	Oct. 19, 1885,	5		26	Jan. 24, "	Tuberculosis Pulmonalis	"	7, "	"
391	Jeremiah McSweeney,	Cathedral, 1,	46	Oct. 19, 1879,	11		13	Feb. 2, "	Double Pneumonia	"	5, "	Widow
392	Thos F. Sullivan,	St. Thomas, 29,	36	Sept. 8, 1881,	9		6	Feb. 7, "	Phthisis	"	3, "	"
393	Michael Killilea,	Leo, 5,	58	May 18, 1880,	10		9	March 17, "	Fatty Degeneration of heart	"	7, "	Mother
394	Daniel Cronin,	Cheverus, 6,	52	Jan. 18, 1881,	10		3	March 18, "	Pericarditis	"	3, Mother	Widow
395	Martin Havey,	St. Francis, 4,	50	Dec. 18, 1879,	11		2	March 21, "	Empyema	"	7, "	"
396	Terence McGowan,	Sarsfield, 48,	31	March 26, 1889,	2		17	April 13, "	Phthisis	"	6, Widow and child'n	Widow
397	James H. Fox,	Constantine, 49,	35	Oct. 11, 1888,	1	10		Aug. 20, 1890,	Pneumonia	"	6, "	"
398	Patrick Quinn,	St. Joseph, 11,	58	May 14, 1880,	10		8	April 22, 1891,	Drowning	"	6, "	"
399	William F. Hastings,	St. Anne, 47,	32	July 2, 1889,	1		4	Nov. 10, 1890,	Phthisis Pulmonalis	"	6, "	"
400	William Clancy,	St. Joseph, 11,	43	Feb. 14, 1881,	10		8	April 27, 1891,	Peritonitis	"	8, "	"
401	John Ready,	Erin, 28,	39	Dec. 12, 1889,	1		5	April 9, "	Phthisis Pulmonalis	"	6, "	"
402	Michael Dunphy,	St. Francis, 25,	48	Jan. 15, 1881,	10	10		April 24, "	Pneumonia	"	4, "	Guardian
403	Francis Kenny,	Charles River, 55,	35	Jan. 7, 1884,	7		26	May 7, "	Chronic Bronchitis	"	3, "	Widow
404	Hugh Foley,	Fitzpatrick, 13,	60	June 23, 1880,	10		23	May 16, "	Acute Tuberculosis	"	9, Moth, sis's & bs.	Sister
405	Jeremiah Lane,	St. Columbkille, 63,	26	March 20, 1888,	3		1	May 23, "	Heart Disease	"	7, "	Son
406	Thomas F. Meagher,	Cheverus, 6,	60	Feb. 17, 1880,	11		2	May 29, "	Phthisis	"	1, Child	Guardian
407	Michael McCready,	Canton, 67,	34	Jan. 26, 1888,	3		9	Oct. 3, "	Tuberculosis	"	1, "	Uncles
408	Daniel J. Claxton,	Cathedral, 1,	34	Feb. 8, 1882,	9		4	June 2, 1890,	Phthisis	"	2, Uncles	Widow
409	Daniel H. Drew,	Sheil, 35,	37	May 27, 1881,	10		24	June 10, 1891,	Phthisis	"	4, Wdw and child'n	"
410	Patrick Flynn,	Hamilton, 1r,	48	July 6, 1880,	11		29	July 21, "	Typhoid Fever	"	5, "	"
411	Thos O'Flynn,	Highland, 52,	45	April 16, 1883,	8		22	July 8, "	Tuberculosis following accident	"	5, "	"
412	Daniel Keohane,	Cathedral, 1,	29	May 4, 1889,	2		12	July 13, "	Tuberculosis	"	1, "	6 in
413	Daniel Sullivan,	La Fayette, 14,	54	Aug. 1, 1886,	5		8	Aug. 7, "	Cerebral Hemorrhage	"	3, Daughters	Daughters
414	John Goggins,	Fenwick, 3,	57	Oct. 14, 1880,	10		16	March 30, "	Heart Disease	"	5, Wdw and child'n	"
415	Jeremiah Barry,	Canton, 67,	44	Sept. 25, 1890,	11		9	Sept. 8, "	Railroad Accident	"	4, "	"
416	Jeremiah Murphy,	Bass River, 30,	54	Feb. 24, 1881,	10	6	15	Sept. 9, "	Brights Dise	"		

No.	Name, Parish, Age		Date Entered		Date of Death	Cause of Death	$1,000	Beneficiary	Relationship
417	Jeremiah Grady, May,	Williams, 19,	37	Jan. 3, 1881	10 8	Sept. 6, 1891	Bright's Disease	$1,000	3, Children	Guardian
418	Frederick Cox,	Griffin, 66,	23	Sept. 12, 1887	3 5	March 23, "	Accidental blow on hd	"	Father	Father
419	William St. Brennan,	Americus, 34,	48	Dec. 16, 1886	4 9	Sept. 18, "	Bright's Disease	"	4, Widow and child'n	Widow
420	Thos Brennan,	St. Thomas, 29,	46	June 14, 1883	8 8	Sept. 2, "	Bright's Disease	"	10,	"
421	John May,	Phil Sh Ian, 71,	42	Feb. 11, 1880	11 11	Oct. 17, "	Paralysis	"	7,	"
422	James B. Shannon,	Cheverus, 6,	51	dC 5, 1889	8 6	dC "	Bronchitis	"	10,	"
423	Lawrence Campbell,	Essex, 16,	45	April 7, 1886	6 11	dC "	Paralysis	"	7,	"
424	James H. Neagle,	Hamilton, 17,	48	Ag. 5, 1880	11 5	Oct. 18, "	Heart Disease	"	5, Brothers & sisters	Sister
425	Wm. P. McCarthy,	St. 34,	38	May 5, 1881	5 0	Oct. 24, "	Consumption	"	Widow and child'n	Widow
426	Thomas F. Gooley,	St. Lawrence, 61,	44	do 26, 1886	3 11	Nov. 28, "	Intestinal Obstruction	"	7,	"
427	Benj. J. Shorten,	La Fayette, 14,	41	do 7, 1887	11 0	do 24, "	Pleurisy	"	2,	"
428	Thos Murphy,	St. John, 33,	56	March 31, 1881	10 5	do 18, "	Cerebral Embolism	"	4,	"
429	ules Mahoney,	Sherwood, 8,	46	Sept. 22, 1881	8 7	do 16, "	Consumption	"	1, Sister	Sister
430	Thomas O'Neil,	Prospect, 58,	49	Aug. 16, 1885	3 5	Dec. 9, "	Pneumonia	"	1, Widow and child'n	Widow
431	Michael J. Downey,	Gen. Sherman, 80,	35	March 7, 1891	0 9	do 25, "	Heart Disease	"	Father	Father
432	J. J. Ryan,	Canton, 67,	25	March 17, 1890	1 7	Oct. 14, "	Typhoid Fever	"	Mr & brother	Mr
433	P. R. Quinlan,	Mt. Pleasant, 20,	49	Feb. 2, 1888	3 11	do 19, "	Spinal Inflammation	"	Mw and child	Mw
434	Patrick Killion,	St. Alphonsus, 21,	60	Oct. 15, 1890	1 2	Dec. 29, "	Pneumonia	"	6, Widow and child'n	"
435	John Moore, Null,	Taunton, 73,	32	March 20, 1891	11 0	Dec. 29, "	Peritonitis	"	4,	"
436	Hugh,	St. Francis, 4,	60	April 8, 1890	11 0	Jan. 8, 1892	...n of Lungs	"	5, Children	Guardian
437	Thomas F. English,	St. Mary, 43,	40	June 7, 1889	2 1	Jan. 6, "	Phthisis Pulmonalis	"	7, Widow and child'n	Widow
438	James Foley,	Williams, 19,	37	March 18, 1881	10 17	Jan. 24, "	Phthisis	"	6,	"
439	Matthew Hanley,	St. Francis, 4,	44	May 18, 1884	9 7	Dec. 19, 1891	Tuberculosis Pulmonalis	"	7,	"
440	James M. Holland,	Gallacher, 64,	49	Feb. 2, 1888	3 11	Jan. 22, 1892	Ate Jaundice	"	1, Widow and child	Widow & guardian
441	William F. Dugan,	St. Gregory, 24,	29	Feb. 12, 1884	7 11	Feb. 2, "	Paralysis and Phthisis	"	6, Widow and child'n	Mother
442	William Nolan,	St. Peter, 18,	48	March 8, 1883	9 11	Feb. 18, "	Pneumonia	"	1,	Mw
443	John Flanigan,	Charles River, 55,	41	Oct. 8, 1883	8 4	Feb. 20, "	Pneumonia	"	6,	"
444	William Woods,	Iona, 10,	51	do 23, 1880	3 1	Feb. 24, "	...	"	10,	"
445	Joe Burns,	Fitzpatrick, 13,	46	do 7, 1881	9 11	July 21, 1891	Hemorrhage of Lungs	"	1, Dependent	Dependent
446	Michael W. Byrnes,	Griffin, 66,	29	Aug. 7, 1888	3 6	Feb. 23, 1892	Pneumonia	"	1, Widow	Widow
447	Thos A. Byrnes,	Griffin, 66,	31	Aug. 22, 1880	6 19	Feb. 26, "	...	"	Mer	Mr
448	Jere. Chamberlin,	St. Peter, 18,	45	July 25, 1881	16 16	March 24, "	Cancer of ...	"	6, Widow and child'n	Widow
449	Patrick A. Morrissey,	Cathedral, 1,	31	March 25, 1881	11 10	Feb. 6, "	Typhoid Pneumonia	"	4,	"
450	John F. Kerrigan,	St. Thomas, 29,	39	do 11, 1887	6 11	March 6, 1891	Killed by cars	"	5,	"
451	Michael Brennan,	St. Alphonsus, 21,	41	July 2, 1887	4 4	March 4, 1892	Typhoid Pneumonia	"	8,	"
452	Peter F. McBride,	Emerald, 53,	48	do 2, 1883	8 7	do 23, "	Pneumonia [Embolism	"	8,	"
453	Michael Tansy,	Layfayette, 14,	45	March 18, 1891	1	do 13, "	Rheumatism, Heart Disease, Chl	"	6,	"
454	William Garrity,	Iona, 10,	59	March 14, 1880	12	March 2, "	Acute Bronchitis	"	4,	"
455	James R.	Stoughton, 69,	22	Jan. 15, 1891	1	Feb. 1, "	Phthisis,	"	4, Mother	Brother
456	Michael Sheehan,	Mystic, 77,	46	April 14, 1890	11	March 24, "	Bronchitis & Pulmonary Hemorrhage	"	5, Widow	Widow
457	Thomas F. Whalen,	Constantine, 49,	49	July 25, 1887	4 4	April 15, "	Phthisis	"	8,	"
458	Edward J. Brady,	St. Thomas, 29,	39	June 25, 1891	9 18	April 13, "	Pleuro-Pneumonia	"	6,	"
459	John E. O'Brien,	St. Catherine, 62,	39	March 7, 1888	4 11	May 5, "	Erysipelas	"	5,	"
460	John Morrisey,	St. Alphonsus, 21,	43	Feb. 17, 1885	3 17	May 29, "	Bright's Disease	"	5,	"
461	James T. Sheehan,	Erin, 28,	40	do 17, 1883	8 5	May 22, "	Concussion of Brain	"	1, Cd	Guardian
462	John Harrington,	St. Francis, 4,	51	June 10, 1880	11 11	May 14, "	Tuberculosis Pulmonalis	"	3, Widow and child'n	Widow

ENDOWMENTS PAID—Continued.

No.	NAME	COURT	Age	INITIATED	Yrs.	Mos.	Dys.	DATE OF DEATH	CAUSE	Endowment	NUMBER OF BENEFICIARIES	TO WHOM PAID.
463	Dennis Burns,	Layfayette, 14,	39	July 1, 1891	11		2	June 3, 1892	Lobular Pneumonia	$1,000	3, Widow and child'n	Widow
464	John McGrail,	Brockton, 82,	34	Dec. 11, 1891		3	24	April 24, "	Heart Disease	"	2, Father & mother	Attorney
465	William G. Parow,	Leo, 5,	48	Dec. 13, 1881	10	5	1	May 14, "	Heart Disease	"	3, Ww and hild'n	Widow
466	Thomas O'Keefe,	Erin, 28,	54	Nov. 23, 1886	5	6	14	June 7, "	Chr. Bright's Disease	"	4, "	"
467	John J. Gately,	Mt. Pleasant, 20,	37	Sept. 14, 1883	8	10	2	July 16, "	Laryngeal Phthisis	"	5, "	"
468	John L. Carroll,	Sarsfield, 48,	28	Aug. 19, 1884	7	9	10	My 29, "	Paresis	"	4, "	"
469	John Meehan,	Erin, 28,	58	April 6, 1881	11	4	18	Aug. 24, "	Cerebral Hemorrhage	"	1, Mer	Mer
470	Maurice J. McCarthy,	Americus, 34,	49	March 15, 1881	11	4	11	July, 26, "	Sunstroke	"	7, Widow and child'n	Widow
471	John Callahan,	Leo, 5,	44	Feb. 10, 1892		3	24	June, 4, "	Pneumonia	"	6, "	"
472	James W. McGuire,	Cheverus, 6,	62	Feb. 11, 1880	12	6	3	Aug. 14, "	Bright's Disease	"	6, "	"
473	Daniel F. Geary,	St. Francis, 25,	35	June 14, 1887	5	1	6	Aug. 20, "	Phthisis Pulmonalis	"	2, and child	"
474	John Clarey,	Sherwood, 8,	34	Aug. 6, 1886	6	1	9	Sept. 15, "	Asphyxia	"	5, and child'n	"
475	John A. Kelly,	Leo, 5,	62	Jan. 16, 1880	12	6	16	Aug. 24, "	Hemorrhage into the Brain	"	1, "	"
476	John Moriarty,	Erin, 28,	51	March 24, 1891	1	3	16	July 10, "	Nephritis	"	6, and child'n	"
477	Richard Walsh,	St. Francis 25,	53	Dec. 13, 1887	4	10	4	Oct. 17, "	Hel Hemorrhage	"	6, "	"
478	Daniel Hayes,	Leo, 5,	48	Jan. 1880	12	8	15	Oct. 1, "	Apoplexy	"	1, Mother	Mother
479	John A. Kenely,	Taunton, 73,	28	March 12, 1889	3	7	3	Oct. 15, "	Typhoid Fever	"	1, Sister	Sister
480	Henry S. Leonard,	Gallagher, 64,	27	June 16, 1887	5	7	5	Sept. 5, "	Phthisis Pulmonalis	"	1, Ww	Ww
481	James P. Breslow,	St. Columbkille, 65,	39	Feb. 17, 1892		7	25	Sept. 5, "	Nephritis	"	4, and child'n	Daughters
482	Patrick Flynn,	St. Thomas, 29,	38	Feb. 17, 1881	10	2	24	May 11, 1891	Phthisis	"	2, Daughters	Guardian
483	Patrick Flynn,	Iona, 10,	48	April 18, 1889	3	2	11	April 9, 1892	Cirrhosis of Liver	"	1, Widow and	Widow
484	John J. Cahill,	Emerald, 53,	35	Mh 28, 1889	3	1	21	Nov. 4, "	Typhoid Fever	"	6, "	"
485	Patrick J. Desmond,	St. Thomas, 29,	49	Feb. 17, 1881	11	8	25	Nov. 12, "	Acute Nephritis	"	5, "	"
486	Michael O'Brien,	Fulton, 12,	49	March 18, 1880	12	7	11	Nov. 5, "	Valvular Heart Disease	"	3, "	"
487	John J. Doyle,	Amer us, 34,	43	July 19, 1888	4	4	10	Nov. 29, "	Pleuro-Pneumonia	"	5, "	"
488	Michael McCarthy,	St. Lawrence, 61,	34	Aug. 16, 1887	5	3	26	Dec. 12, "	Pneumonia	"	5, "	"
489	David Leahy,	Constantine, 49,	52	April 5, 1883	9	7	19	N. 24, "	Valvular Heart Disease	"	2, Widow and Child	Widow
490	John Flynn,	S.S. Peter and Paul, 15,	50	Feb. 2, 1881	11	9	28	Dec. 30, "	Cancer of Æsophagus	"	1, and child'n	"
491	John J. Webb,	Quincy, 76,	32	March 20, 1890	2		5	Dec. 28, "	Chronic Catarhl Pneumonia	"	1, Brother	Brother
492	Andrew P. Reddy,	J. H. Newman, 88,	21	Dec. 12, 1891	1	1	25	Jan. 7, 1893	Typhoid Fever	"	1, Sister	Sister
493	William J. Kean,	Worcester, 59,	40	Nov. 17, 1885	7	1	8	Jan. 25, "	Pneumonia	"	5, Widow	"
194	Michael Barry,	Mystic, 77,	43	Nov. 13, 1890	2	1	20	Jan. 3, "	Pneumonia	"	8, and child'n	"
495	Charles Doherty,	Americus, 34,	43	May 7, 1892		7	12	Dec. 22, 1892	Meningitis	"	6, "	"
496	John Baird,	Stoughton, 69,	24	June 20, 1889	3	6	11	Jan. 1, 1893	Phthisis	"	1, Mother	Mother
497	Mart. D. Carr,	Iona, 10,	58	Aug. 28, 1882	10	3	5	Dec. 4, 1892	Bright's Disease	"	4, Widow and child'n	iWw
498	Richard Donnell,	Sarsfield, 48,	58	April 8, 1884	8	8	26	Jan. 4, 1893	Typhoid Fever	"	1, Widow	"
499	John Horrigan,	Qualey, 32,	50	Dec. 19, 1881	11		16	Jan. 5, "	Meningitis and Typhoid Fever	"	4, and child'n	"
500	Edward McKenna,	St. John, 23,	56	March 21, 1881	11	9	18	Jan. 9, "	Pneumonia	"	8, Chen	Daughter

	Name		Age					Cause of Death			
501	James Mahan,	Cheverus, 6,	46	Feb.	18, 1889	3	10	22 Jan.	10, 1893	Dementia	$1,000	2, Widow and child	Widow
502	Dennis J. Kelly,	Cheverus, 6,	34	April	20, 1891	1	8	20 Jan.	10, "	Double Pneumonia	"	2, " "	"
503	Michael Cody,	Fitzpatrick, 13,	48	Feb.	26, 1881	11	10	17 Jan.	13, "	Cardiac Disease	"	6, " and child'n	"
504	John E. King,	Merrimack, 72,	35	Dec.	20, 1888	4	1	6 Jan.	26, "	Pneumonia	"	2, " and child	

AMOUNTS RECEIVED FOR INITIATION FEES, COURT DUES AND ASSESSMENTS.

No. of Court.	NAME OF COURT.	Received for Initiation Fees 1892	Received for Court Dues 1892	Received for Endowment Fund 1892	Per Capita for High Court Received 1892	Received for Withdrawal Cards 1892	Received from Other Sources 1892	Received for Reserve Fund 1892
1	Cathedral.	$15.00	$554.25	$ 1,963.60	$135 00	.50	$ 142.55	$98.00
3	Fenwick							
4	St. Francis...........	27.00	882.50	1,374.50	90 00	....	101.20	66.50
5	Leo.................	49.00	365.85	1,334.60	95.25	.25	271.60	68.00
6	Cheverus............	38.00	184.80	1,111.80	77.25	....	245.53	55.50
7	St. Patrick	6.00	132.00	465.55	32.25	1.00	12.70	21.50
8	Sherwood...........	71.00	462.00	1,571.00	......		104.63	74.00
9	Columbus...........	11.00	180.00	432.70	35.00	1.50	10.40	23.00
10	Iona....	55.00	295.00	1,033.70	76.50	....	537.30	55.50
11	St. Joseph..........	26.00	420.50	1,504.70	108.75	.25	....	62.50
12	Fulton.............	18 00	101.75	457.80	29.25			25.50
13	Fitzpatrick.........	25.00	170.25	618.20	41.25	.50	2.33	30.00
14	Lafayette.	68.00	245.40	1,006.75	1.50		94.42	11.00
15	SS. Peter and Paul. ..	36.00	243.75	846 40	54.00	....		42.00
16	Essex...............	87.00	718.30	1,302.60	110 50		19.45	89.50
17	Hamilton....	12.00	197.50	731.50	49 50	.50	....	35.00
18	St. Peter............	....	365.35	1,106.10	72.75			55.50
19	Williams.............	13.00	515.50	906.10	66.75			41.50
20	Mt. Pleasant.........	31.00	247.00	832.80	60.75	....	8.50	43.50
21	St. Alphonsus	9.00	156.00	591.30	34 50		28.60	24.00
23	St. John.............	46.00	173.75	634.10	45.50		690.07	42.00
24	St. Gregory..........	51.00	219.75	809.95	58.00		75.78	43.00
25	St. Francis...........	24.00	349.75	1,316.70	89.25	.25	....	58.50
26	St. Raphael..........	4.00	121.50	484.10		....	49.00	
28	Erin................	5.00	277.00	990.40	66.75	.75	....	46.50
29	St. Thomas..........	129.00	506.00	2,059 70	153.00	1.50	1.082.62	104.50
30	Bass River..........	38.00	152.25	505.10	37.50		90.19	32.00
32	Qualey.............	45.00	194 90	600.50	38.00	....	120.54	37.50
33	St. John............	72.00	189.64	722.50	49.00	....	10.05	34.00
34	Americus..	24.00	250.85	877.65	64.25	.25	20.20	46.00
35	Sheil.	....	60.25	201.90	15.00	....	....	10.00
37	Friendship	3.00	154.35	419.00	28.75	.25	....	16.50
38	St. Joseph..........	4.00	144.70	492.20	34.50		....	23.50
39	Benedict...........	......	....	....	....			
43	St. Mary.....	15.00	68.00	408 00	27.75	.75	....	20.00
44	St. Bernard..........	....	87.50	461.50	32.25	....	50.20	20.00
45	Unity	24.00	155 25	550.20	39.00	.25	9.14	31.00
46	St. Augustine........	39.00	121.50	428.30	27.75	....	7.00	22.50
47	St. Anne.	....	....	....	....		....	....
48	Sarsfield	31.00	264.75	907.80	66.75	....	160.30	48.50
49	Constantine..........	18.00	249.70	659.90	49.75	.75	....	36.50
51	Holy Trinity..........	37.00	250.00	1,393 90	102.00	....	199.99	73.85
52	Highland............	14.00	71.25	239.00	18.00	....	....	13.00
53	Emerald.............	121.00	336.00	118.80	84.25	....	123.12	72.50
54	St. James...........	76.00	186.50	576 60	57.00	.50	10.00	38.00
55	Charles River........	36.00	139.45	1,020.20	78.75	....	49.69	59.50
57	Carroll	30.00	177.85	557.40	42.25	....	218.32	31.25
58	Prospect............	6.00	70.00	399.55	18.50	....	....	23.00
59	Worcester...........	42.00	266 85	1,084.10	69.75	....	292.04	47.00
60	Middlesex...........	30.00	121.00	801.60	54.00	....	128.75	35.00
61	St. Lawrence.........	67.00	270 25	1,044.00	77.25	.25	119.60	66.50
62	St. Catherine.........	26.00	346.20	653.10	44.25	5.00	....	29.00
63	Shields.............	12.00	136.00	271.20	14.40	....	156.30	11.00
64	Gallagher...........	25.00	198.20	690.30	47.25	....	12.11	34.00
65	St. Columbkille........	22.00	183 50	610.70	46.50	....	255.20	33.00
66	Griffin....	76.00	66.40	572.80	40.50	....	98.97	40.00
67	Canton..............	5 00	227.75	801.10	55.50	....	7.25	39.50
68	St. Margaret.........	6.25	81.50	308.40	22.75	....	81.56	15.00
69	Stoughton...........	35.00	195.00	795.40	57.75	.50	343.53	44 00
70	St Michael..........	6 00	113.25	374.50			8.10	21.50
71	Phil Sheridan........	9.00	252.60	840.60	63.00	.75	165.19	43.50
72	Merrimack...........	55 00	227.75	829.60	62.00	.25		51.50
73	Taunton.............	58.00	151.20	1,298 50	97.50	.25	633.27	73 50
74	Hendricken	32.00	117.50	403.70	30.75	....	213.66	26.00
75	St. Jarlath...........	9.00	365.85	619.50	42.75	....	785.82	29.00
76	Quincy.............	7.00	176.50	569 70	29.00		34.50	29.50
77	Mystic..............						....	....
78	St. Monica.... ..,.....	15.00	89.00		22.50	....	125.00	15.00
79	J. B. O'Reilly........	16.00	78.75		00		15.25	12.00
80	Gen. Sherman........	27.00	130.35		24.00	.25	10.00	20 00
81	St. Malachi	21.00	129.20		23.25	....	13.60	17.00
82	Brockton	225 00	162.40		50.25	.25	99.00	73.00
83	J. H. Newman	27.00	125 55		9 25		18.00	34.00
84	Danvers	185.00	125.75				95.30	51.50
85	Geo. Washington......	266.00	130.25		51.00	.25	297.00	72.00
86	Avon...	126.00	81 50		30.00	....	34.10	40.50
87	Robert Emmett.......	97.00	67.75		24.75	....	156.45	33.50
88	Enterprise.				14.25	....	9.85	20.50
89	Union						20.75	23.00
90	Rockland ...							11.50

NAME OF COURT.	Paid Endowment Calls 1892.	Paid H. C. Per Capita 1892.	Paid for Rent 1892.	Paid for Salaries of Officers 1892.	Paid Medical Examiner 1892.	Paid H.C.P. 1892.	Paid for Sick Benefits 1892.	Paid Court Physician for Attendance on Members 1892.	Paid for Other Expenses 1892.	Paid Reserve Fund 1.
athedral..	$2,028.50	$135.00	$ 72.00	$ 188.25			$ 52.15	$ 187.00	$ 249.73	$98.00
enwick.										
t. Francis. ...	1,411.40	99 00	93.00	100.00	$ 15.75	$ 2.25			119.00	202.65	66.50
eo...........	1,418.20	97.50	60.00	50.00	33.25	6.75	110.00	109.75	335.71	68.00
heverus.	1,111.80	77.25	50.50	51.80	26.25	3.75			137.79	56.00
t. Patrick.	466,70	32.25	52.50	49.25	3.50	.50		23 00	56.70	21.50
herwood	1,666.40	117.00	72.00	125.00	35.00	5.00		76.50	382.66	74.00
olumbus..	468 40	33.00	84.00	27.00	7.00	1.00			35.35	22.00
ona...	1,033.70	77.25	67.50	50.00	31.50	4.25	18.00	100.75	610.76	51.00
t. Joseph.	1,590.30	105.00	48.00	62.00	26.25	4.25		139.00	124.76	70.00
ulton.......	457.80	29.25	42.00	20.00	10.50	1.50		51.17	7.00	20.00
itzpatrick....	618.20	41 25	44.00	50.00	15.75	2.25		25 50	60.23	30.00
afayette	909.50	68.00	64.50	32.00	43.75	6.25	3.10	105.00	283.06	53.00
S. Peter & Paul	846.40	54.00	60.00	40.00	21.00	3.00			156.75	41 00
ssex..	1,373.80	105.25	156.00	50.00	56.00	8.50			310.67	80.50
amilton......	731.50	49.50	60.00	60.00	7.00	2.50		50.00	15.80	35.00
t. Peter......	1,117.00	71.25	58.00	70.00	12.25	1.75		97.50	201 80	52.50
Villiams	876.25	66.75	75.00	46.30	7.00	1.75	120.00	88.50	285.83	41.50
t. Pleasant....	831.40	62.25	75.00	53.67	21.00	3.25	24.00	101.25	74.68	41.50
t. Alphonsus :.	591.30	34.50	39.00	47.50	5.25	.75	20.60		67.91	24.00
t. John......	634.10	45.50	81.50		31.50	.25			152.63	42.00
t. Gregory....	851 20	57.75	54.00		29.75	.25			271.80	40.50
t Francis	1,316.70	89.25	120.00	65.00	15.75	5.25		103.75	15 .86	58.50
t. Raphael....	501.90	33.00	15.00					44.00	100.33	22.00
rin.	1,089.70	68.25	78.00	75.00				91.50	37.88	47.50
t. Thomas.....	2,053.00	152.25	426.70	25.00	78.75	11.00	10.00	191.00	851.22	104.50
ass River.....	508.30	37.50	48.00	12.00	22.72	3.25	18.00	50.00	102.20	27.50
ualey........	711.90	46.50	39.00	18.00	26.25	3.75	230.00	39.45	19.85	39.00
t. John......	722.50	49.00	62.00		45.50	6.00	40.00	63.50	60.19	34.00
mericus.......	910 40	58.50	72.00	44.50	15.75	2.25	9.05	80.00	106.30	68.00
ei	231.40	15.00	24.00	12.35					8.65	10.00
'riendship. ...	461.50	33.00	68.50	10.00	1.75	.25			58.59	21.50
t. Joseph ...	498.10	34.50	75.00				15.20	55.25	7.35	23.50
t. Benedict.....										
t. Mary... ...	408.00	27 75	40.00		7.00	3.75			16.47	20.00
t. Bernard.....	474.00	33.00	40.00	15.00					23.25	22.00
nity.........	604.80	39.00	35.00		14.00	2.00		54.00	34.85	31.00
t. Augustine ..	427.30	27.75	63.00		24.50	3.50			46.09	21.00
t, Anne.......										
arsfield......	907.75	69.00	150.00	18.75	19.25	2.7	36.00	131.00	136.25	48.50
onstantine .—	784.85	49.75	54.00	31.85	12.25	1.7			129.77	33.00
oly Trinity....	1,544.70	102.00	95.00	45.00	22.75	3.2			452.20	75.50
ighland	258.10	18.75	27.00		10.50	1.5			4.25	14.00
merald.......	1,209.30	84.25	150.00	25.00	78.75	11.2		50.50	245.18	72.50
t James......	576.60	57.00	70.50	25.25	45.50	6.5			186.12	38.00
harles River...	1,067.50	75.00	75.00	25.00	19.25	2.2			92.45	54.00
arroll....	537.10	40.50	84.00	48.19	10.50	1.55			251.77	28.50
rospect.......	416.40	31.00							39.27	23.00
orcester.....	1,084.10	69.75	75.00	36.15	35.00	5.00	90.00	85.50	35.82	47.00
Iiddlesex.....	834.20	57.00	91.63	95.00	10.50				37.55	39.00
t. Lawrence. ..	1,121.50	77.25	54.00	45.75	35.00	.00	25.00	93.48	177.73	65.50
t. Catherine...	595.80	44.25	68.50	65.00	15.75	.25	12.00	73.76	99.96	30.50
hields	302.50	21.00	48.00	9.90		.75	15.00	52.20	40.25	17.50
allagher......	730.60	45.50	50.00	60.00	15.75	.25			190.55	35.50
t. Columbkille.	610.70	46.50	83.00	42.95		00			436.19	43.00
riffin.......	572 80	40.50	30.00		45.50	50			106.81	40.00
anton	820.00	55.50	90.00	75.00			155.00		191.28	39.50
t. Margaret....	337.90	22.50	40.00			1.0			57.15	16.00
toughton	817.20	57.75	155.00	45.00	21.00	3.00		113.00	310.30	44 00
t. Michael....	393.60	30.00	88.00	15.60					7.60	23.50
hil Sheridan...	840.60	63.00	72.00	33.45			102.00		70.00	43.50
Ierrimack.	859.50	62.25	65.00	10.55	31.50	4.50	43.10		341.20	52.50
'aunton.......	1,293.50	97.50	500.00	50.00	35.00	5.00			238.12	73.50
lendricken.....	403.70	30.75	90.00	60.00	19.25	2.75		32.00	153.02	26.00
t. Jarlath......	619.50	42.75	229.30	31.71	5.25	.75	95.00		271.24	29.00
uincy	573.60	38.25	56.25					31.75	55.00	45.25
Iystic										
t. Monica	294.60	22.50	55.00		8.75	1.25			120.00	15.00
. B. O'Reilly...	273.30	18.00	38 50	8.10	10.50	150			66.06	12.00
en. Sherman...	359.20	24.00	55.00		15.75	2.25		34.25	75.96	17.50
t. Malachi....	341.00	23.25	70.00	9.00	14.00				53.62	17.00
rockton......	698.00	50.25	51.00		131.25	18.75			126.60	73.00
. H. Newman ..	348.30	26.25	45.00		15.75	2.25			67.84	34.00
'anvers........	422 60	36.75	30.00		115.50	16.50			127.26	51.50
eo. Washington	617.00	51.00	150.00		161.00	23.00	5.00		319.61	72.00
von.........	303.80	30.00	29.50		77.00	11.00			104.77	40.50
obert Emmett.	239.60	24.75	41.67		14.00	54.00		17.50	139.40	33 50
nterprise......	111.10	14.25	11.50		40.25	5.75			50.20	20.50
nion..	77.90		9.00		47 25	6.75			48.40	23.00

FINANCIAL CONDITION OF COURTS.

No. of Court.	NAME OF COURT.	Balance on Hand Dec. 31, 1891.	Total Receipts 1892.	Total Expenditures 1892.	Total Balance on Hand Dec. 31, 1892.	Deficit from Business of 1892.	Bal. from Business of 1892.	Endowment Fund on Hand Dec. 31, 1892.	General Fund on Hand Dec. 31, 1892.	Contingent Fund on Hand Dec. 31, 1892.	Special Fund on Hand Dec. 31, 1892.	Court Reserve Fund on Hand Dec. 31, 1892.
1	Cathedral	$337.22	$2,908.90	$3,010.63	$235.49	$101.73			$235.49			
3	Fenwick	16.02	2,041.70	2,100.55	120.51	58.85			119.21			
4	St. Francis	179.86	2,184.55	2,287.16	232.18	102.61	$ 1.30		140.68		$ 87.00	$ 4.50
5	Leo	334.79	2,712.88	1,515.14	283.34				181		181.53	
6	Gus	85.60	671.00	705.90	60.50	34.90			61.50	$ 4.40	100.00	50.50
7	St. Hick	95.40	2,282.63	2,563.50	392.16	270.93	291.16				27.75	
8	Sherwood	663.09	693.60	677.75	76.68		$1.74		30.48	18.45		5.50
9	Bus	60.83	2,053.00	2,044.71	283.09	46.86	15.85		170.94	61.65		
10	Iona	274.80	2,122.70	2,169.56	55.57	6.92	8.29		55.57			
11	St. Joseph	102.43	632.30	639.22	47.17				41.67			
12	Fulton	54.09	887.53	887.18	99.01	141.09	.35		88.79	11.22		
13	Hick	98.66	1,427.07	1,568.16	62.34			62.34				
14	Lafayette	203.43	1,222.15	1,222.15	201.64				206			
15	SS. Peter and Paul	201.64	2,327.35	472	322.06				21.92			
16	Essex	135.43	1,026.00	1,011.80	21.92		186.63		174.62			
17	Hamilton	7.22	1,599.71	1,682.05	211.77	82.34	14.70	40.40	257.64		37.15	
18	St. Peter	294.11	1,542.85	88	298.04	65.53		7.15	106.60			
19	Williams	363.57	1,223.55	1,288.00	117.29	445			78.53			3.50
20	M. Pleasant	181.74	843.40	860.81	78.53	17.41			695.26			
21	St. John	95.94	1,631.42	992.48	755.26		638.94		5.18			57.30
23	Ansus	116.82	1,257.48	1,309.25	5.18	51.77		6.30	114.57			
24	St. John		1,838.45	1,929.06	114.57	90.61			149.70			
25	Gary	95.79	658.60	712	157.03	57.63			100.02			
26	St. Francis	63.41	1,386.40	1,487.88	100.00					95.00		
28	St. Raphael	216.00	4,086.82	3,903.42	94.67	101.43	132.90		17.05		25.48	
29	Erin	25.03	855.04	829.50	95.75	5.50	25.54	50.00	4.72	41.00		
30	St. Thos.	74.48	1,036.44	1,173.70	121.20	187.34			55.02		9.30	
32	Bass River	232.01	1,077.19	1,082.69	55.02	83.64			51.99			
33	St. John	101.25	1,283.20	1,366.84	51.99	14.25						
34	us	204.84	287.15	301.40	73.25	33.24			66.98			
35	Shell	69.27	621.85	655.09	66.98	10.00	16.53	74.54	304.33			3.50
37	Friendship	85.23	698.90	708.90	7.454		44.20	1.50	95.00			8.50
38	St. Joseph	83.25	539.50	522.97	309.33			1.00				
39	Benedict		651.45	607.25	1890	5.31				95.00		
43	St. Mary	50.45	808.84	814.15	20.61		32.91		20.65	30.40		
44	St. Bernard	30.34	646.05	614								
45	Unity	314.64	1,479.10	1,519.25		40.15						
46	St. Augustine	101.99										
47	St. Anne	60.76										
48	Sarsfield											

FINANCIAL CONDITION OF COURTS — *Continued,*

49	Constantine	$234.53	$1,050.60	97.24	28453	$ 46.64		$ 237.43	$ 34.35		$ 3.50
51	Holy Trinity	258.68	2,056.74	2,340.40		24.98					
52	Highland	53.88	355.25	352.10	74.53		$ 5.90	74.53			
53	Emerald	189.77	1,921.67	1,926.68	184.76	5.01		173.86			
54	St. James	261.21	944.00	1,063.47	200.34	60.87	54.00	199.75			
55	Charles River	309.21	1,383.59	1,439.45	282.35	26.86		180.35	305.59	50.00	6.00
56	Carroll	297.09	1,057.07	1,242.06	362.10			23.71		12.00	
57	Prospect	14.98	517.05	527.67	122.36			21.36			
58	Worcester	4885	1,801.74	1,888.32	387.27	55.01		62.23	89.79	192.75	42.50
59	Middlesex	17.50	1,170.35	1,121.98	22.97	39.42		22.97			
60	St. Lawrence	96.85	1,644.85	1,703.21	41.49	5.47		41.49			
61	St. Catherine	54.25	1,103.55	1,314.27	154.53	55.36	60.00	154.53	156.30		3.00
62	Shields	75.22	600.90	614.10	162.02			23.02			
63	Gallagher	154.35	1,007.86	1,130.15	32.06	96.28	2.60	11.61	.75		
64	St. Columbkille	3042	1,150.90	1,153.34	248.12	86.80	19 70	163.57	84.55		
65		81.62	894.67	542 11	1418			26.80			
66	Canton	646.02	1,136.10	1,423.28	356.44	52.56	108.32	6.30	346.13	4.06	
67	St. Margaret	60.86	515.46	475.06	101.27			93.96	7.31	4.01	
68	Stoughton	11.31	1,471.18	1,566.25	241.34	40.41		241.34			
69	St. Michael	331.18	550.35	555.30	3.36			3.36			
70	Phil Sheridan	508.84	1,874.64	1,224.55	481.27	95.07				481.27	
71	Merrimack	690.18	1,226.10	1,470.10	282.55	7.95	150.09	202.05		297.68	
72	Taunton	39.42	2,307.22	2,292.62	704.78	244.00		523.45			
73	Hendricken	182.32	823.61	817.47	45.56	14.60		6.14			
74	St. Jarlath	17.10	1,851.92	1,324.50	709.74	6.14		36.05	151.78	521 91	
75	Quincy		846.20	800.10	57.20	527.42					
76	Mystic		561.10	517.10	114.50	46.10		51.00			
77	St. Monica	70.50	413.30	427.96	30.21	44.00		30.21		36.00	
78	John Boyle O'Reilly	44.87	539.00	583.91	84.09	14.66		38.12	43.47		2.50
79	Gen. Sherman	129.00	545.05	527.87	23.38	44.91	14.93				2 25
80	St. Malachi	6.20	1,306.80	1,148.85	157.95			58.95	99 00		
81	Brockton		584.10	539.39	80.11	157.95	21 60	23.11	108.08		
82	John Henry Newman	35.40	884.85	800.11	84.74	44.71	4.70	80.04			
83	Danvers		1,483.50	1,398.81	34.69	84.74	20.14	9.75		5.00	
84	Geo. Washington		615.90	596.57	19.38	34.69		19.33			
85	Avon		619.05	564.42	54.63	19.33	1.00	.18	53.45		
86	Robert Emmett		259.20	253.55	5.65	54.63		5.65			
87	Enterprise		218.45	212.30	6.15	5.65		6.15			
88	Union		118.10	117.60	.50	6.15		.50			
89						.50					
90	St. Vincent										
	Total	$11,358.52	$87,508.82	$88,229.32	$11,679.33	$3,173.83	$844.08	$6,539.37	$1,749.77	$2,072.89	$ 193.05

$2,704.64

ENDOWMENT FUND.

Dr.

Assessment Call No.	80, 81, 82			$ 30
"	"	"	83	2 10
"	"	"	84	4 40
"	"	"	85	10 40
"	"	"	86	20 60
"	"	"	87	118 40
"	"	"	88	328 80
"	"	"	89	5,956 90
"	"	"	90	6,129 70
"	"	"	91	6,137 00
"	"	"	92	6,232 50
"	"	"	93	6,375 10
"	"	"	94	6,303 20
"	"	"	95	6,529 90
"	"	"	96	6,416 90
"	"	"	97	6,221 40
"	"	"	98	4,672 20

$61,519 80

Balance, April, 1892.......................... 7,629 29

$69,149 09

Cr.

M. W. Byrnes,	of Griffin,	No. 66....	$1,000 00
Thomas A. Byrnes,	" Griffin,	" 66....	1,000 00
Jere. Chamberlain,	" St. Peter,	" 18....	1,000 00
Patrick A. Morrissey,	" Cathedral,	" 1....	1,000 00
John F. Kerrigan,	" St. Thomas,	" 29....	1,000 00
Michael Brennan,	" St. Alphonsus,	" 21....	1,000 00
Peter F. McBride,	" Emerald,	" 53....	1,000 00
Michael Tansy,	" Lafayette,	" 14....	1,000 00
William Garrity,	" Iona,	" 10....	1,000 00
James R. Cotter,	" Stoughton,	" 69....	1,000 00
Michael Sheehan,	" Mystic,	" 77....	1,000 00
Thomas F. Whalen,	" Constantine,	" 49....	1,000 00
Edward J. Brady,	" St. Thomas,	" 29....	1,000 00

John E. O'Brien	of St. Catherine,	No. 62....$1,000 00
John Morrissey,	" St. Alphonsus,	" 21.... 1,000 00
James T. Sheehan,	" Erin,	" 28.... 1,000 00
John Harrington,	" St. Francis,	" 4.... 1,000 00
Dennis Burns,	" Lafayette,	" 14.... 1,000 00
John McGrail,	" Brockton,	" 82.... 1,000 00
William G. Parow,	" Leo,	" 5.... 1,000 00
Thomas O'Keefe,	" Erin,	" 28.... 1,000 00
John J. Gately,	" Mount Pleasant,	" 20.... 1,000 00
John L. Carroll,	" Sarsfield,	" 48.... 1,000 00
John Meehan,	" Erin,	" 28.... 1,000 00
Maurice J. McCarthy,	" Americus,	" 34.... 1,000 00
John Callahan,	" Leo,	" 5.... 1,000 00
James W. McGuire,	" Cheverus,	" 6.... 1,000 00
Daniel F. Geary.	" St. Francis,	" 25.... 1,000 00
John Clarey,	" Sherwood,	" 8.... 1,000 00
John A. Kelly,	" Leo,	" 5.... 1,000 00
John Moriarty,	" Erin,	" 28.... 1,000 00
Richard Walsh,	" St. Francis,	" 25.... 1,000 00
Daniel Hayes,	" Leo,	" 5.... 1,000 00
John A. Kenely,	" Taunton,	" 73.... 1,000 00
Henry S. Leonard,	" Gallagher,	" 64.... 1,000 00
James P. Breslow,	" St. Columbkille,	" 65.... 1,000 00
Patrick Flynn,	" St. Thomas,	" 29.... 1,000 00
Patrick Flynn,	" Iona,	" 10.... 1,000 00
John J. Cahill,	" Emerald,	" 53.... 1,000 00
Patrick J. Desmond,	" St. Thomas,	" 29.... 1,000 00
Michael O'Brien,	" Fulton,	" 12.... 1,000 00
John J. Doyle,	" Americus,	" 34.... 1,000 00
Michael McCarthy,	" St. Lawrence..	" 61.... 1,000 00
David Leahy,	" Constantine,	" 49.... 1,000 00
John Flynn,	" SS. Peter and Paul,	" 15.... 1,000 00
John J. Webb,	" Quincy,	" 76.... 1,000 00
Andrew P. Reddy,	" John H. Newman,	" 83.... 1,000 00
William J. Kean,	" Worcester,	" 59.... 1,000 00
Michael Barry,	" Mystic,	" 77.... 1,000 00
Charles Doherty,	" Americus,	" 34.... 1,000 00
John Baird,	" Stoughton,	" 69.... 1,000 00
Martin D. Carr,	" Iona,	" 10.... 1,000 00
Richard Donnell,	" Sarsfield,	" 48.... 1,000 00
John Horrigan,	" Qualey,	" 32.... 1,000 00
Edward McKenna,	" St. John,	" 23.... 1,000 00
James Mahan,	" Cheverus,	" 6.... 1,000 00
Dennis J. Kelly,	" Cheverus,	" 6.... 1,000 00
Michael Cody,	" Fitzpatrick,	" 13.... 1,000 00
John E. King,	" Merrimack,	" 72.... 1,000 00

——— $59,000 00

$10,149 09

GENERAL FUND.

Dr.

Balance, April, 1892.................................	$704 81	
Sale of Postal Cards, Books, &c.....................	930 84	
Per Capita, 1891	6 50	
" " 1892.................................	4,131 70	
Charters..	261 00	
Benefit Certificates	76 25	
		$6,111 10

Cr.

Estate of James Parker:
Rent of office at 611 Washington St. to April 1, 1892.... $400 00

POSTAGE.

Boston Post Office:		
Stamped Envelopes and Stamps..............	$178 93	
Postal Cards	679 50	
		$858 43

REGALIA.

F. Alford:		
Partial Set.................................	$6 75	
" "	2 25	
" "	3 00	
Repairing 1 Set............................	2 50	
1 Set.......................................	8 50	
2 Sets repaired............................	5 00	
Repairing part sets........................	6 55	
		$34 55

Boston Regalia Co.:	
Repairing Part Set.........................	$5 50
2 Ballot Boxes.............................	2 40
12 Gavels	4 20
1 Dozen Badge Pins.........................	1 00
1 1-11 Sets Jewels.........................	9 27
200 White Ballots..........................	1 50
Quarter Gross each, Black and White Ballots..	60
1 Set Jewels...............................	8 50
1 Set Jewels...............................	8 50

1292.98

3 Ballot Boxes...............................	3 30	
2 Sets Jewels...............................	17 00	
8⅓ Dozen Black Ballots......................	83	
1 Set Jewels................................	8 50	
2 Ballot Boxes..............................	2 20	
1 Set Jewels................................	8 50	
1 Ballot Box.	1 10	
Repairing Jewels.............	1 25	
		$84 15

STATIONERY.

Samuel Hobbs & Co.:

Letter Book...............................	$2 50	
Rubber Bands.............................	4 50	
Letter Book...............................	2 25	
Letter Files..............................	4 50	
2 Boxes Pens..............................	1 25	
		$15 00

SEALS.

S. M. Spencer:

1 Seal Press...............................	$5 00	
1 " "	00	
1 " "	00	
1	00	
1	5 00	
		$25 00

TRAVELLING EXPENSES.

Deputy High Chief Rangers:

D. H. Maguire.............................	$9 00	
W. Condon.................................	00	
P. A. Sullivan	18 00	
"	9 00	
D. F. Buckley..............................	7 00	
" "	5 75	
W. H. Linnehan............................	2 00	
F. S. Sullivan..............................	6 00	
John Vogel.................................	5 00	
John B. White..............................	1 00	
J. F. Reilly................................	3 00	
M. Edmonds................................	5 00	
M. Edmonds................................	15	
J. O'Kane..................................	6 16	
A. H. McDonald............................	11 30	
F. L. Smith................................	11 50	
A. M. Lanigan..............................	17 50	
F. J. McQueeney...........................	1 50	
G. H. Keefe................................	5 85	
J. F. Fleming...............................	3·50	
J. B. Rooney	14 85	
		$140 06

TRAVELLING EXPENSES.

High Standing Committee:

To New Bedford	$4 00
Walpole	2 50
Brighton	5 00
Franklin	2 38
Quincy	50
Dorchester	10 00
W. Newbury	2 20
496 Miles B. & M. R.R	9 92
W. Newbury	20 98
W. Lynn	3 83
" "	45
Whitman	8 20
Boston	76
834 Miles B. & A. R.R	16 68
Whitman	6 65
1,000 Miles O. C. R. R	20 00
Portland, Me	20 75
1,592 Miles B. & M. R. R	31 84
Whitman	6 85
Gloucester	12 55
Portland, Me	26 40
N. Attleboro	2 01
Rockland	1 81
Gloucester	12 90
Boston	2 30
" Cambridge	6 00
Holliston	5 70
Middleboro	7 83
W. Quincy	1 00
Lynn	5 15
Rockland	6 38
808 Miles B. & M. R.R	16 16
Lawrence	1 80
1,000 Miles O. C. R.R	20 00
Springfield and So. Framingham	2 25
Holliston	8 05
1,000 Miles B. & A. R.R	20 00
Boston and Dorchester	13 75
Brockton	1 00
Brighton	6 25
Brockton	4 30
Lynn	3 75
Hyde Park	17 20
Salem	10 70
Newton	10 12
Taunton	12 10
W. Quincy	9 55
Holliston	10 35

Boston.....................................	5 60
Brockton.................................	1 05
E. Bridgewater...........................	7 25
Boston...................................	1 55
1,000 Miles O. C. R.R...................	20 00
Boston...................................	5 00
"	6 25
Worcester...............................	1 50
New Bedford.............................	2 00
Middleboro..............................	1 50
Boston and Cambridge...................	3 50
" "	3 00
Woburn.................................	25
Cambridge...............................	15

$489 45

PRINTING.

L. F. Clarke:

10 Lots Postal Cards......................	$7 05
Assessment Call...........................	4 00
200 Circulars.............................	3 00
300 List Names............................	6 00
2,000 Envelopes...........................	5 00
Statements...............................	5 95
Circulars.................................	1 75
3 Lots Postal Cards.......................	2 10
300 Blanks................................	4 00
3,000 Suspension Blanks...................	4 00
7 Lots Postal Cards.......................	4 90
500 Circulars.............................	1 50
600 Credentials...........................	4 00
150 Circulars.............................	1 75
Assessment Call...........................	4 00

59 00

Eastburn Press :

1,000 Folders and Electro Plate..............	$15 00
2,000 Constitutions.........................	63 00
50 Charters.................................	8 00
Electro.....................................	2 50
1,000 Applications..........................	10 00
300 Circulars...............................	3 00
10,000 Applications.........................	131 00
Menu Cards.................................	14 30
100 Lists...................................	4 00
500 Reports.................................	148 75
2,000 Constitutions.........................	51 00
2,000 Approval Blanks.......................	12 00
4,000 Reports...............................	219 00

$681 55

Farrington Printing Company:

10 Lots Postal Cards	$7	00
100 Blank Books	65	00
200 Circulars	2	50
Assessment Call	5	50
1,000 Cards Medical Examiners	1	25
75 Circulars	1	50
15 Lots Postal Cards	10	50
Medical Examiners Lists	4	00
1,000 Circulars, Occupation, etc.	2	75
Calls for Meeting	1	75
High Chief Ranger	4	00
Assessment Call	4	00
Composition and Printing, Avon 86	1	25
9 Lots Postal Cards	6	30
12 Badges	1	00
300 Circulars	1	75
Portland Meeting		75
4 Lots Postal Cards	2	80
44 Books, Financial Secretary	33	00
2,000 Envelopes	5	00
Assessment Call	4	00
9 Lots Postal Cards	6	30
Change of Endowment	8	00
Letter Heads	5	00
Assessment Call	4	00
Roll of Members	4	00
Deputy High Chief Ranger's List	3	50
Roll of Officers	2	50
Financial Statements	4	00
Roll of Members	4	00
12 Lots Postal Cards	8	40
Bill Heads	6	00
Assessment Call	4	00
17 Lots Postal Cards	11	90
Reserve Assessment	6	00
Assesment Call	4	00
2,000 Envelopes	5	00
30 Lots Postal Cards	21	00
Assessment Call	4	00
1,000 Envelopes	2	50
8 Lots Postal Cards	5	60
Assessment Call	4	00
500 Envelopes		75

$290 05

MISCELLANEOUS EXPENSES.

Preliminary Expenses, Forming Rockland Court No. 90,	$23	00
" " " " Court in Holliston	25	10
2 Bottles Ink	2	00
Convention Expenses	35	50

3077.74

Blank Cards and Wrapping Paper..............	$15	00
Closet for Telephone.............................	5	00
Wrapping Paper and Twine.......................	8	50
Preliminary Expenses, Forming Germania Court No. 93,	7	30
" " " Loyola Court No. 94,		
4 meetings.....	35	50
" " Columbia Court No. 95,		
4 meetings.....	39	55
Copy of Record, Mitchell Case....................	3	00
H. W. Upham, Binding............................	16	00
" "	16	00
" "	2	50
" "	5	00
N. E. T. & T. Co., Rent of Telephone..............	78	29
A. B. C. Pathfinder, 1892	5	00
" " 1893.......................	5	00
Preliminary Expenses forming Germania Court, 93...	9	00
Burr Index Co., 1 Index...........................	20	00
Rent of Lawrence Hall for Convention..............	20	00
P. & J. Besse, Catering " "	172	00
R. T. Purcell, Batons.............................	3	60
Boson Gas Light Co., for Gas......................	14	69
Expressing.......................................	4	85
Messenger and Telegrams.........................	12	14
Cleaning...	25	25

$608 77

Salary High Secretary-Treasurer to April, 1893	2,000	00
Balance on hand.......................	433	89
Due from Courts for Books and Cards.......................	344	72

6.119

6.119.90
433.89
5.686 01 .

DEPUTY HIGH CHIEF RANGERS.

FOR THE TERM OF 1893-94.

DIS-TRICT.	COURTS. No.	NAME AND RESIDENCE OF D. H. C. R.	COURT OF WHICH D. H. C. R. IS A MEMBER.
1	Cathedral........... 1 Fitzpatrick..........13	Garrett H. Keefe, 63 Palmer Street, Roxbury.......	Mt. Pleasant.... 20
2	Fenwick............ 3 Cheverus 6	George F. Lowe, 271 Sumner Street, E. Boston....	Leo.............. 5
3	St. Francis .... 4 Carroll ... .57	P. M. Keating, 33 Pemberton Square, Boston....	St. Joseph.......11
4	St. Patrick.......... 7 SS. Peter and Paul..15	Robert Dwyer, 696 East Third Street, So. Boston.	St. Michael......70
5	Sherwood........... 8 Erin 28	J. B Rooney, Walpole.....................	Robert Emmett..87
6	St. Joseph ....11 Columbus.......... 9	E. F. Chamberlain, Mattapan.....................	St. Peter........18
7	Iona ....10 Qualey 32	J. T. Mahoney, 10 Rand Street, Boston Highlands	Cathedral 1
8	Leo................ 5 Williams...........19	Michael Leonard, 98 East-Canton Street, Boston....	Americus........34
9	Mystic...............77 John HenryNewman.83	J. B. Buckley, Malden....	Iona 10
10	St Alphonsus...... 21 Highland 52	Thomas Lockney, Corner Codman Street and Dorchester Avenue, Milton......	St. Gregory......24
11	Fulton ....12 Friendship..........37	F. Schwab, 31 Avon Street, Roxbury........	Holy Trinity....51
12	St. Gregory.........24 St. James...........54	W. E. Shay, 3 Warren Place, Roxbury........	St. Francis.......4
13	St. Augustine.......46 St. Michael........70	A. M. Lanigan, 664 Harrison Avenue, Boston.....	Cathedral 1
14	St. Thomas.........29 Hendricken.........74	A. H. McDonald, Stoughton.....................	Stoughton........69
15	Lafayette...........14 Essex 16	John Doolin, 211 Third Street, South Boston...	St. Augustine... 46
16	St. John............23 Sheil...............35	J. F. Riley, Dedham	St. Raphael......26
17	St. Raphael.........26..	Hugh Montague, 26 Fayette Street, Boston........	Sherwood........ 8
18	St. Malachi ......81..	W. A. Flaherty, 261 Washington Street, Somerville	Benedict.........39
19	St. John...........33 St. Joseph.........38	T. F. Crosby, Parker Hill Avenue, Roxbury....	St. Francis...... 4
20	Bass River..........30 St. Margaret........68	J. B. McCarthy, 41 Woodman Street, West Lynn..	Geo. Washington.85
21	St. Francis......... 25 Quincy..... 76	D. Connelly, 33 Packard Street, Brockton.....	St. Thomas......29
22	Benedict ... .39 Constantine.... 49	J. F. Gleason, 12 Dorchester Street. So. Boston.	St. James........54
23	George Washington..85 Danvers........... 84	Timothy Donovan, Adams Street, Lynn.......... ...	Lafayette........14
24	Hamilton..........17 St. Peter...........18	M. Edmonds, 13 Gay Head Street, Roxbury....	Cathedral 1
25	Phil Sheridan.......71 St. Monica..........78 Enterprise 88	D. H. Maguire, Bradford......................	Merrimack.......72
26	Prospect ....58 St. Bernard.........44	T. F. Gallagher, Bemis..................	Charles River....55
27	Unity ....45 Harmony 92	T. F. Roach, 13 Bartlett Street, Brockton.....	St. Thomas......29

DEPUTY HIGH CHIEF RANGERS.—*Continued.*

DISTRICT.	COURT.	No.	NAME AND RESIDENCE OF D. H. C. R.	COURT OF WHICH D. H. C. R. IS A MEMBER.
28	Holy Trinity........51		D. A. Cronin, 8 Allen Street, Boston...........	St. Joseph.......11
29	St. Anne. ....47..		D. J. O'Brien, Front Street, Salem.............	Essex............16
30	Emerald...........53..		P. F. J. Carney, 42 Buffom Street, Salem.........	Essex............16
31	Charles River.......55 } Middlesex......... 60 }		M. J. Collins, 10 G Street, South Boston........	St. James........54
32	Worcester..........59..		J. H. Fitzgerald, 21 Spruce Street, Worcester......	Worcester........59
33	St. Lawrence ....61 } St. Columbkille.....65 }		P. O'Loughlin, 23 Court Street, Boston..........	St. Joseph.......11
34	Pittsfield............. } Shields ....63 }		J. J. Leonard, 118 Greenwood Street, Springfield	Gallagher........64
35	Gallagher...........64..		F. F. O'Neil, 441 High Street, Holyoke........	Shields......... 63
36	Griffin.............66 } St. Anthony ....97 }		D. F. O'Sullivan, Franklin ....:............	Griffin...........66
37	Avon...............86 } Union ....89 } Rockland ....90 }		P. McCarthy, 30 Packard Street, Brockton.....	St. Thomas 29
38	Canton............. 67 }		J. F. O'Brien, North Attleboro................	Sarsfield 48
39	Stoughton ....69 } Brockton ....82 }		D. F. Buckley, North Easton..................	Hendricken......74
40	Merrimack..........72 } St. Jarlath..........75 }		James F. Carens, 20 Fair Street, Newburyport......	Phil Sheridan....71
41	Taunton ....73 } Gen. Sherman......80 }		Jeremiah G. Fennessey, New Court House, Boston........	St. James........54
42	St. Mary...........43..		J. T. Lawless, Rockland	Rockland.. 90
43	John Boyle O'Reilly.79 } Sacred Heart.... ..96 }		G. F. Brammer, Taunton.	Taunton.........73
44	Sarsfield .... 48..		P. F. Brady, Canton.........................	Canton..........67
45	St. Catherine........62 } Robert Emmett.....87 }		M. J. Kelley, 107 Paris Street, East Boston.....	Williams 19
46	Mt. Pleasant........20 } Americus...........34 }		J. J. Lannigan, 664 Harrison Avenue, Boston....	Cathedral.........1
47	Loyola.............94 } Columbia ....95 }		R. E. Oldham, Norwood	St. Catherine 62
• 48	Germania..........93..		Conrad Mischler, Braintree, Mass................	Quincy..........76
• 49	St. Vincent........91..		J. J. McLaughlin, 1299 Washington Street, Boston..	
	. AT LARGE...... {		R. Farrenkopf, 108 Kneeland Street, Boston. Cassimer Rieser, 4 Spring Court, Roxbury........ P. A. Sullivan, 19 Wareham Street, Boston. P. M. Riordan, 16 Rantoul Street, Beverly....... J. F. McNulty, 12 Woodward Street, So Boston.. Henry Wesling, 135 Thornton Street, Roxbury... Charles O'Brien, 57 Warner Street, Gloucester.....	

MEDICAL EXAMINERS.

For Term Ending April, 1894.

Dist.	Examiner.	Courts.

1   S. A. Callanan, M. D., Warren Street,
cor. Warren Place, Roxbury....Cathedral 1, Fulton 12, Americus 34.

2   Francis J. McQueeney, M. D.,
35 W. Dedham Street, Fenwick 3, Cheverus 6, Fitzpatrick 13, Loyola 94.

3   Joseph P. Murphy, M. D., 1607 Tremont St., Roxbury,
also at Brookline.......St. Francis 4, St. Lawrence 61, Highland 52.

4   James F. Ferry, M. D., 10 Chelsea St., E. B...Leo 5, Williams 19.

5   W. J. Gallivan, M. D., Broadway cor. L St...St. Patrick 7.

6   J. M. Thompson, M. D., 29 Hollis Street......Sherwood 8, Sheil 35.

7   Wm. G. McDonald, M. D., 221 Shawmut
Avenue........Columbus 9, St. Joseph 11, Erin 28, Constantine 49.

8   C. D. McCarthy, M. D., Malden.............Iona 10.

9   C. A. Ahearne, M. D.. Lynn................Lafayette 14.

10   Wm. H. Devine, M. D.,
599 Broadway, S. Boston......SS Peter & Paul 15, St. Augustine 46,
St. James 54, St. Michael 70.

11   Francis E. Hines, M. D., Salem..............Essex 16.

12   T. J. Broderick, M.D., 114 Main St., Charlestown, Hamilton 17.

13   J. P. Lumbard, M. D . Dorchester...St. Peter 18, St. Gregory 24.

14   E. T. Galligan, M. D., 88 Warren St.,
Roxbury ....,...Mt. Pleasant 20, St. Alphonsus 21, St. Joseph 38.

15   John C. Lincoln, M. D., Hyde Park..........St. John 23.

16   Joseph M. Sheahan, M. D., Quincy..........St. Francis 25.

17   A. H. Hodgden, M. D., Dedham..:............St. Raphael 26.

8   Benedict Donovan, M. D , Brockton........St. Thomas 29.

19   T. J. Hayes, M. D., Beverly...........:Bass River 30, St. Margaret 68.*

20   J. H. Conway, M. D., Woburn...............Qualey 32.

21   C. R. Cavenagh, M. D., Bow St., Somerville...St. John 33, Benedict 39.

22   Thomas M. Shay, M. D., 1 Warren Pl., Rox..Friendship 37, Germania 93

23   D. F. Kinnear, M. D., Randolph.............St. Mary 43.

24   C. J. McCormick, M. D., West Newton......St. Bernard 44, Prospect 58.

25   G. H. Watson, M. D., Bridgewater...........Unity 45.

26   Philip Mooney, M. D., Gloucester...........St. Anne 47.

MEDICAL EXAMINERS — *Continued.*

DIST.	EXAMINER.	COURTS.
27	T. P. McDonough, M. D., North Attleborough	Sarsfield 48.
28	C. W. MacDonald, M. D., Roxbury	Holy Trinity 51, Columbia 95.
29	John Shannahan, M. D., Peabody	Emerald 53.
30	M. J. Kelley, M. D., Watertown	Charles River 55.
31	J. P. Broidrick, M. D., Jamaica Plain	Carroll 57.
32	J. H. Kelley, M. D., Worcester	Worcester 59.
33	F. M. O'Donnell, M. D., Newton	Middlesex 60.
34	L. N. Plympton, M. D., Norwood	St. Catherine 62, Robert Emmett 87.
35	G. H. Clark, M. D., Holyoke	Shields 63.
36	A. J. Dunne, M. D., Springfield	Gallagher 64.
37	H. V. McLaughlin, M. D., Brighton	St. Columbkille 65.
38	C. F. McCarthy, Franklin	Griffin 66, St. Anthony 97.
39	Thomas D. Lonergan, M. D., Canton	Canton 67.
40	Michael Glennon, M. D., Stoughton	Stoughton 69.
41	J. J. Healy. M. D., Newburyport	Phil Sheridan 71.
42	John F. Croston, M. D., Haverhill	Merrimack 72.
43	J. B. Murphy, M. D., Taunton	Taunton 73.
44	T. H. McCarthy, M. D., North Easton	Hendricken 74.
45	J. H. O'Toole, M. D., Amesbury	St. Jarlath 75.
46	S. M. Donovan, M. D., Quincy	Quincy 76.
47	J. B. Mahoney, M. D., Medford	Mystic 77.
48	D. J. O'Sullivan, M. D., Lawrence	St. Monica 78.
49	J. F. Sullivan, M. D., New Bedford	John Boyle O'Reilly 79.
50	Edgar D. Hill, M. D., Plymouth	Gen. Sherman 80.
51	E. D. Hooker, M. D., Arlington	St. Malachi 81.
52	T. P. Conlan, M. D., Brockton	Brockton 82, Avon 86, Union 89.
53	P. J. Conroy, M. D., Everett	John Henry Newman 83.
54	E. J. Magee, M. D., Danvers	Danvers 84.
55	J. A. McGuigan, M. D., West Lynn	George Washington 85.
56	D. D. Murphy, M. D., West Newbury	Enterprise 88.
57	J. D. McIntosh, M. D., Rockland	Rockland 90.
58	F. G. Atkins, M. D., Holliston	St. Vincent 91.
59	A. L. Shirley, M. D., East Bridgewater	Harmony 92.
60		Sacred Heart 96

REPRESENTATIVES.

	REPRESENTATIVES.	COURT.	NO.	PROXY REPRESENTATIVES.
1	J. J. Lanigan	Cathedral	1	T. J. Dunn.
2	M. Edmonds.........	"	"	Jeremiah Sullivan.
3	John T. Mahony.....	"	"	John M. Singler.
4	Michael McBarron....	"	"	C. H. Tighe.
5	John J. Irving.......	Fenwick...........	3	Daniel Gallagher.
6	W. E. Shay..	St. Francis..........	4	T. F. Crosby.
7	Michael J. O'Brien...	"	"	James P. Cleary.
8	Thos. Sproules	"	"	John E. Heslan.
9	John Brant	Leo..............	5	John Gallagher.
10	George F. Lowe.....	"	"	D. F. McCallion.
11	Wm. F. O'Donnell....	"	"	Thomas F. Doherty.
12	Owen A. Galvin......	Cheverus...........	6	William T. Rich.
13	James Cashin........	"	"	Andrew Golding.
14	Thomas F. Twomey..	St. Patrick..........	7	George T. Fair.
15	John P. Dore........	Sherwood...........	8	Rudolph Farrenkopf.
16	D. F. Sullivan......	"	"	John J. Stephan.
17	Hugh Montague......	"	"	Charles E. Colbert.
18	James F. Supple......	Columbus...........	9	Richard J. Brooks.
19	John M. Neville......	Iona	10	M. C. Desmond.
20	James B. Buckley.....	"	"	George E. Cusick.
21	Patrick O'Loughlin...	St. Joseph..........	11	Henry C. Griffin.
22	Daniel A. Cronin.....	"	"	Charles F. Dolan.
23	Patrick M. Keating...	"	"	Patrick F. Garrigle.
24	Henry F. Scanlan....	Fulton.............	12	Michael Nolan.
25	James Cullinane......	Fitzpatrick.........	13	Charles J. Jordan.
26	Michael P. Keenan...	Lafayette..........	14	James J. O'Neil.
27	John Driscoll........	"	"	M. J. Malone.
28	Martin Folan...... ..	SS. Peter & Paul.....	15	Thomas F. Gallagher.
29	Patrick A. Donovan..	" "	"	Peter J. McKenna.
30	James J. Murphy.....	Essex	16	Peter F. J. Carney.
31	Daniel J. O'Brien.....	"	"	John B. Harding.
32	Dr. F. E. Hines......	"	"	Michael A. Dodd.
33	John Hurley........	Hamilton...........	17	Lawrence J. Lyons.
34	James H. Dixon......	St. Peter..........	18	Thomas J. Lane.
35	John J. Curran......	"	"	John F. Brooks.
36	James Douglass......	Williams	19	M. J. Burke.
37	M. J. Kelly.........	"	"	F. N. Kievenaar.
38	Garrett H. Keefe....	Mt. Pleasant........	20	Edward A. Dever.
39	Wm. J. Dowling....	"	"	Michael O'Riordan.
40	Patrick H. Shea......	St. Al h	21	James T. Brickley.
41	Thomas Mulcahy.....	St. Ionsus	23	Thomas Murray.
42	Thomas P. Lockney..	St. Gregory	24	Michael Dunican.
43	John O'Callaghan....	"	"	Joseph H. Blake.
44	J. L. Fennessey......	St. Francis	25	John F. Cole.
45	John Vogel.........	"	"	T. J. Foley.
46	Bernard J. McCaffrey.	St. Raphael.......	26	John F. Reilly.
47	John T. Daly........	Erin	28	Jeremiah Mara.
48	James J. Kane.......	"	"	C. J. Lynch.
49	Patrick McCarthy....	St. Thom s	29	James P. Conley.
50	Daniel Connolly......	" a	"	William H. Linnehan.
51	F. L. Smith.........	"	"	Patrick Gilmore.
52	Timothy F. Roach....	"	"	John J. Morton.
53	P. M. Riordan.......	Bass River..........	"	Philip Fitzgibbon.
54	James Dolan.........	Qualey..............	32	John Bowler.
55	Bernard J. Brogan...	St. John.............	33	Timothy J. Quinn.

REPRESENTATIVES.—*Continued.*

	REPRESENTATIVES.	COURT.	No.	PROXY REPRESENTATIVES.
56	J. J McLaughlin.....	Americus............	34	J. W. Brown.
57	P. J. Gorman..........	"	"	Michael Leonard.
58	William H. Pierce....	Sheil................	35	B. H. Hunt.
59	Thomas H. Duggan...	Friendship	37	J. W. Keenan.
60	Peter Morris.........	St. Joseph...........	38	John P. Ego.
61	John J. McGonagle...	Benedict	39	Joseph D. Couch, M. D
62	Wm. W. Hurley.	St. Mary............	43	Charles S. Dolan.
63	M. J. Duane.........	St. Bernard.........	44	
64	David Cashon........	Unity...............	45	Wm. Condon.
65	John Doolin.........	St. Augustine.......	46	Francis M. Hughes.
66	Charles O'Brien......	St. Anne............	47	John J.Flaherty.
67	John F. Riley........	"	"	Wm. F. Moore.
68	James H. Carley....	Sarsfield...........	48	Patrick Ryan.
69	James F. O'Brien.....	"	"	John P. Zilch.
70	James T. Riley.......	Constantine.........	49	James A. Berrill.
71	J. Torndorf, Jr.......	Holy Trinity.......	51	Martin Hasenfuss.
72	Henry Wesling.......	"	"	Gerhard Kranefuss.
73	F. Schwaab.........	"	"	C. Reiser.
74	H. H. Collins	Highland............	52	John J. Corbett.
75	John J. Sweeney.....	Emerald............	53	James J. McCann.
76	James M. Regan	"	"	James Sherry.
77	Thomas F. Lyons.....	"	"	Wm. J. McCarthy.
78	Jere. G. Fennessey...	St. James...........	54	Michael J. Collins.
79	Thos. W. O'Rourke...	"	"	James F. Gleason.
80	Peter McGrath.......	Charles River.......	55	E. J. Burke.
81	James D. Monahan...	"	"	Thomas F. Gallagher.
82	C. J. Fay...........	Carroll	57	J. D. Fallon.
83	Wm. F. Rooney......	Prospect............	58	David Walsh.
84	James H. Fitzgerald..	Worcester..........	59	John B. Ratigan.
85	Timothy H. Murphy..	"	"	Patrick J. Quinn.
86	James Cannon.......	Middlesex..........	60	Patrick A. Mulligan.
87	John E. Briston......	"	"	Myles J. Joyce.
88	Michael Driscoll.....	St. Lawrence.......	61	Patrick Johnson.
89	James T. Donovan ...	"	"	J. J. Muldowney.
90	Richard E. Oldham...	St. Catherine.......	62	Michael E. Hayden.
91	F. F. O'Neil.........	Sheilds.............	63	J. J. Callanan.
92	Patrick J. Murray....	Gallagher..........	64	John J. Leonard.
93	John J. O'Keefe......	St. Columbkille.....	65	Geo. F. Mitchell.
94	M. F. Conroy........	Griffin.............	66	Dennis F. O'Sullivan.
95	Matthew A. Skelton..	Canton.............	67	Edw. C. Murphy.
96	Lawrence J. Watson..	St. Margaret.......	68	Edward H. Higgins.
97	John E. Tighe.......	"	"	John S. Madden.
98	Archibald H.McDonald	Stoughton..........	69	Daniel E. Lane.
99	Robert Dwyer........	St. Michael.........	70	James H. Coughlin.
100	James F. Carens	Phil. Sheridan......	71	John M. Holland.
101	John J. Dunn........	"	"	A. E. Moylan.
102	Daniel H. Maguire . .	Merrimack..........	72	Bernard Haughey.
103	Richard Dwyer.......	"	"	John T. Desmond.
104	Benj. Morris........	Taunton............	73	Thomas F. Cavanaugh.
105	George F. Brammer...	"	"	J. H. Cosgrove.
106	William J. Hedan....	Hendricken........	74	John E. Blake.
107	T. F. Lynes..........	St. Jarlath..........	75	Patrick Manning.
108	Conrad Mischler......	Quincy.............	76	
109	John W. Lynch......	Mystic.............	77	John Crowley.
110	John H. Cronin.....	St. Monica..........	78	Rev. James T. O'Reilly.

REPRESENTATIVES.—*Continued*

	REPRESENTATIVES.	COURT.	No.	PROXY REPRESENTATIVES.
111	James H. Miskell.....	John Boyle O'Reilly	79	John N. O'Brien.
112	Henry S. Healy......	Gen. Sherman.......	80	John E. Tracy.
113	Edmund Reardon	St. Malachi..........	81	Patrick A. McCarthy.
114	John Kent..........	Brockton	82	Thomas J. Doyle.
115	Charles M. Hickey ...	"	"	John J. Hickey.
116	F. Frederick Driscoll.	JohnHenryNewman	83	P. J. Conroy, M. D.
117	T. J. Lynch..........	Danvers	84	D M. Cahill.
118	J. B. McCarthy	Geo. Washington....	85	James S. Barry.
119	Patrick J. Sullivan...	"	"	John J.McGuigan,M.D.
120	P. E. McGonnigle....	Avon................	86	J. F. Sheehan.
121	John F. Kiley........	Robert Emmett.....	87	John S. Crowley.
122	Daniel Cooney......	Enterprise	88	
123	Montague McKinnon.	Union	89	Alphonse Brouillard.
124	James F. Lawless.....	Rockland...........	90	John D. McIntosh,M.D.
125	Maurice F. Coughlin..	St. Vincent.........	91	John F. Nugent.
126	....	Harmony............	92	
127	Christian Lambrecht..	Germania...........	93	Francis I. Mueller.
128	John A. Ryan........	Loyola..............	94	Michael Donovan.
129	Patrick F. Manning ..	Columbia...........	95	

DIRECTORY.

NAMES OF COURTS, TIME AND PLACE OF MEETING, OFFICERS AND THEIR ADDRESSES.

No. AND COURT NAME.	OFFICERS.		ADDRESS.	
1. Cathedral, Boston. Instituted Sept. 3, 1879. Meets 1st and 3rd Wednesday, St. Rose Hall, 17 Worcester St., Boston.	C. R. R. S. F. S. T.	John W. Sweeney.... John T. Hasey....... Joseph A. Barry.... Patrick D'Arcy.......	1 Bechler Avenue, Minot Place, 99 E. Lenox Street, 53 Roundhill Street,	Boston Neponset Boston Roxbury
3. Fenwick, Boston. Inst. Nov. 14, 1879. Meets 2nd Thursday, Lusitana Hall, 164 Hanover St., Boston.	C. R. R. S. F. S. T.	Daniel Gallagher..... Jeremiah J. Crane.... John Keenan .... John J. Irving.......	68 School Street, 9 Hill Street, 7 North Hanover Court, 6 Hichborn Street,	Revere Charlestown Boston Revere
4. St. Francis, Roxbury. Inst. Dec. 18, 1879. Meets 1st and 3rd Wednesday, Tremont Hall, 1435 Tremont St., Roxbury.	C. R. R. S. F. S. T.	David Magner........ Thomas F. Crosby.... Thomas A. McKenna. J. J. O'Brien.........	Washington Street, Jamaica Plain Parker Hill Avenue, 77 Marcella Street, 4 Vernon Place,	Roxbury Roxbury Roxbury
5. Leo, East Boston. Inst Jan , 16, 1880. Meets 2nd and 4th Wednesday, Knights of Honor Hall, 144 Meridian St., East Boston.	C. R. R. S. F. S. T.	John Brant......... Daniel A. Galvin .... Michael J. Torpey.... Michael Galligan.....	315 Paris Street, 439 Bennington Street, 302 Sumner Street, 81 Webster Street,	East Boston East Boston East Boston East Boston
6. Cheverus, Boston. Inst. Feb. 11, 1880. Meets 1st and 3rd Wednesday, Union Hall, 133 Blackstone St.	C. R. R. S. F. S. T.	Charles F. Smith..... James Cashin........ William T. Rich...... Edward O'Hara......	93 Prince Street, 15 Harvard Street, 44 Cooper Street, 59 Chestnut Street,	Boston Charlestown Boston Charlestown
7. St. Patrick, South Boston. Inst. Feb. 16, 1880. Meets 1st and 3rd Monday, Crys- tal Hall, 384 Broadway.	C. R. R. S. F. S. T.	George T. Fair....... Thomas F. Toomey... J. J. Mahoney .... James J. O'Brien.....	19 Vinton Street, 433 Fourth Street, 282 Bowen Street, 8 Vinton Street,	South Boston South Boston South Boston South Boston
8. Sherwood, Boston. Inst. March 4, 1880. Meets 2nd and 4th Thursday, St. Rose Hall, 17 Worcester St.	C. R. R. S. F. S. T.	Michael Mooney...... John J. McDonald ... A. J. Lill............ Thomas J. Lane......	51 Harvard Street, 1147 Dorchester Avenue, 3 Champney Place, 121 Centre Street,	Boston Dorchester Boston Roxbury
9. Columbus, Boston. Inst. March 9, 1880. Meets 2nd and 4th Monday, Lin- coln Hall, 19 Essex St., Boston.	C. R. R. S. F. S. T.	James F. Farley...... Richard D. Cleary.... M. T. Gleason........ M. T. Milliken......	5 Wall Street, 778 Parker Street, 43 Milton Avenue, 282 E Street,	Boston Roxbury Dorchester South Boston
10. Iona, Malden. Inst. March 15, 1880. Meets 1st and 3rd Thursday, Deliberative Hall, Pleasant St., Malden.	C. R. R. S. F. S. T.	John M Neville...... Dennis Kelliher...... Edmund Flavin...... Paul J. McMahon	55 Hubbard Street, 39 Sherman Street, 130 Commercial Street, 288 Main Street,	Malden Malden Malden Malden
11. St. Joseph, Boston. Inst. March 22, 1880. Meets 2nd and 4th Wednesday, St. Joseph Hall, 60½ Leverett Boston.	C. R. R. S. F. S. T.	John Long.......... John P. McGee...... Charles W. Mullen... Daniel Carney	103 Pembroke Street, 3 Lindall Place, 17 Parkman Street, 378 Washington Street,	Boston Boston Boston Boston
12. Fulton, Boston. Inst. March 18, 1880. Meets 1st and 3rd Friday, Carroll Hall, 375 Harrison Avenue, Boston.	C. R. R. S. F. S. T.	Patrick H. Cronin.... Henry F. Scanlan.... .... Daniel O'Brien.......	456 Parker Street, 117 Union Park Street, 139 Shawmut Avenue,	Roxbury Boston Boston Boston
13. Fitzpatrick, Boston. Inst. May 5, 1880. Meets 2nd and 4th Tuesday, Lusitana Hall, 164 Hanover St.	C. R. R. S. F. S. T.	Patrick F. Reynolds.. Michael Cleary...... Joseph H. McIntyre.. Charles J. Jordan	14 No. Bennett Street, Rear 43 Charter Street, 11 Charter Street, 3 Vernon Place,	Boston Boston Boston Boston
14. Lafayette, Lynn. Inst. June 8, 1880. Meets every Wednesday, Emmett Hall, 71 Munroe St.	C. R. R. S. F. S. T.	Bartholomew Whalen . George E. Monroe.... John Driscoll........ Timothy Donovan....	95 Cottage Street, 149 Broad Street, 53 Linden Street, 105 Adams Street,	Lynn Lynn Lyuu Lynn

DIRECTORY—Continued.

No. and Court Name.	Officers.		Address.	
15. S.S. Peter & Paul, So. Boston. Inst. June 25, 1880. Meets 1st and 3rd Tuesday, Tonta Hall, 327 E St.	C. R. R. S. F. S. T.	Thomas Desmond.... Patrick P. Reardon... Charles P. Bergin..... Thomas Sullivan.....	250 W. Fourth Street, 144 Athens Street, 134 N Street, 13 Mercer Street,	South Boston South Boston South Boston South Boston
16. Essex, Salem. Inst. June 23, 1880. Meets 1st and 3rd Wednesday, Mansfield Hall, 199 Essex St.	C. R. R. S. F. S. T.	John B. Tivnan..... L. A. Doherty....... M. A. Finnegan. .... Michael A. Dodd....	Evening News Office, 18 Ward Street, 23 Summer Street, 5 Flint Street,	Salem Salem Salem Salem
17. Hamilton, Charlestown. Inst. July 8, 1880. Meets 2nd and 4th Friday, Lin- coln Hall, Warren St.	C. R. R. S. F. S. T.	Samuel J. Cochrane.. William Mittlestadt.. Patrick A. Quinlan... James Crowley.......	22 Soley Street, 11 Berwick Street, 19 Medford Street, 70 Ferrin Street,	Charlestown Somerville Somerville Charlestown
18. St. Peter, Dorchester. Inst, July 22, 1880. Meets 1st and 3rd Thursday, Blake's Hall, Field's Corner.	C. R. R. S. F. S. T.	James H. Dixon..... Edward T. Shields ... Martin F. Falion..... John J. Curran	Davidson Avenue, Wesley Avenue, 34 Spring Garden Street, Davidson Avenue,	Dorchester Dorchester Dorchester Dorchester
19. Williams, E. Boston. Inst. Sept. 16, 1880. Meets 1st and 3rd Monday, O. F. Hall, Maverick Sq.	C. R. R. S. F. S. T.	James Douglass..... M. J. Kelly......... Francis M. Kievenaar. Thomas Arthur.....	377 Sumner Street, 107 Paris Street, 304 Sumner Street, Maverick Square,	East Boston East Boston East Boston East Boston
20. Mt. Pleasant, Roxbury. Inst. Oct. 20, 1880. Meets 2nd and 4th Monday, K. of H. Hall, 2319 Washington St.	C. R. R. S. F. S. T.	Frank J. McGrath ... Garrett H. Keefe..... Edward A Dever..... David O'Brien.......	16 Langdon Street, 63 Palmer Street, 120 Eustis Street, 30 Mall Street,	Roxbury Roxbury Roxbury Roxbury
21. St. Alphonsus, Roxbury. Inst. Oct. 13, 1880. Meets 2nd and 4th Wednesday, Gurney Hall, Gurney St.	C. R. R. S. F. S. T.	Patrick H. Shea..... Francis A. Mahan.... John Killion......... Cornelius McCarthy..	62 Whitney Street, 36 Delle Avenue, 8 Oscar Street, Prentiss Street,	Roxbury Roxbury Roxbury Roxbury
23. St. John, Hyde Park. Inst. Dec. 14, 1880. Meets 2nd and 4th Monday, Odd Fellows Hall, Everett Sq., H. P	C. R. R. S. F. S. T.	John H. McKenna .. Fred'k J. McGowan.. Frank Cullen....... John Haskell........	Central Park Avenue, Easton Avenue, 10 Thompson Street, Green Street,	Hyde Park Hyde Park Hyde Park Hyde Park
24. St. Gregory, Milton. Inst. Dec. 20, 1880. Meets 1st and 3rd Tuesday, Fra- ternity Hall, Adams Street.	C. R. R. S. F. S. T.	Patrick J. Moore..... Michael Dunican..... John D. O'Brien..... Patrick Fallon.......	Dorchester Lower Mills Box 87, Milton Street, River Street,	 East Milton Dorchester Mattapan
25. St. Francis, W. Quincy. Inst. Dec. 21, 1880. Meets 2nd and 4th Tuesday, For- esters' Hall, W. Quincy.	C. R. R. S. F. S. T.	M J. Daley......... William P. Hughes... Michael Riley....... Alphonse Reinhalter.	 	West Quincy West Quincy West Quincy West Quincy
26. St. Raphael, Dedham. Inst. Dec. 31, 1880. Meets 1st and 3rd Sunday, Me- chanics Hall, E. Dedham.	C. R. R. S. F. S. T.	John F. Barrett...... John F. Reilly....... Charles J. Hurley.... P. O'Sullivan........	Walnut Hill, Walnut Hill,	Dedham Dedham Ashcroft Dedham
28. Erin, Boston. Inst. Feb. 3, 1881. Meets 2nd and 4th Tuesday, St. Rose Hall, 17 Worcester St.	C. R. R. S. F. S. T.	Alexander Thompson. C. J. Lynch......... Peter D. O'Meally... J. O'Mara...........	Ballard Street, 10 Shelburn Street, Lovis Place, 93 Pembroke Street,	Jamaica Plain Dorchester South Boston Boston
29. St. Thomas, Brockton. Inst. Feb. 17, 1881. Meets 2nd and 4th Thursday, For- esters' Hall, Centre St.	C. R. R. S. F. S. T.	Patrick Gilmore....:... Thomas J. O'Rourke. Angus McDonald..... James P. Conley....	29 School Street, 29 Emmet Street, 19 Bride's Court, 28 Charles Street,	Brockton Brockton Brockton Brockton
30. Bass River, Beverly. Inst. Feb. 24, 1881. Meets 1st and 3rd Thursday, Y. M. C. T. H., 87 Cabot St.	C. R. R. S. F. S. T.	John Geary......... John T. McLean .... Peter M. Riordan ... Timothy Hennessey..	20 Rantoul Street, 14 Rantoul Street, 16 Rantoul Street, 16 Pleasant Street,	Beverly Beverly Beverly Beverly
32. Qualey, Woburn. Inst. March 2, 1881. Meets 1st and 3rd Wedn sday, Hibernian Hall, Main St.	C. R. R. S. F. S. T.	James F. McKenna... John Maguire........ Frank E. Tracey..... Wm. O'Brien........	101 Main Street, 121 Main Street, 59 Prospect Street, 20 Church Avenue,	Woburn Woburn Woburn Woburn

DIRECTORY—Continued.

No. and Court Name.	Officers.		Address.
33. St. John, E. Cambridge. Inst. March 3, 1881. Meets 1st and 3rd Friday, G. A. R. Hall, Cambridge St.	C. R. R. S. F. S. T.	Bernard J. Brogan... Peter Gardner....... John O'Connell...... Joseph J. Kelly......	Cor. Otis and Sixth Sts., E. Cambridge 29 Warren Street, Cambridgeport 143 Gore Street, E. Cambridge 110 Otis Street, E. Cambridge
34. Americus, Boston. Inst. March 15, 1881. Meets 2nd and 4th Wednesday, St. Rose Hall, 17 Worcester St.	C. R. R. S. F. S. T.	John T. Whyte..... P. J. Gorman........ John W. Brown...... J. Henry Gramer....:	1 Andrews Place, Boston 49 Brook Avenue, Roxbury Rear 792 Shawmut Avenue, Boston 32 Thornton Street Boston
35. Sheil, Boston. Inst. March 18, 1881. Meets 1st Friday, Union Hall, cor. Hanover and Blackstone Sts.	C. R. R. S. F. S. T.	C. J. Kelly....... Thomas Mooney...... Thomas Jacobs....... Thomas Jacobs.......	4 Pleasant View Avenue, . Everett 20 Sheafe Street, Boston 3 Lexington Avenue, Charlestown 3 Lexington Avenue, Charlestown
37. Friendship, Roxbury. Inst. March 25, 1888. Meets 1st and 3rd Wednesday, Kossuth Hall, 1009 Tremont St.	C. R. R. S. F. S. T.	Jeremiah J. Buckley.. Edward N. Lee....... John F. Dolan....... Thomas H. Duggan..	2 Rogers Court, Roxbury 3 Reins Place, Roxbury 1335 Tremont Street, Roxbury 130 Camden Street. Roxbury
38. St. Joseph, Roxbury. Inst. March 29, 1881. Meets 2nd and 4th Thursday, K. of Honor Hall, 1319 Washington St.	R. S. C. S. T.	John C. Fox. .... Wm. B. Reardon..... John P. Ego......... M. Lennon..........	Grove Hall, Dorchester 384A Warren Street, Roxbury 411 Warren Street, Roxbury Grove Hall, Dorchester
39. Benedict, Somerville. Inst. March 31, 1881. Meets 3rd Thursday, Temperance Hall, Hawkins Street.	C. R. R. S. F. S. T.	James J. Muldoon.... Harry R. Nolan...... William A. Flaherty.. Cornelius McGonagle.	Dane Street, Somerville 202 Summer Street, Somerville 261 Washington Street, Somerville 16 Linden Street, Somerville
43. St. Mary, Randolph. Inst. Sept. 4, 1882. Meets 1st Monday, Hibernian Hall, Main St.	C. R. R. S. F. S. T.	Charles S. Dolan..... M. F. Cunningham... John P. Brady........ Patrick Brady	Randolph Randolph Randolph Randolph
44. St. Bernard. W. Newton. Inst. Sept. 23, 1882. Meets 3rd Monday, Knights of Honor Hall, Washington St.	C. R. R. S. F. S. T.	M. J. Duane........ Thomas C. Donovan.. John W. Gaw........ D. J. O'Donnell......	West Newton West Newton Sharon Avenue, West Newton Auburndale Avenue, West Newton Auburndale
45. Unity, Bridgewater. Inst. Sept. 12, 1882. Meets 2nd and 4th Tuesday, Young Men's Benevolent Hall, Centre St.	C. R. R. S. F. S. T.	David Cashon........ Michael Cashon...... William Condon..... Thos. Daniher	Cor. Main and High Sts., Bridgewater Box 42, Bridgewater High Street, Bridgewater Bedford Street, Bridgewater
46. St. Augustine. So. Boston. Inst. Nov. 14, 1882. Meets 2nd and 4th Tuesday, Tonta Hall, 327 E. St.	C. R. R. S. F. S. T.	John M. Rigby....... James D. O'Brien.... Alexander McDonald. J. F. McNulty	42 Fifth Street, South Boston 12 Knowlton Street, South Boston 207 Third Street, South Boston 12 Woodward Street, South Boston
47. St. Anne's, Gloucester. Inst. Dec. 22, 1882. Meets 1st and 3rd Tuesday, G. A. R. Hall, 171 Main St.	C. R. R. S. F. S. T.	Farrell Duguo ...... Robert Powers ...... John Kincade ...... Daniel Carroll	49 Friend Street, Gloucester 3 Myrtle Square, Glourester 22 Sadler Street, Gloucester 5 Shepherd Street, Gloucester
48. Sarsfield, No. Attleborough. Inst. March 6, 1883. Meets every Tuesday, cor. East and Elm Streets.	C. . R. . F. R. T.	James J. McGowan... Patrick Grady .... John B Altermath... James F. O'Brien....	N. Attleborough N. Attleborough Mt. Hope Street, N. Attleborough N. Attleborough
49. Constantine, Boston. Inst. April 5, 1883. Meets 2nd and 4th Friday, Carroll Hall, 375 Harrison Ave.	C. R. R. S. F. S. T.	James T. Riley...... William J. Goslin.... James A. Berrill ..... John Carroll	2 Pearl Place, Somerville 1118 Dorchester Avenue, Dorchester Hotel Gloucester, Boston 34 Quincy Street, Roxbury

DIRECTORY—Continued.

No. and Court Name.	Officers.		Address.	
51. Holy Trinity, Boston. Inst. April 13, 1883. Meets 2nd and 4th Wednesday, Dexter Hall, 987 Washington St.	C. R. R. S. F. S. T.	George Wirth .... Gustav Stattuck...... Leopold Kohler ...... Joseph Schneiderham.	170 Fifth Street, 136 Bowen Street, 15 Whitney Street, 36 Vinton Street,	South Boston South Boston Roxbury South Boston
52. Highland, Roxbury. Inst. April 16, 1883. Meets 2nd Monday, Kossuth Hall, Tremont St.	C. R. R. S. F. S. T.	Michael J. Driscoll... Jeremiah Sullivan.... Mark E. Gallagher... John J. Corbett......	22 Burke Street, 29 Davenport Street, 221 Cabot Street, 14 Hallock Street,	Roxbury Roxbury Roxbury Roxbury
53. Emerald, Peabody. Inst. July 2, 1883. Meets every Thursday, Thomas Block, Central St.	C. R. R. S. F. S. T.	James J. McCann .. . John L. McManus.... James B. Carbrey.... John J. Sweeney.....	169 Lowell Street, 5 Highland Park, 10 Shillaber Street, 25 Tremont Street,	Peabody Peabody Peabody Peabody
54. St. James, Boston. Inst. July 2, 1883. Meets 1st and 3rd Tuesday, Carroll Hall, 375 Harrison Avenue.	C. R. R. S. F. S. T.	James F. Gleason .... John J. Desmond .... Theodore J. Mignault. Michael J. Noonan...	12 Dorchester Street, 288 Third Street, 86 Emerson Street, 14 Dean Avenue,	South Boston South Boston South Boston Dorchester
55. Charles River, Watertown. Inst. Oct. 8, 1883. Meets 1st and 3rd Monday, G.A.R. Hall, Main Street.	C. R. R. S. F S. T.	John Flood.......... Michael Hamrock.... M. E. Conroy........ James J. Barnes	Washington Street, Arsenal Street, Beacon Hill, Main Street,	Newton Watertown Watertown Watertown
57. Carroll, Jamaica Plain. Inst. June 30, 1885. Meets 1st and 3rd Wednesday, Jamaica Hall, Centre St., cor. of Burroughs St.	C. R. R. S. F. S. T.	Wm. Rooney........ John H. Cronin...... Charles Mahan...... J. H. Moy...........	Burroughs Street, Hyde Park Ave. Paul Gore Street, Child Street,	Jamaica Plain Jamaica Plain Jamaica Plain Jamaica Plain
58. Prospect, Waltham. Inst. Aug. 25, 1885. Meets 1st Thursday, A. O. H. Hall, Main St.	C. R. R. S. F. S. T.	Thomas H. McCarthy. Michael Bergin. ..... John E. Burke. ..... Timothy F. Buckley..	17 Spring Street, 13 Middle Street, 12 Hall Street, 105 Cushing Street,	Waltham Waltham Waltham Waltham
59. Worcester, Worcester. Inst. Dec. 17, 1885. Meets 1st and 3rd Thursday, I. C. B. Hall, 98 Front St.	C. R. R. S. F. S. T.	Patrick J. Quinn..... Michael J. Madden... John McCullough.... John W. Delehanty ..	26 Spruce Street, 61 Eastern Avenue. 135 Washington Street, 8 Preston Street,	Worcester Worcester Worcester Worcester
60. Middlesex, Newton. Inst. Feb. 19, 1886. Meets 2nd and 4th Tuesday, Brackett's Hall.	C. R. R. S. F. S. T.	Peter R. Mullen...... James Ryan .... Charles E. Hodges ... Francis H. Murray ...	12 Waban Street, 105 Pearl Street, Adams Street, 111 Gardner Street,	Newton Newton Newton Newton
61. St. Lawrence, Brookline. Meets 1st and 3rd Tuesday, Good Fellows Hall, Washington St.	C. R. R. S. F. S. T.	Michael J. Kelly..... Daniel Frawley...... Thomas F. McMahon. John S. Meaney......	Chestnut Street, White Place, Kerrigan Place, Cypress Street,	Brookline Brookline Brookline Brookline
62. St. Catherine, Norwood. Inst. Dec. 31, 1886. Meets 1st and 3rd Wednesday, Union Hall, Railroad Ave.	C. R. R. S. F. S. T.	Thomas Norton...... F. E. Nagle .... John H. Williams .... Richard E. Oldham...	Monroe Street, Pleasant Street, Broadway, Railroad Avenue,	Norwood Norwood Norwood Norwood
63. Shields, Holyoke. Inst. Jan. 14, 1887. Meets 2nd Sunday and 4th Tuesday, Redmen's Hall, cor. Essex and High Sts.	C. R. R. S. F. S. T.	James Bartley .... Michael L. Dowd..... Odilon Moreau....... Dr. Geo. H. Clarke...	643 High Street, 16 Plymouth Place, 62 High Street, 441 High Street,	Holyoke Holyoke Holyoke Holyoke
64. Gallagher, Springfield. Inst. April 17, 1887. Meets 2nd Sunday and 4th Friday, Haurigaria, cor. State and Main.	C. R. R. S. F. S. T.	John J. Leonard. .... John T. Lovett....... John Lawler......... Peter Burke.........	118 Greenwood Street, 100 Franklin Street, 15 York Street, 147 Franklin Street,	Springfield Springfield Springfield Springfield
65. St. Columbkille, Brighton. Inst. May 26, 1887. Meets 1st and 3rd Tuesday, K. of Honor Hall, cor. Washington and Chestnut Hill Avenue.	C. R. R. S. F. S. T.	John H. Greenleaf ... William J. VanEtten.. Robert J. Naghten... George F. Mitchell...	22 Winship Street, 249 Market Street, 247 Market Street, Dustin Street,	Brighton Brighton Brighton Brighton

DIRECTORY—Continued.

No. and Court Name.	Officers.		Address.
66. Griffin, Franklin. Inst. Sept. 12, 1887. Meets 1st and 3rd Tuesday, Hibernian Hall, Central St.	C. R. R. S. F. S. T.	James E. O'Donnell.. M. F. Conroy........ John A. O'Sullivan .. William F. Buckley..	Franklin Franklin Franklin Franklin
67. Canton, Canton. Inst. Jan. 26, 1888. Meets 2nd and 4th Friday, G. A. R. Hall, Church St.	C. R. R. S. F. S. T.	Robert E. Lloyd ..... Matthew A. Skelton.. James E. Grimes..... John L. Collins..... ..	Canton Canton Canton Canton
68. St. Margaret, Beverly Farms. Inst. April 14, 1888. Meets 1st and 3rd Wednesday, Marshall's Hall.	C. R. R. S. F. S. T.	Thomas M. Dix...... John C. McCarthy.... Michael J. Cadigan... Lawrence J. Watson .	Pride's Crossing Beverly Farms Beverly Farms Beverly Farms

(Box 35, — for Court 68)

No. and Court Name.	Officers.		Address.
69. Stoughton, Stoughton. Inst. June 7, 1888. Meets 1st and 3rd Thursday, M. C. O. F. Hall, Washington St.	C. R. R. S. F. S. T.	John B. Buckley..... Michael F. Powers ... John S. Madden...... Timothy Cronin	Stoughton Stoughton Stoughton Stoughton
70 St. Michael, South Boston. Inst. Sept. 14, 1888. Meets 1st and 3rd Tuesday, Gray's Hall, cor. I St. and Broadway.	C. R. R. S. F. S. T.	Louis H. Vincent..... W. G. Cunningham. . J. J. Barry.......... T. F. Shea..........	566 East Seventh Street, South Boston 53A K Street, South Boston 187 Bowen Street, South Boston 144 K Street, South Boston
71. Phil. Sheridan, Newburyport. Inst. Sept. 18, 1888. Meets 1st and 3rd Tuesday, G. A. R. Hall, Charter St.	C. R. R. S. F. S. T.	Daniel F. Buckley.... Albert E. Moylan .... Hugh Hart .... George W. Hussy	38 Kent Street, Newburyport 83 Olive Street, Newburyport 19 Midddle Street, Newburyport 54 Warren Street, Newburyportl
72. Merrimack, Haverhill. Inst. Dec. 20, 1880. Meets 2nd and 4th Thursday, G. A. R. Hall, Court St.	C. R. R. S. F. S. T.	John T. Desmond... David F. Roche...... John J. Murphy..... John B. Sullivan.....	17 Union Street, Haverhill 6 New Street, Haverhill 277 River Street, Haverhill 15 Dudley Street, Haverhill
73. Taunton, Taunton. Inst. March 12, 1889. Meets 2nd and 4th Tuesday, Forester's Hall, Union Block, Main St.	C. R. R. S. F. S. T.	George F. Bramer .. Arthur E. Quillen.... William P. Crowley .. Thomas G. Hankard..	11 Second Street, Taunton 27 Broadway, Taunton 31 No. Pleasant Street, Taunton 114 Weir Street, Taunton
74. Hendricken. No. Easton. Inst. March 29, 1889. Meets 1st Monday and 3rd Thursday, Foresters' Hall, Centre St.	C. R. R. S. F. S. T.	John E. Blake .... Michael F. Heelan.... Patrick Campion..... Jeremiah Carroll.....	North Easton North Easton North Easton North Easton
75. St. Jarlath, Amesbury. Instituted June 12, 1889. Meets every Tuesday, Forester Hall, Main St.	C. R. R. S. F. S. T.	Hugh Kellett, Jr..... Andrew J. Carr...... Albert A. Gallagher.. John Kellett.........	Arlington Street, Amesbury Powow Street, Amesbury School Street, Amesbury School Street, Amesbury
76. Quincy. Quincy. Inst. Oct. 24, 1889. Meets 2nd and 4th Monday, G. A. R Hall, Hancock Street.	C. R. R. S. F. S. T.	John A. McDonnell .. James P. McGovern.. Joseph A. Dasha .... John H. Dinegan.....	16 Jackson Street, Quincy 32 Hancock Street, Quincy 10 Summer Street, Quincy School Street. Quincy
77. Mystic, Medford. Inst. Dec. 12, 1889. Meets 2nd and 4th Thursday, Lawrence Building, Medford Sq.	C. R. R. S. F. S. T.	Thomas Curtin....... John J. O'Brien.. ... John A. Gaffey....... Wm. B. Hellen.......	12 Bates Court, Medford 30 Water Street, Medford 7 Curtis Street, Medford 17 Summer Street, Medford
78. St. Monica, Lawrence. Inst. March 26, 1890. Meets 1st and 3rd Monday, Unity Hall, cor. Essex and Appleton Sts.	C. R. R. S. F. S. T.	Andrew Caffrey...... Terrence J. Kelly .... Dominick P. Flanagan Patrick Hogan.......	301 Water Street, Lawrence 116 Hancock Street, Lawrence 358 Oak Street, Lawrence 16 Acton Street, Lawrence

(Box 392, — for Court 74)

No. and Court Name.	Officers.	
79. John Boyle O'Reilly, New Bedford. Inst. Jan. 24, 1891. Meets 2nd and 4th Wednesday, Young Men's T. A. B. Hall, Purchase St.	C. R. James H. Miskell .... R. S. James Doyle......... F. S. John N. O'Brien...... T. Lawrence J. Durant..	96 South ! New Cc 567 Cottage 405 County
80. Gen. Sherman, Plymouth, Inst. March 7, 1891. Meets 2nd and last Tuesday, Good Templars' Hall, Main St.	R. Henry S. Healy. .... S. George F. Anderson.. C. S. Joseph Ready........ T. John E. Tracey	27 Main S 7 Mill Vi 60 South ! 24 Lothro
81. St. Malachi, Arlington. Inst. Sept. 3. 1891. Meets 1st and 3rd Thursday, G. A. R. Hall, Arlington Ave.	R. Edmond Reardon .... S. John F. McBride..... C. S. Francis Spain........ T. Thomas Kenny.......	Mystic Frankl 57 Hayes
82. Brockton, Brockton. Inst. Dec. 11, 1892. Meets 1st and 3rd Thursday, Foresters' Hall, Bay State Block, Centre St.	R. Charles M. Hickey ... S. Thomas J. Doyle..... C. S. Thomas O'Brien, Jr.. T. J J. Hickey.........	59 Cresce 149 No.M o 30 Perkin 152 No. Wა
83. John Henry Newman, Everett. Inst. Dec. 12, 1891. Meets 1st and 3rd Wednesday, G. A. R. Hall, Everett.	C. R. F. F. Driscoll .... R. S. Francis J. McBride... F. S. Fdward J. Mulligan .. T. Thomas Kirwan	75 Cottage 15 Bradfo 44 Centra 52 Vine S
84. Danvers, Danvers. Inst Feb. 10, 1892. Meets 2nd and 4th Thursday.	C. R Daniel M Cahill..... R. S. Richard T. Finnessey. F. S. John E. Cain .. .... T. Michael H. Barry....	Hobart Hobart
85. George Washington, W. Lynn, Inst. Feb. 22, 1892. Meets every Thursday. Foresters' Hall, 773 Western Ave.	C. R. Richard Nagle .... R. S. Daniel Dunn......... F. S. James F. Kelly....... T. James S. Barry.......	55 Light ! 72 Essex ! 70 Moulto 896 Wester
86 Avon, Avon. Inst. March 16, 1892. Meets 2nd and 4th Friday, Forest Hall. Main St.	R. John Connery........ S. W. F. Feeney........ C. S. J. J. Collins ...... T. J. F. Sheehan ......:	
87. Robert Emmett. Walpole. Inst. April 1, 1892. Meets 2nd and 4th Friday, U. O. Workman Hall, Walpole.	C. R. Thomas O'Donohoe .. R. S. John M. Smith...... F. S. Thomas A. Gookin ... T. William Mahoney....	
88. Enterprise, W. Newbury. Inst. June 2, 1892. Meets 1st and 3rd Thursday, G. A. R Hall, Post Office Sq.	C. R. Daniel Cooney....... R. S. Patrick Curley ...... F. S. Frederick Condon.... T. Thomas J. Murphy...	Nain S Prospe
89. Union, Whitman. Inst Aug 24, 1892. Meets 1st and 3rd Wednesday, K. of L. Hall, Washington St.	C. R. Montague McKinnon. R. S. John F. Murphy .... F. S. Michael J. Holland... T. Alphonse Brouillard..	Stetsor 30 Stetsor Box 14 Temple
90. Rockland, Rockland. Inst. Nov. 21, 1892. Meets	C. R. James J. Lawless..... R. S. Robert W. Young.... F. S. John J. Burns.... ... T. D. M. O'Connell......	Water !

DIRECTORY—Continued.

NAME AND COURT NO.	OFFICERS.		ADDRESS.
91. St. Vincent, Holliston. Inst. Dec. 8, 1892. Meets 1st and 3rd Tuesday, Red Men's Hall, Holliston.	C. R. R. S. F. S. T.	Maurice F. Coughlin . John J. O'Larey...... James J. Barry ...... Michael J. Davoren ..	Mechanic Street,	Holliston Holliston Holliston Holliston
92. Harmony, E. Bridgewater. Inst. Feb. 20, 1893.	C. R. R. S. F. S. T.	Michael H. Lyons.... Samuel J. Kingston .. Michael Fitzgerald.... Michael F. Roach	Grove Street, Spring Street,	East Bridgewater East Bridgewater East Bridgewater East Bridgewater
93. Germania, Roxbury. Inst. Feb. 26, 1893. Meets	C. R. R. S. F. S. T.	Christian Lambrecht. Francis I. Mueller.... Valentine Baier...... William Helmer......	12 Walden Street, 192 Highland Street, 80 Fulda Street, 130 Marcella Street,	Roxbury Roxbury Roxbury Roxbury
94. Loyola, Boston. Inst. Mar. 6, 1893. Meets 1st and 3rd Monday, Union Hall, cor. Hanover and Blackstone Sts., Boston, Mass.	C. R. R. S. F. S. T.	John A. Ryan........ John F. Dolan........ J. H. Bird........... Edward J. Doherty...	18 Cornhill, 21 Billerica Street, 4 Charter Street, 21 North Margin Street,	Boston Boston Boston Boston
95. Columbia, Roxbury. Inst. Mar. 28, 1893. Meets 2nd and 4th Thursdays, Columbia Hall, Centre Street, Jamaica Plain.	C. R. R. S. F. S. T.	Patrick F. Manning.. John J. Tierney...... John J. Needham..... Daniel Hagerty......	939 Parker Street, 112 Minden Street, 7 Bickford Street, 8 Atwood Avenue,	Roxbury Roxbury Roxbury Roxbury
96. Sacred Heart, Middleboro. Ins. May 10, 1893. Meets	C. R. R. S. F. S. T.	Edward F. Doherty... William I. Jeffers.... Thomas F. O'Toole... Michael H. Kelly.....		Middleboro Middleboro Middleboro Middleboro
97. St. Anthony, Medway. Inst. May 23, 1893. Meets	C. R. R. S. F. S. T.	Peter O'Byrne........ Thomas E. O'Donnell Lawrence J. Kenney.. Tobias S. Touhey.....		Medway Medway Medway Medway

Our gain in membership the past year is one of which we may be proud. It has not been spasmodic or due to any extraordinary offorts on the part of any person. Applications have come from nearly all the Courts and in cases where few were received it was due not to want of inclination on the part of the members but some circumstances beyond control, such as change of location of members, moving away from immediate vicinity of Hall and for similar reasons.

The High Standing Committee has held itself ready at all times to respond to calls for assistance in the conduct of meetings. Not only for the purpose of forming new Courts but for spurring on the interest in some of the older Courts.

The work of the High Standing Committee has been considerably increased by such meetings, and when it was possible to go the Committee did all it could to help. Right here perhaps it will be well to mention that the labor of the High Standing Committee could be materially lessened if members would not write so many letters to the High Secretary-Treasurer about trivial matters. It is not fair to the Officers of Subordinate Courts, neither is it fair to the Deputy High Chief Ranger who has the Court in charge to have members continually jumping over the heads of those Officers and applying to the High Standing Committee for settlement of questions that should be settled in the Court Room. The High Standing Committee wishes to answer every call made upon it but the evil is growing and a warning must be given.

The Deputy High Chief Ranger has charge of the Subordinate Court and any question not decided by the Chief Ranger should be referred to the Deputy High Chief Ranger in the proper way. To give some idea of the amount of work passing through the office of the High Standing Committee, it will be, perhaps, sufficient to say that from April 1, 1892 to April 1, 1893 the number of letters sent out by the High Secretary-Treasurer was 1071. This does not include regular or routine work of the office such as notifications to the High Standing Committee to attend meetings, assessment calls, notices of approval or rejection of applications. Each letter received requires time to read and consider and more time to answer. It is hoped that with a membership increasing as rapidly as is ours that the members will be more considerate and send communications to headquarters only when it is imperatively necessary.

One of the best evidences of the growth of our Order and the increased interest in its welfare was the display made by the Order in the celebration of Columbus Day, October 21, 1892, in Boston. When the subject was first broached and the High Standing Committee was invited to place the Order in line, the greatest interest was immediately manifested and members of the Order in every direction offered assistance to the High Standing Committee in any manner in which it might be needed. Notices were sent out to the Courts to send representatives to a meeting to decide if the Order should parade. That meeting was held on September 16, and forty-nine courts were represented. The vote was unanimous to take part in the parade, and Capt. Jeremiah G. Fennessey was selected for Marshall of our division with equal unanimity.

Subsequent meetings were had at which it was decided that all members parading should wear dark clothing, canes and white gloves. Each Court was also invited to elect a member to serve on Capt. Fennessey's staff. A uniform badge to be worn by the members was also adopted. Encouraging reports came in from time to time, and under the able guidance of Capt. Fennessey, arrangements progressed satisfactorily. The following Courts reported on the morning of the parade, the number given is not the full membership of the Courts, but the actual number reported as parading: Cathedral Court No. 1, Fenwick Court No. 3, St. Francis Court No. 4, Leo Court No. 5, Cheverus Court No. 6, St. Patrick Court No. 7, Sherwood Court No. 8, St. Joseph Court No. 11, Fulton Court No. 12, Lafayette Court No. 14, St. Peter and Paul Court No. 15, St. Peter Court No. 18, Williams Court No. 19, Mt. Pleasant Court No. 20, St. Alphonsus Court No. 21, St. John Court 23, St. Gregory Court No. 24, St. Raphael Court No. 26, Erin Court No. 28, St. Thomas Court No. 29, Qualey Court No. 32, St·

John Court No. 33, Americus Court No. 34, Friendship Court No 37, St. Joseph Court No. 38, Unity Court No. 45, St. Augustine Court No. 46, St. Anne Court No. 47, Sarsfield Court No. 48, Constantine Court No. 49, Holy Trinity Court No. 51, Highland Court No. 52, St. James Court No. 54, Charles River Court No. 55, Carroll Court No. 57, Prospect Court No. 58, Middlesex Court No. 60, St. Lawrence Court No. 61, St. Catharine Court No. 62, St. Columbkille Court No. 65, Griffin Court No. 66, Canton Court No. 67, Stoughton Court No. 69, St. Michael Court No. 70, Phil Sheridan Court No. 71, Taunton Court No. 73, St. Jarlath Court No. 75, John Boyle O'Reilly Court No. 79, Gen. Sherman Court No. 80, St. Malachi Court No. 81, John Henry Newman Court No. 83, Danvers Court No. 84, George Washington Court No. 85, Avon Court No. 86, Robert Emmett Court No. 87 and Union Court No. 89, making a grand total of 3,588, with 10 bands and 7 drum corps.

In addition to this many joined the line who had not intended to parade. Each man wore an American flag in his buttonhole, and each Court was provided with a white silk guidon bearing the name and number of the Court. The High Standing Committee provided a banner to head the division, which was carried by a member of the Order on horseback. Too much praise cannot be given to the chief of our division for the executive ability displayed in handling a body of men which had never before paraded. The Order received a great deal of commendation all along the line, and every man who participated has reason to feel proud of the fact that he helped by doing his duty on that occasion to contribute to the success of the affair. This parade

We have a growing organization and one of which we may well be proud. It will continue to grow because the good it has done has been seen and the purpose of the membership in keeping alive the interest is easily seen to be an unselfish one.

We have now 85 Courts, and a membership of 6,300, and with God's help, when another year rolls over our heads, we shall be able to show a gain in membership not less than that of the year just closed. We should have a membership in this State alone of 20,000, and if we follow the same conservative policy we will surely accomplish that end.

Respectfully submitted,

JAMES F. SUPPLE,

High Secretary-Treasurer.

FOURTEENTH ANNUAL CONVENTION

OF THE

Massachusetts Catholic Order of Foresters

HELD AT

St. Rose Hall, 17 Worcester Street, Boston.

APRIL 26, 1893.

The Convention was called to order at 9.30 A. M., by High Chief Ranger Hon. Owen A. Galvin. The High Conductors reported all the officers of the High Court present and in their places. The Call for the Convention was then read by High Chief Ranger Galvin as follows : —

MASSACHUSETTS CATHOLIC ORDER OF FORESTERS.
HIGH STANDING COMMITTEE.
611 Washington Street,

Boston, April 1, 1893.

To the Officers and Members of the Massachusetts Catholic Order of Foresters: —

BROTHERS, — In accordance with the powers vested in the High Standing Committee of the Massachusetts Catholic Order of Foresters (under Art. IV, Constitution of High Court, Page 11,) a call is hereby issued for the assembling of the Representatives of the Subordinate Courts of the Massachusetts Catholic Order of Foresters in Annual Session of the High Court of the Order, to be held in St. Rose Hall, 17 Worcester Street, Boston, to be opened in regular form at 9.30 o'clock, A. M., on Wednesday the twenty-sixth day of April, A. D. 1893, as provided for in the High Court Constitution.

The Basis of Representation shall be as laid down in Art. II, Sec. 3, Constitution of High Court, page 8.

Forms of Credential to the Annual Session of High Court accompany this Call, one to be retained and held by the Representative for use at the Convention. If the Credential be transferred for cause, this should be stated on the back of Credential under the endorsements of Chief Ranger and Recording Secretary of the Court.

By Order of the High Standing Committee,

OWEN A. GALVIN,
High Chief Ranger.

JAMES F. SUPPLE,
High Secretary-Treasurer.

The Convention was then opened in due form, prayer being offered by High Chaplan Rev. Hugh Roe O'Donnell.

High Chief Ranger Galvin appointed the following—

COMMITTEE ON CREDENTIALS.

Bros. Hon. M. F. Coughlin....of St. Vincent Court No. 91
L. J. Watson.........of St. Margaret Court No. 68
Daniel Connolly........of St. Thomas Court No. 29
John O'Callaghan......of St. Gregory Court No. 24
T. H. Murphy..........of Worcester Court No. 59
Dr. J. H. Cronin.......of St. Monica Court No. 78
James J. Kane..............of Erin Court No. 28

The roll was then called and showed that seventy Courts were present, eighty-eight representatives and alternates having answered to their names.

On motion of Bro. John T. Daly of Erin Court No. 28, voted to take a recess of fifteen minutes.

On re-assembling, High Chief Ranger Galvin asked for the report of the Committee on Credentials.

Bro. John O'Callaghan reported for the Committee—

77 Representatives present.
17 Proxies present.

Voted to accept report.

High Chief Ranger Galvin then addressed the representatives on the condition of the order, its prosperity for the past year, its needs and prospects for the future. Much interest was manifested by the representatives as he proceeded, and his hearers were quick to catch the telling points as they fell from his lips.

On motion voted to take a recess at 12.30 P. M. until 2 P. M. for dinner.

High Chief Ranger Galvin appointed the following Committees:—

COMMITTEE ON APPEALS.

Bros. William E. Shay.......of St. Francis Court No. 4
Frank F. O'Neil...........of Shields Court No. 63
George F. Brammer.......of Taunton Court No. 73
Thos. W. O'Rourke......of St. James Court No. 54
T. J. Lynch..............of Danvers Court No. 84
John Doolin.........of St. Augustine Court No. 46
John Hickey............of Brockton Court No. 82

COMMITTEE ON PETITIONS.

Bros. Garrett H. Keefe......of Mt. Pleasant Court No. 20
Dr. C. A. Ahearne.......of Lafayette Court No. 14
Hugh Montague.........of Sherwood Court No. 8
James F. O'Brien.........of Sarsfield Court No. 48
Jas. D. Monahan ....of Charles River Court No. 55
Michael Driscoll......of St. Lawrence Court No. 61
James B. Buckley...........of Iona Court No. 10

COMMITTEE ON SECRET WORK.

Bros. Joseph Torndorf, Jr...of Holy Trinity Court No. 51
F. F. Driscoll of John Henry Newman Court No. 83
Daniel H Maguire......of Merrimack Court No. 72
James Cashin...........of Cheverus Court No. 6
John Vogel...........of St. Francis Court No. 25
Charles O'Brien.........of St. Anne Court No. 47
Michael J. Kelly.........of Williams Court No. 19

COMMITTEE ON STATE OF THE ORDER.

Bros. P. M. Keating.........of St. Joseph Court No. 11
Thomas F. Lyons.........of Emerald Court No. 53
Thomas Sproules......of St. Francis Court No. 4
Patrick J. Murray......of Gallagher Court No. 64
John T. Mahoney.......of Cathedral Court No. 1
J. B. McCarthy of George Washington Court No. 85
James F. Carens.....of Phil Sheridan Court No. 71

High Chief Ranger Galvin asked for the report of the Committee on Constitution.

The chairman of the Committee on Constitution, Capt. Jeremiah G. Fennessey, reported in print as follows : —

To the Chief Rangers, Officers and Members of Subordinate Courts of the Massachusetts Catholic Order of Foresters: —

The following proposed amendments to the Constitution have been considered by the Committee on Constitution, and their report is appended to each. A copy has been submitted to the Subordinate Courts as required by Amendment to Constitution, adopted by Convention, April 22, 1891.

Amend Article IV, Sec. 5, page 44. Strike out "each month" on the second line and insert "January," "April," "July," "October."
The Committee on Constitution voted inexpedient.

Amend Article V, Sec. 1, page 12. Strike out "quarterly" in the fifth line.
The Committee on Constitution voted to adopt.

Amend Article V, Sec. 1, page 46. Strike out "$1000," in the fourth line and insert "$1500."
The Committee on Constitution voted inexpedient.

This would necessitate changing Article V, Sec. 5, page 16, line 6.

The Committee on Constitution recommend the creation of another class to receive $2000 at death.

Amend Article IV, Sec. 10, page 45, and amend Article V, Sec. 3, page 48, by adding at end of Section — "Reinstatement shall always require a majority vote of the members present."

The Committe on Constitution voted inexpedient, and the Committee on Constitution recommend that High Chief Ranger decide if such a vote is not now necessary.

Amend Article III, Sec. 1, page 37. Strike out "male" in first line, and change all places in the Constitution, where reference is made to members, to correspond therewith.

The Committee on Constitution voted to adopt.

JEREMIAH G. FENNESSEY, of St. James	No. 54, *Chairman,*		
JAMES CASHIN,	" Cheverus	" 6, *Secretary,*	
D. F. SULLIVAN,	" Sherwood	" 8	
G. F. LOW,	" Leo	" 5	
A. A. CLARK,	" Hendricken	" 74	
JOHN VOGEL,	" St. Francis	" 25	

Committee on Constitution.

High Chief Ranger Galvin stated the question on accepting the report of the Committee on Constitution (inexpedient) to amend Article IV, Section 5, as proposed in No. 1.

Voted to accept the report.

The Chairman of the Committee on Constitution read the second proposed amendment.

The High Chief Ranger stated the question to accept the report of the Committee adopting the amendment.

Vice High Chief Ranger McLaughlan explained why it was desirable to strike out "quarterly."

Bro. Mulcahy of St. John Court No. 23 said his Court instructed him to vote against the report of the Committee, and he moved to indefinitely postpone, which was seconded by Bro. Dunican of St. Gregory Court No. 24.

High Chief Ranger Galvin stated the question on indefinite postponement.

Motion to postpone was lost.

High Chief Ranger Galvin stated the question on adopting the report of the Committee.

Voted to adopt.

Bro. Fennessey read the third proposed amendment and moved as a substitute motion for the report of the Committee, that a committee of seven be appointed to consider the whole subject and report at the next Convention.

Motion was seconded by Bro. Keating of St. Joseph Court No. 11,

High Chief Ranger Galvin stated the question on the substitute motion offered by the Chairman of the Committee on Constitution.

Vice High Chief Ranger McLaughlin asked the Committee on Constitution to accept an amendment to report to the High Standing Committee, and have a special session of the Convention called next Fall.

The Chairman of the Committee said he had no objection to the amendment.

High Chief Ranger Galvin again stated the question.

Bro. James Cashin of Cheverus Court No. 6, thought we should have an expression of opinion from the Courts.

Capt. Fennessey said that in whatever way it was done he wanted the utmost care exercised.

Bro. Torndorf of Holy Trinity Court No. 51 was not in favor of a change, and hoped the matter would be laid over until next year. He wanted the report of the Committee accepted.

High Chief Ranger Galvin stated the question to appoint a Committee of seven to report to the High Standing Committee and hold a special session in the Fall.

The motion as amended was lost.

High Chief Ranger Galvin stated the question on the substitute motion offered by the Chairman of the Committes on Constitution, that a committee of seven be appointed to consider the matter and report at the next Convention.

The motion was carried.

The Chairman of the Committee on Constitution read the fourth proposed amendment to Article 4, Section 10, page 45, and Article 5, Section 3, page 48, that " Re-instatement shall always require a majority vote of the members present."

Bro. Fennessey said the report of the committee was inexpedient, and recommended that the High Chief Ranger promulgate a decision

High Chief Ranger Galvin stated the question on the motion of the Chairman of the Committee on Constitution to accept the report of the Committee.

Voted to accept the report of the Committee.

High Chief Ranger Galvin then made the following decision:—

"In referrence to Section 10, Article 4, page 45, and Section 3, Article 5, page 48, I now decide that Re-instatement shall always require a majority vote of the members present."

Bro. Fennessey then read the fifth proposed amendment to amend Article 3, Section 1, page 7. Strike out "male" in first line, and change all places in the Constitution, where reference is made to members, to correspond therewith, and reported that the Committee on Constitution voted to adopt.

The High Chief Ranger stated the question on accepting the report of the Committee.

Bro. Fennessey stated that he wished to debate the question.

Bro. Mulcahy, of St. John Court No. 23, moved that debate be postponed until after recess, which was to be taken at 12.30 P. M.

The motion to postpone was carried, and it being now 12.30 P. M., High Chief Ranger Galvin declared a recess for dinner.

The Convention re-assembled at 2.15 P. M.

Bro. J. J. Lanigan, Chairman of the Committee on Finance, reported as follows:—

Annual Convention of the Massachusetts Catholic Order of Foresters:

As by direction, under the Constitution of the Massachusetts Catholic Order of Foresters, the Finance Committee appointed at the last annual session, would respectfully report that they have examined the books, accounts and vouchers of the High Secretary-Treasurer, and find them correct. As the outcome of their examination, and in connection with it your Committee feel warranted in offering the following recommendations:

First, that all indebtedness between the High Standing Committee and Subordinate Courts prior to the time of the present High Secretary-Treasurer taking office be wiped out.

Second, that in future all Subordinate Courts be compelled to forward money for supplies before the delivery of the same, to the High Secretary-Treasurer.

Third, that the High Standing Committee be instructed to ascertain and report to the next session of the Convention, a correct account of the assets and liabilities of the Order.

Fourth, that the High Secretary-Treasurer be instructed to issue Endowment Calls in the future dated from the first of each month, and when an additional Call is necessary it be dated from the 15th of the month.

Fifth, that in view of the fact that $400 a year is paid for rent of headquarters, and to outside parties, when this money might be beneficial to an important branch of our own organization, that the High Standing Committee be instructed to dispose of lease of rooms (611 Washington street) by sale or otherwise, and secure rooms at Knights of St. Rose Hall, from Knights of St. Rose corporation.

Sixth, that a per capita of 75 cents be levied to defray expenses of the High Standing Committee for the ensuing year.

JAMES J. LANIGAN,
FRANK J. McGRATH,
JOHN BRANT.

High Chief Ranger stated the question on the motion to accept the report of the Committee on Finance.

Voted to accept the report.

High Chief Ranger Galvin then stated that the question was on adopting the first recommendation of the Finance Committee.

Bro. Lanigan explained why this was necessary.

Voted to adopt.

Bro. Lanigan moved to adopt the second recommendation.

High Chief Ranger Galvin stated the question.

Voted to adopt.

Bro. Lanigan moved to adopt the third recommendation of the Finance Committee.

High Chief Ranger stated the question.

Bro. O'Loughlin suggested that it include all the expenditures since the present High Secretary-Treasurer took office.

A vote was taken and the High Chief Ranger declared it carried.

Dr. F. E. Hines, of Essex Court No. 16, doubted the vote.

The High Chief Ranger again stated the question, and asked the members to stand.

The count showed 57 yes and 15 no, and the motion was carried.

Bro. Lanigan moved to adopt the fourth recommendation of the Finance Committee.

High Chief Ranger stated the question.

The High Chief Ranger stated the question.

Bro. D. A. Cronin, of St. Joseph Court No. 11, moved to refer to the High Standing Committee.

Bro. John T. Daly, of Erin Court No. 28, objected to adoption of this recommendation, and spoke against making such a radical change in the location of the headquarters of the order.

Capt. Fennessey said the Board of Directors of the Knights of St. Rose would not lease rooms in the building, 17 Worcester street, to the Massachusetts Catholic Order of Foresters. He did not think it wise to do so, as the Knights of St. Rose was a subordinate branch of the order.

Bro. James H. Dixon, of St. Peter Court No. 18, interrupted the speaker and raised a point of order, calling the attention of the High Chief Ranger to Rule 13.

High Chief Ranger Galvin decided the point of order not well taken.

Bro. Dixon appealed from the decision of the High Chief Ranger.

High Chief Ranger Galvin said the question was on the appeal from his decision on a point of order raised by the representative from St. Peter Court No. 18, and put the question, "Shall the decision of the chair stand?"

The Convention voted to sustain the decision of the High Chief Ranger.

The High Chief Ranger gave the floor to Bro. Fennessey, who concluded his remarks.

Bro. O'Loughlin, of St. Joseph Court No. 11, said that 17 Worcester street was a suitable place, and that the time lost by out of town members in going there would be slight.

Bro. O'Rourke, of St. James Court No. 54, said it was absurd to talk of changing the headquarters.

Bro. Ryan, of Loyola Court No. 94, thought a change was unnecessary.

Capt. Fennessey said that in speaking against the change, he had in mind his experience of three years as High Chief Ranger.

Bro. John T. Daly, of Erin Court No. 28, Grand Registrar of the Knights of St. Rose, said that the revenue from the building as now rented was greater than it would be if the headquarters of the Order were placed there.

High Chief Ranger Galvin stated the question on adopting the fifth recommendation of the Finance Committee, and the amendment offered by Bro. Cronin, of St. Joseph Court No. 11, to refer to the High Standing Committee.

The High Chief Ranger said the first question was on the amendment.

The vote was taken and the High Chief Ranger declared the amendment carried.

The vote was doubted and the High Chief Ranger again stated the question and asked the members to rise.

A count showed 75 yes, 17 no, and the amendment was carried.

High Chief Ranger Galvin then stated the question as amended, and declared it carried.

Bro. Lanigan, chairman of the Finance Committee, moved to adopt the sixth recommendation.

The High Chief Ranger stated the question.

Voted to adopt.

Bro. O'Loughlin, of St. Joseph Court No. 11, made the following motion: "That if it could be done without loss, the High Standing Committee be directed to sell present lease of office, and negotiate with directors of Knights of St. Rose."

Capt. Fennessey moved to amend to refer to the High Standing Committee.

Bro. O'Loughlin spoke in favor of his motion at great length.

Dr. F. E. Hines asked Bro. O'Loughlin how he could argue the matter when four of the directors out of seven were opposed to letting the place to the High Standing Committee.

Bro. O'Loughlin said that he was not aware that Bros. Daly and Fennessey constituted four of the directors.

Capt Fennessey replied that at a meeting of the Board of Directors Bros. Mara, Daly, McNulty and Fennessey were not in favor of leasing to the High Standing Committee. He thought Bro. Sproules was also opposed to it, but was not sure.

Bro. O'Rourke, of St. James Court No. 54, said he knew the High

Standing Committee had only one object in view, and that was the best interests of the entire Order. He hoped the motion of Bro. O'Loughlin would not prevail.

Bro. Daly, Grand Registrar of the Knights of St. Rose, said he as a director was opposed to the motion of Bro. O'Loughlin, and hoped the motion would not prevail.

Bro. Lanigan spoke briefly in favor of the motion.

The High Chief Ranger stated the question on the motion of Bro· Fennessey to refer the motion of Bro. O'Loughlin to the High Standing Committee.

Vote was taken and declared carried.

Bro. O'Loughlin doubted the vote.

The High Chief Ranger again stated the question to refer, and asked the delegates to stand. While the count was being made, Bro. O'Loughlin withdrew his doubt.

The motion to refer was carried.

High Chief Ranger Galvin asked for report of any Committee that was ready.

Bro. William E. Shay, of St. Francis Court No. 4, Chairman of Committee on Appeals, reported for that Committee on the claim for the payment of the Endowment to the heirs of Ferdinand Shields deceased, and late a member of St. John Court No. 33,— leave to withdraw.

Bro. Lowe, of Leo Court No. 5, asked for information.

The High Chief Ranger stated the question, which was to accept the report of the Committee, and then read the statement of the case as printed in the report of the High Standing Committee to the Convention.

Bro. B. J. Brogan, of St. John Court No. 33, hoped the report of the Committee would not be accepted. He stated what he claimed to know of the case. and said that in his judgement it was not a case of suicide.

Bro. Shay, Chairman of the Committee on Appeals, said that his Committee had no interest in the matter more than any other member. He then read copy of hospital record, and the result of an interview between Dr. Finnegan and the High Secretary-Treasurer.

By request of Dr. Ahearne, of Lafayette Court No. 14, the High Secretary-Treasurer read the hospital record.

High Chief Ranger Galvin again stated the question on adopting the report of the Committee on Appeals — leave to withdraw on the claim for the payment of the Endowment to the heirs of Ferdinand Shields.

Voted to adopt the report.

The vote was doubted and High Chief Ranger Galvin instructed the members to rise.

The count showed 51 yes and 27 no, and it was a vote.

Bro. H. Montague, Chairman of Committee on Petitions, reported no business.

Voted to accept the report.

Bro. D. A. Cronin, Chairman of the Board of Trustees, presented the following report : —

REPORT OF TRUSTEES OF RESERVE FUND.

To the High Standing Committee of the Massachusetts Catholic Order of Foresters :

Gentlemen :

The Trustees of your Order respectfully present the following report for the fiscal year ending April 20, 1893 : —

Amount of money received to date from James F. Supple, High Secretary-Treasurer, for Reserve Fund - - -	$9,729.98	
Interest -	400.31	
		$10,130.29

Which is invested in the name of the Order as follows :

Mortgage on Estate Nos. 40 — 42 Market Street, Cambridgeport, Mass., at 5 per cent. - - - - - - -	$6,500 00	
Cash deposited in the Union Institution for Savings - -	2,056.49	
Interest to May, 1890 - - - - - - - - - - - - - -	8.52	
" " " 1892 - - - - - - - - - - -	169.37	
Cash deposited in Franklin Institution for Savings - -	1,000.00	
Interest to Feb., 1893 - - - - - - - - - - - - -	82.42	
" on Mortgage of $2,800 00, at 5 per cent., held on above Estate, from April, 1892, to 1893 - - - - -	140.00	
Cash on hand - - - - - - - - - - - - - - -	173.49	
		$10,130.29

Respectfully submitted,

DANIEL A. CRONIN,
JOSEPH TORNDORF,

Trustees.

Bro. Cronin said that at present there were only two Trustees, and he hoped that another would be elected at this session, and he thought the High Standing Committee should have the power to fill vacancies in the Trustees. He also recommended increasing the assessment for Reserve Fund to $1.00. He also recommended the purchase of a building down town, in the vicinity of the present headquarters.

Bro. Torndorf, the second member of the Board of Trustees, said there should be three Trustees, and something should be done to fill vacancies.

High Chief Ranger Galvin stated the question to accept the report of the Trustees of the Reserve Fund.

Voted to accept the report.

Bro. Patrick M. Keating, of St. Joseph Court No. 11, chairman of the Committee on State of the Order, reported as follows for that Committee : —

1st. "The Committee recommend that hereafter the circulars announcing the Assessment Calls do not contain the names of rejected applicants for membership to the Order."

2nd. "The change of Deputy High Chief Ranger after two terms be considered necessary by the High Chief Ranger."

High Chief Ranger Galvin stated the question on the motion of Bro. Keating, Chairman of Committee, to adopt the first recommendation of the Committee.

Bro. Lowe, of Leo Court No. 5, spoke against the report of the Committee.

Bro. Keating explained why he thought it was necessary.

Capt. Fennessey read article in the Constitution requiring the announcement of the names.

The High Chief Ranger asked that the matter be laid on the table for the present.

Voted to lay on the table.

High Chief Ranger Galvin stated the question on the motion of Bro. Keating to adopt the second recommendation of the Committee on State of the Order.

Voted to adopt.

nief Ranger Galvin asked for the report of the Committee on Secret Work.

Bro. James Cashin, of Cheverus Court No. 6, reported for that Committee as follows: —

" We recommend that the power of convening at any time during recess to confer and bring a report at the next Convention be granted this Committee.

Bro. Fennessey moved to accept the report of the Committee and that the expenses of the Committee be paid.

The motion was carried.

High Chief Ranger Galvin suggested taking first recommendation of the Committee on State of the Order from the table.

Voted to take from the table.

Ou motion it was voted to refer this recommendation to the Committee on Constitution.

High Chief Ranger Galvin ruled that the filling of vacancies on the Board of Trustees was an amendment to the Constitution, and should be referred to that Committee.

On motion it was voted to refer to the Committee on Constitution.

Ou motion of Bro. Mulcahy, of St. John Court No. 23, voted to take from the table the fifth amendment proposed.

High Chief Ranger Galvin stated the question — the motion of Bro. Fennessey, Chairman of the Committee on Constitution, to adopt the report of the Committee on Constitution, striking out the word " male " in the first line of Section 1, Article 3, page 7, and to change the Constitution in all places necessary to correspond therewith.

Capt. Fennessey said he had given the matter careful attention; it was not a new matter with him, and if he could not show by argument and figures that women were better risks than men, he would acquiesce in the opposite view. He had looked at the matter in its various aspects, and was met by only two objections; first that women were not a success in other organizations, and second that once in a while a woman died. Some one may say a woman's province was by the fireside. Yes, but make the fireside more comfortable by admitting women to our Order. He held the theory that women were a better risk than men because, if we study the social condition of the nation, we find that women were longer lived than men, and he said his authority was the Encyclopædia Britannica. In most populations there were more women than men, not because more were born, but less died. One hundred and four males were born for every hundred females. The census of Massachusetts for 1890 gives 109 more deaths of males than females, and we have 70,000 more females than males in this state.

Bro. Fennessey spoke for over an hour quoting statistics from various authorities in proof of his argument.

Bro. P. M. Keating, of St. Joseph Court No. 11, was not in favor of the admission of women as the tendency, in his opinion, would be to lower them socially.

Bro. Torndorf, of Holy Trinity Court No. 51, was not in favor of the proposition because it would increase the assessments and would not elevate the women.

Bro. Donovan, of St. Lawrence Court No. 61, asked Bro. Torndorf if the Church was not always seeking to elevate women.

Bro. Torndorf replied that he thought the Church always did.

Bro. Mulcahy, of St. Joseph Court No. 11, asked the privilege of making a statment, but High Chief Ranger Galvin ruled that as Bro Mulcahy was not a delegate he was not in order.

Bros. Ryan, of Loyola Court No. 94, and Dolan, of Qualey Court No. 32, were opposed to the admission of women to the Order.

Bro. Shea, of St. Alphonsus Court No. 21, said he was instructed by his Court to vote for the amendment, and he thought we should have women in the Order, as a matter of business. He could trust his wife and daughters in the Order because they were Catholic women. (Applause.)

Bro. Mulcahy, of St. John Court No. 23, and Bro. Brant, of Leo Court, No. 5, spoke in favor of the amendment.

Bro. Brant said this was a Catholic organization, and we should take them in. The Catholic women of the state would be a great help to the organization.

Bro. Carson, of Sheil Court No. 35, moved the previous question.

High Chief Ranger Galvin stated the question, and the previous question was ordered.

The vote was doubted.

The High Chief Ranger asked the members to rise, and a count showed 85 yes, 5 no, and the previous question was ordered.

A motion was made and seconded that when the vote was taken it be taken by yeas and nays.

High Chief Ranger Galvin stated the question, and the yea and nay vote was ordered.

High Chief Ranger Galvin then stated the question on the motion of Bro. Fennessey to adopt the report of the Committee on Constitution striking out the word "male" in the first line of Section 1, Article 3, page 7, and to change the Constitution in all places necessary to correspond therewith, and instructed the representatives to answer to their names as the roll was called, commencing with Cathedral Court No. 1.

The vote follows —

YES.

Cathedral Court No. 1. J. J. Lanigan, M. Edmunds, J. T. Mahoney, M. McBarron.

Leo Court No. 5. John Brant, George F. Lowe and W. F. O'Donnell.

Sherwood Court No. 8. D. F. Sullivan.

Columbus Court No. 9. James F. Supple.

Essex Court No. 16. James J. Murphy.

Williams Court No. 19. James Douglass.

Mount Pleasant Court No. 20. Garrett H. Keefe and William J. Downing.

St. Alphonsus Court No. 21. Patrick H. Shea.

St. John Court No. 23. Thomas Mulcahy.

St. Gregory Court No. 24. John O'Callaghan and Michael Dunican.

St. Francis Court No. 25. J. L. Fennessey and John Vogel.

Erin Court No. 28. John T. Daly.

St. Thomas Court No. 29. Patrick McCarthy, F. L. Smith and T. F. Roach.

Americus Court No. 34. J. J. McLaughlin.

Friendship Court No. 37. J. W. Keenan.

Constantine Court No. 49.   James T. Riley.

St. James Court No. 54.   J. G. Fennessey.

Charles River Court No. 55.   Peter McGrath.

Worcester Court No. 59.   J. H. Fitzgerald and T. H. Murphy.

St. Lawrence Court No. 61.   M. Driscoll and J. T Donovan.

Shields Court No. 63.   F. F. O'Neil.

Gallagher Court No. 64.   J. J. Leonard.

Stoughton Court No. 69.   J. E. Tighe and A. H. McDonald.

Taunton Court No. 73.   George F. Brammer.

Quincy Court No. 76.   C. Mischler.

Mystic Court No. 77.   John W. Lynch.

St. Monica Court No. 78.   Dr. J. H. Cronin.

John Boyle O'Reilly Court No. 79.   J. H. Miskell.

St. Malachi Court No. 81.   D. P. McNeil.

Columbia Court No. 95.   P. F. Manning.—

43 YES.

NO.

Fenwick Court No. 3.   D. J. Gallagher.

St. Francis Court No. 4.   W. E. Shay, Michael J. O'Brien, Thomas Sproules.

Cheverus Court No. 6.   Owen A. Galvin.

St. Patrick Court No. 7.   George T. Fair.

Sherwood Court No. 8.   John P. Dore, Hugh Montague.

St. Joseph Court No. 11.   Patrick O'Loughlin, Daniel A. Cronin, Patrick M. Keating.

Fitzpatrick Court No. 13.   Charles J. Jordan.

Lafayette Court No. 14.   Michael S. Keenan, John Driscoll.

SS. Peter and Paul Court No. 15.   Martin Folan.

Essex Court No. 16.   Daniel J. O'Brien, Dr. F. E. Hines.

St. Peter Court No. 18.   James H. Dixon, John J. Curran.

St. Raphael Court No. 26.   Bernard J. McCaffrey.

Erin Court No. 28.   James J. Kane.

St. Thomas Court No. 29.   Daniel Connolly.

Bass River Court No. 30.   P. M. Riordan.

Qualey Court No. 32.   James Dolan.

Americus Court No. 34. P. J. Gorman.

Sheil Court No. 35. J. C. Carson.

St. Joseph Court No. 38. Peter Morris.

Benedict Court No. 39. J. D. Couch, M. D.

St. Bernard Court No. 44. M. J. Duane.

St. Augustine Court No. 46. John Doolin.

St. Anne Court No. 47. Charles O'Brien.

Sarsfield Court No. 48. James H. Carley, James F. O'Brien.

Holy Trinity Court No. 51. J. Torndorf, Jr., Henry Wesling, F. Schwab.

Highland Court No. 52. Hugh H. Collins.

Emerald Court No. 53. Thomas F. Lyons, James J. McCann.

St. James Court No. 54. Thomas W. O'Rourke.

Charles River Court No. 55. James D. Monahan.

Carroll Court No. 57. C. J. Fay.

Prospect Court No 58. William F. Rooney.

Middlesex Court No. 60. John E. Briston, P. A. Mulligan.

St. Catharine Court No. 62. Richard E. Oldham.

St. Columbkille Court No. 65. John J. O'Keefe.

Griffin Court No. 66. M. F. Conroy.

Canton Court No. 67. Matthew. A. Skelton.

St. Margaret Court No. 68. Lawrence J. Watson.

St. Michael Court No. 70. Robert Dwyer.

Phil Sheridan Court No. 71. James F. Carens.

Merrimack Court No. 72. R. Dwyer, B. Haughey.

St. Jarlath Court No. 75. T. F. Lynes.

Gen. Sherman Court No. 80. Henry S. Healey.

Brockton Court No. 82. John J. Hickey.

George Washington Court No. 85. J. B. McCarthy. J. J. McGuigan, M. D.

Robert Emmett Court No. 87. John B. Rooney.

Germania Court No. 93. Christian Lambrecht.

Loyola Court No. 94. John A. Ryan.

62 NO.

High Chief Ranger Galvin declared it was not a vote, not having the requisite two-thirds.

High Chief Ranger Galvin announced as the next business the reception of names of Past Chief Rangers for membership in the High Court.

The following names were received:—

Cathedral Court No. 1, J. W. Sweeney, C. H. Tighe.

St. Francis Court No. 4, W. F. Finneran.

St. Patrick Court No. 7, T. F. Twomey.

At this point a motion was made that further reception of names be dispensed with, and that Recording Secretaries forward the names of those eligible to the High Standing Committee.

Motion was carried.

High Chief Ranger Galvin announced the next business to be the nomination and election of High Court Officers.

Bro. G. H. Keefe, of Mount Pleasant Court No. 20, moved to appoint a committee of three to receive, sort and count ballots.

The motion was carried.

High Chief Ranger Galvin appointed Bro. Keefe of Mount Pleasant Court No. 20, Bro. Mulcahy of St. John Court No. 23, and Bro. Lowe of Leo Court No. 5, as that committee.

Bro. William E. Shay, of St. Francis Court No. 4, presented the name of Bro. James J. McLaughlin, of Americus Court No. 34, for High Chief Ranger.

Bro. P. M. Keating, of St. Joseph Court No. 11, seconded the nomination.

Bro. J. J. Leonard, of Gallagher Court No. 64, moved that the High Secretary-Treasurer cast one ballot for James J. McLaughlin for High Chief Ranger.

Voted.

Bro. Keefe for the committee reported that the ballot had been cast as directed, and High Chief Ranger Galvin declared Bro. James J. McLaughlin, of Americus Court No. 34, elected High Chief Ranger.

Bro. J. G. Fennessey, of St. James Court No. 54, nominated Hon. John P. Dore, of Sherwood Court No. 8, as Vice High Chief Ranger.

The nomination was seconded by Bro. Thomas Sproules, of St. Francis Court No. 4.

Bro. Mulcahy, of St. John Court No. 23, moved that the High Secretary-Treasurer cast one ballot for Bro. Dore for Vice High Chief Ranger.

Voted.

Bro. Keefe for the committee reported that the ballot had been cast as directed, and High Chief Ranger Galvin declared Hon John P. Dore, of Sherwood Court No. 8, elected Vice High Chief Ranger.

[Vice High Chief Ranger McLaughlin in the chair.] High Chief Ranger Galvin nominated James F. Supple, of Columbus Court No. 9, for High Secretary-Treasurer.

A motion was made and carried that the chairman of the committee cast one ballot for James F. Supple for High Secretary-Treasurer.

Bro. Keefe for the committee reported that the ballot was cast as directed, and High Chief Ranger McLaughlin declared James F. Supple, of Columbus Court No. 9, elected High Secretary-Treasurer.

Bro. W. F. Rooney, of Prospect Court No. 58, nominated Bro. P. A. Murray, of Middlesex Court No. 60, for the position of High Senior Conductor.

Seconded by Bro. Mulcahy, of St. John Court No. 23, who moved that the chairman of the committee cast one ballot.

Bro. Keefe for the committee reported that the ballot was cast as directed, and the High Chief Ranger declared Bro. P. A. Murray, of Middlesex Court No. 60, elected High Senior Conductor.

Bro. John C. Carson, of Sheil Court No. 35, nominated Bro. John Hayes, of Lafayette Court No. 14, for High Junior Conductor.

Seconded by Bro. Charles O'Brien, of St. Anne Court No. 47, who moved that the chairman of the committee cast one ballot for John Hayes, of Lafayette Court No. 14, for High Junior Conductor.

The motion was carried.

Bro. Keefe for the committee reported that the ballot was cast as directed, and the High Chief Ranger declared Bro. John Hayes, of Lafayette Court No. 14, elected High Junior Conductor.

Bro. A. H. McDonald, of Stoughton Court, No. 69, nominated Bro. Fred L. Smith, of St. Thomas Court, No. 29, for High Inside Sentinel.

Seconded by Bro. Cashin, of Cheverus Court No. 6, who moved that the chairman of the committee cast one ballot for Bro. F. L· Smith for High Inside Sentinel.

The motion was carried.

Bro. Keefe for the committee reported that the ballot was cast as directed, and the High Chief Ranger declared that Bro. F. L. Smith, of St. Thomas Court No. 29, elected High Inside Sentinel.

Bro. John B. McCarthy, of George Washington Court, No. 85, nominated, in a very neat and effective speech, Bro. J. G. Fennessey, of St. James Court No. 54, for High Outside Sentinel.

Bro. T. W. O'Rourke, of St. James Court No. 54, seconded the nomination, and moved that the High Secretary-Treasurer cast one ballot for Bro. Jeremiah G. Fennessey for High Outside Sentinel.

The motion was carried.

Bro. Keefe for the committee reported that the ballot was cast as directed, and the High Chief Ranger declared Bro. Jeremiah G. Fennessey, of St. James Court No. 54, elected High Outside Sentinel.

Dr. F. E. Hines, of Essex Court No. 16, nominated Dr. Joseph D. Couch, of Benedict Court No. 39, for High Medical Examiner.

The nomination was seconded by Dr. Ahearne, of Lafayette Court No. 14, and others, and a motion was made and carried that the High Secretary-Treasurer cast one ballot for Dr. Joseph D. Couch for High Medical Examiner.

Bro. Keefe for the committee reported that the ballot was cast as directed, and the High Chief Ranger declared Dr. Joseph D. Couch, of Benedict Court No. 39, elected High Medical Examiner.

Bro. Lowe, of Leo Court No. 5, nominated Rev. Hugh Roe O'Donnell, of Leo Court No. 5, for High Court Chaplain.

Seconded by a great many representatives.

A motion was made and carried that the High Secretary-Treasurer cast one ballot for Rev. Hugh Roe O'Donnell for High Court Chaplain.

Bro. Keefe for the committee reported that the ballot was cast as directed, and High Chief Ranger Galvin declared Rev. Hugh Roe O'Donnell, of Leo Court No. 5, elected High Court Chaplain.

Bro. J. G. Fennessey of St. James Court No. 54, presented the name of Peter A. Sullivan, of Americus Court No. 34, for Trustee.

A motion was made and carried that the High Secretary-Treasurer cast one ballot for P. A. Sullivan as Trustee.

Bro. Keefe for the committee reported that the ballot was cast as directed, and the High Chief Ranger declared Bro. P. A. Sullivan, of Americus Court No. 34, elected as Trustee.

On motion of Bro. John T. Daly, of Erin Court No. 28, a recess was taken for supper till 7.30 P. M.

The Convention was called to order at 7.30 P. M. High Chief Ranger Hon. Owen A. Galvin in the chair.

High Chief Ranger Galvin announced as the next business in order the election of a Finance Committee.

A motion was made and carried that the High Secretary-Treasurer cast one ballot with the following names:—

J. J. Lanigan, of Cathedral Court No. 1; O. A. Galvin, of Cheverus Court No. 6; W. E. Shay, of St. Francis Court No. 4; W. F. Rooney, of Prospect Court No. 58; G. H. Keefe, of Mount Pleasant Court No. 20.

The ballot was cast as directed, and High Chief Ranger Galvin declared the Brothers named elected Committee on Finance.

On motion of Bro. Fennessey, of St. James Court No. 54, it was voted that the salary of the High Secretary-Treasurer be the same as last year.

High Chief Ranger Galvin announced as the next business the installation of officers.

A motion was made and carried that we proceed to installation of officers.

High Chief Ranger Galvin appointed Bro. William E. Shay, of St. Francis Court No. 4, and Bro. J. J. Lanigan, of Cathedral Court No. 1, to act as High Conductors.

High Chief Ranger Galvin invited Past High Chief Ranger Dennis F. O'Sullivan to perform the installation service.

Bro. O'Sullivan then took the chair, and installed the following officers :—

High Chief Ranger.—JAMES J. McLAUGHLIN, of Americus Court No. 34.
Vice High Chief Ranger.—Hon. JOHN P. DORE, of Sherwood Court No. 8.
High Secretary-Treasurer.—JAMES. F. SUPPLE, of Columbus Court No. 9.
High Senior Conductor.—PATRICK A. MURRAY, of Middlesex Court No. 60.
High Junior Conductor.—JOHN HAYES, of Lafayette Court No. 14.
High Inside Sentinel.—FRED L. SMITH, of St. Thomas Court No. 29.
High Outside Sentinel.—JEREMIAH G. FENNESSEY, of St. James Court No. 54
High Medical Examiner.—JOSEPH D. COUCH, of Benedict Court No. 39.

Bro. O'Sullivan then introduced High Chief Ranger McLaughlin, who said he felt highly honored by the election and that it was possible to realize the wish expressed by High Chief Ranger Galvin, and, with the committee as constituted, it could be done. He thanked the delegates for their confidence in him and hoped it would be merited.

Bro. Patrick O'Loughlin, of St. Joseph Court No. 11, said that some recognition of the services of Hon. Owen A. Galvin should be had, that no man had done more for the advancement of the Order than Bro. Galvin, and he moved that the thanks of the Convention be extended to Bro. Galvin for his services on behalf of the Order.

Carried unanimously by a rising vote.

High Chief Ranger McLaughlin then addressed Bro. Galvin and in the name of the Convention thanked him for the work he had performed.

Bro. Galvin responded feelingly and said he was grateful for the regard expressed by the vote, and that what he had done was a labor of love and he could not have done it so well if each man on the High Standing Committee had not done his share, and that all were equally worthy of thanks. What he had done in these later years was done with the same spirit as in past years. The field was large and we should have a larger membership, and could get it. As a fraternal organization we stood in a high place, as our membership was good and in the best physical condition. He was grateful for the vote cast, but only did what he thought was right. Believing in the Order as he did, he asked the members present to go out and build up the Organization, bring in new members, organize a Court in every parish, and make the membership of the Order what it should be.

Bro. John B. McCarthy, of George Washington Court No. 85, asked permission to say a few words, which was allowed. He then said as a member of the committee on good of the Order for his Court, he had labored early and late to benefit the Court. He had paid special attention to the social side of membership in this Order, and had endeavored to make the members feel they were dealing with brothers. He had also paid some attention to the ritual, which he thought could be improved, and that the present ritual could be made much more effective by a proper exemplification, as he had demonstrated to some members of the High Standing Committee at a recent meeting of his Court, and he invited any one present to attend a meeting of his Court on April 27.

High Chief Ranger McLaughlin appointed Committee on Constitution: P. M. Keating, of St. Joseph Court No. 11; P. F. Manning, of Columbia Court No. 95; D. F. Sullivan, of Sherwood Court No. 8; George F. Lowe, of Leo Court No. 5; John Vogel, of St. Francis Court No. 25; John T. Daly, of Erin Court No. 28.

Past High Chief Ranger Galvin moved that the committee be instructed to revise and classify the Constitution, and present it at the next Convention.

The motion was carried.

On motion of Bro. Dixon, of St. Peter Court No. 18, it was voted that the High Standing Committee take into consideration the improvement of regalia for officers of subordinate Courts.

On motion of Bro. William E. Shay, of St. Francis Court No. 4, it was voted to read the record of the Convention.

The High Secretary-Treasurer proceeded to read the records.

On motion of Bro. Fennessey, voted to dispense with further reading of the records, and that the records be approved.

Past High Chief Ranger Galvin said he hoped the Committee on Secret Work would present a new ritual.

Bro. Fair, of St. Patrick Court No. 7, presented the following amendment to the Constitution: "That no suspended member should be eligible for membership in another Court."

High Chief Ranger McLaughlin said the amendment would be referred to the Committee on Constitution.

Bro. John T. Daly, of Erin Court No. 28, said he had repeatedly asked for suggestions for improving the ritual and nothing had been received by him.

Bro. Conroy, of Griffin Court No. 66, wanted information about dangerous occupations, and moved that a list be prepared and forwarded to the Courts.

On motion, voted to refer to the High Standing Committee.

Bro. John J. Leonard, of Gallagher Court No. 64, called attention to the prospectus recently issued by the High Standing Committee. He said he thought each subordinate Court should have some with the name of the Court printed in.

High Junior Conductor Hayes made a motion that we now proceed to close.

The motion was carried.

High Chief Ranger McLaughlin then closed in due form.

Voted to adjourn.

Adjourned at 9.10 P. M.

JAMES F. SUPPLE,

High Secretary-Treasurer.

Lightning Source UK Ltd.
Milton Keynes UK
UKHW020600120219
337137UK00005B/828/P